ASHGATE
RESEARCH
COMPANION

THE ASHGATE RESEARCH COMPANION TO NEW PUBLIC MANAGEMENT

The Companion provides the first comprehensive overview of the most important changes in democratic administrative reform in the post-War era. This will equip scholars, students and policy makers with a solid foundation on which to build assessments of the new approaches to performance management, accountability and flexibility. Well written and presented, the chapters combine sound theoretical insight with useful overviews of national systems. Whether one is an ardent supporter or determined critic of these reforms, the Companion will serve as a starting point for analysis and assessment.

Mark Considine, University of Melbourne, Australia

New Public Management has swept much of the world in the past 20-30 years, a reform movement fed by its adoption by major governments and its promotion by many international agencies. Much has been written about it, puzzling over its origins, the reasons for its appeal and its consequences. This excellent volume presents a comprehensive, systematic and provocative review of how this happened, what it means, and what its effects have been. A must collection for anyone interested in contemporary administrative reform.

Joel D. Aberbach, Center for American Politics and Public Policy, UCLA, USA

If you want to understand how and why the public sector has changed in the last twenty years, and how and why it has resisted or translated change, this is the definitive account to read. The leading international researches in the field do not only tell what happened, but offer realistic and compelling theoretical explanations.

Werner Jann, University of Potsdam, Germany

What exactly has been discovered about the much debated phenomenon of "New Public Management" (NPM), after nearly 20 years of research? If anything can tell us that, it should be this weighty book, written by nearly 40 academics who have debated the issues in international forums for 15 years or so... the book will be an essential source of reference because most of the world's major scholars in the field appear in it, the references alone run to some 63 pages, and it includes thoughtful and authoritative essays on most of the topics that have been discussed on the NPM conference circuit over the past two decades. ... This collection is definitely an important milestone in NPM research...

Governance

This work helps to bring clarity to the evolution and impact of NPM reform, particularly in Europe and Australia and New Zealand... Each chapter is well written and presents its information in accessible language that can be understood by a non-expert... this is an impressive work and is highly recommended for students and researchers interested in studying the movement.

American Reference Books Annual

ASHGATE
RESEARCH
COMPANION

The *Ashgate Research Companions* are designed to offer scholars and graduate students a comprehensive and authoritative state-of-the-art review of current research in a particular area. The companion's editors bring together a team of respected and experienced experts to write chapters on the key issues in their speciality, providing a comprehensive reference to the field.

Other Research Companions available in Politics and International Relations:

The Ashgate Research Companion to Political Violence
Edited by Marie Breen-Smyth
ISBN 978-0-7546-7752-9

The Ashgate Research Companion to Religion and Conflict Resolution
Edited by Lee Marsden
ISBN 978-1-4094-1089-8

The Ashgate Research Companion to the Globalization of Health
Edited by Ted Schrecker
ISBN 978-1-4094-0924-3

The Ashgate Research Companion to Chinese Foreign Policy
Edited by Emilian Kavalski
ISBN 978-1-4094-2270-9

The Ashgate Research Companion to International Trade Policy
Edited by Kenneth Heydon and Stephen Woolcock
ISBN 978-1-4094-0835-2

The Ashgate Research Companion to War
Edited by Hall Gardner and Oleg Kobtzeff
ISBN 978-0-7546-7826-7

The Ashgate Research Companion to Regionalisms
Edited by Timothy M. Shaw, J. Andrew Grant and Scarlett Cornelissen
ISBN 978-0-7546-7762-8

Continued at the back of the book

The Ashgate
Research Companion
to New Public Management

Edited by

TOM CHRISTENSEN
University of Oslo, Norway

PER LÆGREID
University of Bergen, Norway

ASHGATE

Published by
Ashgate Publishing Limited
Wey Court East
Union Road
Farnham
Surrey GU9 7PT
USA

Ashgate Publishing Company
110 Cherry Street
Suite 3-1
Burlington, VT 05401-3818
England

www.ashgate.com

British Library Cataloguing in Publication Data
The Ashgate research companion to new public management.
  1. Public administration. 2. Public administration--
  Cross-cultural studies. 3. Civil service reform. 4. Civil
  service reform--Cross-cultural studies.
  I. Research companion to new public management
  II. Christensen, Tom, 1949- III. Lægreid, Per.
  351-dc22

Library of Congress Cataloging-in-Publication Data
The Ashgate research companion to new public management / [edited] by Tom Christensen and Per Lægreid.
    p. cm.
  Includes index.
  ISBN 978-0-7546-7806-9 (hardback) -- ISBN 978-0-7546-9570-7 (ebook) 1. Public administration. I. Christensen, Tom, 1949- II. Lægreid, Per.
  JF1351.A84 2010
  351--dc22

2010028235

ISBN 9780754678069 (hbk)
ISBN 9781409462507 (pbk)
ISBN 9780754695707 (ebk – PDF)
ISBN 9781409489092 (ebk – ePUB)

Printed and bound in Great Britain by the
MPG Books Group, UK

Contents

PART VI   NPM AND BEYOND

List of Figures

List of Tables

List of Contributors

Lotte Bøgh Andersen, Associate Professor, University of Aarhus, Denmark.
Rhys Andrews, Senior Research Fellow, Cardiff Business School, UK.
Peter Aucoin, Professor, Dalhousie University, Canada.
Ian Bartle, Research Fellow, Ecole Polytechnique Federale de Lausanne, Switzerland.
Ivar Bleiklie, Professor, University of Bergen, Norway.
Jonathan Boston, Professor, Victoria University of Wellington, New Zealand.
Geert Bouckaert, Professor, Katholieke University Leuven, Belgium.
Nils Brunsson, Professor of Management, Uppsala University, Sweden..
Haldor Byrkjeflot, Postdoctoral Fellow, University of Bergen, Norway.
Anthony B.L. Cheung, Professor, Hong Kong Institute of Education, Hong Kong.
Tom Christensen, Professor, University of Oslo, Norway.
Jürgen Enders, Professor, University of Twente, the Netherlands.
Robert Gregory, Visiting Professor, City University of Hong Kong, Hong Kong,
and Adjunct Professor, Victoria University of Wellington, New Zealand.
Carsten Greve, Professor, Copenhagen Business School, Denmark.
John Halligan, Professor, University of Canberra, Australia.
Hanne Foss Hansen, Professor, University of Copenhagen, Denmark.
Graeme Hodge, Professor, Monash University, Australia.
Oliver James, Professor, University of Exeter, UK.
Torben Beck Jørgensen, Professor, University of Copenhagen, Denmark.
Walter J.M. Kickert, Professor, Erasmus University Rotterdam, the Netherlands.
Benedetto Lepori, Senior Researcher, University of Lugano, Switzerland.
Per Lægreid, Professor, University of Bergen, Norway.
Martin Marcussen, Professor, University of Copenhagen, Denmark.
Christine Musselin, Researcher, Centre for the Sociology of Organizations, France.
Janet Newman, Professor, Open University, UK.
Richard Norman, Senior Lecturer, Victoria University of Wellington, New Zealand.
Stephen P. Osborne, Professor, University of Edinburgh, UK.
Martin Painter, Professor, City University of Hong Kong, Hong Kong.
Thomas Pallesen, Professor, Aarhus University, Denmark.
B. Guy Peters, Professor, University of Pittsburgh, USA.
Jon Pierre, Professor, Gothenburg University, Sweden.
Vital Put, Researcher, Katholieke University Leuven, Belgium.
Paul G. Roness, Professor, University of Bergen, Norway.
Bo Rothstein, Professor, Gothenburg University, Sweden.

Sandra van Thiel, Associate Professor, Erasmus University Rotterdam, the Netherlands.
Koen Verhoest, Associate Professor, Katholieke University Leuven, Belgium.
Steven Van de Walle, Associate Professor, Erasmus University Rotterdam, the Netherlands.

Preface

This companion provides a comprehensive, state-of-the-art review of current research in the field of New Public Management (NPM) reform. Aimed primarily at a readership with a special interest in contemporary public sector reforms, the book offers a refreshing and up-to-date analysis of key issues of modern administrative reforms. It covers not only the New Public Management movement in general but also the driving forces behind the reform and its various trajectories and special features.

The collection offers readers an international perspective on the important public sector reforms related to the NPM movement that have occurred in a number of countries over the past 20–30 years. It takes stock of NPM reforms and comprises a general introduction and 28 chapters divided into six thematic sections, each with chapters ranging across a variety of crucial topics in the field of New Public Management reforms and beyond. The principal themes to be addressed are NPM processes and driving forces, the question of convergence or divergence among countries, NPM developments in specific sectors and policy areas, analyses of specific features and components of NPM, the effects and implications of NPM and post-NPM reforms.

More specifically, Part I examines the 'why' question by focusing on different driving forces and explanatory factors behind the NPM movement. The basic theoretical foundation of NPM reforms are discussed as well as driving forces such as political-administrative design and polity features, historical-institutional contexts and cultural constraints. It also considers the importance of institutional environments, copying, diffusion and translation of reform ideas and solutions among countries. How these driving forces changed during the 20–30-year period when NPM-inspired reforms were being implemented is also discussed.

Part II addresses the question of whether NPM reforms have resulted in a convergence of administrative models among families of countries or whether there is still great divergence and diversity among countries. It asks also if there is more convergence about reform ideas than about the implementation and effects of reform. Four families of countries with different state traditions are examined: Anglo-Saxon countries, Continental Europe, Asian countries and Scandinavia.

Part III examines differences between policy areas such as the 'soft' welfare sector where reforms have taken place in the hospital system, universities and the welfare administration, and the 'harder' sectors like the regulation of utilities in areas such as telecommunications and energy.

Part IV focuses on some specific NPM features. NPM is a shopping basket of different instruments, measures and tools including both market- and management-related features. Some of the main components of NPM are examined, including structural devolution, autonomy and agencification; performance management, auditing and ex post control; managerialism and management models; marketization, competition and privatization; and public–private partnerships.

Part V raises the important question of the effects and implications of NPM reforms. This is difficult to answer, but is addressed by adopting an extended concept of effects. Thus this section analyses both the more direct and the narrower effects on efficiency and the broader impact on democracy involving such issues as political accountability and control, on trust involving questions of satisfaction and legitimacy, on union influence and participation, on corporatism, scientification and on public sector values. It also discusses normative aspects as well as the development from input democracy to output democracy and what the implications are for user participation and service quality.

Part VI goes beyond the NPM movement and asks what new trends are occurring. Is New Public Management still alive and kicking, is it fading away or being replaced by alternative reforms, or is a revision going on in which new reform elements are added to the existing ones to produce a more complex public administration? Such questions are examined by focusing on post-NPM measures like whole-of-government initiatives, Neo-Weberianism and quality of government, and New Public Governance as a new trend.

This book is a result of an international professional network that has developed over the past 15 years. There are a number of individuals and organizations to whom we owe our thanks. An acknowledgement goes to our network of colleagues and friends who share an interest in institutional change, comparative public administration and public sector reform. Without their enthusiastic responses to our invitation to contribute to this volume, it would never have been fulfilled.

We are also grateful to our publisher and especially Kirstin Howgate who approached us with the idea and invited us to embark on this project. Thanks are also due to the Department of Administration and Organization Theory, University of Bergen for generous administrative support. Special thanks go to Kjersti Gjuvsland for excellent technical assistance in supervising the preparation of the manuscript, and to Melanie Newton for very competent language assistance.

We are also grateful for generous financial support from the Norwegian Research Council which has funded a number of research projects over the past decade. Without the cumulative knowledge that has been developed from these projects, it would not have been possible to lead this book project. We also express our gratitude to the Uni-Rokkansenteret and to our home departments – the Department of Political Science, University of Oslo and the Department of Administration and Organization Theory, University of Bergen.

Tom Christensen and Per Lægreid
2010

Introduction

Tom Christensen and Per Lægreid

The Broader Picture

New Public Management (NPM) is a general concept denoting a global wave of administrative reforms that has had an impact on many countries' public sectors over the last 25 years (Pollitt and Bouckaert 2004). Most NPM reform efforts have had similar goals: to improve the effectiveness and efficiency of the public sector; to enhance the responsiveness of public agencies to their clients and customers; to reduce public expenditure; and to improve managerial accountability.

The term 'New Public Management' was coined by Christopher Hood in 1991 (Hood 1991), but it actually referred to a concept that dated back a decade. The first NPM reform ideas and measures were introduced by the governments of Margaret Thatcher in the UK and of Ronald Reagan in the USA from about 1979/80, while Australia and New Zealand followed suit in the mid-1980s. Although the reforms definitely have an Anglo-American flavour (Hood 1996a), they have spread widely around the world, driven partly by the forces of globalization and by international organizations dominated by the same countries, but also nationally by conservative and neo-liberal parties, in some cases in collaboration with mainstream social democratic parties.

The first part of this companion will focus on the driving forces behind NPM. It will analyse the main components of NPM ideology, focusing on the generic aspects of this brand of reform. A distinction can be made between reform ideas and more specific reform measures, and here we emphasize the coupling between the two. A broad transformative approach to public reforms contends that when a political and administrative leadership tries to handle and further public reforms it operates in at least three types of contexts that can both enhance and/or obstruct reforms: the constitutionally laid-down political and administrative structure; the political and administrative culture; and the environment, whether technical or institutional (Christensen and Lægreid 2001b and 2007a). These different contexts will be discussed in separate chapters and their relevance for the NPM process analysed more generally.

The second part of the companion deals with the generic question of whether NPM is about convergence or divergence (Pollitt 2001a). One can argue that some major NPM reform ideas will spread around the world quite easily, while the more specific reform measures will show a pattern of divergence. One main reason for this may be national variations in the three contexts mentioned and the complex interaction between them, for each country has different constitutional/ structural features, a different political and administrative culture, and a different environment (Christensen, Lie and Lægreid 2007). A quite common stereotype is that Anglo-American countries are NPM front-runners, followed by some Asian countries, while Continental Europe and Scandinavia have been more reluctant to take NPM on board. The four chapters examining each of these groups of countries will try to outline whether this stereotype reflects empirical reality or whether there are more similarities between the country groups or more variety within the groups than expected.

The third part will deal with whether there is a difference between 'soft' and 'hard' public policy areas with respect to implementation of NPM. Originally, NPM was often thought to be best applied to harder and more technical policy areas, where it was easier to set unambiguous targets and measure results (Gregory 2003a). In the meantime NPM seems to have spread to most policy areas, but does this distinction still exist?

NPM is said to be a 'shopping-basket' of different reform measures, not all pointing in the same direction. Part IV deals with this question and examines the spectrum of NPM reform measures, ranging from the more structural ones, to performance indicators, management and market elements, public–private partnerships and user-orientation.

Part V focuses on the effects and implications of NPM. NPM is broadly oriented and seems to produce both main effects and side-effects, according to Pollitt (2002). The most typical main effect is efficiency; but side-effects, concerning the larger questions of democracy, legitimacy, trust, accountability, control, professional competence and normative issues, seem to be just as important.

Part VI looks at what has followed NPM in terms of public reforms. Reforms that have emerged more recently have been variously labelled as post-NPM, whole-of-government, joined-up government, quality of government, New Public Governance and so on. A central question addressed in this part concerns what happens when different reform waves meet each other. Will NPM prevail, be modified and pushed back, or combined with newer reform measures?

The Content of NPM

One primary characteristic of NPM is the adoption by public organizations of the management and organizational forms used by private companies. This challenges two traditional doctrines of public administration (Dunleavy and Hood 1994): that public-sector organizations are 'insulated' from the private sector in terms of personnel, structure and business methods; and that they operate in accordance with a precise set of rules limiting the freedom of public officials in handling money, staff, contracts and so on. In contrast the NPM movement ascribes to the generic principle that the formal organization of the public and the private sector should be similar and that managers in public sector organizations should have enough discretion and leeway in their daily work to be able to make efficient use of allocated resources.

Even if NPM fundamentally espouses economic values and objectives, as a concept it is loose and multi-faceted and encompasses a range of different administrative doctrines. It offers a kind of 'shopping basket' of different elements to reformers of public administration (Pollitt 1995). The advantage of having a wide variety of reform elements is that it allows public leaders wishing to introduce NPM to be flexible. They may be able to contextualize a broad reform wave that is presented as de-contextualized, that is, a set of measures that will fit everywhere. The disadvantage is that some of the reform elements may be inconsistent or in conflict with one another. This may create ambiguities, conflicts and problems of implementation.

One important set of NPM reform measures are structural ones, which involve splitting up public organizations through horizontal and vertical specialization (structural devolution), whether inter- or intra-organizational. The main vertical change introduced by NPM was increased structural devolution, meaning a trend towards more autonomous agencies and state-owned enterprises (Christensen and Lægreid 2001c). The other main reform element was increased horizontal specialization, based on the principle of the 'single-purpose organization', which makes different organizational units' roles more 'pure'. In other words, following reforms, each unit deals only with ownership, regulation, purchasing, provision and so on (Gregory 2003b). The combination of these vertical and horizontal reform measures led in many cases to structural fragmentation.

Another basic feature of NPM is managerialism and the management model. Boston et al. (1996) see the inclusion of management models primarily as related to the NPM ideals of further devolution, delegation of authority and autonomy. There seem to be at least two basic management models. The first model – let the managers manage – is connected to devolution. A main component of the NPM philosophy is hands-on professional management, which allows for active, visible, discretionary control of an organization by people who are free to manage; explicit standards of performance; a greater emphasis on output control; disaggregation of units; and private sector management techniques. The second model – make the managers manage – leans more towards the use of incentives to further certain decision-making behaviour. It implies increased exposure to competition, contract management and market orientation (contracting out, purchaser-provider models). A third kind of NPM reform measure, connected to the two mentioned above, involves performance management, cost-cutting and budgetary discipline. The increased use of formal performance indicators represents an attempt to quantify the activities of public organizations more extensively, while *ex post* scrutiny and auditing are ways of connecting and comparing goals and actual results. The underlying principle is that good results should be rewarded while poor results should be punished.

Three types of reform measures deal with the connection to stake-holders in the environment – marketization, competition and privatization, which involves changing the organization of service provision. One NPM idea was that if services cannot be improved in the public sector, they should be privatized (Boston et al. 1996). Competitive tendering, whereby public and private providers compete for contracts, was advanced as one instrument for doing this; another was to get different private providers to compete for services once a decision had been taken to privatize them. The focus in these reform measures was often on service efficiency – that is, on getting providers to fulfil their contracts in the most appropriate way, to improve the service offered by public providers by introducing more competition and so on.

The flip-side of competitive tendering is its perception of citizens as users or consumers and its increased emphasis on service-orientation, user participation and satisfaction, and responsiveness to demands from customers, users and clients. Measures introduced to enhance these features include Citizens Charters and users' declarations. Private–public partnerships, on the other hand, entail a more formalized partnership between the public and the private sectors. Instead of giving public organizations sole responsibility for planning, developing, financing, building and operating large projects, such as infrastructure projects, private actors also participate in funding, building and operating them.

Summing up, one can distinguish four different aspects of NPM: the efficiency drive; downsizing and decentralization; the search for excellence; and public service orientation (Ferlie et al. 1996). NPM promised to integrate these themes, linking efficiency and accountability. Other distinctions are between 'hard NPM tools', which address accounting, auditing and performance measurement, and 'soft NPM tools', which include things like human factors, user-orientation, quality improvement and individual development.

Tensions arising from the hybrid character of NPM, which combines economic organization theory and management theory, are well known (Aucoin 1990). They result from the contradiction between the centralizing tendencies inherent in contractualism and the devolutionary tendencies of managerialism. By advocating both decentralization (let the managers manage) and centralization (make the managers manage), NPM thus simultaneously prescribes both more autonomy and more central control.

Many of the most important and problematic reform elements, such as the relationship between managers and elected officials, reflect the potential tensions in the way these reform elements are combined. Through devolution and contracting out NPM has sought to separate policy-making more clearly from policy administration and implementation. Policy-makers make policy and then delegate its implementation to managers and hold them accountable by contract.

Driving Forces Behind NPM Reforms

A distinction can be drawn between reform ideology and ideas on the one hand and reform practice on the other (Christensen and Lægreid 2001b). The relationship between them may be variously interpreted. First, there may be a clear decoupling between the two, as emphasized in myth theory in general and the theory of 'double-talk' and hypocrisy more specifically (Meyer and Rowan 1977, Brunsson 1989). Second, at the other extreme, if reform ideas are driven by a strong leadership and prove to be compatible with the prevailing administrative culture they may be fully implemented. Third, between these two extremes, we have partial and pragmatic implementation of reform ideas, brought about by mechanisms like 'rational shopping for reform elements', editing or translation of reform ideas, 'short-term failures and long-term successes' (March and Olsen 1983), or a 'virus mechanism' (Røvik 2002).

The institutional dynamics of reforms can best be interpreted as a complex mixture of environmental pressure, polity features and historical-institutional context. These factors define how much leeway political leaders have in making choices about reforms – that is, they may both further and hinder NPM reforms (Christensen and Lægreid 2001a and 2007a). One school of thought points to the fact that different countries have different *constitutional features and political-administrative structures* and contends that these factors go some way to explaining how they handle national problems and reform processes. The constitutional and polity frames relevant here concern first, whether political and administrative leaders are constrained by constitutional factors that limit their ability to implement reforms decisively and swiftly, or whether they have more leeway. The second factor is whether the leadership operates within a homogeneous or heterogeneous political-administrative apparatus. A homogeneous apparatus allows leaders to exercise their hierarchical authority more easily, while a heterogeneous apparatus often engenders turf wars and negotiations among leaders and units (March and Olsen 1983). From a structural or instrumental point of view the reforms may generally be seen as conscious organizational design (Egeberg 2003). This perspective is based on the assumption that political and administrative leaders use the structural design of public entities as an instrument to fulfil public goals (Weaver and Rockman 1993).

According to Dahl and Lindblom (1953) two aspects are important in instrumental decision-making processes – social or political control and rational calculation or the quality of organizational thinking. Major preconditions for instrumental design of NPM reforms are that leaders have a relatively large degree of control over change or reform processes and that they score high on rational calculation or means-end thinking. With respect to constitutional and structural frames, one can say that leaders in political-administrative systems with few constitutional constraints and a homogeneous apparatus will probably be able to exert more control over reform processes and will have fewer problems of rational calculation.

Another view holds that reforms are primarily a product of the *national historical-institutional context*. Different countries have different historical–cultural traditions and their reforms are 'path dependent', meaning that national reforms have unique features. Informal norms and values established in their formative years will influence strongly the paths they follow later on (Krasner 1988). There are two crucial aspects of institutional culture: how strong and influential overall the cultural path is for decision-making and the quality or content of the culture. The reform roads taken reflect the main features of national institutional processes, where institutional 'roots' determine the path followed in a gradual adaptation to internal and external pressure. This view stresses institutional autonomy and internal dynamics.

Thus, the cultural context of reform is important. The cultural features of public organizations develop gradually in institutional processes, giving institutionalized organizations a distinct character or cultural 'soul' (Selznick 1957). How successfully a reform wave like NPM is applied in a public organization has a lot to do with cultural compatibility (Brunsson and Olsen 1993). The greater the consistency between the values underlying the reforms and the values on which the existing administrative system is based, the more likely the reforms are to be implemented. Generally speaking, culturally based adaptation tends to be partial.

The relationship between structure and culture is also of relevance for understanding NPM reform processes. On the one hand, culture can develop gradually in an ever more distinct path and eventually lead to structural adaptive changes. On the other hand, structure may heavily influence the development of the culture, either directly or indirectly (Christensen and Røvik 1999). A third alternative is that the structural and cultural processes may be rather loosely coupled. The potential for controlling NPM reform processes is definitely strongest when either a culture is compatible (reflecting the structure) or else rather weak, while a strong and incompatible culture makes political-administrative control difficult.

A third view regards NPM primarily as a response to *external pressure*. This environmental determinism can be of two kinds: either institutional or technical (Meyer and Rowan 1977). In the first instance a country may adopt internationally based norms and beliefs about how a civil service system should be organized and run simply because these have become the prevailing, ideologically dominant doctrine diffused all over the world. This diffusion process implies isomorphic elements, creating pressure for similar reforms and structural changes in many countries. The institutional environment may exercise one of several types of constraints on the leadership, but may also be rather dominant in certain countries in particular periods. The institutional environment may be either homogeneous or heterogeneous, whereby the latter is the most challenging for both executive control and rational calculation.

The institutional environment generally involves the development of myths and symbols in the macro-environment of public organizations to a considerable degree. In a complicated world, where political-administrative systems, patterns of actors, problems, solutions and effects are complex and difficult to understand, there is a need to have certain 'rules of thumb'. These are supplied by myths and symbols that evolve and spread between countries, sectors and policy areas. They represent a kind of 'taken-for-grantedness' concerning which ideas, organizational structures, procedures and cultures are appropriate. Such myths may be provided by international organizations, like the OECD, the IMF, the World Bank, the WTO and the EU, but also by national organizations working as reform entrepreneurs. They may take the form of broad myths or else they may be narrower institutionalized standards (Røvik 2002). The myth theory stresses that myths imported to public organizations remain superficial, functioning as 'window-dressing', enhancing legitimacy without actually affecting practice (Brunsson 1989). But there are also some more instrumental versions of this theory that talk about the editing and translation of myths.

In the second instance, NPM may be seen as the optimal solution to widespread technical problems – that is, it is adopted to solve problems created by a lack of instrumental performance or by economic competition and market pressure (Self 2000a). In this instance NPM reforms are adopted not because of their ideological hegemony but because of their technical efficiency. Quite often, NPM reforms have been initiated or heavily influenced by the technical environment, because of an economic crisis or changing political or administrative pressure. The technical environment may also be either homogeneous or heterogeneous (Scott and Davies 2006). Overall technically-based pressure on a public organization to reform may be strongest either if it has to reply on one strong actor in the environment or if several actors have demands pointing in different directions.

Summing up, external reform components and programmes are filtered, interpreted and modified by a combination of two nationally based processes. One is a country's political-administrative history, culture, traditions and style of government. The other is national polity features, as expressed in constitutional and structural factors. Within these constraints political and managerial executives have varying leeway to launch NPM reforms via an active administrative policy.

Studies of NPM reform processes around the world reflect many of the theoretical points outlined (Christensen and Lægreid 2001b and 2007a, Pollitt and Bouckaert 2004). Political and administrative leaders are often able to control the processes, even though there is also substantial evidence of negotiations, cultural resistance and pressure from the technical and institutional environment. While political leaders have tended to accept the main norms and values of NPM (which may be regarded as natural since they are the ones responsible for the reform processes), resistance in many countries has come more from the administrative grassroots. Acceptance of NPM among civil servants also varies according to educational background, with jurists most sceptical and business economists most accommodating, while national economists and political scientists are somewhere in between, generally leaning towards the positive side.

NPM processes seem to pose great challenges concerning rational calculation. The complex and turbulent waters of different and changing environments for reform, different cultures and structures, multiple goals, intentions, interests, problems and solutions certainly make organizational thinking problematic. There is a tendency to label many NPM reforms and measures in a similar way, as myths and symbols, even if NPM actually covers a much broader range of reform measures and thinking. The more problematic the rational calculations behind the NPM reforms, the more likely new reform processes are to have symbolic features.

Convergence and Divergence

In terms of the control and organization of public service, NPM represents a global change of paradigm, according to the OECD (OECD 1995). This convergence thesis is, however, contested (Pollitt 2001a). NPM has led to major changes in the public sector in many countries (Pollitt and Bouckaert 2004), yet the process of reform has not been the same everywhere. In some countries there might be a strong element of diffusion of NPM ideas from outside, whereas in others the reform process might be more a result of national or local initiatives that have subsequently acquired an NPM label. Thus, the spread of NPM is a complex process, going through different stages and packaged in different ways in different countries, with each country following its own reform trajectory within a broader framework. In other words, NPM is not an integrated and coherent set of reforms with a specific starting point and following a specific path towards a common destination (Wright 1994).

NPM ideas have been implemented to different degrees, at different paces and with differing emphases in different countries and sectors. A general finding is that the degree of variation between countries and also between policy areas increases when we move away from the world of ideas, talk and policy programmes and look at specific decisions, and even more so when we consider the implementation and impact of the reforms (Pollitt 2001a). One can argue about whether NPM has led to the convergence of administrative systems in different countries, yet there is much to suggest that ideas and policy programmes resemble one another more than the corresponding practices do. One mechanism here is 'double-talk', whereby leaders seek political support by publicly espousing modern principles of government, but in fact experience resistance when they try to implement NPM reform measures. How well broad NPM ideas are received may also vary, depending on cultural compatibility, for example.

In order to better understand the divergence between reform decision-making, implementation and practice, we may combine the insights derived from the three contexts presented – structural, cultural and environmental. An instrumental ideal is for the political-administrative leadership to design systematically the NPM reform system by controlling reform processes, managing organizational thinking well, being able to control potential cultural resistance and utilizing or neutralizing environmental pressure, thus achieving the effects expected from reforms. This combination of factors furthering NPM reforms is more likely to occur in Anglo-Saxon countries where there is 'elective dictatorship, cultural compatibility and often strong environmental pressure for NPM reform' (Christensen and Lægreid 2001b).

At the other extreme, weaker control of processes, cultural incompatibility and low environmental pressure may lead to reforms that are much less NPM-oriented, as has traditionally happened in Continental Europe (Hood 1996a). A wide variety of countries fall between these extremes, however, Asian countries being a case in point. In many cases, for example China, they are eager to imitate some of the main NPM reform measures coming from the West (Christensen, Lisheng and Painter 2008), yet these attempts are often modified by strong traditional cultures that are not compatible with the norms and values of NPM. Another common feature is quite dominant but complex political parties or else a complex coalition of political, administrative and business elites, like in Japan and South Korea, which are not always conducive to reforms.

Whether NPM is a kind of generic reform-wave, or whether it is primarily suitable for particular types of public policy areas is a question that has been debated for some time now. One rather sceptical view is that NPM, with its focus on efficiency, should be used primarily in technically and economically oriented policy areas (Gregory 2003a), while in policy areas like education, health, welfare and environment which are qualitatively different and where it is difficult to quantify and measure goal achievement it is less easy to apply. What is more, certain norms suggest that these so-called 'soft policy areas' should be protected from or not exposed to efficiency reform measures. This view holds that the use and effect of NPM should vary considerably between different policy areas.

The opposite view is that NPM should be applied to all policy areas equally, because public and private organizations are alike and efficiency is equally important in both sectors – in other words, no policy area should be treated in a special way. This view, which advocates considerable convergence in the implementation and use of NPM reform measures, is evident in the efficiency-oriented university reforms that have swept through many countries.

A third way to look at convergence and divergence is to examine the political importance of policy areas. If one assumes that NPM will undermine central political control (Christensen and Lægreid 2001b), political salience may influence the balance between political control and autonomy. The argument then goes that the more important the policy area, the less NPM should be used, because the political leadership will want to have hands-on political control.

Although different countries present their reforms in similar terms and support some of the same general administrative doctrines, closer scrutiny reveals considerable variation. Pollitt and Bouckaert (2004) distinguish between four groups of NPM reformers: the maintainers, the modernizers, the marketizers and the minimal state reformers. Countries like the United Kingdom, Australia and New Zealand fit the marketizer profile; while the Scandinavian countries and even more the Continental Europeans are more sceptical about NPM fitting more into the modernizer profile.

Having begun in Britain, NPM gained strongest hold in the Anglo-American countries. In Westminster-style parliamentarian systems NPM reforms fell on fertile ground and were therefore far-reaching and implemented early (Gregory 2003b). This was due, on the one hand, to strong external economic and institutional pressure and, on the other, to few constitutional and administrative obstacles, a compatible culture and parliamentary conditions that favoured a radical strategy and reform entrepreneurs. By contrast, the Scandinavian countries were reluctant to implement reforms. Environmental pressure was weaker, their *Rechtsstaat* culture and strong egalitarian norms were less compatible with the values of NPM, there were more obvious constitutional obstacles, and parliamentary conditions often characterized by minority coalition governments made a radical reform strategy difficult to pursue (Christensen, Lie and Lægreid 2007).

Thus there is no consistent movement towards a new isomorphic model of civil service systems. Most governments still share some main elements of the traditional system of public administration, but some strong common modernization trends have emerged in public services across groups of countries. One of these trends has been a reduction in the differences between the public and private sectors. Nevertheless, the story is not only one of convergence (meaning that all countries are moving in the same direction); neither, however, is it a story only of divergence (whereby all countries follow their own trajectories constrained by their specific context, legacy and tradition). Instead, what we are seeing is a complex mixture of robustness and flexibility and of reform paths that can hardly be explained by using a single-perspective approach.

Variations in reform practice from one country to another are the rule rather than the exception. Different countries and governments face different contexts, risks and problems and start out with different values and norms. In other words, they have different starting points, are at different stages of reform and face different external and internal constraints (Wright 1994). What we might see is two trajectories (Halligan 2003): one represented by civil services that have been modernized within a state tradition and are therefore rather closed and resistant to external pressure (here the reform process is more hesitant and does not involve major shifts); and the other by civil services that are more vulnerable to external pressure and more open to New Public Management concepts, resulting in more radical reforms.

Effects and Implications of NPM

The main hypothesis of NPM reforms is that increased market orientation and management focus will lead to increased efficiency without having negative side-effects on other goals and concerns. So far this hypothesis has yet to be confirmed as evidence-based fact. While it may be correct under specific conditions, it cannot be said to apply generally to NPM reforms everywhere and at all times. Effects are often assumed or promised, but there are few systematic and reliable studies of whether they actually happen, so hard evidence is often lacking. Attention tends to be more focused on strategies, plans and selective success stories than on systematic analyses of results. Moreover, research has generally tried to find out why reform happens rather than looking at the effects of reform initiatives (Pollitt 2002). We know less about external political learning and societal effects than about internal administrative effects on efficiency (Olsen 1996).

To look at the effects and implications of NPM we need to specify what we mean by effects. Pollitt and Bouckaert (2004) distinguish between operational effects, process effects and system effects. In addition, we may focus on effects on the main goal or on side-effects on other goals; on jeopardy or on bonuses (Pollitt 1995 and 2003a, Hesse, Hood and Peters 2003). The main goal of NPM is related to different aspects of efficiency. One way to measure efficiency gains, for instance – the main goal of NPM – is to look at the major macro-economic performance of a country. However, it is not easy to establish whether improvements in performance are the result of NPM, since there are many other factors that play a role. Nevertheless, few studies have demonstrated a favourable macro-economic effect for NPM.

Another way to look at the effect of NPM on efficiency is to focus on increased service efficiency. Have public services become more efficient as a result of NPM? And if so, is it the reorganization of services or increased competition that has brought this about? The literature disagrees over these questions. Economists often conclude that NPM has increased efficiency, while some political scientists are more sceptical and come up with contradictory findings (Boyne et al. 2003). The latter group also has more of a problem with efficiency studies, pointing to the difficulty of comparing the same services over time, given changes in organization, content, choice and competition.

Putting a greater emphasis on efficiency also raises questions about which factors are included in the equation. Have employees been sacked to make services more efficient, for example, and what are the wider implications of this concerning retraining or possible permanent job losses? Have services increased in efficiency but decreased in quality or created more social inequality (Fountain 2001)? Or has the focus on increased efficiency resulted in a narrower and more economically-oriented view of public policy? Does NPM result in more trust towards the public authorities and hence more legitimacy, or vice versa?

Another question concerns the broader democratic effects of NPM reforms – often seen as side-effects in the NPM literature. One line of inquiry asks whether NPM leads to less emphasis on input democracy and more on output democracy (Peters 2008). The argument here is that people become less focused on participation in the traditional election channel (as evidenced by declining party membership or less participation in elections) and instead try to influence the civil service and the services it provides directly through contact and influence. A counter-argument would be that because executive leaders (whether via political-administrative control or through strong professional competence) still wield more influence over the civil service than users or consumers the election channel is still important. A middle position would be to point to a shifting balance between the channels of influence.

A related question concerns political control, steering and accountability. The bulk of comparative studies of the effects of NPM reforms seem to stress that the control of political executive has decreased as a result of NPM reforms (Christensen and Lægreid 2001b and 2007a, Pollitt and Bouckaert 2004). If this is a fair account, what are the main reasons for this? Is it because of a formal undermining of the leaders' instruments of control? What is the significance of increasing complexity in the structure and culture of political-administrative systems? And what about the increasing turbulence in and pressure from the environment? Is the conclusion that political control has been undermined too sweeping? Do we need to qualify it and find factors that explain variety in control under NPM?

Concerning responsibility or accountability, NPM studies tend to point to a formalization of the relationship between political leaders on the one hand and managers and the administrative grass roots on the other and to an increase in mistrust (Christensen and Lægreid 2001b). This represents a change from a more culturally based relationship, characterized by mutual respect and common values, to a system where subordinates are required to account for themselves and the principal does not have much trust in the agent. These two trends are shown in the greater use of contracts, performance management and incentive systems. If this main trend is significant, what are the effects and implications of it? Will it be more problematic for executive leaders to exert control and implement policies? Will the content of policies change as the influence of administrative leaders and their subordinates grows?

The effects of NPM may not only concern political-administrative relationships or relationships with users, but also the relationship with civil service unions (Roness 2001). Historically most unions have been rather sceptical towards NPM reforms. The strong pressure towards reform has, however, presented them with two equally unattractive options: either they resist reforms completely and try to obstruct them, thus risking losing influence and being seen as old-fashioned and inert. Or else they try to retain their influence by participating in the reform and implementation processes. It is, however, important to analyse what actually happens in practice. Have the unions really been able to influence decisions about NPM reform measures and their implementation and, if so, in what ways? Or have they simply been captured by the reformers?

One conclusion to be drawn is that the design of the various NPM reforms may vary considerably between countries, tasks, sectors and administrative levels and will have consequences for effects studies. The implication is that discussions of the effects of reform must strive for exceedingly precise terminology and must not be conducted at a general level. In sum, it is hard to say unequivocally what the effects of NPM reforms are, and they are often disputed and uncertain. The paradox as stated by Christopher Pollitt and Geert Bouckaert (2004) is that these kinds of reforms do not seem to need results to fuel their onward march.

NPM and Beyond

Currently the central question is whether NPM has peaked, thus requiring us to look beyond, or transcend NPM (Christensen and Lægreid 2007a).

One view is that NPM is still alive and kicking and will continue to be a major force in the near future. The major argument is that NPM has proven successful and has spread all around the world; moreover, it would be difficult to reverse many of the NPM reform measures. A further spread of NPM measures is predicted: either within countries that have chosen to follow the NPM path or from these countries to those that have been more reluctant.

A second view is that there is a new generation of reforms emerging, often labelled post-NPM, but also whole-of-government, joined-up government or New Public Governance (Osborne 2006, Christensen and Lægreid 2007b). This reform wave is seen as either replacing or modifying NPM. The reasons why post-NPM reforms have emerged are complex, but it seems to be at least partly a reaction to a loss of political control, NPM is not delivering on economic measures, and the 'fear factor' – that is, terrorism, pandemics, tsunamis, climate threats and financial recession – has created a greater need for control. There have been strong demands for more central control and capacity and more coordination of sectors, polices and programmes, which is reflected in various features – both structural and cultural – of the new post-NPM reforms.

We will further explore what is typical for post-NPM processes, and what their implementation, effects and implications are. What are the main characteristics of post-NPM and how does it deviate from the NPM measures? What happens when post-NPM meets NPM? Are the reform waves combined in a complex and multi-layered way? What are the consequences of this potential complexity for decision-making?

A main finding in the research in this area is that administrative reforms have not taken place along a single dimension. In practice we face mixed models and increased complexity. It is fair to say that NPM is still very much alive in many countries, and NPM reforms have normally not been replaced by new reforms but rather revised or supplemented by post-NPM reforms. The pace and comprehensiveness of these trends has varied significantly from one country to another and from one policy area to another, and reform activities embrace a wide spectrum. Even though NPM in certain ways has been a success, it is too early to conclude that the old public administration model is unsustainable. It has considerable capacity to adapt and is both robust and flexible, even after a long period of NPM reforms and emerging post-NPM reforms.

Typical for the NPM reforms was that the formal structure changed from an integrated to a fragmented one. The formal levers of steering were weakened, the distance to the agencies grew, political signals became weaker, and horizontal specialization increased according to different principles. The second generation of reforms uses formal structures to regain control or modify the loss of political influence by making them more centralized, complex and varied. Formal structural instruments have been used to modify devolution and vertical specialization, but also horizontal fragmentation and specialization, especially in Australia and New Zealand (Gregory 2003a, Halligan 2007b). Vertical control and levers of control are increasingly being applied, while a 'whole-of-government' approach uses new co-ordination instruments and cross-sector programmes and projects to modify horizontal fragmentation.

PART I
NPM PROCESSES:
DRIVING FORCES

Basic NPM Ideas and their Development

Jonathan Boston[1]

Introduction

As noted elsewhere in this volume, the central features, principles and administrative doctrines of New Public Management (NPM) have been variously defined, categorized and enumerated (Hood 1991, 1995, Osborne and Gaebler 1992, Dunleavy and Hood 1994, Boston et al. 1996, Lane 2000, Barzelay 2001, Pollitt and Bouckaert 2004, Dunleavy et al. 2005). The different categorizations highlight the 'loose and multifaceted' nature of NPM (Christensen and Lægreid 2001a: 19). It comprises neither a unified theory of, nor a random collection of ideas about, public management, but rather embodies a particular kind of administrative argument based upon specific doctrines and related justifications (Barzelay 2001). Furthermore, it has been applied in different ways with variable effects across a range of jurisdictions, and is thus associated with a varied assortment of policy interventions and reform agendas.

NPM's multifaceted nature and diverse manifestations reflect its disparate intellectual origins, together with the varied political, administrative and economic contexts in which it found acceptance. Unlike some reform movements, NPM was more practitioner than theory driven. Nevertheless, the government officials and advisers who helped craft and implement the major NPM reforms of the 1980s and 1990s drew their inspiration from a range of sources, including at least three distinct analytical traditions: the managerialist tradition of administrative theory; 'the new institutional economics' (NIE) or the 'new economics of organizations', with its various tributaries such as agency theory, transaction cost economics (TCE) and comparative institutional analysis; and the public choice (or rational choice) tradition. Additionally, NPM was influenced by a broad ideological movement

---

1   I would like to thank the editors, Derek Gill and Alec Mladenovic for their helpful comments on an earlier version of this chapter.

known as neo-liberalism and the burgeoning field of law and economics, both of which were in the ascendancy during the 1980s and 1990s.

While the main sources of NPM ideas are easy enough to identify, it is harder to determine the nature and magnitude of their influence, whether in specific jurisdictions or more generally. Even more problematic is the task of tracing the intellectual origins of the many distinct policy initiatives associated with NPM. This, of course, does not prevent generalizations being made about how and why the different strands of thinking influenced particular policy initiatives, but such generalizations might not apply to each and every case at the national level. Moreover, NPM was not solely the product of a particular combination of ideas, doctrines and theories; it was also the result of significant political, economic, social and technological forces – as highlighted elsewhere in this volume. In each case where NPM ideas were applied, there were different policy contexts, challenges and constraints – historical, constitutional, institutional, political, fiscal and cultural (see Hood 1991, Aucoin 1995, Pollitt and Bouckaert 2004). Administrative reformers were thus faced with contrasting initial endowments and policy legacies and the ever-present limitations of path dependence. It is unsurprising, therefore, that the application of NPM ideas and the extent of their influence on public policy differed so much (as any comparison, for instance, of NPM in Australasia, North-East Asia, Europe and North America would indicate).

This chapter explores the intellectual origins of NPM and the sources of the main administrative doctrines with which it is associated. Particular attention is given to the key ideas, concepts, behavioural assumptions and values that are central to neo-liberalism, managerialism, public choice theory, agency theory and TCE. Of these, relatively more consideration is given to the latter two theories because they are less well known. While a thorough-going critique of these approaches or the appropriateness of their application in specific contexts is not possible here (see Self 1985, Perrow 1986, Boston et al. 1996), several notable limitations and weaknesses are highlighted.

Neo-liberalism

Policy developments in many democracies during the 1980s and early 1990s were powerfully shaped by the ascendancy of neo-liberalism, including the contributions of its leading exponents, such as Milton Friedman and Friedrich von Hayek. This was particularly evident in Britain and the United States under the Thatcher and Reagan administrations, but also in some smaller jurisdictions like Australia and New Zealand. Aside from nation states, neo-liberal ideas also found favour in major international institutions like the International Monetary Fund, the Organization of Economic Cooperation and Development (OECD) and the World Bank. Informed by the 'Washington Consensus' of the late 1980s (and its injunctions to stabilize, liberalize and privatize), these agencies became influential advocates of neo-liberal prescriptions, including key NPM ideas.

The rise of neo-liberalism can be attributed to a variety of political, economic and social forces, not least the experience of protracted stagflation in many OECD countries during the 1970s and the perceived failure of Keynesian policy levers to ensure low inflation and steady growth. Equally, there were growing concerns that the expansion of social assistance programmes across the developed world following the Second World War had not delivered corresponding gains in social opportunity and mobility. Worse, they were deemed to be causing unsustainable fiscal pressures, undermining work incentives and creating unduly large and inefficient public bureaucracies. Likewise, there was evidence that poorly designed regulatory interventions were reducing economic efficiency and generating compliance costs. To counter these tendencies, neo-liberalism offered a simple panacea: governments must do less, while markets must do more. In short, policy makers needed to exert greater fiscal discipline, reduce the range and scale of government activities, embrace a more targeted system of welfare assistance, broaden the tax base and cut marginal tax rates, encourage greater competition through liberalization and deregulation, eliminate subsidies to commercially-oriented activities, abandon efforts at Keynesian demand management, and reduce regulatory protection for workers. Politically, of course, such solutions were not always easy to implement.

In relation to public sector management, neo-liberal prescriptions from academics and think tanks during the 1980s and 1990s were rarely as well developed as those in other policy fields, but the broad policy contours were clear: state enterprises should be privatized; commercial and non-commercial activities should be separated, with the former subject to normal market disciplines; wherever feasible and appropriate, public agencies should be subject to competitive pressures and responsive to customer preferences; rigorous expenditure controls should be imposed and management freedoms extended; and financial management systems should be improved in the interests of greater transparency and accountability. Plainly, these policy prescriptions contributed to – and indeed provided a strong foundation for – many NPM ideas, including commercialization, corporatization, privatization and expenditure reductions (see Table 2.1). This is not to suggest that neo-liberalism was the sole inspiration. Cost-cutting and a quest for greater efficiency was a feature of public sector management across the OECD during the 1980s and early-to-mid 1990s, irrespective of the ideological orientation of the government. The reason was simple: lower economic growth rates and large fiscal deficits required governments to find expenditure savings, and this inevitably affected the resources available to public agencies. In part, therefore, the efficiency drives associated with NPM were simply a product of the times.

Table 2.1   Origins of NPM assumptions, principles and doctrines

NPM assumptions and principles	Theories that informed NPM
1. A belief that, at least from the standpoint of management, the differences between the public and private sectors are not generally significant; hence, public and private organizations can, and should, be managed on more or less the same basis	Managerialism
2. A shift in emphasis from process accountability to accountability for results (for example, quantifiable output or outcome measures and performance targets)	Managerialism and agency theory
3. A preference for straight-line accountability, with single rather than multiple principals, vertical rather than horizontal accountability, and unitary rather than collective leadership	Managerialism and agency theory
4. An emphasis on management rather than policy, in particular a stress on generic management skills	Managerialism
5. A preference for the devolution of responsibilities and management control coupled with the development of improved reporting, monitoring and accountability mechanisms	Neo-liberalism and some elements of public choice theory; agency theory and TCE influential in relation to the design of contracting and accountability mechanisms
6. A preference for single-purpose organizations over large, multi-purpose (single-roof) organizations; hence a policy of disaggregation including the separation of commercial and non-commercial functions, the separation of policy, regulatory and delivery functions, and the separation of broad, cross-portfolio departments into more narrowly focused departments	Neo-liberalism, managerialism and some elements of public choice theory

NPM assumptions and principles	Theories that informed NPM
7. A preference for independent public bureaucracy (agencies) over classic public bureaucracy (ministerial departments)	Managerialism; agency theory and TCE also influential, but provided grounds for retaining ministerial departments in some cases
8. A preference for private over public ownership, and hence support for privatization and corporatization, and the use of independent rather than public organizations	Neo-liberalism, public choice, agency theory and TCE
9. A preference for classical over relational modes of contracting, and hence a shift from long-term and generally poorly specified contracts to shorter-term and much more tightly specified contracts	Agency theory and TCE, but both approaches also provided grounds to support relational contracts in certain contexts
10. A preference for contracting out over in-house provision	Neo-liberalism and public choice; agency theory and TCE important in providing criteria for guiding decisions in this area
11. A preference for multi-source over single-source supply, including greater competition within the public sector	Neo-liberalism and public choice; agency theory and TCE important in providing criteria for guiding decisions in this area
12. A preference for fixed-term labour contracts over unlimited tenure	Agency theory
13. A preference for monetary incentives over non-monetary incentives, such as ethics, professionalism and status	Managerialism
14. A stress on cost-cutting, efficiency, and discipline in resource use	Neo-liberalism and managerialism

Manageralism

The managerialist tradition can be traced at least to the 1880s and the pioneering work of Frederick Winslow Taylor – the founding father of 'scientific management' (or Taylorism). At least four ideas are central to managerialism. The first is the notion that, to quote Painter (1988: 1), there is 'something called "management" which is a generic, purely instrumental activity, embodying a set of principles that can be applied to the public business, as well as in private business'. This view assumes that organizations, irrespective of their precise legal form, size or purpose, have more similarities than differences. Accordingly, a broadly similar set of management skills, capabilities, methods and procedures are relevant and applicable across all organizations, whether public or private, commercial or non-commercial (Pollitt 1998).

A second important feature of managerialism is the idea that managers can and should be given significant authority and discretion, with decision-making responsibilities and resources being appropriately devolved, albeit in the context of clearly specific outcomes, strong incentives for performance, robust monitoring and unambiguous straight-line hierarchical control. Hence, the familiar slogans: 'Managing for Results', 'Let the Managers Manage' and even 'Make the Managers Manage'.

A heavy reliance on incentives represents a third key element of managerialism. Underpinning this approach is the assumption that individuals respond to rewards and sanctions and that carefully crafted incentive structures can deliver improved performance, both by individuals and organizations. Such incentives might take the form of performance-based remuneration or fixed-term, performance-linked contracts. Whatever the precise form, it is assumed that behaviour is strongly influenced by *financial* incentives; hence, financial inducements are generally favoured over non-financial ones.

Finally, managerialism places much importance on defining and measuring the various tasks that individuals and organizations perform in the interests of efficiency, cost-effectiveness and accountability. This includes close attention to job sizing, work planning and programming, the customization of processes and procedures, and the detailed specification of desired outputs and outcomes.

The influence of managerialist ideas on NPM is strikingly apparent in the contents of David Osborne and Ted Gaebler's widely read *Reinventing Government* – a book which unquestionably shaped public management reforms in many countries during the 1990s, not least the United States. Significantly, they acknowledge the management expert Peter Drucker as the single most influential source of their ideas (Osborne and Gaebler 1992: xi).

Further, of the various administrative doctrines identified by Hood and Jackson (1991a) that are consistent with NPM, a substantial proportion can be attributed, at least partly, to the managerialist tradition. As highlighted in Table 2.1, these doctrines include:

1. a preference for independent public bureaucracy over classic public bureaucracy;
2. a preference for private over public organizations;
3. a preference for single-purpose over multi-purpose organizations;
4. a preference for managerial discretion over tight managerial constraints;
5. a preference for filling management positions with those with generic managerial skills over recruitment based on specific technical skills;
6. a preference for performance-based pay over fixed remuneration systems;
7. a preference for fixed-term labour contracts over unlimited tenure;
8. a preference for control by business methods over control by procedure; and
9. a preference for focusing on results (outputs and/or outcomes) over focusing on good processes (or inputs).

Public Choice Theory

Public choice theory has had a profound impact on the disciplines of economics and political science since the 1960s, and has influenced policy formulation in many jurisdictions across numerous policy domains, including constitutional and institutional design, regulatory policy and public management. Central to public choice theory is the assumption that all human behaviour is dominated by self-interest (Buchanan 1978: 17). This does not mean that individuals lack concern for others, 'but rather that they put their own interests ahead of others when these conflict ... and pursue their goals in the most efficient manner given costly information' (Horn 1995: 7). Nevertheless, the assumption of self-interest conditions how public choice theorists characterize the motivation and goals of individuals and organizations within the political system.

Overall, the public choice literature focuses more on the demand side (for example, the preferences and behaviour of voters and interest groups) than the supply side (for example, the production of government outputs). This is reflected in Dennis Mueller's (1989) seminal analysis of public choice theory, which contains only one chapter on the latter topic. Undoubtedly, the most significant attempt to build a theory or model of the bureaucracy from within the public choice tradition was undertaken by William Niskanen (1971). Drawing on previous contributions by two of the founding fathers of public choice, Anthony Downs and Gordon Tullock, Niskanen examines the possible goals of bureaucrats, such as their salaries, power, patronage and public reputation, the perquisites of office, the outputs of the bureau, the ease of managing the bureau and the ease of making changes. All but the last two of these goals, he argues, are 'positively and monotonically related to size of the budget' (Mueller 1989: 252). Accordingly, Niskanen contends that the primary goal of bureaucrats is to maximize their budgets, since this is the best means of achieving their wider goals. Although empirical support for the budget maximization hypothesis remains limited (Blais and Dion 1991), the proposition significantly influenced how bureaucrats were perceived by certain political elites, especially during the early years of NPM. For instance, Margaret Thatcher apparently urged senior officials in Whitehall to read Niskanen's work, and his analysis strengthened her resolve to ensure that her government was not the victim of bureaucratic manipulation or obstruction: the antics of Sir Humphrey Appleby in the popular television series *Yes Minister* were kept fully in check during her stewardship as prime minister (Aucoin 1995: 33).

But the risk of bureaucrats misusing their positions and 'capturing' a disproportionate share of the nation's resources has not been the dominant focus of public choice theorists. Of more concern has been the risk of politicians favouring narrow partisan objectives and short-term electoral considerations over wider interests and of pressure groups engaging in rent-seeking behaviour at the expense of taxpayers, consumers and citizens. To the extent that such behaviour is inadequately restrained by existing constitutional rules, legislative provisions and institutional arrangements, the likely result will be an excessively large public sector, relatively high taxes, inefficient and inequitable regulation of business activity, and sub-optimal economic performance. In short, there will be government failure and society will be worse off in net terms.

To avoid such outcomes, public choice theorists have supported various countervailing policies (Buchanan and Tullock 1962, Niskanen 1971, Buchanan 1987). These have been designed, amongst other things, to ensure a better alignment between the interests of politicians and taxpayers and between the interests of bureaucrats and those they are employed to serve. Over the years, such proposals have included constitutional rules limiting public expenditure and/or taxation, measures to devolve state responsibilities to sub-national government where they can be better monitored by voters, the privatization of commercial organizations owned by the state, contestability in the provision of public services, policies to enhance governmental transparency and political accountability, and various measures designed to limit budget maximization by bureaucrats (including strengthening the levers through which ministers can exert control over their departments). As will be evident, some of these proposals, with their emphasis on a smaller, more constrained state, are strongly neo-liberal in nature. This is not to suggest that public choice advocates favour a weak state, but rather an effective, efficient and principled one, bound by carefully crafted rules.

Assessing the influence of public choice on NPM is not straightforward. The public choice tradition is broad and diverse, and some NPM doctrines conflict with certain public choice ideas. Nevertheless, it is evident that some NPM policies, at least in jurisdictions such as Britain and New Zealand, drew part of their inspiration from public choice theory, whether directly or indirectly. This included measures to:

1. disaggregate large multi-purpose public organizations into smaller units, including the separation of policy, regulatory and delivery functions – partly in order to minimize the capture of policy advice by service providers;
2. replace unitary purchasing agencies with multiple purchasing/funding bodies, and single-source provision with competitive service delivery units;

3. corporatize and privatize public enterprises;
4. establish more contestable arrangements for the provision of advice to ministers; and
5. enhance fiscal responsibility and the accountability of governments for their medium-to-longer term economic management.

As highlighted in Table 2.1, public choice theory was not the only influence on these and related features of NPM, and its contribution differed across the OECD. Nevertheless, it was undoubtedly important in shaping the broad intellectual climate and administrative landscape in which NPM took root.

Agency Theory

Agency theory has influenced many academic disciplines since the 1970s, including economics, accounting, management, political science and sociology (Eisenhardt 1989). As with most social science theories, it remains contentious and its empirical validity and theoretical significance – including its contribution to organizational theory and public management – is disputed. Briefly, agency theory focuses upon, to quote Eisenhardt (1989: 58):

> the ubiquitous agency relationship, in which one party (the principal) delegates work to another (the agent), who performs that work. Agency theory attempts to describe this relationship using the metaphor of a contract.

The notion of a 'contract' is interpreted broadly by agency theorists: it may refer to a 'classical' contract – that is, a formal, explicit, often comprehensive and legally-binding agreement – or an implicit, obligational or 'relational' contract (Williamson 1985: 72). The latter type of contract tends to be long-term, open-ended and incomplete, like a marriage, with considerable flexibility for both parties. Such contracts typically require considerable cooperation between the parties and a commitment to a long-term or enduring relationship. They thus depend on mutual trust and goodwill rather than legal sanctions.

Initially, agency theory focused on the problems arising from the separation of ownership and control in firms, especially the challenge of ensuring that managers act in the interests of their shareholders. But it was soon acknowledged that similar agency problems – that is, inducing agents to maximize the welfare of principals – arise in most fields of human endeavour. Hence, as Moe (1984: 765) argues:

> ... the whole of politics can be seen as a chain of principal–agent relationships, from citizen to politician to bureaucratic subordinate and on down the hierarchy of government to the lowest-level bureaucrats who actually deliver services directly to citizens. Aside from the ultimate principal and the ultimate

> agent, each actor in the hierarchy occupies a dual role in which he [or she]
> serves both as principal and agent.

Accordingly, the question of how best to construct, monitor and enforce contracts (or agreed relationships) between principals and agents is both extremely common and an issue of enduring significance.

Agency problems arise for various reasons. First, the goals of principals may conflict with those of their agents, thus creating the possibility that agents will not realize the objectives sought by principals. Second, uncertainty can arise over the most efficient way of producing the outputs desired by principals. This can pose problems in designing an appropriate contract. Third, principals often find it difficult and/or costly to monitor the performance of agents and verify whether they have fulfilled the contract. Fourth, principals and agents may have different attitudes to risk, thus preferring different approaches to risk sharing. Typically, agency theory assumes that agents are more risk averse than principals because they have fewer options and resources.

The magnitude of such agency problems will depend on the behavioural assumptions adopted and the context within which such behaviour occurs. Agency theory assumes, like public choice theory, that human beings are rational, self-interested utility maximizers. Obviously, if agents (and principals) are opportunistic, the risks of goal misalignment and breaches of contract will increase. Such problems will be exacerbated if information is incomplete or there are information asymmetries between the parties.

Two concepts arising from information asymmetries have occupied the attention of agency theorists – adverse selection and moral hazard. The former arises in the pre-contract situation where potential agents may have information (for example, about their skills or character) that is not disclosed to, or readily observable by, the principal. This may lead the principal to make an adverse selection. Moral hazard, by contrast, arises after a contract has been negotiated and derives from the fact that not all of the agent's behaviour is observable by the principal. Hence, an agent may perform well in relation to tasks that can be readily monitored but shirk where monitoring is problematic.

Given these assumptions and information asymmetries, agency theory addresses how best to negotiate, specify and monitor contracts so as to minimize violations arising from opportunistic behaviour by agents. Principals have three main 'levers' available: using incentives to align agents' interests with their own; monitoring the behaviour of agents; and negotiating a bonding arrangement whereby agents guarantee to act consistently with the principal's interests or provide compensation if they breach the contract. Of course, each method imposes costs. These, together with the residual losses arising from agents' failure to serve as perfect proxies for the principal, are called 'agency costs'. Designing contracts that minimize such costs is central to agency theory.

Broadly speaking, there are two types of contract available: outcome-oriented contracts (for example, market governance structures, performance-based remuneration and the transfer of property rights) and behaviour-oriented contracts (for example, hierarchical governance arrangements, salaried employment and career structures) (Eisenhardt 1989: 58). Outcome-oriented contracts are preferable where results are relatively easy to specify and monitor, and where contract enforcement is thus straightforward; otherwise, behaviour-oriented contracts may be preferable. Accordingly, agency theory provides helpful guidance on the important issue of contracting out versus in-house provision: other things being equal, contracting out is likely to be the most efficient option when specifying, monitoring and enforcing a contract is relatively easy, while in-house provision will be preferable where these conditions do not apply.

Agency theory undoubtedly helped frame the NPM reform agenda during the 1980s and 1990s (see Table 2.1), but its impact varied greatly across the OECD. In New Zealand it was highly influential within the Treasury (1987), which provided much of the analytical leadership and bureaucratic drive for the NPM reforms (Scott, Bushnell and Sallee 1990, Boston 1995a, Boston et al. 1991, 1996, Scott 2001). In particular, agency theory helped inspire and justify the proposals for corporatization and privatization, including the governance arrangements for the new state-owned enterprises. Likewise, it informed ideas about governance and institutional design within the 'core' public sector, especially regarding the appropriate relationship between the roles of policy advice and service delivery, and contributed to the establishment of (semi-)competing publicly-owned providers in policy domains such as health care and research and development. Agency theory also influenced thinking about human resource management, performance management and financial management (including the distinction between outputs and outcomes and the move to output-based budgeting). It thus informed two crucial pieces of legislation: the State Sector Act (1988) and the Public Finance Act (1989). At a wider constitutional level, it influenced views about the nature of the relationship between ministers and departmental chief executives, and contributed to the proposal for ministers to have 'purchase advisers' in their offices – advising them on what outputs to 'purchase' from their departments and helping them to monitor performance.

Beyond New Zealand, agency theory almost certainly had a less *direct* influence on public management reform. But since New Zealand's NPM reforms were replicated to some degree in many other jurisdictions (Boston 1996a, Schick 1996, 1998), agency theory is likely to have had a significant *indirect* impact. Of course, whether the insights of agency theory were appropriately applied is another matter (Boston et al. 1996).

Transaction Cost Economics

While the principal–agent literature focuses on the contract for labour and the exchange of services, transaction cost economics (TCE) addresses the design of optimal governance structures for various kinds of transactions, including the best way of organizing the production and exchange of goods and services. As Oliver

Williamson (1985: 2), its leading exponent and a Nobel laureate in economics, puts it, TCE entails 'an examination of the comparative costs of planning, adapting, and monitoring task completion under alternative governance structures'. Rational agents, he maintains, will select governance arrangements that minimize their aggregate production and transaction costs. Like agency theory, TCE assumes that human beings are self-interested. But while the two theories have a similar lineage in economics, they differ in several important respects. Whereas TCE focuses on organizational boundaries, agency theory is mainly concerned with contract specification. Likewise, whereas the independent variables central to agency theory are attitudes to risk, outcome uncertainty and information constraints, those at the heart of TCE are asset specificity, frequency of transactions and uncertainty with respect to future contingencies.

An asset – whether labour, capital, land or knowledge – is 'specific' when 'it makes a necessary contribution to the production of a good and has much lower value in alternative uses' (Vining and Weimer 1990: 6). To illustrate, an investment in specialized equipment might result in a supplier having an asset for which there is no readily available alternative use – or at least it cannot be redeployed without a loss to its productive value. Such assets represent 'sunk costs' or, more accurately, a 'sunk investment' (Vining and Weimer 1990: 6). Suppliers of such assets enjoy an advantage over potential competitors, because of the barrier they face to entering the relevant market. Asset specificity obviously varies between markets: where it is largely absent, markets are highly contestable and firms can enter or exit with low costs; by contrast, where asset specificity is pronounced, markets are relatively uncontestable and it is thus inefficient for new suppliers to enter and costly for an existing supplier to exit.

Where the frequency of transactions is low, the notion of small numbers bargaining arises. This refers to a situation where there are few potential buyers or sellers for a particular good or service. Imagine that a new contract is being negotiated for the supply of a particular service. At this stage in the process there may be a reasonable number of willing suppliers. But once the bargain is struck, the chosen supplier may secure certain specific assets, such as a unique location or task-specific skills, thereby giving the supplier a cost advantage over potential competitors. Hence, subsequent competition could be limited to a few potential bidders, enabling the relevant contractors to extract monopoly rents by inflating their prices and/or reducing the quality of their outputs. Williamson describes the situation where large numbers bargaining is transformed to small numbers bargaining because of asset specificity as the 'fundamental transformation'.

From a TCE perspective, while some kinds of activities and transactions lend themselves to market-type arrangements, others are more efficiently undertaken by hierarchical or rule-governed organizations, such as public bureaucracies (Williamson 1975, 1985, Bryson and Smith-Ring 1990). In particular, contracting out is likely to be the best option when the supply of a good or service is relatively contestable and the transaction costs are low (which implies a small number of relatively simple transactions, significant external constraints on opportunism and a low risk of adverse selection). Such conditions apply where the quality and quantity of the desired goods or services are relatively easy to specify and measure, thereby making it simple and cheap to monitor and enforce contracts. Classic examples include cleaning, catering, rubbish collection and laundry services. Against this, in-house provision of goods and services is likely to be the most efficient option when these conditions do not apply. Typical examples include policing, diplomacy, national defence and tax collection.

In-house provision may be preferable in such circumstances because it reduces the need to specify and negotiate in advance all the possible, often complex, contingencies that might arise during a contracting period. The parties can instead rely on 'relational' contracting (that is, informal and more flexible processes that facilitate quick responses to rapidly changing circumstances). Furthermore, direct provision enables the problems associated with uncertainty and opportunism to be managed through the use of hierarchical authority, long-term relationships, policy learning and incremental adaptation. To quote Williamson (1975: 25), 'Internal organization often has attractive properties in that it permits the parties to deal with uncertainty/complexity in an adaptive, sequential fashion without incurring the same types of opportunism hazards that market contracting would pose.'

Of course, while direct provision may reduce the problems associated with opportunism and uncertainty, it does not guarantee good results. Moreover, the large hierarchical organizations that are commonplace in public bureaucracies often face other challenges – coordination issues, organizational slack, mission creep and inadequate internal controls. Compounding this, the performance of government agencies is frequently difficult to specify and monitor, thus creating problems for ministers in controlling their bureaucratic agents.

The impact of TCE on the reforms associated with NPM is more difficult to discern and ascertain than managerialism, public choice and agency theory. Nevertheless, as with agency theory, its influence was certainly evident in New Zealand where Oliver Williamson's ideas were well known amongst the key officials who guided the public management reforms (The Treasury 1987, Scott, Bushnell and Sallee 1990, Scott 2001). More specifically, TCE supplemented the insights of agency theory and provided a helpful framework for considering the comparative merits of different ways of configuring the design of public institutions and the different 'contracting' options available. It highlighted, for instance, the need to consider the nature and magnitude of the transaction costs of securing publicly-funded services through alternative governance arrangements and the importance of giving detailed attention to the issues surrounding contract specification, including the risks associated with asset specificity and small numbers bargaining. In so doing, TCE not merely spurred the drive to redesign existing institutional arrangements in the interests of efficiency and effectiveness, but also provided grounds for justifying, in certain circumstances, both the in-house provision of publicly-funded services and the use of long-term relational contracts rather than classical contracts (Boston 1994).

For instance, when serious consideration was given in New Zealand during the early 1990s to contracting out the policy advisory services provided by government departments to private sector suppliers, TCE provided powerful reasons for maintaining existing advisory mechanisms (Boston 1994). Reliance on short-term contractual arrangements was opposed on the grounds that it would be inefficient and likely to increase, rather than reduce, aggregate public expenditure on policy advice. This is because it would intensify the incentives for policy advisers to act opportunistically, undermine trust between ministers and their advisers, exacerbate horizontal and vertical coordination problems, reduce transaction-specific investments in policy advice, increase agency costs and transaction costs, and heighten the uncertainty and complexity surrounding the policymaking process. A competitive tendering model for purchasing policy advice might also exacerbate opportunistic behaviour by ministers, thus increasing the risk of political corruption. This is not to suggest that the use of hierarchies rather than markets for the provision of policy advice to political executives resolves all the difficulties associated with asset specificity, asymmetrical information, uncertainty and opportunism; but a TCE perspective certainly helps explain why hierarchical arrangements are the favoured option in virtually all democracies.

Regarding NPM, therefore, TCE had three notable impacts. First, it prompted reconsideration of how best to organize and 'purchase' publicly-funded services, and provided a framework to guide this analysis. Second, it inspired efforts to re-engineer existing 'contracting' arrangements in order to enhance the specification and monitoring of contracts. This was not limited to contracts between government agencies and the for-profit and non-profit sectors; it also embraced 'contracting' within the public sector – including relationships between political executives and their bureaucratic agents and the structure of relationships within individual agencies. In this regard, TCE contributed to the development of new types of 'contracts', such as detailed and explicit performance agreements between ministers and their departmental heads and a multiplicity of other contractualist instruments. It thus served to reshape the public service bargain between the political and bureaucratic elites, with agency heads being expected to assume more responsibilities and accept fewer protections in return for modest improvements in remuneration and greater delegated authority. Third, TCE provided grounds for retaining certain policy settings, including the provision of services by government agencies. It thus helped set limits on the scope and scale of contracting out, thereby constraining the more radical tendencies within the NPM reform movement.

Discussion

The preceding analysis has highlighted the key ideological and theoretical underpinnings of NPM as it emerged during the 1980s and evolved during subsequent decades. But the five strands of thinking discussed above were not the only intellectual influence on NPM; nor were they of equal significance; and nor did they exert a similar influence across the many jurisdictions where NPM ideas found expression. Moreover, the fact that the various manifestations of NPM within the developed world differed in crucial ways reflects the wide range of other influences on the evolution of public management during recent decades.

NPM has often been criticized for lacking robust philosophical or theoretical foundations. It is evident, however, that NPM drew inspiration from well-established theories, and that some of its manifestations – most notably the public sector reforms in New Zealand during the mid-to-late 1980s – involved a concerted effort to develop an empirically grounded, theoretically robust and logically coherent approach to public management. The survival thus far of most of these particular reforms – as well as those in many other jurisdictions – suggests that NPM is not as devoid of logical consistency or practical utility as some have claimed. This is not to deny the tensions between the streams of thought that contributed to NPM (Aucoin 1990, 1995, Hood 1990). For instance, whereas managerialism stresses the desirability of public agencies being responsive to their customers and clients, public choice highlights the risks of interest-group capture and rent-seeking behaviour. Nor should it be denied that NPM advocates sometimes used evidence selectively or that NPM reforms produced various unintended side-effects (Hood and Peters 2004). Equally, some of the theoretical traditions that contributed to NPM were not always applied appropriately. As noted earlier, the insights of TCE suggest that there is frequently a strong case for public sector organizations providing services directly rather than contracting out to external suppliers. Yet too often NPM reforms led to risky external contracting and/or the introduction of extremely detailed classical contracts which not only imposed high transaction costs but also limited the scope for innovation and flexibility by suppliers.

Another concern relates to the validity of some of the behavioural assumptions underpinning public choice, agency theory and TCE. To give but one example: agency theory tends to focus on opportunistic behaviour by agents rather than principals, and assumes that principals are competent to choose what it is that they wish their agents to supply. But in a public sector context opportunism by principals can represent a major risk, and principals often need considerable help from their agents to determine what should be done and by whom. In New Zealand, the early NPM reforms assumed (contrary to public choice theory) that ministers were independent, competent and discerning 'purchasers', capable of specifying their desired outcomes and selecting the appropriate outputs to achieve these outcomes, and actively engaged as 'principals' in holding their departmental 'agents' to account. Subsequent experience has cast doubt on such assumptions. Indeed, Simon Upton, the Minister of State Services in the National-led government of the late 1990s, rejected the proposition that ministers 'cheerfully fulfil all of the requirements' of the new administrative order. As he put it:

> The theory ... relies heavily upon Ministers playing their role as principals in a contractual regime comparable to a marketplace. We are expected to be energetic and well-informed purchasers, monitoring output delivery and bringing particular sanctions and pressures to bear as required. The reality is far from a market model. It is characterised more by monopoly supply,

> *compliant demand, arbitrary prices and asymmetry of information. (Upton 1999: 12)*

Although more than a decade has passed since these remarks, the divergence between the theory and reality persists – and seems destined to continue.

How NPM will evolve and what eventually will replace it as the dominant public management paradigm remains unclear. As with NPM, however, any new paradigm is likely to have diverse intellectual origins, be influenced as much by practitioner concerns and experience as by theoretical insights, and exhibit various tensions – whether between the different analytical traditions upon which the paradigm is based and/or between its key theoretical assumptions and the realities of management practice in complex political systems. Such tensions may not be welcome, but they appear inevitable. Moreover, they provide a continuing spur for public management reform and serve to impel the enduring quest for better governance.

The Political-Administrative Design of NPM

Peter Aucoin

Introduction

This chapter examines the political-administrative design of the movement in the Westminster systems that came to called New Public Management (NPM) (Hood 1991). A major driving force behind NPM, if not the major force, was the effort to establish a new structure to the relationship between ministers of the government of the day and the permanent professional public service, especially the senior public service executive cadre (Aucoin 1990). This chapter is focused on the Westminster systems as the locale where NPM first came to the fore.

The chapter first considers the three basic reasons why ministers wanted to change the relationship. First, they did not sufficiently trust the public service to implement their agenda, including the provision of advice that would best advance their agenda. Second, they did not have sufficient confidence in the management capability of the public service, at a time when the fiscal circumstances of all Westminster systems demanded enhanced attention to the economical and efficient management of resources. Third, ministers wanted to ensure that they, and not public servants, were in charge of the government's agenda and its implementation. All this meant that there was a paradox deeply embedded in NPM at its inception. The demand for improved management on the part of the public service required greater authority for managers at the same time that ministers sought to reassert their authority over the direction and control of the state apparatus (Aucoin 1990). The paradox is ignored in much of the literature on NPM, perhaps because the second feature of NPM was not present in other than the Westminster systems, or at least not as prominent as in them, especially Britain and Australia. For this reason it is important to stress that NPM in the Westminster systems was largely imposed on the bureaucracy by the political leadership.

The chapter next considers what this meant in terms of the restructuring of the relationship at the outset of the NPM movement. It examines the ways by which prime ministers and their governments in the Westminster systems sought both to reassert political leadership and control over the public service and to improve public management. These ways included:

1. strengthening the corporate centre of government;
2. strengthening the political arm of government in the form of political staff;
3. controlling the staffing of the senior public service;
4. establishing a more explicit set of mechanisms for distinguishing between policy and administration to put ministers in better control; and
5. requiring public service managers to focus on the management of their resources and operations as well as to accept personal accountability for their performance in delivering to expectations.

Again it is important to note that the first three developments preceded the last two, contrary to much later rhetoric or revisionist history.

By way of conclusion, the chapter briefly considers what has happened in the Westminster systems in terms of the relationship between ministers and the public service over the past three decades. The experience suggests that the relationship has been changed, as originally intended, with ministers securing the upper hand. With some exceptions and variations, centralization of power under the prime minister has been accompanied by more influence for political staff at the centre and in portfolios. The influence and role of the public service has thus been diminished, even though greater authority for the management of resources and operations has been part and parcel of NPM reforms. To the degree that NPM was intended to improve public management, it has done so on a number of fronts. NPM has not necessarily led to improved public governance, however. Rather, the partisan-political dimensions of government have gained an ascendency in ways that have led governments, of various partisan persuasions, to abuse and misuse the public service and public resources well beyond the degree necessary to assert political direction and control for improved public management. A pattern that I call New Political Governance has thus diminished many of the gains that NPM brought about in public management improvement, including even its greater political direction and control (Aucoin 2008).

The Determinants of the New Public Management Design

Distrust in the Public Service

By the 1980s, trust in the career public service by the political class in the Westminster systems had diminished (Boston et al. 1991, 1996, Campbell and Halligan 1992, Savoie 1994, Campbell and Wilson 1995, Aucoin 1995). In Britain, Labour viewed the Whitehall leadership of the public service as conservative and elitist, a not surprising view given the dominance of the Oxbridge educated leadership of the public service. In Australia, Labor was not enamoured of the Canberra mandarins, regarding them as an extension of successive conservative governments. In New Zealand, the responsiveness of the public service to the direction of ministers from either governing party was in doubt. In Canada, both Liberals and Conservatives were wary, even though the Conservatives had much greater reason to be distrustful, given the long tenure in government of the Liberals.

By the end of the 1970s in the Westminster systems (and in the United States), the bloom was also off the rose of the political consensus of the post-war period concerning the virtues of the social welfare state that was accompanied by activist government across a wide range of socio-economic affairs and, with that expansion, an expanding bureaucracy. The ideal of rationality in government policy-making and administration, so pronounced in the ascendency of the 'policy sciences' paradigm, applied to governance that emerged in the 1960s and gave way to traditional ideological divisions between the left and the right.

The left and the right had different reasons for distrusting the permanent bureaucracy. The left thought the mandarins too conservative in respecting the status quo, a status quo that even in its expansion was in a great many respects a design of their own creation. They were thus perceived as an obstacle to progressive reform. The right thought them too committed to an activist rather than the minimalist state. But both the left and the right were increasingly pressured to roll back the state in terms of taxing, spending and economic regulation. In Britain, this agenda was labelled as neo-conservative; in Australia and New Zealand, the Labor governments that brought forward fiscal and regulatory reforms viewed it as neo-liberal. To the degree that the short-lived post-war consensus on the social welfare state had collapsed and partisan ideologies returned to the fore, the influence of the bureaucracy that emanated from assumptions about its capacity to provide impartial and objective (what we now call evidence-based) policy advice was downgraded accordingly.

Trust was also adversely affected by the negative view that the professional public service was merely another collection of self-serving interests that used their power and influence to advance these interests rather than the public interest, as defined by their political masters, let alone the interests of their political masters. The British Broadcasting Corporation's *Yes, Minister* television sitcom series, first shown in 1980, not only brilliantly captured the spirit of this view, but, given the sitcom's enormous popularity in all four Westminster systems, it served to propagate it as a novel kind of public affairs documentary (Borins 1988).

The idea that the self-interests of the bureaucrats individually and collectively took precedence over the interests of ministers as the political executive became a part of conventional wisdom on the part of the political class, notwithstanding the fact that the scripts of *Yes, Minister*, and the propositions of public choice theory about this self-serving behaviour from which *Yes, Minister* drew its thematic inspiration, took direct aim at politicians as well as at bureaucrats. Politicians are depicted in both the series and the theory as self-serving *vis-à-vis* their political masters, namely, the citizens whose interests they are meant to represent. Public choice theory seeks to undermine the moral legitimacy of politicians and public servants, treating both as agents who need to be constrained as much as possible because they cannot be trusted by their principals: citizens for politicians and ministers for public servants (Boston 1996b).

As it turned out, the public service suffered the most from this assault, at least in terms of the relationship between ministers and public servants. The reason was simple, given the constitutional design of the relationship, with ministers the superiors of public servants. Bureaucracy-bashing by politicians, both during election campaigns and in government (increasingly the permanent election campaign) could not be countered publicly by public servants, given the prevailing public service norms of anonymity and neutrality. For public servants to speak against politicians, elected or campaigning, would be to risk being seen to be acting contrary to these norms.

For their part, ministers were not wont to defend their public service, if for no other reason than that bureaucracy-bashing was deemed an effective political tactic. It allowed politicians, even when in government, to divert public criticism of themselves and of government more generally to unnamed bureaucrats. It took little in the way of serious thinking to scapegoat the bureaucracy for the high levels of public angst then experienced virtually everywhere in the Anglo-American systems over the deadly combination of debt and deficits in public finances and public services of dubious quality. Although ministers, along with other politicians, were themselves singled out by critics of big government for living off their access to the public purse, the public service bureaucracy was an equally easy, perhaps even easier, target, especially as the public perception of bloated bureaucracies and overly privileged bureaucrats became widespread. To the extent that ministers began to believe their own bureaucracy-bashing rhetoric their trust in the bureaucracy could not but diminish to new lows.

Lack of Confidence in the Public Service

To make matters worse for the relationship, public service bureaucracy became increasingly compared to private sector management in terms of management capacity and performance, with the comparison painting a thoroughly dismal picture of management in the public sector set against an excessively glowing account of management in the private sector. Just two years after *Yes, Minister* appeared on the scene, *In Search of Excellence* was published (Peters and Waterman 1982). This hugely successful and influential book helped transform the business of management consulting, with an enormous consequence for public administration.

The business of management consultancy grew by leaps and bounds during the 1980s and 1990s as traditional or conventional management thinking and practices were trashed and new theories and techniques heralded (Saint-Martin 2000). A new breed of management gurus (or 'witch doctors' as two editors from *The Economist* labelled them (Micklethwait and Wooldridge 1996)) not only advised as consultants, they began to write best-selling books for what appeared to be an expanding coterie of managers, many of whom were armed with an MBA and fervent disciples of their favourite guru. These same books also marketed consultants' wares to the private and public sectors.

In a booming marketplace brimming with constantly changing fads and fashions in management, the practices of management in public administration and public services delivery could not but look deficient and they were widely denounced for being so. Bureaucracy became a label associated almost entirely with the public sector. The term came to have an exclusively pejorative connotation (Barzeley 1992). In this milieu, ministers came to have little confidence in the managerial capacities of the senior public service. It became a common assumption that, whatever their strengths might be, the capacity of senior public servants to manage large and complex organizations and their public service operations in order to achieve economy, efficiency and effectiveness was not among them. The senior bureaucracy was regarded as amateurish by comparison to their private sector counterparts (Pollitt 1990). This was especially the case in Britain where the educational backgrounds of the senior public service were not thought to have sufficiently prepared them in the modern social sciences, let alone in the modern management disciplines.

Political Control of Administration in Question

A paradox in the development of NPM was the fact that the very same ministers who doubted the management capacity of the public service also tended to think that these public servants were too powerful in the administration of public affairs (Aucoin 1990). This was a second defining thesis in *Yes, Minister*, namely that the minister's senior bureaucrat was all too often, even if not always, successful in having his political master come to agree with him and thus with the preferences of the bureaucracy. In this sense, it was increasingly acknowledged that ministers were not able to adequately direct and control their public servants or to hold them to account. Ministers were constitutionally and politically in charge, that is, responsible for the administration of their departments and the public services they delivered, but they were not in control. Real power to effect what they wanted done invariably eluded them.

A variant of this concern was that even if public service bureaucracies could not have their public policy preferences accepted by ministers, they could and would act as obstacles to ministers being able to have their preferences implemented as they intended. Bureaucrats were thought to be able to obstruct policy implementation in many ways, including causing delays in required administrative decisions, devising subtle shifts in implementation processes that result in a displacement of stated policy goals, and paying inadequate attention to securing the necessary linkages between different elements of interdependent operations.

One reason for this concern was the result of the increasing need for *de facto*, if not *de jure*, delegation of authority to a wide variety of managers and professionals, including so-called street-level bureaucrats who cannot perform their functions at all without the exercise of some discretion. To the degree that this discretion is exercised in ways that make observation by superiors, including political superiors, difficult, if not impossible, there exists room for bureaucrats to make decisions that depart from ministerial policy. Exacerbating this inherent bureaucratic reality was the major expansion to the role of the state in the post-war period and thus the number of state officials who must be allowed to exercise such discretion. In brief, size matters in terms of securing effective control over decentralized power.

Restructuring the Political-Administrative Relationship

Concentrating Power

The Westminster system of parliamentary government gives primacy to the prime minister and cabinet. This is a form of strong executive government with fewer and weaker checks and balances on the part of the legislative branch of government than found in the classic regime of checks and balances with shared executive and legislative powers between the two political branches of government – the American system. But just as the strength of the political executive grew with the growth of modern government, the very centre of government – the prime minister and her/his coterie – has witnessed a concentration of power that has pushed even cabinet and thus most ministers to the sidelines (Savoie 1999). Donald Savoie has described this phenomenon as 'court government' and while his focus has been primarily on the Canadian experience of the past four decades, he has reached the same conclusion for Britain, especially with the Blair and Brown regimes (Savoie 2008). Australia under John Howard, particularly in his latter years, evinced the same pattern (Halligan 2006). New Zealand was once very much in this mould, but the consequence of coalition government, following the dramatic change to the mixed-member proportional representation electoral system, reinvigorated cabinet government.

What has come to fruition in terms of a concentration of power at the centre by the end of the first decade of the present century was already beginning to occur by the end of the 1970s. Prime ministers began to gain ascendency over their cabinets as they sought to reassert political leverage over the bureaucracy. In Canada, this resulted, ironically, from a continuous effort to establish effective collective decision-making structures so that ministers would not be captured by their departmental bureaucrats. This form of capture was regarded as the principal way by which bureaucrats assumed power and influence in the executive branch of government. By acting collectively with their cabinet colleagues in cabinet, and especially in cabinet committees, ministers were expected to be able to reduce the influence of departmental officials over them individually. These collective structures were to help weaker ministers especially. And they were supported by what in Canada are called central agencies, that is, the agencies that perform the corporate (or whole-of-government) policy and management challenge and coordination functions on behalf of and under the direction of the prime minister and the handful of other corporate ministers. These were enhanced to constitute an effective bureaucratic countervail to departmental bureaucrats (Campbell and Szablowski 1979).

This strengthening the centre of government by building the collective structures of cabinet and its central agencies in order to reinforce the primacy of ministers was paralleled in the modern private corporation by various matrix type structures. In both sectors, however, these gave way as chief executives soon grew weary and wary of the complexity, confusion and cost of these excessively complicated structures. In the Westminster systems, increased prime ministerial aggrandizement was the outcome. The collective decision-making capacity of cabinet withered accordingly, and even almost disappeared at times in some governments, and the central agencies that supported the collective cabinet increasingly became the agencies of the prime minister as first minister or chief executive (a similar trend occurred in the private sector under a much more positive spin from the management gurus; here, aggrandizement was characterized as leadership).

This concentration of power did not necessarily rule out bureaucratic influence altogether, for the central bureaucratic agencies were, of course, at the centre. Yet insofar as it meant that bureaucrats from these agencies had to work alongside the partisan-political staff of the prime minister, they were now no longer working alone in providing policy advice; at the centre, and even in departments, they no longer enjoyed a monopoly over this function. At the same time, trusted bureaucrats at the centre became arguably even more powerful than their predecessors, especially, as discussed below, if the prime minister had been personally engaged in their appointments and if the prime minister's political staff shared the prime minister's trust in these senior public servants. They had to be, in Prime Minister Margaret Thatcher's words, 'one of us'. In Savoie's model, they had to become courtiers (2008).

Deploying Political Staff

An even more explicit instrument to change the relationship was the expansion in the number, roles and influence of political staff (ministerial partisan advisers). These staff are not public servants. They are not members of the public service bureaucracy. They are a category of government official on their own. They are appointed at the discretion and pleasure of ministers and thus have no tenure beyond that of their political masters. In the Westminster systems their number varies, but numbers are not necessarily correlated with either roles or influence. In part, political staff are also affected by the concentration of power, that is, the influence of staff is determined primarily by the influence of their ministers. Where power is highly concentrated, as it is in Australia, Britain and Canada, the prime minister's political staff are that much more important and they can be much fewer in number, assuming that the prime minister's court is an elite group.

Political staff constitute another countervail to the influence of public servants. They provide ministers with a partisan-political perspective on public policy matters and this perspective can also serve as a challenge function to the advice of public servants. Political staff is intimately involved in the political communications function and this means that they continuously rub up against, if not covertly run, the public service communications of ministers' departments and the government's corporate communications. They also are central players in the interaction with important stakeholders whose interests are politically salient to ministers.

Political staff in both Australia and Canada had their numbers, roles and influence expanded in the 1980s as a consciously adopted alternative to the overt partisan-politicization of public service staffing in the American fashion. As a result, political staff remain in staff, as opposed to line, positions in the government bureaucracy. Accordingly, while they may have the ear of ministers, they do not have formal authority over the minister's departmental public service. As such, they cannot direct public servants. But they can speak for their minister to public servants, albeit with the proviso, in theory, that public servants have the right to seek confirmation from the minister for any directive. Under the Blair government, exceptions to this prohibition against line authority were made in the area of the government's communication function, exceptions later removed following politically adverse reactions to what was perceived as an excessive overload of political spin in government communications. In practice, of course, the reality does not always conform to formal structure.

Aside from constituting a general nuisance factor for professional public servants, especially on the part of the most junior and inexperienced of these political staff (who, given the nature of their assignments, tend to be very young and to burn out quickly), political staff necessarily add a tension to the relationship of ministers and their public service officials. This is not always negative in its outcome. Political staff can assist in this very relationship by relieving public servants from ministerial demands or expectations of assistance in what are patently partisan-political activities.

The outcome is negative on the other hand to the extent that political staff seek to engage public servants in activities or decisions that are inspired primarily, if not exclusively, by partisan-political interests. Leaving aside anything that is illegal, these activities or decisions are sometimes contrary to administrative regulations, sometimes merely contrary to the values of non-partisanship. What is inappropriate is often a matter of interpretation. To the degree that the grey zone is made to cover a significant range of activities and decisions, political staff have lots of room to intervene in public administration on behalf of ministers. Insofar as NPM witnessed a major deregulation of administrative regulations, in favour of decentralized discretion, the room for intervention without challenge expanded, and is not much constrained by an increased rhetorical attention to public service values.

Staffing of the Public Service Leadership

The independent staffing of the public service has long been a central feature of the Westminster jurisdictions, even if not judged to be inherent in the Westminster constitutional regime itself (Aucoin 2006a). Indeed, failure to observe the dictates of non-partisan, neutral staffing of the public service has a long and continuing history in many, if not most, Australian state and Canadian provincial governments, notwithstanding the formal adoption of merit systems of independent staffing by these constituent orders of sub-national government in these two federal systems many decades ago. In many cases, partisans were appointed to public services posts, some at the most senior ranks, with partisanship being the primary, in some cases the only, reason for their appointment.

A critical factor in the staffing of the public services in each of the central governments in the Westminster jurisdictions has been the exclusion of the most senior posts in the public service from independent staffing, with prime ministers and/or cabinet formally making these appointments. There are differences in both the traditions and the current realities of the different jurisdictions. In every case, nonetheless, there has been increased interest and attention given to appointments to these top public service posts (deputy ministers in Canada, permanent secretaries in Britain, departmental secretaries in Australia, departmental chief executives in New Zealand). As expected, ministers by the late 1970s were no longer content to be on the sidelines, formally or informally, as the most senior positions in the public service were staffed. Even if they agreed that those appointed should come from the ranks of the public service, or from professional public service posts in other jurisdictions, rather than from the ranks of fellow partisans, ministers, and especially prime ministers, wanted them to be fully onside with the government's agenda and/or its approach to public management. Only in New Zealand, and somewhat unintentionally, did the NPM reform effort end up with a staffing process that effectively kept ministers at arm's length. Everywhere else, prime ministers and their political staff gave greater attention to these appointments.

Since then there has been something of a running debate about whether there has been a politicization of the public service as a consequence of this greater political attention to staffing, whether there has been introduced a new type of politicization that is different from traditional understandings of explicitly partisan appointments to the public service, and what the consequences of increased political attention to staffing has meant if the charge of politicization does not hold (Peters and Pierre 2004). These issues cannot be resolved here, but it can be said that since prime ministers and their political staff, advised at times by ministers and their political staff, not only have the decisive say in appointments but that they actually spend time in considering whom to appoint, then it is unrealistic to assume that considerations of expressed sympathy and enthusiasm for the government's agenda and/or management approach, or lack of the same, are ignored. This is especially the case when there are not competitions, open or closed, for such appointments.

The adoption of a more active role on the part of prime ministers in staffing these top appointments was indicative of the aim to change the relationship. These top officials would be the prime minister's public service executives, not officials chosen essentially by the public service leadership itself. Whether or not they were partisans, they would be the prime minister's personal appointees. The prime minister becomes their boss, not simply their political master. Appointment at pleasure, as in Canada, or for term, as in Australia, helps transform an institutional relationship into more of a personal one, a development promoted by the idea that a leader should impose her or his personal leadership paradigm on the organization, to make the senior executive cadre her or his team.

Revising the Policy and Administration Dichotomy

The traditional view of the policy and administration dichotomy was that it did not portray reality, for there is policy in administration and administrative issues can become matters of policy. (Framing the dichotomy as politics and administration does not change the basic dynamic here.) What was at issue in the traditional approach to the dichotomy was whether the attempt to separate the two spheres put ministers at a disadvantage in that it often was successfully used to keep ministers out of administration, except in the making of formal rules as policy governing administrative practices.

The practice varied in the Westminster systems in the post-war period, but by the 1970s ministers in all jurisdictions had begun to reassert their authority as everywhere there was greater appreciation of the extent to which the public service had the capacity to subsume policy under administration. The growth of the state and its bureaucracy was a primary reason, as ministers of the largest and most complex bureaucracies increasingly realized, as public administration scholars had argued for some time, the extent to which the assumption that ministers made policy and public servants administered the policy no longer captured reality. If ministers wanted to direct policy and control administration something else was required.

The something else came in the form of contracts, or contractual-type agreements, between ministers and their chief public service executives. The logic here was straightforward: the ministers specify what they want achieved by way of public services outputs or deliverables as they would in any situation where they contracted with a third party to provide services in place of their department. The assumption here was that contracts between ministers and their chief executives, even when there are no meaningful negotiations, could still elevate the extent to which what is expected of a minister's department, in the form of an expectation assigned to the department's top public servant, would be subject to greater specificity than traditionally was the experience.

NPM thus introduced a new twist to the policy–administration dichotomy. It explicitly exchanged the minister's right to intervene in administration with the requirement that their public service executives administer according to a contract that specified precisely not only what was expected in terms of products but also what level of productivity was expected, given that the resources provided to these executives were specified in the minister's departmental budget.

Enhancing Management Authority and Accountability

As noted, NPM is regarded by many scholars and practitioners as essentially about the delegation, devolution or decentralization of management authority so that managers can actually manage their organizations and their resources, financial and human. This makes public management conform to the paradigm of modern management (meaning management in its generic form, although this almost always means private sector management). This understanding of management goes beyond the traditional notion of the public administration of policies, programmes and activities, insofar as it assumes that managers have discretion in managing resources and operations rather than merely obligations to see that corporately imposed processes and procedures are followed. It also assumes that an enhanced emphasis is given to the accountability of managers, as the incentive (using rewards and sanctions) to secure required levels of management performance (Aucoin and Heintzman 2000, Aucoin and Jarvis 2005).

NPM focused on three aspects of management and accountability. First, there was the devolution of authority from central management agencies to executives of line departments or agencies in order that managers have greater and sufficient authority to manage their operations. Second, there was the differentiation of discrete operational/service delivery organizations from one another in multi-service departments and from departmental policy units (the so-called 'agencification' phenomenon when applied to the British and New Zealand experiences (Pollitt et al. 2004), with more modest versions in Australia and Canada) so that the missions and outputs for which managers are accountable can be (more) clearly identified (Christensen and Lægreid 2006). And, third, there was performance management with transparent measures and evaluations of performance that made it more difficult for managers to hide behind their ministers (Bouckaert and Halligan 2008).

NPM was new insofar as this approach departed from the tradition of strong central management agencies that had developed over time to govern management in government departments and agencies, primarily by way of centrally imposed rules and regulations that applied uniformly across all departments of government. This highly regulatory model for the governance of line management in departments imposed a regime of standardized administration on both departmental ministers and their public servants that provided little or no discretion for line department managers and little or no acknowledgement of the great diversity of operational circumstances faced by the managers of different departments (Pollitt 1990, Aucoin 1995).

One cannot overemphasize the extent to which these central management agencies were dominant in the Westminster systems (but not in all other Western democracies) in the pre-NPM era, and in the sphere of public service personnel administration, especially staffing, virtually independent of ministers. The NPM revolution here was substantial, even though, contrary to some rhetoric, not all centrally imposed rules disappeared. Under NPM the major shift was from bureaucrats in central management agencies to line department managers, especially the administrative heads of departments and agencies. Departmental ministers did not obtain more authority over departmental management as a consequence but they could now demand more of their departmental managers in terms of management performance.

Organizational differentiation (or agencification where it occurred) gave managers a cleaner line on what had to be accomplished, at least to the extent that the organizational context could be characterized by stability in policy objectives, output targets and various performance measures. Greater organizational differentiation, it was assumed, meant that ministers could have greater confidence that their objectives would not be bent by the bureaucratic pathologies extant in all large integrated departments that in most cases are little more than conglomerate organizations with multiple overlapping, and invariably competing, objectives.

Governments everywhere had become big government by taking on an increasing number of roles in an expanding number of policy fields. Given the limits to which the number of cabinet portfolios could be expanded in the Westminster systems, the conglomerate character of ministerial departments had become ever more pronounced by the end of the 1970s. Conglomerate departments were a problem for ministers not only because of their complexity; that could not be avoided under big government and conglomerate departments. In addition, however, there was the exacerbated problem of the traditional departmental hierarchy under which the various major divisions of the department report to the minister through the department's top bureaucrat and not directly to the minister. In this circumstance, ministers could be forgiven for regarding themselves as formally on top but not in effective control. Organizational differentiation expanded a minister's span of control by having departmental agencies report directly to them.

Finally, the performance management regimes introduced with NPM, in combination with the above two developments, sought to position ministers so that they could use performance evaluation as the means to better secure the implementation of their policy objectives. As noted, ministers introduced contractual-type relationships to better specify what they wanted. Performance management was the back end of this arrangement: ministers assess how managers perform and act accordingly, with rewards, such performance bonuses, or sanctions, such as dismissal or refusal to renew appointments.

Conclusion: Politics Trumps Management

Over the past three decades the political side of the political-administrative design of NPM has come to dominate the relationship, even though managers now have greater freedom from central bureaucratic controls. In some critical respects, this is what political leaders and their public management reformers wished to achieve. They wanted ministers to be on top and in charge of the public service to set strategic directions and targets for public service organizations and managers; to measure both organizational and managerial performance; and, then to adjust courses and take corrective action as they deemed necessary. This approach, it was said, would enhance both democratic government and good public management.

In a number of ways the political pressures on the bureaucracy have had their desired effects. Although the evidence is mixed and any evaluation of reform generally is fraught with insurmountable methodological obstacles, various aspects of public management, including service delivery, appeared to have improved in the Westminster jurisdictions over time. The record has certainly not been one of continuous learning and progress anywhere and various correctives have had to be inserted over time. But everywhere a great deal has been achieved in addressing the impoverished management state of affairs that had developed by the late 1970s. Thirty years later there is more attention to efficiency in operations, robust financial management, citizen-centred service delivery, people management and results. The record is nowhere as great as the rhetoric, if only because rhetoric has become a tool of public service leadership, and one can easily find slippage where there once had been progress. At the same time, precious few, if any, advocate a return to past practices across the board, even among those whose experience or knowledge goes back to the past (Pollitt and Bouckaert 2004). This fact undoubtedly constitutes the strongest evidence for at least some advance.

In various other respects, however, the relationship between political leaders and their public services has not improved (Savoie 2003). If anything, it has deteriorated further. Ministers continue to distrust their bureaucracies and do not exhibit much confidence in them in matters related to public policy advice or the management of the politics of public administration. The result has been the strengthening of the political arm of government to assist ministers in directing and controlling public administration. In the process, the politicizing of public administration has actually grown in various ways. The original political impulse of NPM that sought to alter the political-administrative balance in public management as a corrective to what had become a bureaucratic state unresponsive to political direction and control has given way to a new phenomenon, what I have called New Political Governance (Aucoin 2008).

New Political Governance arises as a response to developments that emerged or intensified during the last three decades that have little or nothing to do with the pressures that gave rise to NPM. They include the radical transformation in the media and communications technologies that expose ministers and government around the clock to a more aggressive, assertive and, in most places, more partisan press; the proliferation of organized interest groups, social movements, partisan thinks tanks and advocacy institutions; the huge increase in the number of lobbyists for the most affluent interests; and, not the least, radical changes in the political culture of Western political societies, including a significant decline in deference to authority, a rise in know-nothing populism, a polarization of partisans combined with a decline in partisan affiliation producing high degrees of political volatility.

These forces are much more pressing that the forces that led to the demands for greater political direction and control under NPM. The New Political Governance resulting from them has included the primacy of political staff in advising their ministers on policy, often to the exclusion of any real effort to engage public service advisers and resulting in the diminution of the policy advisory capacity of the bureaucracy; the ability of political staff to dictate to public servants on critical political files in the name of ministers, more often than not that of the prime minister, whatever the formalities of the public service system; and, the politicization of government communications and advertising so that the partisan interests of the governing party override any public service requirements of impartiality, political neutrality and non-partisanship in these matters. Where these developments are most pronounced, the ministerial political staff of the governing party have replaced public servants, assumed power over them, and used them and other public resources to engage in a continuous election campaign against their partisan opponents in the parliamentary opposition. Relations between ministers and public servants are obviously altered by these developments, but none of them advance good democratic government or public management.

The Relevance of Culture
for NPM

Koen Verhoest

Culture and Administrative Reforms as Mutually Influencing Variables?

The extent to which governments are receptive to internationally propagated NPM doctrines, and the extent to which these ideas are actually translated into decisions and actions, is influenced and moulded by the 'implementation habitats' in which reforms are initiated and implemented. One crucial variable of these implementation habitats consists of the cultural values held at the societal level and within the politico-administrative system (Christensen and Lægreid 2001a, Pollitt and Bouckaert 2004). As Bouckaert (2007) states, NPM reforms are not culture-neutral. Studies of OECD countries revealed considerable differences in the way they implemented similar public management reform ideas, which can be explained partly by their different societal cultures and administrative traditions (for example Pollitt and Bouckaert 2004). Moreover, even within countries, similar reform efforts, like the government-wide introduction of specific management tools, are adopted to different extents by public sector organizations (see for example Christensen et al. 2007) because of different organizational cultures. Once institutionalized, the organizational culture acts as a 'filter' and influences in a positive or negative way the receptiveness of organizations to managerial reform ideas and initiatives. Bouckaert (2007: 32) states 'Cultural homogeneity is the strength of NPM but also its weakness.'

This chapter discusses the relevance of culture for NPM reforms. More specifically, it elaborates on how the societal and organizational cultures define the context for NPM reforms and how culture influences the extent to which administrative reform ideas are taken up in public management practices (Schedler and Proeller 2007). While the first part of the chapter clarifies the concept of culture, its layers and main typologies, the second tries to substantiate the mediating influence of societal and organizational culture on the receptiveness of countries and public organizations for NPM-like reform recipes and on the degree of radicalness of reforms. To that purpose, the chapter studies the adoption of several elements of NPM reforms across countries with different societal cultures and, to a lesser extent, across organizations with different cultural profiles. After presenting some empirical data and studies, the chapter goes on to explain theoretically why and how societal and organizational culture affects NPM reforms, by referring to some relevant theories.

Culture as a Concept – Layers and Typologies of Culture

As Jann (2000) states, the popularity of culture as a concept is inversely linked to its precision and unambiguousness. Analysing the different meanings of culture in seven different theoretical strands, Schedler and Proeller (2007: 8–19) show that basically, most definitions share the notion that culture consists of shared values, norms, appropriate behaviour and routines, rules and cognitive scripts, and symbols in a specific social group. A widely-referred conceptualization is that presented by Kluckhohn (1951: 86): 'Culture consists in patterned ways of thinking, feeling and reacting, acquired and transmitted mainly by symbols, constituting the distinctive achievement of human groups, including their embodiments in artefacts; the essential core of culture consists of traditions (i.e. historically derived and selected) ideas and especially their attached values.' Hofstede treats culture as the *collective* programming of the mind, distinctive for one group of people, consisting of rituals, heroes, symbols and, most centrally, *values* (Hofstede 2001: 10).

There are different levels of such mental programming, being universal, collective and individual (Hofstede 2001). Culture refers to an attribute or the characteristics of groups, and scholars have distinguished between two (for example Schedler and Proeller 2007), three (for example Peters 2001a) or more interconnected layers of culture (for example Bouckaert 2007). Peters (2001a: 35–36, see also Koci 2007: 254–256) sees public administration and its position in society as being influenced by three partially interconnected spheres of culture: societal culture, as general value orientations on management and impersonal authority; political culture, as a set of complex cognitive and evaluative structures, generally shared among citizens, about what constitutes good government and proper administration; and administrative culture, as the opinions, presumptions, values and attitudes to which public servants subscribe and which they are expected to follow. Individual public sector organizations can then develop their own distinctive organizational culture within these broader layers of culture. Bovaird (2007) refers also to sectoral and occupational cultures, besides national and organizational cultures in order to explain reforms in UK public sector organizations. The different layers are indeed interconnected, but they can diverge quite substantially from each other. For instance, organizational cultures can develop away from societal cultural patterns, because of sectoral or other influences. Dastmalchian, Lee and Ng (2000) show in a study of similar companies in different countries that the different dimensions of organizational culture are either unrelated, or at best weakly related, to national cultures. The industrial sector to which the companies belong explains better the differences in organizational culture than their national culture.

Several typologies or analytical frameworks have been developed to capture cultural differences at the societal level, and some are particularly interesting from a public management point of view. Most popular typologies or analytical frameworks score high on parsimony and comprehensibility. For instance, Peters (2001a) classifies societal cultures in respect to their relevance for public administration along two dimensions. The first dimension is the acceptability of bureaucracy as a means of large-scale organization in the society, distinguishing societies as being bureaucratic (for example Germany), or entrepreneurial (UK), besides some other types (see Bendix 1956). The acceptance of impersonality and universality of rules makes up the second dimension, leading to a low–high continuum of a barter culture (developing countries), over a pragmatic, inductive culture (UK) to a rationalist or deductive culture (France). Referring respectively to two distinct legal traditions (the Continental system of civil law and the common law system), two basic models of administrative culture are popular in public management literature (Kickert and Hakvoort 2000, Lalenis et al. 2002: 36): the *Rechtsstaat* model, where administrative actions are heavily regulated by a comprehensive body of administrative law, and the public interest model, in which a more pragmatic attitude towards administrative action and individual entrepreneurship within public administration is valued. By now, most scholars would accept that the entrepreneurial, pragmatic cultures and the administrative tradition oriented towards the public interest model present in Anglo-Saxon countries help to explain the speed and radicalness of NPM reform in these countries, in contrast to Latin European and Continental European countries, where *Rechtsstaat* tradition and bureaucratic cultures prevail (Peters 2001a, Pollitt and Bouckaert 2004).

These basic typologies are very appealing and popular because of their simplicity and instinctive connotations with administrative behaviour. But in empirical comparative research, their application does pose a problem of measurability, as well as a problem of classifying a large number of hybrid cases. In terms of more fine-grained international comparative research, subjective measurements along multiple dimensions are more instructive. One important typology is developed by Hofstede (2001). His model and country scores have been replicated or used as variables in numerous comparative studies concerning general management (see for an overview Kirkman 2006). Although nearly neglected in the first two decades after its original development, in more recent years the model has become widely referred to in public management literature (for example Brown and Humphreys 1995, Schröter 2000, Pollitt and Bouckaert 2004, Pillay 2008). There are several reasons for the popularity of Hofstede's study for management studies, notably the large number of countries it covers and the way his limited number of dimensions relate easily to issues of management. These features are less present in alternative large-scale comparisons of societal culture (see Smith et al. 1996). Hofstede measures societal culture via five dimensions and indices (Hofstede 2001):

- *Power distance index* (PDI): measures the extent to which the less powerful members of organizations and institutions accept and expect that power is distributed unequally, for example between boss and subordinates.
- *Uncertainty avoidance index* (UAI): measures the extent to which members of a culture feel threatened by uncertain, unstructured or unknown situations.
- *Individualism index* (IND) (vs. collectivism): refers to the degree to which individuals are supposed to look after themselves or remain integrated into strong, cohesive in-groups, which throughout people's lifetimes continue to protect them in exchange for unquestioning loyalty. In individualistic societies, individual initiative and achievement as well as individualized incentives for performance are preferred.
- *Masculinity index* (MASC) (vs. femininity): measures the extent to which gender roles are clearly distinct in society, with men being tough, assertive and focused on material of life, against the extent to which roles of gender are blurred with an emphasis on the quality of life. In masculine societies there is an emphasis on equity, mutual competition and performance, rather than on equality and quality of life.
- *Long-term orientation index* (LT orientation) (vs. short-term orientation): refers to the extent to which a culture programmes its members to accept delayed gratification of their material, social and emotional needs. Long-term oriented societies stress virtues oriented towards future rewards, like perseverance and thrift, as well as virtues related to the past and present, like respect for tradition.

Hofstede uses survey data on the self-perception of individuals and aggregates these to cultural profiles. However, the main data were collected through surveys within IBM in the early 1970s, and this long time span is one of the major criticisms of his model (see for a summary of the criticisms Smith 2002). Nevertheless, replication studies seem to support his model and main findings (see Kirkman 2006).

In the field of public management studies, the Hofstede study remains the main source for comparative scores on societal culture, with alternative measurements only referred to very sparingly. Moreover, it appears that most public management students using such kinds of datasets take the data for granted, without referring to the underlying issues of measurement, aggregation or unit of analysis, although these issues are major topics of debate in the field of cross-cultural psychology. For example, there is a fierce, but interesting, debate about the correct way to study societal cultures between Hofstede and the protagonists of another major culture study, the more recent GLOBE project which covers 61 countries (see several issues of the *Journal of International Business Studies* in 2006). The GLOBE project (House and Hanges 2004) comes to partially different country scores, compared to Hofstede, based on a more refined set of cultural dimensions and on perceptions of individuals *about others* (instead of about themselves).

Describing the Relevance of Organizational and Societal Culture for NPM Reforms Empirically

Clearly, some *organizational cultures* are more conducive to NPM reforms than others. Comparing 1996 and 2006 survey data of respectively 1,482 and 1,848 Norwegian civil servants, Christensen and Lægreid (2008) found that, in Norwegian ministries, the differences in significance of Management by Objectives and Results, the use of managerial tools, structural devolution and market tools, as well as the number of reforms were all strongly influenced by existing organizational cultures that stressed renewal orientation and efficiency orientation, as well as the extent to which civil servants identified themselves with managers in the private sector. The extent of the use of quality management tools in Flemish agencies seems to be contingent on the presence of an organizational culture valuing customers and innovation, but not related to a detail-oriented or team-oriented culture, among others (Verhoest et al. 2010). It is clear that differences in organizational culture – and even sectoral and occupational cultures – can account to some extent for the divergent adoption of NPM-like reforms across public sector organizations within the same societal culture (Bovaird 2007). Indeed, there are several accounts of failing administrative reforms because of their incompatibility with the prevailing bureaucratic organizational cultures in ministries (see on the Copernicus reforms in the Belgian Federal government, Hondeghem and Depré 2005).

This part looks at some of the empirical evidence regarding the influence of *societal culture* on NPM reforms in different countries. This section combines the discussion of some relevant literature with our own analyses, which focus on the adoption of specific NPM elements in different societal cultures. It considers four relevant aspects: the introduction of specific managerial tools, the liberalization and privatization of public service provision, the structural disaggregation of bureaucracies into semi-autonomous agencies and the type of reform trajectory chosen by countries.

Societal Culture in Relation to Managerial Tools and Liberalization

NPM doctrines prescribe the introduction of private sector managerial tools within public administration, with an emphasis on delegation and performance incentives. By selecting a few managerial tools for consideration it is possible to ascertain to what extent their adoption within the public administration of a country can be linked to societal culture. The selected tools are three human resources management (HRM)-related tools – (1) the delegation of human resource management practices to line ministries in central government; (2) the shift towards a position-based recruitment system with lateral entry of both internal and external applicants for specific jobs, compared to a career-based system, which is characterized by competitive selection early on in the public servants' career with higher-level posts open to public servants only; and (3) the use of performance-related pay in central

Table 4.1 Country scores on culture, managerial tools and regulatory restrictiveness

Countries and clusters included	PDI	UAI	IND	MASC	LT	HRM Delegation	Openness recruitment system	Performance related pay	Executive budget flexibility	Medium term budget perspective	ECTR 2005
Anglo											
New Zealand	22	49	79	58	30	0.705	0.592		0.504	0.667	1.9
United Kingdom	35	35	89	66	25	0.531	0.775	0.938	0.603	0.764	0.9
United States	40	46	91	62	29	0.522	0.508	0.708	0.333	0.528	1.9
Australia	36	51	90	61	31	0.681	0.683	1.000	0.358	0.611	1.5
Ireland	28	35	70	68	43	0.319	0.133	0.729	0.446	0.792	3.1
More developed Latin											
Belgium	65	94	75	54	38	0.431	0.383		0.381	0.583	2.0
France	68	86	71	43	39	0.307	0.050	0.729	0.525	0.833	2.4
Italy	50	75	76	70	34	0.330	0.425	0.667	0.259	0.417	2.0
Less developed Latin											
Portugal	63	104	27	31	30	0.399	0.308	0.000	0.381	0.417	2.7
Mexico	81	82	30	69		0.355	0.392	0.000	0.356	0.556	3.6
Germanic											
Germany	35	65	67	66	31	0.480	0.483	0.667	0.350	0.944	1.3
Austria	11	70	55	79	31	0.371	0.475	0.000	0.375	0.750	1.9
Nordic											
Sweden	31	29	71	5	33	0.699	0.767	0.000	0.544	0.861	1.8
Norway	31	50	69	8	44	0.460	0.458	0.792	0.331	0.500	2.3
Finland	33	59	63	26	41	0.522	0.717	0.698	0.327	0.889	2.3
Denmark	18	23	74	16	46	0.413	0.592	0.792	0.470	0.806	1.2
Netherlands	38	53	80	14	44	0.402	0.783	0.583	0.477	0.917	1.8
(Confucian) Asia											
Japan	54	92	46	95	80	0.426	0.133	0.750	0.142	0.750	2.2
Korea	60	85	18	39	75	0.415	0.392	0.938	0.281	0.694	3.1
Near-East											
Turkey	66	85	37	45		0.256	0.217		0.229	0.833	4.0

Sources: Hofstede 2001, OECD 2009a, and Conway and Nicoletti 2006.

government (see OECD 2009a: 76–80 for operationalization) – and two financial management factors – (1) the flexibility of the executive to make changes to the budget during execution; and (2) the extent to which countries have developed a medium-term perspective in their budget process (see OECD 2009a: 90, 94 for operationalization).

Following Hofstede (2001), one may hypothesize that governments in states with high values of power distance and uncertainty avoidance would tend to prefer rather centralized bureaucracies, in which work processes are strictly prescribed by regulations, civil service systems are geared towards career-based recruitment, and administrative behaviour is directed by hierarchical leadership. Moreover, the combination of high power distance and uncertainty avoidance inhibits the empowerment of lower organizational levels and the extensive delegation of managerial flexibilities (Hofstede 2001: 388–389). The adoption of Management by Objectives and performance-related pay, which are central to performance management schemes, seem to be most appropriate in cultures with rather low values of power distance, low values of uncertainty avoidance, and high masculinity and individualism values (Hofstede 2001: 391). For instance, Brown and Humphreys (1995) found that performance appraisal and performance-related pay as motivational tactics could not be expected to work in Egypt as they do in the UK because of a much higher uncertainty avoidance and lower levels of individualism in the former country. In Egypt, elements like secure pay, workplace environment and employment security were much more important motivating factors (Brown and Humphreys 1995).

A second reform element considered here is the liberalization and privatization of public services. NPM and the affiliated neo-liberal view of public economy stresses the introduction of competition, market-type mechanisms, and private ownership for public services that were traditionally delivered through public state monopolies. The subsequent analysis focuses on the liberalization of public utilities, as inversely measured by the OECD ECTR index. One would expect greater emphasis on competitive market structures and private ownership in public services in countries with high levels of individuality and masculinity and rather low levels of uncertainty avoidance and power distance.

Table 4.1 presents, for 20 countries from different country clusters (as defined by Hofstede 2001), the country scores (Hofstede 2001) on the five cultural dimensions, OECD data on the use of managerial tools, as perceived by high-ranked central government officials (OECD 2009a), and the degree of regulatory restrictiveness of markets (OECD ECTR database).

When plotting the cultural dimensions two by two (see Figures 4.1 and 4.2) most of the country clusters can clearly be located. The Anglo group combines low levels of power distance and uncertainty avoidance with high levels of individualism and rather high levels of masculinity. Nordic countries differ from the Anglo group mainly with respect to their low degrees of masculinity. The Latin cluster of countries is mainly distinguishable because of high levels of power distance and uncertainty avoidance.

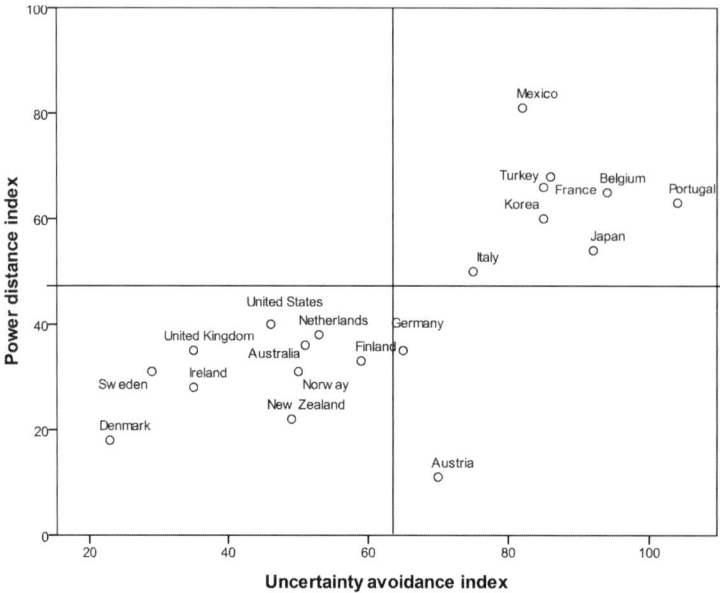

Figure 4.1   Uncertainty avoidance and power distance for 20 OECD countries

Source: Based on Hofstede 2001.

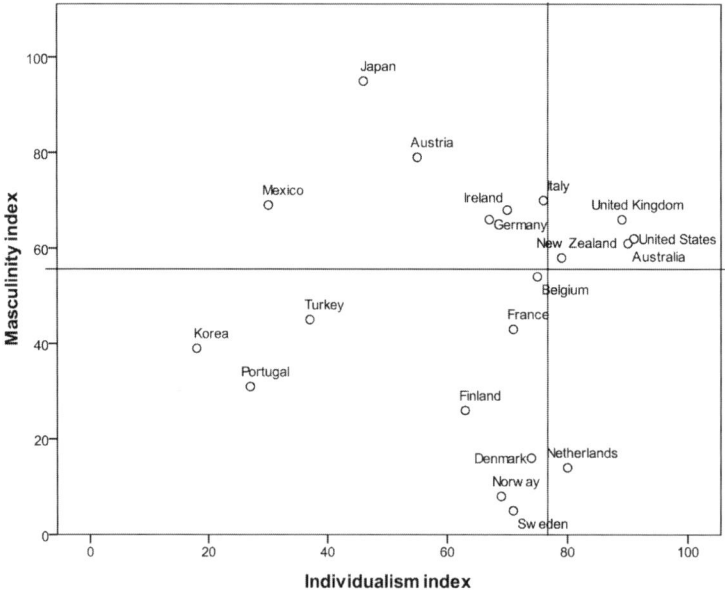

Figure 4.2   Individualism and masculinity for 20 OECD countries

Source: Based on Hofstede 2001.

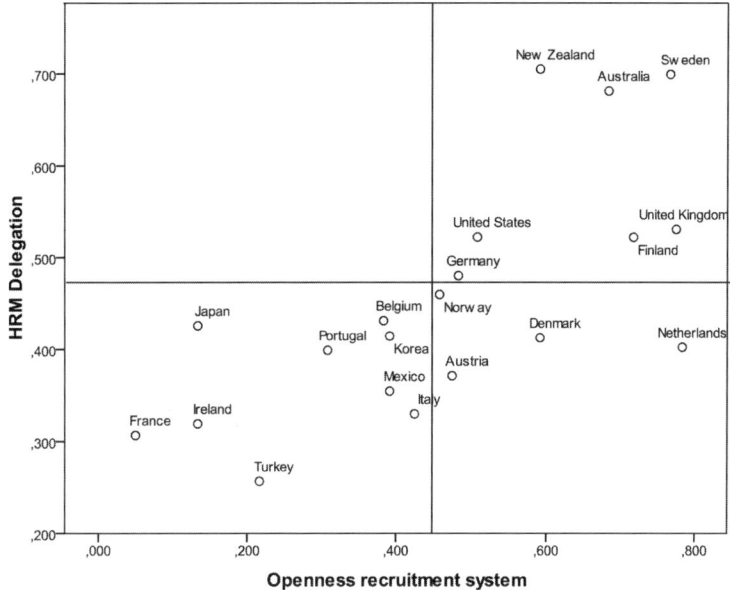

Figure 4.3   HRM delegation and openness of the recruitment system for 20 OECD countries

Source: Based on OECD 2009a.

Plot diagrams in which the respective cultural dimensions are plotted against the different managerial tools or the ECTR data seem to point to some relationships. For illustrative purposes, compare a plot diagram plotting the extent of HRM delegation and openness of the recruitment system (Figure 4.3) with the figures plotting the cultural dimensions.

Countries are situated largely in opposite quadrants of the plot diagrams presented in Figures 4.1 and 4.3, indicating that countries with low levels of power distance and uncertainty avoidance have more extensive HRM delegation and position-based, open recruitment systems, and *vice versa*.

However, the openness of the recruitment system seems to have stronger relationships with the level of power distance and uncertainty avoidance, compared to the extent of HRM delegation, for which relations are rather weak. There are also countries in which these managerial tools are much less present than would be expected, like Ireland. Additionally, open and position-based recruitment systems seem to be practised more extensively in highly individualistic countries (with France and Ireland as clear exceptions), compared to more collectivistic countries.

Figure 4.4 plots the extent of budget flexibility with the degree of regulatory restrictiveness (as the inverse measurement of the degree of liberalization). As Figure 4.4 shows, most countries with low power distance, uncertainty avoidance and high levels of individualism combine considerable budget flexibility with substantial liberalization of public utilities.

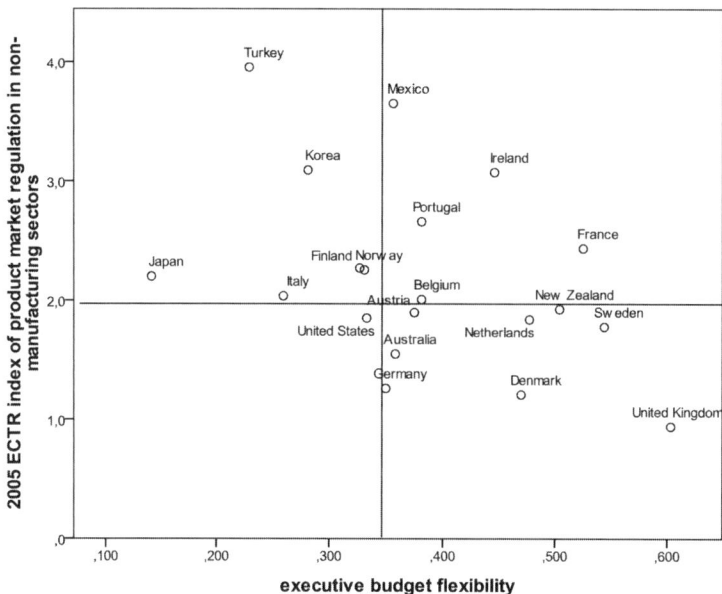

Figure 4.4 **Budget flexibility and regulatory restrictiveness for 20 OECD countries**

Source: Based respectively on OECD 2009a and OECD ECTR data; Conway and Nicoletti 2006.

When plotting the respective cultural dimensions and the other reform variables one to one, plots show that executive budget flexibility seems to have a negative relationship with uncertainty avoidance and seems to associate positively with individualism. The regulatory restrictiveness index (as the inverse measurement of the degree of liberalization) seems to have a positive relationship with power distance and uncertainty avoidance, but a negative one with individualism. These findings are in line with what we expected. However, in all these plot diagrams we find contra-intuitive cases and outliers, indicating that associations between societal culture and reforms are neither direct nor particularly very strong. Moreover, in the plot diagrams we find no indication of any clear relationship between the extent of performance-related pay or medium-term budget flexibility with cultural variables. Nor do the diagrams show any indication of a clear relationship between the masculinity index and any managerial tools or regulatory restrictiveness. Moreover, long-term orientation as a cultural dimension does not seem to relate strongly with managerial reforms or liberalization, also because most OECD countries do not show substantial variance in terms of long-term orientation.

Societal Culture in Relation to Agency Reforms

NPM prescribes the structural disaggregation of large bureaucracies into semi-autonomous agencies that ideally have considerable levels of managerial autonomy and are controlled in a results-oriented way by their minister or parent department (Verhoest et al. 2004). Pollitt et al. (2004) explain the different ways in which agencies are controlled by their ministers in Sweden, Finland, the UK and the Netherlands by referring to path dependency in terms of Hofstede's cultural profiles for these four countries. For example, in the two Nordic countries and in the Netherlands the performance-oriented control of agencies resembles more a model of 'soft contracting', whereas in the UK performance contracts are used in a more 'harsh' way. The relative low level of masculinity in Sweden, Finland and the Netherlands may help to account for this.

Verhoest et al. (2010) compared the managerial autonomy and result control of 226 agencies in Norway, Ireland and Flanders (as a member state of Belgium) based on survey data from senior managers of agencies. The central hypothesis was that a legal tradition in common law, combined with a public interest model, low values with regard to power distance and uncertainty avoidance, and high values with regard to masculinity, would foster agency reforms along NPM lines. Therefore, the authors expected to find agencies with relatively higher levels of managerial autonomy and result control in Ireland, in contrast to Flanders, with Norway holding a middle position (see Table 4.1 for the country scores). Logistic regression analyses showed a significant country effect for most variables, which may be explained partly by the different cultural profiles.

The cultural emphasis in Flanders on uniform and detailed administrative rules and elaborated procedures is reflected in the limited managerial autonomy of Flemish agencies. Additionally, the preference of Flemish ministers to have direct political control over their agencies fits into the cultural profile of high power distance and uncertainty avoidance. In contrast, the characteristics of Norwegian agencies seem to match the consensual, egalitarian societal culture with moderate degrees of uncertainty avoidance. Norwegian agencies have comparatively large degrees of managerial autonomy, and the result control system reflects a system of relational contracting based on frequent interaction, common goals and trust. Furthermore, the virtual absence of individual financial incentives for personnel seems to reflect the lower degree of masculinity in contrast to Flanders where financial incentives are more prevalent.

However, whereas the agency reforms in Norway and Flanders are consistent with the cultural profile in these states, agency reforms in Ireland do not fully match the country's cultural profile. Indeed, in line with the absence of an administrative law tradition, managerial autonomy is not strictly and uniformly regulated. However, it is mainly determined on the case-by-case, rather restrictive, approach of the Department of Finance. Moreover, the trust between ministers and senior civil servants may refer to the low degree of power distance in Irish culture. But the slow and incremental nature of reforms, the strong enduring emphasis on detailed input controls, as well as the virtual absence of performance-related financial incentives contradict the relatively low uncertainty avoidance and high masculinity values.

This study shows again that the relationship between culture and NPM reforms is not a direct one: other factors interfere in the relationship. For example, the reluctance of Irish policy makers to grant large degrees of managerial autonomy to agencies and the strict control of the Department of Finance is very much due to the legacy of the severe economic crises Ireland went through up to the 1990s.

Societal Culture in Relation to General Trajectories of Reform

Several authors explain the different trajectories of administrative reform in countries by referring to societal culture. For example, when explaining the low degree of administrative reform in Germany compared to the UK, Schröter (2000) refers to differences in culture, such as the relatively high degrees of uncertainty avoidance in Germany. Koci (2007) explains the substantially higher reform activity in German-speaking parts of Switzerland, compared to the French-speaking and Italian-speaking parts, by referring to the relatively lower scores on power distance, uncertainty avoidance and higher scores on masculinity. With respect to the overall trajectory of public management reform, Pollitt and Bouckaert (2004: 97–98) distinguish between (in order of decreasing degree of radical reforms) minimizers and marketizers, early and later modernizers, and maintainers. In line with what has been hypothesized above, most radical NPM reforms may be expected in countries exhibiting relatively low levels of power distance and uncertainty avoidance and relatively high levels of masculinity and individualism (Bouckaert 2007, cf. Pillay 2008). As Bouckaert (2007) suggests, the time dimension is harder to hypothesize: 'if there is a focus on quick-wins, there may be a trade off with longer term results which may be more sustainable.'

According to Pollitt and Bouckaert (2004: 98–101), the core group of NPM marketizers contains Australia, New Zealand, the United Kingdom and the USA. All these countries belong to the Anglo group, and indeed combine rather low power distance and uncertainty avoidance, and rather high individualism and masculinity scores (see Figures 4.1 and 4.2). Ireland is a notable exception in this group because of its limited reform record. The Nordic group countries – Sweden, Finland and the Netherlands (one could add Norway and Denmark) – are labelled as early modernizers, who show quite substantial reform efforts despite their low level of masculinity. Indeed, countries with high levels of power distance and uncertainty avoidance show substantially less reform activity. The group of late modernizers contains some developed Latin countries like France, Belgium, Italy, and Continental countries like Germany (at least below federal level). Note that these countries all adhere to the *Rechtsstaat* model. Considering the remaining countries in the sample, Austria, Portugal, Japan and Korea can be seen as rather modest (and, in most cases, late) modernizers whereas Turkey and Mexico could be clustered as maintainers. All these countries score high on uncertainty avoidance and medium to low on individualism (see Table 4.1), although they belong to different administrative cultures.

Discussing the Relevance of Culture for NPM Reforms from a Theoretical and Normative Perspective

The studies and evidence referred to above show that societal and administrative cultures do have substantial relevance when explaining the differences in adoption of NPM reforms across countries. The combination of rather low levels of power distance and uncertainty avoidance and high levels of individualism (within a public interest context) seems to make countries particularly receptive to NPM reforms (Bouckaert 2007). The inverse also seems to be the case. The level of masculinity seems to matter mainly with respect to the extent to which 'hard' aspects of NPM reforms are introduced: low levels of masculinity seem to align with more of an emphasis on relational contracting than on 'hard' contracts, and less emphasis on pecuniary performance incentives.

However, empirical links are, at most, indirect. The causal chain from cultural influences to the specific design and outcome of administrative reforms is very long with many intermediating variables. Cultural values comprise only one element of the larger 'habitats' in which reforms are initiated and implemented. For example, the occurrence of economic or legitimacy crises seems to be a triggering factor in many countries, but other matters concerning polity (for example majoritarian cabinet structures) and actor constellations (for example changes in political parties in power in Sweden), among others, could also be factors. Similar observations can be made with respect to organizational culture.

How can it be explained theoretically that cultures influence public administration reforms, albeit in an indirect way? The idea that societal and organizational cultures influence public management finds its basic theoretical underpinning in the 'logic of appropriateness', which is a major logic of action for actors (cf. March and Olsen 1989). Policy makers and senior bureaucrats choose elements and strategies for administrative reform because they regard them as being in accordance with what has worked well for the administrative system in question in the past, or because they regard them as being acceptable in the environment at the present time (Christensen et al. 2007). This logic of appropriateness is central in most institutional schools, including historical institutionalism with its emphasis on path dependency. Path dependency refers to the tendency of actors to make choices (for example on organizational design) that are consistent with formerly taken 'paths' (Pierson 2004). These 'paths', or legacies, are quite resistant to change, because of the elements both of socialization and of rational calculation (Hall and Taylor 1996). A public sector organization is established at a specific point in time, and is hence shaped by particular cultural contexts or norms and values in the wider environment that leave a permanent impression on it. Both organizational and societal cultures determine what is appropriate behaviour for politico-administrative actors.

Christensen et al. (2007) refer to the cultural-institutional perspective within organization theory. This perspective focuses on organizational culture and organizations as institutions 'infused with value beyond the technical requirements of the task at hand' (Selznick 1957: 17). The organization then becomes a value-bearing institution with its own distinct identities and opinions about what the relevant problems and solutions are. Norms, values and identities are developed gradually and are internalized by the members of an organization through socialization processes. Members will gain experience of an institutional culture by learning what is appropriate. This also implies a form of path dependency, where patterns of behaviour that are seen as appropriate become reinforced over time and are therefore quite resistant to change. Organizational culture also acts as a 'filter', producing different outcomes in different organizations. Internal forces contributing to the organization's robustness and stability will be more important than signals and pressures from superior bodies, and the fate of reform initiatives from above will depend on whether and how they are compatible with established norms and values in the public sector organizations. This line of reasoning holds also *mutatis mutandis* for culture at the societal level. The importance of a good fit between reform initiatives and management models and societal culture is not to be underestimated: Newman and Nollen's study (1996) found that the higher the congruence between the different dimensions of national culture and different general management practices, the higher the organization's performance.

When confronted with external pressures for administrative reforms that do not concur with the existing organizational or societal culture, individuals and organizations may choose to neglect, to resist, or just to implement reforms in a symbolic way due to legitimacy motives. Sociological institutionalism stresses the possibility of 'structural decoupling' (Meyer and Rowan 1977). For example, NPM doctrine advocates an organizational culture with a strong emphasis on goal achievement and customer satisfaction. According to this doctrine, such an organizational culture will encourage, among others, the adoption and use of performance management instruments, that are inspired by the private sector. However, when introduced into organizations with a bureaucratic, detail-oriented and compliance-oriented culture, performance management instruments might not change actual routines and decision-making practices within the organization.

Inspired by these theoretical perspectives, several authors have warned against transplanting NPM public management reforms, which originated mainly within Anglo-Saxon developed countries, straight into other cultural settings. They stress the need for cultural compatibility when applying NPM reforms to different cultural contexts (for example Schick 1998). However, studies of public management reform in developing countries show that 'Western administrative techniques have been introduced without regard to their acceptability and consistency with prevailing mores, customs, values, and norms in the target community', leading to suboptimal outcomes at best (Umeh and Andranovich 2005: 64). As theories on policy transfer and institutional transplantation show (De Jong and Mamadouh

2002), transplanting institutions (like bureaucratic structures) from one donor country to a host country involves a tension between voluntaristic actions by (rival coalitions of) politico-administrative actors that design and create a bricolage of new institutions based on their selection of useful foreign examples on the one hand, and the potentiality of failure, due to a lack of a good fit, on the other hand. Incompatibilities between donor and host societies may lead to hybrid institutional structures, a dubious application and prioritization of rules, confusion, complexity and ultimately failure of the institutional transplantation. Therefore, according to De Jong and Mamadouh (2002: 28), 'a deeper knowledge of the legal, politico-administrative and cultural traditions of both the donor country and the host country, as well as a specific analysis of the congruence between the transplant at hand and its future institutional environment are due'. Similarities between host and donor facilitate the transplantation process, which is demonstrated by the quick transplantation of NPM reforms within the family of Anglo countries in contrast to the much slower transfer to Latin Europe.

However, one could wonder why NPM is so popular around the globe despite its frequent lack of cultural fit. The theory of policy transfer and institutional transplantation point at some potential explanations (De Jong and Mamadouh 2002: 30). First, according to this theory, xeroxing makes the transplantation process less easy than creating a bricolage, that is, adapting to local circumstances. Moreover, considering only one definite model makes the transplantation harder than considering a more loosely defined model or even multiple models. The generic character of a transplant facilitates the transplantation process (for example, general and abstract policy lessons, ideas, and ideologies versus specific legal frameworks or procedures). Most countries have indeed been very selective when introducing elements of NPM doctrines. The nature of NPM as a loose set of (even sometimes conflicting) reform ideas and concepts facilitated this selective approach to a large extent. Most governments have chosen reform strategies which were geared to local circumstances. As the theory of institutional transplantation suggests, special periods of regime transformation characterized by a sense of emergency and urgency create opportunity windows and critical junctures that facilitate the transplantation process, compared to periods of stability. In several countries, severe economic or budgetary crises urged governments to take on radical NPM reforms, as in New Zealand in the mid 1980s and Sweden in the early 1990s. In some countries, particularly developing countries, governments were forced to adopt far-reaching NPM-reforms by the International Monetary Fund or by regional development banks, making the transplantation process much more problematic than voluntary adoption by domestic actors (De Jong and Mamadouh 2002: 30).

In this chapter, culture is mainly examined as an exogenous, inertial factor influencing NPM reforms. However, several management gurus have made it a selling point (see for example Peters and Waterman 1982) that management reforms can also change the culture of organizations. Hence, in empirical research, the 'chicken and egg' conundrum (Bouckaert 2007) is clearly relevant: how can one prove empirically that the organizational culture, which appears to be conducive to NPM reforms, is not a consequence of the latter? Shifting organizational cultures from bureaucratic cultures to performance-oriented cultures has been a central aim in many public management reform programmes. For instance, Parker and Bradley (2000) have hypothesized that NPM reforms would lead organizational cultures in public administration to change from hierarchical cultures (that is, with emphasis on control and internal focus) to more rational cultures (that is, with emphasis on control and external focus), due to the performance of NPM and its goal-orientation, or to more group culture (that is, with emphasis on flexibility and internal focus), because of the increased emphasis on human resources in NPM. This voluntaristic view on cultural change is central to functionalist theories on organizational culture (Schedler and Proeller 2007: 18). Whether or not NPM-like administrative reforms have effectively changed the organizational culture of public sector organizations is still a matter of debate, as empirical research comes to different conclusions. For example, a study on NPM reforms in Switzerland, using data from independent evaluations, concluded that the reforms have led to an administrative culture that stresses cost consciousness, results orientation and entrepreneurial behaviour (Rieder and Lehmann 2002 in Schedler and Proeller 2007: 18). However, others emphasize that administrative and organizational cultures are very persistent. Hajnal (2004) compares the organizational culture of ministries in two countries – Hungary and Australia – with highly distinctive national cultures. Despite the fact that the Australian ministries were subjected to a much higher degree of NPM-like reforms, Hajnal found a surprisingly strong similarity in the organizational cultures of the ministries in both countries. Organizational cultures were still outstandingly bureaucratic, implying that NPM did not cause or involve a de-bureaucratization of government organizations (Hajnal 2004).

Even at the societal level the neo-liberal reforms, demanded by the IMF and development banks when lending to developing countries, have an underlying assumption that public management reforms will even influence administrative and political cultures and values (Bouckaert 2007: 37). However, these effects are very hard to assess empirically, as there would be a need to measure changes in societal culture over time. One empirical question that comes close asks whether or not 'administrative traditions' still have an enduring impact on contemporary administrative systems, despite all NPM reform initiatives (Painter and Peters 2010). Administrative traditions are 'historically based sets of values, structures, and relationships with other institutions that defined the nature of appropriate public administration within society' (Painter and Peters 2010). For example, Ongaro (2009) assesses to what extent the politico-administrative systems in France, Italy, Spain and Portugal currently still share the common traits of the Napoleonic administrative tradition, despite distinct reform patterns in the last two decades. His answer is clearly affirmative; the basic pattern seems to be one of continuity, although some change has occurred. For example, the conception of public officials as managers and accountable for results has gained some ground, but the central focus of both action and accountability remains the law and the way it is administered (Ongaro 2009: 263).

Summary

This chapter has tried to substantiate the claim that societal and organizational culture shapes the context for NPM reforms by discussing some empirical evidence and theoretical perspectives. It stresses the importance of some degree of compatibility between reform initiatives and culture. Future research which considers societal and organizational culture in a systematic and fine-grained way should be stimulated. In particular, future studies could focus on how different layers of culture interact when organizations implement reforms (see for example Bovaird 2007). Moreover, longitudinal studies that could help to disentangle the mutual influence of culture and reforms are highly relevant for future research agendas.

ASHGATE
RESEARCH
COMPANION

New Public Organisations:
A Revivalist Movement[1]

Nils Brunsson

During the 1980s and 1990s, some states, such as the UK, New Zealand and Sweden, underwent extensive, radical reforms in their state administration – their structure, their systems of control and the way they accounted for their activities. In short, the states were given new administrative forms – a phenomenon that was characterised early as a 'new public management' (Hood 1991). Some of these new forms became popular even in less active states (Pollitt and Bouckaert 2004).

In the most active states, one can compare the reforms with a revivalist movement. Within a short time many politicians, administrators and advisors became convinced that specific reforms were needed and that both the need and content were self-evident. Some observers have associated these reforms with neo-liberal agendas, yet governments of various colours have initiated and continued the reform programmes.

Considering the speed of reform initiatives and their radical nature, one could have expected them to be highly controversial and meeting with great resistance from many political parties and interest groups. But even though many academicians criticised the reforms, by and large, this was not the case. Although some specific initiatives raised public debate, the reform programme in general did not spur any broad popular opposition movements. And reformers typically presented the reforms as obvious and unquestionable. They argued, for instance, that all these reforms addressed a necessary modernisation of the public sector. And who could oppose such a project?

The reformers' arguments were ultimately practical. These new forms would change public sector practice; the public sector would work more efficiently and more in line with the needs and wishes of the public. Yet the reformers demonstrated a limited interest for this practice. They chose the indirect method of changing administrative forms rather than changing operations directly. Moreover, they showed little interest in evaluating whether or not their reforms were leading to

---

1   This chapter draws from Brunsson and Sahlin-Andersson (2000), Brunsson (2006) and Brunsson (2009).

higher effectiveness. There was a general lack of empirical investigation of any improvements in operations that may have incurred as a result of reforms initiated early on or of similar reforms in other states; the results of empirical data did not appear to be necessary for creating arguments in favour of reform (Pollitt 2001a, Pollitt and Bouckaert 2004: ch. 5).

In this chapter I argue for the hypothesis that the reform movement, like revivalist movements, was driven by lofty ideas, ideals and principles rather than by practical experiences, and that these roots in the world of ideas can explain the power and the extensiveness of the reforms. It further argues that the central notion underlying most of the reforms was the idea and the ideal of the organisation. The reforms constructed organisations, and modern organisations offer a perfect context for lofty ideas and ideals, making them highly reformist. The construction of organisations increases the likelihood of extensive and continued reforming.

New Public Organisations

In the 1940s and 1950s, there was increasing scientific interest in what was then called administration, and this interest extended to both the private and the public sector. In the 1960s, much of administrative science turned into organisation theory (Czarniawska 2010). Instead of a focus on the activity of administration, emphasis was placed on formal organisations depicted as bounded units within an 'environment', and firms became the main subject of interest. They constituted more obvious examples of organisations than did various subunits of states, which did not have the autonomy and clear boundaries that firms were seen as having. And for the most part, states were not included in the concept of organisation, but were seen instead as one element of the environment of all organisations. Within organisation theory, 'administration' was renamed 'management', and this topic remains a significant and expanding research issue that refers to the management of organisations, the crucial task of which is to maintain and reinforce their existence and their wealth.

The term New Public Management is adequate for describing the public sector reform movement of the 1980s and 1990s, in the sense that it refers to this contemporary idea of management. Yet an emphasis on the concept of management runs the risk of concealing the fundamental underlying concept of organisation – the setting in which all this management is supposed to be taking place. It seems to have escaped the attention of most analysts that a fundamental element of the reform movement in the 1980s and 1990s was the turning of state subunits into organisations. It is through the process of becoming organisations that these subunits were turned into suitable objects for modern management. An even more appropriate name for the reform movement is New Public Organisations (NPO).

Incomplete Organisations

Modern states constitute clear examples of formal organisations, with all the fundamental characteristics of such entities. They are conceived of as units with clear boundaries, a high degree of autonomy, distinctive purposes and tasks, and specific distinguishing qualities (Ahrne 1998, Krasner 1999). They include a hierarchy in the form of a responsible government controlling organisational activities through its decisions, and a right to monitor and sanction relevant behaviour of organisational members (called citizens). And the type of intelligence that fits this construction is instrumental rationality – rationality being a form of processual hierarchy, a procedure by which the tasks of the organisation are expected to transform efficiently into action. States are conceived of as 'actors', having the capacity to do and say things. In these fundamental respects, states resemble other types of organisations such as firms and associations.

Just like other large organisations, modern states are highly complex constructions with many subunits undertaking different tasks. Such subunits have traditionally borne a certain resemblance to their mother organisation, but they have also lacked key organisational characteristics or have weakened forms of those characteristics; they constituted 'incomplete' organisations (Brunsson and Sahlin-Andersson 2000).

Some of the traditional state subunits, such as central or local authorities for police, tax or regional authorities, were part of a large state bureaucracy, where they served as agents for principals higher in the hierarchy. These subunits had weak organisational characteristics. They had unclear and permeable boundaries to higher levels or to other subunits. They were not expected to have their own unique traits; on the contrary, they were expected to be similar to other subunits with similar tasks. They had little autonomy, being directed and controlled from higher levels, where all the important decisions were made, including detailed budget and employment decisions. Responsibility for outcomes lay with higher, political levels. Instead of having autonomous managers, they were run by civil servants who were expected to follow rules that were decided upon centrally rather than making their own rational decisions.

Other subunits, such as hospitals, schools or universities, formed another version of the incomplete organisation. They were arenas for established professions. The importance of common professional norms created strong similarities among such units both within each state and globally. Boundaries among professions were more important than were boundaries among subunits; professionals typically cooperated with each other, regardless of any subunit boundary. Strong professional norms made it difficult for management to control operations; the management of such units were largely decorative rather than real. Responsibility for operations concentrated on professionals, such as individual physicians or teachers, rather than on management.

Constructing Organisations

The fundamental content of the NPO reforms was to turn these subunits into complete organisations, or at least more complete than they had been before. Each state authority, child-care centre, school, university, or hospital was to become a delimited organisation, much more autonomous than and clearly distinctive from other units, with powerful and responsible management of its own and rational systems of decision making and control.

Boundaries were constructed around the units through the introduction of accrual accounting (Olson et al. 1998) and by other accounting techniques that measured the costs, income and result of each unit (Miller and O'Leary 1987, Mouritsen 1997). Categories of people such as patients and pupils with unclear boundaries to the subunits were replaced with the category of customer, a type of person who is clearly outside the units (Forssell and Jansson 1996).

Abolishing detailed rules and budgets and allowing the subunits to control the recruitment of personnel increased the autonomy of the subunits (OECD 1995, Musselin 1997, Lapsley 1997). For many units, allowing them to acquire resources from sources other than central funding increased their autonomy (Schick 1996). The subunits were urged to pay greater attention to their clients, which weakened the authority of higher levels in the state bureaucracy.

Distinctiveness was introduced by requesting each unit to formulate its own goals, policies and profiles (Hood 1996b, Rombach 1997). Even universities were expected to claim that they had unique characteristics and overall goals that distinguished them from other universities (Musselin 1997).

Local managers were given much greater power and responsibility. They were expected to formulate and implement policies for their units (Berrevin and Musselin 1996); and, increasingly, it was managers rather than professionals who were responsible for operations. Efficient coordination was to be achieved by breaking with professional distinctions, and with people from different professional groups working in teams (Sahlin-Andersson 1994). A number of management accounting techniques were installed in order to increase the managers' control over their units (Humphrey and Olson 1995). Politicians argued that the reforms allowed for increased autonomy and freedom at lower levels, yet employees other than local top managers experienced the opposite.

Reformers tried to increase rationality by introducing clear objectives, various forms of management by objectives, systems for follow-up and evaluation and advanced management accounting systems (Power 1997, Olson et al. 1998). Rationality is easier to achieve with fewer goals, and in many cases units were separated into smaller units, each with only one goal (OECD 1995).

Complete organisations can be legally acknowledged as formal organisations. Because complete organisations are possible to buy and sell, some of the new state organisations were sold – privatised. Those remaining turned the state into a conglomerate, which can be described as a case of 'fragmentation' (Pollitt 2009). Interactions among state units were perceived as interactions among organisations rather than interactions among parts of one organisation. In contrast to organisational subunits, organisations are able to advice and legitimately compete with each other. They are also able to cooperate. Before the reforms, fragmentation could be counteracted by attempts at central orchestration within the state organisation; after the reforms, the main method for avoiding fragmentation seemed to be cooperation among the new organisations.

Other than individuals, organisations are the only possible actors in a market. The traditional subunits typically did not have enough autonomy or clear enough boundaries to be market actors. They had to use the state or a local government as the contracting party. By becoming organisations, however, subunits could begin to buy from and sell to others, including other state subunits. Through the creation of new organisations, many new market interactions were made possible.

Not only states were constructing organisations, however. Similar reforms were being initiated in large corporations at the time. They sold or outsourced former departments, and turned other departments into more autonomous business units, each focusing on its 'core business'. And indeed, the creation of more and more organisations can be seen as a major trend in all sectors over the last 60 years or so (Drori et al. 2006). The theories produced by scholars defining their subject as organisation and management rather than as administration seem to have become more and more relevant.

An Institutional Shift

It is not easy to explain why the NPO reforms took place or why that specific content was chosen; although reformers argued differently, there is nothing natural or obvious about constructing organisations within and outside states. One reasonable hypothesis, however, is that a critical factor was the evocation of the *idea* of organisation – that leading administrators, politicians and many others began to perceive state subunits as a form of organisation, and that they succeeded in guiding the thinking of others and the discussion in the same direction. Whereas state subunits had been perceived earlier as administrative parts of the large state organisation, they were now considered to be a collection of organisations – perhaps by direct or indirect inspiration from modern organisation theory.

According to this hypothesis, ideas constituted the driving force behind NPO. The reforms were driven by perceiving reality through a new category rather than by observing a new reality through an old category. A more general category, the organisation, was introduced and reinforced, while more specific ones, such as state authority, school, university or hospital weakened or even became irrelevant. Such reinforcements of general categories are not uncommon in late modernity, and form both a part of and a cause of globalisation.

Organisation is not merely an idea – it constitutes an entire institution consisting of specific ideas, norms and patterns of action that are taken for granted, once we believe that we deal with organisations. These institutional elements differ in substantial part from those characterising the institutions of state authority, school, university or hospital. The introduction of organisation involves an institutional shift from several taken-for-granted worlds to another.

Reforms benefit from problems and solutions. Problems are used to explain why change is required, and solutions are used for arguing that there is a way to change for the better. The concept of organisation can serve as both a problem and a solution. If we classify traditional state subunits as organisations, we create a problem: these units do not fulfil our expectations of what an organisation should look like and how it should behave. And if this is the problem, the solution is both clear and obvious: to make the unit conform better to our ideas about organisations. So once people think of a traditional state subunit as an organisation, they are likely to initiate or accept reforms.

The hypothesis of an institutional shift would explain some peculiarities of the reform processes. Before this reform movement, the fact that state subunits were not complete organisations did not constitute a problem. On the contrary, it was considered to be a problem for achieving political control if individual units had too much autonomy. The shift to the idea of organisation can explain why something that was discussed earlier as a problem could now be perceived as a solution.

The hypothesis of an institutional shift can also explain why it was so easy to launch and defend the reforms – why the reforms had the flavour of something self-evident, and why they met so little resistance. This is the typical pattern of an institutional shift. Once people are convinced that a certain situation should be interpreted as an instance of a certain institution, a whole collection of ideas, norms and actions are evoked and then taken for granted. And the shift can happen quickly if the new institution is well known – which has become the case with the institution of organisation, perhaps partly as an effect of the teaching of organisation and management theory over the past 50 years.

Opponents who want to argue against isolated aspects of an institution have a difficult time, indeed; they try to argue for institutional *change*, for changing ideas, norms and behaviours that are taken for granted. A more effective strategy would be to suggest a different institution, perhaps a return to the old institutions of state authority, university and the like; but this is a difficult strategy, especially when the first institutional shift has been implicit rather than explicit, as has largely been the case with NPO. Although there were some explicit statements that public organisations should be regarded no different than any other organisations (McSweeney 1994), such direct references to the idea of organisation seem to have been the exception rather than the rule.

The hypothesis would also explain why such a large number of radical reforms could be introduced in a relatively short period. Radicalness and swiftness are typical of institutional shifts. A more prudent and slower strategy would have been learning from experience, allowing empirical observations to determine the pace of reform, making one reform at a time, evaluating its effects, and then deciding whether to make more reforms or not. But such an empirical attitude is irrelevant when one compares ideas and practice; the problem is that practice is not consistent with the idea of organisation, and the reforms create such a consistency. Exactly what reforms are to be launched is determined by the logic of the institution rather than by experience. If it shall be possible to measure the results of a unit, for example, it must have clear boundaries. A strong local hierarchy presupposes a high degree of autonomy. If local management shall become responsible for its unit, it must be given strong controlling power. If management is to make rational decisions, it is highly useful to formulate clear objectives. Changing one aspect provides convincing arguments for reforming other aspects. The reform process may seem incrementalistic, but is far from being ad hoc, it has clear logic and direction.

In the World of Organisations

Whatever the *causes* behind the NPO reforms, one of their main *effects* was the increasing perception of state subunits as organisations (even, it seems, by many students of public administration). The subunits entered the world of organisations, a world where ideas and ideals are crucial.

Organisations are decided-upon rather than emergent orders (March and Simon 1958, Luhmann 2000). We expect actions to be connected to decisions by explicit statements describing those actions. Whether made before or after actions, decisions justify actions. Decisions are strongly influenced by rules for talk, by norms for what can and should be said and may therefore deviate somewhat from possible or useful actions (Brunsson 2007: ch. 1). Many decisions made in large contemporary organisations are highly public, and must be adapted to popular ideas in a broader societal discourse, even when it distances them from the special practical problems of the individual organisation. This adaptation is easier for decisions that are one or more steps away from actions – decisions about so-called policies and organisational forms, for instance. Contemporary organisations have an incentive to make and announce that type of decision.

Organisations and their forms cannot be observed in physical terms; they are social constructions. They belong to the world of ideas rather than to the world of materiality. Even if organisations are firmly anchored in a judicial system as legal persons, there is often a need to represent them to members and non-members. Such representations consist of decisions to form the organisation in a certain way, whether these decisions have been made in an earlier period and explain existing forms, or if they are decisions that concern the future of the organisation rather than its present state.

Such representations must convince people that they deal with a 'true' organisation, an entity with all the fundamental characteristics of an organisation. An entity expected to be an organisation but unable to convince about that status may become neglected at best and dissolved at worst.

Modern organisations must also demonstrate that they have virtuous intentions and good results (Meyer and Rowan 1977). Organisations of all types are to be represented as having been designed for achieving such values as sustainability, gender equality and social development. And ideas often become more important organisational outputs than physical products are (Pine and Gilmore 1999).

Furthermore, many organisations actively downplay the material aspects of their physical products, turning them into something more like systems of ideas, like the organisation itself. Through 'branding', industrial firms try to connect their products with the image of the organisation, which presupposes the construction of an (attractive) organisational identity in the form of alleged organisational characteristics, goals, policies and values. Branding also presupposes that people are convinced that the organisation is a 'true' one in other respects as well; only if there is an effective hierarchy is it plausible that the unique characteristics and values of an organisation are affecting its production and products.

In such a world, it is no wonder that there is an ample supply of general ideas and recommendations about the way organisations should be constructed and managed – about the forms they should take (Brunsson and Jacobsson 2000, Røvik 2007). Examples of such management standards propagated by various organisation experts include matrix organisations, management by objectives, quality systems, lean production, process orientation, process reengineering and balanced scorecards – standards that are explicitly directed at 'organisations' of any kind (Henning 2000). There are also standards directed at organisations for corporate social responsibility, environment protection, workplace conditions and the like. And there is much fluctuation – standards are changed, new standards are produced and old ones are forgotten.

Managers of all kinds of organisations must take such standards into account when they make decisions about organisational forms. It is generally easier to justify forms in accordance with, or at least not conflicting with, what leading experts claim to be the right forms. And organisational managers are likely to see the need for reform in order to keep the organisation up to date and to be able to represent the future organisation in accordance with the standards that are popular at the moment.

Comparisons

We compare entities that we perceive as being fundamentally alike, as belonging to the same category. Based on their general similarities as organisations, states and firms have been compared with each other and have inspired each other. Most notably, firms have imitated states by using concepts such as strategy or headquarters, by introducing various forms of industrial democracy and by relating to their environment more broadly, in a way that is typical for democratic states – via such ideas as stakeholder management or corporate social responsibility.

Also, states have imitated firms. But the NPO reforms imply that not only can the state as a whole compare itself with firms; all the former subunits, the new state organisations, can do the same. It is difficult to argue that a traditional administrative unit should learn from firms; they do not belong to the same category. But by placing the subunit in the same general category as firms, such comparisons become much easier.

It is difficult to imitate the practice of other organisations, because it is impossible to observe all their operations. It is easier to imitate the way other organisations are represented by their managers. Firms are powerful models of imitation for other organisations, for several reasons. They have a long tradition of presenting themselves as organisations (Lamoreaux 2004). Large firms have recently placed strong emphasis on and have sunk sizeable resources into representation activities – by involving top management in more and more representational tasks and by creating and expanding large information departments. And most firms are able to present appealing images. These factors make it both easy and attractive to imitate firms' representations of themselves. Thus the construction of organisations tends to create a great deal of 'company-isation', reforms borrowing ideas that firms use in their representations: structures, processes, accounting techniques and ideologies that firms claim are used in their organisations.

More Reformers and Reforms

So by constructing organisations, one is relating to a world with an abundance of ideas, standards and representations describing appropriate and good organisational forms. Constructing organisations also requires the hiring of managers with responsibility for organisational forms and for representing the organisation. The managers, in turn, tend to expand the local administration substantially by hiring information officers, accountants and other administrative personnel who can help to represent and manage the organisation. NPO reforms thereby not only increase administrative costs in the former subunits; they create a management with the resources for, and incentive to reform. The autonomy of the organisation allows it to follow standards, receive advice and buy management consulting services. And like other organisations, new public organisations are under pressure to reform in order to comply with standards and model organisations. When dividing state administration into several organisations, reforms are likely to multiply. The NPO reforms created a fertile ground for further reforms.

Ideas, Practice and Reconstructive Reforms

By making and announcing decisions, organisations lay themselves open to comparisons between their decisions and their actions. Organisational operations are evaluated not only on their own merits, but also on the basis of their correspondence with decisions. As organisational research has demonstrated, there is no guarantee that decisions are easily transformed into actions – a key reason being the idea side of decisions. Decisions that reflect popular standards about organisational forms, for instance, may be unrealistic or inappropriate for the operations of an individual organisation, and therefore difficult to implement.

Even the general idea of organisation suffers from a certain lack of realism. Even if organisations are represented according to the idea of the true organisation, such representations are often difficult to combine with more detailed observations about the workings of organisations. There is often a discrepancy between the idea of the organisation and organisational practice – or even between the idea and what is a possible or useful organisational practice. The institution of organisation belongs to the group of institutions that exert stronger control over what we want and say than they exert over what we do (Brunsson 2006: ch. 1).

A substantial portion of the last 50 years of organisational research, in fact, has been oriented towards the demonstration of this discrepancy. From this perspective, organisations have been described as having unclear boundaries and limited autonomy and as being similar to rather than distinct from each other (Meyer and Rowan 1977, Krasner 1999). In practice, organisations are difficult to control from above. Control is often exerted from below; top management is dependent on the knowledge of activities possessed by lower levels of the organisation. In certain situations, managers talk and decide in a way that is systematically opposite to the way the organisation acts (Brunsson 2007: ch. 7). Coordination is hampered by conflict and inconsistency (Pfeffer 1981). Rationality is limited, and various forms of irrationality are common (March 1978, Brunsson 2000). Organisations also routinely use forms of intelligence other than rationality – forms such as experiential learning, imitation and rule following.

Such discrepancies have been described as examples of a 'de-coupling' (Meyer and Rowan 1977) between talk and decisions on the one hand and practice on the other. The phenomenon of de-coupling protects lofty ideas in organisations. Because operations are little affected by representations, representations need not be tightly adapted to operations and their local idiosyncrasies, but can be more freely adapted to the general idea about what is a true and respectable organisation.

There is a risk of instability, however – a risk that the discrepancy between representation and practice is suspected or revealed. Managers or external parties may learn about activities that are difficult to describe in accordance with decisions and representations. People in close contact with operations may provide information. Those selling organisational standards or consultant services have a vested interest in pointing out that the organisation is not working according to decisions and must therefore be changed. An exposure of de-coupling threatens the image of the true organisation as a coordinated unit under hierarchical control, in which distinctive qualities and purposes are efficiently turned into action.

Doubts about whether or not an organisation's practice really reflects the idea of the true organisation produces a strong incentive for reforms to reconstruct the organisation. Such reforms include attempts at recreating or reinforcing organisational distinctiveness, to create a clearer business concept, clearer objectives and a clearer task; or to concentrate on the core business, focusing merely on one goal or one task. Or the reforms may be aimed at re-establishing or reinforcing hierarchy by installing better control systems or better management accounting systems. Or the reforms may consist of attempts at increasing rationality, for instance, by developing numerical objectives or by introducing better follow-up and evaluation systems or more rational budget procedures. Most popular contemporary management standards build on and are attempts to keep or reinforce the organisation as a true organisation, even if they differ in their detailed methods for reaching this state. Again, reforms are driven by a general idea rather than by the experience of operative difficulties and failures.

Such reforms have the same content as the reforms that created the organisation in the first place. So a newly constructed public organisation is likely to continue reforming in the same direction. But now the purpose is no longer to construct, but to re-construct – to make the practice of the existing organisation more like a true organisation. Constructing organisations involves the radical act of introducing a different institution, while reconstructing involves relatively routine attempts within a given institution to adapt actions to what we want and how we talk. Although identical in contents, construction and reconstruction cannot be expected to have the same causes. As I argued previously, it is difficult to explain why new public organisations were ever constructed; but once they are constructed, it is easy to explain why they – like other organisations – are prone to reform.

Maintaining Hope

A peculiar characteristic of reconstructive reforms is that they do not seem to end. The demand for reconstructive reforms comes not only from newly formed organisations such as the new public organisations. The demand seems to be strong even in old organisations that have previously undergone such reforms, often many times. The repetition is an indication that previous reforms have failed, which comes as no surprise to students of organisation. It is difficult to make organisations work as true organisations. But repeated reconstructive reforms also indicate that people do not lose hope, the hope that these reforms will one day succeed. Hope is a fundamental prerequisite for reforms; without the hope that the true organisation is possible to realise, reconstructive reforms would not take place. Without understanding how hope is maintained or not, we cannot fully understand why organisations undertake reforms.

How can people maintain their hope for realising the ideal of the true organisation? In ordinary organisational life it is easy; de-coupling keeps ideals protected from practical experiences that may threaten the belief that they are possible and useful to implement. But in reform situations, the risks are higher; the very idea of reform is to confront ideals and practice. Even though the purpose of reform is to transform practice in accordance with ideas, the opposite may happen: that reforms change lofty ideas rather than changing practice. By trying to realise our ideas, we may learn about their practical limitations and lose our hope that they can ever be realised. This can happen early in the reform process, when people meet difficulties in transforming an attractive, general standard to more concrete guidelines for their own organisation. Or with attempts at implementation and contact with reformees, reformers may discover that the attractive, simple and obviously correct reform principles turn into a much more complex programme when they are adapted to actual, practical situations – a programme which no longer seems obvious. And losing hope would appear to be a natural consequence of reform failures, especially repeated failures.

Organisations seem rather robust against losing hope, however, even in connection with reconstructive reforms. People can use various cognitive or rhetorical mechanisms to help them to maintain their hope, even for such an elevated project as realising the idea of the true organisation in organisational practice. One reason, again, is the ability of organisations to relate to the world of ideas and to de-emphasise practical experience. There is no reason to expect less hopefulness in new public organisations than in other organisations, and they are likely, therefore, to be as reformist as organisations in general are. This section exemplifies some mechanisms by which organisations maintain hope, collected from my own empirical studies of reform processes in public and private organisations (Brunsson 2006).

Avoiding Practice

One mechanism for maintaining hope is to avoid dealing with practice, even in reform processes. In spite of the fact that reforms are initiated in order to change practice, people successfully avoid relating to practice, thereby maintaining their hope.

Reforms may be used for the purpose of representation, for example, and this purpose may overshadow the purpose of changing practice. In early stages of a reform, a model of the future organisation is represented, and this model is attractive because it conforms to the idea of the true organisation. The top managers I studied found this model to be useful when they represented their organisation to external audiences. Managers at lower levels found the reform model to be a handy tool for describing their department to other people, such as job applicants and newly hired employees. The pre-reform situation was perceived as complex, confused and embarrassingly difficult to describe. The reform model offered a clear, logical and consistent image of the organisation, and provided a much better fit for representation.

Although the reform had not been implemented, and most of these people did not change their own operations in accordance with the reform principles, they found the reform highly useful and successful. Because their experience with the reform was positive, there was no reason to lose hope.

Representations based on reform content can be formulated in a particularly attractive way because they describe an imagined future, and are not limited by empirical knowledge. Because of the futuristic nature of reforms, there are more ways to avoid relating to actual practice. Many people involved in reforms turned out to be concentrating on future practice rather than the existing one; and this was the case not only when the reform started, but also long after, when it had been under implementation for a long time. Any practice that could be observed after the initiation of the reform was extraneous. The argument that a reform had had almost no practical consequences or that it had had unintended negative consequences could be refuted as irrelevant. It was always the future consequences that counted. And the future can always be positive because it can be constructed without being tied to actual practice. Indeed, in the future there would be a true organisation. There was no reason to lose hope.

Choose the Right Practice

Sometimes people cannot completely separate themselves from knowledge about practice or about practical problems. But they can still be selective, choosing to consider only practices that fail to challenge the reform principle. This selection of practice is the key element of several mechanisms of hope.

To take just one example, reformers can avoid learning from their own experience, of which they have first-hand knowledge, and concentrate on the practices of others, about which they know much less and which therefore seems much easier to change according to the reform principles. In this way they can maintain their hope that the true organisation is a realistic and useful project.

In my studies, I have found no reformers who practised what they preached. Most of the external consultants worked in a way that was contrary to the principles for which they argued. Yet they did not compare their reform principle with this practice, which might have undermined their hope about the realism of the reform principles. They saw only the need for their clients to reform. And top managers who had decided upon reform were poor followers of even the initial steps of the reforms. Yet their own lack of adherence did not lead consultants or managers to doubts or to reduce their hope that the reforms were realistic, useful and highly needed – for others. Similarly, many people on lower levels of the organisation who reported that they did not and could not use the reform model in their own departments, had not lost hope; other departments had great potential and need for becoming orderly and rationally organised in accordance with the reform content.

Hopeful Interpretations

In spite of many attempts at avoiding and selecting information about practical problems, information about serious problems or the failure of the reform sometimes reaches reformers and reformees. The remaining strategy for maintaining hope, then, is to interpret the information in a way that is not threatening to the principle – by looking on the bright side. There are many ways of doing that.

For example, one may cling to the idea of the first successful step. Even if a reform has met strong obstacles to implementation, people remember their original level of aspiration as being low, so it corresponds to the small things they have actually achieved (merely creating some documents, perhaps). Thus the reform seems to be a success so far. There is no reason for doubt. And the aspirations for the continued reform process may again be set as high as they actually were from the beginning – great hopes can be revived. Because of the flexibility of aspirations, the otherwise difficult task of combining success and continuation is solved; a reform is already a success because it meets the low aspirations that people believe existed from the start; yet it must still be continued, because aspirations for the future are higher.

Or hope can be maintained by considering oneself, one's department or one's organisation as a unique case. Even if one must admit that the reform principles have not worked in the present context, it is not necessary to admit that the reform principles are wrong or unrealistic. People who had found it impossible or inadequate to implement reconstructive reforms in their own department or their own top management group argued in my studies that the principles were realistic and useful in other departments. Other cases are unlike one's own case. Other cases are general rather than unique, and people in general could, of course, benefit from general reform principles because general principles fit the general case.

In short, people can avoid generalising from their own cases. The general rule can be considered valid, even if it does not fit their unique experience. In this way, general truths can be maintained even if they do not fit the experience of many people. The more extraordinary we consider ourselves to be, the less relevant are our failures to realise the true organisation and the more hopeful we can be.

Organisations and Hope

These are a few examples of mechanisms of hope. By applying them and many other mechanisms, people succeed in escaping the influence of practical problems and failures, and are able to maintain their hope about the true organisation, even when the reform situation puts it to the test. And maintaining hope makes it possible to launch new reforms in the same direction.

Organisations seem to be environments in which it is critical, even required, that one is hopeful. Organisations are projects, the very existence of which expresses a certain level of hopefulness. They are attempts at achieving things – not results. Attempts, projects and decisions are based on a measure of hope – on the assumption that a desired state may be attainable in the future. Organisations are, in part, failed projects; there is extensive experience within them of things not going according to plan. But it appears meaningless to organise and to mobilise organisational action if there is no hope of future success. It is difficult to organise on the basis of the opposites of hope: despair or apathy. A certain degree of hopefulness would seem to form part of our role as members of organisations. And that hopefulness stimulates organisational reform.

A Revivalist Movement

The main hypothesis in this chapter has been that the movement of new public organisations was driven by ideals rather than by practical problems and considerations. In many ways, it was similar to religious revivalist movements. It did not start as the effect of empirical changes, but was initiated by a new interpretation of reality using an existing abstract and a well known concept – in this case the concept of organisation. This concept was interpreted in its pure form, and was the inspiration for a great shift. The aspirations were high; one strived to create true organisations from units that, from the new perspective, had been serious failures in the past. There was great enthusiasm and little resistance to this project among those who had seen the light. Because practical experiences and empirical data were not critical for the great shift, there was much decisiveness and vigour in the process.

Once entered into the world of organisations, there were many more abstract ideas to find and many propagators of such ideas. There was also a great deal of experience with reforms and reforming. As in any eschatological movement, there was a strong need for hope. But organisations provide a context in which hope is facilitated. And when confronted with practical problems or failures, people in organisations have access to a number of mechanisms of hope that prevent them from losing their faith and allow them to continue working for lofty and elevated ideals – even if they do not achieve them. Although the heyday of the NPO movement is long past, the movement constitutes a fascinating and instructive empirical case, not only for students of public administration, but for any student of organisation.

PART II
CONVERGENCE
AND DIVERGENCE
AMONG COUNTRIES

NPM in Anglo-Saxon Countries

John Halligan

Introduction

This chapter examines the concept of New Public Management (NPM) as it emerged in Anglo-Saxon countries, and its life-cycle over the reform era from its origins in the 1980s through to the mixture of models in the 2000s as countries added to and subtracted from NPM features. After more than two decades of activity by the Anglo-Saxon countries – the early reformers – the products of that activity have become clearer: the more stark manifestations of NPM now have less prominence in practice. A more elusive matter is how to characterise NPM's successor, and the ways in which NPM continues to exercise an influence.

The original formulations of NPM are accepted by observers as the starting point (Pollitt 1990, Hood 1991), bearing in mind that these English authors were responding to what was occurring in Anglo-Saxon countries, the original pathfinders that first displayed archetypal NPM features. This chapter first addresses the nature of the Anglo-Saxon group, examines how their systems evolved following the adoption of NPM, and then considers the fate of NPM.

Anglo-Saxon Countries

The four Anglo-Saxon countries of Australia, Canada, New Zealand and the United Kingdom have been regarded as a coherent group by way of a common tradition and historical and continuing close associations and interactions (Halligan 2007a). The 'old Commonwealth' – or the 'Westminster democracies' – has formed a natural group of industrialised democracies with institutional roots in the British tradition. However, given that national factors and prevailing politics have shaped traditions historically and provided for substantial variation in significant areas, there have long been debates in the former British colonies about the derivation and ongoing significance of the Westminster model (Patapan, Wanna and Weller 2005).

Nonetheless, beyond institutional traditions, a number of factors have reinforced the identity of the Anglo-American group over time. The continuing patterns of interaction – historically formed and culturally supported – have been highly significant. There has been a tradition of exporting and transferring British institutions, within the Empire and later the Commonwealth, which has provided a mechanism for communicating among the four with a basis in a common language, cultural legacy and institutions. Furthermore, endogenous communication channels influence members of this group through networks and bilateral relations between countries. Moreover, the formal networks that originated in relationships developed between Britain and its colonies were maintained following decolonisation, and have included agency-level exchanges of staff, regular meetings and the circulation of ideas. Even alliances for defence and war – most recently in Afghanistan and Iraq – have been entrenched features for members of the group.

A differentiating feature of the Anglo-Saxon tradition has been the lack of a well-developed concept of the state, which produced the contrast between the 'stateless' tradition of these systems and the 'state' tradition of Europe. Hence, a more fluid view of the relationship between state and society has existed in Anglophone countries. Moreover, while European observers tend to recognise different state traditions, and the Anglo-Saxon as a distinct and meaningful category, others may focus on the Westminster system or model (Aucoin 1995) and the fusion of the executive and the legislature under this form of responsible government.

The group's distinctiveness was reaffirmed early in the reform era of the last three decades. Administrative change of great magnitude occurred as reform was discovered to be viable and often effective, in contrast to the previous incremental change. Despite substantial variations between countries in the process, type and impact of the reforms, the strong similarities were evident among Anglophone countries. The early identification of NPM came from British writers who first discerned the trend under Thatcher (Pollitt 1990, Hood 1991). In addition to specific reforms in Britain (for example privatisation and executive agencies), individual country programmes gained international significance with New Zealand's 'public management model' being influential (Boston et al. 1996). Early parallels were drawn among them, and Australia, New Zealand and the United Kingdom were grouped because they adhered more to the precepts of NPM than other OECD countries (Hood 1996a). At the peak of the OECD's fixation on NPM, Anglophone experiments were upheld as the ideal (OECD 1995).

The emergence of this distinctive set of reforms in the Anglo-Saxon countries resulted from a pattern of interaction that accorded legitimacy and relevance to initiatives but importantly a tradition that facilitated the rapid transmission and acceptance of ideas and practice (Halligan 2007a). The reform movement therefore served to reinforce the notion of a distinctive Anglophone group identity contrasting with that of other traditions (Halligan 2010a). At the same time this close identification of NPM with Anglo-Saxon countries obscured the fact that there were variations in the acceptance of approaches and in the timing and process of implementation. They ranged from New Zealand's abrupt entry to Canada's slow engagement over several decades.

Comparing NPM across Four Countries

The group of four countries considered here is regarded as reasonably homogeneous for analytical and comparative purposes even though there are some differences in governmental institutions. All maintain parliamentary systems, but two are unitary systems while the Australian and Canadian constitutions combine federalism with responsible government along Westminster lines.

The four have different sized public sectors with New Zealand's being small in absolute terms while Australia's is relatively small as a proportion of GDP, the rest falling in the middle range for the OECD. Canada has occupied an intermediate position for some purposes between its North American neighbour, the US, and the others. The United Kingdom system has greater complexity because of its size and long history of institutional development.

The long-term impact of major reform programmes can be examined over several generations of reform in the Anglophone group. Distinctive models of reform can be distinguished: managerialism (Pollitt 1990), in which management is the central concept; and NPM, in which the market element is prominent and disaggregation, privatisation and a private sector orientation are at the forefront (Hood 1991). How to characterise the 2000s is less clear, although variations on integrated governance are apparent through the renewed focus on modes of coordinating and control designed to produce greater coherence and capacity for the public sector. The four countries experienced these models of reform, but with different emphases.

United Kingdom

The United Kingdom was first to implement a management reform agenda. Margaret Thatcher reasserted the political executive's role and questioned the role and operation of the state in Anglophone countries with considerable success. Furthermore, the UK has regularly renewed the reform agenda under successive prime ministers and consequently has passed through several phases of reform (Pollitt and Bouckaert 2004). In many respects it can claim to have engineered one of the most comprehensive series of NPM-type reforms over three decades centred on management, performance, executive agencies, public–private experiments, privatisation and devolution (Richards 2003). The UK has also ranked highest in the OECD for outsourcing of government services (Blöndal 2005). In addition, the audit 'explosion' was most explicit in Britain (Power 2005), although the institutionalising of a broader role for auditing also occurred in the other three countries (Bouckaert and Halligan 2008). In the 2000s consumer choice has provided an extension of NPM, reflecting market principles.

The mid-2000 formulation of public service reform by the Cabinet Office (2006a) distinguished four elements, three of which can be linked to NPM: top-down performance management; the introduction of greater competition and contestability in the provision of public services; the introduction of greater pressure from citizens including through choice and voice; and measures to strengthen the capability and capacity of civil and public servants. However, the constant restatement of the reform agenda has attracted claims of chronic reformism (Pollitt 2006).

In this formulation, the British performance management framework became highly elaborated with a top-down design, covering targets, service standards and performance assessments that included inspection and direct intervention. Additionally, the public service agreements (PSAs) regime constituted a new tool for steering and coordination that was designed to pull central government together under one performance framework, and to enhance the Treasury's influence over priority setting by organisations outside central government. Limitations to the regime included frequent changes to targets, weak links with systems where relevant activity occurred, and presentation strategies for blame avoidance. Moreover, objectives were not necessarily clear on priorities and PSAs appeared to have weak incentive effects (James 2004a). There was meant to be streamlining of the PSAs in the 2007 spending review, but the continuities between spending reviews were reported as considerable (C. Talbot to Treasury Committee 2007).

Two prominent trends in the 2000s included first, the fate of disaggregation through the use of executive agencies with the reversal of this central reform theme well advanced (Talbot and Johnson 2007) and second, attempts to strengthen central control mechanisms that reflected a Westminster model (Richards and Smith 2006).

In the reversal of the disaggregation theme, the UK has entertained joined-up government since the 1990s as a means of reducing fragmentation. Since 2007, public service agreement (PSA) targets for departments have been cross-departmental; the performance targets are shared by more than one department. A survey of officials indicated that most thought Whitehall was not particularly joined-up and had mixed judgements about the effectiveness of the PSA system. The concept was regarded positively, but seen as containing gaps and system blockages. The factors limiting its impact included the complexity of issues, a lack of hard accountability mechanisms and weak support for sharing (Parker et al. 2010).

As one of the countries affected most by the global financial crisis, the UK revived programme review, efficiency dividends and asset sales. The scale of the deficit confronting the government has meant that spending cuts on public services and other constraints of an 'age of austerity' dominate other considerations.

New Zealand

New Zealand has also experienced several phases of change, but two models: late 1980s–early 1990s and the revision of the first in the 2000s (Boston and Eichbaum 2007, Gregory 2006). The original New Zealand model combined standard management reforms pursued in other OECD countries with distinctive, often unique features based on ideas derived from public choice and institutional economics, and which addressed *inter alia* the questions of agency and transaction costs. The New Zealand model won international admiration as a unique case of public sector reform that employed a sophisticated and coherent framework that was theoretically informed (Boston et al. 1996).

The core public service was subjected to the application of new principles in reformulating the departmental structure, the two most important being the separation of responsibilities for policy and delivery, and the identification of specific functions with specialised organisations. A range of financial management reforms were introduced, two distinctions being between inputs, outputs and outcomes (with the emphasis on outputs), and the definition of government roles as either the purchaser of outputs from agencies or the owner of agencies with an interest in the return on its investment. A new legislative framework for trading bodies enabled corporatisation (eventually a step towards privatisation) and defined principles for state-owned enterprises to operate like a business. Also central was the redefinition of ministers' relationship with departmental chief executives based on associating outcomes with the former and outputs with the latter. The relationship was seen as being contractually based: the government (the owner) purchased outputs from departments. The renamed chief executives (formerly permanent officials) took contract appointments based on performance agreements. Another element was the general reliance on contracting out the delivery of services to the private and voluntary sectors.

Much of the 1990s was spent implementing, reviewing and refining the reforms, although there was difficulty with producing sustained improvements. The strategic capacity of government had been neglected in the framework, producing a short-term focus and inattention to the collective side of government. Strategic and key result areas were introduced for specifying government priorities and focusing performance, but weaknesses in planning and results subsequently became apparent (Scott 2001).

The official evaluation of the system determined it to be sound and successful, but criticised the economic principles that accounted for the system's uniqueness (Schick 1996). While management practice and discourse were transformed, perennial questions of public administration remained with questions outstanding in the areas of incentives and performance measurement, public service ethics and strategic management (Boston et al. 1996). A decade later the list of problems was still extensive, and included fragmentation, domination of the purchase function over ownership, lack of an evaluation culture, service quality variations, and the weak alignment of both agency and system needs and political and managerial accountability (Boston and Eichbaum 2007). There was also the need to factor in more directly the political executive, which was partly supported by a strengthening of its advisory capacity (Eichbaum and Shaw 2010).

In the third phase, system rebalancing and the renewal of public management became central, if cautiously and incrementally pursued. Several themes emerged after 1999 covering capability, outcomes, integration and central agency roles within a philosophy supportive of the public sector. New Zealand concluded that the public management system provided a foundation to work from, but that significant shifts in emphasis were needed. Specific issues requiring attention were products of fragmentation under an agency system: the need for integrating service delivery, cross-agency coordination, improvements to public service culture and central agency responsibilities. As a result, there has been a rationalising and refining of systemic elements to align them with government goals; measures to readdress organisational fragmentation and coordination gaps; and more emphasis on horizontal integration.

The result is that NPM has been adapted and modified, even though basic features remain, and is likely to be further challenged as horizontal issues receive more attention (Chapman and Duncan 2007, Gill et al. 2010). The central agency-driven assessment of all agencies using a performance improvement framework, which commenced in 2010, is a reminder that the focus on high performance remains central.

Australia

The Australian experience can be summarised with reference to three models of reform each associated with a generation, and coinciding with the decades 1980s–2000s. Managerialism best reflects the first phase in which management became the central concept and reshaped thinking. This was succeeded by a phase that came close to the mainstream depiction of NPM, in which the market element was favoured and features such as disaggregation, privatisation and a private sector focus were at the forefront. In turn, NPM was followed, although not displaced, in the 2000s by an emergent model that emphasised integrated governance (Halligan 2006).

The initial period of reform displaced traditional administration with a package of reforms based on management. Over about a decade, a new management philosophy was developed and implemented which emphasised results rather than inputs and processes. The main elements of the reform programme concentrated on the core public service and improving financial management, followed by corporatisation and later privatisation. The Financial Management Improvement Program dominated the reforms of the 1980s. The Australian focus on results, outcomes and performance-oriented management dates from this time, although the emphasis was on programme budgeting and management. The flagging reform momentum in the mid-1980s produced new directions that were linked to an emerging micro-economic reform agenda (Campbell and Halligan 1993).

The first phase displayed incipient NPM in several respects, but the dominant theme was management improvement. The high commitment to neo-liberal reforms in the 1990s, following the advent of a conservative Coalition government, led to the public service becoming highly decentralised, marketised, contractualised and privatised. The agenda centred on competition and contestability of service delivery, contracting out, client focus, the application of the purchaser/provider principle, a deregulated personnel system and greater use of the private sector. A new financial management framework was introduced that included budgeting on a full accrual basis from 1999/2000, implementation of outputs and outcomes reporting, and extending agency devolution to budget estimates and financial management.

The devolution of responsibilities from central agencies to line departments and agencies was highly significant, with a diminished role for central agencies being one consequence. The Department of Finance was heavily downsized, the Public Service Commission's role was modest while interventions by the Department of the Prime Minister and Cabinet were constrained and displayed disinterest in public service leadership.

The Australian experience has been notable for the willingness to experiment and to respond to reform limitations, which was illustrated by the Coalition government's pragmatism (1996–2007) when it moved from an NPM reform agenda during its first two terms to refinements and revaluation of the worth of the public service. Having driven neo-liberal reforms, the government confronted the contradictions of complex reform programmes and how to ensure that their priorities were reflected in programme implementation. Whereas NPM led to fragmentation and vertical structures, underlying the new direction were control, coherence and performance. The integrated governance approach of the 2000s involved rebalancing centre and line, whole-of-government and integrating agendas, central monitoring of agency delivery, and reconfiguring of portfolio organisation. The agenda now placed greater emphasis on strengthening internal capacity through improving implementation and performance. One expression of this was the use of the traditional machinery – cabinet, central agency and the department – but within a performance management framework (Halligan 2006, Bouckaert and Halligan 2008).

The Rudd government introduced its own interpretation of the issues with new policy agendas for transforming public dialogue and emphasising national approaches to improving delivery and performance and objectives for improving the public service, accountability, performance, financial management and intergovernmental relations. Less constrained than other Anglophone systems by the impact of the financial crisis, a blueprint for reform was produced that emphasised high performance and a renovation of internal capacity (Advisory Group 2010).

Canada

Despite the regular grouping of Anglo-American countries as distinctive expressions of NPM, such categorisations disguised differences in pathways and the limitations of a NPM focus. Canada and the United States fitted the category of partly reformed systems, until the 2000s produced a more explicit agenda at the centre. Canada has been the most enigmatic of the Anglophone systems with a public service system that reflects both the Westminster tradition and the influence of the United States, but an administrative tradition and a public service that is distinctively Canadian.

The US influence has been much more significant on Canada than that of other systems. For example, the Glassco Royal Commission on Government Organization (1962–64), to which the origins of modern Canadian management can be traced, was regarded as the counterpart of the US Hoover commissions (Dwivedi and Halligan 2003). And an examination of significant innovations introduced by the federal and the provincial governments between 1960 and 1990 reported that ten were directly based on US influence (Gow 1994).

In terms of management reform, two features were well established: the innovative, creative quality that has produced significant management ideas over the decades; and the lack of assurance when it came to implementing new initiatives systematically over time.

Canada was one of the first Anglophone countries to explore management reform but was slow to incorporate and institutionalise it. In some respects the public service remained unmanagerialised; yet it eventually acquired standard management features. NPM was not introduced rapidly or through a sustained reform programme. The Audit Office sometimes filled the vacuum left by a lack of sustained leadership from senior politicians and lead central agencies (Aucoin 1995).

The verdict in 2000 (Aucoin 2001) identified weaknesses in the management reform process and divided responsibility for human resource management. The Office of the Auditor General continued to raise issues about performance data, and scepticism about the agenda continued (Clark and Swain 2005). With performance management there has also been considerable movement in the 2000s in using information for improved results and with developing a scheme for departments. Indeed, Canada acquired a performance management framework which had the formal attributes of an official performance management model along with other Anglo-American countries (Bouckaert and Halligan 2008). Furthermore, the management and accountability framework has been extended (for example, organisational performance was linked to deputy minister performance) with a more sustained approach to implementation and eventual rationalisation of human resource management agencies.

With the move towards a governance approach there have been interesting experiments that have tested the potential of flexible and focused organisation such as alternative service delivery and horizontal management (Zussman 2002, Bakvis and Julliet 2004). In this regard, Canada had an early focus on citizens and new modes of governance, in particular integrated service delivery, e-governance and other smart practices (Borins et al. 2007, Kernaghan 2009, Marson and Heintzman 2009).

With its tradition of pragmatism and moderation, Canada 'mildly embraced downsizing and the new public management … and avoided over committing to one or two radical reforms' (Gow 2004: 21). This pattern is seen as consistent with 'a pragmatic, evolutionary approach to public sector reform, informed by a collegial, corporate approach involving deputy ministers and other executives' (Lindquist 2006: 61). However, insufficient political commitment and excessive political conflict are said to explain why implementation of reform has been problematic (Pollitt and Bouckaert 2004). Since politicians have not been inclined to lead on reform, it has been left to the public service leaders (Aucoin 2002), which has allowed them greater scope than elsewhere to pursue agenda (Good 2003). This was apparent in the latter half of the 2000s, when, despite minority governments, there has been sustained implementation of the performance management framework (Halligan 2009).

Durability of Elements of New Public Management

Performance and markets have posed the big questions in international public management during the last 15 years, both being central to NPM. Also widely debated has been disaggregation through the use of agencies and contractual relations with third parties.

Towards Market Steering and Regulation

The belief in superiority of the market was once pronounced in several jurisdictions, but this had long passed by the time the global financial crisis forced the issue to an unusual degree. Conviction politics and ideology had been replaced by pragmatism. Though while the unrelenting drive for market testing, outsourcing, disaggregation and competition has been substantially dissipated, the use of market approaches was not discarded.

Despite the different patterns of change between Westminster countries they found themselves confronting broadly similar issues by the turn of the century. Their neo-liberal reforms provided substantial potential in the 2000s for corrective mechanisms for the excesses and limitations of NPM. Reflection on the results of an intense neo-liberal reform agenda produced refinements and a re-evaluation of the worth of the public service under new leadership that suited different agendas. The features of NPM – disaggregation, devolution, outsourcing and multiple services providers – supported specialisation but also encouraged fragmentation and reinforced vertical structures.

Of all four systems, the United Kingdom under Tony Blair appeared to remain closest to a variant of NPM. Markets were still evident in British conceptions with a reform model that combined top-down performance management, competition and contestability in providing public services, and citizen choice (Cabinet Office 2006a). The same government had previously proposed that the provision of services should be 'through the sector best placed to provide those services most effectively, whether the public, private or voluntary sector, or partnerships' (Chancellor of the Exchequer 1998: sec. 4). The UK, however, was the only one of the four Anglo-Saxon countries not to experience a recent change of government prior to 2010.

Another formulation of the place of markets emerged in Australia partly in response to the impact of the global economic environment. The prime minister argued for the replacement of one orthodoxy by another, and contrasted 'competing political traditions … on the role of government and the market', identifying neo-liberalism and anti-regulation with his political opponents. The message was for an activist state and a central role for government in regulating markets and providing public goods (Rudd 2009: 21). This did not preclude bringing together flexibility and markets in design. The approach propounded by one Australian politician, self-styled the 'Minister for Markets', is to embrace the use of markets that are 'properly designed and well regulated' (Swan 2008: 2, 8). While there are precedents for this approach (for example, the Job Network for the delivery of employment services), the conscious articulation of this thinking forms part of a systemic approach that has been applied in different ways. Commonwealth–state government relations have been redesigned using 'a more market-driven framework' that has both incentives and accountability. Additionally, designed and regulated markets have been used for areas such as health, water and rental housing by governments wanting to specify policy objectives and then design an appropriate 'market'.

More generally, the range of options available for public agencies in delivering services was enhanced as they drew on third parties in the private, voluntary sectors and sub-national government. Consequently, networks were pronounced as a universal trend (Lane 2009). Moreover, the acceptance of more flexible approaches to deliver systems for public services and the move beyond the traditional monolithic departmental structure was an important change in thinking, which broke the nexus of integrated policy and implementation and led to a greater use of specialised agencies.

A range of interesting experiments have tested the potential of flexible and focused organisations such as alternative service delivery and horizontal management. Canada, for example, became well known internationally for its focus on citizens and its emerging modes of governance centred on e-governance and integrated service delivery. However, the countries have also been combining commitments to devolution with reviewing and rebuilding core capacity. The debate continues over the costs of capacity deficits and the financial tradeoffs and transaction costs of using agents to perform basic tasks.

Disaggregation and Rationalising Public Bodies

The NPM phase of reform produced greater arm's-length management including the creation of agencies (Pollitt and Talbot 2004). The pattern was not, however, consistent in Anglophone countries despite their reputation for being foremost exponents of NPM, with New Zealand and the United Kingdom opting for systemic separation of policy and execution, and Australia and Canada favouring more ad hoc approaches. Nevertheless, the general direction was towards devolution and experimentation with a range of bodies (executive agencies, statutory authorities and other non-departmental organisations).

In the 2000s, there was movement away from arm's-length agencies and management as political agendas changed in all four countries. The intensification of central coordination and moves towards the reintegration of agencies within the core public service, and new mechanisms for controlling and regulating agencies, pointed to a swing of the pendulum. The general direction was away from emphases prevalent under NPM as re-aggregation succeeded disaggregation. The partial reversal of the agencification trend internationally was appropriately most apparent in Britain (Talbot and Johnson 2007), as the country that had originally led the fashion for executive agencies (Massey and Pyper 2005). The 're-aggregation' prevalent there could not be reproduced in Australia and Canada, which had not systematically followed the British path, yet broadly similar movements were underway elsewhere reflecting a mood to review and tighten oversight through the restructuring and rationalisation of public bodies. The Australian agenda centred on the governance and extent of non-departmental organisations. The more comprehensive ministerial department was resurrected through absorbing bodies and applying tighter control over public agencies (Halligan 2006). In Canada, government response to the Gomery inquiry into the 'sponsorship scandal' was to address control over crown corporations and accountability in general (Aucoin 2007). Similarly, the New Zealand focus on creating arm's-length bodies was succeeded by some restructuring and consolidation and moves to more effective control of crown entities (Gill 2008).

While the trend towards a central resurgence has been apparent, the role of the centre was being attended to much earlier in countries like the UK (Burnham and Pyper 2008). Depending on context, the reform era in some countries can be seen either as a steady oscillation between attention to reforms designed to expand performance and attention to those for steering or sometimes simultaneous adjustments to line and central agencies.

Managing for Performance

Long-term trends have supported the ascendancy and durability of performance as a dominant force. Indeed, the Anglophone systems were highly committed to performance management over two decades during which they refined their measurement and performance framework and increased their capacity to monitor performance. Nevertheless they have, of course, followed different pathways with their frameworks and employed implementation styles that have differed in terms of how relationships between outputs and outcomes are conceived, the responsibilities given to chief executives and the roles of central personnel agencies in handling performance oversight. As a consequence, the exigencies of reform agendas have produced a considerable convergence on public management during the 2000s (Bouckaert and Halligan 2008).

Yet a common element is that practice has fallen short of aspirations, and significant questions remain about the quality and use of performance information in the budget process, internal decision-making and external reporting, and agency engagement. Moreover, there continue to be issues about the use of performance information by public managers and politicians, challenges to accomplishing performance management and a heavy reliance on this approach. The limitations of country approaches have included questions about how well the framework is working; the level and quality of implementation; and top-down complexities and dysfunctional results (Bouckaert and Halligan 2008, Van Dooren et al. 2010).

Nevertheless, the performance movement continues to exercise a pervasive influence on governments that are wrestling with complex issues of public policy. Consequently, Anglophone performance management systems have been substantially refined and continue to be fine-tuned to improve operability. However, unless performance management better serves internal and external needs, particularly those of politicians, their legitimacy and centrality may eventually be undermined.

Comparative Perspectives

The reform era has been remarkable for producing sustained transformations in public administration in countries internationally. The Anglophone systems represented both early and long-term reforming countries by OECD standards, displaying some distinctive features of their own as well as including 'Anglo-Saxon' members that have been most identified with NPM.

The results of extended reform indicate that the strongest examples of NPM have less prominence in practice. This is not of course a revelation for scholars who have been pronouncing on NPM for some time, but a greater challenge has been how to characterise its successor. Some interpretations have recognised the complexities by distinguishing tiers of NPM or contending models based on traditional control and autonomy tensions. What was apparent was that a set of trends had emerged with commonalities across Anglophone countries (Halligan 2007c).

The synthesis of elements in the 2000s suggests that system integration and performance became central. This broader conception addresses mechanisms for more effectively integrating and controlling the components of the executive branch. The results suggested that integrated governance had become the prevailing approach during the mid-2000s. It was also apparent that such a model was an amalgam of new elements and design features derived from previous models.

Consequently there has been a rebalancing of the centre, reform corrections, realignments of different components and the introduction of new horizontal relationships. Furthermore, the strong reassertion of the centre has reversed central agency weaknesses by giving them greater capacity for leadership and direction. The corresponding commitment to integration and whole-of-government was designed to counter the reinforcement given to vertical, functionally-constituted departments and agencies. Further, the renewed interest in capacity and capability reflected in large part the limits to extensive outsourcing experienced during years of contraction.

It is clear that new conceptions of governance address a different mix of features than those previously fashionable. Reaction to NPM features produced similar responses in several countries (Christensen and Lægreid 2006), but there are now a number of country interpretations that reflect local conditions. What is also common is the co-existence of several features derived from different models. In some cases there has been a reaffirmation of components of the traditional system: cabinet, central agency and the department, and the revival of features such as risk aversion in fields with an external orientation. However, there are a number of significantly different features from the earlier hierarchical model of integration. The public service is operating under a political executive with more instruments for securing and sustaining control and direction and for working the system strategically and at several levels (Savoie 1999). Furthermore, the empowered departments have greater responsibilities than traditional arrangements and performance is conceived differently. This can add up to a formidable apparatus for control, scrutiny and performance.

Under integrated governance, elements of NPM persist, and may be central. This is especially the case with performance management, which continues to provide a cornerstone of the public management framework despite continuing debates about how to extract performance for the managers, politicians and the public (Halligan 2007b). Indeed, there has been growth in, and continuing commitment to, performance management despite the fate of the NPM model. Furthermore, under the broader agendas of integrated governance, aspects like contracts and markets are less prominent, while others, such as outcomes and evaluation reviews, have come more into focus. Additionally, the use of regular performance reviews of departments and agencies (variously know as capability or performance improvement assessments) is now uniform across the four countries, and is a product of comparative reviews.

Across the reform generation, there has been both divergence and convergence in the different countries' approaches. Interestingly, the long-term consequences of reform can be seen to have partly come full circle through the rebalancing of constituent features, but there is also a sense of movement along new pathways. Governments have experimented with new models and found them to offer a mixed bag of benefits and deficits. The NPM model of the 1990s has now been succeeded as the trends of the 2000s have either moderated key NPM features or represented new agendas (Christensen and Lægreid 2007a). Nevertheless basic NPM elements are still present within a hybrid system.

Conclusion

Many states never came to grips with a full-blown version of NPM, while the more committed NPM countries, which include Anglo-Saxon systems, have wound down their hard-edge variants while rediscovering old values. NPM-type principles continue to be apparent and this is exemplified by 'flexibility' in design and sourcing expertise. Having expanded both the range of instruments and the regularity of their use, it is relatively easy to resort to them should circumstances require it. The principles of evidence-based and policy design support choosing the most appropriate solution, whether using quasi-markets or internal provision.

The question is not, of course, whether hybrid approaches will remain significant for they will continue to be a source of experimentation and even growth in areas such as collaboration with third parties. Rather the pattern of engagement can be expected to be uneven and dependent on experience with specific arrangements in different sectors and countries.

Public Management Reform in Continental Europe: National Distinctiveness

Walter J.M. Kickert

Introduction

New Public Management (NPM) was a worldwide reform trend that took place all over the Western world. That does not mean that in all countries the same reform took place. In different countries diverse forms and degrees of public management reform occurred. This chapter offers some explanations for this national distinctiveness.

Allegedly NPM reform was mainly successful in Anglo-Saxon countries, with Great Britain and New Zealand presented as the typical 'success stories'. Under the regime of the neo-liberal, right-wing prime minister Margaret Thatcher, the British state was 'hollowed out'. Part of the 'new right' ideology of the time was the belief in wholesome effects of management. The circumstances were different in other European countries. Public management reform took diverse shapes in different countries. In many small Continental European countries that have a consensual political system (Lijphart 1984) and corporatist state–society relations (P.J. Williamson 1989), such as the Netherlands, Switzerland and Austria, the public management reforms were less ideological and more pragmatic. Reform there was not about ideology and belief, but about effectiveness, efficiency and modern management techniques. In Continental European countries with a predominant legalistic 'Rechtsstaat' tradition, such as Germany and France, the public management reform hardly succeeded to break through the monopoly of legalistic thinking. In Southern European countries with a legalistic and formalistic administration, and above all with a highly politicised administration, such as Portugal, Spain, Italy and Greece, public management reform also had a hard time to break through (Ongaro 2009).

In this chapter attention will be paid to a number of Continental European countries. As there is no space for in-depth case studies about what happened in various countries (Kickert 2007, 2008) the following exposition will restrict itself to certain types of states: first the large European states with a Napoleonic or Germanic tradition, then the small European states with a consensual and corporatist tradition, and finally the Southern European states.

An attempt will be made here to explain the differences in administrative and public management reform between countries from the national context of state, politics, government and administration. Historical traditions in state and administration have a conserving influence on current developments. Current administrative reforms are dependent on the historical path that led to the present state and administration, which is the core message of the theoretical framework of 'historical institutionalism' (Thelen 1999, Pierson and Skocpol 2002). Other approaches to explain the national distinctiveness of public management reform are also possible. That will be returned to in the final section.

Napoleonic State: France

State and Administration

Let us first pay attention to the Napoleonic type of state (Wright 1990) with France as the typical example. Spain and Italy are also considered to belong to this type (Kickert 2007, Ongaro 2008), as is Belgium. The nation state is united and the state serves the general interest. The administration is centralised, hierarchical, uniform, accountable and controlled. The administration consists of highly trained and qualified civil servants, who are organised in professional 'corps'.

The origin of the highly qualified and esteemed French administration lies in the period of Napoleon Bonaparte's reign. The administration of Imperial France under Napoleon was transformed into a highly qualified bureaucracy (Thuillier and Tulard 1984). Public offices required formal entrance examinations, and high qualifications were needed to acquire the function. Public officials were qualified, effective, and furthermore cost-efficient and hard working. Officials were organised in various professional corps, a small number of which are the so-called 'grand corps' incorporating the administrative elite. These professional corps were self-regulating as to recruitment, appointment, promotion and payment. Since Napoleon the 'haute fonction publique' gained high popular esteem. In view of the tradition of strong central state steering ('étatism') France gradually became an 'administrative state' run by an elite of high officials, organised in the 'grand corps'.

Another characteristic of French administration is the rather fluid osmosis between politics and administration. There is no strict separation between politics and administration. Members of the 'grand corps' can acquire a political function and afterwards return to the administrative functions of the corps. As a matter of fact many ministers, premiers and presidents are former 'haut fonctionnaire public', member of a 'grand corps' and 'ancien élève' of the Ecole Nationale d'Administration (ENA). Moreover the frequent political nominations of top officials and the 'cabinets ministériels' illustrate the close links between politics and administration.

Another argument adding to the claim that France is an 'administrative state' is the custom that top officials near the end of their career acquire (well-paid) top positions in private business, that is, they are appointed by the government as 'président-directeur-général' of one of the many large nationalised state companies – the so-called 'pantouflage' (Rouban 1998). Thus, a small elite of ENA-trained top officials run both the public administration and the private business sector. In other words, in France the administrative elite governs the whole state, economy and society. Hence the allegation that France is an 'état administrative'.

The traditional French form of public governance ('gestion publique') is strongly juridical, based on principles of equality and the general interest ('intérêt général'), highly centralised and uniform throughout the whole of France. It possesses 'tutelage' over other instances. Public personnel have a legal 'statut de fonctionnaires'. There is strict financial accountability.

Besides the strong central state steering, other characteristics of the 'specific French model of administration' (Muller 1992) are its strong sectoral corporatism and compartmentalisation, and the typical 'territorial administration' of regions, 'départements' and municipalities. The professional corps, especially the 'grand corps', together with the trade unions, have an enormous influence on the personnel management of the French state in terms of entrance examinations, recruitment, promotion and payment. The corps and unions effectively defend their legal privileges. French civil service is based on a strong legal statute ('statut de fonctionnaires'), which is carefully safeguarded and can only be reformed at very high cost.

Administrative Reforms and Public Management

The traditional Napoleonic model has undergone great pressure (Wright 1990). Some characteristics have remained unchanged, like the strong role of administration, uniformity, the expertise and 'grand corps', but the administration has also had to adapt to external pressures, first to the political and social pressures on its fragmentation and juridification. However, due to the economic recession and budgetary crisis, and above all to the pressures on efficiency and productivity, privatisation, contracting-out and deregulation were also carried out in France. The fiscal crisis and budget retrenchments forced French administration to introduce a more businesslike, managerial style of governance.

Rouban (1997) distinguished four periods of modernisation. First was the period 1984–86, when the economic crisis ended the illusions of the Socialist government. The growth of the civil service was severely reduced, modernisation initiatives were taken and a policy of better quality and lower costs was introduced in the public service.

Second came the period of 1986–88 when the Right came to power and explicitly developed a neo-liberal reform programme. The civil service was severely criticised for its excessive costs and archaic culture, and hence developed a defensive response that prevented major reforms from actual realisation.

The third period, 1988–92, when the Socialists returned to power and Rocard became prime minister, formed a break-through in modernisation. A major landmark in the reforms was the 'Renouveau du Service Public' launched by the 'circulaire' of Prime Minister Rocard in February 1989. This reform consisted of a cluster of micro-reforms: 'cercles de qualité' [similar to total quality management], 'projets de service' [increase of managerial autonomy for executive agencies] and 'centres de responsabilité' [management contracts between ministry and agency, plus client orientation]. According to Rouban (1997) this modernisation was a compromise between the progressive introduction of public management and the preservation of the traditional public legal and financial framework.

In the following fourth period attention shifted from administrative to state reform ['réforme de l'Etat']. The 1994 report on state reforms, the 1995 commissariat for state reform and the tri-annual plan on state reform in 1996 confirmed this shift. The subject gained increasing importance within the administration, and was increasingly institutionalised (Bezes 2002). It became a political hot issue. Several prime ministers put 'réforme de l'Etat' on their own political agenda. The reforms were not only of the public management type, such as result-oriented budgeting, customer orientation, management contracts, human resource management and more, attention also shifted towards more fundamental state reform. Deconcentration and decentralisation of central state functions were addressed (for example through the 1992 Act on Territorial Administration). The 1994 report on state reforms addressed questions about the future global role of the state, and a commissariat for state reform was created in 1995, which published a tri-annual plan on state reform in 1996.

After the Juppé government in 1995 added the more fundamental issue of 'state reform' to the 'public service reform', the Jospin government in 1997 opted for a 'state reform' based on two main missions: proximity of the state (deconcentration and decentralisation) and a more effective state. The Raffarin government continued along these lines, and announced in 2002 its three main reform objectives: a better effectiveness based on the diffusion of a managerial culture in administration, an improvement of human resources management, and an improvement in customer satisfaction by the simplification of regulations. The Raffarin state reform consisted of three core-themes: effectiveness, proximity and simplicity.

Chevallier (2004) characterised the state reforms by three essential aspects. First, a reconsideration of the missions of the state. The role of the state in economy, social security and more, has become more modest. The 'regulating' state devolved its operational executive tasks to independent bodies. Second, the principle of proximity. The traditional centrally controlled territorial administration has been enforced by deconcentration and decentralisation. Third, the need for effectiveness, such as the three E's of public management, value for money, service quality, customer satisfaction and result oriented budgeting.

According to Chevallier (2004) and Rouban (2003), French state reforms were not cosmetic and superficial but quite fundamental. However, the strongly institutionalised counter-forces against reform, such as the legal civil service statute, the mighty corps and trade unions, and the close links between the political and administrative elite, remain intact in France.

Germanic State: Germany

State and Administration

Germany has a strong and particular tradition in the development of its concept of the state (Benz 2001). The German philosopher Hegel in 1812 published his theory on the state based on legal philosophy. In his view the state stands above the civil society. Contrary to the particular interests of individual citizens, the state serves the general interest. In Hegel's view the state is the 'Verkörperung der sittlichen Idee' [the embodiment of the moral value]. The state stands for harmony and unity. The individual citizen is 'Untertan' [state subject, literally meaning submissive].

With the establishment of the democratic state after the Second World War, Germany gradually departed from this state tradition (Jann 2003). The democratic failure of authoritarian Nazi governance brought Germany the determined will to establish a democratically controlled 'Rechtsstaat'. In post-war Germany a neo-corporatist type of social market economy ('Soziale Marktwirtschaft') developed. In the 1960s and 1970s the German state, like many other Western welfare states, became more and more involved in government planning. This was also the heyday of reforms in government and administration. The economic recession and fiscal crisis of the 1980s also hit the German welfare state. Retrenchments, privatisation, deregulation and debureaucratisation were to lead to a 'lean state' ('Schlanker Staat').

Germany is a federal state, consisting of the federal government and sixteen 'Länder' governments. The federal government itself is relatively small (about 10 per cent of the total public sector workforce), with limited executive tasks of its own (for example military defence or customs). The federal level is primarily responsible for policy-making, legislation and overall policy coordination. All governmental units have to follow common regulations set by the federal government with regard to public finance and budgeting, civil service and formal procedures.

Local government is relatively strong in Germany, at least from a legal point of view. All local affairs are to be managed autonomously by the communes themselves. In reality, however, this principle is less strong, primarily because of the dependence on state funding and federal and state ('Länder') regulations. Although there is a vertical division of powers between the different layers of government, the amount of joint policies and of vertical policy linkages has considerably increased. In many policy sectors, federal and state governments fund tasks on a mutual basis.

Administrative Reform and Public Management

German administration has, on the one hand, shown a remarkable continuity over the last two centuries. It was, and continues to be, an example of classical Weberian bureaucracy. Its central features have not changed a great deal over time. Hierarchy is still the dominant structural principle. Steering with precise regulations and with the classical cash-based and detailed budget is still the standard. On the other hand, both the contexts and the tasks of administration have changed considerably. After the Second World War and the establishment of the federal republic, German public administration underwent several distinctive phases of development. Reichard (2008) distinguished six phases:

1. A first phase of reconstruction, re-hierarchisation and consolidation (1947–63). Establishment of federal government, restructuring of the 'Länder', re-establishment of the traditional civil service system, first attempts to achieve administrative simplification.
2. A second phase of active policies and of local territorial reforms (1964–75). Public finance reforms, some functional task reforms (devolution to local level), some experiments with programme budgeting; attempts to achieve comprehensive administrative reforms and civil service reforms, amalgamation of municipalities.
3. A third phase of de-bureaucratisation and citizen orientation (1978–89). Extensive reform attempts to reduce bureaucratic burdens and to improve services to the citizens; additionally, some privatisation programmes.
4. A fourth phase of reunification and of transformation of Eastern administration (started in 1990). Technical and administrative assistance to East German administrations, restructuring of the Eastern 'Länder' and local governments, introduction of the (traditional) West German system of administration; in parallel, moving parts of the federal government from Bonn to Berlin.
5. A fifth phase of managerialisation (started early 1990s). Experiments with NPM-type reforms ('neues Steuerungsmodell' [new steering model] (Reichard, 2003)), particularly at the local level, and later with e-government approaches.
6. A sixth phase of reorientation of state functions (started in 1998). Debating on new perceptions of the state (activating, enabling or ensuring state), rearrangement of labour and social policies, more emphasis on civic society, liberalisation and deregulation of utilities.

According to Reichard (2008) phase four (reunification) was an exception in the reform trajectories. This unpredictable project of transforming the state and local administration in the East arose under strong time pressure and did not allow for a great deal of reflection and conceptual development. In the end, the transformation in the East to a Western-type democracy succeeded to a large extent. After a couple of years, the Eastern authorities were working according to the principles and procedures of the (West) German politico-administrative system. However, the price of such a forced transformation programme was that it was nearly impossible to combine the transformation with reform attempts. The West exported the old Weberian models and structures to the East, but there was no opportunity to implement modern concepts (Reichard and Röber 1993). As a result, East German administrations are still much more reluctant to implement elements of the new steering model compared with the West.

The still ongoing phase five (managerialisation) has so far shown some modest positive results. Some elements of the 'new steering model' have been widely practised in operative government for several years. At the local and partly at the 'Länder' level, several managerial instruments have proved to have positive effects (for example budgeting, performance measurement, cost accounting). On the other hand, many expectations have not been met and some critical side-effects of NPM have been observed (for empirical results of German NPM reforms, see Bogumil et al. 2007).

German administrators followed, with some delay, the worldwide fashion of NPM and introduced – at least at the local level – the 'new steering model', believing in the positive effects of managerialism. After about ten years of managerialism the administrators felt disillusioned with the meagre results and turned to new, fashionable reform topics: e-government and issues of governance became the latest reform trends. Altogether, the focus of administrative reform has changed quite considerably in Germany during the last decades. Internal and external pressures, but also international fashions, seem to have been the main driving forces for reform (Reichard 2008).

According to Reichard (2008) the historical developments, the legacies and the characteristics of the German statehood and administration have had distinct consequences for the perception and design of public management. The etatism, the legalism and the related cultural patterns did not form a very fertile climate for a management approach. Interpreting administration as a management problem is not common in this country. Thus the preconditions for applying management concepts and instruments to public sector structures were not very positive.

The legalistic culture of the civil servants seems to be a major hindrance to strengthening managerial thinking in public administration. Rule-based steering is a deeply-rooted practice in all public sector organisations. The legalistic and specialised education of mid-level civil servants in the internal staff training colleges and the preferred recruitment of lawyers to senior civil service classes contribute to this perpetuation of the legalistic culture. To think and to behave in managerial categories is by no means a relevant value or attitude for most of the public sector personnel. The two-centuries-old German civil service system maintains these patterns. Its structures and incentive mechanisms are highly inflexible and demotivating. They do not provide attractive incentives for well-performing or reform-oriented employees.

Nevertheless, there have been some reforms and innovations in the field of public management. Most local authorities and several 'Länder' governments have introduced NPM-related concepts and instruments in the last 10–15 years (see phase five above). However, the design of the concepts and the implementation strategies of public management reforms have been affected by the institutional particularities of the German public sector. The concept of the 'new steering model' for municipalities had a rather narrow and one-sided structure (Reichard 2003). It emphasised a naïve 'product' orientation and cost-cutting tendency, but it neglected strategic steering aspects and market mechanisms. Thus the concept was unable to exploit the potential of a modern public management concept.

The process of implementing public management elements in Germany was also influenced by institutional particularities. The federal structure, with large administrative bodies at the 'Länder' level, explains why there have been different approaches of public management reforms. Each state aimed to design and implement its own specific public management reform concept. The strong principle of local self-administration in Germany points in the same direction: despite the integrative role of the KGSt (Kommunale Gemeinschaftsstelle für Verwaltungsmanagement [Municipal Community Office for Public Management]) as a local government think tank and innovator of the 'new steering model', local governments have had the freedom and opportunity to implement quite diverse public management reform elements. As a result, there is a wide variety of public management approaches in the German public sector.

Small Continental European States: The Netherlands

State and Administration

Many of the smaller states in Continental Europe are highly similar in three respects that are relevant for the type of public governance:

1. They all have a consociationalist type of consensus democracy (Lijphart 1984). Contrary to the majoritarian Anglo-American two-party system of democracy, they have a multi-party system with proportional elections where governments consist of coalitions between more parties. The search for compromises and consensus is a main ingredient of their political culture. The search for consensus in the post-war 'Große Koalition' in Austria, in the 'Proporz' system of division of seats in government in Switzerland, in the coalition governments between the Flemish Christian-Democrats and Walloon Socialists in Belgium, in the varying coalitions between the Social-Democrats, Christian-Democrats and conservative Liberals in the Netherlands, these forms of consociationalism explain the political stability in these societies.
2. They all have a neo-corporatist type of democracy. Contrary to the American pluralist type of democracy, in a neo-corporatist type of democracy interest representation is performed by a few, well-organised groups which are recognised by the state and to which various public tasks and state authority has been delegated (P.J. Williamson 1989). The Netherlands has

a confessional type, Belgium a linguistic, regional and confessional type, Austria again another type, but all are variations of the same basic type of neo-corporatism.

3. They all have socio-political cleavages and fragmented political and social subcultures. Austria has its Christian and Socialist 'Lager'. Switzerland has its regional and linguistic fragmentation into 'Kantons'. Belgium has the linguistic cleavage between Flanders and Walloon and the political cleavage between Socialists and Christians. As a consequence of its confessional history the Netherlands has a 'Verzuiling' [pillarisation] into Protestant, Catholic, Socialist and Liberal-Neutral pillars.

The Netherlands, Belgium, Switzerland, Austria – all have these three characteristics in common, albeit in greater or fewer degrees and in different variations. This section will concentrate on the Netherlands, a highly institutionalised example of a consensual and corporatist state.

The Dutch political system is a consensus democracy. No single party ever wins an absolute majority in elections, so that governments are always coalitions of two or more parties. Deliberation, consultation, reaching compromises and consensus are the characteristics of Dutch politics. Revolutionary fundamental changes are virtually impossible in the Dutch political system.

One of the consequences of this political system is that governmental and parliamentary decision-making is normally preceded by extensive consultation. The first step in governmental problem-solving usually consists of appointing an advisory committee, nominally consisting of independent experts, but its members usually representing the major social and political interest groups. Such an advisory committee produces a report, which is the compromise and consensus between the various interests. This political culture is also reflected in Dutch administrative reform. The past decades of civil service reform are marked by a long sequence of many different advisory committees and few explicit programmes on civil service reform.

Another consequence of the eternal deliberation, compromise and consensus is that radical abrupt reforms are virtually inconceivable in the Dutch civil service. For a reform to be successful it had better be a small, gradual, incremental one. More structural and fundamental reforms have been proposed in the past decades, but they have hardly ever been successfully carried out. And as soon as the proposed civil service reform has political consequences, the probability of successful implementation becomes very low. Rational-technical, politically neutral, small and gradual reforms are the most successful (van Twist et al. 2009).

Administrative Reform and Public Management

Financial management at central government level has undergone major developments since the mid 1980s (Kickert 2000). At that time the need was felt to drastically improve the control of expenditures. The budget deficit was high and the yearly deficits had to be countered. Retrenchments were carried out, the so-called 'open-ended' regulations were closed off, and certain tasks were decentralised to municipalities. Control of expenditures was an important issue. In the mid 1980s demartmental The Hague realised that an orderly financial administration is an absolute precondition for successful expenditure control. At the time some ministerial departments did not even succeed to obtain a positive auditor's certificate. The 'Operation Comptabel System' operating in the second half of the 1980s has succeeded in getting the financial administrations of the departments 'in order'. Strict regulations were issued by the Ministry of Finance for the administrative organisation and the internal control measures. Since 1993 all departments have obtained approving auditor's certificates.

After the financial administrations had successfully been reorganised, the emphasis shifted from 'rightfulness' to 'effectiveness and efficiency'. The improvement of effectiveness and efficiency followed three main lines: promoting result-oriented management, introducing an accrual cost-accounting system, and the use of market-like mechanisms.

Personnel management also underwent reforms. In the 1980s two measures were taken to break through the automatism of every year awarding every official a so-called 'periodical salary increase'. Possibilities were created to differentiate payment within the salary scales. The legal payment system for central state officials was changed in 1987 to allow for a 'labour market bonus' in order to be able to hire or keep personnel in scarce functions. The bonus was meant to 'bind' scarce personnel that could earn much higher salaries outside government (ICT personnel, accountants, fiscal lawyers and so on) to the department for a certain period. A second measure introduced in 1989 into the payment system was performance-related payment. The line manager had to assess the performance of the official before deciding whether to give a salary increase or not. Another measure was the introduction of an additional salary increase to very well or excellently functioning officials.

In the labour conditions of the Dutch civil service a shift has taken place towards the labour conditions of the private market sector. This policy, to give personnel in Dutch (central) administration similar treatment to that received by personnel in the market sector, has been called the 'normalisation' of government personnel policy.

In the Netherlands, ministerial departments traditionally contain both policy preparation and executive tasks. Unlike the United States, where executive agencies are usually independent of cabinet departments, or Sweden with its independent executive 'ambetsverk', in the Netherlands both policy preparation and execution fall under ministerial responsibility. A remarkable reform trend took place in Dutch central government: the 'autonomising' of executive parts of ministerial departments, the distinction between policy making and policy execution, the organisational separation of executive task units from the policy-making department, and the increase in managerial autonomy of executive units (Kickert 2000).

In the past varying attention has been paid to different forms of autonomisation in different periods of time. In the early 1980s privatising and contracting-out dominated the reform debate. In the mid 1980s the idea of 'self-administration' (contract-management) led to some experimental experiences. At the end of the 1980s the debate on functional decentralisation and the use of independent administrative bodies (an organisation established by public law) gained renewed impetus (van Thiel and van Buuren 2001). Autonomisation in the early 1990s took the form of agencies, with contract-management and a new financial regime as major issues.

The 'great efficiency operation', which was launched in the Dutch national administration in 1990, resulted in many departmental proposals in which the autonomising of executive task units played a prominent role. The idea was that putting an executive agency at arm's length of politics and policy-making would enable the agency, being freed of interference from politics and policies in The Hague, to concentrate on its actual main executive task and thus lead to improvement of the agency's task fulfilment. Managerial autonomy would lead to better quality and efficiency of the public service delivery.

The development of internal autonomous agencies was actively supported by the ministries of Finance and Home Affairs in the form of a report published in 1991 containing several proposals to increase substantially the flexibility and autonomy in financial and personnel regulations for the new autonomous agencies.

In 2002 the newly formed cabinet installed a minister for the renewal of civil service (De Graaf, also Minister of Home Affairs and Vice Prime Minister) who appointed a project director-general and installed a programme bureau for the project. This was a rare example of an explicit and centrally coordinated reform programme in the Dutch civil service.

Another example of an explicit reform programme, aiming at the renewal of the Dutch civil service as a whole, was the instalment in 2007 of a project secretary-general subordinated to the Minister of Home Affairs. This time one of the main objectives of the reform programme was a budget cut imposed on all ministerial departments.

Southern European States

State and Administration

Formalism and legalism are major reasons for the rigidity and inefficiency of Southern bureaucracies. Management reforms are based on an economical frame of reference in terms of effectiveness and efficiency, which is contradictory to the juridical frame of reference in terms of legal accountability. As management reforms have to be formulated in juridical language in order to become legislation, the legalistic monopoly remains unbroken. Government policy-making always takes place in the form of laws, regulations and provisions. That also holds true for government reform policy. Hence, public management reforms had to be reframed in legal terms (Capano 2003, Ongaro 2008, 2009).

In Greek, Italian, Portuguese and Spanish administration the factor of overriding importance is politicisation (Sotiropoulos 2004, 2006). Political control of administration, relations between politicians and bureaucrats, political nominations of officials, party patronage and clientelism (Eisenstadt and Lemarchand 1981, Piattoni 2001) in Southern European countries fundamentally differ from the political practice that is usual in Western Europe.

First one should realise that political parties in Greece, Italy, Spain and Portugal differ from Western European ones. Political parties in Southern Europe are not only advocates of policy and ideology, but are primarily organisations that provide jobs, pensions, payments, subsidies, insurances and more to party members. Although Southern European countries legally have the Napoleonic system whereby officially public jobs can only be obtained after professional training and competitive entrance examination, many civil servants bypass that path with a political shortcut. Normal practice in Spain (Alba 1998), Italy (Cassese 2002), Greece (Spanou 2001) and Portugal (de Sousa 2001) is that political appointees, who only receive a temporary contract, soon have their contracts changed into permanent positions, thus bypassing the official examination and qualification path.

The higher the public jobs, the more important party affiliation becomes. Although the practice of political appointments of higher ranking officials formally exists in the United States (spoils system) and Germany ('politische Beamten'), and informally exists in other countries like Belgium and France ('cabinets ministériels'), the extent of party politicisation of career top officials in Southern Europe is higher (Sotiropoulos 2006).

Administrative Reform and Public Management

If one concentrates on Southern Europe, the study of reforms should not be restricted to public management reforms, but broadened to include institutional sorts of state reform (Kickert 2007). The transformation to democracy in Greece, Portugal and Spain since the mid 1970s has led to fundamental state reforms in terms of new democratic constitution and building-up democratic institutions like the legislative, the executive and judiciary. Although the reform and modernisation of the administration were not carried out with likewise rigour, institutional state reform in terms of regionalisation and decentralisation did take place in Spain, Italy and Greece.

In Spain, following the death of Franco, the new democratic constitution of 1978 provided for regional autonomy by creating 17 'autonomous communities' (regions). It was a response to the regional separatism that had been central in Spanish politics for ages (especially in Catalonia and the Basque country), and had become highly violent during the repressive Franco regime (ETA terrorism). In Italy, following the massive popular and political turmoil at the beginning of the 1990s because of the corruption scandals, regional decentralisation became a major political reform issue (in response to Northern separatism) and resulted in state reform at the end of the 1990s. In Greece decentralisation was also carried out, by transforming regional prefectures into directly elected bodies and by merging the multitude of small municipalities into larger and stronger entities. In Portugal regional administration seems mainly to be the vehicle for administering the EU regional funds. A proposal to enlarge the authorities of regional administration was turned down in a referendum.

According to Sotiropoulos (2004) three sorts of reforms can be discerned in the South:

1. First 'rationalisation and professionalisation' in the Weberian bureaucratic sense, the introduction of 'Rechtsstaat' types of rules and procedures. The effect was juridification and legalistic dominance. In Spain this 'juridification' type of reform was already introduced under Franco in the 1950s and 1960s (Subirats 1990) by the 'Opus Dei' technocrats. In Italy juridification of the administration was a reaction to the strong post-war politicisation, in order to protect administration from political interference and to ensure job and career security of civil servants. Another explanation for the strong degree of formalism and juridification is that in Southern Europe most civil servants traditionally used to be and still are administrative lawyers.

2. Secondly 'democratisation' in the sense of getting rid of the old regime reactionary forces in administration: replacing the supporters of the former dictatorships with supporters of the new democracy. In reality purging of the civil service hardly happened. After the transition to democracy in Spain and Portugal the administrative elite remained in place and in charge. In Greece the democratisation of the civil service was mainly political symbolism and rhetoric. What did happen was that after elections the winning party replaced the former officials with its own followers. In Greece, Portugal and Spain a spoils system exists.

3. Thirdly 'modernisation' in the public management sense (Ongaro 2008, 2009). The recognition that budgets were to be cut and efficiency to be increased in Southern Europe was mainly due to external pressure from the EU (Maastricht Treaty on maximum debt and deficit) and started only in the early 1990s. The high degree of politicisation of administration implies that public management reforms, like privatisation, contracting-out and public–private partnership, were sometimes abused to generate party incomes (political corruption) and that HRM reforms were abused to increase political interference and political appointments. Public management reforms can turn out to have little or even adverse effects.

Reforms in Southern European countries, irrespective of their form and content, hardly ever seem to have had significant effects (Alba 1998, Subirats 1990, Cassese 1995, 1999, Spanou 1996, 2001). Failure of administrative reforms has a long tradition, and is not restricted to recent public management reforms. An important explanation for reform failure is the long historical pattern of strong political polarisation between left- and right-wing political parties. After an election the new incoming government not only undertakes a massive replacement of the officials, but often also cancels the reforms of the previous government and replaces them with its own. Hence, before reforms can have any effect, they are cancelled and replaced. Political polarisation has also often led to parliamentary and government instability, thus making it virtually impossible for governments to carry out major reforms. Political polarisation between rival and conflicting parties has a long tradition in the South. For example, nineteenth-century Spain witnessed conflicts between Liberals and Christian-Monarchists, and a deep left–right polarisation marked the political landscape, with the Spanish Civil War as an extreme example in that case. The Greek post-war civil war against the communists was also a savage example.

Another main reason for reform failure is the far-reaching politicisation of the administration (Sotiropoulos 2004, 2006). In Southern Europe the civil service is not only about providing high-quality and low-cost public services to citizens, but also a reservoir of jobs and favours to be distributed by political parties to their supporters. Top officials of the party previously in office are replaced by loyal followers of the new incoming government. So there is political clientelism at the bottom of the civil service and at the top. Moreover, bureaucracies in Southern countries were, and still are, notorious for their rigidity, inefficiency, bad service delivery and lack of client orientation.

Administrative modernisation in terms of improving the quality, efficiency and client-orientation of the provision of public services by the state seems to make little sense in a state which is not so much aimed at providing services to citizens, but primarily aimed at providing jobs and favours to party members (Kickert 2007).

Discussion and Conclusions

This chapter has nuanced the view that public management reforms are mainly a success in Anglo-Saxon countries, and less successful, or sometimes even a failure, elsewhere in Europe. It has shown that such normative judgements about success and failure would be better replaced by the more neutral view that public management reforms are different in different countries, and explained those variations.

In many small Continental European countries that have a consensual political system and neo-corporatist state–society relations, public management reforms may seem at first sight of the more modest 'modernise' type (Pollitt and Bouckaert 2004), but the non-ideological, non-political, pragmatic, technocratic management reforms were most successful in terms of the number of modern financial, organisational, personnel and informational management techniques introduced in Finland, Sweden, Norway, Denmark, the Netherlands, Switzerland and Austria.

The legalistic type of state and administration found in Germany, where most top officials are still public lawyers, formed a hindrance to the introduction of the economic frame of reference of managerial thinking, but at the sub-national level of 'Länder' and especially the municipal level the German equivalent of NPM, the 'neues Steuerungsmodell', was widely introduced. Moreover it should be realised that the German reunification was a much more fundamental and urgent type of reform. Likewise were public management reforms introduced in the legalistic and strong central state in France. But in France more fundamental reforms of the state ('réforme de l'Etat') were considered of greater importance.

In Southern European countries like Portugal, Spain and Greece the transformation from dictatorship to democratic 'Rechtsstaat' since the mid 1970s also formed a much more fundamental and urgent reform. In these countries modern West European types of welfare states have only been built up since the 1980s. Cutting back the long awaited, newly created welfare state expenditures was for native politicians hard to sell to their constituencies. Public managaent reforms were more or less imposed on Portugal, Spain and Greece by the European Union. No wonder that successful implementation of such reforms is hard to expect. The more so as Southern administrations are highly juridified, legalistic and politicised.

In this chapter the differences in public management reforms in different countries were explained by addressing the context of their states and administrations. Legalistic, juridified administrations are less equipped to handle economical managerial reforms. Centralised administrations handle reforms differently from more decentralised or federal ones. Politicised administrations are less equipped to handle effectiveness and efficiency.

Other explanations for the different sorts of public management reforms do exist. Not only the context of state and administrations, but also the socio-economic and socio-cultural context can account for variations. For example, while it was the economic crisis in the 1980s that triggered public management reforms, it was the financial-economic criteria of the EU Treaty that triggered the public management reforms in the Southern countries. Further, the predominant individualistic civic culture in Southern Europe differs from the more collectivistic culture in the Nordic countries. Another external factor that was influential in introducing public management reforms was the ideational context of worldwide NPM-reform. Top officials were influenced by this apparently very successful worldwide reform trend to introduce such modernisations at home.

The explanatory model for public management reform of Pollitt and Bouckaert (2004: 25) mentions more factors. Public pressure, especially in the case of disasters, crises and scandals, can trigger reforms. The corruption scandals in Italy in the early 1990s led to a major landslide in the political system, and opened a window of opportunity to carry out reforms that until then had always failed, such as public management reforms. Not only contextual external factors can account for the different forms of reform, but also the internal characteristics of the political and administrative policy- and decision-making system itself. In France the existence of a highly influential elite of top officials also explains the path that state and administrative reform took. The authority of the British prime minister also explains why reform was much more swift and comprehensive there than in decentralised, consensual countries where many more actors had to be consulted and persuaded. Viewing matters from the perspective of the management of the change process would be yet another approach to explaining the path and outcome of reform (Kickert 2010).

NPM in Scandinavia

Hanne Foss Hansen

Introduction[1]

Seen from abroad the Scandinavian countries Denmark, Norway and Sweden look very similar. All three are small countries situated in Northern Europe. All three have in international comparison very high public sector sizes, as around one third of the total labour force is publicly employed. Accordingly, the levels of taxation are high.

There are also common structural features. All three countries are unitary decentralized states where local governments take care of many functions. All have constitutional but almost exclusively ceremonial monarchies, the executive power resting with the prime minister and the cabinet. Living standards are relatively high. Central and local government influence the everyday life of citizens through welfare state institutions and programmes.

In all three countries public sector reforms based on what later became framed as New Public Management (NPM) thinking were launched in the 1980s. Observers have characterized all three countries as modernizers rather than marketizers, following managerial and user-responsiveness strategies rather than competition, marketization and incentivization strategies (Pollitt and Bouckaert 2004).

This chapter challenges both the conception of similarity across the three countries and the characterization of their reform strategies. The focal issues are: If we take a closer look at the three countries, are they really so similar? Have they followed the same reform trajectories? Are they still primarily modernizers? Or have they adopted additional or new reform strategies, for example competition strategies or post-NPM strategies such as reintegration?

The structure of the chapter is as follows. Firstly, the theoretical analytical perspective and the concepts of NPM and post-NPM are discussed. Secondly, the reform histories of the three countries are analysed one by one. The analysis concerns the questions of who are the central actors pushing reforms, which

1   I warmly thank Mads Kristiansen for helpful comments on a draft for this text.

reform components have been adopted and implemented and what are the results reported. Finally, similarities and differences across the three cases are discussed.

It appears from the research questions that the analysis departs from a classical country comparative approach. This is in line with administrative policy being a national responsibility. In spite of this it is relevant to reflect upon the European and the wider international context. Denmark (since 1973) and Sweden (since 1995) are both members of the European Union (EU). Norway is not an EU member but has entered into the wider Agreement on the European Economic Area (EEA). The EEA agreement means that Norway has no influence on EU decisions but is obliged to put EU directives concerning the internal market into force in Norwegian law. The comparative section briefly returns to the question of whether and how European and international involvement influences administrative policies in the three countries.

Theoretical Approach, Methodology and Central Concepts

The adoption and implementation of public sector reforms may be explained using several theoretical perspectives. This analysis will combine three perspectives: an actor-oriented political perspective (Scharpf 1997a), a rational organizational perspective (Scott and Davies 2006: ch. 2) and an institutional, cultural perspective (Selznick 1996).

The actor-oriented political perspective perceives public sector reforms as ideology- and interest-driven. Different political parties subscribe to different reform components. Political parties in different countries work in different polities involving other actors such as public organizations, interest organizations and experts. Some countries have homogenous systems with stable dominating power coalitions, while others have more fragmented systems. Homogenous systems may stay on the 'path', maintaining public organizations rather than reforming them, or they may radically implement reforms if new reform ideas match political ideologies and interests. Fragmented systems probably seldom implement radical reforms as reforming is an on-going negotiation process.

The rational organizational perspective perceives public organizations as instruments providing regulation, products and services. If problems arise with the functionality of the system, there will be a pressure to reform. Public sector reforms are thus perceived as problem driven. Marketization and managerial reforms may, for example, be defined as solutions to effectiveness problems, re-integration reforms as solutions to political ungovernableness.

The institutional, cultural perspective finally perceives public organizations as institutions reflecting norms and values. Structures may be changed overnight but norms and values develop across time. Countries may differ concerning administrative cultures and values. Reflecting the 'right' norms and values is important to ensure legitimacy. If new international fashions in public sector reform are perceived as successful and modern, they may be rather easily adopted and implemented. But if travelling reform ideas are inconsistent with national administrative cultures, they may be ignored or edited.

These three perspectives are combined in the current analysis as none of the perspectives are expected to be able to stand alone in explaining public sector reforms. Public sector reforms are dynamic and complex transformation processes; they involve many actors and are influenced by political, rational and technical as well as cultural logics.

Methodologically the analysis builds primarily on secondary material in the form of former analyses and research on reforms. Documentary material on reform plans such as modernization programmes are only included to a limited extent, the reason being the intent to focus more on reform practice than on reform talk.

The lack of clarity in the concepts of NPM and of post-NPM creates a definite challenge. Comparing the definitions of the NPM concept as given by Hood (1991), Dunleavy et al. (2005) and Pollitt (2007a) reveals the common feature that NPM reforms introduce primarily managerial and economic principles over bureaucratic principles. Additionally there is a difference in, for example, the importance attached to incentivization and whether or not to couple disaggregation not only to specialization but also to lean, flat and small organizational forms.

In recent years the concept of post-NPM has been discussed (Christensen and Lægreid 2007a). In some of the NPM pioneer countries, consequences of reforms such as greater social inequalities and political ungovernableness have caused concern and initiated further reforms aiming at enhancing the capacity for national central governance (Gregory 2006, Halligan 2006, and Richards and Smith 2006). Reintegration (for example, the rollback of agencification and the creation of joined-up government), needs-based holism (for example, client-based reorganization and one-stop provision) and digitalization in the form of increased use of the World Wide Web, the internet and e-mail have been presented as components of post-NPM reforms (Dunleavy et al. 2005). Post-NPM thinking aims at re-establishing the primary of representative government over managerial and economic principles. In this way the oscillation between NPM and post-NPM can be partly interpreted as the swing of a pendulum between different classical paradigms of administrative reform (Aucoin 1990).

The analysis here will focus on six components. Four of these are NPM components:

1. disaggregation (including agencification)
2. management practice (including emphasis on performance)
3. user responsiveness
4. competition (including free choice, competitive tendering and marketization)

while two are post-NPM components:

5. re-integration (including rollback of agencification and merging)
6. needs-based holism (including client-based reorganization and one-stop provision)

Using these categories means that digitalization and e-government will not be included in the analysis. Whether digitalization is a NPM or a post-NPM strategy is not obvious. Digitalization may support NPM strategies, for example creating transparency in service delivery in order to support free choice, but it may also support post-NPM strategies, for example enhancing the documentation of activities in order to strengthen central control.

Country Reform History

The following section analyses the reform histories of Denmark, Sweden and Norway one by one. As mentioned, the analysis concerns actors pushing reforms, reform components and results.

Denmark

Central actors
Public sector reforms including NPM components saw the light of day in Denmark in 1983, when the then Conservative prime minister launched a Modernization Programme. The preparation of the programme, which was a reaction to the problems related to the planning regime of the 1970s, had been started under the former Social Democrat government. Since then, shifting governments have launched a number of modernization and renewal programmes (the latest being the so-called 'quality reform'). Danish modernization and renewal programmes have been rather loose collections of reform ideas and components and not unified strategic plans. They have nevertheless played an important role in setting a discourse on administrative policy.

Administrative policy has been characterized as concentrated, weakly formalized and integrated into the expenditure policy (Pedersen and Lægreid 1994). Two actors have been reported as the most important reform entrepreneurs. One is the Ministry of Finance, the other the interest organization of the municipalities, Local Government Denmark (Christensen 2009: 282). Many reform initiatives have been initiated by the Ministry of Finance often as voluntary pilot projects subsequently rolled out first in central government and later (to some extent) in local government.

Local government has a strong democratic foundation with directly elected councils. Local government went through a large-scale reorganization in 1970 and once more in 2007. The 2007 reform was a merger reform but it also transferred responsibility for several tasks across administrative levels. Municipalities (before the reform some 270, now 98) have the right to levy taxes. The 14 counties existing until 2006 also had the right to levy taxes, whereas the succeeding five regions do not. The above-mentioned Local Government Denmark, but also the interest organization Danish Regions, are key actors for the Ministry of Finance to negotiate with in order to implement public sector reforms.

The Danish model of central government is based on ministerial accountability. Within the limits of law and the budgetary framework decided by the parliament, the minister has decision-making power in every matter. Implementation of reforms is dependent upon negotiation with the rather strong sectoral ministries.

The Danish administrative culture is pragmatic. This also applies to the use of commissions. Sometimes commissions play a role in preparing public sector reforms but commissions are used ad hoc. Danish commissions are most often dominated by civil servants and representatives from interest organizations. Experts are often members as well, but they seldom take the head of the table.

Reform components
Disaggregation has not been a prominent feature of Danish reforms. Besides the principle of ministerial accountability, the Danish organizational public administration model is weak on principles. Ministries are organized differently, some as large unitary departments, others divided into a department and several agencies. In the 1960s and 1970s the ideal model of a ministry was based on the idea of dividing political from operational tasks and organizing with a small department and large agencies. The ideal model was never fully implemented and is no longer an ideal.

Agencification was in this sense more popular before Denmark embarked on NPM-inspired reforms than it has been since. Restructuring activities in central government since the 1980s have not followed any overall pattern. There are both examples of ministries being reorganized according to agencification – agencies, however, still being ascribed to ministerial accountability – and examples of ministries rolling back former agencies into departments.

Furthermore, in local government there is room for individual choices of organizational models. Some municipalities have a classic committee structure characterized by sectorization, others try to combat sectorization by strengthening the centre and introducing a unitary model with a board of directors.

Public organizations have become more autonomous in relation to budgetary and staff decisions but at the same time they are often rather tightly controlled through the use of contracts. Regulatory agencies have to some extent become reorganized with boards with relatively high degrees of autonomy. In some sectors disaggregation has been important at the institutional level. In the educational area, for example, upper secondary schools and university colleges have been corporatized as they have been turned into self-governing institutions.

Changing management practice, on the contrary, has been a very important reform component. Contracts based on a management by objectives and results concept have become widely used first in central government and later in local government. In the beginning of the 1990s the content of contracts was mostly qualitative. Even though focus over time seems to have shifted towards quantification of results and putting more weight on the evaluation phase, contracts seldom include objectives related to the societal effects of organizations. A recent analysis shows that contracts are used by ministries to hold organizations politically accountable on a number of dimensions (Binderkrantz and Christensen 2009a and 2009b).

Focus on efficiency and the documentation of results has been intensified. In recent years a budgetary reform in central government has introduced a cost-based accrual accounting system. The goal is to raise cost-consciousness and intensify benchmarking activities. Observers conclude, however, that agencies and institutions have not (yet) taken the opportunity to compare costs across organizations (Jensen and Fjord 2010). In some sectors, for example in higher education and to some extent hospitals, results-based funding systems have been developed.

Since the first modernization programme in the 1980s a number of initiatives have been implemented with the aim of increasing user responsiveness. User evaluation and user satisfaction analyses have been institutionalized in most welfare areas. Some have been designed bottom-up primarily as learning tools, others have been standardized and implemented top-down, as, for example, in the hospital sector, where nationwide user satisfaction analyses are now carried out once a year.

Denmark has a long tradition, dating back to the 1850s, for locally initiated service delivery, for example schools and day-care, organized by giving groups of citizens the right to establish their own institutions largely financed by public money. Despite its long history, this system may be considered a market system. As such competition is not something completely new. However, competition has been further promoted in the rhetoric of NPM-reforms since the 1980s. For many years competition however slowly gained importance. Denmark has never had many nationalized industries and the privatization potential was in this way limited. In the 1980s the Social Democrats were critical of the privatization ideas of the Conservative-headed government but in the 1990s, when they came in to head the government, they changed their view. Consequently, in the 1990s a handful of state-owned companies were privatized, probably due to the political potentials of the revenues.

Outsourcing was for many years heavily discussed but little happened. In local government the relative share of contracting out was, in two decades from the mid 1980s, unchanged around 12 per cent. One of the aims of the structural reform in local government in 2007 seems to have been to make municipalities more attractive for private providers. After the structural reform the government and Local Government Denmark agreed to increase the private delivery share to 26.5 per cent in 2010 and 2008 figures show the share had in fact by then increased to around 25 per cent, differing between 15 per cent to well above 30 per cent across municipalities. Free choice was introduced first within the hospital field and later within other fields. Recently there has been a rapid growth in publicly funded private health treatment. Moreover, private hospitals receive an increasing number of patients funded by private health insurance or from their own pockets (Vrangbæk 2008).

The Liberal–Conservative government, in power since 2001, has thus clearly pursued radical NPM components but it has also pursued post-NPM components. Governmental control with local government has strengthened both in relation to budgetary control and municipal taxes and in relation to monitoring service delivery through the development of systemic evaluation systems, such as benchmarking, accreditation and indicator systems. Some of these activities are initiated by the Steering Group for Cross-public Collaboration, established in 2005, and consisting of heads of departments from central ministries and the directors of Local Government Denmark and Danish Regions. The establishment of this group reflects that re-integration is considered important.

NPM and post-NPM components are not always easily distinguished. In many initiatives following the idea that bigger is better – for example merger reforms and shared-service initiatives – NPM and post-NPM elements have been integrated. Merger reforms not only in local government but also, for example, in the hospital and educational sector have increased organizational competition but at the same time facilitated central control. Likewise the adoption of the idea of shared service, where administrative units with support functions such as financial control, wages and IT, formerly located in departments and agencies, are amalgamated in large administrative service centres, on the one hand makes departments and agencies leaner, on the other centralizes control. The many merger reforms reflect a belief in large-scale benefits but these are seldom documented.

Results

It is not easy to assess the overall results of all the reforms. Evaluations have been carried out in relation to some, but far from all, reform components, and knowledge on reform effects is sparse (Hansen 2005). In the 1980s an aim was to slow down public sector growth. This has been achieved but the public sector has not been slimmed down. Public employment has been stable, taxation and governmental expenditure likewise (when the ongoing financial crisis is not taken into account).

Another way to approach the question of results is to ask what has been gained and what has been lost? User responsiveness has increased. At any rate this was a conclusion in an extensive study on the development of the Danish democracy (Magtudredningen) initiated by parliament and published in 2003 (Togeby et al. 2003). What else has been gained? A shift in attitudes towards change: organizational change has become ordinary, no longer something special. Finally, economic values as well as organizational individualism have gained importance, maybe at the expense of democratic values and solidarity.

Norway

Central actors

Reforms including NPM components were launched in a Modernization Programme in 1986 by a Conservative-headed government and followed up in 1987 by a social democratic government, in Norway the Labour Party. Numerous programmes have been launched since then by shifting governments. For most years since the mid 1980s, governments have been headed by the Labour Party but there have been important interruptions in the late 1990s and the mid 2000s when coalition governments have been right-leaning.

In Norway the actors reported as being important in pushing and shaping public sector reforms are the ministries and the government on some occasions in interaction with the parliament (Christensen and Lægreid 2009). Norway has had ministries for government administration since the 1970s. They have been reorganized and their names have changed but administrative policy has been a visible issue in the ministerial landscape. As in Denmark, Norwegian modernization and renewal programmes have tended to be loose collections of reform ideas and components rather than unified strategic plans. They have, however, played an important role in setting a discourse. Since 1999 administrative policy has been debated regularly in the parliament (Stortinget) as the ministers of government administration have given separate statements and accounts of the government's administrative policy.

In relation to budgetary reforms the Ministry of Finance has been a central actor, and when reforms have targeted local government, the Ministry of Local Government and Regional Development has been involved. Norway has a two-tier local government structure with 430 municipalities and 19 counties. At both levels the governing bodies are elected directly and constitutionally guaranteed the right to levy taxes.

As in Denmark the Norwegian organizational model of central government is based on ministerial accountability. The strength of the sectoral ministries has made it difficult to build up ministries with horizontal co-ordination responsibility such as the Ministry of Government Administration.

Public commissions including experts and representatives from civil service unions have also played a role in pushing public sector reforms. Civil service unions have been most strongly involved when the Labour Party has been in power.

Reform components
NPM-influenced reforms were in Norway first suggested and to some extent implemented in local government (Tranvik and Fimreite 2006). During the 1980s a series of reforms aimed at municipal devolution were implemented and culminated in 1992 in a new municipal act. The genesis of the reforms lay in a criticism that the welfare state project had turned local authorities into unresponsive bureaucratic organizations. The hope was to get rid of sectorization, increase local autonomy, flatten municipal hierarchies and develop more individualized public service delivery.

In central government disaggregation in the form of agencification has been an important reform element. Ordinary agencies have gradually been autonomized through internal delegation of authority in personnel and financial matters and to some extent also in substantial policy issues.

Furthermore, regulatory agencies have to some extent been autonomized but this has been more controversial. In 2003 the conservative centre-right minority government, inspired by the OECD, proposed radical changes to regulatory agencies. Regulatory agencies were to be streamlined as regulators and their independence from ministries increased. After negotiations in parliament a hybrid solution was reached. Regulatory agencies were to be reformed on a case-by-case basis not across the board (Christensen, Lie and Lægreid 2007, Roness 2007).

Disaggregation has gone hand in hand with changes in management practice. A formalized system of management by objectives and results (MBOR) has been developed. Agencies are controlled by MBOR in combination with a yearly letter of allocation and a formal and informal dialogue. In recent years MBOR has been further developed including an element of risk management. In addition, evaluations are increasingly used to follow-up and further develop activities. Studies carried out at the beginning of the 2000s show that in both the political and administrative leaders' experience, the control system works rather well (Christensen, Lie and Lægreid 2007).

The infra-structure area has been radically reformed through competition and marketization. Until 1992 major public domains such as railways, telecommunications, the power supply, postal services and so on were organized as central agencies or as more integrated government-administrated enterprises. Since then the commercial parts of these have been corporatized as various types of autonomous state-owned companies and two of these, Telenor (telecommunications) and Statoil (oil), were partially privatized at the beginning of the 2000s. The development towards marketization began when the Labour Party reluctantly and not without conflict changed its view on administrative policy in the direction of neo-liberalism.

In the welfare fields Norway for many years stuck to political control, professional expertise and participation by affected groups counting less on economic norms. From the mid 1990s onwards market principles gained momentum. Market orientation, contracting out, leadership contracts and service declarations saw the light of day. User-responsiveness was an important issue in the 1980s and was revitalized by the end of the 1990s now giving more weight to the rights of users. In 2009 a large national user survey was carried out.

In important areas competition has been increased as quasi-market models have been introduced through the adoption of the 'money follows the user' system and other types of performance-based financing. This applies to higher education and hospitals. In 2002 one major reform was the government takeover of the hospitals from the counties, turning the hospitals into health enterprises. However, the hospital reform, as it also introduced a more centralized structure, potentially increasing political control, can be said to combine NPM reform components with post-NPM reform components. Another example of a combined reform is the merging of the employment administration and the national insurance administration into a new agency for work and welfare collaborating with the social services run by local authorities in local one-stop shops.

The transformation of Norway in the 1990s from a reluctant to a more committed NPM reformer seems to have increased political polarization with the conservative parties strongly pursuing radical NPM components and the left-leaning parties being more sceptical and oriented more towards post-NPM reform components. Consequently there are examples of NPM reform initiatives being rolled back. One example is the Directorate for Public Management, subordinated to the Ministry of Government Administration. The directorate was in 2004 turned into a state-owned company (Statskonsult) and in 2008 rolled back to being an agency (now called difi). Other examples include changes in the law on private schools, making it less easy to establish private schools with public support, and attempts to strengthen political control of the central immigration administration which was reorganized and autonomized in 2001. Currently government documents do not signal strong NPM ideas. A recent white paper, titled 'A Public Administration for Democracy and Solidarity', issued by the Labour-headed government (St. meld.nr. 19 2008–2009) argues that administrative policy initiatives should be anchored in the fundamental values of democracy, the rule of law, professional expertise and effectiveness (notice the order).

Results

As in Denmark it is not easy to assess the overall reform effects. Some observers have characterized the reforms in local government as failures as aims have not been achieved (Tranvik and Fimreite 2006). Municipalities have become less, not more autonomous as they are still more tightly regulated nationally and in recent years also by individual rights regulation.

Others report that Norway has gradually moved away from an integrated state and towards a more fragmented one (Christensen, Lie and Lægreid 2007). Political control of state-owned enterprises has decreased giving higher priority to cost-efficiency, professional norms and user interests. The same but to a lesser extent is evident concerning agencies. Institutional and professional autonomy have become more important than political control. Management by objectives and results has given agencies more leeway in using allocated resources and selecting means to fulfil political goals. Corporatist features are reported to have been slowly weakened (Christensen and Lægreid 2009: 308).

Norway has historically been characterized as a country with a high political consensus on administrative policy. This consensus seems to have decreased. Political polarization and pendulum swings between on the one hand increasing competition and marketization and on the other increasing political control anchored in community values have been evident in recent years.

Sweden

Central actors

In Sweden public sector reforms, including NPM components, were initiated by the Social Democrats in the 1980s as a reaction to limitations and problems of the planning regime of the 1970s (Pollitt and Bouckaert 2004, Eklund 2008). The former right-wing government had, however, already prepared for reforms (Premfors et al. 2009). Key components in reforms at that time were decentralization to counties and municipalities, management by objectives, managerialism and increased choice and user-responsiveness. Privatization was rejected as this was thought to lead to injustices.

Swedish administrative policy has been characterized as de-concentrated but highly formalized (Pedersen and Lægreid 1994). In Sweden four actors are reported as being important in pushing and shaping reforms: the central government, the state agencies, the independent commissions and local government (Eklund 2008).

The central government decides on national policies and determines goals and guidelines for the civil service. Apart from some years in the first half of the 1990s and recent years (since 2006), Sweden has had Social Democrat governments since NPM was adopted.

Swedish Government Offices (Regeringskansliet) including the ministries and the Prime Minister's Office are internationally comparatively small as all operational tasks are delegated to relatively autonomous agencies. Some agencies, such as the Swedish Agency for Public Management (Statskontoret) and the Swedish National Financial Management Authority (Ekonomistyrningsverket), play important roles in cross-cutting reform initiatives.

Sweden has a highly institutionalized system of commissions of inquiry (Statens Offentliga Utredningsväsen, SOU). SOU commissions are regularly tasked by government with investigations into overall reform issues. Commissions have considerable freedom to explore issues and their reports are submitted broadly for opinions. The system is perceived to contribute to elements of rationality, legitimacy and consensus to the processes of reform.

Sweden has a two-tier local government structure with 290 municipalities and 20 counties. At both levels the governing bodies are elected directly and constitutionally guaranteed the right to levy taxes. It has been proposed to merge the counties into a smaller number of regions. It seems that Sweden is moving in this direction even though the topic is politically controversial.

Reform components

Disaggregation has not been a very prominent feature of Swedish reforms, but the disaggregated Swedish agency model has been a source of inspiration for reforms in other countries. A clear division of departments and agencies was designed long before anyone had thought about NPM components. The aim of the division was not to enhance efficiency or give managers better chances to manage, but to constrain the powers of the King after a long period with autocratic monarchy (Pierre 2004). Agency autonomy is in Sweden protected by the constitution. Contrary to Denmark and Norway, where ministerial accountability as mentioned above is a key mechanism, cabinet members in Sweden may be reprimanded by the parliament if they give agencies detailed instructions on decisions and actions. Agencies are governed by overall regulatory frameworks and by annual budgetary allocations ('regleringsbrev') in which government and parliament can give agencies advice and direction by targeting financial resources to specific programmes.

In defiance of – or maybe because of – this institutional construction, there are in Sweden recurrent debates on the 'politicization' of agencies. Government appoints the director-generals of the agencies through the departments. These decisions are politically sensitive in nature. Also informal networks between departments and agencies are well developed. Probably networks constitute the key mechanism for policy coordination. One could argue that the operation of the Swedish system is based on principles inconsistent with the original design of the system.

As already mentioned, changing management practice and introducing management by objectives was an important reform component already in the 1980s. In the late 1980s and the beginning of the 1990s a series of financial management reforms were implemented including results-oriented budgeting and accruals-accounting. Results-based management is still important and has become supplemented with risk management. As in Denmark, analyses have revealed challenges as to, for example, how meaningful objectives are specified and results measured (Ekonomistyrningsverket 2007). In 1993, a new system of central government grants to the municipalities strengthened the latter's autonomy due to fewer central regulations, but at the same time permitted central government to fix tight budgets.

Agencies used to be organized with boards dominated by the representation of organized interests and with shared responsibility between boards and the director-generals. As such, agencies were part of a corporatist model of policy making. In recent years the managerial structures of agencies have been reformed. In most agencies the director-generals have overall responsibility and boards have become advisory, in some agencies boards have been given overall responsibility in a more corporate-like model.

User-responsiveness, focusing on service and quality, was also on the reform agenda early on (Premfors et al. 2009). Sweden has a long tradition for carrying out evaluation activities and this has been further developed during the period. A variety of evaluation and service quality improvement schemes have been adopted. Recently evaluation activities have gained a renewed interest for evidence and effects.

Free choice was also on the early reform agenda. In the late 1980s, when a second phase of reform began, free choice for citizens was increasingly emphasized especially in local government where purchaser–provider arrangements spread and a climate of competition developed. Due to fiscal crisis, an administration programme aimed at reducing the size of the public sector by 10 per cent was launched in 1990. The focus on economy continued as a conservative government took over in 1991. Extensive privatization schemes were put on the agenda and to some extent implemented. When the Social Democrats returned to power in 1994 they had abandoned their opposition to privatization and were prepared to accept it on a selective basis. In the 1990s a considerable number of agencies were turned into public companies. To understand how Sweden could follow a rather radical NPM reform trajectory in a period when the Social Democrats were in power, requires looking to the role of central agencies. Bureaucratic and professional actors seem to have a stronger influence on administrative policy than political.

Competition is well developed in local government where service delivery is organized in a variety of ways. Nongovernmental production and delivery are performed by non-profit organizations, by cooperatives set up by users, by employees in a specific area or by private companies. Furthermore, public–private partnerships have gained ground. The development has caused discussions on inequality across municipalities.

What then about the importance of the post-NPM reform components of re-integration and needs-based holism in Sweden? In Sweden coordination has been a recurring topic in discussions about administrative policy, probably due to the historically disaggregated system. Moreover there has been a discussion on the effects of results-based management on collaboration across public administration bodies. Public organizations have been described as withdrawing into themselves, giving priority to production objectives rather than the development of cross-cutting collaboration (Statskontoret 2005). In continuation of this, more process-based management approaches, aimed at getting two or more actors to deliver services to users through collaborative networks, are being tried out.

Results

Assessing reform results is no more easy in Sweden than elsewhere. Decentralization has meant that welfare state functions are first and foremost local affairs. Municipalities are reported to have become more fragmented (Montin 2000), and the intensified competition climate seems to have increased local differences in service delivery. The national administration has shrunk and former government-administrated enterprises have been corporatized and privatized. The organizational identity of public organizations has strengthened, causing discussions on the risk of suboptimization and the need for developing coordination. On the cultural dimension, observers point to value shifts from solidarity-collectivism to solidarity-individualism.

Similarities, Differences and Interpretations

Table 8.1 summarizes the findings of the country analyses. First of all it is evident that in all three countries public sector reforms are developed through negotiation processes including several actors. But partly different actors are reported as central reform entrepreneurs. In Denmark and Norway administrative policy has been more concentrated than in Sweden. In Denmark reforms have been implemented first in central government on the initiative of the Ministry of Finance and later on spread to local government partly through negotiations between the ministry and the interest organization of the municipalities. In Norway a ministry with special responsibility for government administration has been an important entrepreneur although largely dependent on acceptance from other ministries. In Sweden, where reforms at first were implemented in local government, the administrative policy constituency is more fragmented. In Denmark administrative policy is integrated with spending policy. This is to a lesser extent the situation in Norway and Sweden (except during the crisis period in the 1990s). In Norway the parliament seems

Table 8.1   Reform actors and components

Contents of reform	Denmark	Norway	Sweden
Central actors	Ministry of Finance, Local Government Denmark	Ministries and government	Central government, agencies, independent commissions and local government
Components: NPM			
Disaggregation	Agencification modern before but not after NPM. Disaggregation to some extent important in relation to regulatory agencies	Agencification important in relation to ordinary agencies and to some extent in relation to regulatory agencies	Agencification modern long before NPM. Disaggregation primarily important in relation to regulatory agencies
Management practice	Management by objectives and results through contracts and accrual accounting very important	Management by objectives and results as well as risk management very important	Management by objectives and results as well as accrual accounting and risk management very important
User responsiveness	Quality improvement practices and user satisfaction analyses very important and institutionalized	Quality improvement practices and user satisfaction analyses important and institutionalized	Quality improvement practices and user satisfaction analyses very important and institutionalized
Competition	Corporatization and privatization in the infrastructure area. Competition through result-based funding, contracting out and free choice becoming increasingly important in welfare areas in recent years	Corporatization and partial privatization in the infrastructure area. Competition through result-based funding and free choice important in some welfare areas but partly rolled back in others	Corporatization and privatization in the infrastructure area. Competition climate institutionalized in local government through privatization and free choice
Components: post-NPM			
Reintegration	Re-integration initiatives are important and often combined with NPM reform components	Fragmentation is discussed as a problem. Re-integration initiatives seem to be increasingly important. Examples of NPM roll-back initiatives	Several commissions have discussed fragmentation and argued for furthering integration in both central and local government. But re-integration action seems limited
Needs-based holism	Needs-based holism used as an argument for the 2007 local government reform but in practice it seems to be of limited importance	Needs-based holism important principle in reform in employment administration	The need for needs-based holism is discussed

to be more involved in overall reform discussions than is the case in Denmark and Sweden. Commissions are used in all three countries, on an ad hoc basis in Denmark and more systematically in Norway and especially Sweden.

Analysing the implementation of reform components reveals both similarities as well as differences across the three countries. Overall the three countries have implemented NPM reform components to a large extent. Especially components related to management practice and user responsiveness have been very important. In relation to management, especially performance measurement, broader international comparisons also show that the three countries are among the countries having the longest experience in this field (Curristine 2005). In Norway there seems to be higher acceptance and less criticism than in Denmark and Sweden of the way management practice has been changed in central government.

Furthermore all three countries have developed public sector competition climates but in different ways and at a different pace. Sweden was the early mover when it came to introducing large-scale competition, while Denmark and especially Norway were more reluctant but later on moved rather rapidly in this direction. Are the three countries still modernizers rather than marketizers? The answer depends on what they are being compared to. There is, however, no doubt that competition and marketization are much more prominent features today than they were in all three countries, and Sweden has gone the furthest in this direction.

In relation to the disaggregation reform component there is considerable difference across the three countries. Agencification was modern in all three countries prior to NPM reforms. Agency autonomy was especially well developed in Sweden. Agencification as a reform component has been most important in Norway. In relation to regulatory agencies all three countries have to some extent followed the international trend to transform regulatory agencies into single-purpose organizations.

When it comes to post-NPM reform components these seem to be more important in Denmark and Norway than in Sweden. In Denmark re-integration initiatives go hand in hand with furthering NPM competition components. In Norway there are examples of both re-integration initiatives being combined with furthering NPM components and the use of re-integration in attempts to roll back NPM reforms. In Sweden the discussion on fragmentation and the need to further integration has been ongoing for many years but re-integration practice seems to be limited.

Theoretical Explanations

Three theoretical perspectives were employed here to explain public sector reforms. The first – the actor-oriented, political perspective, implying that reforms are ideology- and interest-driven – has shown to have some explanatory power. In all three countries differences in political positions explained why the countries became modernizers and not marketizers when NPM reforms were initiated. Marketization and privatization were points of conflict between right- and left-leaning political parties while other NPM reform components gained broad political support. Later in the 1990s the left-leaning parties, to some extent and not without internal conflicts, changed positions and marketization and privatization to some extent were implemented. Lately the differences in political positions have become revitalized first and foremost in Norway. It is common for the three countries that right-leaning governments put more pressure on implementing radical reform components, which, however, does not preclude, as the Danish case shows, the possibility of these being combined with post-NPM components.

The actor-oriented, political perspective cannot, however, stand alone. The rational organizational perspective, implying that reforms are problem-driven, also has explanatory power. In both Denmark and Sweden NPM reforms were developed as reactions to problems related to the planning regimes of the 1970s. Furthermore, reforms in Denmark in the 1980s and in Sweden in the 1990s were attempts to move away from economic problems related to public sector growth. In Norway reforms in local government in the 1980s and at the beginning of the 1990s were clearly problem-driven (although the solutions chosen did not solve the problems recognized). Likewise the post-NPM reform initiatives in recent years, especially in Norway, may be seen as reactions to fragmentation problems stemming from prior NPM reforms.

But these two 'hard' theoretical perspectives do not explain all aspects of the reforms. The institutional, cultural perspective also has considerable explanatory power. In Denmark cultural resistance has meant that the agencification component has not been adopted, as agencification was no longer a norm. In Norway NPM thinking for many years met cultural resistance in the collectively-oriented political-administrative culture, resulting in Norway being a more reluctant reformer than Denmark and Sweden. And after some years characterized by more radical reforms, the cultural resistance in Norway in recent years seems to have become re-vitalized.

As mentioned in the introduction to this chapter, the EU and the EEA agreement do not directly interfere in questions related to the organization of the nation states and thus the content of administrative policies. But the EU and wider international collaborations, including the OECD are important backdrops for the development of public sector reforms.

First of all, pursuing the idea of the internal market brings about demands for market regulation. Especially in fields where prior national monopolies have been phased out there are demands for establishing independent regulatory bodies. But also in other fields such as environment, food safety and higher education, the EU or broader collaborations such as the Bologna process, increasingly demand well-developed national control regimes. It is not stated in detail how the regulators have to be organized and work, but there are demands that regulators have to be in place and capable of enforcing common rules.

Moreover, international organizations, probably first and foremost the OECD, are important discussion clubs, where public sector reform ideas and norms are developed and experiences with good practice are spread. To understand fully the development of public sector reforms in this way requires an international perspective and an eye for how ideas are edited and translated across boundaries, which has not really been possible to pursue in this analysis.

Conclusion

In the introduction four questions were raised. Two questions concerned whether public sector reforms in Denmark, Norway and Sweden have followed similar patterns as one would expect. The analysis has shown that there are similarities but also many differences. Historical differences in the organization of central government, different administrative cultures, different challenges met at different points in time, as well as differences in political constituencies in power have all shaped public sector reforms in different ways. Each country has developed its own reform profile with different combinations of reform components.

Two other questions concerned whether the three countries can still be characterized as primarily modernizers as concluded in international studies some years ago, or whether they have adopted additional or new reform strategies, for example competition strategies or post-NPM strategies such as re-integration. The analysis has shown that all three countries are more than just modernizers defined as countries following managerial and user-responsiveness strategies. All three countries have increasingly followed competition and marketization strategies even though these have not been uncontroversial. In recent years especially Denmark and Norway have also followed post-NPM strategies. While Denmark has been combining competition and re-integration strategies, Norway has seen a struggle between the two.

In both Denmark and Sweden public sector reforms have at different points in time been speeded up as a consequence of economic crisis. The world is currently in the middle of a financial crisis and it has hit Denmark and Sweden much harder than the oil-rich country Norway. What will be the implications of the financial crisis for Scandinavian public sector development and reform in the years ahead? In Denmark politicians have begun to discuss the need for downsizing the public sector. We may in the coming years face a development where differences between Denmark and Sweden on the one hand and Norway on the other may become widened.

NPM in Asian Countries

Anthony B.L. Cheung

Introduction

Since the 1990s, Asian countries had been increasingly riding on the global movement of public sector reforms. After the 1997 Asian economic crisis, which cast doubt on the 'East Asian miracle' (World Bank 1993), there had been calls for institutional reforms in some Asian countries in order to cope with the impact of globalization and to catch up with some recognized 'best practices'. For those countries relying on the assistance of international organizations or developed donor-countries, such as Indonesia, Sri Lanka and Bangladesh, they were particularly prone to imposed conditions of aid in the form of requirements on specific reform targets and strategies. Broadly speaking, two dominant paradigms have the most impact on Asian institutional reforms: the New Public Management (NPM) and 'good governance' models. In addition to economic and fiscal pressures, domestic political changes and regime transition have also induced a new articulation of governance and institutional configurations. 'Socialist' countries like China and Vietnam have also embarked on major economic and administrative transformations as part of their journey of systemic reform and ideological reversion.

All this, however, does not occur in an historical vacuum. 'History matters', as path dependence theorists would say (for example Wilsford 1994, Greener 2000a, 2000b). Innate influence of national administrative traditions aside (such as the colonial, military or imperial legacies of some countries), Asian administrative reforms have also been closely linked to political evolutions arising from decolonization, democratization and nation building. They are as much influenced by the global trends of administrative reforms and government reinvention, as by regional and national institutional logics shaped by local history, culture, context and administrative thought, and motivated by domestic politics inasmuch as external inspirations and lessons (Cheung 2005). Behind some common rhetoric and external appearance lies a diversity of evolutionary tracks and reform pathways. To this extent, Asian NPM is not really the same as NPM in Western Europe, North America, or Australia, whose experiences have largely defined the rationale and substance of the global NPM agenda, and set the prescriptions for 'good governance'. What appears to be similar may merely be 'fundamentally alike in all unimportant aspects' (paraphrasing Wallace Sayre, quoted in Allison 1986a). With the recent outbreak of the global financial crisis, Anglo-American capitalism is at a crossroads. NPM, rooted in neo-liberal pro-market ideology, is facing a legitimacy crisis of its own as many nations (especially developing countries) begin to seek lessons from alternative developmental models. The rising challenge to the market paradigm will likely see a growing interest in 'Asian NPM' which is in effect a hybrid of Western and Eastern traditions, combining state-led development strategies and the instrumentalities of public administration.

Dominant Paradigms of Public Sector Reforms in Asia

New Public Management

NPM began as a reform trajectory of mainly Western liberal democracies seeking to use pro-market strategies and measures to cope with economic and political challenges since the 1980s, by seeking remedies from the market to deal with the many failures discovered in the bureaucracy as well as para-governmental outgrowths during the heydays of nationalization and the welfare state (Hood 1991, OECD 1995, Lane 2000, McLaughlin, Osborne and Ferlie 2002). Much of the NPM reform agenda has to do with: streamlining the structure of the civil service; efficiency improvements especially in human and financial resource management; decentralization; and ultimately cultural transformation of public service organizations from their traditional hierarchical and bureaucratic *modus operandi* to one more aligned to the private sector principles of competition, performance rewards and customer orientation. Many of the reform experiences and theorizations found in the international literature are based on those initiatives and their impact in Europe, North America, and Australia and New Zealand, where such reforms were first pioneered. NPM has since informed public sector reforms in many developed OECD countries (Manning 1997: 5) but other parts of the world have also been exposed to its influence (Turner 1998, 2000, Haque 2001, McCourt and Minogue 2001). Asian nations, and many other developing countries, are seemingly at the learning end of the policy diffusion and policy transfer process (Common 2001).

Good Governance

The 'good governance' goals have been advocated by regional and international organizations – such as the International Monetary Fund (IMF) and World Bank – for less developed nations, sometimes modelled on Western pro-market instruments and sometimes with greater emphasis on equity and development. The United Nations

Economic and Social Commission for Asia and the Pacific (UNESCAP), in its paper *What is Good Governance?* (2006), sets out eight characteristics of good governance, namely: accountable, consensus-oriented, effective and efficient, equitable and inclusive, participatory, following the rule of law, responsive, and transparent. The World Bank's World Governance Indicators measure six aspects, namely: control of corruption, voice and accountability, rule of law, regulatory quality, political stability and absence of violence, and government effectiveness (World Bank 2010). In Asia, the Asian Development Bank (1998) sees accountability, transparency, openness, predictability and participation as the principal qualities that governments should aim to attain. In the post-Cold War era, with the concomitant rise of neo-liberalism, the 'good governance' call is often associated with an ideological drive from international organizations to promote convergence to a global economic order supportive of a neo-liberal agenda. Such a drive is sometimes referred to as the Washington Consensus.[1] To that extent, there is a shared impact of the NPM and 'good governance' paradigms.

Asia is a huge land mass with long and diverse histories and traditions, civilizations and cultures, and social, political, administrative and economic systems. There exist developed economies in East Asia and Southeast Asia (represented by Japan, South Korea, Taiwan, Hong Kong and Singapore), as well as developing ones, amongst which China and India have become two of the fastest-growth economies of the world in the twenty-first century. Within Asia, different countries or sub-regions display different domestic political, social and economic conditions, and face different challenges to their governance. The Asian Development Bank (1999: 18, Table 1), for example, has identified different sets of governance problems faced by different subgroups of Asian countries at the turn of the century, ranging from an overextended and over-centralized state, weak administration and rigid regulation, to outright cronyism. Such diversities determine their reform actions and trajectories amid the global NPM trends and international reform models.

Putting Asian Public Sector Reforms in Regional Context

The Political Economy

Some commonalities can be observed of public sector reform experiences in different Asian countries (Cheung 2005). Inheriting legacies of colonial rule, military rule,

---

1   The term 'Washington Consensus' was initially coined by John Williamson (1989) to describe a set of specific economic policy prescriptions constituting the 'standard' reform package promoted for crisis-wracked developing countries by Washington D.C.-based institutions such as the IMF, the World Bank and the US Treasury Department. The term has since been used as a synonym for market fundamentalism, and become associated with neo-liberal policies in general.

or one-party authoritarianism or dictatorship, they have shared a strong tradition of bureaucratic rule and hierarchical values. A paternalistic, authoritarian and centralized brand of bureaucratic culture thus defines the nature and features of public administration. Nation building, economic planning, and the predominant status and role of the bureaucracy (playing as the modernizers and reformers) have been key to administrative organization and reform. As newly decolonized, independent and emergent states in the last century, many Asian countries have sought to strengthen the state as part of their 'nation building' enterprise. Their historical and cultural traditions have tended to favour statist solutions to solve social and economic problems and to cope with political challenges. China and Vietnam – previously state-planned – are now state-directed marketized/ marketizing economies. Japan, South Korea, Taiwan, Singapore and Malaysia are well-known examples of developmental states. Hong Kong, though seen as an East Asian exception and long cherished as the last bastion of classical market capitalism (Friedman 1981), has been actively engaged in regulatory controls and social policy interventions (Schiffer 1983). Even India had for a long time operated a highly regulated economy through bureaucratic licensing controls.

The economic objectives of the 'developmental state' requires centralized systems with centralized power to mobilize and direct resources, in order to drive state-directed industrialization through state-owned enterprises (SOEs) and an active industrial policy. The interlocking state/economy/society systems and interlocking elites have for a long time underpinned the core of governance in East and Southeast Asia (notably the communist party-states of China and Vietnam; former one-party or military authoritarian states in South Korea, Taiwan, Thailand and Indonesia; and 'illiberal' democratic regimes like Singapore and Malaysia). Unlike Western countries, the relatively weak market and weak civil society in many parts of Asia have rendered it impossible for society-driven or market-driven reform forces to bear upon the state. Since the market is also a socially-embedded institution, the impact of marketization or privatization is not exactly creating the same result as in Western market economies. In some cases, the market is largely created and regulated by the state and still needs the latter's support and patronage (such as in China and Vietnam), whereas the private sector is weak and not really independent of the state.

The Reform Logic

Administrative reforms in Asian countries thus seek to empower rather than denigrate the bureaucracy. NPM-like reforms have been adopted not to erode bureaucratic power, but instead to cement or reinvent it as a modernizing and developmental bureaucracy, so as to enhance the state's capacity in economic development and nation building. The fact that there exists a dual agenda of bureaucratic improvement and economic development implies a reform logic quite the reverse of NPM. Instead of decoupling the state and market, and using the market to drive all things including the state's performance, the logic is inverted to enable a capacitated state to drive the economy. While the bureaucratic elites are largely looked upon to drive reform and modernization, they are often also the cause of problems of governance (such as patronage, corruption and government–business collusion) that administrative reforms are supposed to deal with, thus becoming at the same time the main countervailing force to fundamental change when it comes to upsetting their fundamental interests. Coalitions of interlocking interests have remained intact under a state-managed economic strategy, and reform policies like privatization have often been adopted not to confine the role and scope of the state, but rather to strengthen state capacity in alternative ways via political agents and power brokers.

The Western NPM logic is characterized by a market-led, private sector-oriented ideology of administrative change or reinvention, involving rolling back the frontier of the state, and seeking solutions from the lessons and precepts of private sector management. In comparison, the East and Southeast Asian experiences have pointed to rather contrasting values and orientations: state-led; public sector-led; building state capacity; newly acquired governance values in democratic transition; and solutions from strong and 'competent' state institutions in some cases. The East Asian growth model – to denote the impressive economic performance of Japan and the four NICs (newly industrialized countries, namely South Korea, Taiwan, Singapore and Hong Kong) during the 1990s – was driven by an alternative logic of what Wade (1990) described as 'governing the market'. There is, of course, no singular Asian NPM 'face'. However, prominent Asian countries (like Japan, South Korea, Taiwan, Singapore, Malaysia, China and Vietnam in terms of the chronological sequence of their economic development) have tended to adopt a state-planned, state-led or state-managed approach to economic and social development, whether in a capitalist or socialist setting, resulting in the proliferation of the para-governmental public sector, interlocking with businesses and major social elites, and in some cases involving networks of government (including military) patronage and public employment for social-distribution purposes. The private sector-oriented and neo-liberal rhetoric commonly taken to characterize the global NPM logic does not square with the inherent statist and bureaucratic nature of many Asian administrative systems. The 'old' administrative regime of Asia has continued to be firmly entrenched, despite the 'new' public management wrappings and techniques.

The Domestic Politics of Reform

The politics of Asian administrative reform was once diagnosed by Moon and Ingraham (1998) within the context of a tripartite framework between politics, bureaucracy and society, depicted as a 'political nexus triad' (PNT). In Western NPM, apart from party politics and ideological shifts, popular/electoral sentiments and pressures from the private sector often provided part of the impetus for reform – the social habitat factors according to Hood (1996a). However, such 'societal' factors have not featured prominently in the Asian scene, where the growth of a strong free market and an autonomous civil society, to form the pillars of governance along with the state, has yet to be realized in many countries. The paternalistic and centralizing traditions of Asian administration mean that central agencies are reluctant to devolve power, particularly to non-state institutions or those institutions that the state finds difficult to reach and control in some way. Despite all the rhetoric about devolution, partnership and power-sharing, the actual extent of decentralization and power-shedding is limited (Cheung and Scott 2003: 13). Governance reforms are mostly bureaucracy-led rather than market-led or civil society-led.

The role of the bureaucracy in any public sector reform is well recognized in the academic literature. For example, Hood (2002a) has pointed to the importance of 'public service bargain' in terms of politicians–bureaucrats negotiation over the agenda and pace of reform. PNT in Asia is significant more in terms of the inconspicuousness than intervention of either an active civil society or influential private economic sector. The bureaucracy is synonymous with the state; it is both the 'problem' and the 'solution' of governance. To reform the state and state–society and state–economy relationships through the agency of the state constitutes the main paradox of governance reform, so that 'the answer must also lie in the problem' (Cheung and Scott 2003: 17). Because of the close intermingling between the state and economy, and between the state and society, with the state being the dominating force, it is impossible to talk of economic reform without state reform, or of state–society partnerships when the society is still largely dependent on or subservient to state power. The dilemma is: bureaucrats have to be 'reformed' in order for reform to be successful, *and yet* they have to be 'relied upon' for driving the reform; but reforms may be easily 'captured' by the bureaucracy for rent-seeking purposes. The politics of reform has to strike a delicate balance between the forces for regime change and the forces for stability and authority, otherwise regime capacity would become so weakened that it is unable to direct anything.

Impact of Globalization and Learning from the West

In this era of globalization and cross-national policy transfers, Asian institutional reforms just cannot be immune to the global waves of public sector reforms. However, being exposed to a general environment of global reforms displaying a dominant ideological direction or agenda does not necessarily mean that national and local reforms will conform to the same institutional logic. Even among advanced nations pioneering the global wave of reforms, clear diversities have been detected (Cheung 1997, Christensen and Lægreid 2001a, Common 2001). Path dependence explanations fit public management reforms rather well (Pollitt 2000: 185), as these countries do not share the same uniform past in terms of administrative structures, traditions and instruments, but operate in political and legal frameworks that condition their policy choices in responding to change, as well as their political motives and calculations behind reforms (Kettl 2000).

It has always been debated how far Asian reformers have learnt and borrowed from Western reform paradigms and models such as NPM. Conceptually in any process of reform within a country, there exist both exogenous and endogenous factors; there would be both domestically-generated needs for change as well as externally imposed or globally driven directions through policy learning and transfer, or simply policy emulation (Ikenberry 1990). While acknowledging the importance of internal, contextual factors, Christensen, Lisheng and Painter (2008) go for a 'multi-causal' model in which both internal and external factors are present, and the flow of reform ideas and the reinforcing impact of technical and institutional pressures render it difficult for national leaders to avoid imitation and the temptation to pursue them. As opposed to a 'home grown agenda' thesis, they argue along the lines of Spence (1980) that 'learning from the West' had a long history in modern China and Japan, with a tradition of emulating the West in order to 'catch up' and to accelerate the country's development. They see imitation as part of a process of external legitimization for renewed internal momentum, though constrained by internal institutional and cultural factors.

There is some validity in such observation. However, one should also note that East Asian countries seeking to modernize by learning from the West have always insisted on not losing their own identity. For example, despite China's enormous and strenuous reform process in pursuit of a modernization agenda grounded in learning from the West, all along there has been no leadership intention to dismantle or dilute its pre-existing Communist Party rule, or to transplant the Western liberal democratic model as the preferred form of governance. One may, of course, point to China's importation of Soviet-inspired communism as evidence as giving up its traditional political system, but Chinese communism is arguably more *Chinese* than communist in essence. The importation of 'Western' tools and systems would be allowed and encouraged so long as these could serve the best interests of the establishment. Such utilitarian reform thinking is in fact reminiscent of the notion of 'Chinese study as the essence, Western study as the tools' ['zhongxue weiti, xixue weiyong'] espoused by imperial modernizers in the late Ching Dynasty at the end of the nineteenth century, in which the 'tools' were always considered subordinate to the 'essence'.

The overall environment of administrative reforms and the impacts of domestic and external factors, as well as their inter-relationships, are illustrated by Figure 9.1.

Comparing Public Sector Reforms across Asian Countries

Typology of Reform Patterns

There exists a diversity of motives, imperatives and constraints pertaining to public sector reforms among Asian countries. It is impossible to pack these reforms into a single paradigm. Still, at least several significant clusters of Asian reform countries

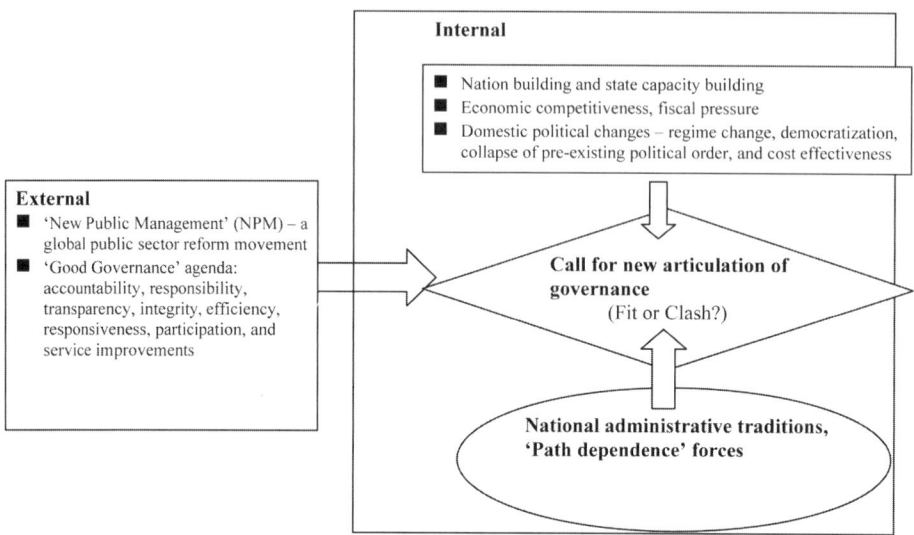

Figure 9.1   Environment of administrative reforms, the impacts of domestic and external factors, and their inter-relationships

can be identified, based on the administrative traditions and legacies, political economy, state role and capacity, salience of administrative reform, and forces and progress of change (see Table 9.1). In terms of agenda setting and the speed of reforms, at least four reform types can be distinguished, namely: (a) *an essentially bureaucrats-led modernization agenda* (in Japan, South Korea, Taiwan, Singapore and Hong Kong, even though politics have featured more prominently in the past decade in some of them as explained in the next section) – with generally a slow pace (except in Singapore, and to some extent Hong Kong); (b) *a politics-led political agenda* (in developing countries in Southeast Asia like Malaysia, Thailand and the Philippines) – with a slow or mixed pace; (c) *a party-state-led legitimacy and capacity building agenda* (in socialist transition states like China and Vietnam) – with a mixed pace; and (d) *a politics-led politicians–bureaucrats bargain agenda* (in sub-continent countries like India) – generally with a slow pace.

Reviewing the adaptation of the NPM menu by Southeast Asian countries at the beginning of this decade, Turner (2002) identified three sets of countries with a different degree of enthusiasm for reform: the 'enthusiastic' diners (namely Singapore and Malaysia), the 'cautious' diners (namely the Philippines, Thailand and Indonesia) and the rest who knew little of NPM (such as Vietnam, Laos and Cambodia). Things might have changed since then. In the case of Vietnam, there has been a more ambitious Public Administration Reform programme, partly driven by the party-state's desire to institutionalize and legitimize the transition to a socialist market economy within a centralized state-management framework, and partly upon the advice of international aid organizations and donor countries urging an

Table 9.1 Clusters of Asian reform countries

Regional sub-groupings	Japan and East Asian 'NICs'	Southeast Asian developing states	Socialist 'transition' states	Sub-continent states
Administrative traditions and legacies	Strong, centralized bureaucratic tradition; politics-administration fusion (Singapore and Hong Kong are typical 'administrative states')	Mostly post-colonial (and some also post-military) regimes, with strong bureaucratic state having close links to business	Communist one-party authoritarian bureaucratic rule; politics in administration (state and bureaucracy are one)	Post-colonial regimes, with relatively strong, centralized bureaucratic tradition
Nature of political economy	Developmental state – 'governed market' model (with the exception of Hong Kong which displays a semi-interventionist model)	'Government in business' model with highly institutionalized government–business relations	From state-planned to state-dominated economy and development	State regulative controls
State role and capacity	Historically strong capacity; highly interventionist (less so in Hong Kong)	State capacity largely dependent on regime control over economy and society	State capacity in question as economy transits towards market	State capacity in question due to political and bureaucratic corruption
Salience of administrative reform	Bureaucratic modernization and self-improvement; state capacity enhancement	Bureaucratic modernization and efficiency improvement; better subservience to political control	Bureaucratic modernization and rationality building, within context of regime consolidation and institutional reconfiguration	Political control and bureaucratic modernization
Forces for change	Mainly bureaucrats-driven, until most recently when politics and societal demands pushed for greater pace of reform (In Singapore, there is a joint politics-bureaucracy agenda)	Mainly politics-driven (to enhance bureaucratic efficiency), coupled with societal demands (In Thailand and Indonesia, regime change has brought about political desire to subdue bureaucratic power)	Party-state driven, to enhance regime capacity to cope with legitimacy and efficiency crises	Formally politics-driven, though bureaucracy has inherent interest and say over substance and pace of reform
Reform outcome	Bureaucratic domination of reform agenda, with slow progress (Successful 'public service bargain' à la Hood (2002a) in Singapore, hence minimal bureaucratic resistance)	Results slow and mixed; problematic 'public service bargain' and bureaucratic scepticism and resistance at times	Party-dominated agenda for reinvigoration of existing regime; reform not allowed to dilute regime control	Unclear 'public service bargain' or lack of it (as in India); slow progress and politicians–bureaucrats rivalry in agenda-setting

Source: Cheung (2005)

accelerated liberalization programme (Painter 2002, 2003). Samaratunge, Alam and Teicher (2008: 42) observe that South Asian countries, represented by Sri Lanka and Bangladesh, have opted for selected reform programmes which suit the short-term interests of the ruling elites. The policy prescriptions of international development agencies have influenced changes, but narrow partisan politics have acted as a force against comprehensive reforms. Although South Asian countries had introduced some major pro-market public sector reforms in order to improve performance, it was found that such reforms had not succeeded in improving performance but had even led to more adverse consequences on equity and citizenship rights, favouring the vested interests of political and business elites (Haque 2003).

The East Asian Pioneers and Enthusiasts of NPM Reforms

Hong Kong and Singapore

Hong Kong and Singapore are arguably the pioneers of NPM in Asia. Indeed they have undertaken similar public sector reforms since the 1990s. Being a former British colony before 1997, Hong Kong had a longstanding tradition of pursuing administrative reforms as substitutes for political reforms. A Public Sector Reform programme was launched in 1989, embracing an NPM-like agenda. Apart from managerial initiatives such as budgetary devolution, contracting out, self-accounting trading funds, customer-oriented initiatives and performance pledges, this reform was also significant in reconstituting the centre of policy management, redefining the policy management-delivery relationships between the policy secretaries (the equivalents of ministers) and various executive agencies. After reunification with China in 1997, major initiatives have been introduced in the areas of civil service reform, efficiency enhancement, performance management, contracting out and outsourcing, one-line budgets and financial devolution, and the introduction of political appointments (at Secretary, Undersecretary and Assistant levels). Economic restructuring, the challenges of globalization and regional competition, regime transition, and the need to meet rising public expectations for better responsiveness within a partial democracy have together shaped the public sector reform agenda (Cheung 2009).

Singapore's administrative reforms can be traced to its post-colonial efforts to rebuild a new civil service in the 1960s. Since the 1990s, the government has sought to bring the best into the civil service by linking the salaries of ministers and top civil servants to the highest paid professionals and corporate executives. In 1995, the Public Service for the 21st Century programme (PS21) was launched to nurture an attitude of service excellence, and to foster an environment for greater efficiency and effectiveness (Quah 2007a). Accompanying reforms included: budget reforms and devolution, the establishment of autonomous agencies and client orientation (Quah 2007b). Despite public sector divestment in the late 1980s, the government has been keen to reinvigorate 'Singapore Inc.' (that is, the government plus government-linked corporations, together forming a formidable political-economic foundation of the developmental state) through an ambitious regionalization strategy, in order to meet the challenges of globalization. In the aftermath of the Asian financial crisis, it has focused on economic restructuring and the 'Remaking Singapore' initiatives in political, social and cultural aspects, underscoring a paradigm shift towards community development and cohesion.

Comparing the two city states, Lee and Haque (2006: Table 2) found that Singapore had attained a greater extent of reform (in terms of scale and effectiveness) in the areas of economic and administrative governance, whereas Hong Kong had achieved a greater extent of reform in the area of social governance, such difference being explained by domestic political and civil society conditions, and social policy philosophy and traditions. Still there are important similarities. Both Singapore and Hong Kong are administrative states essentially enjoying fiscal surplus and economic boom (except in the aftermath of the Asian finance crisis), unlike Western NPM reform countries, and have largely embraced a pro-civil service reform agenda. Public sector bodies have remained efficient, thus privatization and corporatization have been pursued more for non-efficiency-related reasons (Cheung 2002). Public sector reforms have been largely bureaucrats-driven though there is a more prominent politicians–bureaucrats coalition – or 'public service bargain' (Hood 2002a) – in Singapore than in Hong Kong.

Japan, South Korea and Taiwan

The three East/Northeast Asian states – Japan, Korea and Taiwan (dubbed by some as 'Jakota') – share some common administrative heritage, with the latter two being former Japanese colonies until the end of the Second World War. They were initially laggards in public sector reform because of their unduly rigid administrative and organizational culture. Since the late 1990s, thanks to democratization and regime change (in Taiwan and South Korea), but more importantly due to globalization, economic pressure and the impact of the Asian financial crisis, these states have undertaken more wide-ranging reforms in the fashion of the American 'reinvention' movement.

Japan is a developmental state (Johnson 1995). The motives of public sector reform can be linked to its economic and fiscal crisis which has continued for two decades. As early as the 1980s, an Administrative Reform Council was established as the vehicle of reform. However, given the nature of a strong politicians–bureaucrats alliance under the former Liberal Democratic Party rule, administrative reforms were essentially top-down, slow-paced and designed with bureaucratic consent. The pace of reform has quickened since the Asian financial crisis. Over the last decade, major reforms pursued include: privatization of public enterprises; devolution, decentralization and deregulation; fiscal and budgetary reforms; and, most crucial, central-government restructuring and downsizing (Nakamura 1998, Masujima 2005). More recently there have been moves to curb the power and influence of national bureaucrats – such as changing the longstanding political culture where ministers merely confirm policies formulated by their ministry bureaucrats, and ending the practices of *amakudari* (golden parachuting, that is, placement of national civil servants in post-retirement jobs with entities supervised by their former ministries) and *watari* (movement between such jobs) among national civil servants.

Like Japan, South Korea is also a developmental state with a competitive party system since democratization in 1997. The Korean administrative culture as inherited from over half a century of Japanese colonial rule and another three decades of military dictatorship has been a rather closed and top-down one. The Asian financial crisis of 1997–98 and the resulting IMF pressure for deregulation and fiscal reforms, as well as the challenges of globalization, had together induced a strong impetus to a reassessment of the role of the Korean public sector and its management structures and policies. This, in tandem with the newly elected democratic administration of President Kim Dae-jung (1998–2003) put administrative and governance reforms at the forefront of the political agenda at the turn of the century, especially in revamping government–business relations and the civil service system. Reforms since then have been more wide-ranging: the breakup of the monopoly powers of *chaebols* (the business conglomerates previously associated with and groomed by the former military governments as strategic corporate partners to drive industrialization and economic development); privatization of public enterprises; central and local government restructuring and downsizing; agencification; introduction of a new Senior Civil Service; performance management reform; budgetary and financial management reforms; anti-corruption reforms; citizen convenience initiatives; and deregulation and simplification of procedures (Cho and Kim 2000, Ha 2004, Kim 2007).

Taiwan, another newly industrialized and democratized state and former Japanese colony, only ended half a century of Kuomintang (KMT, Nationalist Party) authoritarian rule in 2000, when the opposition Democratic Progressive Party (DPP) came to power, which in turn was replaced by the KMT in 2008. It is still in the process of regime transition from one-party authoritarianism to a competitive party system. The bureaucratic culture has inherited the legacy of half-a-century Japanese colonial rule as well as authoritarian traditions brought from the KMT's rule in mainland China before it fled to Taiwan after defeat by the Communists in 1949. Anti-KMT activism over the years, especially after the lifting of martial law in 1987 and the tolerance of opposition political parties and a free press since then, had led to political liberalization and a democratic political culture in the 1990s. These undercurrents in the society and polity, together with the challenge of globalization and the need for Taiwan to remain competitive, have together induced the government in power (whether KMT or DPP) to pursue public sector reforms (Cheung 2003). Since the 1990s, 'government reinvention' – emulating the US administrative reform slogan – has been put at the forefront of the policy agenda by successive administrations, supported by rounds of government reinvention programmes aimed at reorganization, restructuring and downsizing, deregulation and privatization of SOEs, and citizen convenience initiatives. Despite enthusiasm and rising expectations in society for change, the actual pace of reforms has been slow due to the political gridlock between the two main political camps and legislative delay, causing uncertainties and anxieties in the bureaucracy which used to dominate the administrative agenda. Sun (2008) describes this as a mismatch between the supply and demand of administrative reform.

Concluding Discussion

Asian responses to change remain to be shaped by domestic conditions and institutional dynamics. Asian public sector reforms, even if donning imported NPM or 'good governance' clothing, or subscribing to the language and rhetoric of global reform fashions, are still essentially policy instruments to shore up and sustain the existing pro-state, and very often also pro-bureaucracy, regime. The lack of a major ideological or paradigm break with the past means that governance reform or the reinvention of public administration is pursued only to the extent of preserving pre-existing interests and institutions. This is observed not only in market-socialist states but also in more developed and newly industrialized countries. Granted, reforms have often turned out to be the means for political objectives, whether of the old or new political elites, or of the bureaucracy.

The conventional wisdom under the neo-liberal agenda has it that improved governance is conducive to economic growth, a goal much treasured by Asian and other developing countries, with the corollary that economically more affluent nations are in turn able to afford the costs associated with a competent bureaucracy and better entrenched institutions of good governance, thereby inducing a virtuous circle. However, such causal relationship is more ambivalent on the ground. Kaufmann and Kraay (2002, 2003) found out from empirical studies that there was actually negative feedback from per-capita incomes to governance. Firstly, when the institutions of the state are 'captured' by vested interests (as is the case in some Asian developing countries), those entrenched elites could benefit from a worsening status quo of mis-governance and could successfully resist demands for change even as income rises. Secondly, economic growth could sometimes be achieved despite the lack of what neo-liberals define as elements of good or democratic governance – some would point to China and Singapore as examples; hence Kaufman and Kraay's (2002) suggestion of the possibility of 'growth without governance', which directly challenges the 'good governance' paradigm. The post-Cold War enthusiasm for a singular route towards good governance grounded in neo-liberalism has come to its demise partly because of the diverse experience of reforms across the globe, contrary to the one-size-fits-all prescription, and partly because the recent global financial crisis emanating from the most advanced economies in the United States and Europe has exposed the intellectual and practical vulnerabilities of the NPM doctrine.

The tide of opinion is now fast changing, calling for more critical reflections. Andrews (2010), for example, argues that 'good government means different things in different countries', and that effective governments are actually more likely to display better practice characteristics than implied in one-best-way models. In the aftermath of the global financial crisis, the superpower domination of US capitalism has been seriously eroded, leading to the questioning of not just its economic might, not also its cultural superiority. As *The Economist* (2009a: 9) remarked, while globalization and economic interdependence will continue to be fundamental forces of development, at the same time cultural differences and economic nationalism will likely form the basis of rivalry and conflict. The globalization discourse previously dominated by neo-liberalism is being challenged on two fronts – the emerging post-neo-liberal debates which advocate emancipatory, inclusive and re-regulatory roles for the state (Brand and Sekler 2009), and the critics of the 'Washington Consensus' championing an alternative 'Beijing Consensus' based on the Chinese path of pragmatic developmentalism (Ramo 2004). This is not the place to explore and debate such rival paths and claims. Suffice it to say that a culturally diverse public administration scene at the global level is increasingly recognized to be the norm rather than the exception, and the Asian countries' distinct and varied NPM reform experiences and trajectories attest to such diversity.

PART III
SECTOR STUDIES

Healthcare States and Medical Professions: The Challenges from NPM

Haldor Byrkjeflot

Introduction

Scholars of public administration have noted that during the last 20–30 years, hospital reforms have become a global phenomenon. More recently, they have also noticed that healthcare is in a state of permanent 'dis-reorganization' (Stambolovic 2003, Pollitt 2007b). This chapter starts with the assumption that although New Public Management (NPM) refers to a rather diverse set of reform ideas, it is nonetheless meaningful to use the label as a point of departure for analysing the reforms that have been undertaken in healthcare since the 1980s. The chapter will outline a few common characteristics of such reforms and use them as the starting point for presenting and discussing alternative frameworks for understanding and making sense of recent reform trends. It will then discuss what happens when these frameworks and the empirical realities to which they refer are challenged by NPM.

It is not unusual to hear the claim that as a consequence of NPM, there is now a movement towards convergence among healthcare systems, in particular, within the nations categorized as having National Healthcare Systems (NHS) (former UK area and the Southern European and Scandinavian systems), and also between the NHS systems and the corporatist continental systems of healthcare (Germany and France). The recent healthcare reform in the United States (Tanne 2010) may be a further indication of a stronger role for the nation-state in healthcare governance on a world-wide basis (Freeman 2000).

In an attempt to make sense of recent healthcare reforms, this chapter presents an analysis of reform dynamics, with a particular emphasis on southern, continental and northern Europe. From the NPM perspective, the stated aims of the reforms have been to improve cost control and to distribute health resources more equally across regions and municipalities. Furthermore, in the official rhetoric, NPM reforms have aimed at reducing the size of government and constraining professional control, in order to develop a more decentralized system and to empower patients and consumers of healthcare. From another point of view, a framework I have called a profession-state perspective, it has been pointed out that doctors (in this chapter often referred to as the medical profession) may also play a central role in such reforms, and that NPM may just as well be seen as a movement towards a new and more centralized medical regime. From a third perspective, however, one called the healthcare state perspective, one could argue that the NPM reforms bring about a further strengthening of central state governance. These three perspectives will now be presented with a discussion regarding to what extent each one makes sense of the recent reform events. The discussion will also address how each perspective may help explain long-term development trends in healthcare governance.

New Public Management in Healthcare

The NPM perspective argues that purchaser–provider arrangements and independent regulatory agencies are necessary for articulating and differentiating various roles in the public sector. From this perspective, the smart thing for the state to do is to withdraw from its predominant role as the producer of public services, either by allowing for competition between private or public providers, or by transferring responsibilities for service provision to independent agencies and enterprises. The distinctive components of these reforms have been identified by Hood (1991) as a results orientation, a shift to quantification, incentives for managers and a 'voice' for the citizen as a consumer. A popular way to describe the dynamics of NPM reforms in the early 2000s was through a 'stage theory', in which the modernization of the public sector was to take place in three stages (Harding and Preker 2003: 27–28). The first stage is government divestiture of commercial activities; the second stage takes place when infrastructure services are privatized or placed at 'arm's-length' from the state; the third stage is the current move towards applying marketizing reforms to core functions of the state, social and health services. The prediction is that there will be a necessary movement towards the increased use of privatization and contracting out in healthcare. This will lift some political and financial burdens from the state's shoulders.

More specifically, the NPM perspective suggests three ways to deal with the present and the future. First, it recommends a strong emphasis on management. The state ought to establish managerial identities and create space for managers to act as entrepreneurs. Secondly, the state must develop market instruments and transparency, also in sectors where markets *per se* do not exist, in order to achieve the aims of health politics. Thirdly, there is a need to establish organizational autonomy, where enterprises and other independent organizational units take care of the production and provision of services, but where it is the role of government to purchase, regulate and control. The following discusses these three kinds of

NPM reforms and gives examples of their uptake and impact in various national settings.

Management

Professional management and the management of professions are central to the debate on NPM's impact on public hospitals. While the first initiatives in the UK came in the 1960s and concerned the general management of hospitals, it was the Griffiths Report of 1983 that led to the development of a more consistent programme for turning the NHS into an organization similar to any large private corporation. Hospitals were to be managed by general managers with responsibility for a devolved budget. Few doctors volunteered to take up such management posts, however, and the majority of them came to be filled by old style administrators or managers imported from the private sector (Kirkpatrick et al. 2009). A new class of NHS managers then developed, making it more difficult to integrate doctors in managerial functions. Recognition of this has led to the introduction of a second generation of management reforms seeking to put clinicians back into management; the so-called clinical management reforms (Kirkpatrick et al. 2009).

In other cases, such as in the Scandinavian countries, the general management reforms have been less prone to push doctors and nurses out of management positions. This is partly because the first generation of NPM reforms had developed a dual management structure in which doctors and nurses managed their own professional hierarchies. However, the idea that management must be conceived as a profession in its own right, independent of the traditional notion of a profession, has been widely circulated and institutionalized in national management development programmes (Jespersen and Wrede 2009).

The 1992 healthcare reform in Italy introduced a shift from a politico-representative to a technical-managerial type of healthcare administration (Mattei 2009). Also in France, the 1996 health reform established a stronger position for hospital directors (Freeman and Moran 2000). In Germany in the late 1990s, there were experiments in Hamburg and Berlin that changed the role of the medical director from *primus inter pares* to an assistant of the executive board. The continental and other southern European countries have undertaken management reforms later than the UK, Italy, Denmark and Sweden, and, perhaps due to the continued representation of local politicians and representatives of workers at hospital boards, at least in France and Germany, there have been less demands for clinical management models.

Quasi-Markets: Transparency and Performance Measurement

The introduction of an internal market, or a quasi-market, in UK healthcare was announced and implemented by the Thatcher government in the early 1990s.

Henceforth, intermediaries, such as General Practitioner fund-holders or the Health Authority, were to purchase care on behalf of patients. Similar purchaser–provider models were introduced in New Zealand and in many counties in Sweden.

Changes in payment systems have also been a key part of NPM reforms. From the perspective of the reformers, it was seen as problematic that certain treatments for patients were being carried out at the expense of other patients who may have had a more urgent need for treatment. Previous models had encouraged hospitals in NHS systems to maintain long waiting lists, while in the corporatist systems the costs were running unnecessarily high. The new payment systems that were introduced were Diagnosis Related Payment Groups (DRGs), as in Germany, or systems based on similar ideas, such as the 'payment by result' system in England. These systems reward providers for productivity, since an increase in activity will subsequently increase payment. They also provide the payer and the provider with vital information about activity.

When scholars reviewed the international spread of the DRG system, they found quite an extraordinary expansion in its use on a global basis. In general the experience is that once the DRG instrument is introduced, it tends to take on multiple, although somewhat different purposes, but, in the long run, is likely to be used for similar purposes (Kimberly and Pouvourville 2003, Kimberly et al. 2008).

There has also been a convergence towards emphasizing patients' rights and free choice of hospitals, along with the introduction of new quality development schemes and standardized clinical guidelines. Quality data makes it possible to evaluate changes in effectiveness over time and to compare institutional performance. In order to make it possible for patients to choose between hospitals, it is necessary to demand from hospitals that they provide the public with correct information. A range of national quality criteria has been introduced and user evaluation surveys are produced regularly. Hospitals are evaluated on a regular basis and sometimes ranked. Such rankings and standards have been met with criticism, but authorities have responded by promising to improve them in order to achieve the stated goals (Jespersen 2008).

Organizational Autonomy and the Separation of Roles

The precondition for an effective healthcare sector, reformers argue, is to establish more specialized provider-organizations that have a certain amount of autonomy and flexibility. Reformers have sought to develop new healthcare enterprises that are not part of the public-governmental chain of command, but which nonetheless are open for political intervention. Officially, the policy has been to intervene only in matters of principle, but it has become apparent that it is hard to distinguish between matters of detail and principle (Danielsen et al. 2004, Byrkjeflot and Grønlie 2005).

In most countries, the aim has been to create systems for healthcare governance and planning on a regional level. While regionalization is most commonly seen as a means for devolution, it may historically have been even more important as a means for centralization. Such processes of centralization are highlighted by Daniel Fox (1986) in his theory of 'hierarchical regionalism'. This refers to the attempt, based on scientific criteria, to establish a division of labour and status-hierarchy between hospitals within a given geographical area. The establishment of healthcare regions has nevertheless been a very political process, particularly in systems with a strong tradition for welfare localism, and where centre–periphery relations have been important during processes of nation-building. This is the case in Norway, a country that underwent a major hospital reform in 2002. Citing the problems of keeping within budgets and the recurrent 'blame-games' played between counties and the health ministry, the Norwegian central state took over hospital ownership from the counties. The justification for this reform was very much based on NPM ideas, for instance the need to develop more autonomous hospitals with stronger management and performance criteria. The reform, however, has also strengthened the hands of the state in a more explicit way than many other reforms in Europe have done. In Italy, for instance, there was a similar longstanding struggle between the central state and the regions. Italy underwent a healthcare reform in 1992, which settled in favour of the regions. The Italian health districts were also established as autonomous 'public enterprises', run by general managers rather than by local committees (Freeman 2000: 43, 68). Similar reforms in other countries have 'instigated processes of scaling up from the district or locality as well as down from the centre, aggregating local administrations and interests as well as disaggregating national ones' (Freeman 2000: 80).

More business-like hospital boards were also introduced in many countries. In Norway, reformers argued for a stronger representation of managers with experience from private firms, who supposedly would be able to improve the economic governance of hospitals. Other countries, like Germany and France, have kept representatives for local authorities on supervisory boards. The NHS foundations trusts, introduced in the UK in 2003, represented a break with one of the main characteristics of the British NHS, namely, that up to this point, NHS trusts were directly accountable to the Secretary of State for Health. In the new model, a board of governors has been introduced and the management board is directly accountable to it. The board of governors consists of elected representatives of members of the trust. This new system of devolved accountability to local 'stakeholders' is intended to replace the traditional political accountability (Mattei 2009). One of the most problematic aspects of this new kind of participatory accountability is that the board of governors may become dominated by specific client groups whose interests are concentrated and intense.

Divergence and Convergence in NPM Reforms

There are interesting variations between the respective European countries in terms of the extent to which they have introduced instruments and reform ideas associated with NPM and the ways in which they have introduced them. For example, purchaser–provider models were an important part of the early reforms in the UK and in Sweden, but have been used much less in later reforms carried out in Denmark and Norway. In some cases, for instance in the UK, the aim of purchaser–provider arrangements was to develop competition. In Sweden, on the other hand, such arrangements were used to promote more accountability and transparency in the use of resources (Ham 1997).

Researchers have also observed a great deal of variation in how countries use quality control instruments. This variation shows up even in countries with similar systems such as Denmark and Norway. In Denmark, the autonomy of the medical profession has been sustained in the national programme for quality control, while the quality programmes introduced in Norway challenge the traditional autonomy of the medical profession (Jespersen 2008: 23).

A force for convergence may be found in the trend towards developing an international and transnational means for mutually exchanging ideas. This enables countries and institutions to learn from one another's experiences. On the transnational level, international organizations and intergovernmental agencies are carriers of ideas. In the field of healthcare the World Health Organization (WHO) and the United Nations Children's Fund (UNICEF) has been central, but increasingly organizations that are less specifically focused on healthcare, like the OECD and the World Bank, have also been spreading the healthcare reform message. Accordingly, there has been a change from dealing with social and political aspects of healthcare towards focusing on technical and managerial issues (Mattei 2009, Schiller et al. 2009). During the 1990s, the World Bank began devising reform schemes for developing countries. These schemes, however, have been heavily criticized (Okuonzi 2004, Homodesa and Ugalde 2005). The inspiration for NPM and consequent convergence also comes from think tanks and lobbyists with similar purposes across national borders, and from the evidence-based-medicine movement that has led to the institutionalization of a whole range of organizations seeking to influence decision-making in healthcare (Hansen and Rieper 2009).

The aims of the reforms are to limit costs by introducing various means for 'managed care'. However, there are variations between countries as far as what kind of NPM reforms they emphasize. Reforms play out differently depending on the nature of the particular healthcare system into which they are introduced. The reforms may be seen not only as a consequence of a change of politics in a neo-liberal direction, but also as an attempt to defend the public health sector against privatization. But it is worth noting that governments with different political compositions have actually sought to reform healthcare in much the same ways. During the NPM era, they all have tended to see professional dominance as a problem, arguing that it is necessary to constrain the influence of the professions. The phrase 'iron triangle' was used to indicate that the medical profession dominated education and research, central administration and service provision. This professional power constellation was regarded as one important driver for expansion in welfare state expenditures. Consequently, new organization designs and steering tools were introduced to reduce the impact of the 'professional complex' on service provision. It is to the story of the rise, and claimed fall, of this complex that we now turn.

The Profession-State

The profession-state perspective originally emerged as a criticism of what was presented as the established theory of professions (Parsons 1964, Freidson 1970). According to this established theory, the state and the professions were understood as antithetical phenomena, with states being a threat to professional autonomy. The critiques of this theory argued that the professions are part of any state formation; moreover, it is the relationship between the state and the professions that ought to be the key issue in the study of professions (Johnson 1972, Burrage and Thorstendahl 1990). Medical doctors, they went on to point out, had been somewhat unique in achieving a 'regulative bargain' with the state. One consequence of this kind of bargain was that the medical profession became 'self-regulating', or even an integrated part of the state, particularly in the continental countries of Europe. The premise of the profession-state perspective is that any study of the rise of health systems must focus on the relationship between doctors and the state, and that it is possible to construct a rather unique story in the case of each nation-state (Johnson et al. 1995, Dent 2003).

In the history of the rise of the Scandinavian hospital-centred systems, for instance, emphasis is placed on the simultaneous rise of the health bureaucracy and the medical profession; they are seen as twin partners at the centre of the national health system (Erichsen 1995). This story about the rise and fall of medical self-governance has been a popular narrative (Berg 1997). The 'rise' here refers to the growing autonomy of medicine and to medical management as an 'extension of the medical clinic into the state' until the 1970s (Berg 1997). Since then, their position has been threatened by NPM. A movement has emerged which aims to establish effectiveness and quality in medical services. This movement 'offers medicine the hope that its work can be placed more squarely on the altar of scientific rationality, but at the risk of incursions by outside experts into its domain' (Hafferty and Light 1995). The focus, then, in this story of the profession-state, is on how the professions cope with challenges from NPM, and how reforms lead to changes in the state-professional networks and the way professions are regulated. This story may be a narrative about how the roles of professions in society have been transformed as they face challenges from NPM.

Profession-States and Challenges from NPM

What are the major challenges NPM poses to the profession-state? First, there is the challenge posed by unitary management structures. This triggered some dramatic episodes in the UK in wake of the 1983 Griffith Report, but also in Norway in 2003, when doctors resisted the idea that any professional other than a doctor could be appointed as a clinical manager in a hospital. In Norway there was a round of negotiations on the issue between the Norwegian Medical Association and the Health Ministry. The president of the medical association claimed that the outcome was a victory for his organization's point of view (Byrkjeflot 2005). The Health

Ministry, he claimed, had gone as far as it could in demanding that the hospital enterprises must only put qualified doctors in management positions. But was it indeed the case that the medical profession at the centre of the health system again strengthened its position? It has been argued that this was what happened after the structural reform in Denmark. The current fear among Danish nurses certainly is that the idea of unitary management will entail that they lose some influence as a result of the implementation of ever larger regions and hospitals (Jespersen 2005).

Secondly, instruments for quality control, evidence-based medicine and a system for free choice of hospitals clearly represent challenges for the medical profession. The doctors seek to preserve, on one hand, the high level of trust the state has granted them, and on the other hand, trust from the public and the mass media. They also need to develop strategies for maintaining their predominant position within the respective health systems, and to avoid weakening their position as a result of differentiating their profession into too many roles. The new healthcare regimes in Europe seek to develop a more specialized, diversified and evidence-based structure for healthcare provision, and they may depend on the medical profession to develop and provide them with the quality criteria and arguments needed for making legitimate decisions.

Thirdly, in the profession-state narrative, it is not reform ideas and their circulation that are central, but the way different actors make use of them in attempts to establish autonomy. In the case of regionalization and enterprise reform, there may indeed be ways in which doctors can make use of ideas that benefit their projects for professional autonomy. According to historical comparisons of the medical doctor profession in the Nordic countries, the Danes were shown to have a more local orientation and to rely less on the state in their strategies for professionalization than their Norwegian counterparts (Riska 1993). Yet the Norwegians' orientation towards the nation-state may have proved advantageous in the transfer of hospital ownership from the counties to the state. It has also given the Norwegian doctors a strong position in their relationship with the new and relatively inexperienced administrations and boards in the regional and local health enterprises, a factor which has also rewarded them with a solid pay increase.

The Danish doctors, meanwhile, arguably less integrated in the state than Norwegian doctors, may have exercised stronger influence on the way medical services are organized. We have already noted the cases of the stronger role of Danish doctors in hospital management and quality programmes. Finn Borum, for instance, studied how the Danish doctors, in the early 2000s, were able to set the premises for a new regional organizational framework for Danish healthcare: the so-called function-bearing units. These geographical units were developed purely on the basis of recommendations from medical doctors. The medical means-end frameworks became the basis for geographical organization in much the same way as Fox found in the UK and the USA (Fox 1986, Borum 2004).

The following looks at a perspective that puts a stronger emphasis on other actors within the field of healthcare politics. This perspective differs from the two just discussed, both in its view of the way in which the healthcare system is embedded in society and in how NPM reforms affect healthcare governance.

The Healthcare State

As in the profession-state perspective, the state is also central in the healthcare state perspective. The difference now is that the medical profession is seen as less central, and just one of several stakeholders. Since hospitals are embedded in the political, economic and physical infrastructure, they should not be analysed as merely part of a medical system or an administrative system, but also as technological infrastructures and democratic systems (Moran 1999: 74).

Freeman has distinguished two phases in the rise of the healthcare state: the first phase (1880–1980) consisted of establishing and universalizing a public presence in healthcare. The second phase, beginning around 1975, has been concerned with establishing new mechanisms of governmental control (Freeman 2000: 31). The transition from phase one to two may be associated with the rising cost of the health system, a situation that makes it necessary for the state to intervene in order to narrow the 'health gap' between the ever-increasing demand for health services and the state's ability to develop sufficient capacity and cost control in the public health sector.

In comparison with the NPM story, this plot works almost in the opposite way; the 'healthcare state' story is one of state advancement rather than state withdrawal. NPM predicts that the state will need to privatize a great deal of its current activities, whereas the 'healthcare state' presents a narrative of a movement from 'private government' towards an advancing state:

> For cost containment, management, competition, quality controls are all predicated on public (state) intervention in what once was thought of as a realm of private government. If formerly the role of the health care state was simply to finance and administer health services provided by medical professions, these changes imply that, far from being in retreat, the state has made significant advance. (Freeman 2000: 75)

A strikingly similar view of the dynamics of change was presented on the official webpage of the Norwegian Directorate of Health:

> An increasing degree of standardisation of medical processes and the electronic registration and reporting of all medical activities have 'changed the clinic from a private chamber to an open stage'. It gives the term 'medical monitoring' a completely new meaning. From close political control through political presence in the county municipal model, this development has given central government genuine opportunities to gain insight into most aspects of the production of medical services. Thus, it is possible for an essentially peripheral central government owner to exercise shrewd overall control. (Hellandsvik 2001)

What are the dynamics behind the expansion and development of this 'shrewd' state? We need to understand the dynamic of politicization, for it is this dynamic that may lead to the expansion of the healthcare state. As shown in several studies and in the recent US reform, politicians who seek re-nomination and re-election rely heavily on events related to healthcare. In a comparison of political agenda-setting in the USA and Denmark – countries whose healthcare systems are organized in radically different ways – Green-Pedersen and Wilkerson (2006) found that the level of attention paid to health politics had increased substantially in both countries, but that the level of attention was about the same across systems at the same points in time. They explain this by arguing that health politics affect everyone, they are about life and death, and are therefore particularly attractive to politicians who are trying to drum up voters.

Studies of election campaigns and party programmes show that healthcare has become a much more contested issue among political parties since the 1980s. A report on the daily press coverage of welfare issues concludes that healthcare is now the predominant topic; 'The welfare state is increasingly positioned as a healthcare state' (Bay and Saglie 2003). This increased attention paid to healthcare and its regulation may be related to the new role health plays as a kind of 'modern religion', shaping individual lifestyles and giving inspiration to a new kind of health consumerism, which governments may take advantage of in their efforts to constrain the power of professions. A great deal of modern politics concerns issues related to healthcare and how to provide citizens and consumers with information on the costs, quality and criteria for making decisions about healthcare services. In addition, the political debate has focused on how healthcare services are regionally distributed. Hence there has been a development away from the implicit rationing associated with decision-making based on medical autonomy, towards explicit rationing associated with a policy for implementing clinical guidelines and policy-making rooted in evidence-based medicine (Harrison and Waqar 2000).

In most countries, the new system is rather more hierarchical than the previous one, and this means that local problems may easily end up as problems needing to be dealt with at the central level.

The Healthcare State and Challenges to and from NPM

The healthcare state perspective focuses less on the relationship between professions and management, and less on administrative techniques associated with quasi-markets than do the NPM-perspective and the profession-state perspective. Moreover, regardless of the administrative system in place, whether it was established before NPM or as part of NPM reforms, only seldom will the system be entirely abandoned or radically changed. This gives rise to several standards being maintained simultaneously. Hence, when viewed over time, the division between management and professionalism seems to be stable. From a healthcare state perspective, there are multiple path dependencies and accountabilities aligned with such systems that add to their complex character. This makes it less likely that NPM reforms will necessarily lead to convergence.

In a framework that takes an interest in the role of the state in healthcare over a long time and across various contexts, it cannot be taken as a given that processes of regionalization are indications of either centralization or decentralization; clearly, regionalization can be a symptom of both kinds of processes (Lægreid et al. 2005). For instance, Byrkjeflot and Neby (2008) have contrasted the Norwegian and the Danish experience of decentralization in healthcare over a period of 100 years and find interesting contrasts within the two healthcare systems that have often been treated as compatible. Although Denmark and Norway experienced much the same transfer of responsibility from local authorities and municipalities, relationships in Denmark between local interests and counties have been easier and less bitter because of small distances and easy communication. Denmark therefore experienced more gradual shifts from localism to county- and regional organization. Due to the much higher level of self-financing of hospitals in Danish counties than in the Norwegian counties, there was, in the 1970s and '80s, also a much higher degree of correspondence in Denmark, between the economic, administrative and political aspects of decentralization. Thus, when comparing the Norwegian and Danish hospital systems, we see that the Norwegian counties have had a relatively weaker position than the Danish counties, which may partly account for the breakdown of regional accountability and the very rapid move towards centralization in Norway during the early 2000s. The transfer of hospital ownership in Denmark was not from the counties to the central state, as in Norway, but from counties to regions that were still to be held accountable to voters in regional elections. Correspondingly, we may conclude, the impetus towards political centralization had been less strong in Denmark than in Norway (Byrkjeflot and Neby 2008).

Several researchers challenge the account of history given by NPM reformers in their arguments for reform (Mohan 2002, Paton 2006, Harrison and McDonald 2008). In particular, the NPM reformers' claim that there has been a movement away from a system of command and control towards decentralization and autonomy is a bone of contention. This claim has been questioned in many scholarly studies of the UK's NHS, supposedly one of the most centralized systems in the world. There have been many criticisms of the NPM version of history on this point. To begin with, the UK system was actually quite decentralized when it was re-formed in 1948 with the establishment of the NHS. The fragmented and conflict-ridden structure did not disappear overnight. Elements of localism, markets, and partnerships with local communities 'never really went away', at least not until the New Labour government (Mohan 2003). The truth, Calum Paton argues, is that 'from 1948 to 1991, the NHS was the antithesis of "command and control"' (Paton 2006: 131). An investigation of the history of the more decentralized Norwegian healthcare system also raises doubts about how strongly the state was involved in hospital governance during the heyday of the profession-state, as compared to the contemporary situation (Byrkjeflot 2005).

When comparing this way of sketching the flow of events with the profession-state perspective, it may be argued that the professions play different roles during two particular phases. The profession-state perspective may be most useful during the phase when there is an increasing public presence in healthcare, but in the current phase of political-professional reconfiguration, it may be necessary to allow several other actors on stage in order to study the reform dynamics. Iron triangles may then need to give way to looser issue-based networks (Heclo 1978). All sorts of experts and knowledge institutions now serve as facilitators for change. They speak on behalf of the generalized patient-consumer and rely on techno-scientific systems like the DRGs and various devices and schemes for quality control, evidence production and accreditation in order to acquire status and authority.

Conclusion

Viewed at a European level, NPM reforms represent many things to many people, and they also have variable impacts on healthcare systems. Differences in traditions for governance among countries may even become more apparent as the issue of controlling healthcare costs becomes even more urgent. There has been a convergence among European healthcare states in the direction of managed competition, and this is important because many of the ideas and instruments used in modern healthcare systems are associated with such a model of governance. Insofar as such models are maintained and developed by transnational organizations and policy communities, they may work in the direction of a further integration of European healthcare systems.

Other forces for integration are the new EU regulations, the increasing international trade in health services and the associated trend towards 'health tourism'. Although health policy is formally under the jurisdiction of individual member countries, the impact of the EU, particularly on NHS systems, is profound and far reaching (Martinsen and Vrangbæk 2008). Several court rulings have opened the possibility for including healthcare services as 'free goods' within the EU. In Europe, healthcare under government control is generally not regarded as a service and thus not subject to competition law. Even so, the recent rulings in favour of citizens being reimbursed for healthcare provided in another country may signal a change. But whether or not they do signal change, a huge number of the problems hospitals deal with are acute and therefore local in nature.

Cross-national health organizations have so far not played a major role in regulating healthcare systems. On the other hand, medical systems have been interlinked and influenced by international networks for professional development and research.

The argument all these factors engender is therefore not that NPM reforms are most likely to lead to further divergence, but rather that it is difficult to predict what the impact of the various kinds of NPM reforms will be in the longer run. This is because the reforms are used differently; they have provoked resistance and given way to post-NPM ideas for how to reform healthcare systems. The broader and more long-term consequences of NPM are difficult to foresee, especially if researchers concentrate mainly on detailed studies of how different systems take up NPM ideas, or on the ebb and flow of particular reform movements. It is therefore important to do studies of path dependencies and evolutionary patterns in healthcare systems. The healthcare state and profession-state perspectives offer alternative views to those provided by the literature on specific NPM reforms. They also diverge from the neo-institutional literature on the spread of reform ideas. The two perspectives are additionally useful for focusing more explicitly on how state authorities and the medical profession make use of reforms and how the reforms therefore affect healthcare systems and societies differently.

Professions are still important in setting the direction and pace for organizational change. Medical doctors and other healthcare professionals are present at all levels of healthcare governance, and it will be useful to explore further under what circumstances the medical and other healthcare professions serve as a force for convergence, rather than as a force for divergence in the development of healthcare systems.

Finally, a main concern arising from NPM is the problem of accountability. This partly relates to the problem of the fragmentation of power and control arising from NPM, but also to the strong belief in managerial accountability, in many cases at the expense of political and professional accountability. Consequently, political leaders often find themselves in situations where they have the responsibility without the corresponding power and control. This scenario goes hand in hand with the long-term development away from welfare localism, whereby healthcare providers are held accountable to local authorities, and towards central state control and regionalization. In the UK there is much talk about a 'new localism', where the premise is that the local population can become members of quasi-public institutions, like the foundation trusts in healthcare, and exercise their influence by voting in elections for boards of governance (Allen 2006). Such arrangements have not been much of a success thus far and may lead to further discussions about accountability problems in the healthcare sector. The challenges NPM poses to political and professional accountability in healthcare have been formidable and may be seen as one of the major reasons for the current talk about a post-NPM era, also in healthcare.

NPM, Network Governance and the University as a Changing Professional Organization

Ivar Bleiklie, Jürgen Enders, Benedetto Lepori

and Christine Musselin

Introduction

For most authors, the numerous higher education reforms that have been implemented during the last decades in most EU countries (Eurydice 2000 and 2008), are the consequence of the dissemination of New Public Management (NPM) rhetoric and narratives. These reform processes were accelerated by the central role knowledge and innovation were expected to play for economic development in contemporary societies. As a result higher education and research systems progressively reached the top of the governmental agendas at the national, regional and European levels in the mid 1990s. In a time of budgetary restrictions, solutions aiming at increasing the productivity, efficiency and relevance of academic activities have been launched, and progressively implemented in European higher education institutions.

Ferlie et al. (2008) identified five main NPM reforms that have been commonly implemented in Europe. First, market-based reforms have flourished. This first of all concerns reforms aimed at increasing the level of competition among institutions, staff, students and territories. In many cases, increasing competition comes with economic valuation and exchanges of goods and services that previously were not considered to be of economic value, thus leading to the constitution of markets or quasi-markets (Musselin 2010). Second, budgetary constraints have been tightened through reduced funding or by the introduction of new budgetary instruments based on indicators and output rather than on inputs. Third, budgetary reforms often implied heavier emphasis on performance and explicit performance measurement, assessment and monitoring in research and teaching. Fourth, there is a concentration of funds in the best performing higher education institutions and a broader vertical differentiation among higher education institutions. Finally, institutional governance has become a crucial issue. University leaders are expected to play managerial roles. Executive leadership has been strengthened at the expense of collegial power in deliberative, representative bodies, while the academic community has been transformed into staff and submitted to human resource management.

Nevertheless, if one sticks to a delimited definition of NPM, one will observe that other conceptions influenced higher education reforms over the same period of time (Ferlie et al. 2008). In particular the vertical form of steering inspired by NPM has been challenged or complemented by reforms aiming at developing forms of network governance. First, some policies encouraged the inclusion of stakeholders in academic affairs and thus widened the networks of actors involved in decision-making as well as the introduction of non-academic criteria, principles and preferences in such processes. Second, centralized ways of steering have been challenged by the participation of inter- and supra-national actors in higher education. As a result, most teaching or research projects mobilize a combination of resources from different sources and rely on multiple levels and actors. This has been conceptualized as multi-level governance. As shown in the book edited by Paradeise et al. (2009), in order to understand recent higher education and research reforms in one country, one has to look at the relative influence of NPM and network governance, their interplay and sometimes conflicting influence.

This chapter compares four countries coming from different traditions, of different size, built on national or federal political systems and more or less infused by NPM. It concentrates on how NPM and network governance reforms aim at affecting the academic profession, and on their effects on academic activities, the management of faculty members, and academic power. The first part presents the main reforms in the four countries in a comparative perspective. Their impact on academics is considered in the second part.

Reforms Aiming at Transforming Academic Work and the Academic Profession

This section starts by presenting the four cases in a sequence beginning with the country usually considered an NPM forerunner, the Netherlands, followed by France, Norway and finally Switzerland, the NPM laggard. It ends with a comparison of the four countries' reform histories.

Netherlands

The Dutch experience of higher education reform can be identified as a mixture of elements of NPM and network governance. The two are not seen as alternatives, but rather as complementary models or narratives. Reform was increasingly inspired by an NPM narrative, while the 'Dutch polder model' of network governance had a role to play, though partly with different parties at the table. At the same time, 'Rechtsstaat' principles have been maintained, coupled more closely with stakeholder guidance. Thus the path dependency of the 'Rechtsstaat' and neo-corporatist traditions in the Netherlands deflected and constricted a change toward hard NPM (Westerheijden et al. 2009). Since the 1970s, major waves of higher education reform were, however, partly inspired by NPM and most of them had direct or indirect effects on academic work and the academic profession. Three broad policy areas will be emphasized: funding and market oriented reforms, government steering and institutional governance.

Retrenchment, reallocation and reorganization

Until the end of the 1970s coordination of Dutch higher education and research was a mixture of state- and academic self-regulation, a closed system, in which outsiders or society at large, hardly had a voice. From the mid 1970s, belief in strong and detailed top-down regulation weakened, leading to disappointment with 'central steering'. Moreover, problems could no longer be concealed behind a veil of growing budgets. Dutch higher education and research were faced with increasing demands to contribute to the recovery and restructuring of the economy. In the early 1980s the government promulgated a range of unilateral reforms. 'Remedial' or 'corrective' policies, as they euphemistically were called, included cutbacks and dominated the higher education and research scenes. They included 'conditional research funding' to enhance the size, efficiency and quality of research. This can be regarded as the first large-scale market-inspired reform as institutions had to compete for research grants. Further corrective policies were the introduction of a two-tier university degree structure (1981), reallocation of programmes and departments (1981), college mergers (1983), personnel structure reform (1981) and a second reallocation and retrenchment operation (1986). The mid 1980s brought fundamental changes promised in the preceding years, and they had lasting effects on the coordination of the university sector.

Steering from a distance

In 1985 the government introduced the concept of 'steering from a distance', in which firm beliefs in the virtues of detailed regulation, planning and government coordination was replaced by the idea that government's role ought to be confined to setting boundary conditions while leaving higher education institutions room to manoeuvre as they see fit. This may be seen as a shift from a 'regulatory' to a 'facilitatory' state (Neave and Van Vught 1991) inspired by a network governance philosophy, but also as a move towards an 'evaluative state' (Neave 1998) inspired by NPM. The new policies consisted of a mixture of:

- reduced direct control of administration and use of financial resources;
- development of semi-structured interventionist policies, where a relatively tight frame exists, within which institutions enjoy freedom to make decisions;

- establishment of a system of positive and negative sanctions based on criteria and procedures whereby goals are partly defined by the government, partly left to academics, institutional policies, or to the market; and
- detailed input control was replaced by checking afterwards whether self-regulation of higher education institutions led to satisfactory outputs. If they lived up to expectations, institutions were given more autonomy.

The new governmental steering philosophy thus opened the door to more pronounced competition. Universities were expected to display more competitive and managerial behaviour including the introduction of full cost thinking in all university affairs. They should establish distinct profiles. Mission statements and strategic planning became common, universities were stimulated to create their own niches, and were 'invited' to intensify their efforts to increase private funding. In sum, the rules of the game, which used to be determined by government and academics, were increasingly affected by a completely different regime, that is, competition and performance and the logic of looking at the bottom line of results.

Control at home

One of the most profound effects of the governance shift has been the increased importance of the university as an organization in system coordination (de Boer et al. 2007) and of hierarchical leadership and management within the universities. Already in the 1980s, the Minister stated that institutional management had to be strengthened if universities were to succeed in a competitive world. Moreover, the introduction of institutional strategic plans justified more active central management. The formal authority distribution within the university, however, did not change substantially. The real tilting of the power balance within universities would not happen until 1997.

The Act 'Modernising University Governance' (MUB) introduced the new governing system that concentrated executive and legislative powers. All members of crucial governing bodies – the supervisory body, the central executive board, and the dean – are appointed by the body at the superior level. Appointments replaced elected representatives; the previously powerful departments were abolished. The 1997 Act was characterized by integration, coherence, hierarchy and centralization of powers. This was at odds with traditional academic self-governance, and a further turn towards NPM. The MUB also means enhanced institutional autonomy, since universities have more discretion to design their own structure, within the limits of the government legal framework.

Since the 1980s, certain financial and staffing matters have been devolved to the universities, 'creating' opportunities for university central management to increase their influence in strategic decision-making and budget allocations. In addition, internal monitoring has increasingly been used as a steering device for university managers. Overall, actors and mechanisms of supervision and management are getting closer and closer to the shop floor level of academic work in order to increase the quality and efficiency of the primary processes in universities.

France

In most comparative analyses of NPM, France is considered a latecomer and a rather reluctant disciple of NPM reforms. As shown by Bezes (2009), the influence of NPM as a coherent doctrine associated with specific tools and solutions started to develop after 1995 and did not spread across the French public system before the 2000s.

If one looks at the specific sector of higher education and reforms, four main reforms reflecting the diffusion of NPM can be identified in the 2000s. All of them are of interest to this comparison as they aim (explicitly or not) at transforming the organization and regulation of the academic community, the management of academic careers, the way research is led and funded, and the organizational settings in which academic activities develop. They thus impacted academic life directly. These reforms and what they intend to change will be described first, before other transformations related to other influences that took place at about the same time are addressed.

LOLF (2002 Act) – increasing budget and performance constraints

The LOLF (Loi Organique relative aux Lois de Finance) does not specifically apply to higher education, but to French public administration as a whole. It aims at transforming public budget procedures, and translates public policies into programmes for which annual objectives must be set. The following year programmes have to report and explain what has been achieved with the budget received. Universities were initially exempted from the provisions of LOLF, but in 2008, the Ministry (MESR) developed a new software and algorithm (Sympa) for the allocation of university budgets that partly introduced performance-based allocations. Another step in the same direction was the introduction of global budgets in 2007, requiring universities to formulate targets and report on performance one year later. Since performance budgeting is just starting, it still does not weigh directly on the individual academic, but this will soon change as the new budgeting mode progressively diffuses within higher education institutions.

AERES (2006 Act) – more evaluation and publicity about performance

A second important transformation consists in the creation of AERES (Agence d'Evaluation de la Recherche et de l'Enseignement Supérieur). This new agency concentrates all evaluation processes that previously were dispersed among different actors: the independent agency for institutional evaluation, the CNE; the Ministry and national research institutions. More importantly, AERES transformed the nature of evaluation by making it publicly available and simpler to read. It also transformed the use of evaluation by providing the Ministry with information for decision making and strategy development. The link between evaluation and university budgets could then develop and may be used by the Ministry to determine the size of university budgets, and by universities for internal budget allocation.

Thus more transparency and publicity are trained on the activities of the academic profession.

More competition and concentration: the ANR, the Grand Emprunt and others …
The emphasis on performance comes with increased competition for funds. A first major step was the creation of the national research council ANR (Agence Nationale de la Recherche) in 2007. The novelty of the ANR lies in increased formalization of application procedures and project execution. Although still far from the bureaucratic form of EU research projects, applications have to follow a rather formalized structure. Furthermore, the ANR transforms French research by the amount of money it manages, and the increasing competition for funding. This reinforces concentration of resources to a limited set of units. The trend towards competition and concentration also characterize recent calls launched by the MESR and one being prepared by the Prime Minister's office. Through this highly selective call, up to ten university campuses shall be labelled 'excellent' and receive a significant amount of money. Institutional differentiation is therefore expected to increase, but also the difference between the academics employed by institutions of 'excellence' and the rest.

The LRU Act (2007) strengthening governance of higher education institutions
A last important transformation concerns the empowerment of universities as institutional actors. The main objective of the LRU Act is to strengthen executive university leadership. Presidents are provided with more internal power and more autonomy. They now manage a global budget, including operating and payroll budgets, of which the latter was previously managed by the Ministry.

Many decisions previously made by the Ministry are now transferred to the university level. The allocation and size of bonuses for academic excellence are now devolved to each university. Research funds previously allocated directly to research units are now given as a global amount to the university which allocates funds to the labs. In a near future, the CNU (Conseil national des universités) will evaluate individual academics every four years, enabling presidents to negotiate a redefinition of duties with individual academics. Thus the university level is gaining importance in many decisions directly affecting academic life.

Other reforms
Without contesting the recent impact of NPM on French higher education, it is necessary to mention some limitations to this global trend.

First, some aspects of NPM have clearly been avoided in higher education as in other sectors. The proposal to create a higher education budget allocation agency was rejected in June 2008 by an inter-ministerial committee. In this and other cases, it seems that the Ministry was strongly against establishing intermediate agencies and was afraid to lose power if they were created.

Second, the dispersion of the higher education system into many institutions has been seen as a weakness rather than a strength, and the 2006 Act provided the opportunity to create meta-structures, comprising different institutions, which in some cases led to mergers.

Third, recent NPM-based reforms did not question what is called the 'territorialization' of higher education and research policies, that is, the increasing role of local actors in this sector. Although the reforms described above aim at a re-verticalization of the system as a whole, forms of multi-level governance are at the same time sustained and encouraged.

Norway

Internationally Norway has often been presented as a reluctant reformer whether we speak of public policy in general (Olsen 1996, Christensen and Lægreid 2007a) or higher education reform in particular (Kogan et al. 2006). Reformers have been careful not to infringe on academic territory and inflict unwanted changes. Reforms have tended to be piecemeal, granting individual institutions considerable freedom to interpret and implement reforms as they see fit (Bleiklie et al. 2000, Bleiklie 2009), and characterized by insignificant moves towards competition (Hood et al. 2004). Some rather mild efforts were made during the 1990s to introduce management by objectives, and strengthen institutional autonomy and leadership (Bleiklie et al. 2000). However, the introduction of the Quality reform in 2003 heralded more drastic changes combined with a stronger determination to implement them forcefully (Bleiklie 2009).

The Quality reform – complex reform, mixed record

Most changes in Norwegian higher education in the last decade have been introduced in connection with the Quality reform. The main justification for the reform was that students were neglected, that they had a right to succeed and that higher education institutions had an obligation to ascertain that this right was fulfilled. The government proposal that introduced the reform in 2001, made these concerns part of a more general political agenda. Norway was to become 'a leading nation of knowledge', and higher education was to be generously funded and fundamentally transformed through radical changes of teaching programmes, funding and steering patterns, organizational structure, institutional autonomy and institutional strategies. The following will look at different elements of the reform with a particular view to the way in which they relate to New Public Management and network governance.

Study programme reform

The study reform introduced the Bologna two-cycle degree system and course-credit-based study programmes throughout the higher education system in 2003. The main goal was to make degree studies more efficient by shortening time to degree and increasing compliance with programme schedules and completion rates.

Several tools were supposed to help achieve these aims, such as contracts between student and institution, more coherent study programmes, better use of the entire, enlarged academic year, more varied and better adapted teaching methods and more teacher–student contact. While this reform as such has little to do with NPM, its goals of efficiency and student mobility are easily associated with NPM.

New funding system

The reform was sustained by a new funding system that was clearly consistent with NPM policies. The funding system had a considerable incentive-based and output-oriented component (about 40 per cent), two thirds of which was based on teaching load and efficiency, and one third on research related activity. In the following years the incentive-based component increased, underscoring the importance of this NPM tool to the overall goal of the Quality reform.

New system for accreditation and quality assurance

A third element, clearly consistent with the NPM idea of 'steering from a distance', was the establishment in 2003 of a new system of accreditation and quality assurance. The reform requires all higher education institutions to have an internal quality assurance system. A national agency, NOKUT, was established simultaneously with two main tasks: to evaluate institutional systems of quality assurance and the accreditation of institutions and study programmes in cases where ministerial approval is required. Furthermore, criteria were established that any institution aspiring to obtain university status must fulfil. Thus institutions were enabled to devise relatively predictable strategies in order to achieve university status. The establishment of NOKUT represented a new buffer between ministerial oversight and the institutions, in principle enhancing the autonomy of the latter.

New system for leadership and institutional steering

As part of the Quality reform a new system of institutional governance was proposed whereby higher education institutions would change status from 'special civil service institutions' to 'public enterprises'. The traditional system of elected leaders at all levels of higher education institutions would be replaced by a system of appointed leaders, and representative deliberative bodies would have their role transformed from decision making to advisory functions. The goal was to create more autonomous institutions with stronger strategic capabilities. At the institutional level the rector would be subordinated rather than heading the university board much like a CEO in a business enterprise. Half the board would be external representatives appointed by the Ministry after proposals from the university and the other half elected internal representatives.

The question of the formal status of institutions and their internal organization turned out to be the most contested aspect of the Quality reform and the reform proposal was rejected by a majority of Norwegian professors (Bleiklie 2009). The parliament finally introduced the new legislation in 2005. Institutions were to keep their status as special civil service institutions. It was left to the institutions to decide whether and to what extent they would keep their traditional internal organization or introduce the new system. The only mandatory change was the size of external representation on institutional boards. Most institutions chose mixed solutions. A clear majority kept elected rectors at the institutional level and introduced appointed leadership at faculty and department levels. However, all theoretically possible combinations of elected and appointed leaders are represented among Norwegian higher education institutions. The ambition to standardize the internal organization of higher education institutions resulted in the opposite: more diverse internal organizational patterns, mainly due to opposition from academics.

Switzerland

In the context of higher education reform, the Swiss case stands out as specific, raising questions about widely held beliefs about the impact of new policy rationales, like NPM. Rather wide-ranging reforms have taken place since the late 1990s, but they led mostly to a weakening of state steering and stronger delegation of authority to the institutions, as well as to a renewal of academic values and practices rather than their replacement by more managerial approaches (Lepori and Fumasoli 2010). Switzerland stands out in our context as a very successful case of implementation of network governance.

Despite some attempts at integration, authority over higher education institutions is still divided between the Confederation and the cantons, with corresponding variation as to how state–institution relationships are managed. French-speaking cantons still partly hold on to traditional bureaucratic control, while the Confederation and many of the German-speaking cantons devolved more autonomy to institutions (Fumasoli 2008). Moreover, with the creation of the Universities of Applied Sciences (UAS) in the late 1990s, the Swiss system became binary with a strong divide between the university and non-university sectors in terms of missions, activities, governance setting and management culture. The UAS sector displays more bureaucratic and hierarchical steering than the university sector (Lepori 2008).

In the context of public management it is useful to keep in mind that Swiss higher education is composed of three types of institutions:

1. two university level Federal Institutes of Technology (FIT);
2. ten cantonal universities under direct authority of their home cantons (Fumasoli 2008); and
3. seven public and two private UASs with a mandate of professional, mostly bachelor-level education and applied research (Lepori 2008).

The following presents NPM reforms in Switzerland from 1995 to 2010, since some of the most important reforms took place in the late 1990s.

Funding policies and modest market-based reforms

In the last two decades some incentives for institutional competition have been introduced especially through funding reforms. Since 2000 federal subsidies to cantonal universities are calculated on a formula based on student numbers and third-party grants, while they receive flat federal subsidies for out-of-canton students. These incentives and the introduction of the Bologna system pushed the smallest cantonal universities and to some extent UASs, to a more active student acquisition. Three other factors limit the scope of market-based competition: the generous funding level, the negligible role of private providers, and the fact that existing institutions do not risk being closed down.

The current Swiss situation has two relevant characteristics. First, there is a soft state pressure for some competition, moderated by a high share of non-competitive institutional funding and an emphasis on cooperation among institutions. Second, there is a strong component of cooperative behaviour among institutions, which tend to agree on some division of tasks and specific focus of their activities without direct state intervention.

The political discourse on higher education has been dominated by the need for maintaining or increasing the quality rather than the efficiency of the system. This was the basis for a rapid increase of funding to institutions from 2000. The overall political preference was to provide additional money in exchange for self-managed internal reforms. In the most recent federal university plan (2008–2011) the combination of increasing resources and soft pressures still applies. However, one specific performance-related mechanism was introduced in the University Act, whereby 30 per cent of federal subsidies to cantonal universities are distributed on the basis of third-party funds.

Soft emphasis on performance: development of audit and quality assurance systems

Quality assessment has essentially taken place inside higher education institutions aiming at improving their operations. Most institutions now have a well-developed system of internal quality assurance mainly based on peer review. At the federal level, a quality assurance agency was created at the end of the 1990s (Perellon 2001). Its main task is auditing internal quality procedures in institutions and accreditation of new ones. Overall, this seems a relatively soft approach to evaluation, essentially in the hands of academics and the institutions themselves. The situation is different in the UAS sector, where both institutional accreditation and accreditation of study programmes are performed systematically and used as a steering tool by the responsible federal authority.

Higher education institutional governance and management

Internal governance has changed, but does not necessarily reduce the role of academics and academic autonomy. While the traditional governance mode combined bureaucratic state control of the administration and wide autonomy of individual chairs in academic matters, the tendency has been to transfer management authority from the state towards rectorates and to some strengthening of their position internally. In most universities management practices have certainly become tighter, including detailed strategic plans, budgeting and facilities management (Fumasoli and Lepori 2010). The trend is also reflected in rapid expansion of central administration in most universities, although the degree of delegation is very different from university to university. Nevertheless, the influence of academics in institutional governance remains substantial, and the main institutional positions – rectors and deans – are still strong symbols of academic identity and filled by university professors. Although positions of presidents and rectors certainly include a stronger management component, such skills are still learnt on the job rather than being initial job qualification requirements. The situation is quite different at the UAS, owing to their more hierarchical organization and stronger bureaucratic culture. Management processes are clearly tighter and organized more top-down. The positions of UAS directors and department directors have mostly a managerial function and are filled by people who tend to come from public administration and private companies.

Changes in employment and human resource management
Overall, human resource management in Swiss institutions is traditionally characterized by a two-tier policy. A rather strong public regulation of permanent positions is combined with a much more liberal policy for non-permanent staff such as post-doctoral and Ph.D. students. The main recent changes have affected the intermediary level after the doctorate, where a number of universities have moved towards a model based on temporary positions and access to the professorial level through assistant professor appointments. To our knowledge, most salaries are still based on fixed scales depending on academic degree, even if universities have somewhat larger space for negotiation than in the past. The situation is partially different in UAS, which were originally subject to much tighter public sector requirements. There has been a strong tendency towards deregulation of employment conditions and private sector practices have been introduced to some extent, especially for hiring a large number of part-time teachers with their own professional activities.

Four Reform Histories Compared

Comparing the role of NPM in higher education governance in countries with public higher education systems serves to illustrate how new reform ideas tend to blend with nationally distinct higher education and civil service traditions. Higher education reformers have often adapted modern NPM ideas in nationally specific ways to historically established practices, balancing values of academic autonomy and quality against those of efficiency and government control. In other cases, for example competitive research funding, NPM brought little new in practical terms and reformers have dealt with familiar problems and solutions under new names provided by the jargon of a new reform ideology. Network governance had an impact in our cases in two ways. First, network governance affected the design and implementation of higher education reforms as we argue in the cases of the Netherlands and Switzerland. Second, network governance may be part of the outcome of change processes justified in terms of NPM policies, illustrating some of the ambiguities and tensions within the NMP doctrine.

In very broad terms all four countries introduced NPM reforms that fall under the five categories presented in the introduction: mechanisms that shall increase competition between institutions and budgetary constraints are represented by budget formulas designed to make institutions compete for students and research funds, formulas that gradually have become tougher as performance-based budget elements increase over time. Budget reforms are also important instruments that train and amplify public attention and scrutiny on performance. Crucial additional instruments in this connection are the development of systems for assessment and monitoring of teaching and research performance. One implication is the establishment of intermediate agencies for evaluation and accreditation and internal units for evaluation and quality assurance in institutions. The various measures taken in order to concentrate resources among the best institutions or research groups and institutional governance have been crucial issues, with mixed results in terms of implementation and outcomes. However, the question remains about what changes the reforms have brought about on the 'shop floor' of academic institutions. This is the question addressed in the last part of the chapter.

Effects on Academic Work and the Academic Profession

Although the timing and specific form of NPM governance reforms varied, we found major structural changes that potentially affect academic work and the academic profession in all four countries. The following will look in particular at how these changes have played out in the following areas: professional self-regulation, academic work, careers, tasks and the configuration of academic power.

Academic Self-Regulation

Traditionally professional self-regulation has been considered a necessary condition for the quality of academic work and for universities to operate properly. If by self-regulation we understand the degree of control academics have over their work conditions, it depends on conditions such as: the position and influence of academics within the organization in which they work, the freedom they enjoy in formulating their research and teaching agendas, reward systems, and influence over operating conditions that affect research and teaching inside and outside their institution.

The organizational changes reported in the four countries clearly demonstrate that conditions have changed, but in a far from uniform way. New governance arrangements have clearly reduced the collective influence of academics over decision making in academic institutions, but apparently more so in the Netherlands than in France, Norway and particularly Switzerland. It is still an open question whether the reforms need more time to penetrate academic organizations properly or whether they are unlikely to amount to more than symbolic structural changes that are easily absorbed by existing informal routines and established practices. However, it is striking that the effect on NPM policies that have been in place since the 1980s seem to have penetrated Dutch universities more thoroughly than in the other three countries where similar changes occurred the last 10–15 years. The loss of power and self-regulating ability should also be considered in connection with the reconfiguration of academic power which is taking place within higher education. This will be discussed further below.

Academic Work

The changes that seem to affect academic work the most have to do with changes in funding, quality assurance and evaluation practices. In all four countries we have seen changes in institutional funding and external research funding where incentive-based, competitive funding make up a substantial part of institutional budgets, particularly for research activities. These new funding and evaluation practices affect academics in all four countries. They are expected to, and do spend more time on funding acquisition, writing research proposals according to specified formulas including work packages, deliverables and deadlines. They also spend more time reporting on their activities as part of internal reporting, quality assurance and budgeting procedures at their own institutions where the activities and productivity of every individual academic now affect the funding available for their own research group, or their own department or unit within it. These reporting procedures are making the contributions of academic units, but also of individual academics publicly available and visible. Since they tend to present the outcome of the activities of universities and the departments within them in easily accessible tabular form, it is possible for administrators, politicians and the public at large to evaluate and compare the quantity and quality of academic work.

One may hypothesize that these pressures make academics more dependent on their institutions as subordinate workers under constant pressure to produce and bring in fresh funding. External funding acquisition may on the other hand have the opposite effect for academics that are members of inter-institutional, international research groups and make them more independent of their own institution. As shown by Barrier (2010) the traditional institution-based hierarchical division of work by which academic mandarins looked for funding and allocated work to their group of assistants, has been replaced by teams of academics who each participate in the race for funding and are all involved in various partnerships allowing development of the research programme of their group. While the relationships among permanent staff become more horizontal, relationships with doctoral and post-doctoral students are transformed and become more hierarchical. Ph.D. candidates are no longer disciples but knowledge workers engaged in the production of specific results that form the basis of their Ph.D. but are also individual elements of the research programme of their supervisor. Similar trends are likely to affect research universities in all the four countries.

Academic Careers

The tension between teaching and research is a characteristic of academic work. The distribution between teaching and research obligations for permanent positions used to be part of the formal definition of the academic position or decided informally as academics within a department agreed on the distribution of a given set of teaching obligations (Bleiklie and Michelsen 2008, Musselin and Becquet 2008). The increased visibility of individual performance will probably make the difference between research active and non-active staff more visible, intensifying traditional tensions within the teaching–research nexus in academic work (Leišytė 2007), and create a pressure to solve this at the institutional level. Furthermore, the increase in external research funding has led to an increase in non-permanent staff. This is likely to increase competition for permanent positions and status differences among academics on different types of employment contracts.

New Tasks and Academic Roles

The idea that core activities, traditionally considered to be teaching and examining students, undertaking and disseminating research in academic publications, is clearly challenged. The ability to raise money and manage research teams based on external grants has become a core criterion in system-wide evaluations as well as in performance monitoring and hiring policies of institutions. Activities around teaching have evolved and represent a larger scope. For example, market research for teaching, advertising schools and programmes, attracting and selecting students, designing e-learning tools and programmes, building partnerships for joint programmes, finding financial support for curriculum development, and student exchange and internships also belong to the diversifying work portfolio of modern academics. Finally, new tasks emerge because of the 'third mission' of universities. Technology and knowledge transfer of all kinds, patenting and licensing, community service and regional development, policy advice and business consultancy are examples of a long list of activities that academics are expected to undertake. This multiplication of tasks and expectations is one driver towards a further division of work within the academic profession (de Weert 2004).

Changing expectations and new structures also imply the rise of new and more varied managerial roles for academics and other staff. Such staff include the academic manager and other professionals now employed to meet university needs in areas such as external and internal funding, information systems, human resource management, marketing and public relations, knowledge transfer and public–private partnerships.

Reconfiguration of Academic Power

At a more aggregated level, the increasing role of research in terms of publications, grants and evaluation increase the role of academic gatekeepers: academics sitting on review and selection committees, reviewing papers, selecting projects, and making authoritative judgements on the quality of institutions or disciplines. The impact of their decisions will increase and they are likely to constitute a new academic elite. The same holds true for the university leaders who progressively constitute a specific professional group within the academic profession, with their own trajectories and rewards, as predicted by Freidson in his analysis of the future of professions (Freidson 1984). The position of the members of this new elite is based not just on full professorship and similar academic top-positions, but on network position gained through participation on academic peer review panels of all sorts, research funding panels, evaluation bodies, hiring committees, editorial boards and so on. Although many of the decision arenas in question consist of academic review panels, others, such as research funding bodies, often draw their members from a wider set of backgrounds, including politicians, civil servants, business representatives and so forth. In such cases the decisions are based on criteria that represent compromises between more diverse sets of considerations and decision premises than purely academic ones. Individual members would usually acquire the positions that make them elite members based on research reputation. Within individual universities such elites may be highly influential, at the same time as rank and file academics find themselves in a politically gradually weaker position.

Conclusion

The four cases analysed in this chapter are usually considered quite different in terms of adoption and implementation of NPM policies. Traditionally the Netherlands has been considered an early starter and relatively forceful implementer in a continental European context (Paradeise et al. 2009). Yet it is shown here that characteristics of traditional Dutch consensus-oriented 'polder' politics, manifesting itself in the modern shape of network governance, nevertheless have limited the impact of NPM. Both France and Norway have been reluctant reformers, slowly adopting and partially implementing NPM elements in higher education governance during the 1990s. However, in the 2000s both countries implemented reforms introducing NPM features that are reshaping higher education governance in more fundamental ways. Network governance and a federal political structure in which cantons play a prominent role in higher education policy making and governance are an important explanation behind the Swiss position as the latecomer to NPM policies in this four country group. Thus the early starter and the latecomer interestingly share network governance characteristics that limit and mitigate the impact of NPM policies, although in different ways. In spite of the path dependencies that seem to characterize the various national NPM reform movements it nevertheless appears that all four countries now have changed their systems' funding, evaluation and institutional management in ways that potentially at least fundamentally alter how academic institutions and their activities operate.

In addition to limiting and modifying the extent of NPM-policies, network governance enters the analysis in another interesting way. Whereas one may safely assume that informal networks have previously played an important role in higher education policy making in earlier days, NPM policies have contributed to formalizing new kinds of policy networks related to external research funding mechanisms, evaluation and accreditation agencies, and institutional governance. This may illustrate one of the ambiguities of NPM policies. Thus the usual assumption that NPM reduces the influence of academics in higher education governance overlooks the fact that this reduced influence within academic institutions may have been paralleled by the opening up of new arenas of academic influence. Thus it may be more correct to say that NPM policies have contributed to a reconfiguration of academic power. Where academic power in the 1970s and 1980s was confined to increasingly egalitarian power structures within academic institutions, it has become more limited within increasingly hierarchical institutions and is increasingly based in more elitist arenas of research funding councils, evaluation panels and institutional boards.

Thus all four nations analysed here are cases where NPM policies never represented the radical and rapid break with the past that we know from the UK in the 1980s, yet it seems that governance patterns nevertheless have changed in fundamental ways that have had significant effects on academic work and the position of the academic profession over the last 30 years.

NPM Ideas and Social Welfare Administration

Richard Norman

Introduction

Social welfare systems are magnets for criticism. In developed countries, social welfare payments and their administration are near-constant targets for reform prescriptions due to their share of the total budget and the politics of redistributing wealth. Social welfare is an 'impossible job of public management' (Hargrove and Glidewell 1990), in the sense that no issue is ever 'solved' but only temporarily 'resolved'. Far more than public spending on health and education, welfare involves redistributing wealth from one group of taxpayers to a different group – beneficiaries who are 'at best out of sight and at worst deeply unpopular' and include 'drug abusers, child molesters, unemployed welfare recipients, teenage mothers, destitute residents of urban ghettos, and minority-group members' (Lynn 1990: 136–137).

To add to the 'impossibility' of the welfare administration role, outcomes from this government funding can be slow to emerge and difficult to observe. Public agencies, non-profit providers, beneficiaries and taxpayer lobby groups have differing views on whether the results show funding to be a 'fair entitlement' or 'wasted spending'.

Given these clashes of political and social values, it is inevitable that social welfare has been a high-profile target for New Public Management (NPM) prescriptions during the past 30 years. Reform initiatives in three countries – New Zealand, Australia and Norway – are analysed in this chapter, providing insights into the stages of change that NPM strategies can create. At opposite ends of the world, these long-established democracies, with their mature and comprehensive welfare systems, have used different elements of the set of prescriptions labelled as NPM. These cases provide examples of the use of private sector cultural change techniques, structural separation of policy and delivery agencies, performance specifications for competition-based delivery, and what has come to be seen as a post-NPM agenda in which coordination and collaboration are more important.

The experiences of New Zealand and Australia suggest that NPM reforms result in predictable stages of change. First, the emphasis on measurable indicators – reinforced by the use or threat of competition, and the separation of policy and delivery roles – provides a form of shock treatment for bureaucratic systems. Concerns about coordination and collaboration tend to arise later, when measurement and accountability alone fall short by failing to foster longer-term and difficult-to-measure relationships underpinning coordination and collaboration. The country cases in this chapter illustrate dilemmas described by Kaufman (2001). The use of marketplace competition-based techniques can overcome some dysfunctions of inward-looking bureaucracy, but 'markets are seldom perfect'. Coordination through one-stop shops is a form of centralisation which 'may advance consistency in policies but delay action as the centre gets inundated with detail'. Structural separation of policy and delivery means 'pitting bureaucrats against each other and slows the decision making process.'

Finding a perfect one-size-fits-all organisational model for social welfare administration is an elusive and unattainable goal. But the specific lessons arising from cases of determined reforming can illuminate theory, and provide inspiration and encouragement – or warnings – for would-be imitators.

The Impetus for Reform

The NPM prescriptions of the 1980s were a reaction against the dominant public administration model of the previous century – standardised services delivered through a monopoly model, using hierarchical and lifetime career organisations that were a world apart from the rest of the economy. NPM prescriptions sought more responsive and tailored services, aiming to keep up with the cost and customer service efficiencies increasingly possible through information technology. The services being reformed in each of the countries under study had long traditions. New Zealand had been the first country to create a Department of Labour in the 1890s, initially mainly to regulate relationships between employers and unions, but progressively to help with access to employment. Social welfare of a 'cradle to grave' nature came as a result of the hardships of the 1930s depression. Norway's employment and insurance agencies dated back to the early 1900s. Australia had social welfare provisions from shortly after federal government was established in 1901.

Radical Change in New Zealand

New Zealand was the earliest and arguably the most comprehensive adopter of NPM reforms, using ideas contained in 'Government Management' (The Treasury 1987), a report written by the New Zealand Treasury, which has been described as a major NPM text book.

System-wide change in the late 1980s made possible a period of fundamental change for New Zealand's Department of Social Welfare, which was described by its minister in the early 1990s as 'unclear about its purpose, and unable to meet the needs of New Zealanders in a responsive way' (Petrie 1998). New market-focused hiring processes made it possible to recruit a chief executive who had previously headed a state-owned enterprise, who in turn recruited a change agent for the benefits division. This change agent was George Hickton, a manager who had come from marketing and personnel roles in the motor industry and had experience of reforming employment services.

As the benefits division general manager, Hickton used methods which would have been unthinkable in the pre-1988 public service. He bypassed existing members of the management team to create a management group comprised of individuals who 'hadn't been operating at a senior level before, but had a passion to make a change occur' (Smith and Norman 1997).

Open plan offices, a corporate dress standard, name tags, longer office hours, nationally consistent branding and signage, and a 'clean desk' policy were part of the change strategy. Surveys sought feedback from beneficiaries, who were now to be regarded as clients. The department's traditional 'no comment' was replaced with a policy of active media engagement (Petrie 1998: 22).

At the beginning of the change process, the department's guideline for turning around a benefit application was 21 days, and there were 800 overdue applications. With staff buy-in, an ambitious turnaround target of one day was set. Within two years the goal had been achieved, albeit partly by reclassifying applications (Petrie 1998: 29).

The risk of entrepreneurial management in a public service environment surfaced quickly. After 1993, a new chief executive from a public service background became concerned about 'one page plans', 'wild unstructured growth' and a 'cavalier attitude' to the responsibility to be a 'good employer' under the State Sector Act (Petrie 1998: 59). An Advisory Board for the Income Support Division was introduced to rein in the management, with a not-unexpected result: that the entrepreneurial George Hickton took up a new change role outside the core public service.

Separating Policy and Delivery

In 1998, in response to a rising unemployment rate, the government's 'welfare to work' strategy provided the rationale for combining the income support service of the Department of Social Welfare with employment services from the Department of Labour. A new department, Work and Income New Zealand (WINZ), was created to provide a one-stop shop where case managers would provide clients both with benefit payments and employment-related services – skills training, job and community work placements, and more. A small, structurally separate social policy agency was given responsibility for monitoring the delivery department, which remained within the core public service. WINZ was a merger of two distinct cultures, one 'process-driven, the other relationship-driven; the one stressing uniformity and consistency, the other more free-wheeling and diverse' (Hunn 2000).

WINZ soon became a very visible political target as a result of the management style of its founding chief executive, Christine Rankin, who had gained accelerated promotion during the entrepreneurial era of George Hickton.

In the new department's first year, Rankin invested over $2 million in the organisation's image, including rebranding and staff training road shows. When the media discovered that the department had spent $165,000 to charter a plane to take staff to a national conference, the opposition Labour Party focused on WINZ as a symbol of lavishness and waste in the public sector for its 1999 election campaign. The Labour spokesman on Social Welfare and Employment, soon to become Minister, described it thus: 'WINZ deals with the most vulnerable New Zealanders and its all-glitz style is inappropriate' (Small 1999).

Amidst the political criticism, the department made significant progress in meeting its performance targets. But its style was the major reason why in July 2001, the State Services Commission, Rankin's employer, declined to extend her three-year establishment contract.

To make a fresh start after this controversy, the new Labour Government decided to recombine policy and delivery functions to create a new Ministry of Social Development. By 2006, the ministry was managing all the functions that had been part of the Department of Social Welfare ten years before. The reintegrated policy and delivery services had regular contact with more than 1.2 million adult New Zealanders and nearly a third of all New Zealand children (Ministry of Social Development 2002: 1). Its workforce of about 9,600 represented about 23 per cent of the core public service.

From Transactions to Outcomes

Social welfare administration now moved into a low-profile era. A new chief executive, Peter Hughes, pursued social outcomes rather than the indicator-focused outputs of the previous era. Outcomes were defined as the provision of both social protection for people in difficulty (such as benefit payments and pensions) and also social investment – programmes aimed at achieving better future outcomes, such as those targeting family violence or better parenting (Schwass and Norman 2007).

Social development required MSD to address both immediate problems *and* their underlying causes. Where possible, the Ministry sought ways that people could avoid entering the benefit system, and it took a holistic view of those already in the system, aiming for sustainable employment

When working to a strictly output focus, the staff of WINZ had been able to tick off their job as done once they had matched a job seeker to a vacancy. Now, as Hughes described it:

We start with people's capabilities, we assess their capability. We spend a huge amount of time with people once they go into jobs – helping them sort out their debt, transport, childcare, get out of bed in the morning if it's an issue, housing, health. If they're a sickness beneficiary we're looking at getting them rehabilitated as quickly as possible back to work as quickly as possible. (Schwass and Norman 2007)

Many of the levers to achieve these outcomes were found outside the Ministry, for instance in drug and alcohol rehabilitation and other support services.

As with any service focused on outcomes, proving performance is a challenge. A buoyant economy initially helped. Between 2001 and 2006 the number of working age people receiving income-tested benefits fell by 30 per cent. When people went back to work they stayed there. The number of unemployed also fell significantly; in 2007 it stood at 3.6 per cent of the workforce – one of the lowest rates in the OECD. Since 2008 unemployment has risen to 6 per cent,[1] still lower than the OECD average of 8.7 per cent.[2] By 2010, the Ministry of Social Development was seen as an organisation that politicians could rely on for controversy-free consistency. NPM prescriptions had served their purpose by changing focus and forcing increases in efficiency. But the new agenda was how to extend outcomes-focused delivery, particularly by working with other arms of government such as health, housing, education and immigration.

A Market-Focused, One-Stop Shop for Australia

In adopting NPM techniques, Australia was a sceptical follower (Halligan with Wills 2008). Its single largest NPM experiment was the reform of social welfare administration by creating Centrelink, the one-stop Commonwealth Services Delivery Agency. This was more a pragmatic response to a long-held political concern than an ideological commitment to a form of administration. Australian Prime Minister John Howard commented at the opening of the agency:

From the moment I entered Parliament in 1974 … I began hearing complaints about the number of agencies you had to visit … And what focused my mind at the time was that so many people felt that if only they could go to one place and have all their business done in that one spot it would be a lot more efficient, it would be a lot more human and it would make a great deal more sense. (Howard 1997)

---

1   New Zealand Department of Labour press release, 6 May 2010: http://www.dol.govt. nz/lmr/lmr-hlfs.asp [accessed: 07/06/2010].

2   OECD average in May 2010: http://www.oecd.org/document/1/0,3343,en_2649_34251_ 45174913_1_1_1_1,00.html [accessed: 07/06/2010].

The new agency employed more than 20,000 staff across Australia, and delivered benefits and services to nearly 8 million Australians, more than a third of the total population. It would account for almost one third of Commonwealth expenditure. Centrelink's governance board, which drew on private sector experience, faced two strong pressures from the outset: to save costs through merging of functions from several public agencies, and to demonstrate sufficiently strong performance to fend off competition from potential alternative providers.

Unlike New Zealand, separation of policy and delivery roles has not been a favoured administrative strategy in Australia, perhaps because the federal/state division already contains many such dividing lines. These can bring beneficial clarity about roles, but can also create relationship tensions and the risk that policy-makers become remote from delivery realities while delivery agencies develop tunnel vision. Australian administrations have tended to favour the creation of larger agencies with sector-wide mandates. In 1987, while New Zealand was disaggregating, Australia was consolidating departments horizontally in a search for policy coordination and portfolio rationalisation.

However the transfer of ideas, in particular the operational 'sea change' generated by New Zealand's introduction of private sector-style methods of delivery between 1992 and 1994, was an important influence (Halligan with Wills 2008: 19).

Centrelink was a product of a period in which relatively incremental reforms were followed by the 1996 Howard Government's more radical preference for market methods of delivery. As in New Zealand, pressure was created by performance contracting between a policy-focused ministry and the delivery agency, which was distanced from the traditional public service processes so it could work more entrepreneurially. Centrelink retained the 'attributes of a department of state' while at the same time standing out from the normal Canberra arrangements of integrated agencies. Despite being the largest Australian public service organisation, it was outside the departmental 'club' (Halligan with Wills 2008: 7).

Centrelink was only semi-autonomous – and indeed less autonomous than its departmental counterpart in New Zealand, given the scrutiny by agencies which had previously employed most of Centrelink's staff. The Department of Employment and Workplace Relations (DEWR) proved to be the most active and demanding of these, although the Department of Family and Community Services (DFaCS) accounted for 95 per cent of Centrelink's funding. DEWR had implemented Australia's most contestable programme, the delivery of employment services, and in 1996 had declined to fund the previous monopoly government provider, the Commonwealth Employment Service, when that service failed to offer services at prices competitive with non-government providers.

Centrelink was presented as 'the human face of the Commonwealth government' (Halligan with Wills 2008: 29), with customers spanning a range of areas, such as families and children, retirement services, employment, disability and carers, youth and students, rural and housing. All together Centerlink had more than 6 million customers (Centrelink 1999: 2–3). The biggest categories were retirement services, families and children, and employment.

A fall in unemployment in the period after Centrelink's creation in 1997 meant that the employment segment became a lower priority for the new agency. Just 5 per cent of the agency's total income was now allocated to it, though it took a disproportionate amount of staff time.

An outsider was chosen to head Centrelink. Sue Vardon, the founding chief executive, was initially a community worker and most recently chief executive of the South Australian Department of Correctional Services, where she had reduced costs, changed corporate culture and overseen an improvement in customer service for a group of reluctant 'clients'.

Two potentially conflicting results were expected of Centrelink. Budget savings required major staff reductions and productivity improvements. Service to citizens/customers would require a major change of work style from staff that had come from departments which were predominantly regulatory in their cultures (Halligan with Wills 2008: 84).

Perhaps the most revealing commentary on NPM techniques from the Centrelink example is the impact of complex accountability and reporting mechanisms. This agency was established under a board that drew on 'outsiders', it was given operational autonomy, and was deliberately held at arm's length from the Australian public service 'club'. But its CEO, who was appointed by the board, reported not only to that board but to the ministers of the public service departments which funded and evaluated the agency's work. Moreover, while four of seven members of the Centrelink board were from private sector backgrounds, others were directly from the public service bodies that scrutinised the agency's performance. As Halligan notes, the CEO's role combined some formal autonomy with informal features which sought 'conformity with government policy and preferences in politically sensitive fields' (Halligan 2004).

In 2002, the board commissioned a report on organisational efficiency. It concluded that since the creation of Centrelink, costs had been reduced by 21 per cent per workload unit – an improvement in cost efficiency comparable with that achieved by banks during the period. Customer and staff satisfaction had improved, and more client–agency key performance indicators had been achieved. Corporate and property expenses were lower than public sector standards and generally comparable with the private sector (Halligan with Wills 2008: 58).

Policy Delivery Tensions

But, as Halligan's case study emphasises, there were significant tensions between Centrelink, as the operational agency, and the policy and oversight agencies. Analysed in private sector terms, Centrelink was obliged to work with a very uneven client base. Any fully commercial organisation would have shifted its focus to meeting the needs of the Department of Family and Community Services, which provided 92.4 per cent of funding and was overwhelmingly its most important client. Only 5.3 per cent of Centrelink's business came from the Department of Employment and Workplace Relations (DEWR) and a minimal additional amount was spread between 14 other federal, state and territorial agencies. But despite its small size, DEWR was the most demanding customer, a result of the contracting relationships it had developed with providers of employment services (as opposed to the referral services of Centrelink). DEWR, unlike DFaCS, had retained its own computing systems and had direct information from Centrelink transactions with which to substantiate its views (Halligan with Wills 2008: 125). Moreover, DEWR was enthusiastic about seeking competitive supply of Centrelink services and maintained pressure by commissioning independent surveys of customer responses, something which the largest purchaser didn't do. DEWR was concerned about Centrelink's potential monopoly role, and worked with central agencies (the departments of Finance and Administration, and of the Prime Minister and Cabinet) to limit the agency's independence.

From Centrelink's perspective, these policy departments were trying to micromanage. The costs of maintaining these sometimes fraught relationships and complex contracts proved to be substantial, accounting for more than $107 million of DFaCS's budget provision for 2002–2003 – a figure which Halligan estimates would have been matched by $50 million on the part of Centrelink (Halligan with Wills 2008: 135).

The Department of Finance was concerned that Centrelink was monopolist, and that the purchaser–provider arrangement with DFaCS did not work because the two organisations were not sufficiently at arm's length and pricing was not sufficiently transparent.

But against the purity of a contracting model was the reality of 'very low political tolerance … for income support services to be disrupted for any substantial period or for Commonwealth agencies to enter into public conflict over delivery of government policy' (Halligan with Wills 2008).

A Contestable Market Environment

During the establishment period, Centrelink consciously worked in competitive mode, aware that the politics of organisational survival depended on its performance. It sought additional business, even looking at private sector work. It recognised, for instance, that service functions could theoretically be handled by another government agency, Australia Post. Chief Executive Sue Vardon emphasised the need to retain a competitive edge by delivering on 'cost and quality and excellent customer service'.

But after 2000 (Halligan with Wills 2008: 158), administrative fashion moved from markets towards partnering, governance and whole-of-government. Centrelink, as a horizontally constituted agency, sought new relationships with communities and opportunities to lead on behalf of government, rather than being a contract arm. The heading of Halligan's final chapter, 'Back to the Future', captures this cycle of change at Centrelink. After Vardon finished her eight-year term as chief executive, governance arrangements were changed, the board structure was dropped by

2006, and a new focus was placed on public service collaboration to enable 'joined-up government' that would create 'more efficient and effective linkages' between functions now clustered in a Department of Human Services (Centrelink 2006: 2).

A significant extension of this joined-up approach came in December 2009 with the announcement that Medicare, the government-backed insurance programme for health services, would be amalgamated with Centrelink. The Human Services Minister Chris Bowen echoed John Howard's reasons for establishing Centrelink more than ten years earlier. He stated that 'many Australians find the services offered by the various agencies confusing', and 'better coordination of service delivery mechanisms will result in better services for Australians and savings for Government, some of which can be reinvested in better service delivery.[3]

Norway – Latecomer, but Comprehensive Reformer

Historically, Norway's welfare-oriented institutions and services have been rather fragmented. They have consisted of three types: the national insurance administration, national employment services (both based at central government level and with traditions going back over 100 years) and the social services, based in the municipalities (Christensen, Fimreite and Lægreid 2007). There was a rather low degree of coordination between the services, which meant that users or clients had to deal with several different welfare organisations to obtain their benefits and services. During the 1980s and '90s growing criticism from user groups and their organisations was channelled through the parliament which in 2001 took the initiative to reform the welfare administrative system. The politicians' main aim was to create a more holistic and coordinated service so that users could gain access through just 'one door'. But getting more people into the workforce, having fewer on benefits and establishing a more effective welfare system were other main concerns.

Parliament's initiative was resisted in many ways by the central political-administrative leadership. After an internal review process, parliament rejected this view and appointed a public committee of experts to examine the matter. The committee's report concluded that fragmentation was the best way to organise the various welfare and employment services, but that some more local coordination was possible. The incoming minister for social affairs, now a more coordinated ministry than before, was experienced in this and entrepreneurial in outlook. He rejected a proposal advocating the continuation of fragmentation. Through negotiations with the parliament, and with the national organisation for municipalities, he managed to gain agreement to a partial merger of agencies. The national insurance administration and the employment service were merged to form a national welfare agency with branches on a regional and local level, and a partnership was created between the new agency and social services, creating local welfare offices in all municipalities

---

3   Chris Bowen, Ministry for Human Services, Australia, address, 16 December 2009: http://www.chrisbowen.net/media-centre/allNews.do?newsId=2809 [accessed: 07/06/2010].

(since there was no political support for moving social services away from the municipalities to become part of the central government).

After an interim period, the new welfare agency combining Norway's benefits and employment services – the Norwegian Labour and Welfare Administration, or NAV – was established in 2006. Like its counterparts in New Zealand and Australia ten years earlier, NAV was focused especially on the problems of long-term unemployment and exclusion of groups from the workplace – factors which also provided the major catalyst for the agency's creation. NAV's functions were also the same as those of New Zealand's Ministry of Social Development and Australia's Centrelink: providing unemployment benefits, allowances for rehabilitation, pensions, child benefits and social benefits. Spending in these areas makes up almost a third of the Norwegian budget and covers 15–20,000 employees.

The Norwegian reform had a strong post-NPM flavour, but there were also significant NPM measures. It is thus fair to say that it represented a mixture of NPM and post-NPM elements. A key post-NPM feature is that the catalyst for reform was the desire to coordinate more a fragmented structure (Christensen and Lægreid 2008). Even though the merger finally decided on was only partial, since it did not fully include the social services, this was nonetheless the largest sectoral merger ever completed in the Norwegian central administration. So the holistic aspect of the reform was central. Two of the three main goals of the reform – namely increased efficiency and increased user-friendliness – are also typical of NPM. NPM was also evident in the internal organisation of the new central NAV agency, in which a large provider unit was created within the agency, while the rest of the NAV agency was a kind of strategic purchaser (Askim et al. 2009). This purchaser–provider model was, however, abandoned in 2010. The whole new organisation was also set up with a performance management system. Management by objectives and results was the main steering tool between the ministry and the central agencies, as well as internally between the central and local branches of the agency.

A distinctive difference between the Norwegian experience and that of New Zealand and Australia is the role that local government plays in providing the one-stop shops that serve the Norwegian public. To Askim et al. (2009) this makes the reform strategy adopted in Norway 'post-NPM'. Instead of disaggregation in the interests of creating pressures for performance and independence of policy creation, Norway has merged agencies and formed a partnership between NAV, as the central government agency, and local governments which administer benefits and services. While Australia opted to outsource employment services, the NAV reform has not. Privatisation and public–private partnerships are not part of this reform.

As Askim et al. (2009: 1014) note, the partnership with local authorities is more than co-location. Services are delivered through case handling units which have two 'owners' – central and local government – thereby creating dual accountability systems for staff. The partnership is not voluntary; it is permanent and formalised through contracts and agreements, with minimum standards for what part of the social services and related services could be included (Fimreite and Lægreid 2009). The hierarchy is still clear, with political responsibility for the national insurance service and labour market policy remaining with central government, while financial and social assistance is discretion-based, means tested and under the control of local politicians (Fimreite and Lægreid 2009: 288).

The change process was similar to New Zealand and Australia, with an 'outsider' appointed as leader to mitigate perceptions that any existing agency might dominate, but the new leader was recruited from the public sector and had had many leadership positions both on the central and local administrative levels. This appointment also sought to demonstrate to the Storting (the Norwegian parliament) and to local government that NAV would provide a fresh start for welfare administration (Askim et al. 2009: 1019).

The establishment of NAV was a government reform that aimed to bring together a 'fragmented state apparatus' in the aftermath of NPM reforms. NAV is a hybrid organisation comprising features from traditional welfare structures, and elements also from NPM and joined-up government (Askim et al. 2009). It is what Fimreite and Lægreid (2009) describe as a 'complicated organisational structure'; the use of a mandatory partnership between central and local government is important for coordinating both processes and results, but raises questions about ministerial responsibility. The difficulties of the model lie in combining the legal and local government responsibilities of a traditional vertical organisation with an ambiguous partnership model that has competing lines of authorities, not to mention cultural compatibility challenges:

> *The managers in the partnerships are supposed to be multiply accountable to their superiors in the regional and central NAV-agency, to the local council and political and administrative executives in the municipality as well as to users and clients. Different actors are responsible for different aspects of joint activity and the managers have several lines of accountability – towards the central government political executives but also political accountability to the local government political executives. (Fimreite and Lægreid 2009: 294)*

Social Welfare Administration: An Example of the Emerging NPM Agenda

These three country cases encapsulate the promises and problems of the NPM reform agenda. With their focus on measurable performance, NPM techniques served as bureaucracy-busting initiatives in New Zealand and Australia. In New Zealand, the managerial freedoms given to all public service chief executives made this feasible within a departmental structure. In Australia a special agency was created, although within ten years its private sector-style governance had been replaced with more traditional public service methods emphasising coordination rather than competition. Table 12.1 provides an overview of the trends in reform across the three jurisdictions.

Table 12.1   Trends in reform across the jurisdictions

	Australia	New Zealand	Norway
Structure		1991 Reform of benefits division of Department of Social Welfare.	
	1996–2005 Centrelink: one-stop shop and contestability. Separation of policy and delivery; new agency needing to establish new relationships across and outside public service	1996 Creation of Work and Income New Zealand (WINZ) as a one-stop shop for benefits and employment. Separation of policy and delivery functions	
		2001 Recombining of policy and delivery with benefits and employment	
	2006 Closer integration with core public service	2006 Recombining of child, youth and family functions into Ministry of Social Development	2006– New central agency NAV; merging of long-established benefit and employment agencies and partnership with local government for social services
	2009 One-stop shop concept extended by intention to include Medicare (health payments)		
Governance		1991–2000 Public service departments and ministry, with a private sector advisory board used for income support	
	1996–2005 Board members from private sector	2000 Direct ministerial governance	
	2006 Reverted to reporting direct to minister		2006 Performance management system

Table 12.1 (continued)

	Australia	New Zealand	Norway
Leadership		1991–2000 Two 'outsider' leaders with entrepreneurial focus-led benefits and employment changes	
	1996–2005 Outsider CE chosen for experience of a service orientation towards compulsory 'customers'		
		2000 CE from public service with social welfare and health experience	
	2006– CE with experience of Centrelink as an agency, but also of core public service		2006– Outsider chosen as CE but from within the core public sector
Major focus for agency/ performance measures		1991–2000 Outputs expressed in terms of efficiency, timeliness of benefit payments, reducing administrative costs	
	1996–2005 Performance defined by contracts with policy focused funding departments		
		2000– Outcomes in terms of independence from benefit system/impact on social indicators	2006 Focus on vertical and horizontal coordination
	2009 Stronger emphasis on coordination of Human Services functions		

NPM initiatives of the 1980s and 1990s need to be seen in the context of global ideologies and technologies of that period – a period when the battle between markets and central control seemed to have been convincingly won in favour of markets, dramatised by the fall of the Berlin Wall and the collapse of the Soviet Union. Computer technology, particularly personal computing, enabled decentralised systems that were a radical change from earlier paper-based filing. The dominant managerial philosophy became that of the diversified corporation consisting of semi-independent business units, each accountable for bottom lines monitored by a small corporate office through accounting and qualitative measures. The invention of the spreadsheet in the early 1980s greatly extended the ability of policy-making corporate units to monitor quantitative results, providing the technology with which to implement NPM ideas about accountability and contestability.

The more recent history of administrative reform is less dramatic than the 1980s and 1990s period of crash-through ideology and technology-based change. Instead, governments are seeking the organisational equivalent of the joined-up networks made possible by the technology of the internet and search engines such as Google. Where the NPM recipe of the 1980s sought to disaggregate and foster efficiency through markets and competition, the post-NPM agenda seeks to retain this efficiency to achieve joined-up services and savings to meet the budget pressures created by the 2008–2009 global financial crisis.

The OECD's 2005 report on modernising government (OECD 2005) concluded that delegated and distributed governance, the essence of the NPM approach, was creating new challenges, some of which are shown in the different trajectories taken by the welfare agencies in New Zealand, Australia and Norway. According to the OECD, the main problems that emerged were 'a large number of new organisational forms and governance structures, management regimes and reporting mechanisms', which had resulted in a 'blurred picture of how the system is functioning' (OECD 2005: 118). As a result, overall control by parliament was weakened, potentially shaking citizens' trust and confidence in a system that was, in any event, too complicated to understand. Delegation to arm's-length bodies created difficulties with coordination, and outsourcing resulted in particular challenges of accountability. While bodies' performance was monitored against explicit standards, and ministers had removed the potential for conflicts of interest in the way those standards were set and monitored, the introduction of new delivery agents nonetheless complicated accountability.

Kaufman was quoted with approval by the OECD reviewers, and as a conclusion to this chapter, it is useful to revisit his observations about the cyclical nature of public sector reform at the beginning of this chapter. These extracts capture the tensions that reforms seek to address, and the inevitability that the prescriptions will require different remedies some time later.

> *Pitting bureaucrats against each other complicates and slows the decision making process …*

> *Turning functions back to the marketplace overcomes some dysfunctions, but the factors that induced people to demand governmental intervention in the first place soon generate renewed calls for public programs; markets, after all, are very seldom perfect.*

> *Contracting out public services alleviates some failings, but administering contracts has historically been the Achilles heel of government, a source of corruption and mismanagement.*

Policy planning and coordination and efficiency are furthered by orderly budgeting systems, but budget analysts inexpert in specialized fields often end up second-guessing skilled and experienced professionals ...

Decentralizing authority to field officers generally results in prompter decisions; it may also result in grossly disparate treatment of clients in identical circumstances. On the other hand, centralizing authority may advance consistency in policies but delay action as the center gets inundated by detail. One irritation is alleviated, another is intensified. (Kaufman 2001: 40)

Welfare administration, as illustrated in these three cases, grapples with some of the most intractable challenges of public management. In retrospect, the NPM prescriptions seem a simplistic, but perhaps necessary, method for ensuring new computer technologies and culture change were rapidly adopted during the 1980s and 1990s. New Zealand and Australia illustrate the use of these techniques for breakthrough change initiatives while Norway represents a more cautious approach to reform.

Rather than there being a single template for effective delivery of welfare services, the complex reality is more as Wiggan (2009) observes – that social welfare administration requires a mixture of hierarchical, market and network mechanisms of delivery. The challenge for reformers is to use the strengths of these different organisational forms at appropriate times, and anticipate the weaknesses of each.

Utility Regulation and NPM

Ian Bartle

Introduction

In many ways modern utility regulation can be perceived of as a branch of New Public Management (NPM). Utility regulation shares with NPM an emphasis on decentralised decision making, the use of agencies, a stress on expertise, semi-autonomous decision making, technocratic governance and business-like management practices together with the prevailing belief in as much privatisation and competition as possible. In addition, both developed and diffused across many parts of the world within the same period of history: from the 1980s onwards.

There are nevertheless some important differences. In the UK, the country which pioneered the new utility regulation in Europe and one of the forerunners of NPM, they developed under distinctly different policy programmes despite both being connected to the broad neo-liberal thrust of the Thatcher government in the 1980s. Moreover, rather than being a part of a grand policy programme, the new utility regulation was an afterthought in the drive to privatise the main utility industries (Hogwood 1998, Bartle and Wilks 2002). In addition, NPM and utility regulation have functionally different purposes. The central purpose of utility regulation is the highly technical and specific function of economic regulation and is an aspect of economic policy, while NPM involves the operation of the civil service and public executive and management functions undertaken in separate agencies under the auspices of central government (Moran 2003). In the UK, the 'executive agency', which is a significant institutional manifestation of NPM and undertakes a wide range of governmental and public service delivery functions, is seen as distinct from the utility regulators and other public bodies which undertake specific regulatory, advisory and quasi judicial functions (NAO 2003, Cabinet Office 2006b).

Another key difference is the stress on independence of agencies and the extent to which the independent agency model has diffused across Europe and beyond. There are undoubtedly wide variations in the extent of the separation and autonomy of agencies (Talbot 2004: 9), nevertheless there is more stress on independence from central government of the utility regulators compared to the executive agency. Although the agency model has spread widely, its dispersion across Europe and beyond in utility industries, such as energy and telecommunications, is striking (Levi-Faur 2005). Moreover, while EU directives state that independent regulatory agencies must be established in these industries, there are no similar requirements to set up executive agencies in the many areas of public management. As a consequence, in countries which have been slow adopters of NPM reforms, such as Germany, new regulatory agencies have been established in the utilities, albeit rather reluctantly, but there has not been a similar adoption of agencies for public management functions (Proeller and Schedler 2005); indeed in terms of NPM Germany has been described as a country of 'non-reform' (Toonen 2003: 469).

The aim of this chapter is to explore the connections between utility regulation and NPM, and the problems with the use of agencies and technocratic methods drawing primarily on the experience of utility regulation and NPM in the UK. In the following section a model of independent economic regulation in the utilities is outlined and portrayed as a 'strong' version of the specialisation, decentralisation, unbundling and agencification evident in NPM. The chapter then assesses the extent to which this model has been vulnerable to some of the key problems of NPM such as control and coordination, and reliance on technocratic governance and quantitative techniques such as target setting, performance measurement and cost-benefit analysis. This assessment begins by investigating the development of government–agency relations in utility regulation and the problems of control and coordination. Has practice lived up to the aspiration of the robust model of independent economic regulation espoused by many of its supporters? It goes on to consider the extent to which technocratic methods, such as the regulatory impact assessment and the use of quantitative analytical techniques, have been adopted and become successful. The chapter concludes that despite the narrow technical nature of the utilities and their regulation, as with NPM better control and coordination is required and over-reliance on technocratic methods should be guarded against.

Independent Economic Regulation and NPM: What are the Connections?

The connections between utility regulation and NPM are close. They occurred broadly at the same time (from the 1980s onwards), in response to the same circumstances and context, and are based on closely connected ideologies (Moran 2003: 1–6). The genesis of both was in the economic problems of the 1970s and the perceived failures of the welfare state, big government and bureaucratic excess. Both are focused on increasing efficiency and effectiveness in the supply of public services and based on the same ideological importance attached to the introduction of business practices into the supply of public services. The latter can be undertaken by the privatisation of public organisations, by contracting out to the private sector, or by the introduction of business-like practices into government. Within public management the stress is on decentralisation, de-bureaucratisation and an increase in managerial autonomy of those functions which are, or have to be, undertaken in the public sector, including the provision of certain public services and the regulation of private industry supplying public services.

Some conceptualise the term 'public management' and its reform broadly and connect it to a range of government actions including subsidies, regulation and contracts. In this way NPM naturally includes the utility industries (Hughes 1998). This is evident in the trend away from the use of the term 'public administration', which is seen to be concerned with procedures and following instructions, towards 'public management' which is concerned with the achievement of results and managerial responsibility (Hood 2005a). In more traditional views of public administration, management is a component and subordinate part of administration concerned with the practical implementation of governmental functions (Pollitt and Bouckaert 2004). Public management reform rests particularly on the growing influence of neo-classical and public choice economic theory, and the conclusions 'that the "best" outcome will involve a maximum role for market forces and a minimum role for government' (Hughes 1998: 11). This broad notion of public management and its reform leads to the need to reconsider the appropriate role of government across all areas including public enterprise and the utilities and the possibility of privatisation and the establishment of independent regulatory agencies (Hughes 1998: 81–115). In the UK some have noted the connections between modern regulation and NPM (Moran 2003) making it appear to be a branch in the contemporary trend of NPM.

However, subsuming utility regulation under NPM can mask some important differences and could limit the understanding of utility regulation. In practice 'management' and 'regulation' are often seen to be different functions and activities. A narrower conception of public management can be conceived of as the provision of a public service. These services might be regulated separately but management activity in itself is often perceived as separate from regulation. In the UK, for example, 'executive agencies' are seen as performing public management tasks and as distinctly separate from the regulatory agencies.

The literatures on NPM and utility regulation have also been separate with few overlaps. In two major analyses of agencies there is little or no mention of utility regulation or economic regulation (Pollitt et al. 2004, Pollitt and Bouckaert 2004). Studies of NPM and agencies in the UK mainly focus on the 'Next Steps' agencies initiated in the late 1980s (Löffler 2003, Talbot 2004, Moynihan 2006). This is despite the fact that the independent regulatory agency is seen as a central and ubiquitous institutional innovation in the reform of the utilities since the 1980s. It has spread across the world (Levi-Faur 2005) and, whilst clearly connected to privatisation, has been applied to some utility industries which in some countries have not been privatised. Conversely many analyses of economic regulation and the regulatory state contain little or no reference to NPM. Analysis of economic regulation is primarily concerned with economic techniques, notably the structures and setting of regulated prices (Vass 1998, Newbery 1999). Broader-based analyses of regulation, including those focused on the nature of regulation (Baldwin and

Cave 1999) and politically orientated analyses of 'regulatory state' or 'regulatory capitalism', while drawing on neo-liberal trends, only make fleeting reference to the NPM literature (Moran 2003, Levi-Faur 2005).

In the UK context utility regulation and NPM, while clearly connected to the neo-liberal reforms of the Thatcher government in the 1980s, developed separately. Indeed the model of independent economic regulation was an accidental spin-off from the privatisation of the utilities. There was no blueprint for the design of the regulatory agencies in the run up to privatisation, the stress at the time was on deregulation and competition, not on new regulation and regulatory agencies. The government initially proposed that the regulation of British Telecom, the first major utility to be privatised, was to be undertaken by the competition regulator, the Office of Fair Trading, but this would have meant a large expansion of its duties and was seen as unworkable (Hogwood 1998, Bartle and Wilks 2002). The NPM developments, although connected to the ideology of privatisation and small government, were separate. One of the developments early in the Thatcher government was the Financial Management Initiative, which had the aim to inject greater efficiency into civil service management via greater managerial autonomy accompanied by strong systems of scrutiny and performance monitoring (Pilkington 1999, Löffler 2003). 'Market testing' was also a key initiative, with the aim to contract out as much public service provision as possible, and another was the process of 'compulsory competitive tendering', initiated in the early 1980s, particularly for those services provided by local government. The most significant NPM development in central government in the 1980s was the 'Next Steps' initiative and the proposal to set up decentralised 'executive agencies'. In academic analyses and practitioner proposals of all these initiatives there is little cross reference to utility regulation and the regulators.

Despite the rather accidental establishment of utility regulatory agencies, a clear model of independent economic regulation has developed. Although an *ex post* rationalisation, or at least the ideal type perceived by many analysts and practitioners, represents a 'standard' model of independence and specialisation evident in the NPM ideas. This model of independent economic regulation has arisen with both specialisation and independence from government at its heart (Henry and Matheu 2001, Bartle and Vass 2007). These two 'logics' of delegation derive from principal–agent analysis of the delegation of powers (Majone 2001, Thatcher and Stone Sweet 2002). Specialisation enables regulation to be more effective and efficient, particularly by reducing information asymmetry between the regulated entities and regulators. Independence from government and politicians is a means of ensuring 'credible commitment' to long-run policy objectives without the threat of political intervention for short-term political objectives. These two features are seen as central in utility regulation and underpin not only a standard model but what might be termed a 'strong' model for two key reasons.

First, the function of the utility regulators is derived from a specialist body of micro-economic theory. Since the initiation of modern utility regulation in the 1980s some specialist techniques focusing particularly on regulated prices have become established. An important innovation was 'price cap regulation' which put incentives on regulated companies as price not profit was regulated and profit could be retained (Vass 1998, Newbery 1999, Baldwin and Cave 1999). A related innovation was the 'periodic review' of prices which set and fixed regulated prices within a particular period and specified investment and maintenance requirements on the regulated companies, particularly those providing monopoly infrastructures. In contrast, NPM executive agencies carry out a wide range of managerial tasks which are not based on one type of economic theory. Moreover there is a clear argument for limiting the function of utility regulators to economic matters to ensure efficiency; with others matters such as social and environmental objectives to be handled by other government departments and agencies. Compromising on specialisation, such as by 'adding non-economic objectives to the mandates of regulators may also reduce their overall performance and the degree of clarity concerning their responsibilities' (OECD 2002a: 96). Specialisation on clearly defined core tasks is also a means of ensuring accountability without significant political intervention (Foster 1992: 310–323). The discretion of the regulators is limited by their specialised tasks and they can be held to account by scrutiny of independent experts.

Secondly, independence and credible commitment are particularly important for investment in big industries which are dependent on large, long-term investment and need to keep costs of investment capital low. Costs of capital may rise if there is political risk in the investment, that is, if independence is not perceived to be strong enough (Smith 1997). Price cap regulation and the periodic review also include an understanding that past profits cannot be clawed back by the government (Newbery 1999: 395–396). Reflecting this there is very strong attachment to regulatory agency independence among practitioners and the industry constituency they serve and regulate. This was evident in the UK when the New Labour government in 1997 introduced a one-off windfall tax on the utilities, a politically popular move but one which was seen to compromise independent economic regulation as it clawed back past profits (Newbery 1999: 395). It was also particularly evident in the UK rail industry in the early 2000s when the industry was in crisis and the government initiated a review of industry organisation and regulation in 2004 (Bartle 2005). There had been particular concern about the role of the rail regulator, especially its alleged influence over the level of the large public subsidy. Despite this, during the review there was strong support from industry for maintaining an independent regulator and it was another sectoral agency, the Strategic Rail Authority, responsible for overall planning and the use of the public subsidy, which was abolished after the 2004 review. This strength of feeling about independence is not obviously on display outside the utility regulators, for example, in two major studies of NPM agencies there is little evidence of similar strength of feeling about the independence of the NPM agencies in their social and industry constituencies (Pollitt et al. 2004, Pollitt and Bouckaert 2004).

How does this strong model impact on some of the thorny and often controversial issues associated with specialisation and independence in NPM, particularly those associated with policy coordination and the adoption of technocratic and quantitative techniques? We might suppose that the strong model means a stronger rationale for specialisation and independence and thus fewer associated problems. Conversely, the very emphasis on specialisation and independence in the utilities might mean that the problems are more salient than elsewhere. To investigate these matters we turn firstly to the issue of control and coordination.

Government–Agency Separation and the Problem of Coordination

The separation, both vertically and horizontally, inherent in NPM agencification has led some to perceive a shortfall in coordination (Talbot 2004: 10, Moynihan 2006: 1033). Better coordination might be achieved by fine tuning government–agency relations and agency autonomy, possibly based on a clear split between 'policy' and 'operations' or 'execution' which seems to provide a neat definition of the relations. However, across the world there is great variation in government–agency relations and the appropriate level of autonomy for agencies has proved very difficult to define and achieve: 'the balance between active steering (desirable) and micromanagement (undesirable) is hard to find, and maintain' (Pollitt et al. 2004: 22). A clear policy-execution split has also proved tricky to achieve due to the complexity of the issue and the abiding effects of established organisational relations (Moynihan 2006: 1036).

Decentralisation might have lightened the load on central government, but paradoxically the load has been observed to increase in countries such as the UK and New Zealand which have adopted more radical NPM reforms (Christensen and Lægreid 2005a). This is due to poor connections between adjacent areas of government creating difficulty in handling issues in the lower levels of the hierarchy. The burden on higher levels of government is thus increased as more and more issues have to be channelled up the hierarchy for resolution. One initiative to overcome these problems of coordination has been the promotion of 'joined-up' government to enable greater and more effective coordination between the components of government and agencies. In the UK this has been pursued in central government by vertical links such as 'public service agreements' and various less formal ad hoc arrangements, and horizontally with the promotion of partnerships at central and local government levels (James 2004b, Davies 2009).

The strong model of specialisation and independence in utility regulation could be less vulnerable to coordination problems as the nature of economic regulation is necessarily discrete and specialised. The core tasks of economic regulation – the control of monopoly power and the promotion of competition – use techniques derived from specialised micro-economic theory. These techniques appear to be clearly delineated from interconnecting areas of utilities policy, notably those concerned with social and environmental matters. Where necessary, parsimonious interconnections between the core and other tasks can be set up. Thus, for example, social matters such as maintaining services for the poor can be handled by distribution payments in the welfare system entirely separate from economic regulation. Interconnections can be made by government specifying regulations which, for example, strictly limit the circumstances in which services can be disconnected in cases of non-payment. In environmental matters, economic regulators can work within frameworks and standards set by the government and environmental agencies.

This model of economic regulation tends to be advocated by those who clearly support privatisation, liberalisation and deregulation. Foster (1992), for example, provides an extended analysis of privatisation and competition in this vein, while others describe it as a 'free market' model and contrast it with others (McCrudden 1999). Although its proponents accept that some residual regulation may be required, particularly in the utilities with large networks, they see that regulations are, or should be, transitory phenomena in a movement to full competition. Encumbering and entangling economic regulation and competition with other matters, such as social and environmental regulation, blurs the focus on the specialist task of economic regulation, loses sight of the long-term goal and deregulation, distorts the market and reduces efficiency. Proponents of the free market approach can also point to evidence of a gradual shift towards deregulation. For example, in the UK and other countries there has been significant deregulation and competition in the energy sector. Regulations of the price of electricity and gas have been removed and all consumers are able to change their supplier while economic regulation is left mainly for the natural monopoly network use charges.

However, this model has been contested and there are questions about the extent to which it aligns with practice. It can be contrasted with a 'social market' version whose proponents argue that 'the purpose of regulation by a regulator is to take advantage of the market mechanism where possible, regulate to achieve competition if achievable, but at the same time to moderate the results achieved for the purposes of social integration and the achievement of other non-economic values such as social solidarity and equity' (McCrudden 1999: 276). Environmental protection is another non-economic value connected to the main utility industries with which the regulators might be concerned. There are also good reasons why utility regulation remains substantial despite the move towards competition. As well as the necessity and democratic importance of social, environmental and other issues, regulation is a process of market constitution and regulatory decisions can become more difficult, not easier, in competitive markets (Prosser 1999). Utility regulation, it is argued, is inherently complex: 'it is an essentially open process and cannot, and indeed should not, be reduced to any particular logic, economic or otherwise' (Prosser 1999: 217).

The slimmed-down regulation of the free market model and its parsimonious government–agency relations are not clearly evident in the practice of utility regulation. In the UK the task of utility regulators remains substantial, if measured only by the sizes of the regulatory agencies (Turvey 2001). There are statutory duties placed on the regulators to pursue social and environmental objectives supported by ministerial guidance about what is expected in fulfilling the duties (Graham 2000). Additionally, across Europe in countries such as Germany, France, Italy and the UK, while overt politicisation of regulatory agencies and use of formal powers by ministers over regulators are not widespread, there is evidence of close informal ties between regulators and ministers (Thatcher 2005).

A highly salient area in which utility regulation has become more complex and issues of coordination have arisen, despite the rise in competition, is sustainable development. The need for sustainable development involving the pursuit and integration of economic, social and environmental policy objectives is widely recognised. Policy integration in the energy, water and rail sectors has been pursued in the UK in recent years with statutory duties placed on the regulators to contribute to the achievement of sustainable development (Bartle and Vass 2007). A key reason for this is that in practice it is difficult to disentangle many social and environmental factors from detailed issues of economic regulation. For example, in the energy sector the technical systems set up to facilitate trading and competition can affect the level of renewable energy or energy conservation depending on how they are established (Bartle and Vass 2007: 265). Similarly, in the rail sector many detailed issues, for example the use of on-train electricity meters, have implications for competition and the environment. These are detailed technical issues of which the regulator is likely to have the best knowledge and cannot easily be coordinated by high-level decision makers but which also straddle divides between economic and environmental matters.

Even the process of economic regulation itself, without any connection to issues such as sustainable development, can lead to coordination problems. One of the key activities of economic regulation is the setting of prices for use of monopoly infrastructure. This price setting is related to the investment the network operator is required to make and connected to the prices service providers charge consumers and, in the case of the rail sector, any public subsidy required to maintain the viability of the sector. In many ways this is an arcane technical task, but it can have significant political repercussions – and thus raise problems of coordination – if consumer prices or public subsidy rise too high.

These problems were strikingly evident in the UK rail sector, particularly in the early 2000s during the crisis in the industry. The crisis revealed significant underspend in maintenance of the infrastructure and a review of network access charges concluded in 2003 that a significantly higher public subsidy than the government had allowed was necessary. This placed the government in the invidious position of having to accept the regulator's review or cut rail services (Bartle 2004). There were accusations that the regulator was writing cheques on behalf of the government and a breakdown of cordial relations and effective coordination between ministers and the regulator ensued.

Elsewhere in Europe the introduction of competition and independent economic regulation have led to coordination problems. This is particularly evident in sectors such as railways and energy which have high public interest elements and in which competition has been difficult to introduce. In the German railway sector, for example, although reform has been more incremental and less complex than in the UK, there has been an increase in coordination problems (Bauer 2005). A sectoral body (Federal Railway Agency) was set up in 1994 mainly for the supervision of technical issues but also some federal level financial matters (Böllhoff 2005: 40). However, its responsibilities in the increasingly important area of economic regulation were rather weak and there has been a lack of clarity between its role and that of the federal cartel office.

The Need for Better Coordination and 'Joined-up Government' in Utility Regulation

One response to these coordination problems might be less ministerial involvement in the activities of the regulators and a stress on the core task of economic regulation rather than broader and more nebulous objectives such as sustainable development, that is, an emphasis on the strong model of economic regulation. However, in a survey of regulators, policy makers, regulated companies and other key stakeholders, on regulators and sustainable development in the UK, this position reflected only a minority view while a clear majority said that better government guidance to the regulators was required (Bartle and Vass 2006).

One way of improving coordination is by legal specification. In the UK rail sector, following the problems of the early 2000s, a review in 2004 concluded that there was a need for a legally specified 'iterative process' between the government and regulator which specified how they should interact. It involved when the government should specify its network and service requirements, when the regulator should delivers its verdict on the costs, and how any mismatch and disagreements should be resolved. This set in law a process of coordination between government and regulator which operates fairly smoothly in normal times but without legal backing can collapse in times of crisis.

Another way of improving coordination is to promote more and better interaction. Drawing on sustainable development and the economic regulators we have argued elsewhere that they should have awareness of social, environmental and economic matters and facilitate the best outcomes for all three objectives, if necessary by working more closely with other organisations (Bartle and Vass 2007). This does not mean giving economic regulators significant decision-making powers over social and environmental matters, but ensuring they interact effectively with the appropriate social and environmental ministries, departments and agencies. Low-level technical issues, such as the regulation of energy meters, cannot simply be undertaken by the economic regulator and require coordination across departments and agencies but without being channelled all the way up to the higher levels of government. As in many areas of NPM, this kind of low-level coordination is important but not easy to achieve.

The specialist and apparently discrete nature of economic regulation thus has not meant that there are no significant problems of coordination. This is partly because the utilities and their regulation are suffused and entangled with other issues which inevitably have public and collective concerns, meaning depoliticisation and core task specialisation are not easy. Good coordination is therefore required and can be achieved informally, but UK practice has shown that it sometimes requires a variety of statutory duties and legally specified interactions between regulators and government and other agencies. The regulators' job in interpreting the duties is not easy, and requires pragmatism and working closely with government and others. These initiatives are similar to joined-up government ideas in NPM which include legally specified formal processes, ad hoc initiatives and the promotion of closer networks and partnerships (James 2004b, Moyinan 2006). Whether they resolve the issue is not clear. In another political context, the US, a century of independent agencies of various forms and complaints about lack of coordination have not led to any easy resolution of the problem (Shapiro 1997: 282–283). It all may represent another manifestation of an age old dilemma of government as it cycles between coordination and integration and separation and task specialisation (Pollitt et al. 2004: 329).

Technocratic Governance and Utility Regulation

One of the key elements at the heart of NPM is an aspiration for parsimony, economy and efficiency, and productivity (Toonen 2003: 470). This has resulted in attempts to import business-like techniques from the private sector into public management (Pollitt and Bouckaert 2004: 20). A manifestation of this is the adoption of goals, targets and performance indicators expressed in quantitative terms as much as possible (Hood 1991, Dieffenbach 2009). Reflecting commercial norms and business practice there is a raised cost consciousness, a focus on cost effectiveness and value for money and use of cost-benefit analysis (Dieffenbach 2009: 895).

These developments are also evident in regulation. In regulation since the 1990s there has been a rise in techniques of 'risk-based regulation', 'better regulation' and the adoption of the regulatory impact assessment, all of which are focused on economy and efficiency. Risk-based regulation involves attempts to strictly control regulation and is connected to the deregulatory initiatives and concerns about overregulation. It involves attempts to inject objectivity and transparency into regulation, particularly by moving towards a cost-benefit analysis culture: 'that is a move away from informally qualitative based standard based setting towards a more calculative and formalised approach' (Hutter 2005: 3–4). Better regulation is clearly connected to a risk-based agenda and is about regulatory quality which involves clear articulation of problems to be addressed, setting objectives and use of rigorous analytical techniques to decide on regulatory solutions (Baldwin 2005, Radaelli and de Francesco 2007, Bartle and Vass 2008: 52). The aspiration has been to move away from ad hoc decision making towards more formalised procedures, including analysis of costs and benefits, to ensure regulations are transparent and consistent. Better regulation principles have been articulated including transparency, accountability, consistency, proportionality and targeting, and the regulatory impact assessment has been developed as an analytical tool. The regulatory impact assessment is designed to inform policy decisions and involves 'an assessment of the impact of policy options in terms of the costs, benefits and risks of a proposal' (Cabinet Office 2003: 5). According to the UK government's Cabinet Office the impact assessment process enables policy makers to: think through the full impact of the proposals; identify and assess alternative options; ensure a meaningful consultation process with a wide range of stakeholders is undertaken; determine whether the benefits justify the costs; and determine whether particular sectors are disproportionately affected (Cabinet Office 2003: 5).

The parallels and connections between NPM and risk-based regulation and better regulation are clear. The changes associated with NPM, such as explicit standards and performance measures, private sector styles of management, and discipline and parsimony in resource use have been especially relevant to the rise of risk-based regulation (Hutter 2005: 2). Furthermore, risk-based approaches, better regulation and the regulatory impact assessment have not been limited to utility regulation but are expected to be applied across a wide range of policy-making areas. Indeed, the term 'impact assessment' has now been adopted by the UK government and used elsewhere to reflect the whole-of-government aspiration. However, it is important to note that as with NPM and utility regulation in general, they have developed separately. The connected ideas and discourse do not mean that one has shaped the other. Better regulation has an economic policy orientation and emerged from concerns about economic performance while NPM is focused on the organisation and workings of the civil service (Radaelli and Meuwese 2009: 646–647). It is important to 'make every possible effort to avoid the somewhat obsessive trend to relate any policy innovation to NPM' (Radaelli and Meuwese 2009: 640).

Although the culture of targets, performance measurement and cost consciousness is deeply entrenched, it has also been subject to criticism even in the early years of NPM (Hood 1991). One criticism is that the changes amount mainly to language and emphasis; many of the ideas are not as new as the proponents proclaim and many old problems of public administration remain (Hood 1991: 9, Pollitt and Bouckaert 2004: 14). Another is that although ministers often wish to give the impression that decisions are based on quantitative indicators and technical analysis, and that they are somewhat distant from them, in reality many decisions involve trade-offs in values and are inherently political (Pollitt et al. 2004: 261). In addition, cost consciousness and cost-benefit analysis culture do not always have beneficial consequences: costs can increase and the focus can be on the wrong (and often easier) things (Dieffenbach 2009: 897). Cost-oriented techniques and cost-benefit analysis have also been subject to wide ranging criticism. It has long been known that it is often more difficult to calculate benefits than costs, particularly when the benefits are diffuse and not immediately tangible, such as environmental and social benefits, while costs are immediate and clearly quantifiable (Hutter 2005: 8–9). Moreover, meaningful cost-benefit analyses rely on good data, yet data is often unreliable or absent.

In regulation, there is evidence of similar problems in the use of the regulatory impact assessment (RIA). In many European countries there is a particular difficulty of separating the inherently political aspects of policy making from the technocratic aspects of the impact assessment. This manifests itself in different ways. In Italy, for example, it is not used effectively as there is a clash between the 'rather chaotic process of formulation of new legislation' and the 'idealistic rational-synoptic process' of the RIA (Radaelli and de Francesco 2007: 43). In France there is more central coordination, coherence and direction but the RIA is left to play a 'post-decisional role' to legitimise political choices. Experience in the UK is variable: in some technical and less politicised areas the RIA is undertaken in a rational way but in many areas there is political pressure for particular decisions and a 'tick the box' attitude prevails in the impact assessment process (Radaelli and de Francesco 2007: 43–44, Bartle and Vass 2008).

The whole-of-government organisations in the UK concerned with regulation (Better Regulation Task Force, Better Regulation Commission, Better Regulation Executive) and the National Audit Office (NAO) have clearly been strong advocates of quantitative analysis arguably to the detriment of suitable qualitative analysis. They have been especially focused on more quantification with little consideration of the limits of quantification and the need for complementary qualitative analysis. For example, an impact assessment checklist developed by the Cabinet Office states, in relation to risk assessment policy makers, that they should 'describe and quantify the current situation' without offering practical guidance when the situation cannot be quantified in any meaningful way (Cabinet Office 2003). When costs and benefits are analysed and there is uncertainty, the only advice is to 'use estimates and ranges', which in attempting to create certainty out of uncertainty can lead to a spurious impression of accuracy. The NAO, which has undertaken extensive evaluations of impact assessments about every year over the past decade, appears to suggest that more and better quantification is required rather than considering and assessing qualitative analysis. In 2007, for example, they noted that departments 'should promote the importance of quantification and a renewed emphasis on analytical techniques' but without a similar statement about qualitative techniques (NAO 2007).

Perhaps the nature of the utilities – a high technology industry with narrowly focused and specialised regulatory techniques – lends itself more readily to quantitative techniques. In a critique of risk regulation and better regulation techniques, Hood et al. (2001: 181) concluded that the impact assessment is focused more on technocratic processes of regulation – a narrow 'regulatory craft' – rather than for policy making. Perhaps the world of utility regulation is the most appropriate for 'regulatory craft' and utility regulators might be strong advocates and exponents of the practice.

However, the practice of the UK utility regulators towards quantitative analysis is more nuanced than the whole-of-government organisations and the technocratic nature of the utilities might imply. Interestingly, the utility regulators such as the energy regulator Ofgem, and the rail regulator ORR address the need for qualitative analysis in impact assessments (Bartle and Vass 2008). The ORR, for example, has expressed concern that the governmental guidance on impact assessments has placed too much emphasis on cost-benefit analysis using quantitative techniques and has noted similar feelings amongst other economic regulators. They note, for example, that decision making in practice diverges from economic efficiency and cost-benefit analysis. This is partly for legal reasons: their statutory duties require them to undertake certain activities and strive for certain objectives which differ from pure economic efficiency. They also state that many decision factors cannot easily be monetised and input into cost-benefit analyses. Other factors are considered separately and qualitative judgements are made about trade-offs between different decision factors.

The energy regulator, Ofgem, has also distanced itself from an overly quantitative approach to impact assessments, particularly the approach advised by the Better Regulation Executive (Ofgem 2007). It notes that 'we do not propose to use the BRE's template summary sheet on analysis and evidence. We consider that it places too much emphasis on quantified costs and benefits and overplays the likely role of CBA in Ofgem decisions given our statutory duties' (Ofgem 2007: 4). Later in the same document it notes that while quantitative analysis will be undertaken where appropriate, 'we will avoid spurious accuracy in any quantification where there is little reliable information or where there is considerable uncertainty' (Ofgem 2007: 25). Ofgem also addresses its use of qualitative analysis in impact assessments more explicitly and directly than the NAO does in its evaluations of impact assessments (Ofgem 2007: 25–27).

Utility regulation and its technocratic methods including risk-based regulation, better regulation and quantitative techniques are therefore not free of the problems of similar techniques deployed in NPM. While the broader government bodies such as the Cabinet Office and NAO have pushed for more and better quantification, those at the regulatory coalface, such as the utility regulators, are more nuanced in their response. Undoubtedly they undertake substantial amounts of quantitative analysis, but they also recognise the limits of quantification and stress the importance of good qualitative analysis.

Conclusion

Utility regulation and NPM are both rooted in the same political-economic trends and share many features, but they have developed in different ways and focused on different problems. Although it is important to observe similar trends, conflating the two can limit understanding (Radaelli and Meuwese 2009). They arose with different focuses – one on the economy, economic policy and economic performance, the other on the civil service and the management methodology. In particular, the core task of utility regulation is a narrow area of specialist micro economics, and a clear argument can be made for independent regulation based on the need for detachment from short-term political intervention to ensure long-term private investment by limiting the political risk involved in investment. This can be contrasted to the wide ranging areas of NPM. Compare, for example, the diversity within the management of the prison service, social welfare or vehicle licensing. All of these clearly have specialist knowledge associated with them but not as narrow, discrete or technical as utility regulation.

It could be argued that utility regulation represents a 'strong' model of independence and specialisation and might be free of some of the problems that have plagued NPM, notably the problems of policy coordination and of technocratic and quantitative methodologies. The argument of this chapter is that this is not the case. The specialised techniques of utility regulation and its powerful constituency of support for independence from government do not mean that it stands proud and aloof from the problems that afflict the many other areas of public management.

A central reason for this is that utility regulation is not simply a discrete and technical matter of economic regulation while other matters, such as social and environmental issues, are handled separately by others. Practice in the UK has shown that the many details of economic, social and environmental regulation are inexorably entangled with each other, inevitably leading to significant issues of policy control, coordination and integration. The complexity and interconnectedness of regulation also means that the adoption of technocratic methods, such as impact assessment and quantitative analysis, have their limits. Interestingly, practice in the UK shows the utility regulators are more conscious of these limits than the whole-of-government bodies promoting better regulation techniques.

These arguments do not lead inevitably to the conclusion that the specialisation and independence inherent in utility regulation are wrong in themselves and should be reversed. They do, however, show that there are no easy solutions to the age old dilemma between policy coordination and specialisation, and particularly that the complexity of utility regulation should be recognised (Prosser 1999). In UK utility regulation, the problems have been approached by placing statutory duties on the regulators and specifying procedures in problem areas, but much coordination, such as between the government and regulators in price setting, in practice is informal and has operated satisfactorily much of the time. As in NPM, in regulation there are still some significant problems of technocratic methods, particularly the idea that problems can be resolved with more and better quantitative analysis without qualitative value trade-offs. Despite some recognition of this by regulatory practitioners, many in government have simply strived for more and more quantitative analysis. The impact assessment, for example, is often too focused on 'econocratic' techniques (Baldwin 2005) and can often conceal difficult qualitative trade-offs that have to be made, and often there are 'ad hoc political judgements masquerading as technocratic expertise' (Hood et al. 2001: 184).

PART IV
NPM FEATURES

Structural Devolution to Agencies

Oliver James and Sandra van Thiel

Introduction

As part of the NPM reforms, there has been a major shift in a number of OECD countries to transfer central state activities to various forms of semi-autonomous body, a form of structural devolution often called agencification (Greve et al. 1999, Christensen and Lægreid 2001a, OECD 2002b, James 2003, Pollitt and Talbot 2004). This has led to a plethora of 'agencies' with different organizational, legal, financial and managerial characteristics and degrees of autonomy. Some examples are: Next Steps Agencies and Non-Departmental Bodies in the UK, the Dutch contract agencies and ZBOs, the Australian Statutory Corporations, the EU executive agencies, French Autonomous Administrative Authorities and public establishments (also in Italy and Portugal), and Scandinavian agencies and state corporations (Flinders and Smith 1999, Greve et al. 1999, OECD 2002b, James 2003, Pollitt and Talbot 2004, Pollitt et al. 2004, Allix and van Thiel 2005). These agencies have in common that they are still part of the public domain, perform public tasks and are usually funded by public means, but they differ in their degree of autonomy and in the way in which they are managed by the central government (parent ministries). Establishment and steering of agencies is generally carried out by the executive and/or ministries. Only a few types of agencies report directly to parliament, like the AAIs in France (Allix and van Thiel 2005) or bodies in US Federal Government where strong reporting lines to the legislature are common.

This chapter maps the different types of agency that have been created in a number of OECD countries. The first section discusses the different types of agency that have been established in various countries. The second section presents and discusses a number of explanations for the rise of agencies including the theory of delegation (Majone 2001), rational actor models like principal–agent (van Thiel 2001) or bureaushaping (James 2003), or the more institutionalist approaches such as the task-specific path dependency model (Pollitt et al. 2004) and the transformative perspective (Christensen and Lægreid 2007b). The third section examines the intended and unintended consequences of agencification for performance, especially the need for coordination and re-regulation following the separation of policy and administration, and the responses of the governments, such as the rolling back of agencies, mergers, and the implementation of new and restrictive regulation for agencies such as charter laws.

The fourth section concludes the chapter with an outlook to the future. What are the prospects for agencies and the agency model? While some authors claim that the attempts to reclaim the 'primacy of politics' or restore the 'whole of government' are new waves of reform, other authors challenge the idea that the pendulum is swinging back to the days of the 'old public management' (cf. Lapsley 2008).

Types of Agency

There are many different forms of semi-autonomous agency. In fact, most countries have created several different types of organizations, with different degrees of autonomy and control. The lack of a uniform definition complicates research into agencification, in particular comparative research, but efforts are being made to address this topic, see for example Smullen (2007), Moynihan (2006) and Pollitt et al. (2004). To overcome the definition problem and enable comparative research, a categorization of (groups of) agencies was developed by van Thiel, in conjunction with the CRIPO research network, with funding by COST (EU) (CRIPO 2006). This categorization is developed for agencies at national level only, and draws in part on Greve et al. (1999) (for more details see van Thiel and CRIPO team 2009) (see Table 14.1).

Research into agencification generally focuses on the types of organizations in category 1 and category 2, and sometimes on category 3 as well. We have included examples from a number of OECD countries in the table, which also shows that several countries have 'agencies' of different categories.

Category 1 bodies are characterized by a limited amount of independence, legally they often still belong to the national government, which is reflected for example in the fact that ministerial accountability still applies and/or that employees have retained their legal status as a civil servant. Most category 1 bodies are called agencies, Next Steps Agencies (UK), service agencies (Austria), executive agencies (Australia), Agenzia (Italy), agencies (Netherlands, Belgium), state agencies (Nordic countries) and so on. Category 2 bodies are statutory bodies, usually with legal independence from the state. They have more autonomy than the category 1 agencies, which is often reflected in limited ministerial accountability, financial freedoms and more market-like labour conditions. Typical examples are non-departmental public bodies (UK), ZBOs (Netherlands), public establishments (Italy, Portugal and France), and statutory authorities or bodies (several countries). The establishment of category 1 and 2 bodies is often referred to as 'autonomization'. The number of category 3 bodies – foundations and corporations established and/ or owned by the state (corporatization) – has only recently increased (from the 1990s on), but they are a familiar type of organization in all countries.

Table 14.1   Categorization of public sector organizations

Category	Definition	Examples
1	Unit or directory of the national, central or federal government (not local, regional or state)	Ministry, department, ministerial directorate/directorate general (DG), state institution. Examples found in all countries
2	Semi-autonomous organization, unit or body without legal independence but with some managerial autonomy	Examples: Next Steps Agencies (UK), contract/executive agencies (NL, B, AUS, IRL), central agencies (DK, SW, N), Agenzia (IT), service agency (A), state institutions (EST), central bureaus (HUN), 'Verket' (SW), indirect administration (GER)
3	Legally independent organization/body, based on *statutes* and with managerial autonomy (in some countries sometimes based on private law as well)	Examples: public establishments (IT, POR), ZBO (NL), NDPB (UK), parastatal bodies (B), statutory bodies or authorities (not corporations: A, EST, AUS, IRL)
4	Private organization established by or on behalf of the government like a foundation or corporation, company or enterprise (government owns majority or all stock, otherwise category 5)	Examples: commercial companies, state-owned companies (SOC) or enterprises (SOE), and government foundations. Examples found in all countries.
5	Execution of tasks by regional or local bodies and/or governments (county, province, region, municipality)	Examples: Länder (GER), regions (B, I, UK), states (AUS), cantons (CH)
6	Other, not listed above	Contracting out to private companies and privatization with government owning minority or no stock

Note: Examples taken from countries: Austria (A), Australia (AUS), Belgium (B), Switzerland (CH), Denmark (DK), Estonia (EST), Finland (FIN), Germany (GER), Hungary (HUN), Ireland (IRL), Israel (IS), Italy (IT), Lithuania (LIT), Netherlands (NL), Norway (N), Portugal (POR), Rumania (RU), Spain (SP), Sweden (SW), United Kingdom (UK).

In many countries the use of arm's-length bodies is a longstanding tradition (Schick 2002), for example in the Nordic countries (Christensen and Lægreid 2006), the Netherlands (van Thiel 2001), Belgium (Brans et al. 2006), Italy (Ongaro 2009), Australia (Wettenhall 2005a) and the United Kingdom (Flinders 2008). Their numbers have, however, increased strongly under the influence of the New Public Management (NPM) reforms, from the 1980s on. NPM included the creation of some new types of organizations as well, like the Next Steps Agencies in the UK, the executive agencies in Australia and the agencies in Belgium and the Netherlands (Flinders and Smith 1999, James 2003, Gains 2004, Pollitt et al. 2004, Wettenhall 2005a, van Thiel and Pollitt 2007, Hajnal and Kádár 2008, Verhoest et al. 2010).

Studies into the life cycle of agencies show a low mortality rate, few are abolished, but many move from one category to another (see for example Lægreid, Roness and Rubecksen (2006) on Norway). At the moment of writing this chapter, the most extreme form of such agency-'drift' (cf. Greve et al. 1999) is going on in the transitional Central and Eastern European countries (Beblavý 2002). To meet with the demands for EU membership, CEE countries have been changing the organizational status of many agencies, and imposing new governance regulations for their management, control and accountability. In most Western European countries, agency-drift has been mainly motivated by the debate on the democratic and control deficits of agencies (see also the third section below, on the consequences of agencification). Extensive agencification has led to fragmentation of the public sector because governments lack the instruments and authority to control agencies, make them accountable or intervene in case of ill performance (OECD 2002b, Boyne et al. 2003, James 2003, Pollitt et al. 2004, Vibert 2007). In response, several governments have presented reforms to counter the fragmentation and restore co-ordination. See, for example, the debate on restoring the whole-of-government in the Nordic countries, Australia and New Zealand (Gregory 2003a, Christensen and Lægreid 2007b, Halligan 2007c, Smullen 2007) and joined-up government in the United Kingdom (James 2004b). Nowadays, governments prefer to keep agencies closer to the government than before (cf. van Oosteroom 2002, and van Thiel 2008, on the Netherlands). As a result, many statutory bodies (category 2) have been moved to a category 1 status. However, agencification is still ongoing, including

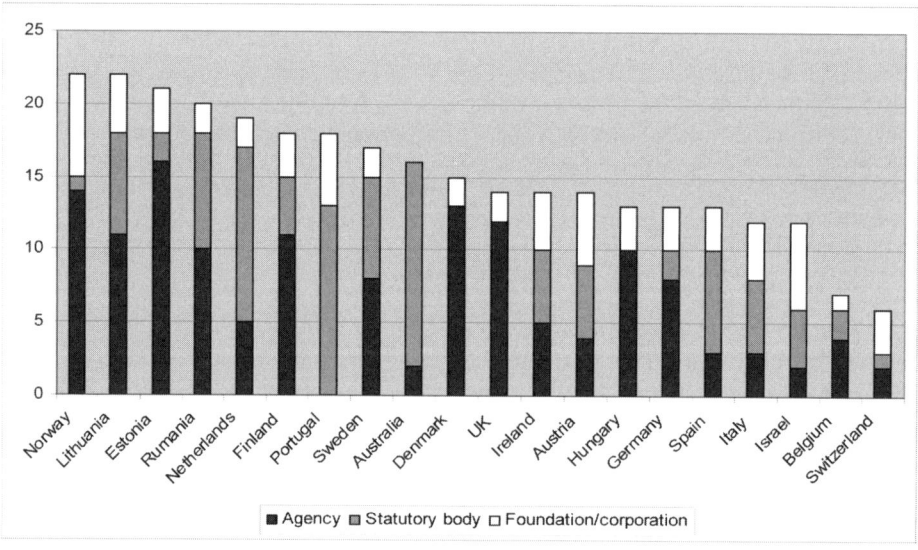

Figure 14.1 The number of agencies in charge of public service delivery, out of a total of 25 tasks in 20 countries

the creation of new statutory bodies (Lapsley 2008, van Thiel and CRIPO team 2009).

There are several noteworthy differences between the trajectories of agencification in different countries (cf. Pollitt and Bouckaert 2004). To illustrate this, Figure 14.1 displays how many out of 25 executive (service delivery) tasks have been agencified in 20 countries (adapted from van Thiel and CRIPO team 2009), but it does not include regulatory agencies which often have more formal legal autonomy.

Figure 14.1 shows that unitary states have agencified more often than federal states; federal states use decentralization and devolution more often to hive off certain tasks. Furthermore, the most frequent agencification is found in the Nordic (Denmark, Finland, Sweden and Norway) and CEE countries (Estonia, Lithuania and Rumania – but Hungary less); they have structurally disaggregated almost *all* tasks that were studied. However, there are big differences in timing; the Nordic countries have always used agencies whereas in the CEE countries many organizations have been established only recently (albeit through mergers and reshuffling of existing bodies). Overall, agencies of category 1 are the most preferred form and particularly in the United Kingdom, Scandinavia and Central Eastern Europe (particularly Estonia, Lithuania and Hungary, with Rumania being a little more diversified). The Netherlands, Australia and Portugal apparently favour statutory bodies most (category 2). However, while the Netherlands and Australia have longstanding traditions in using statutory bodies, the increase in Portugal can be attributed mainly to EU membership requirements, just like in CEE countries (Meyer-Sahling 2009). Finally, there are also countries without clear patterns or preferred agency types: Austria, Italy, Ireland and Spain. This raises a question, how can patterns of agencification be explained?

Explaining Agencification

To explain the existence and development of agencification, several theories have been used (see for example Pollitt 2004 for an overview). This section will discuss some of these, and their strengths and weaknesses. Two broad types of explanations – rather than group theories by discipline – for agencification have been studied by, among others, legal scientists, sociologists, economists, political scientists and public administration or public management scholars: rationalist and institutionalist.

Rationalist explanations focus on the 'utility' of creating agencies for parties involved, such as politicians, civil servants and civil society. Typical examples are theories like public choice, rational choice, game theory and neo-institutional economics. We will discuss three explanations of this type that have been applied to agencification: the theory of delegation (Majone 2001), principal–agent theory (see for example van Thiel 2001, 2008) and bureau-shaping (Dunleavy 1991, James 2003).

Traditionally, the delegation problem refers to the uncertainty of politicians regarding the way in which bureaucrats will execute the policy decisions made by politicians (Bendor, Glazer and Hammond 2001). The delegation problem is in essence a principal–agent problem; because of the information asymmetry between politicians (principal) and bureaucrats (agent) and their potentially conflicting interests, politicians have to decide how much discretion should be delegated to bureaucrats and how policy implementation can be controlled to ensure that outcomes will be as intended (Miller 2005). In economic theory, attention focuses on different forms of contract that might solve this problem, and the difficulties of writing such contracts when agents are not willing to accept the risk–reward contracts that are necessary to align interest. The theories examine, in particular, problems of adverse selection (where agents have private information about their characteristics that is not available to the principal before the relationship begins and which may adversely affect their pursuit of the principal's interests) and moral hazard (where agents may use their information advantage to hide underperformance). In the literature on delegation within the public sector several solutions are presented, mostly contracts, monitoring devices and administrative procedures (McCubbins, Noll and Weingast 1989).

Agencification has led to an extended delegation problem (van Thiel and Yesilkagit 2008), politicians charge bureaucrats with a certain task, which is then again delegated to agencies. This creates a cascade of principals and agents (van Thiel 2001), in which the distance between principal and agent (agency) becomes even longer. Moreover, agencies have more autonomy than bureaucratic divisions (see previous section), with less opportunities for intervention and control by politicians. Delegation theory focuses on two questions: under which conditions will politicians decide to delegate a certain task, in this case to an agency, and how can they reduce their uncertainty regarding agency performance?

There are two 'logics of delegation' (Majone 2001) that can explain why politicians will decide to delegate a specific task to an agency. First, agencification can contribute to the politicians' credibility. Agencification is used to de-politicize a specific task, as it is a testament to the willingness of politicians to refrain from political interference and claims. Second, agencification is expected to lead to an increase in the efficiency of decision-making and implementation. This is a motive which is also often discussed in the literature on NPM (Hood 1991, Hood et al. 2004, Pollitt and Bouckaert 2004). Because agencies are not part of the government bureaucracy, they can operate under different managerial conditions (cf. previous section). Moreover, some agencies operate in a market(-like) environment, which is also believed to contribute to efficiency gains.

The move to agencies is sometimes described as part of NPM borrowing from private sector management practices in an attempt to make services that are not privatized outright, but instead remain in central government control, to operate in a more 'businesslike' way (Lane 2000). However, the 'agency' view of the management control issue resembles a particular model of how business is done, focused on having clear delegated management control, often with a chief executive in command, operating in a clear performance regime, and with formal performance targets. Large multi-divisional companies are often managed in this way, split into specific business-focused accountable units. For example, in the UK, the reformers who created the 'Next Steps' agency reform drew on evidence from Imperial Chemical Industries (a multi-divisional firm) and British Rail (a divisionalized public corporation, James 2003). This model of how to organize big business is, however, different from that found in traditional German or Japanese capitalist models which instead typically focus on more collaborative managerial structures and place less emphasis on formal performance reporting (James 2001).

The following section will discuss the results of agencification in greater depth, but so far there is little clear evidence to support delegation theory. For example, politicians have kept on interfering with agencies, and not only in the case of incidents but also following political changes such as elections, new policy programmes or budget cuts (Pollitt and Bouckaert 2004). This kind of *ex post* haggling (Hood 2002a, Binderkrantz and Christensen 2009b) makes principals unreliable, leading to distrust by their executive agencies (van Thiel and Yesilkagit 2008). Moreover, the need to monitor agency performance has led principals to develop new regulations, appoint regulators and impose audits and evaluations (the 'audit explosion'), all leading to high monitoring costs, which threatens the cost-reduction objective of agencification.

Delegation theory offers an elegant but simplified model of a (one) relation between politicians and bureaucrats whereas the situation after agencification is much more complex. Next to political principals, bureaucrats (that is, ministries) have also become principals to the agencies. The current delegation models do not take such a plural principal problem into account (Miller 2005). Moreover, delegation theory – just like principal–agent theory – focuses most on the misbehaviour of the agent/agency, not that of the principal(s). However, delegation is a political act, and as such subject to political influences like elections, party pledges, unstable preferences and coalitions. Executive politicians may – often and do – decide to change the contractual agreements with agencies, or even retract their decision to delegate a task to an agency in the first place (Hood 2002a). Such (ab)use of their political primacy may, however, not improve their credibility, neither with agencies nor with civil society (van Thiel 2008). To better explain agencification, delegation and principal–agent models should pay more attention to the political aspects of the principals' behaviour and the fact that there are multiple principals. And as politicians and ministries may not have the same preferences, there is also a need for models on the role of ministries *vis-à-vis* agencification.

The bureau-shaping model of agency creation (James 2003), developing the general bureau-shaping theory of Dunleavy (1991) for this context, incorporates a model of politicians and ministries' or civil servants' preferences for the organization of government activity. The model suggests that, within constraints set by politicians, senior officials will apply bureau-shaping strategies to pursue work-related benefits from different organizational forms. The model has been applied to UK central government to explain why senior officials, faced with pressure to spend more time on the management of executive activities, passed on these activities for others to manage in agencies, enabling themselves to concentrate on their preferred policy-making tasks. Some of the apparently dysfunctional aspects of agency creation, notably inappropriate attempted separation of policy from implementation activity in some agencies, are partially attributable to over-enthusiasm for the use of the agency form by senior officials (James 2003).

Institutionalist explanations for agencification focus on the context of agencification, such as existing traditions, structures, norms and values. Whilst many rationalist perspectives acknowledge the existence of structure within which rational action takes place, institutionalist accounts place more emphasis on the context as a determining factor. These institutional variables are expected to influence agencification at all stages, from inception, to implementation, to daily functioning of agencies. We discuss three main forms of such explanations: the task-specific path dependency model (Pollitt et al. 2004), the transformative perspective (Christensen and Lægreid 2001a, 2006, 2007b) and isomorphism (DiMaggio and Powell 1991).

Agencification is an international trend (Pollitt et al. 2004), as shown in the previous section. To explain this convergence, many authors point to isomorphism (cf. Pollitt 2004), a concept originally coined by DiMaggio and Powell (1991) to describe the tendency of organizations to, over time, start to look and act more and more alike. DiMaggio and Powell attributed this mimicry to the need of organizations for legitimacy, in order to survive. By adopting legitimate standards (organizational formats, business techniques) organizations will be accepted by their environment and can thus continue to exist. The need for legitimacy is even more important than the need for efficiency, according to DiMaggio and Powell.

There are three different mechanisms at play. Coercive isomorphism refers to standards being imposed, like in the case of CEE countries that have to establish agencies to comply with EU requirements (see previous section). Mimetic isomorphism refers to the imitation of standards that are perceived to be successful. Agencification became popular at a time when administrative reforms were necessary because governments were faced with fiscal deficit and loss of legitimacy (Pollitt and Bouckaert 2004). Agencies were presented as a solution to both problems (see also above on the two logics of delegation). And finally, normative isomorphism refers to the adoption of standards because they have become 'the' standard, they are transmitted by 'change agents' such as consultants or international networks (like the OECD and the EU), or through the training and networks of bureaucrats and politicians.

Isomorphism thus tries to explain why so many governments, with very different political compositions and for different reasons, all have been very active in creating large numbers of agencies. However, it has proven difficult to really test this explanation, in particular because the three different types of isomorphism are very difficult to operationalize and disentangle (Mizruchi and Fein 1999). Moreover, in practice there is a large variation in the types of agencies, the pace of their establishment, and the conditions under which they work. Governments may use the same label ('agency') but interpret it in different ways (Pollitt 2001b, Smullen 2007). The theory on isomorphism does not offer an explanation for this variation, but the transformative and TSPD model claim they can.

Both the transformative perspective and the TSPD model attribute the shape and pace of agencification processes as well as the form and functioning of a specific agency to a mixture of variables. For example, whether or not a government decides to agencify a certain task (like health care, or more specifically hospitals), depends on the existing politico-administrative traditions (for example, is there a tradition of arm's-length government?), the legal system (for example, procedures for agencification, legal types of agencies), economic conditions (for example, need for budget cuts), the task at hand (for example, does this task require professional expertise which the government does not have, or, can output and outcomes be measured easily?), the history of the sector or organizations involved (for example, have there been many incidents of ill performance, or, is there a longstanding tradition of public–private co-operation?) and so on. These variables relate to different strands of theories, ranging from cultural and organizational studies to public management and institutionalism (Christensen and Lægreid 2001a, 2006, 2007b). And there is a resemblance to path-dependency models (Pollitt et al. 2004).

While these theories offer rich and realistic explanations and can indeed account for differences in agencification processes (described in, for example, OECD 2002b, Pollitt et al. 2007, Ongaro 2009), they also have two disadvantages. First, explanations are limited to (individual) cases. Contextual variables will differ from case to case and can therefore not be generalized to offer systematic explanations of agencification processes. Second, this type of explanation can only be constructed *ex post*, analysing agencification processes over time (see for example, Pollitt 2008). The history, or path, of an organization, task or sector is used to explain the outcome in the present. There is thus no room to make predictions about (differences in) agencification, which could be tested, making it difficult to undertake a systematic empirical evaluation of the relative merits of these theories.

The Consequences of Agencification

There are relatively few studies that have sought to assess the consequences of agency creation for service performance and other outcomes (Boyne et al. 2003, James 2003, Wollmann 2003). Instead, the focus of research has tended to move on to the next set of reforms (Gregory 2003a, Pollitt and Bouckaert 2004). Most of the extensive literature under the label New Public Management describes reform processes rather than evaluating outcomes.

Evaluation is difficult for several reasons. When agencies are established there are often no clear (measurable) objectives or targets set for the agency to achieve. In fact, agencification as a whole has lacked underpinning in most countries (except New Zealand, Boston 1995b). With the advent of newer forms of agency – like the Next Steps in the UK – it became more common to express, for example, expected efficiency gains. However, many evaluation studies still suffer from a lack of quantitative evidence about performance indicators because (i) no targets or norms were set, or (ii) tasks, services and goods cannot be expressed easily into quantifiable outputs. Many evaluation studies are therefore based on qualitative methods only (interviews, interpretation of documentation). Furthermore, as most agencies are monopolist providers of public goods or services, there are few benchmarks against which to evaluate performance and changes therein. Changes in performance can also be attributed to simultaneous other changes, for example other reforms, and changes in legislation or economic conditions (Pollitt 2008). Moreover, the structural disaggregation of the government, and hence decoupling from the budgeting system of the government, and the adoption of new management techniques (copied from the private sector) complicate comparisons of costs and outputs over time as they are expressed in different indicators. For example, the change from a cash payment system to accruals accounting in Dutch agencies (Ter Bogt and van Helden 2000) makes it impossible to compare revenues and expenses from before and after agencification.

The fact that many agencies are monopolists also makes it difficult for a dissatisfied government to impose sanctions, there is no real substitute as there is no market, and all costs of organizational changes will eventually have to be borne by the government (remember that most agencies are paid from public means). However, even if a definitive view of outcomes is difficult, some indication of consequences can be made. The following, therefore, discusses two examples of evaluation studies and their results.

The first example concerns a study of 72 executive agencies in UK government over a three-year period in the late 1990s assessing their economy, efficiency and effectiveness (James 2003). In economy, differences were apparent according to the funding structure of the agency. The creators of the agencies hoped for increased economy from the reform, at a time when the government was seeking to keep public spending in check. Non-trading agencies that were under direct budget control by their supervising ministries experienced a reduction in costs, suggesting the agency model can be used to constrain expenditure. The median score for non-trading agencies was a 5.3 per cent reduction in spending. However, trading agencies that charged customers directly for their services were able to increase their budgets, with a median score of an increase of 8.2 per cent. These findings suggest that freeing up trading agencies allowed them either to increase the services they provided or charge more for services or both. Whilst this did not put additional strain on public finances, it did not shrink the size of the state in terms of a pure measure of central government spending for this type of agencies. Overall, in real terms central government administrative expenditure rose from £12,863m in 1988/89, when the first Next Steps Agencies were created to £15,180m in 2000/2001, a rise of about 17 per cent over the period as a whole (all in 1996/97 prices, James 2003).

Efficiency and effectiveness of agencies is more difficult to assess than economy. However, the bodies were all accountable to ministers who set performance targets for them which provide some indication, although not all aspects of performance were subject to targets. Performance against targets was assessed according to categories for a three-year period between 1995/96 and 1997/98. A large majority of executive agencies achieved most or all targets. However, six executive agencies,

8 per cent of those surveyed, achieved only half their targets or less. A further three executive agencies, 4 per cent, hit very few of their targets. However, targets changed frequently and they give only a partial view of performance, although, being set by ministers, they do at least reflect this important stakeholder group's formally expressed concerns about performance. There were reorganizations to several of the poorly performing bodies. The Child Support Agency was abolished and its functions transferred. However, bodies that performed well under the targets were not immune from change either, see, for example, the Benefits Agency, in part because of their consequences for systemic government performance.

The second example is the meta-evaluation of EU agencies (Eureval 2008), which covers 26 agencies, over the period 2000–2007. It reports in general terms – based on a meta-analysis of individual evaluations – about, for example, the rationale for their establishment, their coherence with EU policies and internal coordination, effectiveness, productivity and management. Some important conclusions are:

- The rationale for establishment is opaque, there is a general reference to the conditions for establishment of an agency, but no explanation why the agency form is considered the best option for a certain policy.
- Agency strategy is coherent with the EU policy agenda, but whether and how agencies (can) contribute to the development of new policies (of good quality) is unclear. The role of agencies in policy making is underdeveloped.
- Cost-effectiveness is hardly ever measured. Individual evaluation reports report on customer satisfaction figures (usually positive) but other measurements are missing, for example about productivity. Internal efficiency is often reported to have been improved though. The management of agencies is, however, evolving slowly, particularly in the field of human resource management and results-based management.

The evaluation study concludes that individual evaluations pay uneven attention to different topics. Problems in previous periods have been addressed and repaired, but there are still some unresolved problems like the assessment of productivity and other performance measures which would enable the Commission to control agencies on the basis of results.

The conclusions of the two examples above are largely indicative of what has been going on in other countries as well (see for example Lægreid and Verhoest 2010). In general, in non-financial terms, agencification has allowed governments to reduce, for example, the number of civil servants (OECD 2002b, Pollitt and Bouckaert 2004) and improve customer service, but has at the same time created extra expenditures because of transition costs, installing new accountability and monitoring mechanisms (Flinders 2008) and investments in quality improvement (see for example van Thiel 2001, on two Dutch cases).

Agencification has also led to some unintended consequences and new problems, in particular increased fragmentation and a heightened need for coordination (cf. James 2003, Pollitt and Bouckaert 2004, Christensen and Lægreid 2006), although there are different patterns in different countries (Bouckaert,

Peters and Verhoest 2010). Depending on state traditions, history with agencies, the size and type of agencification, countries have responded by developing new coordination mechanisms such as coordinating agencies or committees (the UK and New Zealand), exercising more managerial, financial or performance control and increasing accountability requirements (Sweden), setting up more regulations for the establishment of different types of agencies (the Netherlands) or by matching the development of agencification with an increased consolidation of central powers of the state (France, Belgium).

The problems associated with agency structures, especially problems of fragmentation, coordination and systemic performance, have driven reforms in agencified systems. In the most extreme cases this has resulted in reintegration of activities into their supervising department or transfer of the function to another type of body (agency-drift, see for example Lægreid et al. (2006) on Norway, James (2003: 134–136) on UK, and van Thiel (2004) on the Netherlands), or elimination of the function, although these have tended to be rare (but see Ongaro (2009) on Italy where reforms have declined). In most cases, attempts to mitigate the problems of fragmented systems supplement agency structures rather than remove them completely (also known as layering and sedimentation, see for example Christensen and Lægreid 2008).

These supplementary structures have taken on different forms. Figure 14.2 summarizes these in four approaches which governments – the examples are taken from the UK – have used to counter fragmentation (James 2003: 136–146). Sporadic links rely on relationships developing between autonomous agencies on a case-by-case basis. An example of such individual arrangements concerns the appointment of liaison officers or account managers within ministries, to maintain all contacts with agencies (van Thiel and Pollitt 2007). In contrast, regulated networks involve a higher-level authority imposing an element of steering and more formal and enduring relationships being developed between agencies themselves. Agency networks are becoming more and more common, particularly in the field of regulation where even international (or transnational) networks are developing, particularly in the case of regulatory tasks in which the EU is involved. In between these categories are networks of agencies left to develop by themselves, and a regulated approach to encouraging agencies to cooperate from time to time as needed. As agencies have 'matured', they have become self-aware and sometimes powerful actors (see for example Rommel and Christians 2009, and Verschuere 2009, on Flemish agencies). As a result, we can now find examples where agencies have initiated new forms of accountability (Schillemans 2008) or voice their discontent about the relationship with parent ministries openly.

Conclusion: The Pendulum Swing?

This chapter has demonstrated that agencification has spread extensively throughout the public sectors of many OECD countries. The growth has been in

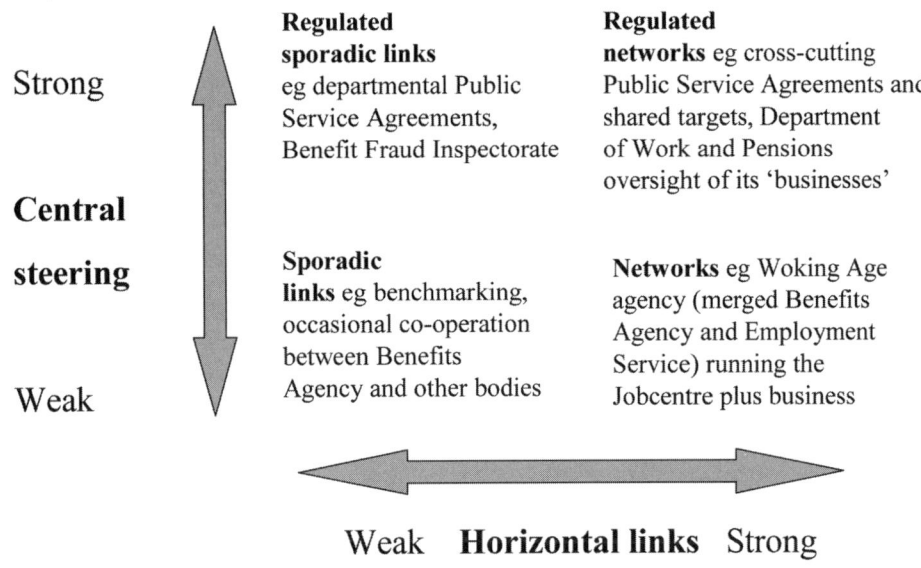

Strong

Regulated
sporadic links
eg departmental Public
Service Agreements,
Benefit Fraud Inspectorate

Regulated
networks eg cross-cutting
Public Service Agreements and
shared targets, Department
of Work and Pensions
oversight of its 'businesses'

Central

steering

Sporadic
links eg benchmarking,
occasional co-operation
between Benefits
Agency and other bodies

Networks eg Woking Age
agency (merged Benefits
Agency and Employment
Service) running the
Jobcentre plus business

Weak

Weak   **Horizontal links**   Strong

Figure 14.2 Structures for coordinating agencies, with examples from the UK
Source: James (2003).

terms of the number of agencies, the budgets they control and the range of policy
sectors in which the organizational form is found. There is considerable variety
of types of agency but all share the feature of structural devolution in some form
to semi-autonomous units. This organizational form structures the way public
policy is developed and implemented. Whilst the evidence about performance is
fragmented, a general pattern appears to be that the agency forms can help focus
attention on the organizations' core business. In some sectors, where the policy
issue requires the agency to be involved in joint working and where coordination
of bodies is required, there is some evidence of agencies contributing to systemic
performance problems, especially where agencies focus on narrow organizational
performance targets or develop idiosyncratic ways of working that can, for example,
inhibit staff transfer and communication across the public sector. In a number
of countries agencification has led to fragmentation and loss of coordination.
Governments have responded in different ways, ranging from consolidation of
state powers, to reducing the number of types of agencies, or by developing new
coordination instruments and mechanisms.

Are agencies here to stay? Based on the analysis, the answer would be 'yes' for
two reasons. First, agencies are not a new phenomenon and most countries had
arm's-length bodies before NPM, although the recent reforms have increased their
use (see the first section, above). Public sector organizations in general tend to have
a long lifespan (Kaufman 1976) and the longevity of earlier agencies suggests that

the more recent, similarly structured bodies may well endure. However, the low mortality rate does not preclude change in their exact form (see the first section, on agency-drift). Second, reforms to mitigate some of the undesirable consequences of agencified systems have been supplementary rather than moving away from the use of agency structures. There has not been extensive de-agencification in the majority of countries, although there have been some exceptions, see Denmark (Jørgensen and Hansen 1995). Reforms such as post-NPM (Christensen and Lægreid 2008), whole-of-government (Gregory 2003a, Halligan 2007c) and joined-up government (James 2003, 2004b) do not appear to be replacing agencies, but instead supplement them. In this way, agencies appear to be here to stay, making academic study particularly important.

Several priorities for research on agencies are suggested. First, there is a need for longitudinal study of structures to track the different transformations that agencies undergo (see for example Lægreid et al. 2006, who use such a design). Second, there is a need for more comparative research. The categorizations discussed in the first section above could be used to compare types of agency and agencification processes across and between countries. Third, a systematic analysis of the contribution of agencies to performance is called for, in terms of economy, efficiency and effectiveness. Fourth, there should be analysis of the contribution of agency management, particularly the phenomenon of the chief executive, to the policy and performance of the agency (Boyne et al. 2010, Boyne, James and Petrovsky 2010). For example, agency managers are supposed to be more accountable for performance than traditional public servants, but are they held accountable for performance? Does the institution of new management at the head of an agency bring about a change in performance? Research in other contexts suggests that senior management change can improve the performance of poorly performing agencies but damage performance when a body is performing well (Boyne et al. 2010). And finally, work should be done to examine the pattern and consequences of bureaucratic-politician relationships across the agency/parent ministry separation and how agencies sit within broader networks of policy making and implementation. Taken together, these questions provide a broad research area on agencies for future research.

Managing Performance and Auditing Performance

Vital Put and Geert Bouckaert

Introduction

The history of public sector performance has been described extensively and demonstrates that there always was a concern for performance in the public sector (Bouckaert 1990, Williams 2003). However, its content, form and importance has changed over time. The history of managing performance has also been described extensively, and received a higher level of attention in the last 30 years with the so-called New Public Management (NPM). NPM has evolved, but the focus on performance and on managing performance has remained. Auditing performance is part of the dynamics of managing performance. This chapter will discuss the interactions of managing performance and auditing performance, more particularly the interactions of recent stages of managing performance, namely NPM, and of external performance audit, namely by Supreme Audit Institutions (SAIs).

Managing Performance

Managing performance consists of measuring performance, integrating or incorporating measured performance information, and using it. The history of managing performance could be summarised in four pure types (Bouckaert and Halligan 2008): performance administration, managements of performances, performance management and performance governance.

'Performance administration' limits its use to administrating data and information on performance which is mostly defined as inputs and processes for the purpose of reporting to internal or external hierarchies. Since inputs refer to financial inputs and processes to due procedures, audit is mostly limited to financial and compliance audits to guarantee reliability of information provided. This type of managing performance is not subject to our attention in this chapter.

'Managements of performances' refer to disconnected systems within segmented organisational silos and/or management functions (personnel, finance, strategy, communication, production and so on). Performance audit is subject to this fragmentation and lacks also consolidation.

'Performance management' remedies the previous deficits in developing a consolidated and coherent perspective on performance which is applied organisation-wide in its measurement, incorporation and use. Performance audit, internal as well as external, has the capacity to be coherent and consolidated, covering all aspects of economy, efficiency and effectiveness.

Finally, 'performance governance' opens the box to the organisation's citizens/ customers, partners and stakeholders. This implies involvement of a range of actors in measuring, incorporating and using, therefore in managing performance, not just the public sector organisations. Performance audit receives a broad, beyond the borderlines, and consolidated focus which includes partnerships, value-added chains, cross-border delivery, shared services, co-production and so on. These performance governance audits are stretched beyond single organisations and become joined up. It is clear that evaluations and broad policy reviews are coming close to this type of performance audit.

A second issue is understanding the changing relationship between managing performance and auditing performance (Figure 15.1). To the extent that internal control systems to manage performance are present, external audits (by SAIs) consist of only the two traditional audits, financial and compliance. In a pure NPM context, which is the most extreme shift, three changes occur. Internal audit is added and moved in between internal control and external audit. Second, part of these three functions may be contracted out. There is outsourcing of internal audit, which does not turn it into external audit, and there is outsourcing of external audits by SAIs. Third and content-wise, performance audit is added to the package of internal and external audit. One question is to what extent external audit is adjusted as a consequence of an emerging and institutionalised internal audit. This

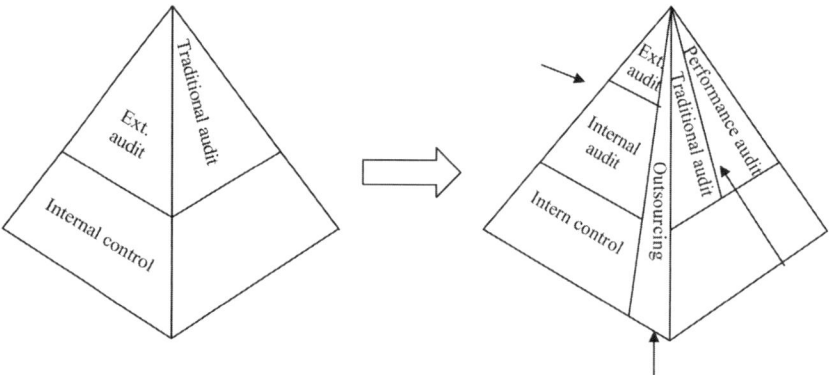

Figure 15.1 Shifts in managing performance and auditing performance

shift between the two pyramids outlined happens in different countries differently according to the variations in managing performance. It is also clear that the second pyramid is not a final position. Tensions between actors, incompatible assignments, administrative overload and reversals of NPM practices have resulted in shifts beyond the second pyramid.

Within OECD countries, even those that were not NPM-fundamentalists or those that have retreated from pure NPM models, the issue of managing and auditing performance remains still very much in the frontline (OECD 2009b, Van Dooren et al. 2010).

Performance Auditing and New Public Management

This chapter is not about the relationship between public management reform and audit in general, it is about the relationship between one particular type of public management reform, New Public Management (NPM), and one particular type of auditing, namely performance auditing (PA) by Supreme Audit Institutions (SAIs). INTOSAI[1] defines performance auditing as follows:

> *Performance auditing is concerned with the audit of economy, efficiency and effectiveness and embraces: audit of the economy of administrative activities in accordance with sound administrative principles and practices, and management policies; audit of the efficiency of utilization of human, financial and other resources, including examination of information systems, performance measures and monitoring arrangements, and procedures followed by audited entities for remedying identified deficiencies; and audit of the effectiveness of performance in relation to achievement of the objectives of the audited entity, and audit of the actual impact of activities compared with the intended impact. (INTOSAI 2004: 11)*

In reality most performance audits concern an assessment of management and/ or policy practices, rather than a direct assessment of effectiveness and efficiency (Pollitt et al. 1999, Put 2006).

A New Public Management environment is characterised by the following elements (Hood 1991, 1995, Pollitt 1995, Shand and Anand 1996, Leeuw 1996):[2]

- reducing the role of the public sector (privatisation, budgetary cuts, deregulation, …);

---

1   The International Organization of Supreme Audit Institutions, the umbrella organisation of SAIs, with currently 186 members.
2   This list is not exhaustive and the mix of these elements varies from country to country. Several elements are not an exclusive characteristic of NPM, but NPM has increased their application.

- shift to more competition by greater use of market-type mechanisms (outsourcing, creating internal markets, public–private partnerships, user fees, vouchers, …);
- disaggregation of bureaucratic organisations into separate agencies or enterprises (very often a separation of the production of public services from purchasing them), often related to the department by a contract, and combined with more managerial flexibility in resource (financial, staff …) decisions ('let managers manage');
- using private sector management practices, for example performance management (results-focused plans, performance measurement, …), risk management, benchmarking;
- greater stress on cost cutting;
- changing incentives in managing people (term contracts, performance-related pay, …);
- increased emphasis on service quality improvement, on treating service users as 'customers'.

In addition to NPM, there are several other factors that shape(d) the evolution of PA and SAIs (see for example Nath et al. 2005, Ling 2007, Lonsdale 2007, 2008) – and which will not be addressed in this chapter, for example: parliamentary expectations, the 'institutional' heritage from financial auditing (for example transfer of concepts such as internal control …); evolutions in information technology; the growing internationalisation (the role of INTOSAI, the growing importance of the European political level in EU countries, the influence of the OECD and the World Bank …); the personal influence of key staff members of SAIs.

The purpose of this chapter is to take stock of the existing knowledge about the influence of NPM on PA and SAIs as well as the influence of PA on NPM. The central question is how NPM reforms effected changes in SAIs and PA and vice versa. In order to answer this question we made a review of the existing literature. We found approximately 50 publications that addressed the relationship NPM <-> SAIs/PA, sometimes extensively, mostly briefly. An attempt to map the variables mentioned in these publications and their stated causal relationships failed because most variables were not well defined and the nature of the causal relationships[3] between these variables were seldom clarified. Therefore we returned to a more classical literature review.

Pollitt (Pollitt et al. 1999: ch. 4, Pollitt 2003b) offers a framework to describe how public management reforms could affect, or be affected by SAIs/PA. He sketches out seven possible connections 'outside-in' (from public management environment to SAI) and two possible influences 'inside-out' (from SAI to public management environment) and illustrates these with anecdotal evidence.

---

3   For example, a 'cause' can be necessary and sufficient or a cause could enable a consequence without being necessary and sufficient, or a cause could be a necessary but insufficient condition; cause and consequence could have a third, common cause; causality can be circular; some causes drive certain changes, other causes inhibit these changes; …

'Outside-in' – effects:

1. Public management reformers could reform SAIs' position or mandate (for example, altering their mandate or powers, restructuring).
2. Management reform might lead to changes in the public sector which alter the audit field (for example, shifting public–private boundaries, decentralisation may increase the number of entities to be audited).
3. The adoption of new management techniques could affect the nature of the auditor's task (for example, specialist skills are required to examine private finance issues).
4. The adoption of new management techniques could affect performance audit by generating new data (for example, the availability of performance information allows new types of analysis).
5. SAIs could decide to apply new management techniques themselves (for example, more contracting out, performance related pay).
6. SAIs could give more attention to performance audit relative to their other activities (for example, increasing number of performance audits).
7. SAIs could apply performance related criteria (efficiency, effectiveness, service quality) more explicitly in performance audits.

'Inside-out' – effects:

1. Individual performance audit reports (or sets of reports) could lead to changes in the nature of management reforms (for example, improvements in the way performance measures are constructed, the imposition of new safeguards in cases of privatisation).
2. The cumulative weight of a series of SAI reports could influence the general atmosphere or debate around a management reform (for example, an increased sensitivity for the dangers that could accompany decentralisation).

In the next sections the existing literature will be read with the help of this framework.

'Outside-in': The Impact of NPM on the Evolution of the Audit Portfolio of SAIs

NPM > an increasing demand for external performance audits?
Performance auditing by Supreme Audit Institutions existed before NPM came into being. In many countries there is an unmistakable move towards performance auditing (Hood et al. 1999, Ruffner and Sevilla 2004, Sterck et al. 2005), however, on a worldwide scale performance audits are only conducted by a minority of SAIs. A survey of INTOSAI, conducted in 2007, revealed that the community of SAIs which conduct performance audits regularly and on a sustainable basis is still relatively

small: 'Probably less than 30 SAIs have well developed and stable approaches to this work'.[4]

Is this growth in performance auditing in certain countries a consequence of NPM? Or is it supply driven? Or is the emergence of NPM and PA caused by common factors (for example the need to control government spending, raising public expectations about the quality of public services, pressure for more government transparency and accountability)?

From a theoretical point of view the relationship between NPM and the demand for performance auditing by SAIs is not so clear:

- Some argue that NPM contributes to the spread of performance auditing, because it stresses the use of audit as a mechanism of control (Mulgan 2001). Even if this is the case, this seems to concern internal auditing: because of NPM reforms the number of principal–agent relationships within the executive increases (more agencies, more private contractors), so there could be an increasing demand for internal auditing to address agency problems. In this NPM environment the role of the external auditor is rather restricted. Glynn (1996) states that under NPM the auditor–auditee relationship is

    increasingly a relationship between the auditor and the contractor, so that performance review can be little more than a review of compliance with the contract. Even if services are delivered in-house there may well be a purchaser-provider split that makes it difficult for the auditor to question key performance standards.

- Another theoretical argument to reinforce performance auditing is that performance auditing is needed to evaluate NPM reforms. Broadbent and Laughlin (1997) argue that NPM reforms do need to be evaluated, among other things because of the considerable public money invested in implementing these reforms and the limitations of the economic reasoning that underpins NPM reforms. Leeuw (1996) argues that performance auditing makes it possible to distinguish the ambitions and intentions of NPM from its realisations and that auditing could unravel possible unintended and undesired consequences of NPM. Of course this information need could also be filled by scientific research or evaluations; performance auditing is not the main source of this kind of information.
- Others argue that NPM creates alternative control mechanisms (financial incentives, competition, …) and in such a way reduces the need for (external) auditing.
- Some authors (Leeuw 1996, Shand and Anand 1996) state that the relationship between PA and NPM is not without difficulties: the focus of auditors on procedures may be too limited to be valuable for performance improvement

---

4   INTOSAI (Professional Standards Committee), PAS draft memorandum to the PSC, 2007, 2–3: http://psc.rigsrevisionen.dk/composite-238.htm [accessed: 09/08/2010].

and the fault-finding approach of auditors does not give a balanced view of performance. The literature on role conflicts, which will be considered hereafter, also illustrates that the relationship between NPM and PA is not so obvious. This also demonstrates that it would be too simplistic to state that the growth of performance auditing correlates with the growth of NPM.

There is not much empirical research that supports or dismisses a causal relationship between NPM and the growth of external performance auditing. Power (1997, 2005) claims that there has been an audit explosion in the UK and attributes this increasing demand to the rise of NPM, increased political demand for accountability and transparency (on behalf of citizens, taxpayers, …) and the rise of quality assurance models of organisational control. Hood's research (2004) puts Power's findings into perspective. Hood studied the evolution of control over the public sector in eight different countries and three different policy domains. His research shows that an audit explosion was not widespread across different countries and policy domains. The development of an audit explosion was especially observable in certain policy areas (schools, universities, health and social care) in the UK.

NPM > new types of audits

The privatisation of public services has led to new types of performance auditing: on the one hand there are audits of the privatisation process (a once-only wave that stops when most assets have been sold) and on the other hand there are audits of the regulatory bodies that have been created after privatisation to protect customers and to promote competition (Hodges and Wright 1995, Hodges 1997, Torres and Pina 1999).

The increasing availability of performance information has also led to a new type of performance auditing to assure the quality of this performance information and/or the underlying systems: the audit of performance information (Barzelay 1997, Pallot 1999, Bowerman and Humphrey 2002, Azuma 2003, 2004, Schwartz and Mayne 2005, Gendron et al. 2007, Lonsdale 2007). This type of audit is very similar to the traditional role of assuring the credibility of financial information. In some jurisdictions (Finland, New Zealand, Sweden, UK) SAIs routinely audit performance reports. In other countries there is no general requirement to audit performance information, and this type of performance auditing is conducted ad hoc as a part of their general performance audit mandate.

NPM > new methods of data collection and data analysis in performance auditing

Lonsdale (2000) studied the development (from the 1980s to the 1990s) of methods used in performance audits in five countries (Finland, France, the Netherlands, Sweden, UK), on the basis of report analysis and interviews, and found that these SAIs employ a wider range of methods in the most recent period (besides the classic techniques such as 'document examination' and 'interviews'), and that there was an increased consultation with users and providers of public services as well as with other interested parties. Several factors that encouraged a wider range of methods relate to NPM:

- improvements in the quality and quantity of performance information opened up possibilities to use methods such as benchmarking and examination of performance measures;
- the importance attached to the quality of public services has led to the use of instruments to measure customer satisfaction.

NPM > changing norms ('audit criteria') in performance audits

Put (2006, 2011) studied the norms used in performance audits of the Dutch Algemene Rekenkamer (ARK) and the UK National Audit Office (NAO) based on an analysis of audit reports. Both SAIs emphasise results-focused management practices (formulating objectives, measuring performance, …) or results-focused policy practices (in case of the ARK), which are associated with NPM. The other characteristics of NPM are less visible in reports of the ARK. By contrast, in reports of the NAO a number of features can be found that are associated with an NPM environment: a strong emphasis on cost cutting, an emphasis on service quality, the importance attached to comparing performance with other organisations and a deal of attention on market-type mechanisms (outsourcing, public–private partnerships, …) without questioning them (Ling 2003). These differences between ARK and NAO correspond with differences in the scale of NPM reforms in both countries, the UK went very far in market-oriented NPM reforms, the Netherlands followed a modernisation strategy (see Pollitt and Bouckaert 2004), but also with other emphases in the mission and strategy of both SAIs (the NAO primarily wants to contribute to performance improvement, for the ARK accountability towards parliament is the ultimate mission). In the same study the relationship between the management environment and the nature of the norms in use is demonstrated (for example, without explicit goals – in strategic plans or performance agreements – and without data on effects, audits of effectiveness are not feasible; if there are no data on costs and outputs, efficiency-audits become difficult; …).

NPM > changing approaches of selection of topics for performance audits

Put and Turksema (2011) show how several features that are associated with NPM also influenced the way SAIs select topics for performance audit. SAIs increasingly tend to inform the process of selecting topics by employing a system of risk analysis to detect (potentially) failing public organisations, policies, functions, … and by using long-range strategic plans (for example, giving priority to certain policy areas, supporting public management reforms of the government, …). Both tools are inspired by private sector management techniques. The availability of performance information also enables a more profound analysis in the selection phase of a performance audit.

'Outside-in': The Impact of NPM on the Functioning of SAIs

NPM > performance management within SAIs and the way SAIs account for themselves

More and more SAIs measure their own performance (Azuma 2004, UN and INTOSAI 2007, European Court of Auditors 2008). INTOSAI is also interested in this topic, as is shown by a recent symposium (UN and INTOSAI 2007) and by the creation of the Working Group on Value and Benefits of SAIs within INTOSAI (INTOSAI 2009). The degree to which SAIs have adopted performance measurement mirrors the extent to which NPM reforms have been adopted in the country concerned: SAIs who are convincingly embracing NPM (UK, Finland, Sweden) give information about the performance of their own work and justify the reason for their existence by the results achieved; SAIs who belong to the 'constitutionalist' camp (France, European Court of Audit) do not (Pollitt and Summa 1997).

NPM > increasing role conflicts within SAIs

Traditionally the mission of SAIs was to assist their parliament in holding government to account. An accountability relationship is a triangular relationship (parliament/principal – auditee/agent – auditor), premised on distrust, in which the auditee is an object of audit; the focus is on accounting for the past, the audit report is made public. Increasingly SAIs add to their traditional mission that they want to improve the performance of the public administration. In contrast with an accountability relationship, this is a one-to-one relationship, based on trust, in which the auditee is a subject that takes part in deciding what happens; the focus is on problem solving for the future, the approach is more delicate. This improvement role is more compatible with the objectives of NPM. But even if a SAI emphasises its improvement mission, it continues to function in structures that are focused on accountability. This creates conflicts and SAIs can employ various strategies towards these conflicts. Azuma (2003, 2004), for example, describes – based on a field survey conducted in 2000–2001 (Australia, New Zealand, United Kingdom, United States) and 2003 (France, Germany, the Netherlands) – how SAIs play a pro-active role in helping to realise the effective implementation of NPM-reforms (privatisations and public–private partnerships, performance-based management, reform of accounting and budget systems). He considers this active incorporation of NPM efforts as natural because the objectives of NPM and SAIs are the same.

However, most articles give a more problematic picture and focus on the role conflicts, dilemmas and so on provoked by NPM reforms. Gendron et al. (2001) show that the role of the state auditor in Alberta (Canada) in the 1990s has significantly changed (compared to its role in 1979–80) from that of an auditor who detects and reports problems in public administration to that of a promoter of a particular accountability arrangement (that is, the 'performance-accountability framework' of Alberta). The office designates auditees as 'clients' and offers help and advice. The office measures the usefulness of its work by the acceptance of the recommendations made. In this case the close association with NPM makes it difficult to sustain the claim that the office is able to provide independent assessments of public sector administration. Mulgan (2001), on the other hand, using federal and state examples in the Australian context, states that the emphasis on results provides a new role for SAIs. But SAIs are not only concerned with effectiveness and efficiency. They also stick to values such as accountability and transparency. This may set up tensions with the more managerialist approach, especially on issues such as outsourcing (with an over-use of 'commercial-in-confidence' disclaimers). Finally, Funnel (2003) states that

> in the exaltation of the three E's of economy, efficiency and effectiveness, tensions between the individual as citizen and the individual as consumer / customer can be forgotten easily.

Funnel argues that a redefinition of service delivery in technical terms emphasises the implementation dimensions of service delivery, rather than the underlying political choices and values (for example 'who gets what', equity, participation, …). Using Australian cases, he argues that NPM encourages a narrow, economic, managerial, conception of accountability which contributes to improved performance at the expense of constitutional, democratic accountability. Auditors-general question this evolution, and especially the consequences of contracting out (because there can be an imbalance between the benefits to private contractors and the government's continued financial exposure, because confidentiality clauses threaten the accountability of the executive to parliament, …).

A strong example of an open clash between an audit office and the government comes from the state of Victoria (Australia). In response to critical reports of the auditor-general (for instance of the governments preference for secrecy in its dealings with the private sector) the government tried to curtail the auditor-general's powers. This political attack was legitimised by an economic discourse on competition policy, which was common across the public sector: analogous with the separation of contracting from delivery, the right to conduct audits was taken away from the auditor-general and transferred to a statutory body, which had to compete with private audit firms for the conduct of financial and performance audits. All audits were put out to competitive tender. The role of the reformed Victorian Auditor-General's Office was reduced to facilitating audits (that is, to determine audit priorities, supervise audits conducted by others, report to ministers and parliament on these audit reports). This reform became a major political issue in the 1999 state election campaign. An alternative government was elected and the newly elected government restored the former powers of the auditor-general and enshrined them in the state constitution (Funnel 1997, Mulgan 2001, English 2003, Funnel 2003).

Jacobs (1998) provides an overview of the changing role of performance audit in New Zealand. Performance auditing was promoted by the Office of the Auditor-General as a solution to the problems of growing government expenditure, as a way to restore public confidence and to address demands for public accountability (1975–91). The Treasury also developed an alternative policy solution, involving radical (NPM) reforms of the public sector. With the change of government in 1984, a window of opportunity emerged. The 'Treasury solution' was implemented from 1984 to 1991. As a result, the Audit Office found itself sidelined. These reforms set off a process of conflict/competition between the Treasury and the Audit Office. In response the Audit Office redefined the role of performance auditing as a service to the parliamentary select committees (1992–97). Pallot (2003) examined the above-mentioned tension between the Treasury and the Audit Office in New Zealand as part of a wider conflict between a 'privatisation' agenda and a 'democratisation' agenda. Central to the tension are their different notions of accountability. The Treasury – dominated by economists – viewed efficiency as the primary goal; accountability is merely one of a collection of instruments to promote efficiency. The Treasury focused on intra-government managerial accountability. For the Audit Office, on the other hand, accountability is not just a means to an end, it is of fundamental constitutional significance in itself. The Audit Office focuses on accountability to parliament and the public at large. The Audit Office facilitated New Zealand's public sector reforms, especially in the development of performance reporting and whole-of-government financial statements, and to this extent can be regarded as legitimating them. But the Audit Office has challenged many aspects of NPM, such as the narrow focus on outputs, and advocated a wider accountability to parliament and the public at large, focused on information about outcomes.

In the Canadian case, Morin (2003) explores the dual role of performance auditors at the auditor-general's level. Based on her article, Table 15.1 provides a comparison of the auditor-general as a 'controller' and as a 'catalyst for change and improvement'.

Table 15.1 The dual role of performance auditors (based on Morin 2003)

	'Controller'	'Catalyst for change and improvement'
Mission	Informing parliament. The mission is accomplished when auditors identified deficiencies and informed parliament.	Encouraging improvement. The mission is to inform parliamentarians, but also to encourage improvement in public administration. Formulating recommendations is considered important.
Client	Parliament Keeps auditees at a distance.	Parliament, but auditees are also important clients.
Modes of influence	Dissuasion and warnings	Persuasion and advice
Relationship with the auditee	Negotiations between auditors and auditees are restricted to the cosmetic aspects of the report. Auditors consider themselves in a position of power in their interaction with auditees.	Open to negotiation with auditees. Do not see themselves in a position of power *vis-à-vis* auditees, feel engaged in an aid relationship with the auditee.

Morin argues that the transition from controlling to improving performance can hardly be expected to happen in the near future, because of several factors that relate to the mandate, knowledge base and culture of performance auditors in Canada. Significant arguments in this context are:

- the mandate of the auditors-general emphasises accountability (the auditor's alliance is with the public and parliamentarians, not with public managers);
- the Canadian performance audit framework has been borrowed from the financial statements audit that has been recognised as an instrument of control;
- the managerial logic that underlings' performance audit is highly influenced by classical organisation theory in which control occupies a predominant position; and
- the culture of performance audit practitioners is highly influenced by that of financial statements audit (most performance auditors have begun their careers as financial auditors).

In a case study of the French Cour des Comptes, Morin (2008b) illustrates how a traditional, judicial culture mixes with modern, performance-oriented culture and practices: the Court positions itself as judge in carrying out performance audits (this appears from the work methods adopted, the language used, the collegial decision-making process).

Saint-Martin (2004), also writing on the Canadian Office of the Auditor General (OAG), addresses the same role conflict and refers to three causes – which also relate to the mandate and knowledge base of performance auditors – of what he calls 'institutional schizophrenia':

- the OAG's mandate in relation to financial and value-for-money audit: when wearing the financial audit 'hat' the OAG focuses on control, processes and respect for rules and procedures; when wearing the value-for-money auditing 'hat' the OAG advocates fewer rules, less bureaucracy, risk-taking and a focus on results rather than processes;
- the combination of the OAG's institutional permeability (that is, it relies heavily on outside professional advice to fulfil its role) and the structure of the management consulting industry in Canada (which is dominated by accountants), so most of the advice comes from the world of 'management expert-accountants';
- the tensions between the 'negative' (paying attention to cases of waste and inefficiency) and 'positive' dimensions (best practice studies) of the OAG's mandate.

Finally, Barzelay (1997) explains why public auditors' commitment to performance improvement is not widespread. The public auditing profession exerts normative pressure to limit the audit body's role to that of strengthening the bonds of accountability. Furthermore, most audit executives operate on the basis of mental models of organisational change in which public criticism is a powerful motive force. Finally, the appropriations process rewards audit bodies for producing large numbers of reports; from the perspective of the audit body performance improvements are externalities.

In summary, it is not so obvious as it seems that NPM makes SAIs move to focus on performance. Issues of knowledge, culture and mandates easily turn the NPM agenda into a conflict of roles.

'Inside-out': The Impact of SAIs/PA on NPM

The performance audit work of SAIs can and does have multiple impacts (Van Loocke and Put 2009): it has an impact on the content and implementation of policies, it has an impact on the way governments account for their actions towards parliament, it can also have an impact on (new public) management reforms. This section focuses on this last category of impact. 'Impact' can mean many things (see, among others, Weiss 1979, Kirkhart 2000, Hanney et al. 2003); performance audits could, for example, have an instrumental, legitimising or conceptual impact on NPM.

PA > instrumental impact on NPM

The recommendations in performance audit could contribute to a better implementation of NPM reforms. For example, Ingraham (Ingraham and Moynihan 2001), based on a survey in the US states, argues that the certification of the credibility of performance information by Audit Offices contributes to the utilisation of this performance information.

Of course, instrumental impact raises the question of circular causality: to some extent auditees may implement recommendations because auditors formulate recommendations that match with the ideas and the current projects of the auditee. There is some research that supports this hypothesis. For example, Radcliffe (1999) illustrates how auditors map out what is possible to recommend (what the auditee is likely to accept) and make recommendations that appeal to local discourse. Morin (2001, 2008a) conducted two impact studies in Canada (on the federal level and on the provincial level in Quebec) and concluded that impact is determined by the nature of the audit process (interaction auditor–auditee), but also by the presence of favourable environmental conditions, such as the existence of a major reorganisation in the body being audited or a reform at the government level.

PA > legitimising impact on NPM

English (2007), substantiated by evidence from the Australian context, suggests that the audits of public–private partnerships offer inadequate independent oversight (so that it is impossible to conclude that Australian public–private partnerships deliver, for example, risk transfer, value-for-money savings) and may have more to do with legitimising government policies than providing that oversight. Broadbent and Laughlin (2003), in the UK context, come to a similar conclusion: they state that the adoption of Public Sector Comparators in NAO performance audits has legitimised the use of Public Sector Comparators to judge the value for money of public–private partnerships.

PA > conceptual impact on NPM
Performance audits can influence ideas about reforms and NPM reforms could be adjusted on the basis of performance audits (for example, being more attentive to the possible trade-offs between performance and ministerial accountability in outsourcing decisions or decisions to create agencies; being more attentive to the limitations and negative side-effects of instruments such as strategic planning, performance measurement; …). The above-cited literature on role conflicts (Jacobs 1998, Mulgan 2001, English 2003, Funnel 2003, Pallot 2003) is also relevant to demonstrate some forms of conceptual impact.

Conclusions

The existing evidence about the relationship between NPM and PA/SAIs may be summarised as follows:

- the (direct) relationship between NPM and the rise and diffusion over the world of (external) performance auditing is not so clear;
- the nature of performance auditing (methods of selection of topics, types of audits, methods of data collection, norms) is probably influenced by NPM;
- NPM has probably influenced management practices within SAIs (for example, performance measurement);
- NPM has probably reinforced role conflicts within SAIs (for example, conflicts between the 'accountability' role and the 'improver' role);
- there is evidence that PA has also had an influence on the implementation and adjustment of NPM reforms.

Figure 15.1 showed a shift from the first pyramid to the second. According to the NPM logic, shifting to the second pyramid constitutes a reform programme. However, some of the 'solutions' have resulted in new problems such as: administrative overload; dysfunctional effects of measuring, incorporating and using performance information; new tensions within organisations (for example, inspecting and counselling); competition for people between internal and external audit organisations; conflicts between public and private actors (SAIs and private sector consulting and auditing firms). As a consequence some countries have reversed this shift partly, for example by reducing internal audit, or by applying the performance logic in a pragmatic and reduced way ('comply or explain' in the Netherlands), or by moving to single audit principles. This proves that the NPM–PA interaction is multidimensional, sometimes ambiguous and definitely dynamic in its changing nature. This makes it a necessary topic for researching public sector reform.

Managerialism and Models of Management

Martin Painter

Introduction

Managerialism is a belief system that highlights the role of management and managers in providing solutions to social and economic problems (Pollitt 1990, Clarke and Newman 1997, Deem et al. 2007). At the root of managerialism is the assumption that in any enterprise or organization, managers are the most important people – more important than bureaucrats, clerks, accountants, teachers, doctors, nurses and so on. Private sector experience is, for the most part, depicted as the fount of most practical management wisdom, as it is argued that only in the face of market competition do core managerial values – efficiency, cost-effectiveness, quality, flexibility and so on – become imperatives, compelling managers to learn from mistakes and to innovate (Downs and Larkey 1986: 20–21).

Management as a distinct function in the modern workplace developed along with industrial mass production and it has been associated primarily with control and coordination of business enterprises. But increasingly in the twentieth century, management became associated with the reform and modernization of public sector organizations, a process which has been labelled 'managerialization' (Clarke et al. 2000: 6–10). Managerialism took strongest and earliest roots with respect to government administration in the USA. From the USA, management doctrines in government spread to other Anglo-Saxon countries and beyond. Generic management models in one form or another have been looked to as answers to many different problems of modern government, including controlling and administering the large-scale, complex mid-twentieth-century welfare state (Pollitt 1990); enhancing the accountability and responsiveness (as well as effectiveness) of conservative-minded public bureaucracies so as to make them better instruments of progressive reforms (Royal Commission on Australian Government Administration 1976); and cost-cutting and retrenchment in the Reagan/Thatcher eras and in the aftermath of the most recent financial crisis.

Managerialism as a movement is thus both older and also more diverse than NPM. NPM comprises a quite specific set of techniques, emphasizing the marketization of public service delivery. It has been labelled 'new managerialism' or 'neo-liberal managerialism' (Deem et al. 2007: 8). In Australia in the 1980s and 1990s, both 'corporate management' and 'market bureaucracy' ('old' and 'new' managerialism) appeared alongside each other as reform themes (Considine and Painter 1997). Following what some saw as the excesses of NPM, we are now in a phase of 'post-NPM' managerialism, emphasizing such things as partnerships, 'joined-up government', 'network governance' and 'collaboration'. The flexibility of managerialism in absorbing or generating new ideas and models is one of its distinguishing features. Indeed, in pursuit of new mechanisms of control and myths of success, managerialism often seems to value 'change for its own sake'.

The rest of this chapter follows four inter-related themes: first, it traces some of the intellectual roots of managerialism and explores the nature of the 'science' of management as a basis for managerial thought; second, it reviews debates about the appropriateness of managerialism in the public sector; third, it looks at some specific models and 'recipes' of managerialist thinking and practice; and fourth, it explores how these models have been translated into public management reforms in recent years in different contexts. The trajectory of managerialist thinking and practice as applied to public sector reform in recent decades is a global phenomenon, albeit with considerable variation in different contexts. Despite the ups and downs and swings of fashion in managerialist thinking, the core beliefs continue to drive much of public sector change and reform.

A Science of Management?

Both scientific research and practitioner wisdom provide managerialism with its doctrines. As Hood (1998: 173–174) points out, any 'what to do' set of ideas about complex social organizations, such as models and recipes for public management, are likely to resort to methods of persuasion other than truth claims based on scientific method – their rhetorical content is just as significant. At the same time, management thought has relied heavily on key breakthroughs in social science research, and we can identify a number of major strands or schools of management thought from these origins. Four such schools of thought will be briefly discussed: scientific management, human relations, system thinking and economic theories of organization.

F.W. Taylor's *Principles and Methods of Scientific Management* provided the basic text for the 'classical management school'. Taylor claimed that the scientific design of working environments, including pay and incentive schemes, could radically increase an individual's productivity and lower costs. Drucker (1976) asserts that Taylor was as important as Karl Marx and Sigmund Freud in his influence on the modern world. Pollitt (1990: 16) argues that 'neo-Taylorist tendencies' strongly influenced the direction of management reform in the UK in the 1980s and beyond, including such things as pay-for-performance. Taylor remains a controversial figure among scholars of management, being accused of 'dehumanizing' the workplace through mechanistic forms of control; on the other hand, he continues to have many defenders (Wood and Wood 2002).

Some of the more seemingly mechanistic tendencies of Taylor's prescriptions for reforming the workplace were challenged by a series of findings from the 'Hawthorne Studies' of the late 1920s. The work of their principal author Elton Mayo (1933) and other industrial psychologists made claims about the importance of informal aspects of organizations, as well as their formal structures and incentive mechanisms. Mayo found that incentive schemes could have opposite effects to those intended, because groups of workers cooperated informally and adopted defensive stratagems. This informal dimension of organization and the emphasis on group relations inspired the human relations school, which argued that managers must give more attention to the human needs of employees. Workplaces contain 'natural groups' and workplace performance rests as much on the satisfaction arising from membership of these groups as on the rewards and sanctions provided by the formal organization. Management techniques favoured from this perspective include flatter structures, more cooperation and greater employee participation. Yeatman (1987) argues that managerialism in its late-twentieth-century manifestations in Australian public sector reforms combined scientific management with human relations approaches, with an emphasis on both economizing and efficiency-related aspects of management and also 'soft skills' such as negotiation, communication, networking and stress management. Total Quality Management (TQM) echoes some of the ideas of the human relations school, seeking to internalize quality control as the responsibility of all workers through teamwork, not something to be imposed by control and inspection (Deming 1994).

The third set of ideas, loosely labelled system thinking, covers a very wide range of theories about decision making and organization. System thinking came to the fore in the 1950s and was particularly influential in government circles, as the origin of some of the ideas was in US military planning. One branch of system thinking, cybernetics (Ashby 1956), gave birth to ideas such as homeostasis, feedback loops and the 'law of requisite variety' as general principles reaching across natural, technical and social systems. System thinking has had wide-ranging impact in both highly technical management disciplines such as operations research and also in 'softer' fields such as human resource development. In organization theory, systems thinking also gave rise to the stress on how organizations adapt to their environments. From this viewpoint, 'contingency theory' attempts to identify the appropriate structures and processes for dealing with specific tasks under a particular set of environmental conditions (Woodward 1965, Pugh and Hickson 1976, Donaldson 1995: 32–41). Rather than a 'one-size-fits-all' approach, contingency theory looks to management solutions that are more tailored to the specific situation facing the organization. A contingency view of management places the onus on managers to scan their environment, strategize and consult stakeholders.

System thinking also led to an emphasis on planning and strategy, including the introduction of programme budgeting, management by objectives and policy analysis in the 1960s and 1970s in US governments. These approaches to public management presumed a collective capacity to make rational, forward-looking decisions and drew on decision-making theory. Herbert Simon's name is the one most often mentioned in the context of organizational decision theory. One of his most influential ideas is the concept of 'satisficing' (March and Simon 1958: 137–172) – that is, the way in which cognitive limits to decision making lead to stratagems that fall short of optimization, but nonetheless are 'organizationally rational'.

The final school of management thought to be mentioned is perhaps the one that has most contemporary relevance and influence: economic theories of organization. This way of thinking about management emerged somewhat independently. Donaldson (1995: 177–179) notes that many of the economists who theorize about management for the most part ignored previous contributions to organization theory. The most influential economic theories of organization are agency theory and transaction cost theory (Jensen and Meckling 1976, Williamson 1985). The first sees most management situations as problems of contracting between principal and agent, both of whom are conceived as self-interested utility maximizers. The trick of successful management is to get the carrots and sticks and the monitoring mechanisms right. Most often, the agent has the power of holding vital information as a result of being on the spot, and thus has many opportunities to cheat and shirk; the principal has the power to command and monitor and must provide the agent the right incentives to align the latter's interests with those of the principal. In transaction costs analysis, organizations are seen as a solution to market failure arising from close inter-dependency between two transacting parties. Such inter-dependency is open to abuses and to the costs arising from haggling, giving rise to the need for various remedies to align incentives and avoid 'rent-seeking'.

Economic theories of organization provide the intellectual inspiration for NPM, through instruments such as internal markets and contracting out. The entrepreneurial manager, whose work is deliberately structured to expose her to competition and risk-taking, is the new exemplar. One authority on management theory argues that this brand of management thought is in fact 'anti-management' (Donaldson 1995). Economic theories of organization treat managers as crooks rather than heroes. Most other schools of management thought by and large presume that managers are motivated by the desire to achieve the purpose of the organization. Economic theories of management may be said to be 'anti-management' also in the sense that all their prescriptions for successful management presume that a market solution would be the best. However, entrepreneurial management and market bureaucracy have become important tools and techniques of managerialism in the public sector.

The existence of a science of management with roots in academic research and social or psychological theories, while it creates a seeming confusion of different ideas and models, is nevertheless a source of respectability for managerialism. Also important for lending legitimacy is the existence of a global industry of management education training, centred on the world's leading universities. They offer a standardized global product, the Master of Business Administration (MBA), marketed on the basis that acquiring a prestige MBA has direct benefits in pay and rewards for the recipient. The MBA is sometimes a prized qualification for public management jobs as well, with a templated multi-disciplinary curriculum that emphasizes practice as much as theory. Indeed, the 'academic' and 'theoretical' basis of management thought is often down-played in these programmes. One feature of MBA education is the use of case studies to exemplify successful practice.

Consultancy firms are also important legitimizing and disseminating instruments of managerialist thought and practice. All large corporations, whether private or public, seem compelled to 'call in the experts' when they have a management problem, or want training in the latest ideas. The history of management consulting is intertwined with the history of business schools, with founders and partners being graduates and professors from schools such as Kellogg (Booz Allen Hamilton) and Harvard (Boston Consulting). The consulting industry boomed in the last few decades of the twentieth century, particularly in providing services to the public sector (Saint-Martin 2000, 2001: 590–594). International consulting firms played an important role in spreading the doctrines of managerialism and in bringing new ideas and fashions to governments across the world.

Management literature is voluminous and widely disseminated among practitioners, ranging from archetypical social science research in academic journals to 'how to do it' 'management guru' texts displayed at airport bookshops. Andrez Huczynski (1993) argues that these guru texts rely for their success on rhetorical devices rather than on the reliability or validity of their truth claims. Hood (1998: 176) makes a similar point, exemplified by the case of Osborne and Gaebler's (1992) best-selling *Reinventing Government*, which makes copious use of anecdote and selective examples, or 'fables' of triumphant managers who turned sleepy public bureaucracies around. Another important source of management texts and manuals is the publications of international organizations such as the OECD and World Bank. They bring together current thinking and they pronounce on the current 'state of the art', seeking to promote 'best practice'.

All these sources of managerialist ideas and models are global in their reach and have had profound effects, particularly in recent times, when the global circulation of people and ideas has accelerated. The clearest example of such a direct transfer of management theory into managerialist practice was the introduction of public choice economics (agency theory and transaction cost theory) into New Zealand state sector reforms by a small group of Chicago-trained Treasury economists in the mid-1980s. The sudden U-turn this represented for New Zealand, from a progressive, corporatist, statist tradition to a radically marketized system of government, was triggered by economic crisis and a change of government, with the radical new ideas ready-to-hand as reform became urgently necessary. What this illustrates, though, is not that managerialism is characterized by enjoying a 'direct line' to the latest 'scientific' theories of management, which in the right circumstances prevail over less 'truthful' or inappropriate models. Hood (1998: 190–191) uses this example to argue that the frequently noted phenomenon of 'fads' and rapid 'pendulum swings' in public administration may be a form of 'cultural shift', with new ideas suddenly becoming attractive at a moment of crisis because they are the polar opposite to an orthodoxy in decline and decay, and hence offer hope.

Managerialism and Government

The role and status of management and managerialism in public administration has often been a point of contention or, at least, of ambiguity (Pollit and Bouckaert 2004: 8–9). Managers as administrative leaders may have to compete for control with others in a way that is not quite the same as in the private sector. The claim that management is the most important function of these leaders is not self-evident. Other spheres of activity – in particular, policy (or politics) and the law – also make this claim. Policy overlaps with politics, so administrative leaders have to compete with political party leaders and other politicians in running government organizations. They routinely have to take politics into account in their own managerial activities. They may also have to compete with various 'policy professionals', some of whom give direct advice to political leaders. Formal roles and administrative cultures acknowledge these complexities, even in the face of managerialization.

As to the law, it is often claimed that the need for 'legality' is an overriding one and that this constrains the role and scope of management as an activity in government (Pierre and Painter 2010). Keeling (1972) embodied this point in his attempt to distinguish between 'administration' and 'management' in government, with the former concerned with review and enforcement of law, and the latter to do with the 'best use of resources'. In most Continental European administrative systems, the notion that high-level administrative and policy work are governed primarily by law and that jurisprudence is the most important dimension of 'statecraft' often leaves managers and management sidelined. Indeed, the penetration of managerialism into the public sector is much more an Anglo-Saxon phenomenon, although in recent decades countries outside this sphere have increasingly adopted public management reforms in one form or another (albeit often with quite different results) (Ongaro 2009). These differences are also reflected in the conception of the nature of the subject as it is taught in universities. Universities in the USA and in the UK, for example, often teach 'public management' (sometimes in Business Schools) whereas Continental European universities are more likely to call it 'administrative science' or plain 'public administration' (Pollitt and Bouckaert 2004: 10).

It has often been argued as well that managerialism misconstrues much of the work of public administrators by conceiving of their work as if it were a 'production process'.[1] Under this conception, the policy-making and administrative processes are ideally decoupled through insisting that political control and accountability should be confined by and large to two functions: first, setting objectives and second, evaluating and adjusting policy based on assessments of results, or

---

1   The following sections draw on Pierre and Painter (2010).

outcomes. Managers are left to get on with the rest of the 'business of government'. In the business production model, each production unit has a core, unequivocal purpose or set of production goals related to its often narrowly defined purpose and a specific set of customers. As a consequence, 'customer rights' and 'service quality' receive primary attention, while wider democratic principles such as citizen entitlements or third-party participation rights are sidelined. Integration of goals and values across related service functions and activities in larger, more 'general-purpose' public service organizations, which are monitored by more diffuse and diverse sets of policies and values, is sacrificed to permit managers to focus clearly on a single set of service objectives and clearly defined clients or customers. The clarity and simplicity of marketplace expectations such as 'good service' and efficient production are preferred to the ambiguity and complexity of conflicting political and social values.

By contrast, in the traditional public administration model, politics and administration are kept distinct in theory but in practice are closely coupled through mechanisms of control and accountability that are in principle unified and consistent across the public sector (albeit in pursuit of multiple and sometimes conflicting goals and values). At the core of this system is a generalized hierarchy of political control focused on the political executive, embodying not only the immediacy of policy control over operational matters but also a clear principle that public administration is regulated through universal attention to procedure for the sake of core democratic values of equity and access. Customers are no more prioritized than the general citizenry or specific constituencies of stakeholders, represented in many guises through multiple accountability mechanisms. Diverse procedural standards are given pervasive but often shifting attention: economy, attentiveness, integrity and probity, accuracy and dispatch, promptness, fairness and equity, anti-discrimination, preserving the environment or local amenity and so on (Dunsire 1986: 337).

In this traditional model, the organization of government is often less concerned with allocating separate service delivery tasks to production units than with collecting together related functions and activities within more common-purpose, inclusive politico-administrative structures. Thus, in traditional public administration, large-scale bureaucratic organizations tend to predominate over more disaggregated units focused on particular clients. They facilitate procedural consistency and, where there is ambiguity, its resolution through hierarchical authority. Where this aggregation becomes too cumbersome, multiple accountabilities are often handled by 'hiving off' or 'tacking on' para-state organizations or local self-governing bodies that reflect particular communities of interest. If these concerns can be handled through a dispersal of authority and power, the democratic principle of organization is often preferred to more technical, efficiency-based managerialist values.

Managerialists in response to such views make two arguments: first, they argue that most of the work of government – for example, service delivery, infrastructure provision, immigration control – is, in fact, able to be conceived and organized as a production process with inputs, throughputs and outputs. There can be no excuse, in this case, not to apply best practice principles of management in order to achieve the desired results at the least cost (Paterson 1988). Second, they argue that many traditional forms of public administration result in inefficiencies and roadblocks that are counter-productive, even for the achievement of values such as legality and equity. Multiple accountabilities create procedural delay and obfuscation; clients and customers lose their way in the labyrinths of multiple jurisdictions; citizens give up and lose trust faced with these complexities and confusions; those in authority lose control of the increasingly complex machinery; managers are deflected from their service delivery and production roles by the tasks of coordination and accountability; and so on.

For the most part, the managerialist view of things has prevailed in recent public sector reforms and the 'traditionalists' have been in retreat. However, as is discussed below, in acknowledgement of the force of some of the criticisms of the universal applicability of a simple production model of public administration, they have been making something of a comeback, arguing for the need to develop a distinctive public sector form of managerialism.

Managerialism and Central Reforms

Managerialism was an increasingly attractive set of doctrines for the organization and staffing of the public sector the faster government grew and the more services it delivered. In the USA in the 1960s and 1970s cost effectiveness analysis, programme budgeting and so on were applied at the same time as the federal government was expanding its role and introducing new programmes in poverty reduction, urban renewal and so on. These techniques were direct descendants of earlier managerial trends, beginning with the Brownlow Report in the 1930s and continuing through post-war initiatives in performance budgeting and efficiency analysis (Downs and Larkey 1986: 149–165). In the UK, a growing emphasis on the need for better management techniques across the senior civil service was evident in the Committee on the Civil Service (the Fulton Report) of 1968. The Report argued that there were 'too few … skilled managers' in the ranks of the civil service, which was dominated by the 'amateur, generalist or all-rounder' (quoted in Saint-Martin 2000: 76). Fulton argued that the civil service as then constituted was incapable of managing the welfare state and needed to learn from the private sector. He recommended more interchange of staff and better management training. Fulton also recommended the setting up of planning units in each government department. Corporate planning was also the main theme of the Bains Report on management in local government in 1972 (Pollitt 1990: 41). In UK central government in the 1960s and 1970s, the Public Expenditure Survey (PESC) process was designed as a rational planning and resource allocation mechanism. A new Conservative Government in 1970, strongly influenced by a group of business advisers when in opposition, introduced a series of measures aimed at bringing better management to Whitehall, including setting up 'super departments' and undertaking more comprehensive rational policy analysis

(Saint-Martin 2000: 85–90). One aim was to bring about better policy control by getting the cabinet to focus primarily on larger, more strategic issues. Similarly, in Australia the Royal Commission on Australian Government Administration (the Coombs Report) stressed the importance of 'accountable management', including greater devolution of management responsibility to department heads coupled with a much enhanced central strategic planning capacity through forward estimates (Smith and Weller 1978). This report was commissioned by an incoming Labor Government, for which managerialist ideas were seen as a way not only of improving efficiency but also of enhancing political control.

Following this wave of interest in managerial reform in the 1960s and 1970s, governments everywhere entered a new phase associated with an era of severe and prolonged financial cutbacks. At the centre, financial management reforms evolved seamlessly from the earlier initiatives, albeit with a new emphasis on cutting and re-directing expenditures. In Australia, for example, the Financial Management Improvement Program was launched in 1983, followed by a succession of measures to strengthen 'outputs and outcomes' budgeting, culminating in the introduction of accrual budgeting and accounting in the late 1990s. These mechanisms were accompanied by a rationalization of the central machinery of government and a tightening of central policy management and coordination processes by the central agencies. A key objective was to improve political control through enhancing the capacity to set priorities and redirect resources. As with programme budgeting, performance evaluation and performance information were built in to these procedures to allow the politicians and central managers to maximize 'value for money' in line with political objectives.

A somewhat similar trajectory occurred in the UK with the introduction of the Financial Management Initiative in 1982. Accrual budgeting and accounting were also subsequently adopted, as they were in New Zealand, and private sector accounting methods were brought in to many other jurisdictions in the same period (Pollitt and Bouckaert 2004: 71). These budgeting and accounting methodologies were supposed to make clear the 'real cost' of all government activities and their 'true economic value' so that managers of separate 'cost centres' and 'business entities' in the public sector could be held fully accountable for operating an efficient production unit. Clean 'purchaser–provider' splits were part of this model, so that managers had a clear, unequivocal interest in getting full value for money. There was an attempt here to mimic the market (often, these measures were closely linked to the NPM reforms discussed in the next section, by exposing managers to market or market-like disciplines from all directions). These measures were accompanied by publication of increasingly 'wide' and 'deep' performance information (Bouckaert and Halligan 2008).

Another managerialist strand in central government reforms was structural reorganization. A consistent theme was managerial devolution in order to free managers to do their job ('let the managers manage'). At the extreme was privatization, which put management into the hands of a new set of owners and freed them altogether from the constraints of government. Less dramatic were various 'corporatization' measures to ensure that government-owned enterprises operated on a fully commercial basis, with no hidden subsidies and under an imperative to show a real 'profit' (or rate of return). The corporate governance models for these reforms were taken from the private sector. For non-commercial bodies, 'agencification' in the UK followed a somewhat similar logic: a large number of semi-autonomous agencies were hived off in order to bring wider spheres of government under a stricter 'results management' regime (Pollitt et al. 2004).

On one reading, this devolution of managerial control was an abdication of political responsibility by political leaders; on another, it was a common-sense 'clearing of the in-tray' so that politicians could get on with the more important matters of broad policy. On the one hand, the result was apparently 'control over less' (Christensen and Lægreid 2001a); on the other hand, it was supposed to bring better control over the most important things. The actual results show that things are more complicated than this. Politicians often prefer the detail, which is where the headlines are (indeed, ministers often intervened in agency management when it suited). In fact, they are generally very poor at forward-thinking and planning. In addition, the devolved agencies probably acquired much less autonomy than appeared on paper. It has been argued that the enhanced autonomization was in many cases illusory, as it was accompanied by new performance audit regimes that opened up another channel of control (Hood et al. 1999).

Managerialism also influenced personnel management. First, we have seen that Fulton in the UK (as well as Coombs in Australia, among others) favoured bringing in more private sector managers to the civil service. This had sweeping implications if taken seriously, as it meant that traditional civil service systems, which relied on promotion through the ranks, would be opened up to 'lateral recruitment' into senior positions. In Australia, Canada, New Zealand and the USA, this was taken further with the creation of a Senior Executive Service in which members were trained in generic management skills as an elite group of executives, with mobility across departments. There would be more or less free movement in and out as well as within, with many on short-term contracts (rather than permanently tenured) and receiving performance pay. In many respects, the life and careers of public managers (on the surface at least) increasingly mimicked that of private managers.

At the same time that these managerialist reforms were taking place in budgeting, personnel management and the machinery of government, a parallel set of reforms was occurring in front-line public service production and delivery. It was here – in the 'rowing' rather than 'steering' parts of government – that NPM may have had the biggest impact. NPM reforms provided an armoury of managerial techniques for transforming public service production in ways that promised to save money, while continuing to provide high-quality service. These transformations were especially sweeping in the case of human welfare services.

Managerialism, NPM and Service Delivery

As a case of the influence of managerialism on public service delivery, the UK local welfare provision system provides a good example. The dominant welfare management model that emerged in the UK welfare state before the 1980s was a so-called 'bureau-professional' regime (Clarke and Newman 1997, Harris 1998). Professional teachers, health workers and social workers shared in a division of labour between 'bureaucratic' and 'professional' work. The 'bureaucrats' were relatively 'hands-off' in practice while the core work of production units was controlled by professionals. Administrators and clerks were there to do paperwork, while the professionals delivered the substance of the service. They often enjoyed considerable discretion and power, including over claims for resources to meet what they defined as the necessary standards of service. For example, social workers in local government enjoyed considerable day-to-day discretionary power as case workers, while local government was not very closely supervised by Whitehall. This 'permissive supervision' led to a 'parochial professional culture' (Harris 1998: 849).

This 'bureau-professional' model reflected a political-cum-administrative settlement in which the providers as professionals were delegated the key production roles. Citizens were cast as taxpayers who footed the bill or 'clients' for whom the services were designed (Deem et al. 2007). One problem with this 'bureau-professional' model was that it was expensive; another was that it gave citizens no active role. A third – acknowledged and tackled in the managerialist measures described in the previous section – was that it militated against central strategic resource planning and control. In the New Right attack on the size of government in the 1980s, this system of professional autonomy was targeted head on at the level of the production unit, both as a source of profligacy and also as a system that stifled choice. Social workers themselves were the objects of criticism as the 'front-line troops' of an inefficient welfare state.

A different model for the production of public services emerged under the Thatcher government in the UK in the 1980s: provider agencies were organized more on business lines and exposed to competition; social workers were constrained to act within targets and under contractual arrangements, rather than purely as autonomous professionals managing their 'case load'; strategic planning was undertaken centrally to set the targets and ensure that social workers followed new priorities of entitlement and service quality and kept to a strict 'bottom line' to ensure savings; and the bureaucratic control structure was 'delayered' so as to produce a leaner, more direct principal–agent system of monitoring of results. Social workers themselves had to internalize managerialist norms and practices so as to be part of the systems of gate-keeping and rationing. Information technology enabled the adoption of standardized on-line procedures and forms to facilitate these new controls, including workload measurement. This 'de-autonomization' of the professional-dominated production units of the welfare state took place in a setting where central government not only mandated marketization but also found new ways to control and squeeze local government authorities more generally. Auditing, league tables and benchmarking were intensified to keep local production units 'up to the mark'.

Post-NPM Managerialism

One problem with neo-liberal managerialism was an illusion of choice when provision was being squeezed and budgets were being cut. NPM alone could not deliver the cost savings (indeed, many argue that there were sometimes cost increases due to some of the measures, such as contracting out (Downs and Larkey 1986)). Marketization did not always result in multiple providers competing on quality but rather in stratagems such as 'creaming' (searching out cheap clients because they would be less of a 'problem' to managers) so as to exceed performance targets. Another problem was that the squeeze on public services, particularly where they were enjoyed by the middle class, brought unpopularity to elected governments. Following the election of the first Blair government in the UK, the new priority was not to cut and economize but to offer better access and higher quality in public services. This brought a change in rhetoric: the highlighted themes were 'personalization', 'co-production', 'localization' and 'partnerships' between public and private actors. Community participation would give consumers real power, unlike the imaginary power of a lone consumer in an imperfect market. New 'hybrid' organizational forms at local level evolved with novel public–private mixes, producing more of a 'network-style' of governance involving complex 'boundary-spanning' activities. The market was still evident, but it was now overlaid at the local level with various forms of collaboration and cooperation. At the centre, a more elaborate set of managerial tools was developed in pursuit of quality – in particular, a proliferation of performance metrics. This was more an intensification of previous trends than a departure, however. Minimum standards were increasingly defined in terms of results and outcomes, such as examination pass rates in local schools, in order to bring about improvements in quality.

Also at the centre, 'joined-up government' became the new mantra, emphasizing the interconnectedness of people's problems and the need for an integrated approach in dealing with them, as distinct from the kind of disaggregation implied by NPM (Bogdanor 2005, Christensen and Lægreid 2007b). A feature of the move towards joined-up government was a reassertion of confidence in government itself after a period of market-leaning thinking (Perri 6 et al. 2002: 42–45). In this sense, joined-up government was part of the post-NPM reaction to some of NPM's failings. But the idea was not revolutionary or profound and promised little staying power as a set of organizing themes for reform. Rather, there was a rediscovery of older themes concerning the need for coordination (Hood 2005b).

One significant feature of post-NPM managerialism is that many of its features are the product of learning from the failings of NPM. In this regard, they are managerial lessons based on public sector experience and models, rather than being yet one more round of private sector imports. Post-NPM might be said to be a 'new generation' of public sector managerialism. It already has its gurus and its texts, most notably Mark Moore's *Creating Public Value* (1995). Moore takes the distinctiveness of public management as the starting point. Topics covered in his text include mobilizing support; advocacy and negotiation; 'political management'; and 'ethical challenges of public leadership'; as well as more conventional managerialist themes such as 'reengineering organizations' and 'defining organizational mission and product'.

Recent writers on public management have associated the 'public value' approach with post-NPM reforms and with such features as 'networked government' (Stoker 2006a, Alford and O'Flynn 2009). Here, post-NPM managerialism has affinities with the rhetoric about 'new modes of governance'. Features such as blurring of lines between public and private sectors are viewed as part of a broader phenomenon. From this standpoint, there has been a set of challenges to the power and authority of the state, one symptom of which is the emergence of new, 'non-state' ways of organizing, such as networks that cross national and state boundaries (Pierre 2000). Such 'network governance' contains elements of new forms of managerialism, calling on the softer managerial skills of negotiation and other modes of networking and on mastery of new internet technologies which permit wider participation, greater spontaneity and enhanced flexibility.

Conclusion

Managerialism has not lost its hold on public sector reform in the post-NPM era. However, it may be the case that managerialism itself is going through a new phase as a driver of public sector reform. Public management as a profession and public managerialism as a body of doctrine may be coming of age. The advocates of 'value management' do not deny the relevance of private sector models and NPM-style delivery mechanisms, but see them pragmatically as one set of tools available in a larger tool bag. To take a longer view, perhaps it is also true to say that public management is re-discovering some of the doctrines of pre-NPM public administration – such as the importance of law and politics – and applying them in the new context of post-NPM, networked governance.

Privatization

Thomas Pallesen

Introduction

In Christopher Hood's now classic article 'A Public Management for All Seasons', privatization is considered to be one of the constitutive elements of New Public Management (NPM), perhaps *the* constitutive element of New Public Management (Hood 1991). Privatization is not only one of the four public sector 'megatrends' that Hood links to NPM. He also dubs privatization as one of the 'doctrinal components' of NPM because NPM is replicating or coloured by private sector thinking. Thus, 'hands-on professional management', 'explicit standards and measures of performance', 'output control', 'disaggregation', 'competition', 'private sector styles of management', 'discipline and parsimony in resource use' are all doctrines more or less taken over from the private sector.

Paradoxically, even though privatization is a prominent element in recent public sector reforms and a constitutive element of NPM, there is no common understanding of what privatization really is. In the literature, we find two digit numbers of different meanings of the concept of privatization. But, even though we are not certain about what privatization actually is, there seems to be a surprisingly broad understanding of why central, state and local governments globally are said to have resorted to privatization: private delivery is considered to be cheaper than comparable government-provided services. Following this assumed competitive advantage of private delivery, it has furthermore been argued in the literature that when governments are fiscally stressed, they are inclined to engage in privatization because privatization is a way to preserve the service level when government resources are strained. In contrast to this apolitical account of privatization, other strands in the literature consider privatization as a right-wing political attempt to shrink government services and demolish left-wing political strongholds.

In sum, there seems to be a great number of different understandings of privatization, and of why and when it is politically implemented. The aim of this chapter is to give an account of the concept of privatization and critically discuss its causes and effects. One of the points of the chapter is that, in this respect, it may be important what kind of privatization we are talking about. Specifically, considering the perhaps most important type of privatization, namely contracting out, it is argued that the driving force of privatization in the public sector is not fiscal strain. Quite to the contrary, it may be 'the politics of good times'.

The Concept of Privatization

Privatization is a multifaceted concept that has been defined in a number of ways. Savas (2000) for example lists no less than nine different meanings of privatization. Prominent among these is the sale of state-owned enterprises (whether the sale of state and government land and buildings also qualifies as privatization is a matter of greater dispute). Contracting out public services to private providers is also considered to be an important example of privatization. Contracting out often takes place after competitive bidding among private providers – occasionally also public providers are invited to take part. If public providers take part in the competitive bidding, it is sometimes referred to as 'competitive sourcing' or 'managed competition', and when the public provider actually wins the auction, it may be called 'contracting in'. 'Contracting in' also takes place when public providers take over privately delivered services. What term is used for when one public provider delivers service to another public organization has yet to be definitely coined.

Furthermore, some government agencies are organized and operate on conditions that are more or less equivalent to private companies. They may have their own boards and raise their revenue by selling their services on the private market. These cases of privatization are called both 'corporatization' and 'marketization' (Christensen and Pallesen 2001a). Finally, Savas notes that the concept of 'public–private' partnership broadly refers to joint operation or collaboration between public and private organizations and more narrowly as private provision of infrastructure and buildings in return for a dividend.

The editor of the pro-privatization *Privatization Watch* and *Annual Privatization Report*, Leonard Gilroy, also notices that there are many different forms of privatization, but he points out that the most common forms of privatization are contracts, franchises and divestiture. 'Contracts' occur when a government contracts with private sector (for profit or non-profit) providers to deliver public services. In 'franchises', a government awards a private firm an exclusive right to provide a public service or operate a public asset in return for an annual lease payment or one-time upfront payment. 'Divesture' takes place when a government is 'getting out of a service, activity or asset entirely, often through outright sales (Gilroy 2010).

Thus, to academics, practitioners-cum-(pro-privatization)-think-tankers, there are a great number of different forms of privatization. Nonetheless, two forms of privatization stand out as the most important: the sale of government-owned enterprises and contracting out of government services.

Even if we narrow the concept of privatization down to two and accept the idea that the most important instances of privatization are the sale of state-owned enterprises and contracting out, there are still marked differences between the two types of privatization. In economic terms, the sale of state-owned enterprises may be considered as the 'major' type of privatization while, in comparison, contracting out is the 'minor'. This is because the sale of state-owned enterprises represents a more profound privatization than contracting out does; when state-owned enterprises are sold, the government is in principle totally out of this business. On the other hand, when governments contract out, they still have the main voice in deciding what kind of services they need because the delivered services are for public use and the public money spent on contracted services is included as public spending.

This difference in government involvement between selling state-owned enterprises and contracting out can also be illustrated by Savas' (1997) classic three-way categorization of government involvement. Savas argues that governments have three distinct roles of involvement, namely a regulatory, a financing and a producer role. Thus, in principle, governments can potentially be involved in eight different ways, from total government control (performing all three roles) to absolutely no government control (performing none of the three roles). In between, there are (six) different combinations of government involvement, for instance regulating but not financing or producing the service (for example, the way taxi-driving is organized is many countries), regulating and producing but not financing (for example, how the issuing of passports and driving licenses is often organized). Furthermore, when this terminology is applied, selling state-owned enterprises is a more profound example of privatization than contracting out because when governments are selling state-owned enterprises they are no longer financing and producing these services, while they may maintain or install some kind of external regulation of the privatized enterprise's activities. In contrast, when governments contract out, they are only cutting off the producer role, but they are still paying for the services (the financing role) and specifying what they want to buy (the regulating role).

But, when we consider the political dynamics of the two kinds of privatization, the 'major' and 'minor' characteristics of the types of privatization may be reversed. By political standards, it may be easier to sell government-owned enterprises than contracting out hitherto government-provided services because of the very different short- and long-term fiscal properties of the two kinds of privatization that are important for policy makers' propensity to engage in them. The argument is expanded below, and it also suggests that there may be different political forces at play behind selling state-owned enterprises and contracting out – and that the 'minor' (contracting out) is perhaps, from some theoretical perspectives, more interesting than the 'major' (selling state-owned enterprises). Notably, because of the different fiscal properties of the two types of privatization, we should expect contracting out to be a more political-ideological endeavour than selling government-owned enterprises.

Moreover, selling state-owned enterprises is a 'sunset industry' because such enterprises are in limited supply. The bulk of the sale of state-owned enterprises in Western Europe took place in the 1980s and 1990s, and privatization of state-owned enterprises in Eastern Europe has peaked since the sale took off in the early 1990s (Megginson 2005). Privatization of state-owned enterprises is still going on in the developing world, but also in these countries, as well as in the developed countries, there is a limited stock of marketable enterprises. On the other hand, contracting out public services remains a viable option in all countries with a public sector that delivers services to its citizens. Moreover, (growing) public sectors are presumably not limited in supply in the foreseeable future. For these reasons, concerning the determinants of privatization, the chapter focuses mainly on the factors that explain the contracting out of public services.

Why Privatize – and When?

The literature points to a number of political and economic explanations as to why governments choose to privatize (Feigenbaum and Henig 1994, Spulber 1997, Feigenbaum, Henig and Hamnett 1998). Prominent among these is the political explanation that right-wing governments privatize in order to shrink the public sector and, in a broader sense, to diminish the impact of a large government sector and to encourage an 'enterprise culture' (Studlar, MacAllister and Ascui 1990). The prime example is, of course, Thatcher's Conservative leadership in the late 1970s and 1980s in the United Kingdom even though Adenauer's sale of shares in Volkswagen in 1961 was one of the first examples of major privatizations in Europe (Megginson 2005).

Another prominent explanation of privatization focuses on the economic rather than the political consequences of privatization. According to this explanation, both left- and right-leaning policy makers pragmatically favour privatization. One strand of this argument is the NPM-toned position that policy makers (should) prefer to shed day-to-day operation of mundane public services and concentrate on setting up goals and overall prioritizing (Lane 2000). In NPM terminology, policy makers privatize because they (should) prefer to steer rather than row.

Another pragmatic line of argument is that both left- and right-leaning policy makers like to privatize because it is a shortcut to spending money on popular vote-increasing purposes without the pain of raising the money on less popular tax increases. In this view, privatization is simply 'a pragmatic solution to immediate problems, for example the need for cash' (Feigenbaum and Henig 1994: 194).

Akin to this argument is the idea that the driving force behind privatization is the need to increase the efficiency of the public sector. Numerous studies theoretically and empirically investigate the possible relative efficiency of private versus state-owned enterprises and private versus public delivery of services. Gérard (2008), Megginson (2005) and Vickers and Yarrow (1988) argue that from a theoretical perspective there are reasons to believe that privatization has a positive impact, but that the increase in efficiency is contingent on sufficient competition and/or proper public regulation.

Empirically, Megginson and Netter investigated a number of companies in various countries and industries that have been fully or partially privatized. Their overall conclusion is that privatization has been successful in terms of sale, profitability, investment, operating efficiency, debt and dividend, but that the success of privatization is contingent on proper market conditions with sufficient competition (Megginson and Netter 2001). Similarly, in a meta-study of nearly a thousand studies, Domberger and Jensen (1997) show that private provision tends to be up to 20 per cent cheaper than public service provision – but replicate Megginson and Netter's caution that a competitive market is a precondition for harvesting any advantages of privatization because private monopolies are no more efficient than single public providers. Hodge's meta-analysis also suggests that costs can be saved by contracting out but notes that the savings are often marginal (Hodge 2000).

One counter-argument against the postulated efficiency advantage of private provision is that private and public services are not comparable (Blom-Hansen 2003). It is argued that public services are more expensive either because the quality is higher or because public employees have better pay and working conditions than their colleagues in the private sector. Either way, public services tend to stand out as more expensive than private services if these differences between public and private services are not taken into account. However, Blom-Hansen shows that private services are somewhat cheaper than public services even if the quality of the services is taken into account but that the savings are often marginal.

In sum, privatization as sale of state-owned enterprises raises substantial short-term revenue and it seems that the enterprises – with sufficient competitive and regulatory conditions – become more profitable when they are privatized. Consequently, privatized state-owned enterprises also become taxable in the long run, but in comparison to the substantial instant revenue from selling the state-owned enterprises, the additional long-term tax revenue is much more limited.

In contrast to sale of state-owned enterprises, contracting out publicly provided services does not generate any short-term extra revenue; in the short run, it may even incur costs on the public authority to set up the contracting out regime. In the longer run, contracting out public services can as a rule of thumb be expected to save the public purse an average of 10 per cent on the outlay on these services.

Assuming a political leadership that takes an interest in overall societal efficiency, we should expect widespread contracting out of public services and steady privatization of state-owned enterprises. However, with this kind of political leadership, it may be difficult to explain why we had publicly-delivered services and state-owned enterprises in the first place. This also suggests that the political leadership is not searching for optimal societal solutions, at least not all the time or perhaps only some of the time. What policy makers maximize is disputed, and the issue will not be discussed here. Whether it is offices, votes, policy goals (Strøm 1990), budgets (Niskanen 1971) or slack (Migue and Belanger 1974), it does seem that policy makers' concerns are much broader than societal efficiency. Also, there are reasons to believe that policy makers focus on short-term rather than long-term political costs and benefits (Christensen and Pallesen 2001b). If this line of argument has some merit, it also suggests that the distributional impact of the two kinds of privatization is important for policy makers' eagerness to engage in this kind of political activity.

Considering the distributional benefits of the two kinds of privatization, they both create marginal long-term benefits but differ in terms of the presence of the substantial instant revenue that is suitable for fulfilling short-term political goals of various kinds (for example, by increasing spending or lowering taxes), whether the reason is maximization of votes, offices or policies. Thus, in terms of both timing and size of the benefit, it is likely that it is much easier to establish a political majority behind privatization of state-owned enterprises than it is to establish a political majority behind contracting out public services to private providers.

In terms of political costs, the impact of both contracting out and selling state-owned enterprises is more uncertain. At first sight, public managers and public employees stand to lose when services are contracted out or state-owned enterprises are sold to private investors. Public managers and public employees often oppose plans to privatize, and they may voice their opposition to the plans to contract out services. This resistance represents a political cost to the policy makers who champion plans to contract out or sell state-owned enterprises, but it may be softened by a number of contingencies, for instance when the private employer is obliged to take over the existing staff and uphold their working and pay conditions. In this way, the political costs of contracting out and selling state-owned enterprises are also diminished (as well as the economic benefits of privatization).

In sum, the political costs of contracting out or selling state-owned enterprises are comparable, and in both cases, there are means to lower these costs. But, taking the benefit side into account, privatization as the sale of state-owned enterprises seems to have a much broader appeal to policy makers than contracting out.

Notably, the very limited, if any, short-term economic gains from contracting out make it much more likely to be the subject of partisan politics. If there is no economic short term in sight, Social Democratic political executives have a very limited incentive to contract out. With limited economic gains, there is no reason to upset the core constituency and compromise their own sceptical ideological view on contracting out.

To conservative politicians, the calculus may be different. Even if there are no economic gains from contracting out, it may nonetheless be an attractive reform strategy to enhance the right-wing ideological policy goal of diminishing the public sector just because they consider it to be a good idea. Exactly because of the often very substantial gains from selling state-owned enterprises, this reform strategy may be blurred in terms of ideological footprints because left-wing governments also are tempted to exploit these opportunities that often comfortably outweigh the cost of privatizing state-owned enterprises.

Moreover, the distributional benefits of the two kinds of privatization raise the more general question of how privatization is related to fiscal stress. The literature traditionally sees privatization as a venue for elevating fiscal stress because of the revenue it generates (Feigenbaum and Henig 1994). But even if the traditional view is taken for granted, it seems relevant to distinguish between the two types of privatization. While contracting out only contributes moderately to dampen fiscal stress, there seems to be much more to gain by selling state-owned enterprises than contracting out in the short run.

Nevertheless, the traditional view is that fiscal stress tends to spur contracting out because public authorities can maintain current levels of services for fewer taxes by replacing more expensive in-house produced services with less expensive privately delivered services (Kodrzycki 1994, 1998). This idea has been questioned, not only due to the general scepticism of policy makers' eagerness to improve societal efficiency (cf. above). A variant of the argument is Ferris and Grady's idea that the possibility to intervene in the specific provision of services is paramount to policy makers who prefer in-house provision that enables this kind of ad hoc intervention rather than externally contracted services that are less flexible (Ferris and Grady 1986). The political reality for policy makers is that there is ongoing public debate and critique of the adequacy and quality of public services, and the policy makers in charge are held accountable for the current adequacy and quality of these services. When policy makers contract out services, they constrain their possibilities for responding to this critique in the short run because the quality and number of contracted out services are specified for a longer period. It may be difficult or expensive to persuade the private contractor to change these conditions. In contrast, there is no legal obstacle to the policy makers in charge if they want to change the provision of in-house delivered services. Thus, also in times of economic austerity, and even if in-house provision is marginally more expensive than contracted services, policy makers may be inclined to prefer in-house over privately delivered services.

Expanding on the Ferris and Grady argument that policy makers are more eager to maintain control than saving a few per cent on the service delivery, it should also be noted that contracting out entails a number of 'transaction' or 'contracting' costs that are often not included in the comparison of public and private services delivery. In principle, it is of course possible to specify responsibilities in detail, that is, to specify performance expectations and the financial or other penalties in case of violation of the contract and so on (Gilroy 2010). However, in the real world of providing public services, it takes a good deal of governmental effort to specify the requirements, simply because it is often difficult to specify exactly what the public buyer wants and what public services precisely entail. This not only seriously complicates the specification and the successive monitoring of the contract. Evidence suggests that contracting out requires employment of highly-skilled juridical and economical expertise (Bhatti, Olsen and Pedersen 2009). These kinds of costs are generally not taken into account when the private and public services delivery are compared. Moreover, there are national or supranational rules of how government biddings should be framed in the first place. If these rules are violated, (supra-)national stipulated fines have to be paid for neglecting the often very dense web of rules governing the process of contracting out in the public sector. These fines may be substantial, and for this reason also, governments may hesitate to contract out even if they aim to increase efficiency and save the public purse for superfluous expenditures.

However, it has been disputed that contracting out is primarily guided by the possibility of marginal savings on public service delivery and that governments do contract out to a greater extent in times of fiscal strain to obtain these savings. On the contrary, it has been argued that contracting out is actually the 'politics of good times' rather than the preferred politics in times of economic austerity (Pallesen 2004, Zullo 2009). This argument rests on the idea that societal efficiency is not the only, and perhaps not even the most important, concern for policy makers (cf. above), who may also be concerned about their public employees and the criticism that plans to contract out publicly-delivered services are likely to attract (Chandler and Feuille 1991, Hefetz and Warner 2004). The line of argument is that while contracting out services delivered in-house is controversial, contracting out additional, new services is less likely to provoke criticism because it does not harm the interests of the existing public employees. Thus it is possible to add new contracted out services to the public sector in times of growth and expansion. In contrast, policy makers often need to cut expenditures in times of austerity, and these spending cuts are not very popular. However, the criticism is often less fierce when it comes to cutting privately-delivered services rather than in-house produced services because of the different impacts on the public employees. It can thus be argued that contracted out services are a buffer in the public sector economy and increase when expansion of the public economy is on the agenda and decrease when spending cuts are on the political menu. In effect, contracting out becomes the 'politics of good times' rather than a remedy to ease fiscal stress.

Of course, the validity of the general argument of the buffer role of contracted out services assumes that public sector employees are significant political actors with whom most policy makers prefer to avoid conflicts. The validity of this assumption may vary with the political-ideological orientation of the political leadership and the political-institutional context in a broader sense. Thus it may be hypothesized to be more relevant in relatively large public sectors with strong unions, predominantly governed by pro-labour Social Democrats in Scandinavia, than in a more conservative Anglo-American setting of a smaller public sector and weaker public sector unions. But, like the general and theoretically more controversial issue of the impact of fiscal stress on the level of contracting out, this is also an empirical question, to which we will now turn.

Empirical Studies of the Political-Economic Dynamics of Contracting Out

As mentioned, it is important to investigate the determinants of contracting out in different political-institutional settings in order to establish whether there is a general pattern or the determinants of contracting out are contingent on the specific setting. Therefore, three empirical studies of contracting out are considered: one from Denmark (a case study of the large Scandinavian public sector) and two from the leaner American public sector. The common denominator of the studies is that they take advantage of public accounting systems that enable a very accurate measurement of contracting out. In this respect, the studies differ from other mainly survey-based studies of determinants and measurements of contracting out. The argument for relying on the fewer studies with accurate measures of contracting out instead of the more numerous studies relying on self-reported levels of contracting out is that contracting is or may be politically controversial and that policy makers and public servants (may) have reasons both to downplay and to exaggerate the level of contracting out when they are asked to report the level. On the other hand, it is rather unlikely that they are willing to fiddle with the figures if there are strict rules of accounting.

The study of contracting out in Denmark investigates Danish localities from 1985 to 1997 (Pallesen 2004). There are pros and cons to sub-national studies, notably in unitary states where central government regulations tend to reduce local governments' autonomy and dampen the possible impact of the explanatory variables, for example party political differences. On the other hand, studies of the numerous local governments, in this case 275 localities, enable a more rigorous test of determinants of contracting out. In this case, the advantages seem to outweigh the drawbacks. First of all, central government regulation of local government contracting out is very modest, and there are only a few examples of central government rules that prevent local governments from contracting out services (or force them to). For example, local governments cannot contract out primary home nursing care of newborn babies to private companies. As a result of this autonomy, there is substantial variation in the level of contracting out in the localities, ranging from 5 to 30 per cent of total local government expenditure with an average of about 11 per cent. Second, the Social Democrats and the Liberals dominate Danish local government; more than 90 per cent of the mayors are either Social Democrats or Liberals, which makes local governments a fertile ground to study the potential impact of partisan politics on the propensity to contract out. Third, as a matter of central government decree, all local governments are obliged to follow the same accounting guide. The guide describes in detail how local governments should account for their expenses, including outlays on services contracted out to private providers. As a result, it is possible to account very precisely for the magnitude of contracting out, both in absolute terms (total expenditure on contracted out services) and relative terms (the share of total local government services). Finally, the local tax base is the conventional and easily accessible measure for the local fiscal situation. Also this measure varies substantially between the rich localities in the northern suburbs of Copenhagen and the poorer peripheral localities.

The test is a pooled analysis for all localities from 1985 to 1997. To verify the results of the pooled analysis, time series analyses have been conducted for each of the 275 localities. It has been argued that local market structure and size of localities are important for the possibility and need to contract out (Ferris 1986, Greene 1996, Stein 1990). The local market structure refers to the access to a competitive market of possible providers. It often requires that the locality is located in or close to an urban area. For this reason, location in the greater metropolitan Copenhagen

Table 17.1   The impact of political affiliation (mayor's party affiliation), economic prosperity (tax base), local government size (number of inhabitants) and metropolitan status on the level of contracting out in Danish localities, 1985–97 (n=3575)

Right-wing impact	Economic prosperity	Local government size	Metropolitan status	Explained variance
-.017	.494***	-.192***	-.237***	.12

Note: Level of significance: ***1%.

Source: Pallesen (2004).

Table 17.2   The impact of an improved local economy on local government spending and level of local government contracting out in Danish localities, 1985–97 (n=3575). After control for local government size, metropolitan status and party political leadership

	Change in local government spending	Change in local government contracting out
Change in local government tax base	.119***	.036***

Note: Level of significance: ***1%.

Source: Pallesen (2004).

area is taken as a proxy for the easy access to a viable private market for services. The size of the locality is another factor that may have an impact on the level of contracting out. Size may, however, impact contracting out in both directions. It can be argued that smaller governments need to contract out because, in contrast to larger localities, they are not able to harvest economies of scale themselves. On the other hand, it may be argued that contracting out requires specialized, highly-skilled bureaucratic expertise to handle the juridical and technical aspects of contracting that it takes a larger government to employ while it is not sensible or possible in smaller localities to employ this kind of bureaucrats. In any case, the size of the locality has been included in the analysis to account for its possible impact on the level of contracting out.

Table 17.1 highlights the result of the study and shows no significant impact of partisan politics. Thus, the proposition that right-wing Liberals tend to contract out more than left-wing Social Democrats cannot be supported. Nor does size of locality or metropolitan status have any great impact on the level of contracting out. Smaller and provincial localities tend to contract out moderately more than larger localities in the greater Copenhagen area. The most significant and unequivocal result of the study is that prosperous localities contract out more than fiscally strained localities.

Table 17.2 shows that there is a positive impact of an improved economic situation in the localities, that is, a change in the local government tax base, on total local government expenditure and the relative share of local government expenditure spent on contracted out services. When the local government's economic situation improves, it spends more in general but even more on contracted services. On the other hand, when the local government tax base deteriorates, total spending is moderated and the level of contracting out is reduced. In this situation, spending on contracted services decrease even more than general spending is reduced. In effect, contracted services have a buffer role in the public economy and the evidence supports the notion that contracting out is 'the politics of good times' rather than a device to counteract fiscal stress.

Many studies of contracting out in America use the International City/County Management surveys of alternative service delivery (Ferris 1986, Greene 1996, Morgan, Hirlinger and England 1988, Morgan and Hirlinger 1991). These surveys report the localities' use of private providers for different services – public works, transportation, public utilities, public safety, health and human services, parks and recreation, cultural and arts programmes and supports functions – and give a crude measure of the trend in local government contracting out (Greene 1996).

The surveys conducted by the Council of State Governments and the American State Administrators Project (Chi, Arnold and Perkins 2003, Brudney et al. 2005) aim to obtain a more precise measure of contracting out by asking the local authorities to estimate the level of contracting out in intervals of 5 per cent (less than 5, 6–10, 10–15 and so on).

Notwithstanding their merits, the surveys show that it is difficult to measure precisely the level of contracting out in this way. A more precise measure requires an administrative system that precisely and routinely registers all expenditures to privately-delivered services, but such budget and account systems are generally not found in the American public sector. An exception is the school districts' budget and account systems, which register outlays to privately-delivered services.

Some empirical studies of the determinants of contracting out take advantage of and focus on American school districts in Texas and Washington (O'Toole and Meier 2004, Pallesen 2006). These studies measure contracting out as the 'purchased services' delivered by private providers, that is, food services, student transportation, maintenance of buildings, facilities, equipment and grounds, security, warehousing and distribution, and information technology services.

Analysing the determinants of contracting out requires variation in the level of privately-delivered services. In Texas, the average level of contracting out is 9 per cent of total current expenditure, but it varies a great deal, from a low 0.6 per cent to a high 54 per cent. In Washington, the average level of contracting out is 10 per cent, but it varies somewhat less, from 3 per cent and up to 30 per cent of the total current expenditure. Thus, both the average level and the variation in contracting out in the Washington State schools are similar to the level and variation in contracting out in Danish localities.

Table 17.3   The impact of fiscal resources, school size, teacher turnover, local
             funds and school bureaucrats on contracting out in Texas state
             school districts, 1997–99 (n=3122)

Revenue per pupil	Enrolment	Teacher turnover	Local funds	School bureaucrats	Central officers	Explained variance
.4080	-.0252	.0374	.0271	.9326	1.3662	.2400

Note: Level of significance: at least 5%.

Source: O'Toole and Meier (2004).

Table 17.4   The impact of fiscal stress, size of school district, metropolitan
             area, urbanization and task difficulty on contracting out in
             Washington state school districts, 1993–2001 (n=888)

Fiscal stress	Size of school district	Metropolitan area	Urbanization	Task difficulty	Explained variance
-.376***	-.244***	-.088	.176***	.053*	.210

Note: Level of significance: ***1%, *10%.

Source: Pallesen (2006).

The School Districts' fiscal situation is in both studies measured as the total resources available per student. To account for the fact that also the task difficulty varies and puts different strains on the school districts with similar total resources available per student, the share of students with English as a second language (ESL-student) is included in the Washington study. The Texan study includes other control variables, such as teacher turnover, since it is argued that low organizational memory may force school districts to rely more on contracted out services. Furthermore, stronger bureaucratic capacity, measured as the size of the central school district administration, may have an impact on contracting out. Moreover, the importance of district size (cf. above) is taken into account in both studies.

As seen in Tables 17.3 and 17.4, the most important result of the investigation of the determinants of contracting out in both Texas and Washington state school districts is the level of fiscal stress. Notably, and similarly to the result of the Danish study, increased fiscal stress significantly reduces the level of contracting out.

Moreover, contracted out services have the same buffer role as in the Danish localities (Table 17.5). When the available resources per student in Washington state school districts increase (decrease) contracted out services' share of total current expenditure also increases (decreases). On average, the budgetary adjustment of the contracted out services is nearly two times higher than the change in total expenditure. By way of example, when expenditure per student increases (decreases) by 3 per cent, contracted out services increase (decrease) by 5 per cent.

Table 17.5   The impact of an improved school district fiscal situation on expenditure per student and level of contracting out, 1993–2001 (n=888). After control for school district size, metropolitan status, urbanization and task difficulty

	Change in expenditure per student	Change in school districts' contracting out
Change in school districts' fiscal situation	.657***	.176***

Note: Level of significance: ***1%.

Source: Pallesen (2006).

In Texas, a school manager explains the very same mechanism this way: 'Some of our contracting is for bells and whistles, a guest conductor for an orchestra or video services for athletic events ... these things are the first to go in a budget crunch. By contracting out we avoid layoffs' (O'Toole and Meier 2004: 348).

Conclusion: 'The Politics of Good Times'

Privatization is a multifaceted concept, but sale of state-owned enterprises and contracting out public services to private providers are considered to be the two most important features of privatization. While the sale of state-owned enterprises has peaked in the Western world, contracting out is likely here to stay because it is possible as long as we have public sectors. The two types of privatization differ in other respects as well. Sale of state-owned enterprises generates instant revenue, which makes it a privatization strategy with a broad political appeal. Because there is no fast money in contracting out, it may have a stronger appeal to right-wing policy makers who want to diminish the role of the public sector. On the other hand, both sale of state-owned enterprises and contracting out are said to improve long-term societal efficiency, at least marginally. The relative cost efficiency of private enterprises and private service delivery is traditionally perceived to spur fiscally stressed public authorities to contract out. The traditional view of the impact of fiscal stress on contracting out assumes that policy makers are rewarded for trying, in this way, to maintain the service level with less spending. This reasoning may be wrong because policy makers – and (because) voters – may have broader priorities. Notably, for political decision makers who are held accountable for public services whether they are in-house or contracted services, enforceable contracts with external providers are likely to reduce the flexibility and therefore the attractiveness of externally delivered services in general. Moreover, it requires specialized and highly skilled government units to handle a complicated contract regime governed by national and sometimes supranational rules as is the case within the European Union. Most importantly, the major lesson of this inquiry is that privatization in the form of contracting out is not attractive to policy makers because it may be somewhat cheaper than in-house produced services and therefore especially interesting in times of austerity. Rather, contracting out is a convenient buffer in a public sector that shrinks in times of fiscal stress and expands in times of public sector growth, basically because it is easier to cut off privately delivered services than public sector employees. In essence, contracting out is politics and, to be more specific, the 'politics of good times'.

A Transformative Perspective
on Public–Private Partnerships

Carsten Greve and Graeme Hodge

Introduction

Public–private partnership (PPP) has become a defining characteristic of modern governance. Interestingly, though, precisely how PPPs fit together with the evolution in recent decades of New Public Management (NPM) is less clear. PPPs can be broadly defined as organizations and institutions that mix elements from both the public sector and the private sector, and interest in PPPs has clearly gained momentum through the 1990s and in the 2000s. This chapter seeks to gain some conceptual clarity regarding just how notions of PPP fit within some of the developing ideas of public sector change.

Basically there have been two arguments as to the relationship between PPPs and NPM. One is that PPPs have been an extension of the NPM agenda, which was itself based deeply on notions of marketization and efficient private sector delivery methods. Under this view, PPPs are seen as privatization in disguise – a way to institutionalize the NPM agenda through the backdoor if you like. The other argument is that PPPs are a whole new phenomenon. Following this line, PPP itself represents a key part of the post-NPM New Public Governance agenda, which seeks networks instead of single organizations, and encourages cooperation instead of competition.

This chapter argues that the appeal and power of PPP lies in its very ambiguity. It is this exact feature of PPP – the uncertainly as to whether it is a NPM or a more post-NPM and governance-influenced agenda item – that makes PPPs attractive. PPPs can represent both types of reform and can therefore be located right at the centre of the transformative perspective on public management reform. PPP represents transformation into new and improved public sector delivery practices, whilst some parts stay the same! And not only does it represent old and new together, it simultaneously represents private sector efficiency hand in hand with political effectiveness. This chapter proceeds by first articulating the breadth of the PPP phenomenon. It then investigates the manner in which PPP has formed part of the NPM marketization agenda as well as part of the new governance (post-NPM) thrust. Finally it analyses PPP through the adoption of a transformative perspective and articulates some of the key challenges such an interpretation brings.

The Public–Private Partnership Phenomenon

The exact history of PPPs is debatable. As sceptics were quick to point out, the PPP idea itself was not so new. Some viewed partnerships in an historical perspective and delineated several long pedigrees of public–private 'mixes' over the centuries (Wettenhall 2005b). Others pointed out that the use of the exact term 'public–private partnership' appeared to have evolved out of the US urban development sphere as early as the 1940s, although it reached its zenith through the 1970s and 1980s (Bovaird 2004). Some have also since pointed to the multiple lines of evolution from which modern PPP notions seem to have arisen (Bovaird 2010). And yet others suggest, with stretched credulity, an association between the long-term French infrastructure contract practice of *affermage* (dating back centuries) and the modern day PPP phenomenon. The partnership concept has also been associated with the rise of interest in networks and cooperation (more about which later).

The idea of PPPs is nowadays often associated with the Private Finance Initiative (PFI) in the UK. Initiated in the 1990s, the notion of PFI as partnership soon spread to other countries around the globe (Terry 1996, Hodge and Greve 2007, 2009). Henceforth, PPP signalled a new form of cooperation between public sector organizations and private sector organizations. The basic principle involved the public sector and the private sector cooperating in designing, financing, building, operating and maintaining public infrastructure. One of the central attributes of PPP was the new role and importance allocated to risk analysis. It was argued that governments should put a suitable price on such risks and ought to be fully aware of just who bears them (OECD 2008). This required considerable technical analysis on behalf of governments.

Considering the notion of partnership more broadly, however, PPPs have been defined as

> *cooperation of some sort of durability between public and private actors in which they jointly develop products and services and share risks and costs which are connected with these products. (Van Ham and Koppenjan 2001: 598)*

Likewise, both Hodge and Greve (2007) and Weihe (2005) have suggested that PPP be thought of not as one particular technical approach but as a wide range of different approaches. Both have suggested five families of activities, one of which is infrastructure delivery through PFI-type contracts. Clear to both here was that there was considerable ambiguity in the very definition of PPP. Moreover, whilst this ambiguity was a serious analytical concern, it was also one of the reasons PPPs appeared to be so popular.

PPPs were in a sense so broad that they could not be opposed. The government in the UK, for example, continues to employ both a broad terminology and a more specific one in relation to PPPs:

> *Public–private partnerships are arrangements typified by joint working between the public and the private sector. PPP can cover all types of collaboration across the interface of the public and private sectors to deliver policies, services and infrastructure. Where delivery of public services involves private sector investment in infrastructure, the most common form of PPP is the Private Finance Initiative.*[1]

At the end of the 2000s the UK could boast of around 600 PFI projects in operation and had a clear policy set out for their development (HM Treasury 2008). Together with Australia and perhaps Canada, the UK case is the most studied in the literature on PPPs.

The practice of the PFI policy soon gained interest in other countries. Australia and Canada were quick to follow the UK. In the US various partnership arrangements had existed for some time, but under a variety of concepts. In the rest of the OECD world, the recent interpretation of the concept was still seen as relatively new in the 1990s. But the idea soon spread to governments in OECD countries (and in developing countries as well). International organizations such as the World Bank and the OECD caught on to the idea (OECD 2008), and the big consultancy firms advocated the concept (Deloitte 2006). There has also been movement towards intensified public–private collaboration within the European Union (for a review see Mörth 2007), even though it had hesitated for a long time, mainly because it could not square the partnership idea with its basic principle of market competition. Perhaps it was also inherently a little more sceptical and unwilling to believe the promises of the PPP salesmen. So by the end of the 2000s, many countries around the world had taken up the PPP concept, particularly in its private finance form, and such projects could be found in Ireland, Spain, France, Germany, the Netherlands and the new member states in the European Union (Hodge and Greve 2007) to name just a few jurisdictions. Interestingly, the Scandinavian countries showed somewhat less interest and hence have comparatively few projects.

One of the biggest questions related to PPP continues to be 'does it work'? It would therefore be logical to contemplate, albeit briefly, the performance record of PPPs. Although results are beginning to surface, much less is known about the performance of PPPs as about contracting out or privatization in the form of the sale of public enterprises. However, preliminary overviews of the recent experience of PFI forms of PPP are now certainly available, such as that published by Deloitte (2006). Hodge and Greve (2009) also looked at 25 PPP infrastructure evaluations

---

1   HM Treasury website on public–private partnerships: http://www.hm-treasury.gov.uk/ppp_index.htm [accessed: 03/02/2010], italics added.

over the past decade, focusing on one crucial aspect of performance – the evidence on value for money (VFM). They pointed out that whilst there was much blatant salesmanship on the one hand and critical and colourful language on the other, there had been no careful meta-analyses or statistical overviews summarizing multiple quantitative PPP performance results to date. They saw the available evidence on the relative performance of fully private infrastructure 'partnership' activities as 'mixed', and noted the existence of many general reviews[2] as well as assessments concerned with particular aspects of performance.[3] Supportive results achieved in the UK formed a major part of this performance data. But there were many critical studies, too, such as that of Pollock et al. (2007) who saw estimates of PPP benefits as overly optimistic. To them, there was 'no evidence to support the Treasury cost and time overrun claims of improved efficiency in PFI', and claims of superiority were simply 'biased to favor PFI'.[4] Economic analyses of actual PPP deals in other jurisdictions, too, have remained sceptical towards the bold claims that PPPs lead to more efficiency, and have advocated measuring not only the production costs of the deals but the transaction costs as well (Vining and Boardman 2005, 2010). Consequently, the PPP performance debate continues.

It is also easy or tempting to overestimate the economic and financial importance of PPPs. Other scholars have therefore quite rightly pointed to the need for a more sophisticated and nuanced way to measure the performance of PPPs (Jeffares et al. 2009) rather than simply to think of PPP in terms of economic efficiency. Indeed, Hodge (2010) has documented some 15 objectives of PPP covering a huge range from at one end broad efforts to better govern and pursue economic development in a country, through to the other end where narrower objectives cover management and project delivery in terms of value for money (VFM) and timeliness. In other words, the very objectives of PPP are as much related to governance and economic development as to matters of management and simpler infrastructure project delivery. Of further importance in respect of understanding the objectives of PPP is the fact that the objectives have altered over time and today remain slippery in the rough and tumble of government policy rhetoric. In the midst of reformist governments advocating the PPP model, therefore, it is perhaps of little wonder that in many countries, outside of those most prolific in terms of PPP, governments still rely on schemes of public investment in infrastructure projects run by the public sector along with more traditional contracting and construction delivery methods.

What, however, can be said of PPP and its place in the recent reforms of governments? It is to this matter that we now turn.

---

2   Aside from Hodge and Greve (2009), see also, for example, Hodge and Greve (2007), Ghobadian et al. (2004), Grimsey and Lewis (2004) and Osborne (2001).

3   See Flinders (2005), Mott Macdonald (2002), NAO (2000), Pollock et al. (2002) and Shaoul (2004) for examples of PPP reviews taking a more specific focus.

4   Difficulties faced by the Pollock et al. team in extracting this research data from behind government claims of 'commercial-in-confidence' also amplified concerns that healthy peer review was not welcomed.

Public–Private Partnerships as Part of the New Public Management-Based Marketization Agenda

PPPs can be seen as part and parcel of the marketization aspect of NPM. PPPs mean that market-based principles will be used in the distribution of public services. US scholar E.S. Savas (2000) exemplifies those who view PPPs as basically an extension of the well-known privatization agenda. PPPs certainly indicate that private sector organizations are willing to become involved in the delivery of public services, but the PPP concept has also been adopted progressively on the basis of it representing best construction practice and a model of good NPM practice. Indeed, the whole notion of PPP has prolonged the life of marketization ideas that were created during the Thatcher era in British politics, and later spread across the globe as part of the NPM story as documented by Christensen and Lægreid (2001a) and others.

The most frequently repeated promise of PPP is its ability to achieve cost savings, compared to traditional methods, in the pursuit of better value for money (VFM). Whether in the form of better VFM, or improved on-budget or on-time delivery, all can be seen as a continuation of cost savings concerns begun earlier in the case of contracting-out reforms of the 1970s and 1980s. Other PPP promises, such as improved accountability and greater innovation, also add to the idea that PPP continues on from earlier NPM reform efforts. To reformers, it ticks all the NPM boxes. But there is more to PPP than simply the hope of economic efficiency. PPP offers the intellectual advantage of the NPM holy grail – the promise of performance measurement through the definition of outcomes, rather than the past obsession with inputs, organizational structures and output services. Enabling government, in the role of purchaser, to specify simply the achievement of particular outcomes such as high-speed road travel or quality building occupancy, the stage was set for PPP to take its place as a management tool of the highest order. The common preference to provide private finance as part of the partnership arrangement and to underpin contract performance incentives in terms of on-time and on-budget project delivery criteria then cemented this place.

The early story of how New Labour in the UK came to embrace the PPP concept is illustrative here. New Labour was in some ways expected to drop the PFI policy once it gained power in 1997. But it kept the PFI agenda going and rebranded it as PPP. One crucial issue was not so much the concept itself, but the signal it sent to the City of London. The message from New Labour in pressing ahead with PPP was that New Labour was not anti-business. On the contrary, it encouraged the private sector to join public sector organizations in the finance and delivery of services, and in the best traditions of NPM, use private sector skills, expertise and capabilities to provide important public sector services. In doing this, New Labour not only demonstrated its mettle as a reformist government, but also confirmed its commitment to the third way and took a step towards shedding the old Labour character (Flinders 2005).

In order to analyse further the suggestion that PPP is an extension of NPM the following considers the former in the light of some of the characteristics commonly associated with the latter. According to some theoretical constructs, NPM has been characterized as having three important elements: disaggregation (or fragmentation), competition and incentivization (Dunleavy et al. 2005). Does PPP have any of these characteristics?

Fragmentation

PPPs were seen as opening up the gates for private sector organizations. In the UK, private sector organizations became involved with school maintenance, hospital maintenance, training courses for unemployed people and the designing and financing of key infrastructure projects in the transport sector such as bridges, tunnels and roads. Infrastructure planning was chopped into smaller pieces.

Competition

Although synergy was always one of the big selling points of PPPs in the rhetoric, PPPs were not freed from competition. In many contracts, and despite all the hype surrounding PPPs, there was often a principal facing one or more agents. Public and private sector organizations in the European Union had to follow the EU public procurement rules when awarding a contract. Private sector organizations had to compete, still, against each other in consortia to obtain the public sector contracts.

Incentivization

Incentivization, as alluded previously, was a key aspect of NPM (see Dunleavy at al. 2005), and was built into the contracts in very sophisticated ways. Put simply, contracts were written in ways that would keep the private sector oriented to the task before them. Fortunately, too, not many contracts were of the 'cosy deals'-type expected from the first round of criticisms characterizing the PPP idea.

Overall, then, it is in many ways plausible to argue that PPPs extended the marketization ideas that were inherent in the NPM agenda. Marketization, as well as private sector ideas and methods were all clearly key parts of NPM. The introduction of PPPs did not mean that markets went away; in some senses they just became more sophisticated or complex by inviting private sector organizations to organize themselves in complex consortia.

Public–Private Partnerships as Part of the New Public Governance

The notion of PPP has always been as much about governing style as it has about anything narrower, such as the delivery of an infrastructure project. So it is with modern-day, long-term infrastructure contract PPPs. They of course demonstrate the willingness and skills of private sector organizations to contribute to the delivery of public services (as noted in the previous section), but they are also an inherent demonstration of governance style and a symbol of government's belief in the crucial role of the private sector – as well as its own – in infrastructure delivery.

All of these broader governance issues were evident in Labour's early adoption of PPP in the UK. As Hellowell (2010) put it, in opposition the UK Labour Party had been attempting to mend its traditionally poor relationship with business when they produced a 1994 paper supporting and expanding the UK PFI scheme. As Hellowell observes:

> ... the paper was a seminal moment in Labour's attempt to develop a new relationship with industry, and in particular those elements of industry that had historically been hostile to Labour, specifically the financial institutions of the City of London and their advisers.

Through PFI, the government's relationship with business, and particularly with financial institutions and their advisers, had been mended. By the mid 1990s, then, what had been 'a high-profile but dysfunctional policy idea' had been transformed into 'an effective financing mechanism', as Hellowell (2010) put it. Moreover, the promotion of PFI both across the UK public sector and internationally was another means of cementing relations with the City. As Hellowell again observes, the UK government committed itself to using its influence to expand PPP in the European Union, as part of a broader push to open up the markets of the continent. Through the provision of professional services for technical procedures and guidance for public authorities, market entry was thereby facilitated by British banks and other businesses in countries such as the Czech Republic, Mexico and South Africa. In other words, PPP was as much about enhancing export services for the UK as it was about infrastructure delivery *per se*.

Another aspect of governance style was the degree to which this new PFI/PPP technique enabled governments simply to deliver investment today without that investment impacting on today's public finance statistics. On this issue, Hellowell (2010) eloquently states that 'this is an advantage that has appealed to Conservative and Labour governments alike, just as it has proved irresistible to governments around the world'.

PPP, in other words, enabled many governance-related objectives to be achieved. These have included: changing the public sector culture; infrastructure delivery away from the Public Sector Borrowing Requirement; improved business sector confidence; greater feasibility to apply user fees in some instances; and even support for business during difficult times. Clearly, PPP has functioned as a governance tool as much as it has functioned as a tool for infrastructure delivery.

From a theoretical perspective, too, there are some additional points worth making. First, PPPs can also be seen as a renewal of the public management reform agenda. PPPs are about collaboration: they mean that no single agency can deal with a problem on its own. This has been argued in many places and perhaps most forcefully by Donald F. Kettl (2009) in his book *The Next Government of the United States*. Kettl observes how no organization can solve any serious public policy problem by itself. Collaboration is needed for most of the important tasks. Other network theorists have embraced the same idea. Indeed, networked governance as a concept has been present in the public management and administration literature for some time now, and is attracting more interest year by year (see Osborne 2009 for a recent overview). Today's public policy world is too complex to be handled by any one organization, or a single organization as envisaged in the NPM agenda. Defining a target for a public leader and charging him or her to form a results-based organization is simply not enough for the complexity of the issues before the public sector. Collaboration is needed.

Second, the creation of a more broadly defined public value (Moore 1995, O'Flynn 2007) could also be seen as an argument for PPPs. To begin with, the levels at which providing such 'public value' is aimed for are many fold, and range from reforms to management and delivery right up to issues of culture change, export services, supporting the role of the private sector as the crucial engine of our economy and ensuring a confident business sector. The ambiguity here is palpable, but perhaps also typical of today's difficult and interconnected political decision making era. Under such circumstances, public value cannot be decided by any one organization, and must be created together in many organizations. Innovation, too, is likely to continue to play an important role here.

Third, innovation in governance (Hartley and Moore 2008) means broadening the mindset and letting other sources be of help in thinking innovatively. A clear attribute of a PPP is its force in that it can create new solutions that neither the public sector nor the private sector can see by themselves. With the innovation debate having been dominant in many discussions about the future of the public services in recent years, PPPs can be the medium for transmitting these new ideas and putting them into practice. As a consequence, the argument about synergy, or getting the best of both worlds, has often been seen as a dominant feature of pro-PPP arguments.

Summing up, then, it can be argued that three governance threads are at the core of the PPP phenomenon; collaboration in governance networks, creating a value that is beyond the immediate output focus associated with NPM, and an emphasis on innovation and finding new solutions to new challenges. All three of these governance threads are as central to understanding the PPP phenomenon as notions of management and project delivery reform.

A Transformative Perspective on Public–Private Partnerships

PPPs can be seen both as consisting of NPM elements, and as belonging to the post-NPM agenda that emphasizes the new governance elements associated with networks, collaboration and innovation towards a broader conceptualization of public value creation. How do we deal with this split in conceptualization? One suggestion is to view the development from a transformative perspective (Christensen and Lægreid 2001a, 2007a). For example, the idea of institutional change mechanisms is a concept found in historical institutional theory (Streeck and Thelen 2005). These various mechanisms include displacement, layering, drift, conversion and exhaustion that will change institutions gradually over time. Similarly, PPP can be thought of as a concept that transcends NPM and moves into the new governance arena. To start with, there are elements in PPPs that are clearly NPM-based and that are grounded in institutions, for example the public procurement rules in the European Union. Although the concept of PPPs may signal partnering and cooperation, this state of affairs cannot be manifested unless there has first been competition (formal procurement processes) according to the European Union rules. Incentivizations in contracts that include both bonuses and punishments are also a part of the contractualization surrounding PPPs, and these are not going to go away any time soon. At the same time, there are clearly movements towards a new governance agenda. PPPs offer a way to think about a complex problem when there is no obvious solution in sight, and the partnership itself can create the conditions for innovative practice between public sector and private sector actors.

So, what is the 'problem' here that PPP offers to solve? In line with the multiplicity of meanings given to the phenomenon and the numerous versions of PPP, there are also a multiplicity of problems to which PPP may be applied. A few examples are sufficient. Much of the early political appeal of PPP came from the initial promise of delivering public infrastructure without raising measured levels of public sector debt in the UK. In other words, PPP in this case functioned as a 'mega-credit card' (as Hodge and Greve 2007 put it), or, in the words of Flinders (2005: 15), a 'buy now, pay later' scheme. The point here is not to make a judgment of worth or preference, but to make the observation that PPP offered a new technical solution to a political problem. Secondly, to the degree that a PPP project may indeed deliver earlier and more timely results than traditional projects, PPP may provide another solution. PPPs may well offer a new project delivery method which cuts through the increasingly laboured and paralysed constraints now placed on governments of most persuasions in local policy making, community consultation and planning. Private energies are mounted to push through projects and achieve project results through new methods. Thirdly, and at the broader level, PPPs involving private finance enable governments to demonstrate progress and deliver impressive and iconic projects to citizens. Government is then seen as 'action-oriented' despite operating in the midst of multiple and expanding accountability frameworks, increased legislative webs of oversight, and simultaneous pressure to reduce staff numbers in public employment lists. Again, a technical tool is being employed to deliver on a government's policy priorities. Fourthly, the broader label of PPP is also useful in the development context as governments struggle to signal their political philosophy and governance directions whilst nurturing a private construction sector from scratch. For example, whilst the notion of PPP projects in China now has common acceptance, even successful PPP projects such as the Line 4 subway project in Beijing may still function essentially as a political statement rather than anything a Western government or bureaucrat might assume. This project, with just over 92 per cent public ownership, would more likely be seen as a 'public–public partnership' in the West!

A PPP is thereby an example of a transformative institution. Theoretically, PPP cannot be labelled as purely belonging to the NPM camp or the post-NPM camp. This is an empirical matter in which the dominant characteristic features will be revealed over time. In the so-called PPP-advanced countries, that is, where the markets for PPPs are 'mature', in other words the UK, Australia and Ireland (according to a Deloitte 2006 survey of global experiences with PPPs), examples or traces of fragmentation, competition and incentivization in the performance contracts signed for actual PPP projects will still be evident. These qualities are currently being retained in the European Union public procurement rules, where competition is upheld as a value. Meanwhile, transformative movements are going on in reaching out to other organizations and partners in various networks, coalitions, alliances or consortia: private sector organizations are constantly engaged in new consortia that bid for new PPP contracts; governments are encouraging public organizations to share knowledge about partnership organizing and thereby also encouraging network-like organizing; private organizations are seeking to establish what will create value beyond the immediate tasks at hand; and some private organizations see themselves as contributing to the creation of public value that does not minimize their own interest in creating private value for their shareholders (Skanska is an example of this, see the official website). Moreover, in the new EU member states and the developed world, private sector organizations are often allocated a role in developing the countries which make their activities more worthwhile to those countries than completing a specific infrastructure project (see for example, the World Bank's interest in the role of PPPs in the evolution of the new member states).

The empirical nature of the matter also makes it complicated to talk about a real 'transformation' from NPM to a post-NPM future dominated entirely by new governance attributes. The NPM elements of PPPs are likely to persist for a long time yet, while the governance aspects of PPPs will develop gradually. There is no specific end-state in sight, when PPP can be interpreted as having reached a total 'post-NPM' stage. The ambiguity of the PPP concept is again at the forefront of the thinking here, and the point made previously is re-emphasized – that the ambiguity of PPP itself is what in many ways is fundamentally attractive about the notion. Language in politics is its lifeblood, and PPP is clearly a warmer and preferable label than traditional techniques such as privatization and contracting out. It has indeed been seen by many as a concept that would make the 'contracting out/privatization' image go away. Yet this has not happened and critics keep on insisting that PPP is a key way for public services to be run on market-based governance principles.

On the other hand, PPPs can be seen as a new way of reaching out to many more organizations to work together to solve complex problems. The possibilities that the PPP concept holds for finding new and smarter ways to cooperate have not yet been exhausted. This is for two reasons. First, most Western governments would argue that a strong economy and thriving community requires a strong and talented private sector as well as a powerful and capable government. Mintzberg (1996) put it nicely when he said that the so-called 'triumph' of capitalism over communism in the 1980s was not so much a triumph of the free market idea over government – but the triumph of balance. Likewise, Herb Simon (1997) over a decade ago argued that Western communities do not want either the domination of business interests over governments or the domination of governments over business interests. By definition, therefore, citizens want a balance of both public-ness and private-ness, and the label of PPP simply reinforces this desire. The second reason for the PPP notion having a bright future is its breadth. It is an infinitely flexible and pliable label and as a consequence can easily adapt to new economic circumstances or challenges. Thus, public finance or private finance could in concept be applied, along with a wide range of differing possible options, as management and political fashions dictate. All versions of 'partnership' would, by definition, involve both public and private efforts to some degree.

Naturally, any assessment of the degree to which PPP has succeeded from a transformative perspective requires some evaluation of the extent to which PPP has performed well in traditional terms as well. On this score, the current rampant performance debates will continue, as will debates on the degree to which private sector preferences under the NPM rubric will continue to be entertained following the global financial crisis of 2008/2009. Three relevant observations might be made here. First, governments were advised to step into the breach quickly and offer financial support to ailing private banks and institutions after confidence evaporated in world financial markets and the capacity of private financiers to look after anything other than their own narrow financial interests was questioned. Moving forward this should of course be cause for questioning the faith in the superiority of private sector ideas. Second, with countries such as the UK and Ireland leading the global PPP bandwagon but also suffering bigger financial and economic shocks than many others, one might rightly question the veracity of advice coming from such countries' financial advisers in terms of outcomes for their citizens. Or as Greve and Mörth (2010) put it, perhaps it is just as well that Scandinavian countries, for example, did not adopt PPPs with the reformist zeal that some others did! The third observation here is that in terms of rigorous assessment of PPP performance, it is early days. But if one were courageous enough to venture a judgement, then on balance, PFI/PPPs probably perform no worse than traditional public sector operations undertaken through contracts with major private sector construction firms, and better than the older institutions in the form of Western public works departments. They also appear to deliver infrastructure quickly compared to traditional methods, in part because new delivery processes are often now possible and cut through conventional delays, and in part also because much of the planning and preparatory work has often already been undertaken over preceding decades. In any event, this logic suggests that PPPs are probably politically effective whilst remaining relatively economically inefficient. Given their complexity, the ongoing battles over evaluation methods and criteria, and the ambiguity of the exact counterfactual in any case, this would hardly be a surprising conclusion. Perhaps it would also be a suitable post-NPM result, as it would meet two of the primary performance objectives of both the public and private sectors – those of political efficacy and profitability!

Moreover, as complex public policy challenges keep popping up and craving more and more of decision-makers time (disasters, financial crises, pandemics and so on), there is likely to be a continuing interest in finding new and innovative ways to work together. The collaboration agenda clearly has a direct appeal to many decision-makers who come to experience that hierarchic-bureaucratic decisions and market-based governance alone do not help solve immediate problems satisfactorily. Therefore, a quest to collaborate and to pursue partnering with relevant organizations will be one of the key features of these coming decades as nobody can manage by just go-it-alone strategies (Kettl 2009).

At the organizational level, the dual split of the PPP also poses challenges for managing and governing. As many have pointed out, the challenges of managing a network structure is potentially more complicated than running an organization with a clear performance goal (Klijn and Koppenjan 2004). Managing partnerships means that many organizations' aspirations and activities have to be coordinated. The management has to find a way to produce value for both the public organization(s) and the private organization(s) involved in the partnership arrangement. Likewise, the governing structure surrounding a PPP is likely to be a complex one. A PPP is not the same as an ordinary contracting out arrangement where a principal directs one or more agents to accomplish the tasks agreed upon. The contractual period is usually longer in a PPP, up to 30 or even 40 years. Moreover, as the governing structures are not developed the same way as in contracting out arrangements there may be uncertainty as to how the *post hoc* regulation should be dealt with. The research has yet to come up with enough empirical evidence for a verdict on how the management of partnerships is developing, but research in public infrastructure projects point to the complex processes and challenges for managers that follow with partnerships (Klijn and Koppenjan 2004).

Conclusions

This chapter has focused on the development of PPPs as part of both the NPM agenda and the post-NPM agenda. PPPs have been an important part of the last decades' policy development in the public sector. They were associated with countries that were also among the most prolific in their employment of NPM, including the UK, Australia, Ireland, the United States and Canada. It has been suggested in this chapter that PPPs can best be understood from a transformative perspective. Present day PPPs have elements of the NPM agenda – fragmentation, competition and incentivization – but also elements that are associated with the post-NPM agenda – governance networks and collaboration, a broader conception of public value creation than just focusing on outputs and the focus on innovation practices.

PPPs are thereby representative for much of the current situation in the literature and analysis in public management reform. Many elements associated with PPPs are still related to NPM, although the recent ideas and discussions may revolve around the prospects of a post-NPM agenda. PPPs retain marketization aspects, but there are also signs that they are part of the network age where organizations need to cooperate with each other to address the public policy challenges that lie ahead. Theoretically, the transformative perspective heralded by Christensen and Lægreid, and the notion of a fine-grained analysis of institutional change mechanisms, put forward by Streeck and Thelen amongst others, may help us to understand better the complex change processes ahead. There is an emerging literature on the empirical experience of PPPs and how they fit into the global reform developments in both developed and developing jurisdictions. PPPs are part of a movement which wants to go beyond NPM, but just how this will happen in practice is currently unclear. The future study of PPPs will therefore also be important in ascertaining just how far we have moved into post-NPM territory.

PART V
EFFECTS AND
IMPLICATIONS OF NPM

NPM and the Search
for Efficiency

Rhys Andrews

Introduction

The belief that large public bureaucracies are inherently inefficient was a critical force driving the emergence of New Public Management (NPM) in the 1980s. To reconfigure the state along more cost-efficient lines, NPM protagonists recommended that the public sector be downsized and opened up to greater private sector influence (Hood 1991). Although the high-tide of the NPM phenomenon has arguably passed, the relationship between NPM reforms and the cost-efficiency of public organizations remains an extremely timely concern for students of public management. Faced with the effects of global recession, governments are once again searching for tools and techniques which can enable public managers to seek out and find cashable cost-savings. In this chapter, evidence on the impact of specific NPM reforms on public sector efficiency is surveyed to provide a preliminary assessment of the successes and failures of the past 20 or so years.

Public management scholars suggest that there are several key features of NPM reforms which are assumed to enhance the relative efficiency of the provision of public services: agencification, performance management, competition, public–private partnership and consumerism (see Part IV of the present volume). The creation of single-purpose agencies to implement certain policies and the use of monitoring systems to evaluate service achievements is thought to reduce the transaction costs associated with controlling and coordinating large seemingly impermeable bureaucracies. Similarly, the introduction of increased competition for service provision, or quasi-competition through the use of benchmarking and league tables, and the development of collaborative arrangements between public and private organizations are all argued to have positive implications for efficiency, since they ensure that bureaucrats are constantly under pressure to search for new ways to drive costs down. In addition, the extension of consumer rights and the involvement of users in service design have been regarded as critical devices for making public services more customer-orientated – an attribute that is claimed to inevitably tend towards better efficiency (Day and Klein 1987).

Arguments for the introduction of NPM reforms have had significant practical, as well as theoretical import, and have been reflected in numerous major reforms in several countries, such as the US Government Performance Results Act 1992, the Service Improvement Initiative in Canada, the Putting Service First scheme in Australia, Strategic Results Area Networks in New Zealand, Management by Results in Sweden, and Regulation of Performance Management and Policy Evaluation in the Netherlands (Pollitt and Bouckaert 2004). However, despite extensive acknowledgement of the worldwide impact of NPM and a growing evidence base on the implementation of NPM reforms, surprisingly few studies have systematically investigated the relationship between these reforms and public sector efficiency (Simpson 2009).

In this chapter, it is the salience of NPM's link with the drive to make public services more efficient which is the main concern. Published empirical studies of NPM-inspired policies and public sector efficiency are surveyed to provide a preliminary assessment of what is known about the connection between the two. To what extent are the relative costs associated with delivering public services attributable to agencification, performance management, competition, public–private partnership and consumerism? Quantitative evidence from across several developed countries is assessed to develop a better understanding of which features of NPM (if any) appear most likely to lead to efficiency savings and which do not. This is a timely and extremely pertinent subject for investigation. In the wake of the global financial crisis, policies to promote public service value for money are again the focus of policy-makers' attention (Broadbent 2010). Governments across the world are increasingly concerned with ensuring that a downsized public sector can still deliver value for money. The management of public organizations and the search for policies to reduce costs while maintaining service standards will thus be subject to ever more intense scrutiny given severe budgetary pressures over the forthcoming years.

In the first part of the chapter, the concept of public sector efficiency is analysed. Next, the hypothetical effects of five key features of NPM are examined. These are: agencification, performance management, competition, public–private partnership and consumerism. In the third section, the results of 18 quantitative studies examining the NPM-efficiency relationship are reviewed. The chapter concludes by discussing which aspects of NPM seem to have mattered most and what additional knowledge is required to fully understand in what circumstances NPM might lead to better or worse cost-effectiveness.

What is Public Sector Efficiency?

Crudely speaking, the concept of efficiency refers to the relative inputs required to achieve desired outputs or outcomes. The notion that the maximization of outputs over inputs is a core administrative value in the public sector has a long pedigree, especially in the United States. The origins of the concept of efficiency can be traced to the influential Progressive Era of social, political and economic reform in the US from the 1890s to the 1920s. During this period, numerous liberal reformers succumbed to the belief that rational planning was necessary to eliminate waste within the economy, society and government, as well as to enhance positively the quality of citizens' lives. Scientific study of the causes and consequences of inefficient administration within each of these sectors would therefore enable experts to identify and design technical solutions to social problems (Mosher 1968).

According to Fredrick Taylor (1911), in particular, it was possible to derive universal principles of efficient work design by amassing a wealth of information about the work routines of individual employees, especially in terms of the amount of time that was required for them to produce a given unit of output. By comparing the performance of individual workers, it would then become apparent what standards it was reasonable to expect workers to attain, and hence what constituted efficient production and the level of training and supervision required to achieve this. Although Taylor's work was largely carried out in manufacturing plants, he nonetheless believed it applicable to any organizational setting, including government. Indeed, he vigorously argued that the scientific organization of government could only be achieved by elevating the principle of efficiency above normative political values (Taylor 1916).

Taylor's ideas about the need for a science of administrative efficiency later influenced the work of scholars such as Luther Gulick and Lyndall Urwick (1937) who urged the development of universal principles of organizational rules and structures in order to maximize outputs over inputs. Herbert Simon (1976) too sought to understand the organizational antecedents of efficiency.

While Taylorism may never really have gone away, advocates of NPM became particularly vociferous supporters of the search for public sector efficiency (Moe 1994). With its focus on data acquisition, apolitical managerialism and performance incentives, NPM has obvious affinities with Taylor's work. However, its explicit rejection of bureaucracy and its penchant for private sector solutions (see Osborne and Gaebler 1992), indicate that it is difficult to draw straightforward comparisons between NPM and previous doctrines of government efficiency (Schachter 2007). Moreover, lost within much of this debate, about the pursuit of efficiency, is considered reflection on the nature of public sector efficiency itself. In particular, theories of government (in)efficiency associated with NPM have not paid much attention to how efficiency should be conceptualized, operationalized or evaluated.

One fruitful lens through which to examine the concept of public sector efficiency is public finance theory. In his classic (1959) work *The Theory of Public Finance*, Richard Musgrave argued that government was responsible for performing three separate but interrelated functions: allocation, distribution and stabilization. The allocative function pertained to the role of government in meeting demands that could not be met through the free market; the distributive function to government's role in upholding an equitable distribution of goods; and the stabilization function, to its contribution to stable economic growth. By dividing the functions of government in this way, it was possible to gain a clearer insight into the relationships between taxation and expenditure within the public sector, and correspondingly the relative levels of government efficiency.

Although Musgrave's three-function framework was originally conceptualized at the macro-level of the state, it can be applied to all levels of government. Thus, assessments of the impacts of specific policy reforms on the public sector should ideally seek to explore their effects on each of the three functions. Indeed, it is possible to identify and measure three general dimensions of efficiency in the public sector that reflect the Musgravian framework: allocative, distributive and productive.

Allocative efficiency can be characterized as the most efficient allocation of resources to reflect the wishes of recipients (Leibenstein 1966). Thus, in the public sector, the responsiveness of service providers, such as local governments, to the demands of service recipients, for more neighbourhood level services, for example, can be set against the inputs required to meet those demands to provide an indication of allocative efficiency (Boyne 2002a). *Distributive efficiency* may be defined as the most efficient process through which goods and services can be distributed to those in greatest need of them (Lerner 1944). This can be measured by gauging the equity of public sector outputs and outcomes relative to the rate of inputs (Boyne 2002a). *Productive efficiency* (or technical efficiency) reflects the classic notion of efficiency as the maximization of outputs and the minimization of inputs (Farrell 1957). When measuring productive efficiency in the public sector, both the quantity and quality of outputs can be set against inputs (Boyne 2002a).

In order to provide a comprehensive review of the evidence on NPM's effects on public sector efficiency it is important to consider the potential relationship of key NPM reforms with each of these dimensions of efficiency, especially since improvements (or deteriorations) in one dimension may not necessarily be reflected in another. The hypothetical effects of NPM on efficiency are explored next.

Hypothetical Effects of NPM on Efficiency

The influence of the search for efficiency on NPM can in many respects be traced to the breakdown of the post-war welfarist consensus in the 1970s. In response to the perceived inefficiencies of 'big' government, economists and libertarian thinkers began to argue for a new settlement based around the need to inject incentive structures into the public sector that would curb seemingly inexorable budget-maximization by bureaucrats. In particular, public choice theory (Niskanen 1971) laid great emphasis on the need to better coordinate and manage public organizations through the application of market mechanisms. At the same time, Taylorism and the scientific management movement experienced a revival in fortunes, as management scholars and gurus increasingly touted the indispensability of professional management expertise (for example Peters and Waterman 1982, see Hood 1991). Thus, the confluence of social, political and economic forces at the heart of NPM came to be inextricably tied to a renewed search for efficiency in the public sector.

Each of the key features of NPM is thought by their advocates to have distinct (though probably interrelated) positive effects on efficiency in the public sector. Although critics of NPM suggested that its focus on efficiency is likely to be detrimental to equity of outcome within the public sector (and thereby distributive efficiency) (Pollitt 1990), it is nonetheless the case that NPM protagonists believed it possible to square this apparent circle (Osborne and Gaebler 1992). For the sake of simplicity and brevity, it is assumed here that the hypothesized benefits of NPM may be observed for allocative, distributive and productive efficiency. The remainder of this section, therefore, outlines the hypothetical positive effects of agencification/disaggregation, performance management, competition, public–private partnership and consumerism on public sector efficiency.

Agencification

Agencification through the disaggregation of units in the public sector is assumed in NPM to make formerly monolithic excessively bureaucratic organizations more amenable to control by professional managers. The devolution of power to lower levels of government and the establishment of single-purpose agencies and arm's-length management organizations are symptomatic of this drive to impart greater control over policy delivery to managers and away from senior civil servants. By according managers greater control over budgets, it was thought that they would seek out and find new innovative solutions to service delivery problems, thereby cutting costs (Osborne and Gaebler 1992). Another important aspect of this process of disaggregation is the attempt to separate the purchasing and providing arms of public organizations. This was thought necessary to enable purchasing agents to drive the price of service delivery downwards (Hood 1991). At the same time, these structural reforms would create clearer lines of accountability and control, thereby increasing the pressure on managers and bureaucrats to deliver results.

Performance Management

Allied to the supposed gains in control associated with agencification was a desire to improve the monitoring of the performance of public organizations. Central to the pursuit of better quality services at a lower cost in NPM has therefore been an emphasis on output controls, with resource allocation and rewards linked to measured achievements (Hood 1991). To enable this process to be carried out effectively and scientifically, it was deemed necessary for public organizations to introduce performance management practices similar to those found in the private sector, such as total quality management (Boyne et al. 2002). Strong performance information systems can be used to formulate, implement and monitor organizational goals. As such, it is claimed by management scholars that performance management ensures that vital information about organizational functioning is not overlooked or insufficiently considered (Huff and Reger 1987). Thompson (2002) suggests that measurement and control systems are essential to enable managers in the public sector to review and analyse how resources are spent and what results are achieved. Thus, the introduction of performance management systems was integral to the attempt to control inefficient spending within the public sector.

Competition

At the heart of NPM reforms is the contention that market mechanisms are required to inject competitive pressures into the public sector. In many cases this has led to the privatization or deregulation of public services (see Swann 1988), and in others attempts to establish either compulsory competitive tendering processes or an internal market for service provision (Eliassen and Sitter 2008). One prerequisite for injecting competitive pressures into the public sector is the existence of multiple service providers who are able to compete for 'customers'. Where such a market of providers is restricted to a set of public organizations, another prominent feature of the public sector reforms across the globe has been the introduction of a range of comprehensive performance classification schemes to establish benchmark (or yardstick) competition into the public sector (Pollitt and Bouckaert 2004). Clear comparable performance information is hypothesized to lead to better services by enhancing the 'voice' of service users and their awareness of 'exit' options (Hirschman 1970). If service users are unhappy with the quality of service that they receive from a particular organization then they may simply 'vote with their feet' in search of a better deal (Tiebout 1956). This, in turn, is hypothesized to generate efficiencies as competition for clients between organizations may become more intense (Salmon 1987).

Public–Private Partnership

Osborne and Gaebler argue that the private sector is 'better at performing economic tasks, innovating, replicating successful experiments, adapting to rapid change, abandoning unsuccessful or obsolete activities and performing complex or technical tasks' (1992: 45–46). By increasing the pressure to reduce the ratio of inputs to outputs, partnerships between public organizations and private firms can therefore generate large savings. Private sector organizations operate in an economic environment of contestable resource markets. Pressure to maximize shareholder value together with the threat of mergers and acquisitions should ensure that value is maximized from resources controlled by private sector organizations (Vining and Boardman 1992). Alongside the discipline of surviving in contestable markets and the absence of conflicting political imperatives, protagonists of NPM have maintained that private sector organizations typically benefit from less 'red tape'. With fewer formal decision-making procedures and less administrative oversight, private sector organizations may conceivably be less hampered by bureaucratic rules and controls (Rainey 1989). They might enjoy, as a result, more managerial flexibility than their public sector counterparts, which, in turn, can enable their public sector partners to reap a comparative advantage in terms of organizational responsiveness, and a corresponding reduction in the costs of inputs.

Consumerism

The drive to enhance the customer orientation of the public sector reflects the managerialist elements of NPM that stress the virtues of the private sector's responsiveness to market pressures. To introduce consumerist principles within public organizations it is necessary to ensure that there is a constant flow of information to service users to enable them to become competent and discriminating clients of public services. At the same time, there is corresponding need for public organizations to establish feedback mechanisms through which customer voice can be heard. Improving communication with service users about what public organizations do can help generate public confidence (Cowell et al. 2005), which may relieve them of the 'burden of enforcing compliance' with legislation, increasing their capacity to improve services (Boix and Posner 1998). Evidence from the US suggests that citizens are able to make discerning judgements about varying levels of service quality and that they often use consultation processes as an opportunity to provide feedback on matters of concern (Swindell and Kelly 2000). Better information on the issues facing public organizations and improved citizen surveying procedures are thus conceived as effective means for 'guiding program management and organisational functioning' (Heinrich 2002: 722). At the same time, involving users directly in service design is also thought to result in efficiency gains as bespoke services are likely to be more responsive to clients' needs (Office of Public Service Reform 2002).

NPM and Public Sector Efficiency: The Empirical Evidence

A growing literature examines the impact of the features of NPM on organizational performance in the public sector. For example, Andrews, Boyne and Enticott (2006) and Walker and Boyne (2006) analyse the relationship between performance management, public–private partnership and consumerism on local government performance. And several researchers assess the effects of competition on the performance of high schools (for example Smith and Meier 1995, Andersen and Serritzlew 2007) and hospitals (Kessler and McLellan 2000, Propper et al. 2004). However, rather less is presently known about the impact of NPM on public sector efficiency, despite the explosion of academic and policy interest in the relationship between NPM and potential cost-savings across the globe during the past decade (see Pollitt and Bouckaert 2004).

Numerous researchers have speculated on the effects of NPM on public sector efficiency (for example Lane 2000, Torres and Pina 2002). Nevertheless, to date, few studies have systematically analysed the links between specific features of NPM and the cost-effectiveness of public services. Research on the effects of contracting out and privatization on public sector efficiency was not included in this review of the available evidence, as these are (arguably) not distinctively NPM policies (see Eliassen and Sitter 2008). Moreover, there are several published reviews of the existing findings on these issues (see, for example, Domberger and Jensen 1997, Hodge 2000). Similarly, to retain the conceptual focus of the review, studies of the relationship between planning and targets and efficiency are excluded (see Boyne 2010 for a review of these).

To identify published studies which analyse the impact of NPM on efficiency, a thorough review of the available evidence requires the adaptation of additional search terms for the key features of NPM analysed here. For agencification: arm's-length control, corporatization and disaggregation; for performance management: performance monitoring; for competition: contestability, market-testing and internal market; for public–private partnership: PFI; and for consumerism: customer focus, consultation and empowerment. This extensive search revealed only 18 studies that sought to quantitatively analyse the relationship between some feature of NPM and efficiency in the public sector. Numerous articles were deemed unsuitable for inclusion with the review because they were theoretical or reviews of existing evidence, drew on inappropriate measures of efficiency (particularly raw costs data), or did not carry out statistical tests for significant differences. The selected studies were all undertaken in single countries, with most being conducted in the UK (six), Germany, Sweden and the US represented on two occasions, and Canada, Denmark, Italy, Korea, Norway and Spain once each. Despite the appropriateness of the content of these studies, they are nonetheless limited.

None of the studies utilize a comprehensive theoretical model of NPM. Rather than adopt the kind of conceptual framework that could deliver a summative assessment of the overall impact of NPM, the available evidence largely focuses on only one feature of NPM, especially competition which forms the subject of 11 studies. At the same time, none of the studies identified here examined all three dimensions of public sector efficiency, or included measures of each of these within the same model to assess potential trade-offs between them. Indeed, the only efficiency dimension that is included within the review studies is that of productive efficiency. To develop and fully test a comprehensive theoretical model of the impact of NPM on public sector efficiency, it would be important to explore the effects of multiple reforms on multiple measures in the same study.

Despite their limitations, the quantitative studies summarized below provide an initial template for developing an understanding of the relationship between NPM and efficiency. The evidence covers several different areas of the public sector ranging from single purpose organizations, such as schools, to multipurpose

Table 19.1   Empirical studies of NPM and public sector efficiency

Study	Organizations and sample size	NPM reform	Efficiency dimension	N of tests	% of tests +	NS	-	Controls
Andrews and Entwistle 2010	46 Welsh local government service departments	Public–private partnership	Productive	1		100		E and I
Bilodeau, Laurin and Vining 2007	11 Canadian federal agencies	Agencification	Productive	2	50	50		E
Boschken 2000	42 US Urban transit agencies	Competition	Productive	1		100		E
Boyne 1996	395 UK local governments	Agencification	Productive	1			100	E
Bradley Johnes and Millington 2001	2567 English secondary schools	Competition	Productive	29	79	21		E and I
Ferrari 2006	52 Scottish hospitals	Agencification	Productive	5		100		I
		Competition	Productive	5	40		60	I
Gerdtham et al. 1999	26 Swedish county councils	Competition	Productive	1	100			E
Gonzalez and Trujillo 2008	10 Spanish port authorities	Agencification	Productive	1		100		E
Hansen 2010	271 Danish municipalities	Competition	Productive	24		87.5	12.5	E and I
Hayes, Razzolini and Ross 1998	1303 Illinois municipalities	Competition	Productive	1	100			E
Jensen and Stelling 2007	Swedish railway system	Competition	Productive	2	100			E
Kuntz and Vera 2007	32 German hospitals	Competition	Productive	3	50	50		I
Lee, Chun and Lee 2008	106 Korean hospitals	Agencification	Productive	1	100			E and I
Macinati 2008	148 Italian health care providers	Performance management	Productive	1		100		I
Pendleton 1999	47 UK local bus service providers	Competition	Productive	5	40		60	
Revelli and Tovmo 2007	205 Norwegian local governments	Competition	Productive	2	100			E and I
Schubert 2009	266 German university research units	Performance management	Productive	4	25	75		I
Söderlund et al. 1997	221 English hospitals	Agencification	Productive	4	100			E and I
		Competition	Productive	2		100		E and I

organizations, such as local governments. Several studies draw on samples of over 100 organizations thereby increasing the generalizeability of the findings. In addition, nearly all implement multivariate techniques to control for the potential effects of other relevant external (E) or internal (I) variables. The findings on the effects of each of the key features of NPM are summarized in Table 19.1, and explored in more detail next.

Agencification

Six studies examine the relationship between some form of agencification and efficiency. Bilodeau et al. (2007) find that corporatization, through the designation as a special operating agency or autonomous service agency, of 11 Canadian federal agencies resulted in improvements in employee productivity, though not for overall cost-efficiency measured as unit of output per cost of input. By contrast, disaggregation of local authority services in England and Wales by breaking up the responsibilities for key functions into smaller geographical units is found by Boyne (1996) to be associated with worse waste management efficiency. Ferrari (2006), however, indicates that the establishment of a purchaser–provider spilt had no detectable effect on the efficiency of Scottish hospitals. By contrast, Gonzalez and Trujillo (2008) provide evidence of a small statistically significant improvement in productive efficiency in the wake of decentralization of further powers to Spanish port authorities. Lee et al. (2008), too, find that the efficiency of Korean hospitals improved as a result of reforms encouraging specialization. Söderlund et al. (1997) suggest that both the introduction of a purchaser–provider spilt and the resulting increase in purchaser power have enhanced efficiency in English hospitals.

To assess the evidence from these studies in detail, it is important to consider how their results should be best combined and synthesized. The method that is used here is based on the percentage of statistical tests that support the hypothesis that competition results in better efficiency. To count as support for this hypothesis, the result must be in the predicted direction and be statistically significant, that is, greater than would be likely to arise by chance alone (at the .10 significance level or better). A support score can then be derived by calculating the number of tests that are consistent with the hypothesis that competition results in higher efficiency as a percentage of all the tests that are reported in the study. The final step in this procedure is to construct an aggregate support score across all the studies that have tested the impact of competition on efficiency. This can be done in (at least) two ways (Rosenthal 1991). First, the support score for each study can be treated equally, regardless of whether it contains 1 or 29 tests, thereby ensuring that studies carrying out a large number of tests on the same data set are not given undue importance. Second, the support score for each study can be weighted (multiplied) by the number of tests in that study. In other words, equal weight is attached to each test rather than each study, ensuring that support scores are not biased by studies reporting only a small number of tests.

For the tests of the agencification–efficiency hypothesis included in this analysis, the unweighted scores tend to support the idea that efficiency is more likely to improve (42 per cent) than deteriorate (0 per cent), though it is more probable that no effect will be observed (58 per cent). This finding is replicated for the weighted scores (43 per cent positive, 57 per cent no difference). Thus, although a positive impact on efficiency for agencification may be observed more often than a negative one, this is not uniformly the case. At the same time, systematic investigation of the effects of agencification on allocative and distributive efficiency is necessary to derive firmer conclusions on the merits of this particular reform.

Performance Management

Two studies address the relationship between the introduction of performance management systems and efficiency in the public sector using quantitative methods. In both cases, the balance of evidence suggests that performance management makes little difference to efficiency. Macinati (2008) uncovers no efficiency gains resulting from the use of new management information systems by Italian health care providers, while Schubert (2009) finds that the introduction of performance evaluation systems is associated with better efficiency for only one out of four measures of the efficiency of German university research units. Although neither study reveals a negative effect of performance management, the meagre evidence of its benefits for efficiency contradicts long-standing theories, such as those embraced by Frederick Taylor, about the merits of strong systems of control and monitoring.

Competition

The literature search uncovered almost twice as many quantitative studies of the impact of competition on efficiency than any other feature of NPM. This may in part be due to its centrality within the reforms made to the public sector, the availability of suitable data for statistical modelling or to economists' greater interest in studying this issue than that of performance management or consumerism. Most of these studies are within a local government setting (7), with all gauging the effects of competition in terms of the existence (or establishment) of multiple providers of the same public service within a given geographical area.

To assess the overall impact of competition on efficiency revealed by the reviewed studies, support scores are again calculated and a meta-analysis of both the unweighted and weighted scores carried out. On this occasion, a positive relationship between the two is found more often than not for the unweighted scores (53 per cent). When these scores are weighted by the number of tests there is more likely to be a positive (44 per cent) than a negative (12 per cent) relationship, though equally likely to be no relationship at all (44 per cent). Once more these findings pertain solely to productive efficiency, so it is important that future studies seek to examine the effects of competition on allocative and distributive efficiency.

Public–Private Partnership

To date, few studies have quantitatively examined the effects of public–private partnership on performance in the public sector. Despite the existence of a massive literature on the relationship between privatization and efficiency (Hodge 2000), and growing evidence on the costs of public–private partnership (especially Private Finance Initiatives – see, for example, Pollock, Price and Player 2007), only a single study provides a statistical test of the connection between such partnership and efficiency. Andrews and Entwistle (2010) find that partnership with private sector has no statistically significant relationship with the productive efficiency of 46 local government service departments in Wales. Given the current vogue for cross-sectoral collaboration (and indeed for partnership *per se*), there is an urgent need for more studies to be carried out on this important topic to ensure that policy-makers are on a firmer footing when extolling the virtues of public–private partnership.

Consumerism

The literature search was unable to uncover any published studies examining the relationship between consumerism and efficiency. This is an area that merits exploration as the potential links between service user consultation and involvement and public service performance in general are poorly understood.

Future Research

The sparse evidence presented here indicates that the features of NPM which appear to be the most likely sources of efficiency gains are agencification and competition. Nevertheless, it is well recognized that NPM reforms may lead to inequitable outcomes for service users (Andersen and Serritzlew 2007). Public sector performance is complex and multidimensional. Public organizations are typically required to meet multiple and potentially conflicting organizational goals (Rainey 1993). Moreover, their achievements are judged by a diverse array of constituencies, such as taxpayers, staff and politicians. The criteria, weighting and interpretation of performance indicators are thus all subject to ongoing debate and contestation amongst key stakeholders (Boyne 2003). This highlights that there is a need for more systematic investigation of the impacts of NPM on each dimension of public sector efficiency, and on the relationship between efficiency and other important aspects of performance in the public sector, such as effectiveness, equity and responsiveness.

The impact of specific NPM reforms on public sector efficiency rarely occurs in isolation from other relevant contextual characteristics. In particular, each of the five aspects of NPM examined here is likely to have important combined as well as separate effects on cost-effectiveness. However, virtually no studies have sought to explore these more complex influences on public service performance. Moreover, it is also conceivable that unintended consequences of NPM reforms are causing the loss of potential efficiencies. There is growing evidence on the negative impact of NPM on job satisfaction and organizational commitment within the public sector (see, for example, Korunka et al. 2003, Noblet and Rodwell 2009). To explore fully how public organizations might benefit or suffer from NPM reforms it would be essential for researchers and policy-makers to trace the relationship between the different features of NPM and other relevant influences on efficiency.

A host of circumstances within and beyond the control of public organizations may also affect their efficiency. It is conceivable that public organizations benefiting from a larger stock of human capital are better able to respond to policy change, or that organizational strategy, structure and process make a difference. Similarly, in countries, regions and communities high in social capital or with a vibrant private sector, public organizations may find it easier to gain the benefits of NPM reforms. Future studies should seek to establish whether human capital and organizational design or civil society and business vitality are key to realizing any potential economies associated with agencification, performance management, competition, public–private partnership and consumerism.

Finally, it is important to note that the reported findings may simply be a product of where and when the empirical studies were conducted. Systematic comparison of the links between NPM reforms and the efficiency of different public agencies in multiple countries could unravel for which policy fields and in which countries NPM has mattered most and in what way. Answers to all these questions could have profound implications for the theory and practice of public administration in years to come.

Conclusion

The issue of public sector efficiency is once again top of the policy agenda across the world. Over the coming years, governments will be subject to an urgent requirement to ensure that resources are used in the optimum way to deliver high quality public services in line with citizens' priorities. The design of policy interventions that will successfully enhance value for money will therefore become increasingly important. This chapter has provided a review of the limited existing quantitative evidence on the NPM-efficiency relationship and identified important areas and topics requiring further research. Although empirical studies are more likely to confirm that NPM reforms have resulted in lower rather than higher rates of input per unit of output, almost nothing is known about whether improvements in technical efficiency are accompanied by better or worse allocative and distributive efficiency. Thus, despite the many claims and counter-claims about the propensity of NPM to deliver efficiency gains, there is presently a dearth of conclusive evidence supporting either position. What little is known about the effects of NPM on efficiency therefore suggests that policy-makers should think twice before embarking on extensive reform programmes to enhance the cost-effectiveness of the public sector.

Unions, Corporatist
Participation and NPM

Paul G. Roness

Introduction

Both administrative policy and corporatism denote certain aspects of the political organization of society. Administrative policy is the type of public policy that concerns the public administration infrastructure. While by nature inward-looking it also aims to affect substantive public policy via the changes it makes in the formal structures, procedures and personnel of public administration (cf. Chapter 1). Corporatism, on the other hand, relates to how interest organizations (particularly trade unions, employers' organizations and other economic-producer organizations) participate in the formulation and implementation of public policy through formal contacts with the public administration. Administrative policy and corporatism may also be linked in the sense that corporatism can play a role in the formulation and implementation of administrative policy, and there may also be elements of corporatism in the public administration infrastructure (Jacobsen and Roness 2008: 145). This chapter, however, will focus on those aspects of corporatism that involve public sector unions as a category of interest organization rather than on corporatism in a broader sense.

This chapter will discuss the effects of certain forms of administrative policy-making and reforms – that is, those related to New Public Management (NPM) – on public sector unions and corporatist participation. In the case of public sector unions, the main focus is on their organizational characteristics – their interests, identities and capabilities – and how they will affect whether and how they take part in the formulation and implementation of NPM reforms. Conversely, the outcome of NPM reforms may also affect these characteristics. While interests are related to the trade unions' goals, identities denote their conception of what kind of organization they are, and capabilities refer to their knowledge and competencies. Taken together these three components will also determine the extent to which public sector unions respond to and have an impact on administrative reforms. In the case of corporatist participation the main focus is on how some elements of corporatism related to public sector unions become part of the public administration infrastructure, that is, as a result of NPM reforms. Here, too, these elements may affect how public sector unions respond to and have an impact on future administrative policy-making.

NPM reforms emphasize certain arguments primarily related to steering and efficiency. They also prescribe certain doctrines that may affect unions and corporatist participation either explicitly or implicitly. The chapter will therefore start by outlining some potential effects of NPM orthodoxy on public sector unions and certain corporatist arrangements. It will then present some actual effects found in the academic literature, distinguishing between union interests and identities, union capabilities and corporatist participation. Some of these effects may be directly related to NPM reforms, while others may be more indirect, revealed only by comparing union characteristics and corporatist participation before and after typical NPM reforms. Since New Zealand and Australia are often regarded as frontrunners of NPM reforms (cf. Chapter 6), the focus will be particularly on these two countries. The chapter will also draw on a previous comparative study on how NPM reforms transformed state employees' unions which likewise involved these two countries (Roness 2001). Further sources include a number of other academic studies as well as government and union documents. The concluding section will also indicate some lacunae for future research.

The NPM Orthodoxy on Unions and Corporatist Participation

In general, two types of arguments may be presented to assess the participation of public sector employees and their unions in administrative policy: arguments based on steering, effectiveness and efficiency; and arguments based on the assertion of democratic rights – that is, the right of representation of the affected parties (Lundquist 1991, Roness 1993). However, according to the NPM orthodoxy, the participation of public sector unions in administrative policy-making and in the public administration infrastructure is only justified if it increases the chances of achieving official goals in an efficient way, and not simply because it asserts the democratic rights of unions and their members. Thus, arguments about steering and efficiency are central to NPM, while arguments about the democratic representation of interests are considered irrelevant.

More specifically, NPM doctrines prescribe that public sector unions should be included in the formulation and implementation of administrative policy and in the result of administrative policy-making if they can contribute important knowledge about the consequences of using various kinds of formal public administration structures, procedures and personnel, or if their participation makes it easier and less costly for the leaders to carry out and apply these types of administrative reforms. If, on the other hand, so the doctrines go, the unions are likely to put obstacles in the way of leaders or make reforms more costly, they should be excluded or their resistance should be overcome.

As noted elsewhere in this book, NPM has a hybrid character, consisting of many components (cf. Chapter 1). According to arguments on steering, effectiveness and efficiency, public sector employees and their unions will be particularly affected by NPM reforms that increase the autonomy of the formal organizational structure and of human resource management (or industrial relations), while reforms related to financial management, for instance, will be less relevant. Thus, the focus here will mainly be on the effects on and implications for unions and corporatist participation of structural devolution and HRM autonomy. Moreover, even if NPM doctrines do not prescribe specific types of effects on public sector union interests and identities, the removal of the distinction between the public and the private sector also implies that public sector unions should not have interests or identities distinct from trade unions in general. With regard to the effects on public sector union capabilities and corporatist participation, the extent to which this will affect the knowledge and power of unions is particularly important.

Effects on Union Interests and Identities

Public sector unions are trade unions whose membership includes public sector employees. Like other trade unions, they attend to their members' interests concerning wages and working conditions. Some unions are also professional associations, that is, organizations that represent and promote the more wide-ranging interests of a profession. Moreover, like many organizations, public sector unions often have not only individuals but also other organizations as members, that is, they may consist of, or be a part of, other unions. For example, many national unions consist of local branches and are part of union confederations. This also means that unions may have several identities at the same time, related to different levels.

The question of whether a union's membership is based on workplace or on qualifications (occupation or profession) may influence what kind of interests and identity are most prominent. When a national union's membership consists almost exclusively of employees within a certain part of the public sector – for example a state agency – the identity of the union and of the public sector organization may coincide and may be quite distinctive. Where membership is based on qualifications that are more widespread throughout the public sector, or that also cover the private sector, the union's organizational identity may be weaker than its occupational or professional identity.

Even for national unions that are affiliated with a union confederation, the importance of hierarchy for interests and identity may vary. Thus, professional associations tend to be more independent of their superior organization than other national unions. There may be historical reasons for this, since professional associations were often founded to represent the interests of a specific profession.

The importance of historical legacy for interests and identity is also evident in the strong and lasting connections between unions and political parties, especially labour parties. Thus, some national unions and union confederations may regard themselves as being part of the labour movement, while others are independent of political parties.

What, then, are the actual effects of NPM reforms on union characteristics? We will first have a closer look at some effects on public sector union interests and identities of NPM reforms in New Zealand. Prior to the introduction of NPM reforms, the existence of the Combined State Unions (CSU, founded in 1932) as a separate union confederation and the Public Service Association (PSA, founded in 1913) as a large national union belonging to the CSU implied that specific interests and identities of public sector employees were built into the trade union structure. While the other union confederation, the Federation of Labour (FOL, founded in 1937), mainly consisted of unions for blue-collar employees in the private sector, and as part of the labour movement had ties with the New Zealand Labour Party (NZLP), the CSU did not have any formal affiliation with political parties. Moreover, the PSA comprised various groups of state employees, while most of the other unions in the CSU were smaller and more specialized according to workplace or qualification.

Until the 1980s, state employees' unions were quite centralized, reflecting the character of the industrial relations system in which they operated (Walsh, Harbridge and Crawford 2001: 185). At first, this also applied to the effects of the State-Owned Enterprises Act 1986. Following the re-election of the Labour government in 1987, the State Services Commission and the Public Service Association agreed to move from a service-wide, occupationally-based bargaining system to a system of departmental agreements (Walsh 1991: 61). However, directly afterwards the government introduced a State Sector Bill containing more radical administrative and industrial relations reforms. The potential for broader-based union action was reduced by the replacement of the separate private and public sector union confederations (FOL and CSU) with the more inclusive New Zealand Council of Trade Unions (CTU) in 1987. This confederation of private and public sector unions and of blue- and white-collar unions did not clearly bind unions to the cooperative approach of its leadership (Bray and Neilson 1996: 78).

Through the State Sector Act of 1988, state employees and their unions became subject to the provisions of the Labour Relations Act, which previously had applied only to the private sector (Boston et al. 1996: 211). The special interests and identities of the public sector were further reduced by the more far-reaching NPM reforms introduced by the new National government elected in 1990. For state employees and their unions, the 1991 Employment Contracts Act (ECA) was particularly important. Under this Act, unions had no special privileges. No employment contract could require workers to join, or not to join, a union. Instead, unions were compelled to compete with one another and with outside consultants selling their services, sometimes with employer support, to potential employee clients (Kelsey 1995).

The reorganization of the internal structure of the PSA may also reflect an attempt to confront the challenges posed by these reforms. While the PSA previously had 24 branches organized geographically, in 1999 it was divided into six sections (called sectors) covering specific parts of the public sector. Within each section (or sector), workplaces and enterprises comprise the basic units, reflecting the fact that these have now replaced occupations as the basis for wage determination. This means that specific union interests and identities within the state sector are now more organization- than occupation-linked. This division of the PSA into six sections has been in place since 1999.

In the Employment Relations Act of 2000, passed by the Labour-led coalition government, collective agreements between registered unions and employers were accorded a more prominent position than under the Employment Contracts Act (ECA) (Shaw 2005: 217). Nevertheless, this new act still covered all employees across the public and the private sector. Thus, unlike prior to the NPM reforms on industrial relations there were no longer any specific legal arrangements for the special interests and identities of public sector unions.

In Australia in the early 1980s there was only one union confederation: the Australian Council of Trade Unions (ACTU). This had recently merged with two other union confederations: with the Australian Council of Salaried and Professional Associations (ACSPA) in 1978, and with the Council of Australian Government Employee Organisations (CAGEO) in 1981. Thus, the ACTU now included unions for federal employees as well as unions for employees in the provinces (that is, states and territories), municipalities and the private sector.

The ACTU was founded in 1927 and has since then had close ties with the Australian Labor Party (ALP). The federal state structure was reflected in the ACTU, where state trade and labour councils were formally branches of the ACTU but generally had a much longer history than the union confederation and displayed a degree of independence and considerable power in their localities (Bamber and Davis 1992: 16). The extent of specialization was also quite high, with 150 affiliated unions in 1980 (Rawson and Wrightson 1980: 16). For public sector employees, some unions were confined to a specific state or territory. Thus, in the public sector specialization based on workplace or qualification was supplemented by specialization based on geographical location.

For federal employees and their unions, agreements on wages and working conditions were most important. As part of the new Accords between the Labor government and the ACTU and the law on industrial relations, some decentralization of wage determination to industry and workplace level occurred between 1987 and 1990. However, this was closely managed within a national framework by the arbitration tribunals (Bray and Walsh 1998: 368). Enterprise bargaining was adopted by the Accord partners as their wages policy in 1990.

By the mid 1990s the Labor government had implemented a series of NPM and industrial relations reforms that had extensive effects on union structure. In return for union approval of enterprise bargaining provided for by the law on industrial relations in 1988, the government passed legislation facilitating the plans of the leadership of the ACTU to reorganize the union movement and drastically reduce the number of unions (Svensen and Teicher 1999: 338). Unlike its predecessor, the new law stipulated that unions seeking registration must have a minimum of 1,000 members and be industry-based. This amendment was an attempt to reduce the proliferation of small, occupationally-based unions. In 1991, the federal government amended the law to facilitate union mergers and further increase the minimum size of federal unions to 10,000 members (Bamber and Davis 1992: 105–106). The number of unions thus fell, though not to the extent planned by the ACTU leadership (Peetz 1998: 133).

For federal employees, from 1989 onwards several older unions affiliated with the ACTU merged and in 1994 joined the new Community and Public Sector Union (CPSU) (Gardner and Palmer 1997: 545, Lansbury and Macdonald 2001: 27). Federal employees are part of the PSU Group, while the SPSF Group covers employees in the state public services. Within the CPSU, the two groups mainly operate as separate unions. The PSU Group has offices in every state and territory, while in the SPSF Group there are separate state-registered public sector unions and branches. Following the prevalence of enterprise bargaining in the public sector, the CPSU was reorganized in 1997. The workplace is now the basic unit of the union structure. All workplaces must be single agencies under the new structure. All members are allocated to a section – that is, a single government department or agency or a group of employers with some common interest. In addition, they are also a member of a geographically-based branch.

While until 1996 service-wide or enterprise negotiations and agreements involved unions and employers at various levels, the new Workplace Relations Act of 1996 initiated by the incoming Liberal-led coalition government made it possible for agencies to exclude unions and to conclude individual agreements (Australian Workplace Agreements, AWA) with employees at all levels of their organization (Thornthwaite and Hollander 1998: 105). Moreover, the Public Service Act of 1999 reconceptualized the framework for employment and management of the public service to allow for the workplace efficiency and flexibility sought under the more general Workplace Relations Act (Halligan 2005: 27). However, since 2008, the incoming Labor government has stopped the individual agreements (AWA) and strengthened the elements of collective bargaining between unions and employers.

The ACTU is still the only union confederation covering the public as well as the private sector, and includes most union members. It currently has 46 affiliated unions and branches (labour councils) in all states and territories. Since its creation, the CPSU has been the principal public sector union (O'Brien and Hort 1998: 48, Lansbury and Macdonald 2001: 26). The division of the CPSU into separate groups for federal and state employees and the existence of branches within each state and territory also imply that geographically-based interests and identities are built into the union structure. Moreover, the establishment of separate sections for government departments and agencies may imply that specific workplace interests and identities have become stronger than those related to the overall federal or state level.

Our main objective here is to find out how the interests and identities of public sector unions in New Zealand and Australia have been affected by NPM reforms. In some instances, the effects have been quite direct, such as abolishing the distinction between public and private sector in employment relations, increasing the importance of individual contracts and agreements, and making the workplace the crucial organizational unit. In others, the effects have been more indirect and linked to other change processes, like the merger of Australian unions (including the public sector) initiated by the ACTU. Moreover, constitutional aspects are still relevant, with the Australian federal system implying that union structure should also reflect geographically-based interests and identities.

The interests and identities of public sector unions after the NPM reforms may also have an impact on whether and how they are affected by future administrative reforms. To what extent they respond and how influential they are will depend on their capabilities, which may also have been affected by the NPM reforms.

Effects on Union Capabilities

To attend to their interests and identities the public sector unions need resources for analysis and action. For example, while a service-wide bargaining system emphasizes the importance of strong head offices at the national level, workplace and enterprise bargaining will put more emphasis on branch offices at the local level. Nevertheless, the head offices and their composition are crucial for being able to respond to and have an impact on future nation-wide administrative reforms. In some unions the head office may include specific positions or units for handling these issues, and some of the people working there may have acquired relevant expertise through their education or previous experience. In addition, public sector unions may draw upon resources from unions they are a member of or have as members themselves. A union's opportunities for having an impact on reforms may also depend on its connections with other types of organizations. For example, links with labour parties may be decisive, especially when those parties form the government.

The capabilities of public sector unions may also depend on the size and composition of their membership. A large membership provides economic resources through subscriptions and forms a basis for mobilization through strikes and other kinds of action. Moreover, the distribution of union members among different levels of the public sector as well as across the public–private divide affects the strength of public employees within their national unions and union confederations. Likewise, the relative strength of the national unions and union confederations depends on their share of the employees in various parts of the public sector or the public sector as a whole. Union density in agencies and the public sector also expresses the extent to which unions may claim to represent all employees.

What, then, are the actual effects of NPM reforms on union capabilities? In New Zealand and Australia, as in most countries that have implemented NPM reforms, there is more systematic information on the size and composition of public sector union membership before and after the implementation of the reforms than on the resources in national or local offices. Thus, we will emphasize the effects on capabilities related to union membership.

In New Zealand overall union density in 1981 was 48 per cent. Public employees accounted for approximately 27 per cent of all union members, indicating that union density was higher in the public than in the private sector. Thus, although membership in state employees' unions like the PSA was voluntary, unlike in (parts of) the private sector, membership levels were quite high. Unions registered under the arbitration system had the exclusive right to represent workers who fell under the jurisdiction of their membership clause (Bray and Walsh 1998: 362). Even if this exclusive right did not apply to state employees' unions (Boston et al. 1996: 227), inter-union competition was not prevalent in the state sector.

Measured by union density, the strength of the unions declined markedly in the 1990s: from 45 per cent in 1989 to 17 per cent in 1999 (Harbridge, Crawford and Hince 2002: 185). Thus, the ECA (1991) seems to have had a major impact on union support (see Walsh and Brosnan, 1999: 107). In 1999, there were about 302,000 union members, of which public employees accounted for approximately 54 per cent. This indicates that union density was much higher in the public sector than in the private sector and that public sector unions lost fewer members than private sector unions after the introduction of the ECA.

The ECA broke the automatic link between trade union membership and representation and created the potential for state employees' unions to be challenged as the dominant bargaining parties in the state sector. Until the mid 1990s, this did not happen as the PSA still negotiated the contracts of most employees. However, many of the PSA's collective contracts covered only a small number of employees, thus stretching its resources to negotiate and service these contracts (Boston et al. 1996: 233–236). Nevertheless, the changes in the industrial relations system in the early 1990s had an impact on how union characteristics affected their response to NPM reforms. Thus, it has been pointed out that it is important for public sector unions to 'not only assert their identity as a mobilising device in the process of bargaining, but also assert a role in the public policy process that determines the environment in which the bargaining takes place' (O'Brien 1997: 503).

Following the introduction of the ECA, membership of the main public sector union – the Public Service Association – at first remained quite stable, increasing to about 67,000 in the mid 1990s as a result of mergers with unions for local government employees (Boston et al. 1996: 234). By 2000, the membership of PSA had declined to less than 40,000 members, but it increased again in the following decade to approximately 58,000 members. Likewise, a large drop in the number of staff at the head office during the 1990s has been followed by an increase in the last decade.

In Australia, overall union density was 50 per cent in 1982, and the difference between the public sector (73 per cent) and the private sector (39 per cent) was quite marked. Measured in terms of union density, the strength of the unions diminished during the 1980s and 1990s, and in 1999 it was 26 per cent for all employees and 50 per cent for public employees. The reduction in the number of union members was less marked, from 2.57 million in 1982 to 1.88 million in 1999 (Griffin and Svensen 2002: 31–32). The decline in the relative share of public sector employment also contributed to a decline in the relative share of public sector union members among all union members, from 47 per cent in 1982 to 40 per cent in 1997 (Peetz 1998: 6).

Until 1996, the bargaining system maintained a central place for unions. In contrast, the coalition government created an industrial relations system that reduced unions to the status of agents of employees and promoted arrangements that encouraged direct agreements with employees, as well as individual contracts. While federal public sector unions had previously been able to use either awards or service-wide agreements to maintain a high level of consistency in employment arrangements, the unions, in particular the main public service union (CPSU), now faced an environment where their capacity to enforce service-wide arrangements was severely constrained (O'Brien and Fairbrother 2000: 63). Thus, while the Workplace Relations Act of 1996 did not exclude unions from representing employees as bargaining agents, employers were given the option of pursuing agreements with employees directly (O'Brien and O'Donnell 1999: 449).

During the 1990s, the form and extent of the delegation of authority and the distribution of capabilities among union levels were disputed in the ACTU (Briggs 1999, 2004) as well as in the CPSU (O'Brien 2000). Thus, the role and the resources of the confederation, the main national public sector union and the local branches changed as a response to structural devolution and HRM autonomy. In particular, enterprise bargaining and new forms of workplace agreements implied the need for public sector unions to transform their strategies to remain relevant and active in workplace resolution (O'Fairchellaigh, Wanna and Weller 1999: 158).

The changing bargaining systems for federal employees introduced by the coalition government contributed to the decline in the number of members in the CPSU (PSU Group) from approximately 110,000 in 1995 to 72,000 in 2000 (Griffin and Svensen 2002: 34). Today, the PSU group reports having approximately 60,000 members, while the SPSF Group have approximately 100,000 members.

Above the question was asked whether and how the NPM reforms in New Zealand and Australia have affected the size and composition of public sector unions. In both countries, the decline in the number of members owing to the introduction of individual contracts and agreements has been quite marked. Moreover, in both countries there have been debates within the trade unions on whether their capabilities should be diverted from those related to a servicing model (where unions organize in order to service their membership more effectively and efficiently) towards those related to an organizing model (where members are active participants in the way unions organize and operate) (cf. Fairbrother and Yates 2003). The form union capabilities take and how they are distributed is also linked to the question of union participation in corporatist arrangements, which is the subject of the next section.

Effects on Corporatist Participation

The discussion by Schmitter (1974) is generally considered to be the first serious attempt to clarify the relevance of the concept of corporatism in recent years. However, even if there is widespread agreement on the core of the concept and phenomenon of corporatism as being related to the existence of close and formal connections between interest organizations and the state, it has been specified in somewhat different ways internationally (for example Cawson 1986, P.J. Williamson 1989, Molina and Rhodes 2002). In some instances, particularly in New Zealand and Australia, the focus is often on the bipartite relationships between the government and the trade unions (for example Easton and Gerritsen 1996: 44–47). Moreover, so far, students of corporatism have only to a limited extent examined the role of public sector unions in relation to corporatism. This is somewhat surprising, since in most West European countries more than 40 per cent of trade union members work in the public sector (Ebbinghaus and Visser 2000). As noted above, the share in New Zealand and Australia is similar.

In general, two main types of corporatist arrangements may be outlined (Nordby 2004). The first is bargaining corporatism, where representatives of the state and affected special interests (employers and employees) jointly determine wages and conditions of employment. The second is corporatism linked to the administration, where representatives of interest organizations from almost all areas of society participate in boards, public commissions and task forces appointed by the government. In both instances, those aspects that involve public sector unions may be regarded as part of the public administration infrastructure. Moreover, here, various arrangements on co-determination between unions and government or agency leaders will also be included as an example of this type of infrastructure.

What have been the actual effects on corporatist participation of NPM reforms? In Australia, the unions began to co-operate more effectively with the Australian Labor Party in the late 1970s and early 1980s. The party became receptive to the possibility of a corporatist relationship, and the unions demonstrated both a reciprocal interest and the organizational capacity to participate in such an arrangement (Bray and Walsh 1998: 366). Just before the ALP entered office, the party and the union confederation had negotiated an agreement on incomes policy. The subsequent agreement (Accord) between the Labor government and the ACTU was the first in a series of eight agreements in the 1983–1996 period. In addition to incomes policy, the Accord also covered elements of economic, social and industrial relations policy (see Bray and Walsh 1998: 358, Peetz 1998: 3, 157). In the federal sector, for example, the Labor government strongly supported enterprise bargaining linked to productivity improvements in the Australian Public Service in the early 1990s. However, the incoming coalition government discontinued the Accord arrangements in 1996, and since then federal governments (including the Labor government from 2008 onwards) have not entered into any formal partnerships with the trade unions involving administrative policy.

As shown in Chapter 6, like in Australia, the first NPM reforms in New Zealand were initiated by a labour government, but in contrast to Australia, the trade unions were not involved (or even informed). After the first radical reforms had been introduced, the leadership of the newly established New Zealand Council of Trade Unions tried in 1988 to seek an agreement (a social compact) between the union confederation and the government, inspired by similar arrangements (the Accord) to those in Australia (Harvey 1992). However, the negotiations between the CTU and the Labour government progressed slowly, mainly because of some opposition and scepticism within the union as well as the government. Instead, the outcome was a less binding 'tripartite Compact Council': 'Such a compact certainly gave unions earlier access to the policy-making process, but only as a lobby group on behalf of a sectional interest' (Harvey 1992: 74). Nevertheless, later on the CTU entered into a more specific wages accord or 'Growth Agreement' with the government. However, after the change of government in 1990 these types of arrangements were no longer relevant: the Employment Contracts Act 'with its atomisation of bargaining structures, is, of course, the complete antithesis of the incomes accord and the Compact' (Harvey 1992: 76).

Since the late 1990s, administrative reform activities by New Zealand public sector unions have focused on workplace relations. Thus, through what it calls the 'Partnership for Quality' strategy, the Public Service Association aimed to strengthen employee participation and workplace democracy, partly in line with the organizing model of unions. In 2000, the PSA entered into an agreement with the Labour-led coalition government, and in some government departments and agencies the PSA entered into more specific agreements (Shaw 2005: 218). According to the PSA, Partnership for Quality is an active relationship based on recognition of a common interest in securing the viability and prosperity of government departments and agencies. It involves a continuing commitment by the PSA to improvements in quality, and the acceptance by government employers and the union as stakeholders with rights and interests in decisions affecting employees' work and employment (cf. Shaw 2005: 219). Thus, these arrangements are more in line with doctrines related to personnel democracy than with NPM doctrines related to steering and efficiency. In 2007, the PSA signed a third partnership agreement with the government and some government departments and agencies. However, in 2008 the new National-led government declined to continue a partnership agreement with the PSA, implying the end of this type of formal arrangement between the union and the government.

As noted above, different forms of corporatist participation existed before and after the introduction of NPM reforms in Australia and New Zealand. However, while many of the Australian reforms were handled through the Accord, similar arrangements between the Labour government and the union confederation came later and were less comprehensive in New Zealand. In both countries, the end of a labour government also implied the end of these corporatist arrangements and of the importance of this type of union capability. On the other hand, while the main state employees' union in New Zealand (the PSA) later entered into other types of partnership arrangements, this was not the case for the main federal employees' union in Australia (the CPSU – PSU Group). Thus, while the NPM reforms related to the bargaining system seem to have led to new forms of corporatist participation for public sector unions in New Zealand, this does not seem to have been the case in Australia.

Conclusion

This chapter took NPM arguments and doctrines as its point of departure, and identified some potential effects of the NPM orthodoxy on public sector unions and corporatist arrangements. Since New Zealand and Australia are often regarded as being among the frontrunners of NPM reforms, the discussion of actual effects on union characteristics and corporatist participation have been restricted to events in these countries. We have found some direct effects on union interests and identities and on union capabilities, particularly related to structural devolution, increased HRM autonomy and the homogenization of employment relations across the public–private divide. We have also found some indirect effects, often linked to internal processes in the unions. In both countries, but particularly in Australia, the public sector unions went through several mergers during the period when NPM was being implemented. Moreover, in both countries, the main public sector union and the union confederation assessed what kind of union model was most effective and efficient or most appropriate, and how their capabilities should be allocated in line with this model. With regard to corporatist participation, the distinctions between New Zealand and Australia seem to be based on the pre-existing relationships between the union confederation and the labour party. At any rate, these corporatist arrangements were discontinued in the 1990s after these parties no longer were in government.

This chapter has sought to illuminate the potential and actual effects of NPM reforms on union characteristics and corporatist participation in these two countries, without trying systematically to explain the form and extent of coupling between potential and actual effects, and the similarities and dissimilarities between the two countries. In some instances, the explanations seem quite obvious. For example, the differences between the Australian Labor Party and the New Zealand Labour Party in their use of corporatist arrangements while in government are based on previous party-union and corporatist relationships. Moreover, the differences between the response of the PSA and of the CPSU can at least partly be attributed to the difference between New Zealand's unitary system and Australia's federal one. However, future research on the effects of NPM reforms (and other types of administrative reforms) should attempt to explain the actual effects to a larger extent than we have done here.

This chapter has drawn on some country-specific contributions on New Zealand and Australia in comparative studies devoted to the changing prospects for trade unionism (Fairbrother and Griffin 2002), the renewal of trade unions (Fairbrother and Yates 2003), the strategic choices in reforming public service employment (Dell'Aringa, Della Rocca and Keller 2001) and staff participation in public management reform (Farnham, Hondeghem and Horton 2005). A number of other comparative studies looking at the actual effects of NPM reforms, for example on public service employment relations in Europe (Bach et al. 1999), have also been done. However, more comparative and longitudinal studies of the actual effects of NPM and other administrative reforms on public sector unions and corporatist arrangements will need to be conducted in the future. Moreover, some more in-depth case studies of specific unions should also be conducted, like the one by Bach and Givan (2008) on the consequences of public service modernization on the British public sector union UNISON. Taken together, comparative studies and case studies may provide more systematic knowledge about and explanations of administrative reforms and their effects on unions and corporatist participation.

NPM: Restoring the Public Trust through Creating Distrust?

Steven Van de Walle

Introduction

Policy makers frequently invoked restoring the public sector's legitimacy as one of the main motivations for public sector reform in the 1980s and 1990s. Low or declining public trust in government and a decline of the public sector's legitimacy (perceived or real) became a central motivation for public sector reform efforts, notably NPM-style reforms. Low public trust worried governments. Not just because of a rise of populist political parties in many Western countries, but also because it was seen to hinder effective recruitment into the public sector, and because low trust required greater government efforts to ensure citizens' compliance (OECD 2000a: 25).

Declining citizens' trust in government has been identified as one of the main forces driving changes in government (McNabb 2009). The public sector in the 1980s was seen to be inefficient, non-transparent and expensive, and was believed not to deliver the services citizens wanted. Dissatisfaction with services was a direct consequence of a low or absent customer service orientation, including unfriendly public officials, incomprehensible forms and long waiting lines.

This chapter first shows how trust and legitimacy entered the reform agenda and became important motivations for public sector reform programmes in the 1990s. Creating congruence between what public services citizens really wanted and the services the public sector provided was seen as the key to regaining the public trust. This section also examines whether the basic assumption of declining trust was correct and whether NPM reforms have eventually contributed to restoring trust.

The following section elaborates on the apparent irony that NPM wanted to re-establish the public trust by introducing distrust-based control and compliance mechanisms. It shows that this is not necessarily a contradiction by distinguishing between three different types of trust and by outlining NPM's effect on these three types of trust. The chapter concludes by discussing the re-emergence of trust-based steering concepts in public management.

Restoring the Public Trust by Reforming Government

Public trust features prominently in many public documents about public sector reform. One often-used example within the National Performance Review in the US, later the National Partnership for Reinventing Government, made a direct link between the functioning of public services and citizens' trust. 'How can people trust government to do big things if we can't do little things like answer the phone promptly and politely?' (Clinton and Gore 1997: ix). The Government Performance and Results Act explicitly linked government inefficiency to low trust: 'waste and inefficiency in Federal programs undermine the confidence of the American people in the Government ...' (GPRA 1993), and many other government reform documents and public speeches from the last decade of the twentieth century show explicit references to trust in government. OECD documents in a similar way posited a relation between public sector performance and public trust, driven by the conviction that trust in government had declined and that therefore a reform was needed (OECD 2000a). Reform programmes were very optimistic about their own impact on the public trust. The National Partnership for Reinventing Government (NPR) in the US boldly stated in 2001:

> *After a 30-year decline, public trust in the federal government is finally increasing. When last measured by the University of Michigan in 1998, the public's trust in government had nearly doubled within a four-year period to 40 percent. While this cannot be totally attributed to the results of reinvention, NPR believes reinvention has made an important contribution in raising the public's trust in the government and creating a better workplace for federal employees. (National Partnership for Reinventing Government 2001)*

Many Western governments produced or commissioned reports exploring levels of public confidence in the public sector. Quite a few of these looked into how the performance of public services influenced citizens' trust, often with mixed results. Examples include a State Services Commission report in New Zealand looking at the relationship between citizens' trust and government performance in a number of key policy areas (Barnes and Gill 2000), a report written for the Auditor General of Western Australia (Ryan 2000), work by the Audit Commission in the UK looking at trust in public services as part of its work on corporate governance (Audit Commission and Mori Social Research Institute 2003a, 2003b), or the Citizens First reports in Canada.

The same period also saw the emergence of systematic measurement of public attitudes towards the public sector (Bouckaert and Van de Walle 2003). Trust and confidence surveys, barometers and monitors of all types became increasingly common. Central governments organised broad surveys of public attitudes, while public organisations such as tax offices or police forces commissioned opinion surveys to complement the already available user satisfaction data. Researchers likewise contributed to an expansion of the evidence base on public trust by organising their own surveys (Vigoda-Gadot and Yuval 2004, Christensen and Lægreid 2005b).

Surprisingly, few of these initiatives explicitly linked up with research done by political scientists looking into voting behaviour or political cynicism, despite the considerably longer research tradition in this field. While political scientists and sociologists in the 1990s had identified several explanations for levels of public trust, including many political and ideological ones, failing public sector performance became a dominant explanation in governments' rhetoric, despite the absence of solid evidence. Dissatisfaction with the political organisation of government was suspiciously absent from many analyses, and it appears political discontent had to be deflected and redirected to discontent with the functioning of public services (Van de Walle et al. 2005b). Deflecting the political discontent to the functioning of public bureaucracies also allowed politicians to strengthen their grip on the bureaucracy and to create support for public sector reform programmes. This despite the fact that politicians and political parties ranked considerably below public officials and bureaucrats on the lists of most trusted public institutions.

What Kind of Trust and Legitimacy Problem?

Government's image has long been a worry for policy makers and political leaders. In the public discourse in the 1990s policy-makers frequently referred to findings from opinion polls to express their concern about the public sector's image, especially when these polls showed a long-term decline in trust. During the NPR in the US, it had become quite common to refer to the longitudinal National Election Studies surveys that indeed showed levels of trust in government in the early 1990s that were considerably lower than those in the late 1950s. Yet, at the same time, arguments about a steady decline of trust are not supported by the data. Still, trust in government was exceptionally low in the early 1990s, giving policy-makers good reason to worry. The stream of academic books on trust in government shortly thereafter also reflects this concern, and not just in the US (Kaase and Newton 1995, Nye et al. 1997, Norris 1999).

In European countries, overall levels of trust can be measured using the European Commission's Eurobarometer which provides a time series starting in 1973. Satisfaction with the way democracy works is in this context generally used as an indicator for broad disaffection from the political system. Despite recurrent rhetoric about declining trust, Eurobarometer data show many fluctuations, but few downright declines in public trust (Van de Walle et al. 2008). In many other countries, including NPM champions such as New Zealand or Australia, solid longitudinal opinion data were simply unavailable in the 1990s when much of the discourse on declining trust was at its height. More specific data on changes in public confidence in the civil service in a series of countries, taken from the World Values Surveys, neither show a coherent universal decline in confidence (Van de Walle et al. 2008).

Neither the absence of proper longitudinal opinion data, nor the absence of clear downward trends where such data do exist should discredit the overall argument that the public sector was suffering from a legitimacy crisis though. Despite considerable differences in absolute levels of trust across countries, most Western countries considered public trust to be problematic. Politicians and civil servants generally dangled near the bottom of lists of most trusted professional groups, many countries suffered from declining voter turnout and an increase in protest votes, and several countries suffered from public scandals laying bare the defective functioning of the public sector. A political discourse about declining trust appealed to many, and served as a mobilising force to put public sector reform firmly on the agenda (Van de Walle et al. 2005b).

Building Legitimacy by Delivering What Citizens Really Want?

The perceived decline in trust was attributed to governments' inability to provide citizens with the public services they really wanted and needed. Not only, it was argued, was government delivering the wrong services, it also delivered them in an inefficient and inaccessible way. Government was seen as out of touch with people's needs. It would have to build trust through providing more choice, democracy and transparency (OECD 2000a: 12).

These strategies to improve trust are actually based on the very straightforward assumption that creating congruence between what citizens want and what government delivers is the surest way to creating more trust. Such responsiveness effectively transforms the public sector into a reactive public sector, and citizens into consumers. The state becomes a supermarket state (Olsen 1988). One other element of public sector reform that featured prominently in, for example, Osborne and Gaebler's *Reinventing Government,* quietly disappeared from the public sector reform agenda: community. Apart from improvements in service delivery, Osborne and Gaebler also promoted a more democratic public sector through more participation and a community-owned public sector (1992: 49–75). Efforts to restore legitimacy, however, almost exclusively focused on transforming government into a business-like government. New communitarian ideas found relatively little expression in public sector reforms, and were largely restricted to (intended) reforms in the political sphere.

Public sector reform efforts to restore trust focused on reducing the distance between government and citizens by creating a new public services mission based on high quality services reflecting the user's concern (Ferlie et al. 1996: 15). One way of doing so was to restore congruence between citizen needs and wants and the supply of public services. A second way was to improve the quality of how services were being delivered, and thus the service orientation of the public sector. These two approaches are largely built on an assumption of considerable homogeneity in the public's demands, and assume that citizens have a clear and consistent idea of what they really want.

Congruence between supply and demand

By delivering those services citizens really wanted and needed, governments hoped to close the gap with citizens. By putting citizens first and giving them choice, citizens would be able to receive the services they wanted, and not those service providers thought they wanted (Kettl 2000: 2). This could be done through introducing competition and other market mechanisms, where the idea was that public organisations would cease delivering those services citizens didn't want anyway. Because of the disappearance of monopolies, (public) service providers would furthermore have to invest in their customer relations.

Creating congruence between supply and demand of services, or delivering what users want, meant an abandonment of standardised services and of rationing services (Clarke et al. 2007). Citizens as customers would be able to choose those services they wanted, from a multitude of suppliers. Doing so required the creation of a public services market, and the provision of market information to inform citizens' choices. Vouchers and service fees gained importance alongside, or even instead of, public services paid through general taxation. The latest addition is the trend towards the differentiation of consumers (Simmons 2009, Laing et al. 2009) and the personalisation of public services (Needham 2009a, 2009b), supposedly intended to create a perfect match between supply and demand through offering customers a tailored service.

A service orientation

The second objective of public sector reforms was to improve the service orientation of public services through customer-oriented reforms. Not only at the basic level of reducing waiting times, improving communications, or pimping waiting rooms, but also at a more generic level by introducing new opportunities for citizens to express voice and exercise choice. Many now common features of a service orientation in the public sector only emerged in the 1990s. Examples include the introduction of user charters such as the Citizen's Charter in the UK and similar charters in many other European countries; a proliferation of complaints handling procedures and of ombudsmen offices; and a strengthening of citizens' opportunities to use administrative law to challenge administrative decisions. Gradually, the idea of the anonymous civil servant was abandoned through introducing name tags and through making direct telephone numbers of case workers available to citizens, in order to reduce the distance between citizens and government. The introduction or strengthening of Freedom of Information laws and the growth of government websites would contribute to making government more transparent. The influence of NPM ideas led to public sector organisations copying service orientation ideas from the private sector.

Performance and Trust

The emergence of NPM-thinking did not just lead to a series of specific innovations. It also led to a shift in the (perceived) drivers of public sector legitimacy. Whereas Weberian bureaucracies derived their legitimacy from due process and the pursuit of the public interest, NPM-style public sectors derive their legitimacy from delivering the services customers want in a cost-effective, efficient and customer-friendly way.

Much of the 1990s reform talk made an explicit connection between the public sector's performance and its legitimacy. Low public trust was seen as due to low efficiency and the absence of a customer service orientation, and to a mismatch between the services government provided and those citizens wanted. Both empirically and theoretically, such a direct link between government performance and citizens' trust in government is difficult to sustain (Van de Walle and Bouckaert 2003). Furthermore, testing such a link leads to considerable empirical and conceptual problems (Van de Walle et al. 2005a, Van de Walle and Bouckaert 2007). Empirical research testing this claim is therefore difficult to find. Where such research exists, evidence of a relationship between trust and performance is not particularly convincing (Bok 2001, Killerby 2005). Derek Bok's study (2001) in which he compared the effectiveness of American government in the 1960s and the 1990s found little evidence of a direct relationship between citizens' trust in government and government performance. Earlier, he had already criticised the idea that public opinion would be the best index of government performance (Bok 1997: 55–6). Suleiman found that patterns of distrust in Western countries did not seem to correspond to patterns of NPM reforms (Suleiman 2003: 65), and that 'Data on public distrust do not adequately explain why reforms have been more comprehensive in some states than in others' (2003: 22).

Did NPM Reforms Create More Public Trust?

The result appears to be widespread scepticism about the contribution of NPM-style reforms and public sector reform in general to public trust. Kettl did a macro-evaluation of the global public management revolution, and concluded, after looking at confidence and trust statistics from the 1980s and 1990s that, 'There is no evidence that the extensive management and political reform efforts have halted the downward slide of public confidence in government' (Kettl 2000: 56). Yet he adds that confidence may need a much longer time to reflect changes in government. Likewise, in assessing the results of public management reform in a set of Western countries, Pollitt and Bouckaert (2004: 131) found no indication that public sector reform has lead to an increase in public confidence: there appears to be no relation between the extent of reforms in countries and cross-sectional differences in confidence, or between the timing of reforms in a country and longitudinal changes in levels of trust.

Critics have even highlighted that particular aspects of public sector reforms may actually have contributed to the public's distrust. Roberts identified the corrosion of public trust as a potential hidden cost of public sector reforms, because reforms have lead to a concentration of executive authority, and contracting has made control harder through decreased transparency. Combined with a possible decline of public service ethics, he claims, the public sector may have become more vulnerable to scandals (Roberts 1998). Specific innovations related to NPM have lead to considerable popular discontent. Higher executive salaries and a new practice of paying off government executives when things go wrong politically (Gregory 2003b: 244), and an increase of unaccountable quangocrats have created considerable distrust. In terms of transparency, business-like operations may have reinforced secrecy, and spin and marketing have been adopted from the private sector. At the same time, new transparency requirements and improved communications have also made public sector deficiencies and government failure more visible (OECD 2001). Despite a growth of transparency-supporting initiatives, government has become more complicated and fragmented making it much less transparent for citizens.

The reform process itself has also been identified as a potential new source of distrust. OECD stated that the large-scale public sector reforms in New Zealand coincided with a decline in public trust because the scope and speed of the reforms made them unpopular, and because the reforms themselves created new expectations (OECD 2000a). Protracted public sector reforms may not always be understood by citizens, and may lead to reform fatigue.

Restoring Public Trust Using a Model Based on Distrust

NPM-style reforms wanted to tackle low public trust in the public sector due to failing performance and opaqueness. Ironically, it did so by introducing distrust-based innovations. Through a complex system of contracts, fragmentation, short-term explicit standards of performance, and audit and control mechanisms, it inserted a degree of institutionalised distrust into the public sector (Dubnick 2005). It has been suggested that NPM-reforms have driven trust out of traditional bureaucratic interactions, and have, as a result, done little to restore the legitimacy of the public sector. This section shows this is only part of the story (Gregory 2003b).

Three Types of Trust

Before expanding on this argument, it is necessary to first elaborate on different types of trust. Lewicki and Bunker (1996) distinguished between three types of trust: calculus-based trust, knowledge-based trust and identification-based trust. Calculus-based trust is based on a calculus of the rewards of being trusting and trustworthy, and the reputation effects of not being trusted. The fear of the effects on trust of certain behaviours thus acts as a deterrent. Where there is calculus-based trust, it is assumed that actors will act in a trustworthy way because of the benefits this brings, or the costs incurred by not being trustworthy. For public officials, such rewards may include receiving a new contract or a promotion, and likely costs are a reputation loss or losing a lucrative job.

Knowledge-based trust is based on information, not on deterrence. Predictability is a key value in knowledge-based trust relations. Actors can only trust each other when they have sufficient information about each other's behaviour and intentions. Knowledge-based trust thus implies that trust is not possible where information and knowledge are limited. In a public sector context, knowledge-based trust can be fostered through inserting more and better information into the system.

Finally, identification-based trust is based on mutual identification and shared values and goals. Unlike calculus- and knowledge-based trust, it is not cognitive, but emotional: 'trust exists because the parties effectively understand and appreciate the other's wants' (Lewicki and Bunker 1996: 122).

Lewicki and Bunker (1996: 124) regard these types of trust as stages, where stable identification-based trust is limited to a few relationships and takes time to develop. Knowledge-based trust applies to many relationships, and takes some time to develop. Just like identification-based trust, calculus-based trust again only applies to some relationships, but in contrast, it can be developed quite rapidly yet remains fragile. It can only apply to some relationships because it requires constant monitoring, as well as consistent and quick action.

NPM as a System Based on Distrust?

It has been argued that NPM is a distrust-based system. This is only partly true. NPM is indeed built on the initial assumption that interests are antagonistic, and that actors can therefore not trust each other. NPM, with its roots in public choice thinking, is based on the idea that public officials cannot be trusted – they are self-interest maximisers, using their administration to fulfil this self-interest (Niskanen 1971). Public choice comes with a 'sceptical or cynical view of the 'public service ethos', and 'articulated a moral economy of mistrust'' (Clarke 2010).

Pre-NPM information deficits and information asymmetries prevented elected officials from controlling public officials and holding them to account. Citizens as well had little information and even less direct links with public officials, making it also for them difficult to check this self-interest. It follows that NPM proponents do not believe in identification-based trust, because such trust assumes commensurability of interests, which is simply thought not to exist. Instead, NPM has focused on creating knowledge- and calculus-based trust. By inserting more control and information in the system, NPM would make it possible for principals and agents to trust each other again.

NPM is thus different from other approaches to the public sector, and especially the Weberian assumption of public officials working in the public interest (an interest that is, furthermore, straightforward to identify), in that it takes distrust as the basic condition of collaboration in the public sector. Principals and agents distrust each other. Ministers are suspicious of the intentions of officials and vice versa, and citizens feel government is not working to their best interest.

This initial distrust between ministers and officials is a central theme in much of the public choice-inspired literature, in public choice-inspired popular culture (see for example the sublime TV series *Yes Minister*), and indeed in many studies on political-administrative relations ('t Hart and Wille 2006). Politicians' and top officials' interests are antagonistic, and relations between top officials and lower-ranking bureaucrats are equally problematic. Likewise for citizens, NPM does not expect them blindly to trust their politicians or officials to deliver high quality services (Christensen and Lægreid 2002: 289), but instead urges them to demand better services and to control government output (for example through relying on publicly available indicators, or through exercising voice and choice). This background partly helps to explain the initial popularity of NPM-style reforms: their anti-government foundation appealed to widespread popular cynicism about government.

Creating Calculus- and Knowledge-Based Trust

The NPM philosophy does not believe in public officials working for the public interest. Antagonistic interests between citizens and public officials make identification-based trust relations impossible. But this does not mean that NPM is an entirely distrust-based complex of reforms. NPM-style innovations focused on reducing information deficits and asymmetries, and on more elaborate control and compliance mechanisms. Even markets cannot work without a certain degree of trust between actors. Otherwise, transaction costs become unsustainably high.

So what we did see following NPM-style reform is a focus on knowledge- and calculus-based trust mechanisms, instead of identification-based mechanisms. NPM dismantled identification-based trust relationships (which took time to develop), because it didn't believe they could exist, and replaced them with some calculus-based trust relationships (control mechanisms, short-term contracts, competition), and many knowledge-based trust relationships (performance monitoring, greater transparency through disaggregation).

Interactions between ministers and top officials or collaboration between public agencies are typically interactions where there is a relatively small distance between principal and agent. Furthermore, they typically concern a relatively small number of relationships. In such relationships, therefore, NPM reforms focused on building calculus-based trust. In interactions between top officials and officials working on implementation; interactions between policy makers and schools and hospitals; or interactions between citizens and service delivery bodies, we are dealing with a large number of relationships, making calculus-based trust relationships difficult. In such situations, NPM reforms focused on facilitating knowledge-based trust through making detailed performance metrics available (Van de Walle and Roberts 2008).

NPM's Effects on Identification-Based Trust

Through focusing on calculus- and knowledge-based trust, and not on identification-based trust – because the latter was according to NPM's philosophy theoretically impossible – NPM may have contributed to the destruction of identification-based trust where such trust existed. Through its focus on control and thus initial distrust in public sector reform, NPM has often been blamed for effectively destroying existing trust relations in the public sector. Modern performance measurement and management systems were often seen to be in direct contradiction to traditional trust-based control and steering systems (Halligan and Bouckaert 2009: 271).

One prominent example is the position of professionals in modernised public services. Whereas professional groups such as teachers and health care workers initially had a considerable degree of discretionary space and extensively relied on self-regulation, distrust-based reforms lead to a (perceived?) decline of autonomy (Ferlie et al. 1996: 11). A system of trust in professional standards and expertise was abandoned and replaced by explicit standards of performance (Hood 1995: 97). An audit explosion replaced trust relationships, and inserted active distrust into the system (Power 1997), creating professionals who no longer felt trusted (Broadbent and Laughlin 2002). When many of such audit and control systems were subsequently found to be ill-designed and promoting dysfunctional behaviour, they actively started to contribute to distrust (Berg 2005).

In interviews with public officials in New Zealand about the effects of public sector reform, Norman observed that trust was a recurring topic. According to these public officials, it was felt that NPM-related fragmentation and distribution almost deliberately lead to low mutual trust (Norman 2003: 203). The introduction of new management tools based on distrust led to decreasing trust between executive leaders and politicians (Christensen, Lie and Lægreid 2008: 25). Indeed, 'Trust has been a significant casualty of systems designed to counter provider capture by using competition as a method of control, and creating distance between principals and agents' (Norman 2003: 203). This distance, and the related absence of mutual trust, contributed to a climate of fear where making mistakes and taking risks is not appreciated and even dangerous (Norman 2003: 161). The managers interviewed by Norman in New Zealand stated that committing to high and ambitious targets requires trust (2003: 203). They also considered strict accountability mechanisms as useless if there is no trust between chief executives and ministers, and emphasised the importance of informality and trust in relations between ministers and chief executives. This sharply contrasts with the control, formalisation and contracts on which many NPM innovations are based (Norman 2003: 147), and with the compliance and control routines which were widely perceived as a burden (2003: 199–200).

The disaggregation of the public sector into autonomous units, or the privatisation of parts of the public sector furthermore led to a decline in cohesion, and possibly of common values (Ferlie et al. 1996: 179). This declining common public service ethic may also mean a disappearance of 'a network of high trust contract relationships across the public sector (reflected in low transaction costs of negotiations between different public agencies)' (Dunleavy and Hood 1994: 12). This disaggregation was followed by an active rebranding of organisations, leading to a wide range of unconnected brands, rather than one single public sector brand, and (public) officials now identifying with their own organisation and less with the public sector as a whole. This made identification-based trust harder to achieve.

Low-trust, short-term contractual arm's length relationships have replaced long-term collaboration (Dunleavy and Hood 1994). Such contracts leave little place for relational trust, even though trust is needed, even in contractual relationships (Lane 2000). Using short-term contracts for executives may create perverse incentives, and replace mutual trust with opportunism (Gregory 2003b: 244). Indeed, the introduction of contractualism, according to Gregory, was based on a 'belief that people cannot be trusted' (2003b: 245). The result of such contractualisation is then that the new institutionalised 'mistrust fosters more distrust' (2003b: 245).

Concluding on NPM and Trust

While NPM has often been blamed for creating distrust, the previous sections show this needs to be put in perspective. NPM appears to have had a negative effect on identification-based trust, but other NPM-related innovations may actually have contributed to building calculus- and knowledge-based trust. The overall evaluation of the effects of NPM depends on the perspective one takes. Some NPM critics equal the pre-NPM period to one where politicians, public officials and government organisations worked harmoniously together guided by a common public sector ethos and mutual trust relationships.

Others, especially public choice scholars and other scholars focusing on bureaupolitics, saw widespread distrust in the public sector, both between politicians and top officials, and between ministries defending their turf. Analysts also remarked that prior to the wave of reforms in the 1990s, there was profound distrust between managers and politicians, between managers themselves, between citizens and government and so on (Osborne and Plastrik 1998). Furthermore, traditional trust-based relations were sometimes too cosy, as is evident from widespread politicisation and corruption which helped NPM ideas to gain prominence, and from scandals involving unaccountable professionals. The increasing demands that emerged for increased audit and control are an expression of the distrust that existed (Power 1997), and should probably not be seen as something that was imposed from above, but as something that fell on fertile ground.

A final observation relates to the fact that prior to NPM reforms, many public sectors already suffered from extensive control and compliance systems. Traditional bureaucratic organisations breathed distrust, and required lower ranking officials to ask permission for everything and explain everything.

This shows that the distrust-creating effects of NPM should not be overemphasised. What is different though is that NPM-style reforms are based on deliberate fragmentation and distribution of functions, and competition, based on an assumption that trust is not possible, while traditional bureaucracy was based on the (mythical?) belief that all officials worked for the public interest.

A Return to Identification-Based Trust?

In traditional bureaucratic organisations, there existed little or no need for permanent trust building, because trust had become a non-issue because of highly formalised rules and interactions (Grey and Garsten 2001). In post-bureaucratic configurations, trust again became an issue, which was initially solved through implementing control and compliance mechanisms. In more recent approaches to public sector reform, we see that identification-based trust has re-entered the public agenda. Recent trends in public sector reform see public sectors moving away from command and control systems to trust-based steering and collaboration. The desire to lower transaction costs and reduce short-term opportunistic behaviours is at the core of this evolution.

This is evident in a number of evolutions. In contracting, we see a move from short-term contracting to long-term, trust-based relational contracting or partnerships (Greve 2008). Highly-specified principal–agent relations are being replaced by collaborative networks, and trust plays an important role in these arrangements (Klijn et al. 2010). Trust is also re-entering relations between ministries and executive agencies (van Thiel and Yesilkagit 2008). The repoliticisation of relations between politicians and top executives in some countries is further evidence of this trend (Halligan 2007c). The new idea appears to be that 'trust may best be fostered by trust' (Gregory 2003b: 245).

Scientization

Martin Marcussen

Science and NPM

The role of science in policy-making – negative and positive – has become a central ingredient in New Public Management (NPM). Depending on one's theoretical point of departure, the scientization of public administration can be interpreted as a process that enhances the efficiency of decision-making, consolidates the depoliticization of entire policy areas, and helps politicians establish an appearance of trustworthy service-providers in the eyes of citizens.

The link between the New Public Management revolution (Kettl 2000) and scientization will be analysed using three complimentary perspectives: a functional perspective, a rational choice perspective and a symbolic perspective. According to a functional perspective scientization improves decision-making. Thus, it makes good sense that experts rather than civil servants or politicians themselves deal with the integrate details of policy preparation and implementation. After all, most administrative issues require technical expertise at a very high level and it will improve the quality as well as the efficiency of the policy process and output if experts are allowed to apply their expertise. Thus, there is a fine split of duties in modern public administration allowing political leaders to lead, public managers to manage, and experts to contribute with expertise. The link to New Public Management is clear: the productivity of the public sector in terms of increased effectiveness is enhanced if decision-makers make decisions based on expert advice.

According to a rational choice perspective, scientization will be seen as an attempt of consolidating the autonomous status of independent regulatory agencies. Essentially, a range of regulatory agencies have been given an autonomous status to protect them from short-sighted politicians. The political business cycle would lead us to expect that political actors will seek to align the natural cycle of the economy with the electoral cycle in order to maximize their chances of re-election. De-politicization of regulatory agencies in a certain policy area can prevent such a political attempt at manipulation. However, de-politicization may be temporary. Politicians can, at any time, and typically with a simple majority in parliament, repoliticize a regulatory agency. To prevent this from happening, civil servants have all kinds of interests in assuming the status of a scientist who presumably is working on the basis of almost divine laws. Scientization can be seen as an attempt of a-politicizing a field of policy-making displacing it from the realm of politics, disavowing the very possibility of deliberation, choice and political action (Hay 2007: 87). Again, the link to New Public Management becomes apparent: policies can be improved if left to autonomous regulatory agencies because these cannot be accused of serving shorter-term political interests. Accordingly, anything, such as scientific authority, that can help to protect regulatory agencies from untimely political intervention in day-to-day regulation should be supported.

According to a symbolic perspective, scientization can primarily be seen as an attempt of 'talking the talk without walking the walk' (Brunsson 2009). On a world-wide scale trust in policy-makers and civil servants is decreasing rapidly. A number of factors, including globalization, mismanagement, biased press coverage and so on can account for such a decline in trust in decision-makers. In contrast, scientists, university professors and certain professions within the field of medicine are benefitting from quite high levels of generalized trust. The symbolic perspective would, therefore, predict that politicians and top civil servants try to borrow some of the decision-making authority that lies in the hands of the trusted professional categories. They would, in other words, try to dress up as evidence-based decision-makers. By inviting experts and scientists into certain stages of policy-making, the appearance of evidence-based decision-making can be secured. This does not mean, that policy-makers necessarily listen to experts, or that policy-makers in practice make better quality decisions. Decoupling would, according to this perspective, be a common phenomenon in the everyday lives of policy-makers (Meyer and Rowan 1977). Expert committees appear, first of all, to be mere window-dressing hiding normal political in-fights, bargains and pragmatic compromises beneath a surface of scientific jargon. Again, the link to New Public Management can be made. Policy-makers need to connect with citizens and their needs. They are being held accountable for their ability to deliver what they have promised. As a minimum, therefore, policy-makers need to establish the appearance that they know what they are doing. In that process, science and scientists come in handy.

In the final section, the question will be asked whether scientization has come to stay or whether it will gradually scale out so as to bring accountable politicians back into business. One such challenge to scientization may take the form of a profound society-wide crisis that fundamentally challenges existing theoretical beliefs and taken-for-granted causal relationships. In terms of example, the financial crisis of 2008–2009 may have challenged the almost sacrosanct authority of central bankers by questioning the usefulness of the analytical tools normally applied in that field of policy-making and not least their capacity and willingness to act as fire-fighters. This brings elected politicians back in charge of policy domains such as financial stability and supervision which have on earlier occasions been passed to autonomous regulatory agencies. The question is whether the financial crisis has been so profound that citizens tend to have lost confidence not only in central bankers and stockbrokers, but also in the political elite in general (Marcussen 2010b).

Another challenge to scientization is more gradual and related to the ways in which the broader population has been intellectually empowered to grasp and react to evidence-based policy-making. With rising levels of education and flows of information it becomes increasingly difficult to impress the population by way of expertise. Expert authority may become devaluated as political legitimation simply because many ordinary citizens are increasingly capable at looking right through the scientistic surface of political rhetoric.

Scientization: The Concept and its Dimensions

Proponents of NPM have sometimes distanced themselves from experts and scientists, hoping to fill the perceived gap between policy-makers and citizens. For instance, when assuming office in 2001, the Danish Prime Minister, Anders Fogh Rasmussen (Liberal Party), promised to fight the 'tyranny of experts'. According to the new Prime Minister the experts had long been exploiting their position as 'authoritative truth-tellers' shaming and blaming everyone who had 'wrong opinions' or even opinions of their own. Time had come to let people run their own lives, he argued. Yet, looking back at the last few decades of Danish policy-making, experts are now more involved in policy preparation than ever. During the 1980s, 20–30 per cent of the members of governmental preparatory committees were so-called 'experts'. During the 2000s expert representation in committees has risen to 50–60 percent (Christensen et al. 2009). Notwithstanding intensions, experts have become indispensable in policy preparation. They are 'speaking truth to power' (Wildavsky 1979).

At the European level, experts have also found their way into policy preparation. For instance, the European Commission has established more than 1200 expert committees that assist the commission in its preparation of policy-initiatives by providing expertise. About a third of these expert committees even have scientists as members (Gornitzka and Sverdrup 2010). In parallel, the Council Secretariat and the European Parliament have expert committees of their own. In consequence, it has been common to align European Union decision-making with the concept of technocracy (Radaelli 1999).

Experts are not only lending their authority to policy-makers. Experts themselves tend to take office as policy-makers. Law and business studies seem to have become a *sine qua non* among top policy-makers in developed as well as less-developed countries around the world (Dezalay and Garth 2002). It is clearly an exception to the rule that the so-called layman walks the corridors of power. The 2009 edition of the international 'Who's Who' database documents that 36 per cent of politicians worldwide have been employed within these two professions alone (The Economist 2009b). If we narrow our focus down to selected branches of policymaking, such as monetary policy, the selection bias among ruling elites becomes even clearer.

Among central bank governors, for instance, there is a clear tendency that previous careers have been in academia as university professors (Marcussen 2006).

The fact that experts and expertise play a role in decision-making is not a new or revolutionary finding. In the field of European studies, for instance, the disagreement is not whether expert involvement is a predominant mode of European Union decision-making, but rather whether this is a good or a bad thing. On one hand, it is argued that knowledge is a key ingredient in enlightened decision-making. It improves the quality of decisions. In fact, in contrast to decision-making made in majoritarian institutions, where lowest-common-denominator compromises need to be made, expert decision-making ideally rests on scientific rules and theory cleansed for ideology. On the other hand, some would argue that technocratic decision-making undermines normal democratic decision-making practices essentially reducing political questions to technical problem solving. Democratically elected politicians are being sidelined, threatening the basic tenets of liberal democracy. Science has become a veritable fifth branch of government. In addition, science can be wrongly directed and politicians can even be hijacked by epistemic communities with almost hegemonic knowledge authority within a field of policy-making.

The relationship between science and politics is two-sided, though. On the one side, scientists and other experts with considerable knowledge authority actually can 'speak truth to power'. The first Secretary-General of the OECD, Thorkil Kristensen, was of the opinion that the organization had a moral and even a democratic obligation to inject new and challenging ideas into national policy-making. OECD experts were employed in steady positions, on average they were much better educated than national experts, they had access to high quality comparative data, and they were independent from the kind of political struggles that characterize most policy-making contexts among the member states. If the OECD could not speak truth to power by confronting policy-makers with the inconvenient truth, he rhetorically asked, then who could (Marcussen 2002)? The Epistemic Communities literature promotes exactly that line of argument (Haas 1992). It regards scientists and experts as free-floating knowledge entrepreneurs detached from national policy-making, enlightening policy processes in all sorts of ways.

However, there is another side to the relationship between scientists and policy-makers. Whereas the first side discussed above focuses on the ways in which politics is being exposed to scientization, this other side considers the inverse relationship and talks about the politicization of science. According to that line of argument, policy-makers may be 'speaking power to truth'. Scientists and science may be purely legitimizing devices enhancing the authority of policy-makers without really improving policy-making. Politicians need to bring science and scientists into everyday practice. However, this does not mean that politicians are puppets in the hands of scientists. It may be that politicians do not have knowledge authority, but they have legitimacy based on delegated authority – something which in democracies may overrule any other kind of authority. Through democratic elections, populations have delegated decision-making powers in the hands of politicians. The dimensions and scenarios discussed so far are summarized in Table 22.1.

Table 22.1   Dimensions of the relationship between science and politics

	Scientization of politics 'Speaking truth to power'	Politicization of science 'Speaking power to truth'
Positive evaluation	Evidence-based policy-making enhances decision quality	Elected politicians make required normative decisions where science is no clear guidance
Negative evaluation	Technocracy is capturing the political process, sidelining politicians	Politicians hide themselves beneath a surface of scientistic jargon, picking and choosing the kind of science which supports their main claims

There are many important reasons why most modern democracies cultivate science in policy-making. The emergence of risk society, information society, increased complexity, increased speed, technological development and so on has fundamentally changed the political game. These developments make science the *lingua pura*. Essentially, scientization is constituted by three core features: rationalization, knowledge authority and professionalization (Drori and Meyer 2006a).

It was Max Weber that referred to a process called *rationalization* according to which rules may take precedence over discretion. As the social world becomes increasingly complex, the social reality starts to conflict with the limited cognitive capacity of human beings to actually cope with all these complex signals in the social world. Such a conflict may trigger a transformative development, a form of profound learning among people. It may force people either to start believing in a God-given destiny, leaving social phenomena unexplained, or to start striving for simplification, categorization, generalized rules about expectations concerning cause and effect and other so-called scientific scripts which make it possible to make sense of a larger unwieldy whole. Both developments can be empirically identified today: complexity is either handled by an increased addiction to classical religious regimes or by an orthodox application of science as a lodestar – a new form of religion (Drori and Meyer 2006b: 46). Through distinct routes, CERN (The European Organization for Nuclear Research) and the Vatican will be providing answers to the biggest questions of our time. According to Max Weber, science would challenge cultural conventions, mystery and religion by analysing patterns, modelling behaviour and deriving laws. If such a process of rationalization unfolds it would become an objective in itself to seek regularity in the natural as well as in the social world. At that stage a phenomenon such as 'risk society' becomes something to be dealt with – a problem that challenges order and civilization and which requires a 'solution'. Everything which is unruly, unexpected, irregular would be seen as a problem and as an exception. Thus, coping with uncertainty would require a considerable dose of risk governance involving rationalization (Renn 2008).

Rationalization, in other words, assumes universality of patterns as a result of which law-like rules of regularity can be deducted. A result of rationalization is that we would expect people to use standards to distinguish success from failure. If measured according to a standard, some issues can easily be characterized as irregular and consequently as a failure, whereas other issues, according to these standards, can be classified as an orderly success. Scientization has a quite radical effect as a tool of standardization – this is expressed in the concept of 'audit society' (Power 1997) but we also see examples of standardization in some of the more generalized governance tools that have been diffused around the world. Benchmarking is just such an example of a tool that applies unified criteria while serving as authoritative input for decision-making.

A second element, contained in the concept of scientization relates to the kind of *authority* that can be deducted from science. There is no doubt that in a public administration characterized by scientization, science can be considered a major tool of empowerment. Scientific knowledge would become the direct justification for political, economic and social choices. One could even go as far as arguing that if scientization is in place, it would require science – scientific data, arguments, references and background – to be constituted as a relevant political actor in the first place. The kind of authority that we are speaking about here is very different from the authority that can be derived from electoral delegation or morality. It is a rational-authority which can be applied to exercise a kind of subtle power that differs from instrumental or violent exercises of power.

Thus, scientization is a prime example of governmentality according to which power manifests itself in the production of knowledge and certain discourses that become internalized in society, become taken for granted and directly guide the behaviour of populations. In contrast to top-down versions of control, governmentality – governance through knowledge production and diffusion – leads to extremely efficient forms of social control since no political contestation takes place. People essentially govern themselves in line with the hegemonic knowledge regime. It would take a paradigm change to alter the criteria for sound knowledge in a society. Benchmarks are only reliable if they measure according to the reigning knowledge regime.

A third element of scientization has to do with *professionalization*. When a certain philosophy (rationalization) has become institutionalized to such an extent that it gives superior legitimacy to decisions that are essentially political (knowledge authority), it becomes necessary not only to standardize problems and solutions, but also to harmonize the kind of people who are employed in public administration. To be a professional requires that a certain scientific curriculum forms the basis for one's role and role perception. This is where management education comes into the picture. Through training and certification a common standard is being established for how to operate and lead a decision-making system. Various teaching programmes leading to a master's degree in public management will pop up, gradually harmonizing the class of civil servants (Hedmo and Sahlin-Andersson

2007). The *métier* of being a civil servant will become accurately defined, as is the case with classical professions such as medical doctors, accountants, lawyers and so on. There will be only a few distinct and certified ways in which management in public organizations can take place. Rules, regularity, predictability, reliability come in as highly appreciated values in national (Beck Jørgensen in this volume) as well as international (Trondal et al. 2010) bureaucracies. Together with a firm belief in efficiency and responsiveness, rationalization has become one of the constitutive pillars of public administration. Civil servants have become professional in the sense that they share certain characteristics from unit to unit, department to department, country to country and even in intergovernmental and supranational organizations. The *métier* of civil servants in a modern democracy is defined by a set of shared rationalized values that imbue them with authority.

Scientization and New Public Management: Three Perspectives

In curious ways, a concept which is central to Max Weber's social philosophy has been promoted by way of marketization in the public administration. This section will argue that New Public Management has helped promote scientization. More concretely, central features of NPM such as effectiveness, autonomization and service orientation seem to have required processes of scientization in public administration.

According to a *functionalist perspective* we would expect that 'what works will grow, what doesn't will fade away'. The public administration should be seen as an organism that strives at growing organically, expelling all elements that do not fit or have dysfunctional characteristics. We would explain functions, roles, structures, relations and philosophies in the public administration by applying a circular argument: 'it is here because it works, and the proof that it works is that it is here'.

In pluralist policy systems such as the European Union, lobbyism is seen in exactly that way. Interest organizations in Brussels are being conceptualized as expert organizations that provide a small European Commission bureaucracy with much needed expertise (Coen and Richardson 2009). In fact, it is typically claimed that a supranational multipurpose bureaucracy is depending on regular high-quality input from expert stakeholders. Had it not been for the injection of relevant high-quality knowledge, the European Commission would not have been able to produce the regular initiatives needed to bring the European integration project forward. One of the more explicit illustrations of this perspective is the European White Paper on Governance in which systematic inclusion of a multitude of groups and organizations in the preparatory stages of decision-making was constituted as a cornerstone of a distinct European way of making decisions (Commission 2001).

The more expert inclusion, the better – simply because it is assumed that better decisions are being made.

The same argument, although operationalized in a different way, is applied in a corporatist decision-making setting. The Danish EU-coordination system, for instance, is organized in three stages (Marcussen 2010a). When a regulatory initiative has been made by the European Commission, a preparatory committee starts working somewhere in the Danish central administration. Constituted by civil servants as well as representatives from the main Danish umbrella organizations, the purpose of these various preparatory committees is primarily to undertake an evidence-based analysis of the scope and consequences of the European regulatory initiative. Thus, umbrella organizations function as experts with a view to improving the quality of the initial analysis. In a second stage, horizontal coordination between different concerned departments takes place. In a third and final stage, just before intergovernmental negotiations in Brussels, a Danish parliamentary committee, the European Committee, gets a chance to veto the ensuing Danish position. Originally, the procedure was meant to create a sound balance between expertise in the expert committees and ideology in the parliamentary committee. As it turns out, the expert part of the Danish EU-coordination system is clearly dominating. The fact that new as well as old members of the European Union are gradually copying the entire or parts of the Danish EU-coordination system is taken as proof that somehow it works satisfactorily.

In the functionalist perspective, the link between scientization and NPM has to do with the emphasis on effectiveness – to reinvent a government that works better and produces results (Osborne and Gaebler 1992). It requires knowledge to identify problems and to develop solutions. Thus, performance is taken to be radically improved if high-quality analysis is being conducted in the preparatory stages. The chances that real-life problems will find their solutions through policy-making is much enhanced if sound, factual and neutral analysis dominates at the expense of ideology. Thus, the evaluation criterion is clearly related to the output side (Put and Bouckaert as well as Peters in this volume). The nature of scientization as well as of NPM is to go beyond semi-religious, ideologically biased and dogmatic sub-optimal policy-preparation in order to focus on 'value-neutral analysis'. The experts play according to the apolitical scientific rules of the game as a result of which solutions will be produced that are optimal for the entire population. In short, a functional perspective will help us understand that the focus of any public administration would be to actually deliver the kinds of services that the population demands at any time. The public administration exists to service people, and any qualified service is based on healthy expertise. The more focus is on delivering effective solutions to real-life problems, the more we would expect that expert analysis would prevail in public administration.

According to a *rational choice perspective* any public administrative agency will seek autonomy and growth. When established, a public agency will have a purpose, a set of instruments and resources to achieve that purpose, and some outer limits for its activities. Thus, there will be a set of formal institutions that will constrain and enable the agency in its tasks. Over time, however, we will expect that, gradually, an agency will displace its goals, reconfigure its roles and relations, and maximize its resources. It will seek to push the outer limits for its activities in order to consolidate its position. The objective of realizing its initial purposes will be supplemented by other objectives with a view to avoiding political intervention and to striving for growth.

In consequence, public organizations that are being supervised by politicians will strive towards formal autonomy. They will, in other words, seek to de-politicize their policy field (Flinders and Buller 2006). By sheltering a policy arena from political supervision, the administrative agency will have obtained freedom to pursue its own agenda. This movement towards de-politicization is characterizing many fields of public policy in modern democracies around the world. As an integral element of a neo-liberal Washington consensus, the autonomous regulatory agency as a distinct organizational form has been diffused by international financial institutions such as the International Monetary Fund and the World Bank to all sorts of places in the world. The same recipe has been used everywhere: free politics from politicians and let the experts do their job. De-politicization is wrapped in a more general concept such as good governance and applied as a condition for development loans. In that way, international financial institutions have presumably had considerable impact on public sector convergence world-wide (Cheung in this volume).

The rational choice logic does not end here. Once a policy sector has been de-politicized, the involved bureaucratic actors will have an incentive to further protect themselves and their organization from external intervention. It requires no more than a simple majority in parliament to change the legal status of any public agency. Formal autonomy can easily be granted, but it can also easily be withdrawn. Therefore, complete freedom can only be obtained if a policy field is moved entirely beyond the political sphere, into a domain in which politicians cannot define the rules of the game. Such a sphere is the scientific sphere in which no political deliberation, choice and action is possible. One could choose to refer to such a transformation as being a matter of second-order autonomization or simply as a-politicization. De-politicization can make it difficult, although not impossible, for politicians to intervene on a policy issue. A-politicization goes much further than that. It disavows all kinds of political reflection on a certain issue area. To illustrate, it is to be expected that most national politicians will have formulated a coherent strategy with regard to the shape of the welfare state. They are expected to act in that area if they are to be re-elected. It could concern matters of schooling, health, pensions and so on. However, when it comes to monetary policy, this is an area which in many countries to a smaller or larger degree is formally sheltered from political intervention. Politicians are allowed to have an opinion about monetary policy, but they are not directly allowed to intervene in that area. This would be an example of de-politicization. When it comes to a-politicization, a second-order of autonomy, we should imagine political issues that have obtained a status akin to a law in physics. Politicians do not get elected on disputing such laws. In fact they do not even think about contesting scientific theories. A-politicization is about making one's policy field a matter of non-contestation. In short, what we would expect from a rational choice perspective is that public agencies would continue to strive for being completely disassociated from political deliberation on an issue area.

In practice, we would expect that one strategy that could be applied in order for a policy area to obtain a status of second-order autonomy could be to securitize that area. Securitization is about transforming a policy issue into a matter of security enabling the use of extraordinary means in the name of national security. Normal democratic procedures can then be circumvented and a few trusted actors – in this case experts – can be entitled to do the necessary to solve this existential problem. If something is successfully labelled a veritable security problem it becomes illegitimate to engage seriously in a political debate on that subject. Normal political contestation would be brought to an end. In cases of terror attacks, for instance, we would listen uncritically to security advisors and provide ample resources to those agencies that contribute to upholding a sense of security in the population. In the case of international pandemics, the dynamic is the same. An international health organization like the WHO would have ample possibilities to expand and position itself as a veritable standard-setter world-wide.

In short, a central element of NPM concerns de-politicization in various ways. Autonomization of public agencies is based on the idea that policy-makers are acting on the basis of a shorter-term political election cycle, whereas the broader society follows another cycle of development. Therefore, to make optimal decisions bureaucrats ought to be protected from narrow-minded politicians. A rational choice perspective would be able to understand why politicians act the way they do, but it does more than that. It will also be able to explain why autonomous agencies will seek a second-order of autonomy including a movement out of the political sphere altogether by way of scientization.

According to a *symbolic perspective* we would expect that civil servants 'are talking the talk, but not necessarily walking the walk'. Much modern politics and administration is about public relations, priming and framing. It is about creating visions, perspectives and identities just as much as about handling real-life day-to-day problems. Today, to be a top civil servant requires more than legal and economic expertise. It requires a fine-grained sense of the present day political climate and the broader public sentiment. In addition, it requires that leaders and managers excel in rhetoric. Top leaders act in a multitude of social spheres simultaneously. A talent for communication is necessary to handle political dialogue legitimately inside as well as outside the political organization. From the perspective of the top civil servant the same truth will have to be presented in many different ways, with different kinds of intonations. From an outside perspective, the borderline between the truth, the full truth and half a lie becomes blurred. In some contexts political communication of the sort that we discuss here is analysed in terms of decoupling. One thing is being said, something else is being done. In other related contexts there is talk about hypocrisy (Brunsson in this volume).

The link to NPM concerns the focus on service orientation. Public managers are urged to be in more direct dialogue with customers in order to obtain a better idea about needs and preoccupations on the receiving side of public service provision. The public manager is also expected to be in regular contact with sub-contractors, political leaders, the media, her personnel and other relevant groups of actors in a certain policy area. In addition to getting to know the policy field with a view to better targeting and gauging policy initiatives, the objective is also that the public manager can communicate and explain her initiatives to the relevant audience. There is a two-way communication going on here requiring a very pro-active and socially competent personality.

In combination with the requirement for performance management, the public manager is somehow being placed in a dilemma. On one hand she is supposed to grasp what the customers want her to deliver. On the other hand she is rewarded for delivering what she promises. It sounds simple: 'Don't promise more than you can deliver.' But it is more complicated than that. According to the symbolic perspective, part of the legitimacy of a public manager is based not on what she delivers, but on what people think she can deliver – her appearance. Is she visionary? Is she innovative? Is she concerned? The answers to questions such as these are decisive for whether the public manager is considered to be a success or not. Therefore, there will be a temptation, first, to pass on different messages to different audiences in order to please everyone. Second, when composing political initiatives and programmes she will be constrained by political, economic and administrative realties and resources. She is far from always able or willing to deliver what she promises as a result of which there will most likely be a smaller or larger gap between what is being said and what is being done.

In official rhetoric much legitimacy can be gained by applying either a scientistic story-line or, alternatively, actively engaging scientists around a problem of concern. For instance, frequent references can be made to the OECD PISA studies when initiating reforms of public schools. This does not necessarily imply that the OECD has provided the needed tools for carrying through that particular reform of the national education system. The OECD may simply be providing the policy reformer with knowledge authority and a momentum for reform. Additionally, when investigation committees are established whose membership contains Nobel prize-winners, they constitute, according to the symbolic perspective, clear examples of decoupling. Each time an ad hoc committee is established with high-profile international high-fliers, it has – next to a sincere wish to make evidence-based policy-reform – a legitimizing and attention-maximizing purpose. From a symbolic perspective, inviting international scientists from the Nobel prize class can be seen as pure name-dropping. The purpose is to enhance the authority of public managers caught in a dilemma between being open to all kinds of demands for services, on the one hand, and administering scarce resources that prevent fulfilling all these demands, on the other.

To summarize, the functional, rationalistic and symbolic perspectives have some important contributions to make in terms of an explanation for why NPM has helped promote the scientization of public administration. There have been elements of scientization in public administration for many years, but public management reform over the last couple of decades containing elements of NPM has further expanded scientization. The question is whether this will continue or whether there are signs that indicate an end to scientization.

Scientization in Demise?

Public sector reforms around the world indicate that we may already be transcending NPM. Alternatively, elements of NPM exist side by side with a whole-of-government approach to public administration (Christensen and Lægreid in this volume). It is relevant to ask, therefore, whether scientization is gradually withering away with NPM. There are at least two factors that support such a claim: one concerns the flawed status of science as a result of profound crises, the other concerns the empowerment of citizens, enabling them to look right through scientific jargon.

It could be argued that profound and sudden crises may seriously challenge our fundamental beliefs and theories. This is not something that happens on an everyday basis. After all, a paradigm change is exactly recognized by the fact that it is relatively rare and quite substantial. An obvious example is the end of the Cold War, which rightly challenged the field of political science. Very few scientists were able to predict this happening and very few had answers that could help us react appropriately to this historic event. Another more recent example is the financial crisis of 2008 and 2009. Ordinary citizens, the media and other interested parties started to ask critical questions to the economic theories that had formed the basis of our action so far. Did 'science' work when it was needed? Were economic scientists able to predict the crisis, take action during the crisis, and prepare for the future in sustainable ways? The answer seems to be negative. Science was not of much immediate help before, during and after the crisis (The Economist 2009c).

The question here, though, is whether the crisis of science somehow spills over into the political field. If very large amounts of political legitimacy have been deposited in the hands of science, a crisis of science becomes a political crisis. This does not seem to have happened, however. During crisis situations, political and administrative elites are re-conquering the political scene, withdrawing all kinds of first- and second-order autonomy. A 'New Normal' will be established with political elites displaying statesmanship and taking charge for a while (The Economist 2009c). The pendulum swing between rules (science) and discretion (political leadership) seems to be a recurrent phenomenon (Marcussen 2007: 146). The fact that science and those who represent science – neo-classical financial economists, for instance – find themselves in a situation requiring serious rethinking does not mean, however, that science has disappeared from the political scene. There is a time after the crisis in which the 'normal' becomes to establish new scientific rules for the social world. In dealing with the issue of global climate change, for instance, science has regained its place right in the middle of political debate (The Economist 2009e, 2010).

Another potential challenge to scientization is more gradual and rooted in the political resources accumulated by the population. Now and again, the OECD publication *Education at a Glance* documents that the general level of education is steadily rising, in the developed as well as in the developing world. More and more money is being spent on general education. In addition, we know that the share of the population that has access to information via the internet has increased radically over the last decade. This does not mean that all segments have equal access to information, but it is safe to argue that we are approaching something that can be referred to as a veritable information society. The paradox is that globalization has contributed to scientization of our public administration through increased complexity and increased sense of risk and uncertainty. At the same time globalization is related to the development of the information society. Doctors report that their patients, in contrast to earlier times, are extremely well-prepared, almost on a specialist level, when they consult with their doctor. The same goes with the economy and the inner working of the public administration. People today are much more aware about what is going on in society than before. The chance that ordinary citizens are aware of their rights, possibilities and obligations is much larger today than before. They are more difficult to impress with knowledge. Science is maybe not as prestigious today as it used to be, simply because knowledge monopoly has become increasingly difficult to uphold. Knowledge authority has become devalued as a source of political legitimacy.

At the same time, however, the sense of uncertainty seems to be increasing with improved access to information! It may be that patients are much more aware of various possibilities of treatment and have gathered enough information to ask the right sorts of questions of their doctors. But there is a clear tendency around the Western world that people are seeking much more medical attention today than before. The fact that citizens have become empowered by free access to knowledge does not mean that they are self-governing, on the contrary (Stoker 2006b)! They still need governance – meta-governance. Maybe even more than before. It is a different kind of knowledge governance. They need coaching by their doctors, politicians, civil servants and other relevant personnel in the public sectors. They do not need classical forms of knowledge governance in the form of instructions and good advice. This is where politicians still need scientists. Image surveys quite consistently underpin the fact that 'scientist' is considered to be one of the most trustworthy, reliable and prestigious professional occupations in society while professional politician ranks just ahead of journalist (The Harris Poll 2009).

Taken together, it seems that Max Weber is still alive and relevant for our analysis of public sector transformation. Rationalization, knowledge authority and professionalization have become central features of modern public administrations, and there are not many indicators that this is going to change any time soon.

An Aftermath of NPM: Regained Relevance of Public Values and Public Service Motivation

Torben Beck Jørgensen and Lotte Bøgh Andersen

Introduction

In 1991, Christopher Hood wrote an article entitled 'A Public Management for All Seasons?' about how New Public Management (NPM) challenged fundamental features of the public sector (Hood 1991). Indeed, an array of managerial and organizational mechanisms inspired by private sector practice has since invaded the public sector. Firstly, greater emphasis has been put on efficiency – although efficiency is hardly a new value in public sector reforms. Secondly, the mechanisms to achieve efficiency have been altered. NPM introduced a new conception of the modern public sector and modern public organization that did away with hierarchy, monolithic systems, politically neutral administrative bodies, standardized personnel systems and standardized regulation of citizens and companies for the benefit of a market-like, deregulated system of pseudo-corporate, autonomous service producers and enthusiastic public managers (Peters and Wright 1996, Brunsson and Sahlin-Andersson 2000, Peters 2001b). Thirdly, NPM brought us a new time spirit including a changed perception of humankind. Neo-liberalism provided this development with an ideological soundboard, which favoured values such as freedom of choice and individuality in sharp contrast to collective solutions and solidarity but in accordance with the rational choice approach which models reality on the assumption that people seek to maximize personal benefit given the rules of the game.

Framed by these currents of thought, reformers of the public sector have questioned the existence of public employees who are loyal to the state, the organization they work for, ethical principles, professional standards or the users. NPM-inspired reformers refuse to see them as altruists and expect them to be loyal only to themselves and their respective careers. When the public sector grows, it is therefore not because citizens need more service, but rather because those who make their life in an organization live better if it is growing (Niskanen 1973) or if it is 'bureau-shaped' so that the work becomes more interesting and less routine (Dunleavy 1991). The way to manage such egoistic public employees is to manipulate their self-interest, which brings us to performance-related pay, contractual relations, market control and so on. Correspondingly, citizens are no longer beneficiaries to be cared for; they are individuals capable of making rational, fully informed decisions about which services are to their greatest benefit, which leads to individualization of public services and free choice. In Le Grand's (2003) words, reformers no longer see public employees as 'knights', but rather as 'knaves', while the citizens have been transformed from pawns to queens – the most powerful piece in chess.

The NPM perspective has not gone unchallenged. In the UK, the home of NPM, the counter-reaction was prompt and strongly focused on values. The dangers of one-sided values and of efficiency crowding out other – classical – values were pointed out (Stewart and Walsh 1992, Butler 1994, Greenaway 1995), and a common denominator was the attempt to rethink the normative foundations of the public sector and to reinstate 'disconnected' service producers in a greater structure marked by values such as solidarity, democratic responsibility, stability, ethics and rule of law (Smith 1991, Frederickson 1997). Even the OECD, which has been among the foremost advocates of NPM-inspired modernization, has noted dangers such as a possible erosion of the sense of statehood and responsibility (OECD 1996, 2000b, 2005).

In terms of research areas, two different literatures challenge the NPM view of public employees as purely self-interested and loyal only to themselves. The public service motivation (PSM) literature argues that public service motivated individuals want to work on the mission of public organizations because of their altruistic motivation to do good for others and society. The public values (PV) literature insists that the desirable, not only the desired, is important. Both are central as an aftermath of and beyond NPM, and the next two sections will discuss them in more detail, following three tracks (cf. Beck Jørgensen 1999: 581–582):

- The conceptual track: What are PSM and public values?
- The empirical track: How do PSM and public values affect decisions and behaviour in the public sector, and how has NPM affected PSM and public values?
- The 'beyond-NPM' track: What are the enduring and basic questions?

The chapter ends with a discussion of what the two research areas can offer, compared to NPM. Although we refer to NPM and counter-reactions throughout the chapter, the reader should bear in mind that we are dealing with a timeless dilemma between self-interest, duty, altruism and values.

Public Service Motivation

In contrast to the NPM perspective, the public service motivation (PSM) literature expects individuals to vary in the extent to which they prioritize their own utility relative to societal considerations. Some might even attach so much concern to public policy and service delivery that they will sacrifice other important goals to improve it. This stands out against the NPM perspective, but before we discuss the relationship between PSM and NPM in detail, we need to discuss what we mean by PSM.

The Conceptual Track

Public service motivation (PSM) is a type of altruistic motivation linked to the delivery of public service. Until recently, the PSM literature was primarily based on American research, but the tendency has spread to the rest of the world in the last five years. In the US, the trend was sparked by an article by James Perry and Lois Wise, in which they defined PSM as 'an individual's predisposition to respond to motives grounded primarily or uniquely in public institutions and organizations' (Perry and Wise 1990: 368). As the definition indicates, the concept was originally related closely to organizations in the public sector; in other words, the expectation that this type of motivation is primarily found among public employees was almost built into the definition. However, more recent research does differentiate between public service motivation and public sector motivation (Perry and Hondeghem, 2008a: 3). The latter concerns the motivation found among public employees (Wright 2001), and the reference to public organizations has been removed from recent definitions of the former. Vandenabeele (2007: 547) defines public service motivation as 'the belief, values and attitudes that go beyond self-interest and organizational interest, that concern the interest of a larger political entity and that motivate individuals to act accordingly whenever appropriate'. He thereby explicitly works values into the definition. This is not entirely unproblematic as it is difficult to capture value conflicts in a one-dimensional concept. Nevertheless, we agree that PSM must be distinguished from self-interest and organizational interests, and we therefore work with Hondeghem and Perry's (2009: 6) understanding of the concept as 'an individual's orientation to delivering service to people with the purpose of doing good for others and society'. This definition understands PSM as altruistic motivation tied to the production of service. The service must be collectively oriented in one form or another; PSM is hardly relevant in relation to the provision of hairstyling services. Provision of services is not supposed to have a user-oriented character alone; it must also have a general character directed at the public at large (Blau and Scott 1963, Beck Jørgensen et al. 1998).

In the 1990s, PSM research worked towards developing a good measuring instrument as well as accounting for variations in PSM. As far as developing a measuring instrument, the central contribution was James Perry's index construction (1996), which demonstrated that the concept can be subdivided into dimensions

Table 23.1   Overview of the public service motivation dimensions

Dimension	How the dimension is understood	Originator
Commitment to public interest (public values)	Obligation- and loyalty-based motivation for providing public services and thereby serving society	Perry (1996) / Kim and Vandenabeele (2009)
Compassion	Emotion-based motivation for providing services for others or society	Perry (1996)
Attraction to policy making (public participation)	Motivation to improve the political decisions (and participate in the public sphere) in order to improve conditions for others or society	Perry (1996) / Kim and Vandenabeele (2009)
Self-sacrifice	Willingness to disregard own needs in order to help others and/or society via the provision of public services	Perry (1996)
User orientation	Motivation to help the specific other via the provision of public services	Vandenabeele (2008)
Democratic governance	Motivation to provide public services in accordance with central public values	Vandenabeele (2008)

(the upper four rows in Table 23.1). Kim and Vandenabeele (2009) interpret the 'public interest' dimension as being more about a 'commitment to public values' and suggest that the 'attraction to policy making' dimension is re-interpreted in terms of an 'attraction to public participation'. In addition to the traditional four dimensions, Vandenabeele (2008) suggested two new dimensions: democratic governance and client/user orientation. Democratic governance is about providing services while respecting central democratic principles such as responsibility, equality and neutrality. The user orientation dimension is more in line with NPM; although it is altruism, the recipient is an individual.

Reflexive indexes consisting of Likert format questionnaire questions have been developed for all dimensions in Table 23.1. The tradition is based on survey research, but other methods are being introduced into the field, including register data (Andersen and Serritzlew 2009) and qualitative interviews (Kjeldsen 2010).

The Empirical Track

Although the PSM dimensions and measurement remain under discussion, the literature deals extensively with the effects of public service motivation. This research is structured by three expectations presented by Perry and Wise (1990) (see Box 23.1).

Box 23.1   Perry and Wise's (1990: 370–371) original propositions

> 1.   The greater an individual's public service motivation, the more likely they will seek membership in a public organization.
> 2.   In public organizations, public service motivation is positively related to individual performance.
> 3.   Public organizations that attract members with high levels of public service motivation are likely to be less dependent on utilitarian incentives to manage individual performance.

Concerning the first proposition, the empirical results are consistent with the theory. PSM is higher among employees working in the public than the private sector, but the literature is still exploring the causal processes underlying the differences (Perry and Hondeghem 2008b: 296). Public employees might be attracted to the public sector due to their initial high level of PSM or public organizations might increase public service motivation through socialization. The major point is, however, that public organizations differ from private organizations, and this implies that private sector management tools cannot (as sometimes claimed in the NPM perspective) be transferred directly to public organizations.

NPM sees public organizations as 'a chain of low-trust principal/agent relationships (rather than fiduciary or trustee–beneficiary ones), a network of contracts linking incentives to performance' (Dunleavy and Hood 1994: 9). This implies that public employees (the agents) will only exert themselves to produce the public services sought by the politicians (the principals) if they are rewarded specifically for their effort or results. That is not always possible, given that output and outcome are difficult to measure in many public organizations (Wilson 1989: 159–171). Gailmard (2010: 40) argues that PSM alleviates this problem by bringing in individuals who want to work on the mission of the public organization due to altruism; they will exert themselves without merit pay. The findings concerning the second PSM proposition indicate that this is true, at least for some specifications of performance. The literature finds that employees with higher levels on the public interest dimension consistently have higher levels of individual performance (Vandenabeele 2009, Leisink and Steijn 2009, Andersen and Serritzlew 2009). Although some studies suffer from self-reported performance measures, these findings indicate that we might miss something valuable if NPM blinkers limit our vision.

Based on a review of the literature, Perry et al. (2009) discuss whether public service motivation theory is a more applicable lever for improving performance in public agencies than the NPM-based performance-related pay systems. They argue that performance-related pay can potentially reduce overall motivation, as confirmed by the results from the motivation crowding literature (Frey and Jegen 2001, Andersen and Pallesen 2008, Weibel, Rost and Osterloh 2009). Especially for interesting work, NPM-inspired systems should be used cautiously. Work is perceived to be interesting if it is felt to be challenging, enjoyable or purposeful

(Weibel, Rost and Osterloh 2009: 5). For example, implementing strict control systems for research activity (which most researchers regard as challenging and enjoyable as well as purposeful) can be counterproductive (Frey and Osterloh 2006, Jacobsen and Andersen 2009). Based on a meta-analytic review of previous experimental studies on the impact of performance-related pay on performance, Weibel, Rost and Osterloh (2009) find that while performance-related pay has a positive effect on performance in the case of non-interesting tasks, it tends to have a negative effect in the case of interesting work. They argue that performance-related pay strengthens extrinsic motivation for behaviour and simultaneously weakens other types of motivation. The net effect on effort and performance depends on the strength of these two opposing effects and the initial level of motivation (Weibel, Rost and Osterloh 2009: 18). The providers of public services generally have a high level of PSM and intrinsic motivation alike, and performance-related pay can therefore potentially reduce PSM and intrinsic motivation.

To know whether reduced PSM is a problem, we need to discuss whether high PSM is necessarily a good thing in the public sector. PSM might, as mentioned, help to solve some principal–agent problems, but it can also create new problems (Gailmard 2010). There is often more than one way to 'do good for others and society', and highly motivated public employees will hardly subvert their own values and accept organizational values determined by democratically elected politicians. Given that conflicting values between agents and organizations reduce work effort (Brehm and Gates 1997, Gailmard 2010: 41), this is a potential problem. We must therefore retain our critical faculty in relation to PSM and not trust public employees to work automatically towards organizational goals just because they have high PSM. Still, we should not go to the opposite extreme and not trust public employees at all.

The 'Beyond-NPM' Track

Given that a one-eyed focus on self-interest is problematic, one of the central questions 'beyond NPM' concerns the association between different types of motivation. How do we design robust incentives and regulatory systems, which ensure efficiency and responsiveness and do not crowd out PSM (and intrinsic motivation)? Very few public employees act like pure egoists unless treated as such. At the same time, it is naive to assume that we are all altruists. The solution is hardly to transfer the entire decision making authority and the keys to the treasury to public employees, but the years with NPM-inspired regulatory instruments have demonstrated that we should avoid addressing the employee's wallet narrowly. As Le Grand (2003) writes, it is about discovering robust incentive systems that speak to the knight and knave alike. The same incentive system can apparently be perceived in very different ways according to the signals on how it is implemented. The key is to implement regulatory systems that simultaneously ensure that the knight is recognized for the effort he makes of his own accord to the benefit of society and that the knave does not exploit the system. The public service motivation literature can help us achieve this end, as it helps us understand the knight's motivation.

We might not only want to maintain the existing level of PSM; we might also want to increase it via strategic recruitment and socialization. But can public managers select employees with high PSM, and can they affect the PSM of the existing employees? The literature has begun to ask these questions (Paarlberg, Perry and Hondeghem 2008, Park and Rainey 2008), but they have not yet been answered conclusively. The discussion (ibid.) is very much focused on how PSM can be made useful in the production of public service, but the question is whether PSM should be used instrumentally in this way. The employees may sense that their motivation is promoted not as a value as such, but rather as an instrument to achieve external goals. This may reduce rather than enhance their motivation; overt instrumental usage may thus endanger the very possibility of creating and maintaining public service motivation (Steen and Rutgers 2009).

Public Values

NPM has provoked an intense debate not only on the shortcomings and the advantages of modern economizing measures in the public sector but also on the more general cultural impact of NPM.[1] This is in essence a discussion about values: what are we talking about when we discuss public values (the conceptual track); which values actually guide decisions and behaviour in the public sector (the empirical track), and what are the basic questions in the public values literature (the 'beyond-NPM' track)?

The Conceptual Track

Public value research can be divided into two perspectives: the *generative* perspective and the *institutional* perspective (Davis and West 2009).[2] The first perspective focuses on *creating* public value as output and outcome and is represented by, among others, Moore (1995) and Stoker (2006a). This perspective seeks to develop a paradigm for public value management as a broader network-related approach to public management compared to NPM's market approach (O'Flynn 2007). The

---

1   See for example Christensen and Lægreid (1999). For a recent overview of the debate on NPM and public values, see Van der Waal (2008).

2   The concept of value has attracted attention from philosophers, economists, sociologists, psychologists, anthropologists and political theorists, and it is hardly a surprise that the concept is contested. Here, it is sufficient to define 'value' as expressing the *desirable* as opposed to the *desired* (Van Deth and Scarbrough 1995). For further discussions on value definitions, see Bozeman (2007), Van der Waal (2008) and Hodgkinson (1996).

Table 23.2   The public value universe

The structure of the universe	Public values (examples)
The contribution of the public sector to society	Public interest/the common good, social cohesion
Interests converted to decisions	Majority rule, protection of minorities
The politicians–administration relationship	Political loyalty
The relationship between the administration and its immediate surroundings	Openness, balanced interests, impartiality
The internal relations within the administration	Reliability, innovation, productivity
Public employees	Professionalism, accountability, integrity
The relationship between the administration and citizens/users	Rule of law, dialogue, user orientation, fair treatment

generative perspective as a normative approach to public management has become very popular lately among both practitioners and researchers.

Within the institutional perspective – the point of departure in this chapter – public values are defined as the ideals, coined as principles, to be followed when producing a service and thus *provide direction* rather than *drive action*. According to Bozeman (2007: 13) public values specify:

- 'the rights, benefits and prerogatives to which citizens should (and should not) be entitled;
- the obligations of citizens to society, the state and one another; and
- the principles on which governments and policies should be based.'

The latter – systemic or institutional – element in the definition is important, as it indicates that values can be considered as the basic building blocks of the public sector (Beck Jørgensen 1999: 581).

Public values defined, the next question is: which public values can we talk about? Is there a definitive number of 'eternal' public values, or are we dealing with an expanding (or diminishing) universe? The value discourse often equates public values with 'classic values' such as integrity, accountability and honesty.[3] But can other values be labelled 'public' apart from these few classic 'boy scout' values?

In order to attain a broad perspective regarding the 'possible providers of direction', Beck Jørgensen and Bozeman (2007) registered public values referred to in the relevant academic literature.[4] The registration provided a total of 72 values,

---

3   Cf. the recommendations of the Nolan Committee on Standards in Public Life (1995).
4   For a similar and very detailed registration of possible public values, see Van der Waal (2008)

which indicates a considerable breadth in the total public values universe. To create order out of this chaos, they applied a classification focusing on the aspects in the administration or the public organization that the value in question related to or was directed towards. Table 23.2 provides an oversight.

The Empirical Track

This classification leads up to the basic empirical question: which values are actually followed in the public sector? Can we find differences between sectors and countries? And has NPM caused a change in a public value profile? Unfortunately, very few empirical studies address these questions and none in a satisfactory way. We will sum up the results from a Danish and a Dutch investigation.

The Danish Democracy and Power Study conducted relatively comprehensive empirical studies in 1999–2001, including an analysis of long-term changes (1850–2000) in the legal rules regulating and governing public organizations, a survey of public managers at all levels and sectors, analysis of mission statements, and case studies of service-producing organizations, regulatory organizations, as well as public debates on outsourcing.[5]

While the study of value changes in legal rules pointed to the emergence of a market state (Henrichsen 2010) the most commonly reported values in the survey were the classic values: accountability to society, public insight, the rule of law and independent professional standards.[6] Characteristically, the lowest ranking value was 'listening to the public opinion'. The answers to questions about important personnel competences and motivating factors supported an almost classic ideal regarding authority and the role of a civil servant: The civil servant is above others in order to serve others. The case studies at the agency level pointed to professional standards as *the* important value. All told, a general public ethos emerged, not NPM values (Beck Jørgensen 2007, Vrangbæk 2009). As Shakespeare put it: 'Thou art not for the fashion of these times, Where none will sweat but for promotion' (*As You Like It* II.iii).

But this is not entirely in accordance with the results from the analysis of mission statements. Most popular values were *responsibility, respect, development, cooperation, quality, openness, trust, commitment* and *professionalism*. To some extent these values reflect the values in the general public ethos. On the other hand, judicial values and accountability to society were rare guests in value statements and many of the most popular values – respect, openness, trust, cooperation, dialogue – were found in private companies as well and may simply reflect a human resource fad (Beck Jørgensen 2007).

---

and Van der Waal and Huberts (2008).

5   The study and its main results are summarized in Beck Jørgensen (2007).

6   Renewal and innovation also scored high and could be an indicator of a changed value profile. However, it is absurd to think of renewal and innovation as values related *only* to NPM.

In 2007, a structural reform in Denmark merged municipalities from 271 to 98. This was an opportunity to investigate whether a major reform would influence public values. In short, local top managers in the 98 municipalities expected the reform to give more importance to both 'modern' values (renewal and innovation, career opportunities, networking, flexibility and efficiency) *and* a few classic values (judicial values and professional standards), while accountability to society ranked quite low. Looking further at factors of motivation and employee competences the general impression was that individualism and flexibility were expected to be favoured by the reform, for example strategic thinking and adaptability ranked higher than personal integrity and loyalty to rules (Asboe Kristensen and Beck Jørgensen 2008). These results might indicate that NPM-related values have slipped into the municipal world, even though the reform in itself had little to do with NPM. On the other hand, changes in value rankings may just as well reflect what is considered useful (for example adaptability) and natural (for example career opportunities) during a major reorganization.

In 2009/2010, a near-replication of the 2000 survey was carried out, and interesting value changes were identified. Efficiency, networking and career opportunities all scored higher in 2010; indeed, efficiency was ranked as the most important value. On the other hand, satisfying users' immediate needs scored lower and, most important, the aforementioned classic values all scored the same or higher in 2010. Has NPM caused a change in the value profile? Maybe, but so far NPM has apparently not crowded out other values although there might be a time lag between changes in steering instruments and changes in institutionalized values.

The Danish studies had one important shortcoming: comparisons between public and private organizations were not included. In contrast, differences and similarities between public organizations and private companies are systematically explored by Van der Waal (2008) and Van der Waal and Huberts (2008). Specific public values are lawfulness, impartiality and incorruptibility, while private companies score high on profitability and innovativeness. Conversely, both public and private organizations score high on expertise, efficiency and accountability to relevant stakeholders (stakeholders not specified) and low on obedience, social justice and responsiveness towards citizens and customers. Not only is it difficult to see NPM as a predominant set of institutionalized values; on some points, it is even difficult to recognize the image of private companies described by the theory and ideology. Neither customers (responsiveness) nor personnel (self-fulfilment) obtain high scores.

The Danish and the Dutch studies implicitly take us to the next question: can we find differences between countries? Van der Waal, Pekur and Vrangbæk (2008) have compared public values from three countries: the Netherlands, Denmark and Estonia. One of the primary results is that the Netherlands and Denmark are more result-oriented, while Estonia places greater emphasis on formalities, duties and principles. One interpretation is that the Netherlands and Denmark have adopted NPM instruments more comprehensively than Estonia; another interpretation is that Estonia needs to enshrine a neo-Weberian style in the relatively young bodies of administration or to demonstrate to the outside world that 'we are a Rechtsstaat' in connection with EU admission negotiations. Values thus can – and must – be interpreted contextually (West and Davis 2010).

The 'Beyond-NPM' Track

At least three central areas in public value research take us beyond NPM. The first focuses on which mechanisms or structures can promote or inhibit certain values. How is it possible to organize towards rule of law, political loyalty or, indeed, efficiency? This question, earlier addressed by Hood (1991) and Beck Jørgensen (1993), has gained focus for example in infrastructure sectors on the background of the significant EU deregulation in recent years (De Bruijn and Dicke 2006, Jones 2009). A related question is how to get public employees to follow specific values. A classic instrument is taking an oath (Rutgers 2009), manifest today also in the form of codes for good governance, good public management, good public service and so on. Closely related studies investigate the extent to which the institutional heritage and socialization frame employees' value perception (Pratchett and Wingfield 1996, Stensöta 2010).

Value changes – or value dynamics – are the second important area. Clearly, NPM has provoked an interest in value changes but the phenomenon itself is certainly not new (Charles, de Jong and Ryan 2010). Which shifts in values can we observe and which explanations can we find? Explaining public value changes is a theoretical playground. Many theories can be brought into play as illustrated in a special issue on public value changes in infrastructures (Bruijne, Dicke and Veeneman 2009). Various value changes are explained by path dependency, pendulum dynamics, fashions, mimetic isomorphism, strategic calculations, and changes in institutional contexts as well as in deeper societal structures. The study of value dynamics represents a challenge, not least empirically because of the obvious difficulties in obtaining data that shed light on shifts in values over time.

The third area is the normative analysis. The normative discussion of which values ought to be selected as providing behavioural direction is crucial to the evaluation of any administrative reform. These considerations are also central for the practical development of documents that contribute to a formal or informal constitutional foundation for a system. Part of the normative discussion has an analytical flavour: what are the relations between values? Are they in conflict, can they live together in harmony, or are some values instrumental to other prime values (Beck Jørgensen and Bozeman 2007, Martinsen and Beck Jørgensen 2010)?

The message from research on public values is clear: the desirable has significance and cannot be reduced to 'the desired', as NPM has attempted. The next section couples this insight with the discussion of PSM and relates the two research areas to NPM.

Public Service Motivation, Public Values and New Public Management

Both public value and public service motivation are occupied with phenomena that are above self-interest (duty, fidelity, altruism and values). In that sense, they are both part of the reaction to NPM. But what can the two research areas offer compared to NPM other than being more virtuous and politically correct?

Firstly, PV and PSM offer *realism*. It might be regarded as sensible to maintain a so-called realistic belief that people ultimately act selfishly. Then you won't be disappointed. But what if public employees do not merely act to maximize their self-interest? Or worse, what if the perception of public employees as pure egoists (via the implementation of steering techniques that send the wrong signals) becomes a self-fulfilling prophecy because employee motivation is undermined? In that case, you are generating your own disappointment. The empirical study of employee motivation in the public sector can provide a more subtle sense of what drives people to act and thereby avoid the development of perverse incentive systems. Even from the question of efficiency, one can further ask whether it is particularly appropriate, via the use of self-interest-based incentive systems, to break down other sources of motivation. Correspondingly, more accurate knowledge about the competing values NPM is up against increases the realism of reforms. PV counteracts one-sided values and value blindness and turns the attention to the possible impact of institutional heritage in various sectors and national political cultures on present-day reforms.

In addition to realism, PSM and PV offer *vision* – a broader normative orientation. For NPM, the societal obligation of the public sector is practically irrelevant. If you only think in terms of NPM, you cheat yourself of both realism and the ability to assess *how* and particularly *why*. Steering techniques are rarely value-neutral, and an understanding of values opens up for a normative assessment of whether global ideas on 'smart' administration are appropriate and desirable in a given context. Indeed, we should ask ourselves whether we will let a one-sided approach such as NPM dominate our view of human nature. In the long term NPM presents a risk of losing the imagination necessary to develop the public sector and society itself. PV and PSM offer a greater normative context, of which NPM is part. It may seem like NPM has colonized values and motivation, but the argument presented here is that NPM is in fact a special case within the broader normative context provided by PSM and PV. Consequently, it is far too narrow to see PV and PSM as a reaction against NPM. The broader normative context encompasses NPM. Without this broader normative context, NPM is meaningless.

Research in values and public service motivation has considerable potential, especially combined, as contributions 'beyond NPM'. In many ways, they are each other's proverbial blind spots. PSM research has a narrow focus; PV research has a broader scope. PSM considers the effects to a greater extent, while some value research assumes effects. Finally, PSM is primarily occupied with the driving force behind the actions while PV deals with direction: what is, could be or should be desirable. The combination of PSM and PV thus provides a conceptual frame to understand goals other than promotion of self-interest, and it allows us to analyse systematically how much energy individuals are willing to put behind achieving these goals, why this energy varies, and how it is directed by values.

Whether they are combined or applied separately, the claim in this chapter is that the interplay between NPM on one side and values and motivation on the other is important. It is also a manifestation of the far more fundamental and timeless relationship between self-interest, duty, altruism and values.

Serving the Public? Users, Consumers and the Limits of NPM

Janet Newman

Introduction

Many of the features of NPM discussed in this volume have been introduced in the name of the service user or consumer. Structural devolution is claimed to bring management decisions closer to the customer and thus to enable more responsiveness to service users. Managerialism itself challenges professional power bases and is strongly associated with the consumerist turn in public services. Marketisation and competition are viewed as empowering users by enabling them to have greater choice of provider. And New Public Management has produced important developments around service quality, flexibility and responsiveness. The question of how far these developments enable organisations to better serve their publics and deliver public value is, however, more problematic (Newman and Clarke 2009). The aim in this chapter is threefold: first, to trace the genealogy of developments such as quality, consumerism and public participation; second, to explore their capacity to 'empower' the service user and wider publics; and third, to challenge their continued relevance in the face of contemporary economic, social and political challenges. In doing so it returns to the matrix of governance regimes I first developed to explain developments associated with the first New Labour administration in the UK, which was strongly associated with the rise of NPM; but then rework this around current ideas of a 'new synthesis' in public administration that challenges many of the NPM orthodoxies.

NPM, Service Quality and Organisational Change

NPM is a shorthand term used to describe the rise of managerialism in the context of attempts to reform public services through the 1990s and beyond. One of the targets of reform was the mix of bureaucratic and professional power that had characterised the growth of the public sector in modern welfare states. Bureaucracies were viewed as wasteful and inefficient, and organisations were made subject to a range of marketising pressures, from internal purchaser–provider splits through market testing, quasi markets, outsourcing and outright marketisation.

The competitive pressure on organisations required them to place more emphasis on service quality. Quality measures were essentially a managerial tool, subject to managerial technologies of measurement and audit; as such they presented a major challenge to professional power. The implicit knowledge base of professionals was no longer enough to justify the ways in which they delivered a service. Professional criteria of judgements were codified into quality and audit measures (which hospitals perform best in terms of patient deaths following surgery; which schools deliver the best exam results, and so on). Such measures provided greater public knowledge and could of course be used to inform choice where users had a choice of provider. But in the process, the recourse of staff to professional judgement and/or to a wider public service orientation were subordinated to organisational norms of performance and efficiency. One strand of this transformation of knowledge reflects broader social trends: in some contexts people no longer believe that 'professionals know best', and the authority enjoyed by professionals has become more fragile or contingent. But a second strand has been the subordination of implicit, informal and experiential knowledge – whether of staff or service users – to the requirements of 'evidence-based practice', and the transformation of professional standards into a proliferating array of audit, inspection and regulatory regimes. Much has been written about the deficits of the 'target culture' in which governments set standards and targets and introduce inspection and audit regimes and league tables of performance. The result tends to be game playing on the part of organisations, with 'cream skimming' and 'boundary management' games enacted to select certain customers (the 'cream') and to ensure others are shunted to the province of a different organisation (Clarke and Newman 1997). Targets and centrally imposed standards have other perverse consequences, not least the stifling of innovation outside the 'core business' of what gets measured, and the undermining of the capacity of organisations to respond to local circumstances and need – precisely the features needed, some might argue, to enhance the voice of the service user and wider public in shaping public service delivery.

The development of quality systems were overlaid on these tensions rather than resolving them. The turn to quality took different forms. Some organisations developed quality control systems whose aim was to assure consistency – the doctrine of getting it 'right first time' in the delivery of a product or service. Others attempted to position themselves in the new contract culture by emphasising the 'value added' their service delivered to a particular client or customer group – especially to the most frail or difficult users whose needs could be better met by a high value (and cost) service rather than through standardised services to the general user. Most organisations became subject to the new commitment to quality assurance, quality control and the (then) new ethos of total quality management. These all offered a contested field of practice with purchasers and suppliers, managers and staff, users and providers negotiating about what quality might mean and whose version of quality was to be pre-eminent. To some extent quality standards stabilised these contested meanings through the use of quality technologies. Service user charters – the standards of service a user might expect and a statement of their entitlements to service – filled a similar function. But Kirkpatrick and Martinez-Lucio, writing in 1995, nevertheless highlighted the contested 'politics of quality' as quality measures designed for business and industry were applied to the public sector. Such measures tended to be made in the name of the service user but with little actual user voice included in their definition or the forms of their application.

Consumerism and its Limits

So how far, and in what ways, has the voice of the service user been enhanced as professional power has been challenged? The primary focus of NPM was on transforming organisational cultures and systems and on enhancing managerial prerogatives in order to maximise organisational efficiency and competitive success. At the same time it installed a succession of reforms that attempted to place the service user at the centre of the service relationship. These included service charters, user involvement, and the reconfiguration of service design into 'one stop shops' and 'co-production' systems.

The neat equivalence between NPM and the growing emphasis on the importance of the service user is, however, too neat a story. The 'user' of public services is a complex entity. She may be an individual simply seeking the best quality of service among competing providers, as in the commercial world. But she may be someone reliant on professional power to make judgements about the best intervention or treatment in a particular circumstance: the doctor diagnosing an illness, or the police officer intervening in a disturbance or attending the site of a burglary. She may not be the direct service user but may be mediating the user relationship on behalf of someone else: the carer or relative negotiating care services for an elderly or dependent person, or the parent concerned about the performance of the school attended by her child. It may be a collective rather than an individual entity: the local community wanting someone to help them tackle crime or antisocial behaviour, the carers group wanting more of a voice in how care is resourced and managed, the users of a local park or library wanting a stake in how that facility is designed or wanting to protest about its potential curtailment.

However the dominant image of the service user within NPM is as a consumer. This needs a little unpacking. The consumer is an individualised entity capable of and desirous of choosing between alternative products and providers. The consumer's relationship with a service is as a customer, with a focus on repeated transactions rather than an ongoing relationship. The consumer's entitlements and rights are those of the entitlement to choose and the right of redress. The consumer relationship takes different forms in different nations, for example, between those with social insurance models such as Germany and those with state funded services such as the UK (Newman and Kuhlmann 2007). And consumerist orientations can sometimes provide the rationale for political campaigns to restore rights and entitlements (see for example Vabø 2010, on the 'elder revolt' in Norway following the 'modernisation' of welfare services). However there are also considerable deficits to the spread of consumerist logics of public service delivery. In research on the rise of the citizen-consumer in the UK in the 1990s we examined the impact of the consumer culture on different services (health, social care and policing) and investigated the implications for users themselves. Our study revealed that people using public services in England were reluctant to identify themselves as consumers or customers. Respondents stressed identities as users of particular services (such as patients) or as members of publics or local communities (Clarke et al. 2007, Clarke and Newman 2007). Other research has highlighted the tensions between consumerist and relational approaches to care giving (for example Anttonen and Häikiö 2010).

This indicates something of the troublesome character of the user in relation to public services. Singular narratives of change that propose a wholesale shift from solidaristic attachments to individual interests, or from citizens to consumers, are unfounded. People have complex relationships with public services, sometimes wanting care and support, and at other times prioritising independence and choice. Compare, for instance, the expectations that an individual might have when lying in the street waiting for an ambulance having had a serious accident, and those expectations that the same individual might have some months later when attending a hospital as an outpatient for a check up on how well the broken bones are healing. Or compare the needs of the relative of a frail older person who is becoming unable to care for themselves with the needs and desires of the older person herself. How does choice work in these circumstances? In the first example choice of ambulance service is not a priority but choice of treatment and possibly of provider may be relevant in the aftercare stages. In the second example, whose choice is to count? The development of individual budgets in social care offers some measure of 'empowerment' for service users, but may place additional burdens on families. Users may not see themselves as consumers or users at all but as citizens with entitlements and rights, or, as our study showed, as members of the public. However relationships are complex: people bring multiple expectations to the service relationship, with some identities dominant in some contexts but not in others, and with priorities at one moment giving way to others as needs and expectations change. The result is a series of 'unstable encounters' (Clarke 2007) which do not fit the standardising tendencies of quality management nor the efficiency imperatives of NPM.

From Consumers to Publics?

The supposed exhaustion of NPM is opening up spaces in which both professionals and managers are talking the language of democratisation, involvement, co-production, empowerment and choice (Duyvendak et al. 2006). The suggestion that there is evidence of a move 'beyond' NPM is not necessarily convincing, but nevertheless attention needs to be paid to the different ways in which such concepts are emerging and being deployed. One innovation over the last decade that is sometimes viewed as a development or evolution within NPM is that of public participation. This covers a range of practices, from consumer consultation exercises to deliberative forums, from user involvement in service design to public engagement on policy priorities and choices, from participation in ongoing governance arrangements to one off events such as participative budgeting exercises. There have been important experiments focused on engaging communities and civil society organisations as the co-producers of effective policy outcomes – drawn into the management or governance structures of initiatives to improve health or well being, to regenerate deprived communities, to enhance community safety or local environmental sustainability, or to recover from some kind of disaster or trauma. This begins to expand the focus of attention beyond efficient service delivery to take account of issues of democratic control and accountability (for example Sullivan 2001, Skelcher Mathur and Smith 2005, Sørensen and Torfing 2008) and wider issues of citizenship (Neveu 2007). At the same time the growth of the World Wide Web and other new technologies has enabled experiments and innovations, from the e-petition to the on-line discussion forum (Morison and Newman 2001). And increasingly public policy actors and public managers are turning to the national and local media to help them engage publics more actively.

But does this take us *beyond* NPM? In Barnes et al. (2007) we noted four key discourses that shaped developments in public participation: an 'empowered' public discourse, a 'consuming' public discourse, a 'stakeholder' public discourse and a 'responsible' public discourse. These offer very different images of the publics who are summoned for the purposes of public participation, and offer very different relationships between publics and public services. The consumerist discourse is the only one that is highly consonant with NPM, with the stakeholder discourse partly compatible with the proliferation of new governance arrangements in a dispersed field of power. The dominance of these discourses is now being challenged from at least two directions. The empowered discourse challenges the subordination of democratic principles to managerial logics. Here public participation offers a means of reconnecting citizens to the polity through their engagement in quasi-democratic practices: the citizens jury, the deliberative forum, the participative budgeting exercise. But as is shown elsewhere (Newman and Clarke 2009) the ways in which the technologies of public participation are elaborated and deployed may render such initiatives more compatible with managerial logics and the repertoires of NPM. The 'responsible' public discourse reflects the growing policy emphasis on the need for more 'active citizenship', with citizens participating through their contribution to civil society and in taking responsibility for forms of provision formerly the responsibility of the welfare state (Newman and Tonkens 2010). The role of the state, and of public service bodies, shifts from that of efficient delivery to that of capacity building and/or an engagement with new pedagogies of citizenship – teaching and 'nudging' individuals to take responsibility for their own health and well being, for those of their children and relatives, and for those of the communities in which they live.

Challenging the Dominance of NPM

Such developments challenge the dominance of NPM assumptions and practices in several ways. First, the focus shifts from organisational management in the name of output efficiency. Although efficiency remains important, attention turns to wider issues of effectiveness in the use of increasingly limited resources; and public engagement – although costly to develop in the first instance – is viewed as a means of ensuring effectiveness by enrolling the public (in its various forms) as co-producers of service and policy outcomes. Second, the focus shifts from transactional to relational models of service delivery. While NPM and service quality models can be used to improve the effectiveness of individual service transactions, making them more responsive, introducing a measure of flexibility, making them more timely and accessible, this is only ever a partial contribution to effectiveness because of the relational dynamics of most public services. What tends to be valued by the public – as users, citizens and communities – is an ongoing relationship with the service in question, and often with a particular practitioner. This is particularly significant in some services – for example in the delivery of domiciliary social care – but applies to others too, including health (where users tend to want access to their regular doctor) and policing (where an ongoing relationship with a 'bobby on the beat', a visible police presence on the street, remains highly valued even where there is little evidence of their impact on crime reduction or control).

Third, notions of public participation and engagement challenge the dominance of both professional and managerial forms of knowledge. The knowledge and experience of service users, communities and publics is regarded as something that is of value to the organisation. Accessing such knowledge and experience helps it to adapt to new needs, demands and expectations. And the acknowledgement of the voice and experience of users and publics helps organisations to gain legitimacy, both among the publics directly served and in relation to the wider field of competition and performance. For example, a health service that uses web-based systems to enable young people to talk about their experience of health problems and of using health services is likely to be able to develop services better tailored to the needs of young people, to improve take up and preventative work, and to be able to involve them in the development of new models of service design.

Fourth, public participation and engagement can challenge the forms of organisation and models of control associated with NPM. They do this by opening up questions of democratic and political participation that are antithetical to the business ethos and to managerial autonomy. They suggest the need for greater degrees of devolution and differentiation (in order to respond to both local and specific publics) that are inimical to NPM trends towards the consolidation of strategic and resource decisions to achieve economies of scale. The result may be the increasing remoteness

Table 24.1   Challenging NPM

NPM	Public participation and engagement
Quality of service	Quality of life, of relationships
Consumers	Citizens, publics, members
Choice of provider	Continuous relationship, co-production
Delivery	Sustainability
User as shadow presence	User with voice
Managerial power	User, citizen power
Enhancing (consumer) choice	Enhancing (public) engagement

of users and citizens from decision making, opening up the potential for loss of legitimacy and trust. Challenges to such models often come from the global South; not only the famed Participative Budgeting experiments in Porto Alegre but a range of other initiatives and developments (Cornwall and Coelho 2007). Where these are translated in the North in line with established institutional practices and NPM rationales, however, the results may be impoverished: it seems that it is not only the ideas behind innovation that matter but also the mediums through which they are enacted (Mahony 2008).

So far this chapter has set up a potential duality between NPM and public participation and engagement. On the one hand it might be argued that public participation and engagement are the logical extension of the service user focus, extending the user to encompass each of the categories listed earlier; proxy users, collective users and citizens entitled to a voice in how public resources are used, even where they themselves may not be a direct user of the service in question. Here public participation and engagement are viewed as *adaptations* of NPM. On the other hand it might be argued that public participation and engagement represent a challenge to many of the dominant assumptions and practices of NPM: challenges that cannot be accommodated by adaptation. The tensions between the two paradigms are presented in the binary oppositions listed in Table 24.1.

However there is a fifth development that challenges NPM in more fundamental ways. This results from the perceived problem of sustaining welfare and cohesion in the face of an array of contemporary challenges to welfare states. Western governments are searching for ways of shifting responsibility for health and well-being onto citizens, communities, social enterprises, volunteers, the 'third sector' and other entities. A range of analytic framings for this search have emerged: the emphasis on the importance of 'civil society' propounded by Robert Putnam and others; the focus on 'community' as a resource for and focus of governance (Mooney and Neal 2009); the development of interest in the 'social economy' (Amin 2009); work on enhancing the 'capability' of citizens and communities (Sen 1999, Bonville and Farvaque 2007); and the current turn by political leaders in the US and UK to strategies of 'nudging' individual behaviour through the restructuring of choice architectures (Thaler and Sustein 2008), together with a range of behaviour change programmes directed at improving diet, parenting or civic participation, with the long-term goals of reducing reliance on increasingly pressurised services.

These direct attention *beyond* the public services that were the dominant focus of NPM, and thus are not readily amenable to processes of adaptation. The next section offers ways of conceptualising the tensions between different managerial and governance regimes rather than working with a single image of NPM; then go on to explore possible developments to this model emerging from the work of those promoting a 'new synthesis' in public administration.

Mapping the Shifts

In an attempt to map different understandings of the relationship between publics and public services this section returns to the model of governance tensions that I first used to analyse the shifts associated with the first New Labour administration in the UK in the late 1990s. This mapped forms of governance along two axes (process and outcome legitimacy; weak and strong control) and produced a typology of four regimes of governance:

- hierarchical governance (process legitimacy, strong control)
- managerial governance (output or results based legitimacy, strong control)
- network governance (output or outcome legitimacy, weak control)
- self governance (process legitimacy, weak control)

Hierarchical governance is linked to the kinds of bureaucratic organisational forms and to the producer dominance which NPM successfully challenged. It is still an integral part of public management since it assures accountability and forms of control that seek to secure compliance to laws, rules and regulations. At first sight it has little to do with quality improvement or public participation: indeed the latter is sometimes viewed by politicians as undermining proper representative channels, short circuiting relationships between publics and their representatives. However it is strongly associated with representative democracy, an essential channel through which the public expresses voice and choice (Du Gay 2005).

Managerial governance underpins the templates of NPM. It is associated with consumerist conceptions of the service user and with a concern to enhance service quality in order to compete effectively in governance fields characterised by contracting and competition (Clarke and Newman 1997). This is strongly linked to the consumerist discourse of public participation noted above.

Network governance has been the focus of an extensive literature that posits a shift from old-style government, based on the state, to emerging systems of governance appropriate to dispersed systems of power and a plural polity (for example Rhodes 1997). It challenges many of the precepts of NPM in its focus on the importance of relationships and the centrality of trust to effective network building. And it is viewed as an essential means of addressing the kind of 'wicked' problems discussed

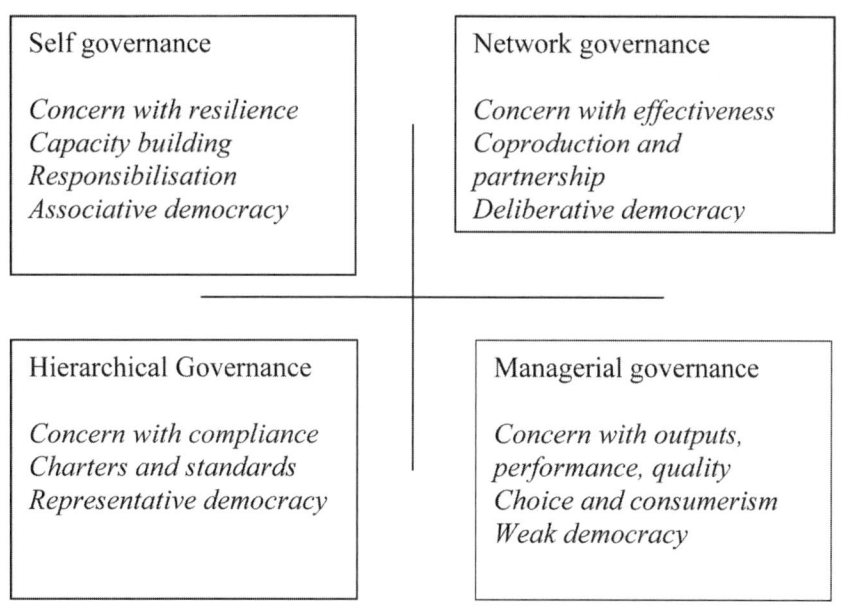

Figure 24.1 Competing images of the service relationship

at the end of the previous section. While the managerial emphasis is on efficient outputs, network governance seemingly promises whole system outcomes. It is associated with the stakeholder discourse of public participation but also to emerging discourses of co-production as users are drawn into networks and partnerships with professionals and service providers. To the extent that networks unlock traditional forms of patriarchal and paternalistic power this model may also offer some forms of empowerment: though power equity within networks and partnerships is notoriously elusive.

Self governance has become an increasingly significant policy orientation as the capacities of the state have supposedly reached their limits and alternatives to state-provided welfare are sought. It is paradoxical in its political orientation, being associated both with the empowered discourse of public participation and with the responsible discourse: in offering empowerment it simultaneously responsibilises citizens to take action on their own (and others) behalf rather than to rely on the state.

Turning to Figure 24.1, the vertical axis represents a tension between tight and loose control, or hard and soft forms of power. The horizontal axis reflects different forms of legitimacy, with process legitimacy on the left of the axis and output/outcome legitimacy on the right. Newman (2001) used the model to illustrate tensions in governance systems in relation to partnership working, public participation, performance and the overall governance shifts associated with so called Third Way politics.

The value of this model is its capacity to highlight tensions. There is, for example, a significant line of tension between hierarchical and network forms of governance: the shift towards networks in which publics and citizens become involved in shaping policy decisions, become stakeholders in partnership arrangements, or become co-producers of services confronts elements of the hierarchical regime that demand compliance with standards or that require responsibility to be clearly allocated for the purposes of accountability. As a result, many so-called power sharing forms of public engagement become limited by bureaucratic requirements that stifle the extent to which the public can exert their voice effectively and see positive outcomes from their involvement. The result may be disenchantment and a reduction of, rather than extension of, trust. A second key line of tension is that between managerial governance and self governance. How can an organisation driven by NPM requirements for short-term results and/or efficiency savings invest in long-term capacity building? And perhaps more importantly, what are the effects of a decade or more of treating people as individual consumers when they are suddenly required to become self-sustaining communities? And of course there are significant tensions between managerial and network forms of governance: NPM requires organisations to be 'selfish', prioritising competition over collaboration, organisational performance over system effectiveness.

Conclusion

So what of the future? The economic downturn facing most mature welfare states means that the fate of NPM and its focus on the citizen consumer is uncertain. It may be that there is a resurgence of NPM strategies and technologies as organisations face the need for deep cuts and significant efficiency savings. These may well restore the managerial 'right to manage' in the face of what were emerging challenges to the NPM orthodoxies in recent years. But at the same time there is likely to be more emphasis, rather than less, on self-government, responsibility and citizen 'empowerment' as the state looks for ways of reforming social welfare away from citizen reliance on state-provided services. Beyond the current crisis and its paradoxical effects there is a growing emphasis on the need to invest in enhancing the resilience and sustainability of communities and even states in the face of the challenges of climate change, the increase in natural disasters and threats of terrorism, as well as long standing problems of a growing elderly population, the exacerbation of inequality and growth of social divisions. In response to such issues there has emerged a series of debates about the possibility of a 'new synthesis in public administration'. The role of the New Synthesis project is 'to explore what is different about serving in the 21st century, what is new and what is of enduring value; how this will transform the role of government going forward; what new systems, skills and capacities will government need to live up to citizens' expectations and the challenges of their times?' (Bourgon 2007, 2008, Bourgon 2010: 31). The key concepts of the new synthesis project are those of 'emergence' and 'resilience'; but these do not displace the traditional concepts of performance (associated with NPM) and compliance (associated with bureaucracy, hierarchy and democratic control). The point is to consider how the traditional concepts need to be transformed in the light of the need for a greater focus on emergence and resilience in the twenty-first century.

Hereby hangs the future of NPM: can it adapt or does it need to be abandoned in favour of new paradigms more fitted to contemporary challenges and demands? The problem with this question, however, is that NPM is not a singular entity that is either present or absent, evolving or static. Rather, it comprises multiple elements that have been assembled in different ways, and aligned with other rationalities and institutional sedimentations, in different nations, regions and sectors (see Newman and Clarke 2009, on assemblage). There is, then, no singular *it* that can either evolve/adapt or be transcended.

However as this volume testifies, 'the NPM' remains central to discussions of the fate of public services. We need to move on from affording it this central symbolic place for at least two reasons. The first elates to the rise of new governmentalities of the self and community that rest on notions of personal and social responsibility rather than reliance on the state and its services. NPM, it might be argued, solved the problems of the past (the presumed dominance of bureaucratic and professional power) but in doing so created new problems (often the perverse consequences of choice and competition and of cascading targets and unrefined regulatory methods). But even if we solved these perverse consequences, the question remains as to how far NPM is able to address the problems of the present and future rather than the past. This brings us to the second reason for abandoning the idea of NPM as a desirable governing rationale. The key challenges facing welfare and post-welfare states are no longer those of delivering effective and efficient services but those of responding to climate change, natural and human related disasters, the care of the elderly, obesity, responses to the growth of chronic diseases, social cohesion, the new flows of both people and resources in a globalising world, and deepening inequalities. These require both a different time-frame of governance and new governing architectures. To the extent that the state still provides services then performance and efficiency will remain important drivers; but as the state looks beyond its public sector architecture in the search for new solutions, the application of old templates and technologies will surely stifle the generation of coherence, capacity and resilience – all qualities needed to serve the public and the public interest beyond the narrow confines of the service relationship.

Responses to NPM: From Input Democracy to Output Democracy

B. Guy Peters

Introduction: Bureaucracy and Democracy

In most models of democracy (Held 2006) the actions of government are legitimated through the electoral mandate they have received from the voters. The policy choices of government are further legitimated by the constitutional and legal processes through which they are made, so that even if decision-making is delegated, there is a clear legal basis for the delegation and substantial oversight of the actions of the agents by legislatures or ministers. The argument of this chapter is that this neat model of democratic governance is becoming somewhat suspect, and that increasingly governments are legitimating their existence through their outputs. This shift in legitimation, in turn, places the public bureaucracy at the center not only of delivering services but also of political legitimation.

The development of New Public Management (NPM) was to a great extent a reaction to bureaucracy. The reaction was a response both to the reality of formal public organizations and to many of the conventional stereotypes of bureaucracy. Furthermore, although the relationship is perhaps less clear, there was also some reaction against democracy given that political leaders were not seen as particularly skilled in running public organizations and hence should perhaps be sidelined in favor of greater influence from skilled public managers.

The terms bureaucracy and democracy are usually thought of, in both the academic and the popular literature, as antithetical approaches to providing governance for a society (see Etzioni-Halevey 1983). On the one hand public bureaucracies are typically conceptualized as necessary for the effective administration of public programs, but as being legalistic and largely indifferent to the wishes and demands of individual citizens.[1] Bureaucracies also tend to be associated with hierarchical

---

1   These views of public organizations are, of course, stereotypes and do not reflect the real nature of many or even most public bureaucracies (see Goodsell 2004, Du Gay 2000).

and even authoritarian forms of governing, even though at least part of the logic for institutionalizing the bureaucratic form of governing was to ensure equal treatment of citizens. Further, formal institutions can provide clients with records and justifications for the decisions being made about them within the public sector and thus may enhance the accountability of the public sector.

On the other hand, democratic governance institutions are assumed to be responsive to the wishes of the public, and to be attempting to map those preferences of the public into positive outcomes for their citizens. Richard Rose (1974) and other scholars have pointed out that the linkage between voting and policy choices in conventional representative democracy is not as clear as most democrats might like to believe. Further, the public may vote for inconsistent goals, or have unrealistic expectations that will require leaders – elected and bureaucratic – to make policy decisions on their own (Caplan 2007). Still, for some good reasons, democratic governance is assumed to be able to adjust more effectively to the needs and wants of the public than most other forms of governing. Further, democracy contains the mechanisms for enforcing accountability over bureaucracies and hence permit those institutions to perform more effectively in the public interest.

Although it is easy to consider these two sets of institutions, and these two sets of institutional values, to be contradictory, they are both necessary for effective government, given the accepted values of public control over the public sector. In particular, bureaucracy is necessary for effective governance, including effective democratic governance. Most democratically elected officials are not experts in the policy areas about which they must make decisions and therefore, much of the work of the public bureaucracy is advising government about policy. While usually associated with the senior public service, this policy advice function is actually more widely distributed throughout the public bureaucracy (Page and Jenkins 2005).

In addition to providing policy advice, the bureaucracy rather obviously is involved in implementing public policy (Winter 2004). This function is the historical function of public administration but is also important to effective democratic governing. The public bureaucracy is the primary locus of contact between state and society and therefore much of the image that citizens have of government is shaped by their interactions with public administrators.[2] Further, those public administrators have substantial discretion as they implement the law (Hawkins 1992) and the manner in which they exercise that discretion will influence not only the style of governing but the real outcomes for citizens.

Bureaucracies were in part devised, at least in Weber's ideal type, as a means of ensuring greater equality and greater transparency in the public sector. Those positive aspects of formal organization in the public sector are often forgotten and the negative stereotypes of bureaucracy prevail (Olsen 2006, 2009). Although any effective democracy will depend upon an equally effective bureaucracy (see Rothstein

---

2   The good news is that most citizens report that their interactions with civil servants are for the most part acceptable, and in general as good as their interactions with the private sector. That does not, however, prevent citizens from having negative stereotypes of public bureaucracy, and indeed of government more generally.

2009), the contributions of the bureaucracy to governing are forgotten or denigrated. Further, as governments are at least in part evaluated by their capacity to deliver services, the bureaucracy plays a central role in legitimation, and that role continues to expand.

To this point we have been discussing bureaucracy as an institution, but it is important to remember that increasingly public services are delivered through non-governmental actors. Therefore, to understand the focus on output democracy it is crucial to understand how these organizations produce public services and how the public is capable of delivering services. On the one hand, the logic of utilizing these non-governmental organizations is to improve service delivery by eliminating the stereotypical problems of bureaucracies. In addition, many citizens find the non-governmental organizations are more congenial by virtue of being less 'bureaucratic' and simply because they are not in the public sector.[3]

NPM has attempted to provide a number of alternatives to the formality of public bureaucracies. Many if not most of these alternatives to bureaucracy involve private actors – market or non-market – providing public services. Further, NPM is designed to focus on the outputs of government rather than the procedures within government, and the proper means of assessing government and public organizations is what they focus on as much as or more than how the decisions are reached. Further, the emphasis on the role of public managers and their allies in governing to some extent displaces an emphasis on the role of political leaders.

Despite the emphasis on the use of alternative means of service delivery in NPM, and in many other repertoires of reform of the public sector (see Pollitt and Bouckaert 2004), these mechanisms may pose more of a problem for democracy than does the public bureaucracy. This is in part because most members of the public bureaucracy have been inculcated with some values of public service and probity, while for non-governmental actors providing public and private services are essentially the same thing.[4] Further, there are fewer formal mechanisms for controlling non-governmental actors than there are for controlling the public bureaucracy, and indeed some of the reasons for using these instruments is to minimize the extent of control over their actions.

Decline of Input Legitimation

In a democratic society there is a strong assumption that public policies and public governance should be controlled by the people through the voting process. That

---

3   Groups such as illegal immigrants may be threatened by government officials, even those not officially charged with enforcing controls; private service providers are much less threatening no matter the quality of the service they provide.

4   The idea of generic management is central to the logic of NPM, but as Graham Allison and others have pointed out, this underestimates the difficulties of public management and also tends to deny the importance of democratic values in governing.

capacity of the public to control governing is, in many ways, only a pious hope given the number of impediments to that control. Rose (1974) demonstrated rather clearly that even in majoritarian political systems such as the United Kingdom politicians may have limited will and even less capacity to implement the programs for which they campaigned during elections. That capacity is even less for politicians in coalition governments given the difficult bargaining necessary to forge and then maintain coalitions (Müller and Strom 2003).

Even if there is no direct control of public policy through voting, then the choices made by governments may still be legitimated by the willingness of the public to vote, and to engage in other forms of conventional political participation. If voting is not an instrumental act it may still be emotive and symbolic, and the turnout of voters in elections provides diffuse support for the political system and its policy choices.[5] Even when voters are aware that they are not actually choosing policy through their votes, political leaders can still claim to have attained a mandate (Powell 2002) from the public through elections.

Although voting is the most common means of legitimating government and policy, there are other forms of participation that may also be important for providing support for the system. In particular, in most industrial democracies interest groups may provide an alternative source of involvement and influence for the public (see Rokkan 1967). While this form of participation may help to channel public demands to government, it tends to lack the broader legitimating capacity of voting, and may be seen as the pursuit of particular interests at the expense of the public interest. This negative conception of interest group involvement in government is especially true for systems with a pluralist orientation in which interest groups are not considered as appropriate participants in politics as in more corporatist societies (McFarland 2007).

Legitimation through voting and political parties continues to be important, but its viability is declining in many contemporary democratic systems (Pharr and Putnam 2000, Norris 2002). The most important element in this decline is the reduced level of voting in the established democracies. Except for a few notable exceptions, for example the French presidential election of 2007 and the American presidential election of 2008, voting has been declining over the past several decades. The decline has been perhaps more extensive in the newer democracies of Central and Eastern Europe as the initial enthusiasm for voting as a mechanism for addressing governance problems has diminished. In short, citizens appear to be losing interest in, and commitment to, the electoral process.

The decline in voting is significant in many countries but the decline in political parties as instruments for representing the demands of the public has been even more dramatic in most democratic political systems. The decline in membership and identification is especially marked for the mainstream political parties that have been central in governing for decades. These parties have become 'cartel parties' which are intimately linked with government and to some extent have become part of the governing process (Katz and Mair 1995, 2009). In contrast to

---

5   This is in the sense of diffuse support in David Easton's model of the political system.

these more conventional parties, 'flash parties' that reflect single issues or the leadership of particular individuals have been successful electorally, although they fail to institutionalize the linkages between the public and their government (Taggart 1995).

The changing nature of political parties and their behavior in government has tended to accelerate declining public membership in parties. The Katz and Mair (1995, 2009) argument concerning 'cartel parties' advanced the thesis that political parties in most industrial democracies have changed their fundamental motivation. They argued that cartel parties have as their primary motivation maintaining their position in the cartel of parties that control government. Thus, the parties have a greater interest in perpetuating their involvement with government than they do in representing their constituents. This commitment to remaining in government is accentuated by public funding of existing political parties, creating this cartel that is relatively insulated from the public they are meant to represent.

A loss of confidence in public institutions has been associated with the decline in voting and the decline in party membership. The loss of confidence extends across a range of political and governmental institutions and has been true even in countries such as the Scandinavian countries that have a history of effective and benevolent government. There has been a general loss in confidence in government and a sense that those political institutions are not capable of doing the job necessary for effective governance. Interestingly, the decline has been less marked for the bureaucracy and for other output institutions than it has been for political institutions. This relative success of the bureaucracy is particularly remarkable given the generally negative view that the public holds of the public bureaucracy.

Samuel Huntington (1974), rather early in the development of this apparent democratic malaise, identified a fundamental paradox of modern democracy that was emerging and affecting the involvement of the public in government and the legitimation capacity of voting and other conventional forms of political participation. On the one hand, political participation should be increasing substantially as populations become on average better educated, more exposed to media and have more leisure time for involvement in politics. In addition, the diffusion of post-industrial values including authentic participation should make the public more interested in active involvement in politics.

On the other hand, however, the issues that governments must now confront are more complex, more technical and less familiar. Further, and paradoxically, the vast increase in the information and communications technology may in fact be decreasing public attention to the complexity of policy issues, and especially diminishing any common understanding of the issues. As the public increasingly consumes 'narrow casting' rather than broadcasting, and newspapers continue to face economic problems in producing serious journalism, the public may think they know more but may actually know less.

Although many people around the world struggle to institutionalize electoral democracy, many citizens who already have functioning democratic systems appear to have lost some commitment to those institutions. This does not, in most cases, appear to be rejection but rather apathy. Some critics of representative democracy argue that the public are searching for more direct involvement in governing, while others argue that the public no longer see the relevance of politics for their daily lives. Whatever the reasons, political leaders cannot depend upon input forms of legitimation for their policies in the way that they have been able to for some decades, and must consider alternative means of legitimating public action.

This discussion has been primarily in terms of changes within established democratic systems, but we need also to consider the uses of output legitimation, and output democracy, for transitional regimes. Even when a single hegemonic party may prevent effective political democracy, there may still be opportunities for citizen involvement and some citizen control at the level of individual institutions or local government. For example, in China citizen reactions to policy failures appear to have some influence on local government without threatening the domination of the Communist Party (see Zhao and Peters 2009). It is difficult to determine the extent to which this style of output involvement can influence a system more broadly but it does provide some opportunities for democratic action.

NPM Cuts Some of the Links with Input Legitimation

Changes in the behavior of citizens and political parties has, as already pointed out, a good deal to do with the declining capacity for input legitimation in contemporary democracies. Other changes in the prevailing ideas about governing, however, also influence the capacity of input institutions and processes to legitimate government action. In particular, the spread of the ideas of NPM (Christensen and Lægreid 2001a) has tended to emphasize the role of public managers in providing governance while at the same time denigrating the role of elected politicians. To the extent that this connection is broken, much of the emphasis is shifted from legitimating government by its performance (see Scharpf 1999).

There are several points within NPM that tend to reduce the capacity of input mechanisms to legitimate public action. Most importantly, this approach emphasizes the importance of public managers as the source of high quality government. The mantra of the approach 'let the managers manage' emphasized the importance of empowering managers to make and implement their own decisions. Rather than being subordinate to their nominal political masters, as in most models of political democracy, senior public managers should be expected to, in essence, provide the direction in public governance.[6] The assumption of NPM has been that managers as professionals can provide better governance than the amateur politicians.

As well as emphasizing the role of public managers, whether career public servants or not, NPM has also put forward structural recommendations that have

---

6   Although he certainly accepted the subservience of public servants to their political masters, Woodrow Wilson's writing emphasized that administration was superior to politics because administration could be a science while politics was only an art (see Wilson 1887).

tended to reduce the capacity of input democracy to exercise effective control over policy. The most commonly used, and most important, of these recommendations has been the creation of 'agencies' as autonomous or quasi-autonomous organizations designed to deliver public services (Pollitt and Talbot 2004). The logic, typical of NPM, is that by removing direct political control and by allowing organizations to focus on a single purpose,[7] higher levels of performance will be generated.

In addition to the use of agencies, the reforms associated with NPM have tended to use a variety of instruments outside the public sector to deliver public services. Contracting out, the use of market mechanisms and developing public–private partnerships are all seen as means of improving the performance of government and also reducing the direct costs to the public sector. All of these devices involve some form of delegation to non-governmental actors who can exercise authority on behalf of the state, which tends to lessen the amount of democratic control over their actions (Gailmard and Patty 2007). These instruments may have some virtues of efficiency but operate at two stages of delegation of authority and hence are less directly accountable to political control.

Performance measurement and management is the final element of NPM that is important for understanding why the locus of democratic activity may have shifted to the output side of the political system. Despite the numerous pitfalls in performance management (see Bouckaert and Halligan 2008), the focus on what the public sector does, and how well it does those things, does emphasize the outputs of the public sector. In addition, the widespread availability of performance information enables citizens to understand what is being done for and to them, and provides a potential impetus for political mobilization. That mobilization may, however, be directed toward output institutions rather than through parties and input mechanisms in the public sector.

NPM is more than just a set of ideas about public administration; it is in reality a theory of governing. The political dimension of NPM is also illustrated by the language used to describe the members of a society. In particular, the members of the public are commonly referred to as 'customers' rather than as 'citizens' in this literature. This characterization of the public tends to deny the public their political role and reduce them to consumers of public services. The intention of this characterization is to emphasize the need to treat the public as if they had some other place to go for public services and hence they must be provided with high quality services. That said, this characterization also tends to assign the public a rather inferior role within the public sector.

All of these recommendations and ideas coming from NPM are subject to challenge. Some of the challenges are on democratic grounds, most notably that the dismantling of the state and the denigrating of elected politicians (Suleiman

---

7   One of Niskanen's (1971) standard critiques of large government departments was that it was difficult to determine the costs of delivering each of the multiple services delivered, and to hold the organization accountable for those services. The advocates of NPM have picked up this point, and argue that by creating autonomous organizations the chances of creating greater accountability will be enhanced.

2003), that tend to undermine political democracy. Further, public services may involve values of equality and probity that are not necessarily compatible with the efficiency criteria stressed by NPM. Other challenges to the orthodoxy created by NPM are empirical. It is not always clear, for example, that non-governmental actors are better are 'rowing' and providing services. Likewise, the breaking down of the state into large numbers of autonomous organizations imposes coordination costs that may exceed any benefits created through improved efficiency of the individual organizations (see Christensen and Lægreid 2007a).

Despite these numerous challenges coming from the direction of accountability and control, NPM has had a pervasive impact on the way in which contemporary political systems are organized, and the ways in which they function. The emphasis on the central role of managers, on performance management, and on providing services to 'customers' all tend to depoliticize the processes of governing and to emphasize the production of services rather than the democratic mechanisms for selecting policies, making them function well and then holding the individuals involved responsible for their actions.

'Presidentialization' Arguments

Another of the political patterns pressing governments in the direction of output legitimation is the shift within governments away from conventional parliamentary dominance toward control by the cabinet and the prime minister. Many democratic governments are referred to as 'parliamentary' because holding the position as the chief executive in government depends upon being able to command a majority in parliament. That title also implies that parliament is the dominant source of authority in these systems. Parliaments, however, have been losing powers relative to the executive, and within the executive the full cabinet is losing power relative to prime ministers.

This discussion of the changing role of parliaments is important for understanding contemporary politics but it is also important for understanding the locus of legitimation and democracy in those contemporary political systems. If this characterization of the declining capacity of parliaments to control the bureaucracy is indeed correct, then the chain of legitimation leading from voting through parliament and then to policy choices is largely broken. In this conception of contemporary democracy parliaments are merely rubber stamps for the executive[88] and the focus of contemporary democracy is on the executive and the performance of public programs. Thus, again, input and process legitimation of public policies is weakened.

---

8   This is hardly a new position and some scholars have been arguing that this has been occurring for decades in European democracies (see Grosser 1967). More recently see Poguntke and Webb (2005).

Although the 'presidentialization' label that has been applied to this phenomenon is fundamentally incorrect – executives in parliamentary governments presently have greater powers than most presidents – the logic does point to the importance of the output side of the political system. If the real action in government is in the executives, as it increasingly appears to be, then those executives can be seen as influencing the public through the outputs of the public sector. Further, as executives tend to have substantial control over their political parties as well as over parliaments, they can minimize the challenges to their controls over policy.

However these changes in governing are typified, there is a basic democratic issue of how citizens and parliamentarians can control the executive. This is important for limiting the possible excesses of presidents and prime ministers but it is more relevant in the context of this chapter in terms of controlling the public bureaucracy. If legislative bodies have lost much of their capacity to exercise control over elected executives, then their capacity to control the unelected executive may be weakened even more.

Bureaucracy as a Locus of Democracy

This chapter has already argued that bureaucracy and democracy are not incompatible, as often thought, and indeed the two concepts may be complementary. Further, given that many conventional instruments of democracy have become less viable in many democracies, there is a need to consider alternative formats for involving the public in policy decisions and for creating greater capacity for enforcing accountability. Moreover, the public appears to have become more concerned with the performance of government and with the actual production of goods and services, rather than with the procedures by which those benefits (and burdens) may be created. Indeed, many of the traditional procedures of government may appear arcane and outdated in the contemporary technological era, creating the impression that governance is one of the most important democratic elements of the public bureaucracy given that its members are in much closer contact with the public than are elected officials. The average citizen rarely meets with his or her member of parliament or even local councilor, but is in frequent if not daily contact with the bureaucracy.[9] Although members of legislative bodies generally find it important for their careers to engage in a great deal of constituency service, these contacts tend to be intermittent and generally are oriented around some very particular problem. The representative nature of democracy tends to be exercised at some distance from the actual citizens, except at election time.

The actual decisions made by these officials may help to shape the opinion of citizens about the legitimacy of government, but the style may be more important. How the average citizen is treated by public officials appears important in shaping

---

9   This includes postmen, school teachers, policemen, postal clerks and the host of other lower echelon officials in the public sector.

public perceptions and in creating efficacy among citizens. This is true even though in many cases the outcomes appear contradictory. Most studies have found that citizens believe that they are well treated by the public bureaucracy (Bovens and Zouridis 2002) but at the same time many negative perceptions of government persist. Indeed, over the past decade governments have invested a great deal of effort in improving service to the 'customer' while at the same time public confidence in the public sector has continued to fall (Aberbach and Christensen 2005).

In addition to having frequent contact with citizens as individuals, the public bureaucracy also has frequent contact with groups in civil society. Again, interest groups may lobby with members of parliament or other political officials but they have continuing and often close contacts with the bureaucracy. For example, contemporary network mechanisms for governance tend to rely heavily on connections between those networks and ministries or agencies. Indeed, many networks are sponsored and supported by the bureaucracy and are intimately intertwined with that public bureaucracy.

To the extent that networks and analogous structures in civil society have become complementary forms of democracy (Sørensen and Torfing 2005), their connections with bureaucracies provide a good deal of capacity to affect public policies. Public participation is an important value in itself but democracy also needs to be capable of shaping policy decisions. For policy networks their capacity to exert that influence depends largely upon the powers delegated to them by bureaucracies (Hansen 2007) or on their capacity to influence bureaucracies and their programs.

Some of the shifts in the public sector resulting from adopting NPM also facilitate the capacity of bureaucracies to fulfill some of their democratic potential. For example, the emphasis on performance management in NPM has provided very large quantities of evidence for individuals and for organizations that want to influence policy or to improve the services already being delivered to them. Most of the performance indicators available to the public are linked to a particular agency, program or institution so that citizens can identify the locus of inadequate performance and use that information as part of the political process attempting to influence government.

The information from performance management, as well as the more general activity of networks and civil society organizations, becomes a source of political mobilization. If the public can see readily if a school or a hospital is failing, then they are likely to mobilize to challenge the school board or the hospital management. At times that political mobilization is individual. The logic of No Child Left Behind in the Bush administration was to permit parents to exert some individual power *vis-à-vis* the educational bureaucracy. In other cases the information may lead to developing political movements and indeed to activating social networks to press their case for enhanced performance.

The availability of a good deal of evidence on the performance of government institutions and programs also enhances the capacity to hold those organizations accountable. Indeed the logic of accountability may be shifting away from traditional forms of political accountability toward performance based accountability. To some extent this has been occurring within formal political organizations, for example the Government Performance and Results Act in the United States, but it has also been occurring more generally with the public. Governments now regularly publish 'league tables' on how well individual schools, hospitals, water departments and the like are performing and citizens can see clearly how their public services compare with those received by other citizens.

With more information available to them, citizens can focus more on the actual performance of governments on average and over time, rather than concentrating attention only on more egregious examples of governance failure.[10] Parliamentary debates on accountability may be about grand issues of policy, but they often revolve around relatively minor errors and nonfeasance. If, however, accountability debates are focused more on questions of performance and improvements of performance then there are greater opportunities for citizens (as well as the officials) to enhance the manner in which governments and their agents are able to deliver services to the public.

Is it Really that Easy?

The logic of citizens becoming more informed and more involved in holding government organizations accountable again points to a shift in democracy toward the output side of the political system. Presumably citizens should be able to assess how well their governments are performing and then to mobilize to impose changes in those governments. This is a nice, optimistic model of democracy, but like all such rather simple models it does make a number of assumptions that may be difficult to support in the real world of governing. The question is whether such a simple model of political involvement is adequate for the complexities of contemporary governing.

The first and most basic problem is that although the citizens may be given a great deal of information about performance of public programs, it may not be sufficient to motivate them to political action and effective democratic control over these public organizations. The public are already given a number of opportunities to participate politically and, as noted above, they tend to find many other things to do with their time and energy. While the proximity of a local facility may motivate greater levels of activity, the assumption of political mobilization may still be a heroic assumption about political action. Voting is a very simple act taking in general only a few minutes but citizens seem to find this too taxing so why should we expect them to spend long hours in meetings about their local school?

---

10 The extreme failures are important, but a more salient question may be: how well is government performing on average, and is it improving? Similarly, all organizations, public or private, have their failures, but the more pertinent question may be: what is the average error rate?

In addition to the general difficulties in generating high levels of political mobilization, the levels of citizen mobilization that do result may vary markedly with class and education. One of the standard critiques of representative democracy has been that it is dominated by the more affluent and by citizens with substantial organizational capacity. The same critique can be made about social networks that are often considered an alternative format for democracy (see Hansen 2007), as well as about citizen mobilization against failing institutions. Indeed these are the groups who might have the most to gain from their political opposition to failing institutions and public programs.

Thus far the argument of this chapter has been attempting to develop an empirical case for the shift of democratic activity to the output side of the public sector. The question is whether concentrating on this form of legitimation is sufficient to maintain the sense of the legitimacy of public action, and whether it is sufficient to maintain levels of citizen involvement with government. Having already said that the public appears to have lost some confidence in the traditional input-oriented forms of legitimating policy making is there really much to be gained by placing a greater emphasis on the output side of government?

The output legitimation argument may be successful for a multi-national structure such as the European Union that has no real history, and little real pretension, of being democratic in the conventional sense (Scharpf 1997b, Hix, Noury and Roland 2007). It is not clear, however, that a concentration on political mobilization directed to the output side of governing will be adequate for more traditional national democracies where citizens expect to be directly involved in choosing policy. Democracy and governance are still about selecting policies as well as monitoring the outcomes of the policy process, so unless the bureaucracy and other objects of delegation become also more central in making policy then there the focus on output legitimation becomes part of the solution but not the entire solution.

The decline of the traditional forms of democracy and the increased interest in output democracy raises questions about other issues in contemporary democracy as well. Deliberative democracy and direct democracy have been proposed as possible alternatives, or supplements, to the traditional forms of democracy that would be central for making policy if the traditional institutions continued to face challenges – especially the challenge of apathy. These devices are designed to bypass institutions such as political parties and engage the public more directly in making policy. Both of these forms of democracy have well known problems, yet both may be capable of addressing some of the problems that have become identified in parties and legislatures.

One should not expect an end to political parties, voting and parliaments. These structures are too deeply institutionalized in democracies and perform far too important functions that are indispensable for any conception of modern democracy. That said, it has already been demonstrated that the public is losing confidence in these institutions and that they are participating less in these traditional opportunities for democratic action. Therefore, unless these institutions can find ways to revive public confidence, they may be destined to remain in a long twilight in which they continue to exist and to carry out their nominal functions while the real activity of democracy and governing occurs elsewhere.

The vision of this change in democracy may well satisfy many critics of the conventional representative form of democracy. Those critics have hoped for a more continuous and more direct involvement of the public in making policy decisions, and in monitoring the performance of the public sector. The emphasis on involvement with local service-providing institutions may provide some capacity to shape policy on an on-going basis. The emphasis may well remain on monitoring performance, however, given that the potential impediments to deliberative democracy, and even direct democracy, are so daunting in practice (Budge 1996, Dryzek 2002). Still, developing active practices of monitoring policy may be the precursor to developing equally active habits of participation.

Summary and Conclusions

Democracy remains an important value in most contemporary societies, but it is clear that there are important transformations under way in the manner in which democracy is being practiced. It appears that the conventional mechanisms of democracy, such as voting and political parties, are now weaker than in the past. Therefore, if democracy is to continue to be a successful means of steering the economy and society then some development and modification of the basic format for popular control over public policy must be institutionalized.

This chapter has discussed 'output legitimation' as one alternative to the traditional, input-oriented model of democracy. Bureaucracies are not usually considered the natural locus for democratic action, but there is reason to consider the necessity of a well-functioning bureaucracy for democratic government. Further, as the performance of political systems becomes both more apparent to citizens and more important, a good deal of political action in even well-functioning democratic governments shifts to the output side. This transformation is by no means a panacea for the ills of contemporary democracy, but at the same time the development of participatory instruments on the output side of the political system does help augment other aspects of democracy.

These shifts in the nature of democracy also represent some reaction to, and perhaps even extension of, the logic of NPM. While NPM tended to drive power and control away from elected politicians and to develop alternative instruments for service delivery, it also emphasized performance. That emphasis on performance has produced opportunities for citizens to understand better what their governments are producing and this in turn can serve as an impetus to greater public involvement on the output side of government. The familiar problems of mobilization and motivation remain, but these may be countered by the clear connection between political activity and services delivered.

Normativity and NPM: A Need for Some Theoretical Coherence

Robert Gregory

Introduction

As shown elsewhere, and in this volume, 20 years since the wave of NPM reform began there have been so-called second-generation or third-generation changes, in different jurisdictions, in different ways, at different times (Christensen and Lægreid 2001a, 2007a). In all of this, rigorously conducted empirical evaluations of the impacts of NPM are hard to come by. For its part, one of the leading international institutions behind NPM, the OECD, has itself been highly ambivalent about the general impact of NPM on member states (Manning 2006). Despite claims that NPM has enhanced efficiency and improved the standard of public service delivery, the evidence to support such claims remains mixed and ambiguous. Ultimately, assessments as to whether governmental reforms have achieved the aims espoused by their designers remain largely impressionistic and rhetorical, shaped as much by the beliefs and ideological perspectives of those making the judgements as they are by hard data and information (Boston 2001).

If that is true of empirical evaluations of NPM, it is obviously true of normative evaluations of the phenomenon. There is, as would be expected, widespread agreement among academics and practitioners that both 'good government' and 'good governance' ought to embody high standards of ethical probity, fairness, honesty, impartiality and so on. Few, if any, would openly advocate increases in efficiency or effectiveness, for example, to be achieved at the expense of fairness, honesty and impartiality in the delivery of governmental goods and services. Yet if empirical evidence were to show conclusively that such an outcome has in fact occurred – generally or in particular jurisdictions – then it would be necessary to be able to justify such an outcome in normative terms.

However, phenomena like NPM have to be evaluated simultaneously in both empirical and normative terms, since – as in all areas of public policy – empirical facts seldom speak for themselves, and must be evaluated against normative criteria, and vice versa. If it has produced demonstrable gains in governmental efficiency, why is this good, if the principal means of achieving that outcome – the marketization of goods and services – has had an adverse effect on standards of ethical probity in government, or on the accountability of public officials?

Before the emergence of NPM there existed a reasonably coherent body of theory which went a long way towards explaining important relationships between empirical and normative dimensions of governmental administration. One key aspect of this theoretical framework, which may loosely be called traditional public administration (TPA) was the widely accepted position that bureaucratic hierarchy (the so-called Weberian model) was essential in achieving and maintaining central technical values such as efficiency, effectiveness, accountability and – largely through unified career systems – normative values, notably high levels of commitment to and ethical probity in public service. NPM, however, was driven by a concern to enhance some of these values, notably efficiency and accountability – through marketization – rather than others. Consequently, there has emerged a theoretical gap, since it has become unclear as to the effects of these changes on normative values, and whether or not any such effects can be considered justifiable.

The purpose of this chapter is not to try to offer empirical evidence as to the actual effects of NPM on normative values that were for a long time accepted as being sustained by TPA. Instead, it will traverse some of the main issues relating to normative theorizing about NPM. It concludes that there is still a long way to go in developing a much needed coherent theoretical paradigm that seeks to explain key relationships among empirical and normative dimensions of NPM-inspired governance and public management.

NPM, Normative Theory and the Rise of the Market Model

In his comparative analysis of complex organizations, Etzioni (1975) identified three main types of power: coercive, remunerative and normative. He also observed three types of organizational member involvement: alienative, calculative and moral.

These categories in turn produce nine types of compliance, three of which – coercive/alienative, remunerative/calculative and normative/moral – are found most frequently because they are 'congruent', one with the other in each case.[1]

While virtually all large modern organizations combine all three of Etzioni's types of compliance, it is the relative balance among them that matters in particular cases. Generally speaking, neither TPA nor NPM have been characterized by strongly coercive/alienative compliance modes, any more than most organizations

---

1   'When the kind of involvement that lower participants have because of other factors and the kind of involvement that tends to be generated by the predominant form of organizational power are the same, we refer to the relationship as *congruent*. For instance, inmates are highly alienated from prisons; coercive power tends to alienate; hence this is a case of a congruent compliance relationship' (Etzioni 1975: 12, emphasis in original).

in other sectors, though there have certainly existed many individual public sector organizations in which this mode has been dominant, if only for limited periods of time. State coercive agencies like prisons rely predominantly on this type of compliance, but even in these the coercive/alienative mode dominates the relationship between prison managers and prison inmates, not necessarily that between managers and prison staff. The more relevant modes when considering any general effects of NPM on public sector organizations are the remunerative/ calculative and the normative/moral ones. There has clearly been an apparent shift to remunerative/calculative compliance in the management of public organizations, away from the normative/moral type. The effect of this shift on the behaviour of public officials constitutes a pressing empirical question.

The normative/moral compliance base of TPA was sustained by public service career systems, in which public sector employees were inculcated with key values and norms in the early stages of their careers and could be relied upon to adhere to them during long careers of up to 40 years or more, before retiring on a pension. There was much in this that was strongly reminiscent not only of Max Weber's (1947) 'ideal-type' bureaucracy with its monocratic hierarchical form, but also of Barnard's (1968) emphasis on the need to build a common sense of organizational purpose, of Selznick's (1957) distinction between an organization as a technical system, on the one hand, and an institution, valued not for what it does as much as for what it is, for what it represents as an exemplar of key values and norms, and of 'neo-institutionalists' like March and Olsen (1989), who distinguish between what they call 'aggregative' and 'integrative' political processes.[2] While scholars like Barnard, Selznick, and March and Olsen were writing of individual organizations (whether public or private), the same strongly normative foundations of organizational compliance were relevant to the establishment and maintenance of a unified public service career system, transcending employees' commitment to any particular organization within that coherent and integrated whole. Membership within an integrated governmental service, as distinct from one's employment in a particular government organization, was a key feature of the normative/moral foundations of a career-based public service.

As Boston has argued in this volume, NPM was strongly influenced by agency theory and transaction costs economics, especially in the three Westminster jurisdictions which were regarded as NPM leaders—New Zealand, Britain and Australia. Agency theory promotes the use of formal contractual relationships between principals and agents, in addressing the perennial issue of combating 'moral hazard' and 'adverse selection' on the part of public officials. The former career-based personnel systems that were typical of TPA relied overwhelmingly

---

2   'In an aggregative process, the will of the people is discovered through political campaigns and bargaining among rational citizens each pursuing self-interest within a set of rules for governance through majority rule. In an integrative process, the will of the people is discovered through deliberation by reasoning citizens and rulers seeking to find the general welfare within a context of shared social values ...' (March and Olsen 1989: 118).

on relational 'contracts' which were largely implicit, open-ended and dependent on agents' willingness to behave according to an ethos of dutiful and ethical public service. NPM, on the other hand, vigorously promoted the abolition of unified public service career systems and their replacement with position-based systems within which principals (employers) and agents (public employees) entered into specific, usually fixed-term employment contracts.

Agency theory has been central to the adoption of contractualism not just in personnel recruitment and management but also in the delivery of public goods and services. As Lane (2009: 72) observes, 'The idea that government could get the job done through buying and selling entailed a revolution in the thinking about public management.' Such buying and selling was to be carried out, of course, in markets or quasi-markets. The former are markets which provide for the competitive tendering between government principals and non-government agents, whereas the latter involve competitive procurement processes within a network of government agencies. In both cases, but especially in the former, 'Tendering/bidding and cost efficiency are linked to each other through powerful theorems in economics ...' (Lane 2009: 74).

The widespread adoption of markets in governmental service delivery has greatly reduced – though by no means eliminated – the explanatory force of Weber's 'monocratic' bureaucracy as the dominant mechanism of governmental organization (Gregory 2007). However, Weber well understood that his 'ideal-type' bureaucracy was a formal system, uncomplicated by the realities of value conflicts that were typical of actual human relationships. He distinguished between 'associative' and 'communal' social relationships. In the former, social action rests on 'a rationally motivated basis of rational judgement be it absolute values or reasons of expediency ...', while in the latter, social action is based on the subjective feelings of the parties that they belong together (Weber 1947: 136). These distinctions in fact presaged the 'aggregative' and 'integrative' political processes of March and Olsen (1989). Weber's bureaucratic model was machine-like in the directness and certainty of its control. It did not envisage the rise in the twentieth century of professional knowledge as a source of authority in bureaucratic organizations, and the perennial tension between the imperatives of managerial control, on the one hand, and the desire for professional autonomy, on the other. In general, it did not well explain important differences in organizational authority relationships, both formal and informal, that stem from the diversity of tasks that organizations perform.

Weber's monocratic bureaucracy rests largely on Etzioni's coercive/alienative compliance, but – like Etzioni – Weber also recognized that this could never be a sufficient foundation for cooperative organizational enterprise. Indeed, total reliance on this form of compliance would be ultimately self-defeating, and would undermine the compliance that necessarily flowed from communal and associative relationships. If the organization were to be effective, as well as just technically efficient, it had to ensure that those who worked in it felt a strong sense of belonging, as well as a sufficiently strong vested interest in cooperative action.

The main difference, however, between the likes of Barnard, Selznick, Etzioni, and March and Olsen, on the one hand, and those who provided the main theoretical foundations for NPM, on the other, was that the former did not subscribe overwhelmingly (if at all) to narrowly economistic assumptions of political and bureaucratic behaviour. They were more attuned to the multi-faceted, human and non-rational sources of organizational compliance, and were much less inclined than were the latter to assume the universal importance of remunerative/calculative compliance.

Assuming that all governmental officials were, in Le Grand's (2003, 2007) metaphorical terminology, essentially knaves rather than knights, NPM theorists saw contractualized appointments, and rigorous performance management systems that were closely linked to incentivized pay for performance as the optimal means of harnessing employees' narrow self-interest to the goals of the organization's owners. In this, the pursuit by organization members of their narrow self-interest would not transform them into knights, acting altruistically in pursuit of the public interest – a sort of 'guided invisible hand' perhaps – but it would ensure that the negative effects of knavish behaviour, such as waste, inefficiency, cynicism and incompetence, would be minimized, even though there existed (in the reformers' conceptual framework) no concept of 'the public interest' as a normative standard against which to judge officials' behaviour. Scholastically, the essential difference between the two approaches to public administration theory is epitomized in two important books, each of which exemplified the dominant Zeitgeist of its time. The normative/moral tradition is represented by Kaufman's (1960) classic study of the US Forest Service, showing how the organization can rely on 'pre-formed' decisions by forest rangers working in a large physically decentralized public organization. The remunerative/calculative paradigm of NPM is clearly exhibited in Horn's (1995) innovative theoretical work, which adopts an economistic interpretation of political-bureaucratic behaviour. Both works are exemplars of their own particular ages.

Assessing Consequences

In their emphasis on the remunerative/calculative mode of compliance, the theoretical underpinnings of NPM seemed to many to contrast refreshingly with long-standing public administrative scholarship, which in the eyes of public choice theorists had failed to produce any rigorous theoretical framework within which to build and maintain efficient, accountable and productive public organizations. However, while there was no 'rigorous' TPA theory as such, there had always been a certain coherence among the elements which comprised the TPA paradigm. With the advent of NPM, some semblance – if not the reality – of theoretical rigour may have been gained at a practical cost. The question is whether or not the application of the remunerative/calculative compliance mode in the transformation of public organizations has had the unintended consequence of undermining the normative/moral foundation of public service. To what extent has the operational assumption that all public officials are essentially knaves rather than knights been self-fulfilling? Has it resulted not only, or even primarily, in curbing the behaviour of knaves, the assumed majority? In a working environment in which public service-oriented knights, characteristically displaying normative/moral compliance, have – especially through marketization and the out-sourcing of goods and services – been increasingly provided with opportunities to act knavishly, have normative/moral commitments been adequate in discouraging them from doing so? In countries like Britain, Australia and New Zealand strong normative/moral compliance had underpinned public service career systems for many decades, and has undoubtedly continued as a path-dependent constraint on the emergence of opportunistic behaviour resulting from NPM reforms. Furthermore, as Schick (1998) has argued, the so-called 'New Zealand model' with its heavy reliance on legal contractualism, is unsuited for developing countries which have not first secured solid and enduring legal-rational foundations. On the other hand, trust in public institutions, built up over a long period of time, can dissipate relatively quickly if politicians and government officials begin in their own various ways to betray it.

There are as yet no conclusive answers, and there may never be. Commentators in different countries make their own observations and draw their own, varied, conclusions. They can see knavish behaviour in many forms: personal or official corruption; unethical behaviour; and the 'gaming' of the same performance management systems that are intended to ensure purpose-oriented (as distinct from rule-oriented) compliance. Personal corruption – the illegitimate use of public office for personal gain – has been and remains the worst form of public service dereliction, or 'moral hazard', while official corruption occurs when officials exercise their authority illegitimately in pursuit of the interests of their organization, rather than themselves (Banfield 1975). In other words, they cease acting as trustees who in knightly fashion can be relied upon to promote and preserve the public interest, in the face of opportunistic behaviour by their political principals (Hood and Lodge 2006). Unethical forms of behaviour by politicians and bureaucrats commonly involve such activities as the surreptitious leaking of information for tactical political purposes, and failures to disclose real or potential conflicts of interest in their work. Officials 'game' performance management systems when they devise ways to ensure that targets or other objectives are met, even though such activity may actually subvert the purposes and outcomes which these targets and objectives are intended to serve (Hood 2006).

It is difficult to know with any certainty whether or not NPM, and its shifting of the emphasis from normative/moral to remunerative/calculative compliance, has in fact resulted over the past 15 to 20 years in governmental services which have become more prone than in earlier times to such behaviour. In Britain, Australia and New Zealand a public service ethos was strongly institutionalized over many decades, but may have eroded incrementally since the abolition of the unified career services, though even if that is the case, the causes are likely to be manifold and difficult to attribute solely to elements of state sector reform. In recent years New Zealand's central state services agency has re-institutionalized a formal code of conduct and integrity for all state officials, and similar steps have also been taken in both Britain and Australia. There has, however, been no official acknowledgement that these steps result from any growing concern over any attenuation of the public service ethos or of standards of ethical probity.

'Bureaucracy', in the pejorative sense, has always had a 'bad press', and still today, in a post-NPM era, news media stories about bureaucratic failings, inefficiencies and absurdities are not far to seek in most countries. Whether warranted or not, whether arising out of any prejudice against public organizations, or whether such stories are seldom if ever 'balanced' by those which show public management in a favourable light to a sceptical citizenry, very little of this critical commentary is directed at NPM-styled state sector reform itself.

The use of agency theory and transactions costs economics in designing new institutional arrangements was intended not only to enhance efficiency in the delivery of governmental goods and services, but also to ensure robust systems of political and managerial accountability. Again, however, outcomes have been rather opaque and ambiguous. On the one hand, bureaucratic mechanisms have been favoured because of the apparently clear lines of accountability that are embedded in hierarchical systems, as depicted in the Weberian 'ideal-type'. However, ensuring accountability in complex multi-organizational governmental systems has always been problematic. If accountability is understood as the requirement that subordinates be answerable to their organizational superiors, then the bureaucratic mechanism has generally been able to ensure this. But if accountability is taken to mean, as it commonly is in political discourse, that when something goes awry someone, somewhere should be held to be culpable and sanctioned appropriately then even in the pre-NPM era there were very often problems in fulfilling these expectations.

There is certainly no conclusive evidence that either notion of accountability has been enhanced by NPM reforms. On the contrary, it is not difficult to find evidence suggesting that the shift from hierarchies to markets and quasi-markets in the delivery of governmental goods and services has exacerbated such problems of accountability. This is because contractualized out-sourcing, in which lines of accountability can be simultaneously both vertical and horizontal, often blurs questions of who is accountable to whom, when and for what (Mulgan 2003, 2006).

Organizational Disaggregation

As others have commented in this volume, the political-bureaucratic nexus is one of the most paradoxical dimensions of NPM. On the one hand, NPM promotes more of an 'arm's-length' relationship between the political and bureaucratic components of executive government, but on the other, it was supposedly designed to make bureaucrats more 'responsive' to their political superiors, less able to usurp power and authority in their own bureaucratic interests (Aucoin 1990, Maor 1999, Hood and Peters 2004). At one level, NPM can be understood as a means employed by politicians to transfer risk and blame to their bureaucratic subordinates rather than as a means of enhancing accountability per se. Horn's (1995) theoretical arguments are consistent with such an interpretation, and the rise of NPM and the marketization of public services has provided fertile ground for insightful theory-building about governmental risk and blame games (Hood 2002b, 2007).

The application of public choice theory, in particular, in an effort to reduce 'provider capture' (whether real or perceived) has arguably led to a loss of institutional integration. Both vertical and horizontal disaggregation caused governmental systems to become progressively fragmented, 'agencified', or 'siloized', as large conglomerate multi-purpose organizations were disaggregated into a host of small agencies with single, dedicated missions (Pollitt et al. 2004). This disaggregation, whatever its benefits, is likely to exacerbate age-old problems of facilitating inter-agency cooperation and collaboration in pursuit of complex governmental policy outcomes. This is essentially a strategic problem, which has resulted in ongoing attempts to reconnect the institutional dots in the form of 'joined-up government' or 'whole-of-government' initiatives. However, as an issue of normative unity it invites reflection on the extent to which NPM has been a contributing factor to the emergence in recent decades of 'the hollow state' (Milward and Provan 2000, Rhodes 2000). It has raised questions as to whether any recognizable entity called 'the government' prevails in the face of blurred distinctions between 'public' and 'private' organizations interacting as networked 'governance', and whether these developments have undermined the felt presence, if not the sense of legitimacy, of the state in the lives of citizen-subjects, who are now more likely to be thought of as 'consumers' of public goods and services.

It is important to distinguish the rhetoric of reform and change from the substance. While staunch advocates of NPM have naturally been loath to concede that NPM places more emphasis on some traditional public service norms than on others – as if NPM could be expected to maximize all key values and norms simultaneously – in fact it has generally placed significantly more importance on what can be called *mechanistic* rather than *organic* norms and values (Gregory and Hicks 1999). The former relate to organizational structures and technical/managerial systems, and emphasize efficiency, effectiveness and economy in the formulation and implementation of policy designed to engineer specifiable 'outcomes'. The latter, on the other hand, place the emphasis on democratic processes, fairness and equity, impartiality, and ethical and moral probity in public service. The organic perspective focuses on institutions valued for what they are rather than organizations designed just for what they do (Selznick 1957). It sees organizing as collective 'sense-making' (Weick 2001), rather than as rational and technical design. In the conceptual terminology of March and Olsen (1989), 'aggregative' political processes are aligned with mechanistic perspectives, while 'integrative' ones are associated with organic approaches; mechanistic with remunerative/calculative compliance and March and Olsen's 'logic of consequentiality'; organic with normative/moral compliance and March and Olsen's 'logic of appropriateness' of obligatory action.

Such organic values and norms were not uppermost in the minds of NPM advocates when they set about transforming what they saw as inefficient and unaccountable government organizations. But the jury remains out on whether or not some central elements of NPM, such as marketization and the abolition or attenuation of public service career systems, have had an adverse effect on standards of ethical probity and the idea of public service (Gregory 1999). Whatever the evidence, ethical probity in government is a two-way street. In the language of agency theory, politicians as principals have strong moral and ethical duties of obligation to their bureaucratic agents, just as the converse is true. As Hood and Lodge (2006) argue, there is plenty of scope for 'cheating' on both sides of this relationship. The idea of 'public value-seeking leadership' by politicians and public managers (Wallis and Gregory 2009) is strongly normative, even idealistic; but speaks to a need to enhance political and bureaucratic behaviour which is primarily self-denying rather than self-interested.

It is ironical that the man whose name will be forever associated with what he called 'bureaucracy' as an analytical category rather than as a normative standard, Max Weber, well understood that rational political action usually produced unintended consequences and reverse effects. Radically instrumental transformations of complex organizational and human systems are bound to have such consequences. But in the absence of a body of coherent theory of causal relationships among the relevant variables it is not possible to predict with any surety what the outcomes will be. Much reformist zeal, as desirable as it may often be, rests on faith rather than hard evidence, and the stronger the faith in their theories the less reformers are willing or able to see evidence that challenges their beliefs. Notably, whether or not the 'privatization' of state utilities, or the decoupling of policy ministries from their relevant operational agencies, enhances efficiency or results in less rent-seeking by bureaucrats and their clients are questions that remain strongly disputed well after the heyday of NPM. It is doubtful, however, whether evidence is itself sufficient to change the minds of strong advocates on either side of these arguments.

In their empirical research into public service motivation (PSM) Moynihan and Pandey (2007) have found that higher levels of employee education and professional membership were the most powerful predictors of PSM. They found that bureaucratic excesses weaken PSM, and – perhaps counter-intuitively – their findings suggest that it could be wrong to assume that the acculturation over time of career officials in a public service ethos, or commitment to the public interest, is an important element of PSM. Moynihan (2008) makes a clear distinction between the normative model and the market model, arguing that the conundrum is how to 'square the circle', how (in Le Grand's terminology) to design compliance systems that appeal simultaneously to both knights and knaves. Moynihan argues that the market model reduces the intrinsic public service motivation that is needed to ameliorate its flaws.

PSM is clearly associated with Etzioni's normative/moral compliance. However, the congruence between PSM and normative/moral compliance should not be overstated. High PSM can mean a misplaced desire to do what an official considers to be in the public interest but which may not be sanctioned by legitimate political authority. Or it may give rise to the proverbial 'can-do' mentality, which results in overly zealous activity even when carried out with the best of public service intentions. As many a politician has found, the road to a political hell can often be paved with the best intentions of rational public servants. Moreover, the 'gaming' behaviour which often arises from the application of management systems which set performance targets can be seen as a form of perverse PSM (Bevan and Hood 2006, Hood 2006, 2007).

Task Differences Do Matter

While it is not possible to draw incontrovertible conclusions about the actual effects of NPM on the normative foundations of public service, a generalization that can be made with much greater confidence is that NPM tended to adopt a 'one size fits all' approach to state sector reform, anticipating that the differences among the various tasks required of different public organizations were not really crucial in shaping the behaviour of people who worked in them (Wilson 1989, Gregory 1995). But task matters (Pollitt et al. 2004). Both politically and managerially, running a taxation department is a far cry from running a child protection service, and managing a postal service is profoundly different from organizing a forestry service, a police department, or a prison. In ushering in the era of the 'generic manager', NPM's insensitivity to the peculiarities among public organizations' diverse tasks, which are as often about changing people's behaviour as they are about producing or delivering goods and services, meant that it failed to comprehend how different approaches to organizational compliance stemmed from the nature of the organization's central task and also shaped how that task would be carried out. In other words, by their nature different tasks require different mixes of Etzioni's three models of compliance. There is no one best way. On top of this, NPM was borne along on an ideological wave of anti-public service, and pro-market, rhetoric, which is unlikely to have had a positive effect either on the morale of public employees, or on any quest for a more discerning understanding of how public organizations could in fact be better managed within their inevitably political context, and especially where they are required to carry out tasks which by their very nature border on the undoable. As some have observed, the surprising thing is not that public organizations often do things badly, but that they are able to do them at all.

In looking more closely at the importance of differences among organizational tasks insights are available from a tradition of scholarship that was ignored, if not actively discarded, by NPM architects wedded largely to economic interpretations of political and bureaucratic behaviour. It is not necessary to canvas these insights in detail here, only to reaffirm that prominent scholars in this tradition have indeed been prepared to balance mechanistic and organic interpretations of public organizations, in considering how they ought to be managed. Mintzberg's (1996: 81) 'normative model-control model of managing', for example, in which control is 'rooted in values and beliefs', in which 'attitudes count, not numbers', and which 'muted the negative effects of bureaucracy' should be aspired to more than the 'old machine model'. In Mintzberg's model people are recruited on the basis of their values and attitudes rather than their credentials; they are socialized into an integrated social system; they are guided by accepted principles rather than by imposed plans, by visions rather than targets; they accept responsibility and feel trusted and supported by leaders 'who practice a craft style of management that is rooted in experience'; and their performance is 'judged by experienced people, including recipients of the service, some of whom sit on representative oversight boards'.

This model is, of course, idealistic, strongly normative rather than descriptive. It is hard to imagine any organization, anywhere, at any time, displaying total conformity with this image. People, whether inside or outside of organizations, are not always – or perhaps even usually – motivated by principle, totally trustworthy, and ready to accept personal or collective responsibility for their actions. Public choice theorists may place too much emphasis on the so-called self-interested utility-maximizing behaviour of politicians and bureaucrats, for example, but only someone who has never observed or experienced political and organizational behaviour could believe that their interpretation is a purely cynical one. Further, Mintzberg's model itself, which 'hasn't exactly worked badly for the Japanese', has its own potentially dark side in that it conjures up an image of an organization or institution in which the individual is totally subsumed by the system – at worst, a kind of organizational totalitarianism. This is scarcely in keeping with the normative constitutional requirement that a public organization should be responsive to an elected political executive in what it does and how it does it. Notwithstanding this, Mintzberg argues persuasively against NPM's strong normative inclination to hold up the business model as a universal template in public sector transformation.

The trick of intelligent organizational design is to know when and under what circumstances it can be applied and when and under what conditions it cannot. There is a marked similarity between the arguments of Mintzberg (1996) and Wilson (1989) regarding the need for a more discerning approach in understanding the managerial implications that flow from the variety of tasks that public organizations are required to undertake. In speaking of a 'craft style of management', Mintzberg is echoing Wilson's idea of a 'craft organization', in which the work (outputs) undertaken by employees is not easily observable by their managers, while the outcomes produced in the community by that work is, on the other hand, readily observable. Craft organizations usually are strongly dependent on professional norms and values in the execution of their tasks. NPM, however, had a strong tendency to try to change all public organizations into what Wilson calls 'production' organizations – which is the type typical of corporate business, where both the work carried out and the outcomes produced by it are readily observable by managers (Gregory 1995). The sort of managerial controls that can be applied in a production organization cannot work so readily when confronted by professionals' need for legitimate autonomy in craft organizations.

In other words, whereas NPM placed a heavy normative value on the production model typical in the corporate world in seeking its general application to the public sector, a theme that is apparent or implicit in the representations of Mintzberg (1996), Wilson (1989), Moynihan (2008) and others is that the craft model of public organization is more attractive as a general, though by no means exclusive, normative ideal for public organizations. Nevertheless, it should not be a case of holding one or the other up as a normative ideal, but of using greater insight and discernment in designing public organizations which can combine both mechanistic and organic dimensions dependent on the nature of the tasks that they carry out.

The rise of NPM brought with it little theoretical development to this end – not unsurprisingly, given its commitment to the corporate/market model. Nor has this challenge yet been adequately taken up by scholars who are acutely aware of the different demands made on managers in the public and private sectors, or who find distinctions between 'public' and 'private' organizations in an age of networked governance to be increasingly irrelevant. In regard to maintaining high standards of ethical probity in government organizations, and the problem of maintaining and even fostering knightly behaviour when assuming that all are knaves, both rule-based and normative approaches to compliance are required in most organizations. Neither model can guarantee optimal outcomes under all circumstances and at all times.

As Moynihan (2008) has argued, performance-based management systems incorporating financial incentives may 'crowd out' intrinsic motivation, thus leading to a net reduction in overall performance. Apart from this, they are usually based on the mistaken assumption that performance is easily measurable (or observable, in Wilson's terms) and can be linked directly to pay levels. However, for a variety of reasons, which are not far to seek in the nature of the work carried out by many public sector employees, this is often not so. Especially but not exclusively in Wilson's craft and coping organizations, they include the problems of specifying contracts for work which is not readily specifiable, multiple and conflicting goals, the need for inter-agency cooperation and collaboration, and the importance of 'contextual goals' – that is, powerful constraints of due process, impartiality, equity, transparency, fairness and so on in the ways public money is spent and public authority is exercised.[3]

Contextual circumstances can demand that one type of organizational function be transformed into another type in order to ensure effectiveness – Wilson (1989) gives the example of an army being largely a procedural organization in peacetime and a craft one when in battle. An army trying to fight a battle by way of parade ground drills is unlikely to win it. However, if governmental reformers believe that all public organizations ought to be transformed readily into what Mintzberg calls machine organizations, and Wilson calls production ones, then reverse effects are inevitable, to the point of actually creating what it is originally intended to

---

3   In Wilson's (1989) typology, a 'coping' organization is one in which, by the nature of its task, neither outputs nor outcomes are readily observable.

avoid, limit or abolish. Targets for performance management can beget gaming, too detailed specification of contracts can beget too many transactions costs, and the selection of too many people who are motivated by remunerative/calculative considerations rather than by normative/moral ones can erode commitment to generic public service values and norms which transcend narrower individual and organizational ones. Agency theory has been applied in order to control behaviour in organizational and market circumstances where the behaviour of agents cannot be directly observed by principals, that is, in Wilson's craft and coping conditions. But trying to turn craft and coping functions into production ones (where principals can readily observe agents' behaviour) is likely to diminish the discretion that agents need in order to carry out their work effectively, which leads to self-defeating outcomes.

In such circumstances high levels of mutual trust are required between both principals and agents, often based on principals' respect for the professionalism of their agents over time, rather than in short-term, formally specifiable contracts entered into in a competitive market. When outcomes are hard to specify and to monitor over time, in conditions which are shaped by changing social and political circumstances, agency theory – in so far as it prefers formal contractual arrangements – has much less to offer that is conducive to sensible and effective governance. But because NPM has essentially favoured markets over hierarchies as an article of almost blind faith among its adherents, there has been a strong tendency to favour agency theory for all cases rather than just for those where it was best suited. Little has been heard, by contrast, about the relevance of stewardship theory, which is nested in normative/moral rather than remunerative/calculative models, in developing and maintaining trust over time in relational 'contracts' suited to the delivery of public services of the craft and coping types, especially in pursuit of social policy outcomes (Dicke and Ott 2002, Cribb 2006).

There is nothing new in NPM's production of unintended consequences or reverse effects. It is the equivalent of the type of 'goal displacement' that has always been characteristic of bureaucratic organizations that are overly rule-driven. Ironically, this was the situation that NPM sought to overcome in its endeavours to marketize the formerly bureaucratic delivery of goods and services. However, because the theoretical underpinnings of NPM were so strongly shaped by economic interpretations of political and bureaucratic behaviour, and were insufficiently balanced by insights from TPA and organizational scholarship and experience, those who were bent on transforming bureaucracy have simply reinvented it.

Conclusion

There is a pressing need for coherent theoretical development on the key normative issue in public management and administration, which is: how to ensure that public service institutions are not only efficient and effective but also simultaneously accountable, fair, impartial, non-corrupt, imbued with a service ethos and ethically robust. This is a daunting research task as the relationships among these and other key variables are not only complex but also untestable in any controlled public sector setting. Instead, as is apparent in the preceding discussion, we have a range of theoretical and conceptual tools – public choice theory, agency theory, stewardship theory, accountability, normative/moral compliance, aggregative and integrative political processes, corruption, transparency, PSM, public service bargains and so on – which are invaluable in organizing speculative thinking and analysis of normative dimensions of public service, but which singly and collectively have so far been inadequate in gaining any firm understanding of the conditions under which and in what circumstances changes to the structures and processes of governmental systems will affect these variables. As it has been so it will probably continue to be: any such transcendent theory will remain elusive, to say the least. In its absence state sector reformers of various political and ideological persuasions, pursuing a variety of agendas, will continue to act pragmatically as they see fit, and the consequences of their actions will be examined and analysed as they are subsequently revealed or perceived, sometimes giving rise to further pro-action or counter-action. It should be clear, however, that in any such theory-building much more care should be taken than was apparent in the heyday of NPM to adopt an eclectic approach that is inclusive rather than exclusive of traditions of academic inquiry and of practical experience.

Finally, NPM should never be considered, as it so often has been, within a frame of reference that excludes the wider political, constitutional and democratic context of which it is but one part.

PART VI
NPM AND BEYOND

Beyond NPM?
Some Development Features

Tom Christensen and Per Lægreid

Introduction

One of the insights gained from studying reforms in public organizations is that the political-administrative system is not – as is popularly believed – in a state of inertia, but actually in a state of flux. As internal and external preconditions and constraints change, so does the view of how to tackle problems, and of what the goals, solutions and consequences should or might be. In addition, reforms are producing countervailing reactions that are paving the way for new reforms. Light (1997) describes reforms in terms of tides that have ebbed and flowed over the decades as different reform philosophies have prevailed.

This chapter builds on two central suppositions. The first is that the NPM reform wave has stalled and is no longer as strong as it was previously. The second is that NPM is still of vital importance in many countries, existing alongside new reforms and developments that go beyond NPM. These are labelled whole-of-government (WG) or joined-up government (JUG), but referred to here more broadly as post-NPM (Polidano and Hulme 2001).

How NPM and post-NPM reforms are combined will vary according to many factors. Analytically, we can say it will be determined by polity, cultural and environmental factors, which also influenced how easily NPM was adopted and implemented in the first place (Christensen and Lægreid 2001c and 2007b). Empirically, we can state that the Anglo-Saxon countries embarked on NPM reforms rather early, in the 1980s, but were also the first to move beyond NPM in the late 1990s (Hood 1996a, Gregory 2003a, Halligan 2010b). Scandinavia and Continental Europe, on the other hand, were more reluctant to take NPM on board and did not go all the way down the NPM road; yet they were also later in adopting post-NPM measures (Christensen, Lie and Lægreid 2007). In these countries NPM ideas collided with existing systems of public administration, so that a process of selection and re-interpretation took place, with different elements of NPM being implemented in different national and sectoral contexts across Europe (Pollitt, van Thiel and Holmburg 2007).

In the USA we see an interest in collaborative public management emerging, focusing on how to manage boundaries and networks in American administration, on the collaboration process itself and on the design and implementation of cross-sector collaboration (Agranoff 2006, O'Leary, Bingham and Gerard 2006). Interestingly, this renewed focus on collaborative public management in the USA seems to be loosely coupled to a similar development launched under a different label in other Anglo-American countries.

This chapter will focus on four questions. First, why has NPM stalled? Second, what is typical for reform trends pointing beyond NPM, the post-NPM development? Third, is post-NPM really transcending NPM, or more broadly, what happens when NPM and post-NPM reform measures meet? Fourth, what are the effects of combining NPM and post-NPM measures?

Why has NPM Stalled?

In considering whether NPM has stalled or not we need to consider two structural dimensions – the vertical and the horizontal. When NPM was introduced reform entrepreneurs promised that political control would not be weakened, merely that the control instruments might change. Vertically it was argued that structural devolution was the answer to central capacity problems because it would allow leaders to focus more on strategic questions (Christensen and Lægreid 2001b). There were many new forms of structural devolution: giving traditional agencies more leeway, that is, moving them further away from the political executive, and/ or relaxing certain rules constraining their activities; establishing more regulatory agencies with strong institutional and professional autonomy; giving state-owned enterprises stronger autonomy, with a lot of barriers towards any political involvement; and paying more attention to market norms and values (Spicer et al. 1996). However, Boston et al. (1996) argue that the theoretical background to the reforms, which was derived from a combination of new institutional economic theory and management theories, also included control elements stipulating that devolution should be balanced with re-regulation and new control measures. NPM supporters still believe this strategy has been implemented in reality and they claim it has been successful.

The mainstream of research on NPM sees the matter quite differently. A major claim is that political control has indeed decreased, and that this is a major reason why NPM has stalled (Pollitt and Bouckaert 2004). NPM favoured strategic steering by the political executive and arm's-length control, meaning that structural devolution or a formal weakening of the control instruments of leaders was introduced (Christensen, Lie and Lægreid 2007). In practice this, combined with strong normative cultural pressure to abstain from political interference, led to a real undermining of political control, which tilted the balance of influence and power away from executive political leaders.

It is a paradox of NPM that political executives are more frequently being blamed when things go wrong, even though they actually sought to avoid blame through devolution (Hood 2002b, Hood and Lodge 2006). Not surprisingly, they consider that being criticized and embarrassed politically while at the same time being deprived of influence and information is a bad combination. In addition, they are unhappy about the loss of central capacity to solve societal problems.

A central principle of NPM was 'single-purpose organizations' (Boston et al. 1996). The argument was that organizing public organizations into distinct and separate units with specialized roles, functions and tasks would make them more efficient, avoid overlap, produce clearer role enactment, assign accountability and lead to systematic changes (Christensen and Lægreid 2001b). But after two decades of NPM the horizontal challenge is regarded in some countries as even more important than the vertical, because the large number of sectoral pillars or 'silos' created, appear to be obstructing the solution of cross-sectoral problems (Pollitt 2003c). Instead of cooperation, horizontal specialization and fragmentation have produced turf wars among competing public organizations with expansive ambitions, hence hampering effectiveness and efficiency (Boston and Eichbaum 2007). Post-NPM responses to disaggregation have been to introduce more horizontal coordination and more integrated governance (Halligan 2010b).

Taken together, the increased vertical and horizontal specialization brought about by the NPM reforms seems to have produced overall fragmentation in public organizations, leading to more problems of control and coordination. Structural devolution undermines control, while horizontal fragmentation undermines coordination and creates more problems of capacity at the top (Christensen and Lægreid 2001b).

A second major reason for NPM stalling relates to the critical issue of efficiency. NPM focused on efficiency as a central objective, claiming that there were major efficiency problems in public organizations. There are different aspects to this. One of them is the macro-economic aspect. The reforms in Australia and New Zealand, for instance, were introduced against the background of economic crisis. But it has been difficult to prove that countries that embarked on NPM early or implemented it more extensively have been doing better than NPM laggards (Self 2000b). Overall, it is difficult to establish a connection between public administration reforms of this kind and macro-economic measures because there are so many other potentially influential factors. We face a general problem of attribution, meaning that it is almost impossible to isolate the effects of NPM reforms from the effects of other reforms and changes happening in public administration and in society at the same time (Pollitt 1995, Pollitt and Bouckaert 2004).

Another efficiency aspect of NPM is the micro-economic one, which concerns the efficiency of public services. The argument – which became almost a mantra among economists – was that more competition would produce greater efficiency in service delivery, and indeed they claim that efficiency has increased by about 15–20 per cent. Most political scientists are more cautious in drawing such conclusions and they claim that the results are much more divided and inconclusive (Boyne et al. 2003). They point, for example, to the variation between sectors, which may be connected to the differing complexity of services and tasks, that is, it is easier to make less complex services more efficient. They also doubt whether comparisons can be drawn between one service and another and over time, pointing out that one simple way of increasing efficiency is to sack people, whereby the costs of retraining and of paying unemployment or other benefits are transferred to other parts of the state budget. Another point is that increased efficiency may produce lower-quality services or more social inequality (Stephens 1996). In other words, while there may have been some positive effects on responsiveness and individual freedom in choosing services there may also be negative effects on equity and equality.

To sum up, one major motivation for moving beyond NPM is scepticism about how efficient NPM really is. This concerns not only structural measures, market analogies and competitive tendering, but also the emphasis on efficiency as such, given the potential problems of delivery and the negative social effects.

Third, as terrorist attacks, natural disasters and pandemics become more frequent and the world is perceived as increasingly insecure and dangerous, the 'fear factor' has an increasing role to play. The concerns raised by terrorist attacks have had important repercussions for public sector reforms in the USA, the UK and Australia in particular, but in other parts of the world too (Kettl 2003, Halligan and Adams 2004). The new threat of terrorism has underlined how crucial it is for governments to avoid contradictory outcomes and for agencies to share information. Natural disasters, like tsunamis, or pandemics, like SARS, bird flu and swine flu, have also highlighted the need for concerted and coordinated government action, as have other more long-term issues like climate change and the global financial recession. This has led to a tightening-up of government, or what some Australians refer to as a 'thinking up and out' strategy, which includes post-NPM measures. In New Zealand, for example, bio-security is very high on the political agenda (Gregory 2006).

Reform Trends Pointing beyond NPM

The concept of working across boundaries is gaining increasing currency in public administration and in management theory and practice. This is first and foremost a response to the greater complexity and fragmentation that NPM reforms have brought about, which strain political and administrative leaders' capacity to solve societal problems (Christensen and Lægreid 2007b). As a result there is currently an enhanced focus on the notion of increased coordination, integration and connecting the knots. Such efforts are typically referred to as joined-up government, whole-of-government, holistic government, networked government, connected government, cross-cutting policy, horizontal management, partnerships and collaborative public management (Gregory 2003a). A common feature is the notion that working across organizational boundaries will enable more efficient and/or effective policy development, implementation and service delivery. Such modes of operating are supposed to counter 'departmentalization' and fragmented modes of working. However, while they promise much, there are actually a number of challenges associated with using them in practice. Like NPM, post-NPM efforts aim to find 'one size to fit all', which is rather unrealistic.

When some countries, primarily the NPM trail-blazers, started to move beyond NPM in the late 1990s, executive leaders tried consciously to redesign their civil service apparatuses. The typical reorganization measures adopted were seen as a reaction to the undermining of vertical hierarchical control experienced as a result of NPM. The repertoire of structural changes included more control of reform processes, aiming at vertical integration and hierarchical control; a reassertion or strengthening of the centre through vertical structural integration; strengthening political control of subordinate units; and increasing the central political and administrative resources and capacity. Generally there was a greater focus on performance audit, regulation and control.

There are many examples of these vertical post-NPM reform measures. The Blair government in the UK implemented rather aggressive top-down style whole-of-government initiatives (Stoker 2005). The UK has also led the way in strengthening the role of central government, establishing structures such as strategic units, reviews and public service agreements. Labour's first move towards joined-up government was the creation of the Social Exclusion Unit in 1997 and the Strategic Communication Unit one year later (Kavanagh and Richards 2001). Both the UK and New Zealand have a clear hierarchical component in their style of 'joining-up' (Perri 6 2005). Labour governments have tried over the last decade to improve service delivery by enhancing central control mechanisms while at the same time continuing to argue for more autonomy for the officials charged with delivering services, which shows hybrid features (Richards and Smith 2006). The best example of the shift in vertical emphasis in the USA is the creation of the Department of Homeland Security (Kettl 2004).

The hierarchical strengthening of the centre has also led to a stronger prime minister's office, in both a political and an administrative sense, as seen in the UK, Australia and New Zealand. It also implies stronger audit systems, tightening up financial management and strengthening governance and accountability regimes, as in Canada (Aucoin 2006b). Measures like this are primarily concerned with strengthening central political capacity, potentially making subordinate agencies and companies less autonomous. Even though the Prime Minister's Office in Australia has been strengthened (Halligan and Adams 2004: 86) and the specialized agencies brought back under greater central control (Halligan 2006), this represents more a tightening-up than major restructuring.

The horizontal dimension of post-NPM efforts is regarded as even more important than the vertical one. In Australia and New Zealand, for example, new organizational units, such as new cabinet committees, inter-ministerial or inter-agency collaborative units, inter-governmental councils, circuit-breaker teams, super networks, task forces and so on, as well as cross-sectoral programmes or projects, tsars and a lead agency approach have all been established with the main purpose of getting government units to work better together (Halligan and Adams 2004, Gregory 2006). In 2003, a new Cabinet Implementation Unit was established in Australia to support whole-of-government activities. Creating coordinative structures inside existing central structures, increasing the strategic leadership role of the Cabinet, and focusing more on following up central decisions are typical hierarchical efforts in Australia. Their aim is to put pressure on the sectoral authorities to get them to collaborate and coordinate better (Halligan 2006). In Norway a new minister of coordination was established in the Prime Minister's Office in 2009. Other examples are merging agencies to form larger bodies, such as the Department of Homeland Security in the USA or the new welfare administration in Norway.

The horizontal dimension typically concerns policy areas that cut across traditional boundaries, so called 'wicked issues'. The Canadian government launched what were labelled horizontal management initiatives from the mid-1990s to tackle policy issues such as innovation, poverty and climate change (Bakvis and Juillet 2004). Other examples of these were seen in Australia in 2002, where attempts were made to bring more coordination to such areas as national security, demographics, science, education, sustainable environment, energy, rural and regional development, transportation, and work and family life (Halligan and Adams 2004).

Procedural efforts have also been made to enhance whole-of-government initiatives. In New Zealand there is a stronger emphasis on effectiveness, broader long-term 'ownership' interests and outcome in contrast to the shorter-term and narrower 'purchaser' efficiency and output focus that characterized the NPM reforms (Boston and Eichbaum 2007).

The whole-of-government approach will necessarily have *negotiative features*, whether inside the cabinet, between ministries and departments involved in inter-sectoral task forces, programmes or projects, or specialized agencies involved in collaborative service delivery, as in New Zealand. Whole-of-government seems generally to be more about working together in a pragmatic and intelligent way than about formalized collaboration. This is especially true in Canada where working horizontally has been an issue of ongoing importance since the mid-1990s (Bakvis and Juillet 2004). The approach to major stake-holders in the environment, including private actors, is more heterogeneous and involves joined-up governance efforts and the use of networks and partnerships.

The collaborative efforts, like, for example, Australia's one-stop shops aimed at delivering a seamless service, can be seen both as control from above and as a real local collaborative effort requiring autonomy from central control (Halligan 2006). A comparative study of service delivery organizations in the UK, New Zealand, Australia and the Netherlands concludes that procedural bureaucratic models are being superseded by network governance to cater for the whole-of-government approach (Considine and Lewis 2003).

Several features of this approach can be understood using a *cultural perspective*. Post-NPM reforms are also about cultural change or the dynamic relationship between structural design and culture. When public organizations are exposed to reform processes, the reforms proposed must go through a cultural compatibility test (Brunsson and Olsen 1993). This shows the importance of path-dependency and historical trajectories and traditions (Krasner 1988). Balancing fragmentation and integration, individualization and common identity, and market pressure and cultural cohesion is a big challenge in public sector reforms (Lægreid and Wise 2007).

The post-NPM reforms focus more on cultivating a strong and unified sense of values, teambuilding, the involvement of participating organizations, trust, value-based management, collaboration, and improving the training and self-development of public servants (Ling 2002). There is a need to re-establish a 'common ethic' and a 'cohesive culture' in the public sector because of the reported corrosion of loyalty and increasing mistrust brought about by NPM (Norman 1995). All agencies should be bound together by a single, distinctive public service ethos, as emphasized in Australia (Shergold 2004). Under the slogan 'working together', the Australian government has emphasized the need to build a supportive public sector culture that encourages whole-of-government solutions by formulating value guidelines and codes of conduct.

In New Zealand, too, there has been a renewed focus on value-based management and ethical standards. Ethical guidelines around the world cover a host of values: more general values like integrity, fairness, accountability, loyalty, excellence, respect, honesty and probity in the organizational context; democratic values such as rule of law, neutrality, openness, responsiveness and representativeness; professional values such as effectiveness, efficiency, service, innovation and quality; and people-related values such as caring, tolerance, compassion and humanity (Kernaghan 2003). Some claim that public value pragmatism will be the next phase of public management reforms as a way of counteracting the 'one best way' orientation of NPM (Alford and Hughes 2008).

Post-NPM is also more preoccupied with leadership aspects which show the importance of combining structural and cultural factors. There is an increasing demand for pro-active leaders, instead of leaders who only react to problems. Post-NPM leaders should also have a broad competence, rather than focusing on narrow institutional interests, care more about collective goals, norms and values, and accordingly also counteract sub-cultures. Leaders should also aim to further pragmatic cooperation between public organizations, for example in service delivery.

A *myth perspective* sees reforms and their main concepts mainly in terms of myths, symbols and fashions (Christensen, Lægreid, Roness and Røvik 2007). Reform concepts often imitate practices in the private sector and are 'sold' by private consulting firms and international reform entrepreneurs primarily in order to increase the legitimacy of the political-administrative system and its leaders rather than to solve particular instrumental problems (Sahlin-Andersson 2001). 'Window-dressing' is important, as is pretending to act in a successful way. In such a perspective whole-of-government is primarily a buzzword and a counter-myth to NPM.

It is not difficult to imagine that a whole-of-government approach would have myth aspects. NPM was 'sold' as an efficient instrument, but so was post-NPM, which may seem a paradox unless we regard this more symbolically than literally. Very few actors would dispute the advantages of an integrated governmental apparatus or of taking anything other than a wide and collaborative view. A rather cynical view of the whole-of-government approach in Australia would be that it is a fashion and that it suits political and most especially administrative leaders to be seen to be thinking big ideas (Mulgan 2005). The concept of 'value-based government,' which seems to have been imported and spread as a fad, is one aspect of reforms in Australia that could be understood from a myth perspective.

Gregory (2006) sees the recent reforms in New Zealand and the whole-of-government approach to some extent as rhetoric. There is a gap between talk and action that may be attributed to a certain weariness with structural reforms, to the fact that the civil service has taken NPM on board and adapted to it, and to a general move to the right politically. As a result, he sees the new generation of reforms as 'treating the effects rather than the cause'.

Transcending NPM?

A further central question is whether post-NPM is transcending NPM, that is, moving beyond the NPM reform measures. There seem to be rather different views on this. One would be basically to answer 'yes' to this question but to add that we are seeing a process of substitution and pendulum swings. Dunleavy et al. (2005) claim that NPM is dead and has been replaced with digital-era governance. Just as NPM was a substitute for the 'old public administration', they say, post-NPM will replace NPM, simply because the time is ripe for it. This Zeitgeist approach focuses on the deinstitutionalization and (re)institutionalization of reforms, rather than combinations of reforms (Røvik 2002). Another possibility is simply that political priorities have changed and that leaders therefore decide to scrap one set of reforms and start with another, or that dominant coalitions are renegotiated and decide to move beyond NPM.

A related question is whether substituting one set of reforms for another also involves a pendulum swing back to older reform principles. One argument for this would be a cultural one, namely, that path-dependency would tend to make actors nostalgic for the 'good old days'. Old norms and values are over-represented in current structures and cultures, regardless of new reform waves, and they have proven to be resilient (Boin and Christensen 2008). Moreover, when NPM fails to work, it is more convenient and resource-saving to resort to old principles and norms. A counter-argument would be that since structural and cultural conditions are continuously changing, it is impossible to turn the clock back.

A rather different view takes it for granted that different reform waves will be combined. In reality reform waves influence the development of public organizations and their activities in a gradual change process, so that it is difficult to identify the end of one reform wave and the beginning of another. The claim is that NPM is by no means over (Pollitt 2003a), but is being challenged and supplemented with other reform initiatives. The next question is then how we may characterize this combination, that is, what kind of dynamics and mechanisms does it involve? Some would say that NPM is the dominant reform wave and that post-NPM has simply supplemented or modified certain aspects of it. Another view is that both reform waves are important and are used in different ways according to policy area or just combined differently in different reforms.

Another take on how reform waves interact is inspired by a combination of structural, cultural and myth perspectives and sees the different reforms as a process of layering or sedimentation (Streeck and Thelen 2005, Olsen 2009). If we look at the historical development of public institutions, we see that at certain points in time elements of their basic structures and cultures are either pushed aside and deinstitutionalized when a new reform wave comes along or else manage to remain viable and influence the further development of the organization, regardless of new reform waves. This layering of various elements from the 'old public administration', NPM and post-NPM makes public organizations increasingly complex.

One reason for layering processes may be the simple instrumental and hierarchical fact that executive leaders decide to keep reform elements they support or like when introducing new reforms. Another reason may be that a diversity of reform elements from different waves makes it easier to make political compromises, decrease conflicts and increase legitimacy. A third and more culturally-oriented reason could be that path-dependent mechanisms make it difficult to remove all elements from an old system or reform when a new one emerges. It is never easy to start from scratch, and continuity in norms and values help a public organization to cope with periods of transition. A fourth and more symbolically-oriented reason is related to the labelling of reforms. Often reforms are sold as new, modern and efficient, whereas in actual fact there is far more continuity than reform entrepreneurs would have us believe. Continuity that incorporates some new structural and cultural elements – sold as modernization – may be a better option than reforms that turn an organization up-side down.

Summing up, we would tend to subscribe to the argument that reform movements are characterized by combining, complexity, layering and hybridization, rather than by dominance, substitution and pendulum swings. Our main argument is that public reforms are driven by a number of different forces. Public administration is faced with increasingly complex environmental and internal conditions, reflected in multifunctional organizational forms, and the administrative reforms in the public sector can be understood as compound reforms that combine different organizational principles based on multiple factors working together in a complex mix (Egeberg and Trondal 2009). Compound administrative reforms are multi-dimensional and represent 'mixed' orders and combinations of competing, inconsistent and contradictory organizational principles and structures that co-exist and balance interests, values and claims to power (Olsen 2007).

Multi-dimensional orders are considered to be more resilient to external shocks and therefore preferable to uni-dimensional orders (March and Olsen 1989).

Compound reforms thus depart from 'either/or' theorizing by assuming that executive governance rests on the mobilization of multiple and complementary sets of institutions, actors, interests, decision-making arenas, values, norms and cleavages, reflected in what we call a transformative approach to reforms (Christensen and Lægreid 2001c and 2007b). In a pluralistic society, where there are many criteria for success and different causal understandings, we have to go beyond the idea of a single organizational principle to understand how public organizations work and are reformed and look at them as composite organizations (Olsen 2006 and 2007).

The argument here is that we face a dialectical development in which the old public administration has been combined with NPM and post-NPM features to create new hybrid organizational forms. The central component in the old Weberian bureaucratic model is sustainable and robust, but in the strong modern state it has been supplemented with neo-Weberian components such as performance management and user participation, responsiveness and professional management (Pollitt and Bouckaert 2004).

Effects of Combining NPM and Post-NPM

One rather bright outlook on combining NPM and post-NPM elements in public organizations is that it offers leaders more flexibility. Public leaders have to balance a lot of diverse norms, values and interests, and are well trained in that respect, so combining reform measures from different reform types is a viable option, even though the challenges of doing so are growing (Christensen and Lægreid 2007b). The underlying view here is that this is a systemic feature in the public sector that leaders have to relate to. The legitimacy of government will be determined by how well the balance between different considerations is organized. Executive leaders should be able to cater to different interests without undermining the overall objective of realizing public goals, so there must be certain limits to how diverse and inconsistent this balance is.

There are various strategies for dealing with complexity in a flexible manner. One is to trade off different norms, values and interests at different points in time. This involves reconciling different interests rather than assigning clear priorities. Leaders may then portray this compromise or trade-off in different ways, for instance, pointing more to how each interest has received a fair share than stressing the balance with other interests. This can be done via double-talk, whereby symbols that appeal to certain actors are stressed, whereas in reality the picture is less favourable (Brunsson 1989). Another way is to realize and prioritize certain norms, values and interests at certain points in time and others at other times. As Cyert and March (1963) point out in their seminal work, this is an easier way of creating consensus and legitimacy, but may be beset with potential long-term conflicts and inconsistencies.

Another view would stress that the increased complexity and potential hybridity resulting from combining NPM and post-NPM would exert much more pressure on political and administrative leaders (Christensen and Lægreid 2007b). NPM created more fragmentation and complexity, while under post-NPM leaders have focused more on coordination measures. This might lead actors to sharpen their priorities and identify the important goals, problems and issues. Increased complexity may, however, lead to problems of accountability, attention and capacity, making it difficult to maintain clear priorities in practice.

Third, given that leaders have shown themselves more able to control reform processes than to think rationally about them, increased complexity may increase the pace at which new reforms are introduced in public organizations. Since executive leaders are constantly adopting new reforms that have problems delivering but still control change processes quite well, they may tend to demonstrate their power and their change-oriented policy by introducing even more reforms (Christensen and Lægreid 2007b). This may be one reason why reform decisions are often symbol-ridden decisions and why many reforms are rather shallow and do not last very long. This may also mean that the evaluation and scrutiny of reforms becomes a political process, where it is important to control the interpretation of effects, that is, impression management acquires greater significance.

A fourth possibility is that increased complexity resulting from combining NPM and post-NPM reforms may simply result in increased institutional confusion and ambiguity (March and Olsen 1976). Complexity requires greater control and attention, making actors less able to decide on reforms capable of fulfilling public goals. In line with Dahl and Lindblom's (1953) classical distinction between control and rational calculation, reforms may produce both conflicts and confusion concerning participation, but also acute problems of clear organizational thinking. And the more confusion and ambiguity, the greater the problem of legitimacy – that is, getting civil servants and external stake-holders to accept and support reforms.

Accountability is a central concern, and a key question is how one can have post-NPM joint action, common standards and shared systems, on the one hand, and vertical accountability for individual agency performance on the other. The challenge is to balance vertical accountability, horizontal accountability and downward responsiveness better (Ryan and Walsh 2004). Even if governments set budgets, programmes and objectives that cross organizational boundaries, post-NPM activities might still be limited unless there are fundamental changes in accountability systems, dominant cultures and structural arrangements.

One lesson is that if one wants to encourage more collaborative working practices, one size does not fit all (Page 2005). A critical Canadian study of horizontal management recommended that horizontal arrangements should be entered into only after careful thought and estimate of the costs involved. Departments working horizontally in the same policy area may well engage in competition and rivalry rather than cooperation (Bakvis and Juillet 2004).

Another lesson is that high-level politics and changes in central government organizations are not necessarily the most important reform tool for promoting 'whole-of-government' initiatives. Whole-of-government is to a great extent about lower-level politics and getting people on the ground in municipalities, regions, local government organizations, civil society organizations and market-based organizations to work together. Whole-of-government needs cooperative effort and cannot easily be imposed from the top down (Pollitt 2003a).

Conclusion

The argument here is that administrative reforms are based on a combination of different driving forces. Public administration is faced with increasingly complex and multifunctional organizational forms. The proliferation of semi-autonomous organizational forms in the public sector is one of the reasons why many countries have now launched initiatives to enhance coordination and to manage 'cross-cutting' and 'whole-of-government' issues (Christensen and Lægreid 2007b). In such initiatives, strengthening the link between individual public sector organizations and the larger objectives of government as well as with other public sector organizations seems crucial.

Structural complexity in public organizations enables them to cope more easily with complex societal problems and heterogeneous interests and demands. Political and administrative leaders thus have a repertoire of responses to complex and diverse problems at their disposal. Culturally, complexity may indicate that a hybrid culture, catering to diverse traditions and sub-cultures, has developed, enabling organizations to be flexible in adapting to internal and external efforts to bring about change. Complexity determines how reforms are decided and implemented, but also makes it difficult to get them to yield the expected effects.

Increasing complexity makes control more problematic for political and administrative leaders. Complexity means having a variety of actors and institutional norms and values to attend to, which may make it more difficult to influence 'local' activities and implementation. The more complexity, the more potential capacity and cognitive problems leaders will have, a problem that can be coped with by delegation, making administrative leaders more powerful. Political leaders have to divide their attention and process more information than before, while policy questions may become more technical and complicated, which makes politicians more reliant on experts. The down-side of complexity may be that it includes incompatible elements, leading to uncoordinated or countervailing actions and creating chaos or stale-mates (Boston et al. 1996). The ultimate question is whether it is possible for executive leaders to choose many roads at the same time, going in the direction of both control and autonomy, without getting lost or encountering problems.

Post-NPM initiatives differ according to the starting points and administrative cultures in different countries. But a common characteristic is that post-NPM reforms do not represent a break with the past, nor do they fundamentally transform existing organizational modes. Rather it is a question of rebalancing existing administrative systems without changing them in any fundamental way (Gregory 2006, Christensen and Lægreid 2007b).

Summing up, post-NPM reforms imply an increased focus on integration, horizontal coordination and enhanced political control (Pollitt 2003a, Lægreid and Verhoest 2010). The emergence of post-NPM reforms can be understood as a combination of external pressure from the technical and institutional environments, learning from NPM reforms, and deliberate choices by political executives. This counter-reaction of increased central control and coordination to organizational proliferation has been observable in many countries (Bogdanor 2005, Bouckaert et al. 2010). External and internal pressures have questioned the effectiveness of a proliferated public sector. These include internationalization and Europeanization, security threats and crisis management needs, as well as a call for more integrated service delivery and holistic policies, e-government and regulatory reform initiatives, and the loss of a common civil service culture. These post-NPM reforms have, however, not replaced the NPM reforms. Rather they can be seen as supplementary adjustments producing increased complexity in public sector organizations. Countries show complex combinations of organizational autonomy on some issues, increased centralized control, and network-like coordination mechanisms, alongside remnants of traditional hierarchical controls (Bouckaert et al. 2010).

An increasing number of scholars are arguing that these post-NPM trends are a reaction to the organizational proliferation and resulting fragmentation induced by NPM doctrines (Pollitt 2003c, Pollitt and Bouckaert 2004, Gregory 2006, Halligan 2006, Boston and Eichbaum 2007, Christensen and Lægreid 2007b, Bouckaert et al. 2010). However, it remains unclear what these 'whole-of-government' initiatives imply in terms of the actual autonomy, control, coordination and performance of public sector organizations. One take is that this is a new 'one best way' orientation with a great deal symbolic flavour. Another is that such post-NPM initiatives have made a substantial contribution to a better organized public sector.

The question is whether whole-of-government will continue to be a strong reform movement or whether it will gradually fade away and be supplemented or replaced by new reform initiatives (Page 2005, Stoker 2005). Seen from a myth perspective this might easily be the case. We have seen a shift from 'joined-up government' to 'whole of-government' and post-NPM, and new reform concepts such as multi-level government and New Public Governance are gaining currency.

Reinventing Weber:
The Role of Institutions in
Creating Social Trust

Jon Pierre and Bo Rothstein

Institutional Trust and the Administrative Side of the State

This chapter starts from recent research results showing that the state, by virtue of its legality, impartiality and accountability, is critical to producing macro-level social trust in society. Such trust, which is a central component in social capital, has been shown to be important for a large number of social outcomes that are usually deemed important such as economic prosperity, tolerance and population health (Zmerli and Newton 2008, Rothstein and Stolle 2008, Herreros 2009). While micro-level trust is seen as a requirement to reduce transaction costs and thus to support economic growth, it is suggested here that macro-level trust is a requirement for the legitimacy of the state and therefore critical to democratic governance (Gilley 2009). In this, institutional trust is the key link between citizens and the state for creating legitimacy (Rose-Ackerman and Kornai 2004). In a recent study based on the World Value Study survey data from 72 countries, Bruce Gilley concludes that that 'general governance (a composite of the rule of law, control of corruption and government effectiveness) has a large, even overarching importance in global citizen evaluations of states'. According to Gilley, governance factors are more important than democratic rights when citizens express their opinions about the legitimacy of their states (Gilley 2009: ch. 2). Although low levels of trust do not necessarily cripple government – there are plenty of examples of efficient governments despite low levels of institutional trust – they raise transaction costs and complicate the process of governing (Braithwaite and Levi 1998).

From this larger problematic, the present analysis is focused on three particular aspects. First, the chapter explores what appears to be a puzzling and quite unexpected revival of Weberianism – as shorthand for a model of a public administration system that puts emphasis on legality, hierarchy, impartiality, due process, rule-following, transparency and accountability – in three fields of academic research and reform practice. One such area is development economics, where there is today a growing interest in institutional design and legality as instruments of curbing corruption.

A second and related field is the analysis of transaction costs and 'good governance'. This line of research has mainly been explored by neo-institutional economists who argue that variation in institutional configurations is what explains the huge variation in economic prosperity (and social well-being) among nations (Acemoglu and Robinson 2008, North, Wallis and Weingast 2009). In this research, the Weberian ideals are seen as one of the central forces for creating economic prosperity.

The third area, finally, is contemporary administrative reform, particularly the implementation of the system of public administration known as New Public Management (NPM). When it was originally launched, NPM was mainly seen as a direct assault on Weberian models of administration arguing that they were too rigid and inflexible to meet increased demands for economic efficiency and adaptation to new demands from citizens (Dunn and Miller 2007). However, in this process of change, we can today witness a debate on to what extent market-based reforms *are contingent on pre-existing Weberian structures*. In all three fields of research, and practice, the previous denouncement of Weberian models which were seen as excessively rigid and inefficient has given way to what appears to be a reaffirmation of the norms and values that the Weberian model of administration represents.

The argument explored in this chapter is thus that Weberianism's coming into vogue is not so much related to its model of institutional design, nor to its focus on structure and process, but rather because it, directly or indirectly, creates and reproduces trust between the state and its citizenry and also in markets. A central conclusion that follows from the neo-institutional theory in economics is that in order for market models to work, a fair amount of social trust is needed and this can be created by a Weberian type of rule-bound administration that creates security against arbitrariness and favouritism, respect for contracts and transparency (Rothstein 2005, Rodrik 2007).

Although there is consensus – at least among the Western democracies – regarding the core, baseline functions of the state, there are contending views about how the state should pursue these collective goals. It is argued that we live in a post-bureaucratic era in which the traditional type of legalistic, rule-bound and disengaged Weberian mode of government organization is seen as outdated (see Olsen 2008a, 2008b). Today's public administration, in the predominant reform vernacular, should be goal-oriented instead of rule-bound; emulate private sector management techniques; privatize and contract out as much as is possible of its service production; use evaluation and performance management and measurement instead of *ex ante* evaluation; focus on outcomes instead of focusing on process; and so on. Instead of rule following and due process, utilitarian-based efficiency has become the yardstick with which contemporary public administration is evaluated (Moore 1995, Christensen and Lægreid 2007a).

Scholars of public administration and public management recognize this as the NPM model of public administration. This anti-Weberian development has not only been influential in countries governed by neo-liberal agendas but also in polities that have been strongly influenced by social democracy (Christensen and Lægreid 2007a). While the success (and drawbacks) of the anti-Weberian model is a disputed topic (see Du Gay 2000, Olsen 2008b), it is safe to say that anti-Weberianism has become almost hegemonic as a model of reform or practice in the advanced Western liberal democracies. This goes both for policy-makers and for large parts of the scholarly work in public administration; if nothing else, NPM has become the standard model of administrative reform among practitioners in most advanced industrial countries. Although the current debate on the virtue and pitfalls of market-based reform substantiates some profound problems in this reform strategy, it remains the implicit model against which all other models are compared (Pierre and Painter 2010).

NPM is part and parcel of the neo-liberal 'turn' that took place in the Western world during the 1980s and 1990s, which witnessed a sortie of such prominent social theorists as Keynes and Weber. Indeed, it could well be seen as the application of neo-liberalism on public administration; the basic tenets of NPM are directly or indirectly derived from neo-liberal economic theory and public choice models of administration. The normative foundation is that there is nothing that differentiates the operational logic of market agents and public officials; market choices are not fundamentally different from 'public choices' when it comes to what motivates agents and how they calculate what is in their interest. In relation to the question 'how should the state behave', NPM has a clear answer: its institutional setup and *modus operandi* should emulate that of for-profit corporations acting in competitive markets with economic incentives as the driving force. Citizens should be regarded as customers and local managers of (publicly financed) services should compete for these customers. If dissatisfied with the service they receive, instead of appealing to rules guarding their rights, citizens should 'vote with their feet' by exercising market choice and turn to another service provider, thus providing local managers with market-like incentives for making changes in the services. For the providers of public services, flexibility and customer satisfaction are seen as more important than rule-bound behaviour and results are valued higher than correct procedures. Instead of life-long employment, employees providing public services work on short-term contract, and so forth (Peters 2001b).

The Revival of Weberianism

How should we understand the seemingly unlikely revival of Weberianism in an era when there has been such a strong emphasis on reforms inspired by neo-liberal and largely anti-government ideas. In the midst of this dominance for neo-liberalism in the discourse about 'how the state should behave', as argued above there is also a growing interest in the economic and societal roles of the formal and legal government institutions. Most prominent is the increased interest in corruption and corruption-related problems (such as clientelism, cronyism and nepotism) as the major obstacles for economic and social development (Rodrik 2007, Holmberg, Rothstein and Nasiritousi 2009, North, Wallis and Weingast 2009). Needless to say, corruption and its related problems are of course the anathema of Weberianism. This change, which started in the mid-1990s, is dramatic since it is not so long ago that most economists and political scientists thought that corruption and related problems were of minor, if any, interest in the study of economic and social development. For example, the 17 volume (!) *International Encyclopedia for the Social Sciences* published in 1968 does not offer a single entry for 'corruption'. Even more interestingly, the same goes for the *Handbook of Development Economics*, published in the mid-1990s.

There are many reasons behind this development, not least the 'institutional revolution' in the social sciences inspired to a large extent by the work of Douglass North. In addition, new empirical research measuring corruption (and related problems) has given empirical support for its negative impact on economic development (Mauro 1995, Kaufmann 2004, Holmberg, Rothstein and Nasiritousi 2009). Furthermore, studies show a positive effect of Weberian traits in a country's civil service on economic development (Evans and Rauch 2000, Henderson et al. 2007). Other studies show that trust in institutions such as the courts and the police have a positive effect on social trust, as does trust in the fairness of institutions that implement social policies (Kumlin and Rothstein 2005, Stolle and Rothstein 2007). Thus, the conclusion in this research is not only that corruption is bad (which, given what we now know about the importance of institutions, seems rather obvious) but also that good old-fashioned Weberianism may be much more important than has been realized in the NPM movement. The result of this development is that, as has been stated by Johan P. Olsen, 'the enthusiasm for a universal de-bureaucratization cure and the pressure for global administrative convergence have diminished since the early 1990s' (Olsen 2008b).

This research also challenges the predominant idea in neo-liberal economics that it is the size of the government that is the key problem. For example, prominent economists still argue (using only formal-deductive logic), that 'a large government increases corruption and rent-seeking' (Alesina and Angeletos 2005: 1241). However, several empirical studies show that it is not the size of government that is the problem, but rather the qualitative dimension of how it operates. Thus, Gerring and Thacker (2005: 235) 'find no consistent relationship between the aggregate size of the public sector and political corruption'. Similarly, La Porta et al. (1999: 42) found that high-quality governments had higher public spending and thus warned that 'identifying big government with bad government can be highly misleading'. In sum, this indicates that there is something about the qualitative dimension of Weberianism that, contrary to its many critics, supports economic development and the reduction of poverty. If so, the success in the developed world of the anti-Weberian NPM approach – or at least the IMF's and the World Bank's aggressive marketing of that model of administrative reform – becomes something of a mystery. We will return to this issue later in the chapter.

Several important international organizations engaged in policy making in this area, most notably the World Bank, the European Union, and the United Nations, have put 'good governance' (read: anti-corruption) very high on their agendas. Today, this has become so prominent and involves so many powerful national and international actors that it is possible to speak of a new international 'anti-corruption regime' (Bukovansky 2006, Smith 2007). In any case, this 'international regime' launches recommendations that are clearly Weberianism-oriented such as the importance of precise and unambiguous rules; merit-based recruitment; personnel that clearly distinguish between their interests as private citizens and their duties as civil servants; a salary system which is sufficiently generous to make public officials less susceptible to bribery; and a transparent system of responsibility (Fjeldstad and Isaksen 2008).

As stated above, on a more theoretical level, this development has been propelled by the 'institutional revolution' in economics and political science spurred most prominently by the work of Douglass North. The effects of variation in institutional characteristics have become central in such various fields as evolutionary game theory, political history, comparative politics, policy analysis, and in the study of organizational effectiveness and, not least, organizational culture (Peters 1999). For example, Weberian 'rule-of-law' institutions must secure property rights through the enforcement of legally produced private contracts and must safeguard market agents against arbitrary actions by the various branches of the state apparatus. Such institutions can, following George Tsebelis, be labelled 'efficient' because they are not enacted in order to redistribute resources to a special group or certain agents known beforehand. Contrary to 're-distributive' institutions, efficient institutions are supposed to serve the collective interest of all agents by lowering their transaction costs (Tsebelis 1990). One effect of such institutions is that market agents can trust that other market agents will respect agreements they have entered into; they know that if they do not, the agent can turn to an impartial court or other type of Weberian civil service for remedies. They also know that tax rules and other government regulations will be implemented in a way that does not give improper advantage to some agents (because of their personal contacts, ability to pay bribes or political connections).

In relation to development research, this problem has been captured poignantly by economist Dani Rodrik who argues that 'the encounter between neo-classical economics and developing societies served to reveal the institutional underpinnings of market economies' (Rodrik 2007: 153). Among such institutional underpinnings Rodrik lists a specified system of property rights; effective regulation that prevents monopolies from dominating markets; uncorrupted governments; the rule of law; and social welfare systems that can accommodate risks. Interestingly, Rodrik also emphasizes the importance of informal societal institutions that foster social cohesion, social 'rust and cooperation. Criticizing neo-classical economics for disregarding the significance of such institutions, Rodrik (2007: 153–154) argues that 'these are social arrangements that economists usually take for granted, but which are conspicuous by their absence in poor countries'. As can be readily seen, many of the institutional characteristics that Rodrik points at are distinctly

Weberian. Thus, the puzzle is this: while many public administration scholars and international organizations for a long time have pointed to the shortcomings of the Weberian model and to a large extent argued that it is outdated and should be replaced, there are clear signs of an opposite approach in institutional theory in general and in development studies in particular. That having been said, it should be added that there is no automatic correspondence between pointing to the importance of institutions on the one hand and Weberianism on the other. To the contrary; institutions can be of many sorts, and as all students of public administration know, Weberian institutions are quite particular.

The point should be clear. For all its rigidities and hierarchical features, Weberianism, or neo-Weberianism, is a model of public administration and government that also brings some degree of stability, legality, predictability and continuity to a country. Recent research suggests that in developing countries with 'soft' institutions, low levels of education among the public servants, patronage-based recruitment and thereby low levels of institutional trust, that model is more efficient than market-based models of administration. Indeed, it seems as if it is the very rigidity and legality in the Weberian model that curb corruption and increase institutional trust. This theme is not confined to the problem of creating economic growth in developing countries, but relates also to the problem of democratization. The problem was taken up at a conference held in 2007 celebrating the establishment 25 years earlier of the US-based *National Endowment for Democracy*. At this conference, where the spectacular success of democratization over the world was lauded, Larry Diamond, one of the most prominent scholars in the field of democratization studies, stated that 'there is a specter haunting democracy in the world today. It is bad governance .... Governance that is drenched in corruption, patronage, favoritism, and abuse of power' (Diamond 2008: 119). Diamond further argues that the idea that the pathologies of 'bad governance' can be cured with more 'democracy assistance' is not convincing because such assistance does not reach the deeper levels of the political culture in societies that are dominated by clientelism or endemic corruption. Since such practices are often 'deeply embedded in the norms and expectations' of what political and economic exchanges are seen as, improvement will, according to Diamond, require nothing less than a 'revolutionary change in institutions' (2008: 119). It is difficult to see this not as a cry for more Weberian ethics in developing countries.

Shortly the chapter will look further into the peculiar development that while the Weberian mode of 'being a state' has become much less popular in the developed world, it has become a centrepiece of understanding of what is lacking in developing and transition countries. Before that, there is a need to look more closely at the relationship between NPM and Weberian models of administration.

The Success and Demise of New Public Management

As stated in the introductory section above, the past two decades or so have witnessed the rapid diffusion of a variety of market-related models of administrative reform across the world (Pollitt and Bouckaert 2004). This is not the place to rehearse all the finer details of such reform; suffice it to say that this reform strategy emphasizes clear separation of policy and operations, deregulation, managerial autonomy, customer choice, privatization and contracting out, internal markets, empowerment of lower organizational levels and performance management and measurement (that is, incentive-based output controls). It is often argued that NPM emerged as a problem-driven solution to bureaucratic rigidities, inefficiencies and poor public services. To some extent, the NPM cure for these, and other, shortcomings in the public sector was to abolish those features of the public sector that made it different from the private sector. By focusing on management and efficiency, the normative discourse of public administration shifted from legality and public ethos to corporate and managerial values, philosophies and objectives. To be sure, that shift in discourse had already begun when the concept of 'public management' emerged. As Rosenbloom (1998: 16) argues, '(T)hose who define public administration in managerial terms tend to minimize the distinctions between public and private administration.' This change in discourse is no accident; as mentioned earlier, it represents an essential shift in the normative foundation of public administration in order to pave the way for managerial reform.

Thus, if the chief problem haunting public administration was low performance, the NPM strategy to ameliorate that problem was to introduce philosophies and styles of management and external relationships from the corporate world where they (purportedly) had already proven successful. The NPM campaign of the 1980s and 1990s was not the first attempt to look to private enterprise for solutions to problems in the public administration; administrative reform in the US had tried that strategy already in the 1960s. The main difference between that context of reform and that of the latter decades was that the previous case lacked the discursive and normative foundation to sustain it. In the 1980s and 1990s, that foundation was firmly in place, thanks to the Reagan administration in the United States and the Thatcher government in the UK. Others (Canada, Australia, New Zealand) were to follow suit. With those countries on board the NPM wagon there was a critical mass, and yet another group of countries – encouraged by transnational organizations like the World Bank, the IMF and the OECD – joined the crusade.

With this rapid diffusion of NPM, the causal linkage between problems in the public administration and solutions was gradually confused. NPM was implemented or at least seriously considered by a very large number of countries, not so much because it was believed to be the best strategy of reform to address problems in the public administration but because a number of other countries had adopted the philosophy. The fact that countries which had gone down the NPM road were often competitors in international trade probably helped propel the diffusion of NPM further. Although there was little evidence that NPM in and of itself had any significant effect on national competitiveness, it appeared sensible to follow the behaviour of your competitor to level the playing field. Indeed, the notion of bringing the market into the public sector had not been systematically attempted before and this novelty alone was probably instrumental in boosting its attractiveness. In many countries, efficiency problems in service production and delivery had become 'wicked' and resilient to reform. NPM offered a new strategy to solve those problems, or at least so it seemed.

However, while the implementation of NPM was a smooth process in the public interest-based public administration systems of the Anglo-American systems, the tradition of legality, equity and accountability in the 'Rechtsstaat' systems of Western Europe and Asia proved much more resistant to market-based reform. In spite of strong pressure from international organizations, the implementation of NPM reforms in many Asian countries was fragmented and partial (Turner 2002). In Western Europe, the picture is more scattered, although it appears safe to say that public administration has proven more entrenched and institutionalized than what was perhaps expected. Furthermore, the values of legality, accountability and transparency loom large in this part of the world, not least in the Scandinavian countries where institutional trust is high by all international comparisons. As Peter Munk Christiansen (1998) argues, the corporatist tradition that is typical to these countries does not provide the necessary social micro-foundations for market-based administrative reform.

Today, administrative reform seems to be designed with somewhat more consideration to the nature of the specific problem to be resolved. Although the World Bank and IMF continue to emphasize deregulation of domestic markets, the demands for a marketization of the public service have been downplayed. OECD has terminated its Public Management Section, and the current view on NPM is rather mixed. In 2007, the position held by the Swedish National Financial Management Authority (ESV), as given in an interview to one of the present authors, is firm: 'NPM is out'.

In addition, the discussion of the causes behind the financial crisis that hit the world in the autumn of 2008 has increased focus on the importance of the Weberian type of firm regulations and impartial authorities that oversee markets. A number of prominent economists (including several Nobel Laureates) have stressed that a central causal factor behind the collapse of the financial market has been lax regulations and far too close relations between the large investment banks and the authorities that were supposed to regulate and oversee their operations (Johnson 2009).

When will NPM Work?

The argument so far in this chapter has not been that NPM-style public administration is generally a failure but that it should not be seen as something than can replace Weberianism. What we see in the literature is that while NPM seems to have passed its peak in the developed world – there is now a search for administrative models that combine Weberian features with NPM-style market solutions (Christensen and Lægreid 2007a) – the developing countries are still wrestling with the issue of whether or not they should adopt NPM as a philosophy of administration. However, introducing a model of public administration whose efficiency is predicated on some degree of social trust in a political, social and institutional context where such trust is low is essentially asking for problems. NPM, with its arm's-length relationship between elected politicians and the senior level of the public administration is, to reiterate a point made earlier, contingent on some level of trust between politicians and managers. It could well be argued that principal–agent theory, which is at the heart of NPM, assumes essentially no trust; it is a rationalistic model of hierarchical control and command. However, a low degree of trust will generate high transaction costs for output measurement, surveillance and audits, something which will impair the efficiency of the NPM model. Managers will have to be monitored more closely than the model states, politicians will have to devote time and resources not just to formulating long-term goals but also to create new authorities that oversee the operative elements of the public administration. As Gary Miller has shown, 'incentives-only'-based systems of steering are very unstable and probably inefficient since they tend to destroy trust (Miller 1992, Falaschetti and Miller 2001).

There is also the problem of low micro-level trust in developing countries. The NPM-style empowered front-line civil servant in a developing country does not enjoy the same level of trust from his client as his colleague in a Western democracy. The client, or customer, will not trust the integrity of the civil servant and thus has incentives to offer side payments to ensure a positive treatment. The alternative modernization strategy would be not to rely on market-based reform but rather to adopt a neo-Weberian model of public administration. The main problem with this strategy is that it to a large extent requires what is to be the goal of modernization, that is to say firm, coherent and insulated institutions staffed by a trained, professional civil service. This paradox of administrative reform haunts a number of countries in the developing world.

Thus, we do not see how NPM would be a viable reform strategy in the developing world. Instead, it is a reform strategy which is predicated on the pre-existence of Weberian-like administrative features which may or may not be present. A number of studies show that NPM will not work, at least not without costly side-effects in development or transition countries (Schick 1998, Bately 1999, Nickson 1999, Polidano 1999, Manning 2001, Peters 2001b, Sarker 2006, McCourt 2007). According to one of these studies in countries that lacked an established Weberian ethos, 'privatization became a popular source of income for corruption and patronage distribution' (Samaratunge et al. 2008: 41). What comes out of this research is that NPM style reforms cannot be an alternative to Weberianism in developing or transition countries. Instead, they seem only to work if they can rely on the type of institutional and social trust that an already existing Weberian state generates. As Nick Manning suggests about the need for a Weberian foundation for NPM reforms, 'NPM proponents did not see the need to spell out how these good things had come about – but clearly relied on them to continue as foundations for their reforms' (Manning 2001: 302).

NPM is in fact more dependent on professional managers and skilful politicians than the Weberian model of public administration. Weberianism emerged as a model of public administration in a social context characterized by moderate legality and moderate professionalism in the public service. The solution to those problems was to make legality the backbone of the public administration and to ensure that individual civil servants had a minimum of discretion. Thus, Weberianism was probably just as problem-driven as NPM; it offered a model of public administration which resolved or by-passed the key obstacles to modernization at that time. By emphasizing legality, standardization and hierarchical command and control systems, Weberianism devised a model of public administration which works reasonably well in the social and political context of institution building, democratization and increasing public services. Also, Weberianism was probably a congenial solution to a lack of trust in public officials, or the public administration as a whole.

On reflection, Weberianism is the perfect model of public administration in political and social settings where trust in institutions and public officials is low. By focusing on legality, hierarchy and impartiality, the Weberian philosophy of public administration essentially allows the citizen to engage the public bureaucracy without trusting its officials, since those officials have a minimum of latitude and discretion on the administration of specific matters.

This, of course, is another way of saying that in the NPM model of public administration, with its extensive decentralization, managerial autonomy and clear separation of policy and operations, trust in the public sector becomes essential. As soon as lower-level, front-line bureaucrats are given increased discretion to tailor services to the needs of their clients (or 'customers'), trust becomes key since with discretion comes the possibility for abuse. Trust, in this model of public administration, cannot be derived from legality, equality and due process, since the very objective of NPM is to escape the iron cage of legalism. Instead, trust is derived from performance (Scharpf 1999). As clients, we might not trust a public servant because s/he conducts administration strictly in accordance with a legal framework, but rather because s/he offers tailored services. Still, there is always the risk that NPM reforms will tempt the public service managers to engage in practices that are detrimental to the integrity of the public sector and thereby destroy institutional and also social trust (Rothstein and Eek 2009).

A case in point is the day-care and pre-school system in Sweden and Denmark. These are major public undertakings in financial terms that serve many important policy goals, not least to enable both parents with small children to work fulltime and thus increase gender equality. These institutions are either public, operated by local governments, or private but for the most part financed by public money in exchange for operating according to the same general rules that apply to the public pre-schools. The 'private' pre-schools should thus be understood as 'charter-schools' in the sense that they are fulfilling a public policy under public rules and with tax money. However, the managers and personnel at both the private and public pre-schools have a wide discretion for what type of pedagogical model they want to follow, and many parents choose pre-schools accordingly. Private pre-schools can be for-profit or non-profit and operated by groups of parents, commercial companies or non-profit civil society organizations. Most children are at public pre-schools but the number of private (or charter) ones has been growing for quite some time.

Thus these public services are to a large extent organized according to what the NPM model suggests. The managers are managing and enjoy considerable discretion regarding how to organize the service. There is choice between different service providers that compete for customers with different types of services (Björklund 2005). Moreover, the managers and teachers at these institutions, whether public or private, do not think of themselves as rule-bound Weberian bureaucrats that follow a strict palette of universal rules which they apply in an impersonal way. Instead they seem to follow a (semi-) professional logic and they apply different 'styles' of teaching and care-giving. It is also safe to say parents do not want the personnel to act according to a set of strict impersonal rules in an emotionless way towards their children. It is simply taken for granted that teachers use their professional knowledge to adapt in a flexible way to the specific needs of each and every child. It is thus more a 'logic of care' than a 'logic of justice' that dominates these public undertakings (Stensöta 2004). Still, there would be an uproar among the parents (and the public in general) if they were to find out that pre-school teachers had paid extra attention to some children because the parents had offered them cash for such services, or because they belonged to a certain religious or ethnic group, or if the content in their teaching followed the dogmas of a religious group that they belonged to instead of what was stipulated in the curriculum. Managers would instantly be fired if they had accepted bribes to let children in the waiting line jump the queue and they would be heavily criticized if they refused to take children from low-income or single-parent families. The moral of this example is this: the successful NPM character of this (hugely popular) publicly financed and regulated service depends to a large extent on an underlying – tacit or just taken-for-granted – acceptance of the type of institutional trust that follows from the Weberian mode of impartial or universal standards. Another way to express this is to say that the parents and citizens in general accept NPM-style solutions like this one provided they feel that their rights to impartial and fair treatment and equality before the law and so on are not violated. This development in the Swedish welfare state is not unique to the pre-school sector but has impacted the basic and secondary school sector, the provision of basic health care and to some extent care for elderly persons. The right for citizens to choose service providers within the universal welfare state system and the idea that service providers should 'brand' their services according to what managers/personnel deem their professional standards has been widely accepted. This is not to say that there is no criticism of the NPM system in the provision of public services, but it seems confined to situations when impartial/universal/equality standards are not respected. For example, when the system increases social segregation of students, when homes for elderly people do not meet established standards of care or when private/charter pre-schools refuse to accept children with special needs because of economic restraints (Blomqvist 2004).

Conclusions: Are New Weberianism and New Public Management Alternative Paths to a Better Quality of Government?

It has been argued in this chapter that when designing administrative reform, policymakers need to consider factors exogenous to the public administration just as much as endogenous variables. In particular, different societies offer quite different ethical and normative underpinnings of what public administration should be and they have very different types of institutional configurations for public services. Our tentative conclusion is that the NPM style of 'how the state should behave' should not be seen as an alternative to Weberianism. On the contrary, it appears as if NPM reforms can be made to work only if they rely on an already existing strong Weberian ethos in the public administration, something that is missing in most developing and many transition countries. This ethos can either exist as a 'basic norm' within the public services that are to work according to the NPM model, or in the public administration that is to ensure that the NPM-organized services adhere to rules and regulations for how and with what they can compete.

In an article criticizing the type of institutional reforms that the EU have demanded a country like Romania introduce for combating corruption, Alina Mungiu-Pippidi (2006) argues that such policies miss the heart of the problem, which, according to her, is the underlying political culture. It is a lack of an ethos of *universalism* and the dominance of what she labels particularism in the political culture that is the main obstruction to establishing 'good governance' in countries like Romania. Another suggestion for such a basic norm has been presented by Douglass North, John Wallis and Barry Weingast (2009) in a recent book subtitled *A Conceptual Framework for Interpreting Recorded Human History*. They distinguish between societies with 'open access orders' and those with 'limited access orders'. In the former, access to politics is open to everyone and the exercise of public policies and laws is based on an *impersonal* notion of public power. A third suggestion for how to describe this basic norm has been put forward by Rothstein and Teorell (2008), namely *impartiality* in the implementation of public policies. The differences between these three conceptualizations of 'good governance' are in reality mostly terminological since they all point to the same basic norm for the relationship between the government and its citizens. It may be that NPM-style reforms can only work if they are layered upon a state that has as its *modus operandi* a Weberian understanding (universalism, impersonality, impartiality) of 'how the state should behave'.

Public Governance and Public Services: A 'Brave New World' or New Wine in Old Bottles?[1]

Stephen P. Osborne

Introduction

More than a decade has passed since the publication of Christopher Hood's influential piece that codified the nature of the New Public Management (NPM) paradigm (Hood 1991). At that time it seemed likely, certainly within the Anglo-American research community, that this paradigm would sweep all before it in its triumphal re-casting of the nature of our discipline – in theory and in practice. One hundred-odd years of the hegemony of public administration in the public sphere seemingly counted for nothing in this momentous shift. Since then, though, the debate on the impact of NPM upon the discipline, and indeed about whether it is a paradigm at all (Gow and Dufour 2000), has become more contested.

This chapter argues that NPM has actually been a transitory stage in the evolution from traditional public administration to what is here called New Public Governance.[2] A note upon terminology is important here. The term 'public policy implementation and public services delivery' is used here to denote the overall field of the design and implementation of public policy and the delivery of public services. Within this, public administration (PA), New Public Management (NPM)

---

1   This chapter is a revised, abridged and adapted version of S. Osborne (2010a), 'The (New) Public Governance: A Suitable Case for Treatment' and 'Public Governance and Public Services Delivery: A Research Agenda for the Future', both in S. Osborne (ed.), *The New Public Governance?* (London: Routledge).

2   Ever since Hood's influential essay on NPM, there has been a tendency to herald every shift in public services provision as the 'New Something-or-other'. Whilst there are clear limitations to this approach it is nonetheless the one adopted here – primarily to differentiate it from the other diverse approaches to 'governance' and 'public governance' discussed below.

and New Public Governance (NPG) are then denoted as policy and implementation regimes within this overall field.

The argument advanced here is that public policy implementation and public services delivery has passed through three design and delivery regimes – a longer, pre-eminent one of PA, from the late nineteenth century through to the late 1970s/early 1980s; a second one, of NPM, through to the start of the twenty-first century; and an emergent third one, of NPG, since then. The time of NPM has thus in fact been a relatively short-lived and transient one between the statist and bureaucratic tradition of PA and the embryonic plural and pluralist tradition of NPG. The remainder of this chapter will first expound upon the extant natures of PA and NPM. It will then explore the nature of public governance and NPG before considering the new challenges that it poses both for the theory and practice of public policy implementation and public services delivery.

At the outset it is important to emphasize that such a tripartite regime model is inevitably a simplification – elements of each regime can and do coexist with each other or overlap. Many network governance systems often operate in the shadow of, or in spite of, the dominant regime of hierarchy, for example, whilst both PA and public governance contain strong, if differentiated, elements of hierarchy (Klijn 2002). The current economic recession is also requiring intense attention to the effective management of public service organizations whilst at the same time as requiring the effective governance of the public service delivery systems that they exist within. The intention here is not to reduce such complexity to sophistry but rather to tease out three 'archetypes', in the Weberian tradition, that will assist and promote analysis and discussion of the conceptual and practical development of public policy implementation and public services delivery. It will draw strongly upon UK experience in undertaking this task.

The Shadow of the Past...

Public Administration

The key elements of PA (Hood 1991) can be defined as

- the dominance of the 'rule of law';
- a focus on administering set rules and guidelines;
- a central role for the bureaucracy in policy making and implementation;
- the 'politics-administration' split within public organizations;
- a commitment to incremental budgeting; and
- the hegemony of the professional in public service delivery

Developing out of the early years of the public sector in the late nineteenth and early twentieth centuries, PA, as an academic field of study has been a strongly 'grounded', rather than theoretical, discipline in the UK (the classic early statement being Robson 1928) – and at variance with its cousins in mainland Europe and the US which are more firmly located within administrative theory.

As a field of practice it reached its high-point in the UK in the 1945–79 era of the welfare state, when the state was confidently expected to meet all the social and economic needs of the citizenry, 'from the cradle to the grave'. PA was to be the instrument of this heroic aspiration, with a focus on administrative procedures to ensure equality of treatment. Predictably, perhaps, such a vision was doomed to failure – public needs inevitably outstripped the public resources available to meet them. In the latter days of their hegemony both the welfare state and PA came under increasing fire – first from their academic critics (for example, Dunleavy 1985) and eventually from the political elite (see Mishra 1984 for an overview of these critiques). Most damagingly Chandler (1991) argued that PA had now entered terminal decline as a discipline, whilst Rhodes (1997) asserted that it had become a 'bystander' to the practice of public policy implementation and public services delivery. This paved the way for the rise of NPM.

New Public Management

The spread of NPM, from the late 1970s onward, saw the growth of a new discourse of public policy implementation and public services delivery. In its most extreme form, this asserted the superiority of private sector managerial techniques over those of PA and with the assumption that the application of such techniques to public services delivery would automatically lead to improvements in the efficiency and effectiveness of these services (Thatcher 1995). The key elements of NPM (Hood 1991) can be summarized as

- an attention to lessons from private sector management;
- the growth both of hands-on 'management' (in its own right and not as offshoot of professionalism) and of 'arm's length' organizations where policy implementation was organizationally distanced from the policy makers (as opposed to the 'inter-personal' distancing of the policy – administration split within PA);
- a focus upon entrepreneurial leadership within public service organizations
- an emphasis on inputs and output control and evaluation and upon performance management and audit;
- the dis-aggregation of public services to their most basic units and a focus on their cost management; and
- within the Anglo-American and Australia/New Zealand regions at least, the growth of use of markets, competition and contracts for resource allocation and service delivery within public services

In the research community, this led to a focus upon the management of public services and of public service organizations (PSOs) as a distinct field separate from the public policy process – public management as opposed to public administration. At a practical level, it led to the evolution of management as a coherent and legitimized role and function within PSOs, in contrast to (and often in conflict with) the traditional professional groupings within PSOs.

In the years since it first contested the territory of public policy implementation and public services delivery with PA, though, the nature and/or success(es) of NPM have been questioned on a range of grounds (see McLaughlin et al. 2002 for an overview of these critiques). Critics have argued, *inter alia*, that:

- NPM is not one phenomenon or paradigm, but a cluster of several (Ferlie et al. 1996) – and has a number of distinct personae, dependent upon the audience, including ideological, managerial and research-oriented personae (Dawson and Dargie 1999);
- the geographic extent of NPM is limited to the Anglo-American, Australasian and (some) Scandinavian arenas, whilst PA continues to remain dominant elsewhere (Kickert 1997);
- the nature of NPM itself is also geographically variegated with, for example, the British and American variants actually being quite distinct from each other in their focus and locus (Borins 2002);
- in reality, NPM is simply a sub-school of PA that has been limited in its impact by the lack of a real theoretical base and conceptual rigour (Frederickson and Smith 2003);
- the benefits of NPM are at best partial and contested (Pollitt and Bouckaert 2004); and
- NPM was a 'disaster waiting to happen' (Hood and Jackson 1991b) and was a failed paradigm (Farnham and Horton 1996).

NPM has been criticized most devastatingly for its intra-organizational focus in an increasingly plural world and for its adherence to the application of out-dated private sector techniques to public policy implementation and public services delivery – and in the face of evidence about their inapplicability (Metcalfe and Richards 1991).

...And the Shadow of the Future

New Public Governance

At the outset it is important to be clear that NPG is being presented here neither as a normative new paradigm to supersede PA and NPM nor as 'the one best way' (Alford and Hughes 2008) to respond to the challenges of public policy implementation and public services delivery in the twenty-first century. Rather it is being presented as a conceptual tool with the potential to assist our understanding of the complexity of these challenges – and which reflects the reality of the working lives of public managers today.

Moreover, 'governance' and 'public governance' are not new terms – they come with considerable prior theoretical and/or ideological baggage. Following Rhodes (1997), it is possible to differentiate three broad schools of governance literature: corporate governance, 'good' governance and public governance.

Corporate governance is concerned with the internal systems and processes that provide direction and accountability to any organization. In public services it has most often been concerned with the relationship between the policy makers and/or trustees of public organizations and the senior managers given the task of making these policies a reality (for example, Cornforth 2003).

'Good' governance is concerned with the promulgation of normative models of social, political and administrative governance by supra-national bodies such as the World Bank (Leftwich 1993) and which invariably has placed a premium upon market-based approaches to the allocation and governance of public resources.

Public governance, which is the focus here, can itself be broken down into five distinct strands:

- *Socio-political governance*, concerned with the over-arching institutional relationships within society. Kooiman (1999) argues that these relationships and interactions must be understood in their totality in order to understand the creation and implementation of public policy. In this approach government is no longer pre-eminent in public policy but has to rely upon other societal actors for its legitimacy and impact in this field.
- *Public policy governance*, concerned with how policy elites and networks interact to create and govern the public policy process. Marsh and Rhodes (1992), Börzel (1997) and Klijn and Koppenjan (2000), building upon the work of Hanf and Scharpf (1978), are good examples of such explorations of the workings of policy communities and networks. Most recently Peters (2010) has explored 'meta-governance' instruments as a way by which to re-assert political direction within multi-stakeholder policy networks.
- *Administrative governance*, concerned with the effective application of PA and its re-positioning to encompass the complexities of the contemporary state. Thus, for example, Salamon (2002) uses governance almost as a proxy term for the generic practice of public policy implementation and public services delivery, whilst Lynn et al. (2001) also use it as a catch-all term to try to create an holistic theory of public policy implementation and public services delivery in conditions of the 'hollow state' (Milward and Provan 2003). More provocatively Frederickson (1999) contends that governance, taken together with the theory of 'administrative conjunction', is in fact a way to re-position PA as the continuing pre-eminent discipline for the realities of the modern world.
- *Contract governance*, concerned with the inner workings of NPM, and particularly the governance of contractual relationships in the delivery of public services. In this vein, Kettl has argued that public agencies in the

modern contract state have become 'responsible for a [public service delivery] system over which they [have] little control' (Kettl 1993: 207, see also Kettl 2010).

- *Network governance*, concerned with how 'self organizing inter-organizational networks' (Rhodes 1997, see also Kickert 1993) function both with and without government to provide public services. In contrast to public policy governance this is focused upon those networks that *implement* public policy and deliver public services (for example Denters and Rose 2005, Entwistle and Martin 2005).

All of these theoretical perspectives on governance make an important contribution to our understanding of public policy implementation and public services delivery. The intention here is to argue that, from being an element within the PA and NPM regimes of public policy implementation and public services delivery, public governance has become a distinctive regime in its own right that captures the realities of public policy implementation and public services delivery within the plural and pluralist complexities of the state in the twenty-first century.[3]

The State of the Art

As outlined above, therefore, PA is situated firmly within the political studies discipline. Influential theorists include Woodrow Wilson (1887) and William Robson (1928). It has at its core a concern with the unitary state, where policy making and implementation are vertically integrated as a closed system[4] within government. It focuses upon the policy making and implementation cycle, with an assumption that effective public administration and management is comprised of the successful implementation by public managers of policies decided 'up stream' in this system by democratically elected (and, it is implicitly assumed, accountable) politicians. Because of its vertically integrated nature, hierarchy is the key resource allocation mechanism for PA, with a focus upon vertical line management to ensure accountability for the use of public money (Simey 1988). The value base is one based in an explicit assumption of the hegemony of the public sector for the implementation of public policy and the delivery of public services.

Some writers, of course, have long recognized the fallibility of the PA paradigm without entirely dismissing it as a framework for the design and delivery of public services. The theory of 'street level bureaucrats' (Lipsky 1979), for example, seeks to explain the breakdown of the 'policy maker–administrator' divide in conditions of resource shortage, but without dismissing in its entirety the framework of PA for the provision of public services (see also Schofield 2001 for a good overview of this range of arguments).

---

3   For a counter-argument to this position see Hughes (2010).
4   See Scott (1992) for a full discussion of systems theory.

By comparison, NPM[5] is a child of neo-classical economics and particularly of rational/public choice theory. Influential writers include Tiebout (1956) and Niskanen (1971). It is concerned with a disaggregated state, where policy making and implementation are at least partially articulated and disengaged, and where implementation is through a collection of independent service units, ideally in competition with each other. The key role of the state here is regulation, often within a principal–agent context (Vickers and Yarrow 1988). Its focus is almost wholly upon intra-organizational processes and management.[6] Drawing upon open rational systems theory, it models the production of public services as an intra-organizational process that turns inputs into outputs (services) within a mediating environment, and with an emphasis upon the economy and efficiency of these processes in producing public services. As already noted, it assumes competitive relationships between the independent service units inside any public policy domain, taking place within a horizontally organized market place – and where the key resource allocation mechanism is a variable combination of competition, the price mechanism and contractual relationships, depending upon which particular variant of NPM one chooses to expound. Its value base is formed around 'the logic of accounting' (Broadbent and Laughlin 2002) and is contained within its belief that this market-place, and its workings, provides the most appropriate place for the production of public services. An extreme form of this argument is made by Pirie (1988).

In contrast to both the above, NPG, if it is to be situated as a paradigm of public policy and public services delivery, is rooted firmly within institutional and network theory and draws much from the influential work of Ouchi (1979), Powell (1990), and Nohria and Eccles (1992). It posits both *a plural state*, where multiple inter-dependent actors contribute to the delivery of public services, and *a pluralist state*, where multiple processes inform the policy making system. Drawing upon open natural systems theory, it is concerned with the institutional and external environmental pressures that enable and constrain public policy implementation and the delivery of public services within such a plural and pluralist system. As a consequence of these two forms of plurality, its focus is very much upon inter-organizational relationships and upon the governance of processes, stressing service effectiveness and outcomes that rely upon the interaction of PSOs with their environment. The central resource allocation mechanism is the inter-organizational network, with accountability being something to be negotiated at the inter-organizational and inter-personal level within these networks (Osborne 1997).

---

5   NPM, as discussed here, is very much the market-driven variant that emphasized the efficacy of inter-organizational competition in the delivery of public services. It is the model prevalent across the UK, the US and Australia and New Zealand in particular. An alternative version, that is common across mainland Europe, does not place such an emphasis upon an external competitive environment. Rather, it emphasizes contractual mechanisms *within* rather than *without* government (Schrijvers 1993).

6   Though Ostrom and Ostrom (1971) do offer a more explicitly *inter-organizational* approach to public choice theory as a basis for NPM.

Importantly, such networks are rarely alliances of equals but are rather riven with power inequalities that must be navigated successfully for their effective working. Hence the value base in such networks is often dispersed and contested.

NPG is thus both a product of and a response to the increasingly complex, plural and fragmented nature of public policy implementation and service delivery in the twenty-first century (Haveri 2006). Again, this does not deny the importance of issues of public policy and accountability or of the internal management of key organizational resources. Rather it positions them within the reality of the plural and pluralist state, as discussed above.

Now significant work has already taken place that might legitimately be said to fall within the boundaries of the emergent regime of NPG. This includes work upon the nature and governance of the policy process (Klijn and Koppenjan 2000), the issue of 'managing outward' for PSOs and managers (O'Toole et al. 2007), the development of key management skills in an inter-organizational context (Mandell and Keast 2008), expanding the nature and impact of accounting within PSOs to embrace a more holistic approach to their environment (Marcuccio and Steccolini 2005) and the governance of inter-organizational relationships themselves (Huxham and Vangen 2005). Invariably, though, the focus has been at the organizational rather than the service system level.

However, it has become increasingly apparent that the public policy implementation and public services delivery research agenda, certainly within the UK, is one where its parameters and questions have been set within the previous regimes – and particularly within that of NPM. This research agenda is asking old questions about public policy implementation and public services delivery. These questions are epitomized within the ESRC Public Services Programme in the UK. This programme has been a vital one for the research community and has produced some outstanding research findings. Nonetheless, as a research agenda, it is characterized precisely by these 'old questions' of intra-organizational efficiency and effectiveness. These old questions can be summarized as:

- How do we manage public policy implementation to ensure that the political will is carried out in practice? (the policy implementation question);
- How do we ensure organizational and individual service performance? (the audit and targets question);
- How do we ensure that individual PSOs can work in partnership most effectively? (the partnerships question);
- How do we hold public managers accountable? (the scrutiny question);
- How do we 'incentivize' staff for optimal productivity? (the rewards question);
- How do we ensure organizational sustainability? (the change and innovation question).

The argument here is that, if we are going to develop NPG as a conceptualization of public policy implementation and public services management, then it is necessary to move towards an integrated body of knowledge about NPG. This requires our research community to start asking a series of 'new questions' about the fundamentals of NPG. These questions are focused upon the underlying principles of public services delivery in the plural and pluralist state and upon the public service system, rather than upon individual PSOs. These new questions have been elaborated on in more detail elsewhere (Osborne 2010a). The intention here is to focus on four in particular:

- What should be our basic unit of analysis in exploring public policy implementation and public services delivery – and what are the implications of this for theory and practice? (the fundamentals question);
- What organizational architecture is best suited to delivering public services in the plural state? (the architectural question);
- How do we ensure sustainable public service systems – and what does sustainability mean? (the sustainability question);
- What values underpin public policy implementation and services delivery in such systems? (the values question).

It should be emphasized that these new questions are not a simple replacement for the old ones. Again, the imperatives for responsive policy processes and for intra-organizational efficiency remain – and hence the 'old questions' still remain pertinent also. However, such responsiveness and efficiency, by themselves, will not engender the delivery of successful public services in the contemporary plural and pluralist state. These core 'new questions' require to be addressed also, therefore, if our research community is to remain relevant to public policy implementation and public services delivery in the future. These are now discussed in more detail below.

The New Questions

The Fundamentals Question

As discussed above, within PA, the unit of analysis was the public policy system as a *closed system* with a focus upon the efficacy and impact of this system in its own right. The key questions in this regime were about the effectiveness of the policy-making process and the extent to which public policy implementation addressed the aspirations of their extant public policy origins (see for example Hill and Hupe 2009). Within NPM, the unit of analysis shifted to the individual public service organization (PSO) as open rational systems and to individual public service managers within these systems. It modelled public services delivery as an intra-organizational process that turned inputs into outputs (services) within a mediating environment, and with an emphasis upon the economy and efficiency of public services delivery.

Within the NPG paradigm, a systemic approach is required that views public services delivery from an open natural systems perspective. This focuses attention upon the institutional and external environmental pressures that enable and constrain public policy implementation and the delivery of public services within such a plural and pluralist system. Borrowing from the services management literature (for example, Gronroos 2007, Vargo et al. 2008), it is suggested here that the fundamental unit of analysis should be the public service system. This includes not just the public policy process and PSOs (including their personnel and hard and soft service delivery technologies), but also the involvement of services users as the co-producers of public services and the wider institutional land environmental contingencies of public services delivery. Such an approach moves beyond the concept of 'simple' inter-organizational networks as the focus of attention for analysis, as in open rational systems. Rather it moves our attention to the inter-relationships between a number of inter-dependent elements of the public service system (Osborne 2010b).

Co-production is a core element here. Public policy has included this as a policy aspiration for several decades now (Brandsen and Pestoff 2006), yet it has rarely understood its role as a core and unavoidable element of services delivery – and one that shapes the nature and impact of these services. New work, drawing upon services management theory, is now evolving that will help our understanding of co-production as precisely such a fundamental and inescapable element of the delivery of any public service (for example, Strokosch and Osborne 2010a).

In this context, the key 'fundamentals' questions for our research agenda include:

- What can we learn from the services management literature that will help to illuminate the nature of public delivery within the NPG regime or paradigm?
- What are the core elements of the service delivery system and how do they inter-relate?
- What types of public service systems are there – and do they require a differential approach to their management and governance?
- What are the implications of the implicit element of user co-production within public service systems?

The Architectural Question

The architecture of public services delivery within PA was relatively straightforward. This involved all elements of service provision being vertically integrated within PSOs – and with these bodies invariably being part of the government sector. The structure and functioning of these governmental bodies was broadly similar for all services.

Within NPM, the architecture became more complex with the plural provision of public services both from a range of PSOs and from a range of societal sectors (government, the third sector and the private sector). The architecture of these organizations could vary in size, structure and functions, but was often broadly similar within societal sectors. Moreover, the market acted as an isomorphic force to encourage homogeneity within organizations providing similar services.

Such vertically integrated and sectoral approaches to organizational architecture have broken down as the fragmentation and pluralism of NPG has progressed. Increasingly the unit of analysis is not distinct organizations. Now it includes both networks of public managers and of PSOs working in concert to provide public services (O'Toole et al. 2007) and hybrid organizational forms that do not fit neatly within one distinctive societal sector and that have a fragmented and intermingled architecture (Evers 2008).

The concept of hybrid organizations is not a new one. There has been a longstanding debate about 'publicness' in PSOs and the blurring of the boundaries between public and private organizations. What is distinctive now is the growing complexity of this hybridity. It is not simply a blurring of the boundaries between the public and the private. Rather it is the evolution of genuinely new forms of organizational architecture that are not bound by sectoral limitations and that engender new forms of accountability. Social enterprises are one example of such hybrid organizations that mix social ends with a business orientation to income generation (Vidal 2008).

In this world, there is no 'one best way' or prescribed approach to organizational architecture. It becomes a contingent process. Such new architecture needs us to ask questions such as:

- What organizational architecture is best suited to deliver what sorts of public services?
- What are the key contingencies of the contemporary architecture of PSOs and what are their implications for public services delivery?
- How do PSOs develop organizational architecture that goes beyond simple organizational survival to tackle the issues of 'boundary spanning' and 'boundary maintenance' in sophisticated service delivery systems that rely upon multiple elements for the successful delivery of public services to local communities?

The Sustainability Question

To date, sustainability has often been viewed in public services delivery research either as concerned with the organizational ecology of PSOs and the sustainability of individual PSOs or as concerned with issues of environmentalism and ecological sustainability. The contemporary architecture of public services, as discussed above, requires a more sophisticated approach. This needs to consider sustainability across a number of dimensions. These include the development of sustainable income streams and funding for public services and the impact of these income streams upon their wider environment (perhaps through ethical investment strategies), the ecology of PSOs and their sustainability as discrete entities, the sustainability of services delivered by PSOs and public service delivery systems, and their impact upon their users and host communities, and the effect of public services delivery systems upon environmental and ecological sustainability.

Research has also noted how the logic of the 'old questions' has subverted and incorporated sustainability within the existing 'status quo' rather than allowing it to challenge this status quo (Ball 2005, Ball et al. 2009), whilst others have argued for approaches to sustainability that creates a new paradigm of accountability within public services and PSOs (Gray et al. 2009). Drawing upon this emerging body of research, some preliminary questions in this area are:

- What is sustainability? There is a need to move beyond the 'simple' definitions of the Brundtland report.
- What are the key dimensions of sustainability for public service delivery systems – are the ones suggested above the correct ones, or are there alternatives or additional ones?
- To what extent is sustainability a marginal or mainstream issue for PSOs – and is it being 'backwards incorporated' into existing service-led agendas from the NPM paradigm?
- How has concept and practice of sustainability evolved over the period of PA – NPM – NPG?

The Values Question

The discussion about the role of values in public services has a long lineage. Within PA, there was an assumption of distinctiveness in the values of public, as opposed to private, sector management – and often an assumption of moral hegemony of the former. One of the first statements of the 'public value thesis' was Sayre (1958) and the argument was developed by, among others, Rainey et al. (1976) and Murray (1975) – though the classic statement was probably Allison (1986b: 234) who argued that 'public and private management are at least as different as they are similar, and that the differences are at least as important as the similarities'.

As market and business disciplines came to have a greater influence on public management within NPM, however, this hegemony of public values was challenged. A number of studies argued that public and private sector values and managerial practice were either not as differentiated as had earlier been argued or were converging (for example Posner and Schmidt 1996, Boyne 2002b). Several studies also argued that public values had been replaced by new public sector entrepreneurial values (Llewellyn et al. 2007), whilst Mark Moore has coined the term 'public value' as the equivalent of 'shareholder value' within public organizations (Moore 1995).

Within the field of public governance, however, the debate about values has become a contested one. Hoggett (2006: 192) has argued that PSOs now have

> *... multiple tasks which are often in contradiction; they are certainly beset by conflicting notions of what they should be doing and ... for some organizations, paradoxically, it is important that they fail in order to maintain their contested legitimacy by serving the public's unresolved ambivalence.*

Because of this contested terrain in which PSOs now operate, and also because of the hybridity discussed above, public values have become contested also. Further, the evolution of the co-production of public services also poses new challenges both for the way that service users are perceived by the staff of PSOs and for the value base of PSOs themselves. The competing discourses of 'client', 'consumer', 'customer' and citizen', to name but a few, all imply different modes of service delivery for PSOs and a different set of values underpinning this service production (Strokosch and Osborne 2010a).

For managers working in hybrid organizations their values may need to span different societal sectors and be able to embrace the pradoxicality of their new organizational architecture and logic. Thus, for example, Poole et al. (2006) found both convergence and divergence in public and private sector managerial practice and values, whist feminist critics have challenged the public and private dichotomy as irrelevant in contemporary society (Nickel and Eikenberry 2006). As a consequence of these critiques, it is important now to ask some fundamentally new questions about public values within the plural state and within public service systems:

- What values do public service managers and public service users hold and how can the potential contradictions between these be governed?
- Does co-production require a distinctive set of values to underpin public services delivery – and what might the basis of these values be?
- What is the impact of contested values within public service systems upon the delivery and use of these services?
- Do individual public services have distinctive values and how can these be negotiated in complex service delivery systems?

Conclusions

This chapter began by questioning the extent to which a 'New Public Governance' exists or not. It has been argued here that it does indeed exist and is a defining element of public service delivery systems in the twenty-first century. Its meaning may continue to be contested, and at its worst, it can mean 'all things to all people'. Nonetheless the concept does capture the challenges of the delivery of public services within fragmented service delivery systems around the world. The challenges may not be the same in all parts of the globe, but relational values are at their core.

This chapter has concluded by suggesting that a new research agenda is required to capture fully the complexity and diversity of public governance in this global context. It is an ambitious one. However the argument here is that it is one that must be embraced if we are to move forward and consider the realities of public policy implementation and public services delivery within public governance. Again, this is a not a 'boosterist' agenda that argues for NPG as the 'one best way' to implement policy and deliver public services. Nor does it suggest that the need for effective public policy processes and for effective organizational management have gone away. Manifestly they have not. Rather it asks how these challenges can be approached within the fragmented, inter-organizational and contested space that now comprises the delivery of public services.

This subsequent discussion about what these new questions might be has not been intended to be either exhaustive or conclusive. Rather it has been intended as a contribution to fire a debate about the research agenda on public governance for the next decade and beyond. The research community must embrace this new research agenda if it is to stop asking 'old questions' that do not reflect the reality of public services in the twenty-first century. The 'new questions' suggested here do not, of course, negate the need to continue exploring some of these 'old questions' – but only in a context that reflects the new context of public governance. These 'new questions' are ones that must be addressed in order to drive forward evidence-influenced public policy implementation and public services delivery in the twenty-first century.

References

6, P. 2005. Joined-Up Government in the West beyond Britain: A Provisional Assessment, in *Joined-Up Government*, edited by V. Bogdanor. Oxford: Oxford University Press, 43–106.

6, P., Leat, D., Seltzer, K. and Stoker, G. 2002. *Towards Holistic Governance: The New Reform Agenda*. New York: Palgrave.

Aberbach, J.D. and Christensen, T. 2005. Citizens and Consumers. *Public Management Review*, 7(2), 224–246.

Acemoglu, D. and Robinson, J. 2008. *The Role of Institutions in Growth and Development*. Washington D.C.: The World Bank on behalf of the Commission on Growth and Development.

Advisory Group on the Reform of Australian Government Administration 2010. *Ahead of the Game: Blueprint for the Reform of Australian Government Administration*. Canberra: Commonwealth of Australia.

Agranoff, R. 2006. Inside Collaborative Networks: Ten Lessons for Public Managers. *Public Management Review*, 66(Special Issue), 56–65.

Ahrne, G. 1998. Stater och andra organisationer, in *Stater som organisationer*, edited by G. Ahrne. Stockholm: Nerenius & Santérus Förlag, 123–156.

Alba, C.R. 1998. Politique et administration en Espagne: continuité historique et perspectives. *Revue Française d'Administration Publique*, 86(April–June), 229–241.

Alesina, A. and Angeletos, G-M. 2005. Corruption, Inequality, and Fairness. *Journal of Monetary Economics*, 52(7), 1227–1244.

Alford, J. and Hughes, O. 2008. Public Value Pragmatism as the Next Phase of Public Management. *The American Review of Public Administration*, 38(2), 130–148.

Alford, J. and O'Flynn, J. 2009. Making Sense of Public Value: Concepts, Critiques and Emergent Meanings. *International Journal of Public Administration*, 32(3–4), 171–191.

Allen, P. 2006. New Localism in the English National Health Service: What Is It For? *Health Policy*, 79(2–3), 244–252.

Allison, G.T. 1986a. Public and Private Management: Are They Fundamentally Alike in All Unimportant Respects?, in *Current Issues in Public Administration*, edited by F.S. Lane. 3rd edition. New York: St. Martin's Press, 184–200.

—— 1986b. Public and Private Administrative Leadership: Are They Fundamentally Alike in All Unimportant Respects?, in *Leadership and Organizational Culture:*

New Perspectives on Administrative Theory and Practice, edited by T.J. Sergiovanni and J.E. Corbally. Champaign, IL: University of Illinois Press, 214–239.

Allix, M. and van Thiel, S. 2005. Mapping the Field of Quasi-Autonomous Organizations in France and Italy. *International Journal of Public Management*, 8(1), 39–55.

Amin, A. (ed.) 2009. *The Social Economy: International Perspectives on Economic Solidarity*. London: Zed Books.

Andersen, L.B. and Pallesen, T. 2008. 'Not Just for the Money?' How Financial Incentives Affect the Number of Publications at Danish Research Institutions. *International Public Management Journal*, 11(1), 28–47.

Andersen, L.B. and Serritzlew, S. 2009. *Does Public Service Motivation Affect the Behavior of Professionals?* Paper to the 2009 International Public Service Motivation Research Conference, Bloomington, Indiana, 7–9 June.

Andersen, S.C. and Serritzlew, S. 2007. The Unintended Effects of Private School Competition. *Journal of Public Administration Research and Theory*, 17(2), 335–356.

Andrews, M. 2010. Good Government Means Different Things in Different Countries. *Governance*, 23(1), 7–35.

Andrews, R., Boyne, G.A. and Enticott, G. 2006. Performance Failure in the Public Sector: Misfortune or Mismanagement? *Public Management Review*, 8(2), 273–296.

Andrews, R. and Entwistle, T. 2010. Does Cross-sectoral Partnership Deliver?: An Empirical Exploration of Public Service Effectiveness, Efficiency and Equity. *Journal of Public Administration Research and Theory*, 20(3), 679–701.

Anttonen, A. and Häikiö, L. 2010. From Social Citizenship to Active Citizenship? Participation, Responsibility and Choice in Finnish Elder Car, in *Summoning the Active Citizen: Participation, Responsibility and Choice in Western Europe*, edited by J. Newman and E. Tonkens. Amsterdam: Amsterdam University Press.

Asboe Kristensen, A. and Beck Jørgensen, T. 2008. Fremtidens kommuner – lokale statskontorer? En undersøgelse af kommunale topledere forventninger til opgave – og strukturreformens mulighedsrum. *Politik*, 11(3), 79–93.

Ashby, W.R. 1956. *An Introduction to Cybernetics*. London: Chapman & Hall.

Asian Development Bank 1998. *Annual Report*. Manila: Asian Development Bank.

—— 1999. *Governance in Asia: From Crisis to Opportunity*. Manila: Asian Development Bank. [Online] Available at: http://www.adb.org/Documents/Reports/ Governance/default.asp?p=gvrnance [accessed: 04/08/2010].

Askim, J., Christensen, T., Fimreite, A.L. and Lægreid, P. 2009. How to Carry out Joined-Up Government Reforms. *International Journal of Public Administration*, 32(12), 1006–1025.

Aucoin, P. 1990. Administrative Reform in Public Management: Paradigms, Principles, Paradoxes and Pendulums. *Governance*, 3(2), 115–137.

—— 1995. *The New Public Management: Canada in Comparative Perspective*. Montreal: Institute for Research on Public Policy.

—— 2001. *Comparative Perspectives on Canadian Public Service Reform in the 1990s*. Ottawa: Office of the Auditor General of Canada.

—— 2002. Beyond the 'New' in Public Management: Catching the New Wave?, in *A Handbook of Canadian Public Administration*, edited by C. Dunn. Don Mills: Oxford University Press, part I, chapter 3.

—— 2006a. The Staffing and Evaluation of Canadian Deputy Ministers in Comparative Perspective: A Proposal for Reform. *Research Studies*, 36(1), 297–336.

—— 2006b. Accountability and Coordination with Independent Foundations: A Canadian Case of Autonomization, in *Autonomy and Regulation: Coping with Agencies in the Modern State*, edited by T. Christensen and P. Lægreid. Cheltenham: Edward Elgar, 110–133.

—— 2007. *Public Governance and Accountability of Canadian Crown Corporations: Reformation or Transformation*. Paper to the Canadian Political Science Association Annual Conference, University of Saskatchewan, 31 May.

—— 2008. *New Public Management and the Quality of Government: Coping with the New Political Governance in Canada*. Paper to the Conference on New Public Management and the Quality of Government at the SOG and the Quality of Government Institute, University of Gothenburg, Sweden, 13–15 November. Available at: http://www.qog.pol.gu.se [accessed: 10/03/2010].

Aucoin, P. and Heintzman, R. 2000. The Dialectics of Accountability for Performance in Public Management Reform. *International Review of Administrative Sciences*, 66(1), 45–55.

Aucoin, P. and Jarvis, M.D. 2005. *Modernizing Government Accountability: A Framework for Reform*. Ottawa: Canada School of Public Service.

Audit Commission and Mori Social Research Institute 2003a. *Exploring Trust in Public Institutions*. London: Audit Commission.

—— 2003b. *Trust in Public Institutions: New Findings: National Quantitative Survey*. London: Audit Commission.

Azuma, N. 2003. The Role of the Supreme Audit Institutions in NPM: International Trend. *Government Auditing Review*, 10(March), 85–106.

—— 2004. Performance Measurement of Supreme Audit Institutions. *Government Auditing Review*, 11(March), 65–94.

Bach, S., Bordogna, L., Della Rocca, G. and Winchester, D. (eds) 1999. *Public Service Employment Relations in Europe: Transformation, Modernization or Inertia?* London: Routledge.

Bach, S. and Givan, R.C. 2008. Public Service Modernization and Trade Union Reform: Toward Managerial Led Renewal? *Public Administration*, 86(2), 523–539.

Bakvis, H. and Juillet, L. 2004. *The Horizontal Challenge: Line Departments, Central Agencies and Leadership*. Ottawa: Canada School of Public Services.

Baldwin, R. 2005. Is Better Regulation Smarter Regulation? *Public Law*, Autumn, 485–511.

Baldwin, R. and Cave, M. 1999. *Understanding Regulation, Theory, Strategy and Practice*. Oxford: Oxford University Press.

Ball, A. 2005. Environmental Accounting and Change in UK Local Government. *Accounting, Auditing and Accountability Journal*, 18(3), 346–373.

Ball, A., Mason, I., Grubnic, S. and Hughes, P. 2009. The Carbon Neutral Public Sector: Early Development and an Urgent Agenda for Action. *Public Management Review*, 11(5), 575–600.

Bamber, G.J. and Davis, E.M. 1992. Australia, in *Industrial Relations around the World*, edited by M. Rothman, D.R. Briscoe and R.C.D. Nacamulli. Berlin: de Gruyter, 11–30.

Banfield, E. 1975. Corruption as a Feature of Governmental Organization. *Journal of Law and Economics*, 18(3), 587–605.

Barnard, C. 1968. *The Functions of the Executive*. 30th anniversary edition. Cambridge, MA: Harvard University Press.

Barnes, C. and Gill, D. 2000. Declining Government Performance? Why Citizens Don't Trust Government. *State Services Commission Working Papers*. Working Paper No. 9. February 2000. Wellington: State Services Commission. Available at: http://www.ssc.govt.nz/display/document.asp?Docid=4549&pageno=3 [accessed: 15/04/2010].

Barnes, M., Newman, J. and Sullivan, H. 2007. *Power, Participation and Political Renewal: Case Studies in Public Participation*. Bristol: Policy Press.

Barrier, J. 2010. La science en projet. Ph.D. thesis in sociology. Paris: Sciences Po.

Bartle, I. 2004. *Britain's Railway Crisis: A Review of the Arguments in Comparative Perspective*. Occasional Paper No. 20. Bath: University of Bath, School of Management.

—— 2005. *The 2004 Rail Review: Towards a New Regulatory Framework*. Occasional Paper No. 24. Bath: University of Bath, School of Management.

Bartle, I. and Vass, P. 2006. *Economic Regulators and Sustainable Development: Promoting Good Governance*. CRI Research Report No. 18. Bath: University of Bath, School of Management.

—— 2007. Independent Economic Regulation: A Reassessment of its Role in Sustainable Development. *Utilities Policy*, 15(4), 261–269.

—— 2008. *Risk and the Regulatory State: A Better Regulation Perspective*. CRI Research Report No. 20. Bath: University of Bath, School of Management.

Bartle, I. and Wilks, S. 2002. Utility Regulation, Competition Policy and Regulatory Reform in Britain, in *Reforming Public and Corporate Governance: Management and the Market in Australia, Britain and Korea*, edited by A. Byong-Man, J. Halligan and S. Wilks. Cheltenham: Edward Elgar, 123–142.

Barzeley, M. 1992. *Breaking through Bureaucracy: A New Vision for Managing in Government*. Berkeley, CA: University of California Press.

—— 1997. Central Audit Institutions and Performance Auditing: A Comparative Analysis of Organizational Strategies in the OECD. *Governance*, 10(3), 235–260.

—— 2001. *The New Public Management*. Berkeley, CA: University of California Press.

Bately, R. 1999. The New Public Management in Developing Countries: Implications for Policy and Organizational Reform. *Journal of International Development*, 11(5), 761–765.

Bauer, M.W. 2005. Administrative Costs of Reforming Utilities, in *Refining Regulatory Regimes: Utilities in Europe*, edited by D. Coen and A. Héritier. Cheltenham: Edward Elgar, 53–88.

Bay, A.H. and Saglie, J. 2003. I verdens rikeste land. Pressens dekning av velferdsstaten 1969–1999. *NOVA Rapport*, 25/03. Oslo: Nova.

Beblavý, M. 2002. Understanding the Waves of Agencification and the Governance Problems They Have Raised in Central and Eastern Europe. *OECD Journal on Budgeting*, 2, 121–139.

Beck Jørgensen, T. 1993. Modes of Governance and Administrative Change, in *Modern Governance: New Government–Society Interactions*, edited by J. Kooiman. London: Sage, 219–232.

—— 1999. The Public Sector in an In-Between Time: Searching for New Public Values. *Public Administration*, 77(3), 565–584.

—— 2007. Public Values, Their Nature, Stability and Change: The Case of Denmark. *Public Administration Quarterly*, 30(4), 365–398.

Beck Jørgensen, T. and Bozeman, B. 2007. Public Values: An Inventory. *Administration and Society*, 39(3), 354–381.

Beck Jørgensen, T. and Hansen, A-M. 1995. Agencification and De-Agencification in Danish Central Government: Contradictory Developments, or is There an Underlying Logic? *International Review of Administrative Sciences*, 61(4), 549–563.

Beck Jørgensen, T., Hansen, H.F., Antonsen, M. and Melander, P. 1998. Public Organizations, Multiple Constituencies, and Governance. *Public Administration*, 76(3), 499–518.

Bendix, R. 1956. *Work and Authority in Industry*. New York: Wiley.

Bendor, J., Glazer A. and Hammond, T. 2001. Theories of Delegation. *Annual Review of Political Science*, 4(1), 235–269.

Benz, A. 2001. *Der moderne Staat*. München: Oldenbourg Verlag.

Berg, A.M. 2005. Creating Trust? A Critical Perspective on Trust-Enhancing Efforts in Public Services. *Public Performance and Management Review*, 28(4), 465–486.

Berg, O. 1997. Meta-Medicine: The Rise and Fall of the Doctor as Leader and Manager, in *The Shaping of a Profession: Physicians in Norway, Past and Present*, edited by Ø. Larsen. Canton: Science History Publications.

Berrevin, R. and Musselin, C. 1996. Les politiques de contractualisation entre centralisation et decentralisation: Les cas de l'équipement et de l'enseignement supérieur. *Sociologie du Travail*, 4(96), 575–596.

Bevan, G. and Hood, C. 2006. Have Targets Improved Performance in the English NHS? *British Medical Journal*, 332(7538), 419–422.

Bezes, P. 2002. Aux origines des politiques de réforme administrative sous la V-ème République: la construction du 'souci de soi de l'état'. *Revue Française d'Administration Publique*, 102(April–June), 307–325.

—— 2009. *Réinventer l'Etat. Les réformes de l'administration française (1962–2008)*. Paris: Presses Universitaires de France.

Bhatti, Y., Olsen, A.L. and Pedersen, L.H. 2009. The Effect of Professionals on Contracting Out. *Governance*, 22(1), 121–137.

Bilodeau, N., Laurin, C. and Vining, A. 2007. Choice of Organizational Form Makes a Real Difference: The Impact of Corporatization on Government Agencies in Canada. *Journal of Public Administration Research and Theory*, 17(1), 119–147.

Binderkrantz, A.S. and Christensen, J.G. 2009a. Delegation without Agency Loss? The Use of Performance Contracts in Danish Central Government. *Governance*, 22(2), 263–293.

—— 2009b. Governing Danish Agencies by Contract: From Negotiated Freedom to the Shadow of Hierarchy. *Journal of Public Policy*, 29(1), 55–78.

Björklund, A. (ed) 2005. *The Market Comes to Education in Sweden: an Evaluation of Sweden's Surprising School Reforms*. New York: Russell Sage Foundation.

Blais, A. and Dion, S. (eds) 1991. *The Budget Maximizing Bureaucrat: Appraisals and Evidence*. Pittsburgh, PA: University of Pittsburgh Press.

Blau, P. and Scott, W.R. 1963. *Formal Organizations: A Comparative Approach*. London: Routledge and Kegan Paul.

Bleiklie, I. 2009. Norway as Higher Education Policy Maker: From Tortoise to Eager Beaver?, in *University Governance: Western European Comparative Perspectives*, edited by C. Paradeise, E. Reale, I. Bleiklie and E. Ferlie. Dordrecht: Springer, 127–152.

Bleiklie, I., Høstaker, R. and Vabø, A. (eds) 2000. *Policy and Practice in Higher Education: Reforming Norwegian Universities*. London and Philadelphia, PA: Jessica Kingsley.

Bleiklie, I. and Michelsen, S. 2008. The University as Enterprise and Academic Co-determination, in *From Governance to Identity*, edited by A. Amaral, I. Bleiklie and C. Musselin. Dordrecht: Springer, 57–78.

Blom-Hansen, J. 2003. Is Private Delivery of Public Services Really Cheaper? Evidence from Public Road Maintenance in Denmark. *Public Choice*, 115(3–4), 419–438.

Blomqvist, P. 2004. The Choice Revolution: Privatization of Swedish Welfare Services in the 1990s. *Social Policy and Administration*, 38(2), 139–155.

Blöndal, J.R. 2005. *International Experience Using Outsourcing, Public-Private Partnerships and Vouchers*. Washington D.C.: IBM Centre for the Business of Government.

de Boer, H., Enders J. and Leišytė, L. 2007. Public Sector Reform in Dutch Higher Education: The Organizational Transformation of the University. *Public Administration*, 85(1), 27–46.

Bogdanor, V. (ed.) 2005. *Joined-Up Government*. Oxford: Oxford University Press.

Bogumil, J., Grohs, S., Kuhlmann, S. and Ohm, A.K. 2007. *10 Jahre neues Steuerungsmodell – eine Bilanz kommunaler Verwaltungsmodernisierung*. Berlin: Edition Sigma.

Boin, A. and Christensen, T. 2008. The Development of Public Institutions Reconsidering the Role of Leadership. *Administration and Society*, 40(3), 271–297.

Boix, C. and Posner, D.N. 1998. Social Capital: Explaining its Origins and Effects on Government Performance. *British Journal of Political Science*, 28(3), 686–693.

Bok, D. 1997. Why People Don't Trust Government, in *Measuring the Performance of Government*, edited by J.S. Nye, P.D. Zelikow and D.C. King. Cambridge, MA: Harvard University Press, 55–76.

—— 2001. *The Trouble with Government*. Cambridge, MA: Harvard University Press.

Böllhoff, D. 2005. Developments in Regulatory Regimes: Comparison of Telecommunications, Energy and Rail, in *Refining Regulatory Regimes: Utilities in Europe*, edited by D. Coen and A. Héritier. Cheltenham: Edward Elgar, 15–52.

Bonville, J-M. and Farvaque, N. 2007. A Capability Approach to Individualised and Tailor Made Activation, in *Making it Personal: Individualising Activation Services in the EU*, edited by R. van Berkel and B. Valkenburg. Bristol: Policy Press, 45–66.

Borins, S. 1988. Public Choice: 'Yes, Minister' Made it Popular, but does Winning the Nobel Prize Make it True? *Canadian Public Administration*, 31(1), 12–26.

—— 2002. New Public Management, North American Style, in *The New Public Management: Current Trends and Future Prospects*, edited by K. McLaughlin, S. Osborne and E. Ferlie. London: Routledge, 181–194.

Borins, S., Kernaghan, K. and Brown, D. 2007. *Digital State at the Leading Edge*. Toronto: University of Toronto Press.

Borum, F. 2004. Means-End-Frames and the Politics and Myths of Organizational Fields. *Organization Studies*, 25(6), 897–921.

Börzel, T. 1997. What's So Special about Policy Networks? An Exploration of the Concept and its Usefulness in Studying European Governance. *European Integration Online Papers* (EIoP), 1(16).

Boschken, H.L. 2000. Behavior of Urban Public Authorities Operating in Competitive Markets: Policy Outcomes in Mass Transit. *Administration and Society*, 31(6), 726–758.

Boston, J. 1994. Purchasing Policy Advice: The Limits to Contracting Out. *Governance*, 7(1), 1–30.

—— (ed.) 1995a. *The State under Contract*. Wellington: Bridget Williams Books.

—— 1995b. Lessons from the Antipodes, in *The Next Steps: Improving Management in Government*, edited by B. O'Toole and G. Jordan. Dartmouth: Aldershot, 161–177.

—— 1996a. Origins and Destinations: New Zealand's Model of Public Management and the International Transfer of Ideas, in *New Ideas, Better Government*, edited by P. Weller and G. Davis. St Leonards: Allen & Unwin, 107–131.

—— 1996b. The Ideas and Theories Underpinning the New Zealand Model, in *Public Management: The New Zealand Model*, edited by J. Boston, J. Martin, J. Pallot and P. Walsh. Auckland: Oxford University Press, 16–40.

—— 2001. The Challenge of Evaluating Systemic Change: The Case of Public Management Reform in New Zealand, in *Learning from International Public Management Reform*, edited by L. Jones, J. Guthrie and P. Steane. Oxford: Elsevier, 103–132.

Boston, J. and Eichbaum, C. 2007. State Sector Reform and Renewal in New Zealand: Lessons for Governance, in *The Repositioning of Public Governance:*

Global Experience and Challenges, edited by G.E. Caiden and T-T. Su. Taipei: Best-Wise Publishing, 127–179.

Boston, J., Martin, J., Pallot, J. and Walsh, P. (eds) 1991. *Reshaping the State: New Zealand's Bureaucratic Revolution*. Auckland: Oxford University Press.

—— 1996. *Public Management: The New Zealand Model*. Auckland: Oxford University Press.

Bouckaert, G. 1990. Public Productivity as a Classical Movement. *Public Productivity and Management Review*, 14(1), 33–34, 53–89.

—— 2007. Cultural Characteristics from Public Management Reforms Worldwide, in *Cultural Aspects of Public Management Reforms*, edited by K. Schedler and I. Proeller. Amsterdam: Elsevier, 29–64.

Bouckaert, G. and Halligan, J. 2008. *Managing Performance: International Comparisons*. London: Routledge.

Bouckaert, G., Peters, B.G and Verhoest, K. 2010. *The Coordination of Public Sector Organizations: Shifting Patterns of Public Management*. Basingstoke: Palgrave Macmillan.

Bouckaert, G. and Van de Walle, S. 2003. Comparing Measures of Citizen Trust and User Satisfaction as Indicators of 'Good Governance': Difficulties in Linking Trust and Satisfaction Indicators. *International Review of Administrative Sciences*, 69(3), 329–344.

Bourgon, J. 2007. Responsive, Responsible and Effective Government? Towards a New Public Administration Theory. *International Review of Administrative Science*, 73(1), 7–26.

—— 2008. The Future of Public Services: The Need for a New Balance. *Australian Journal of Public Administration*, 67(4), 390–404.

—— 2010. *The New Frontiers of Public Administration: The New Synthesis Project*. Ontario: Public Governance International, University of Waterloo.

Bovaird, T. 2004. Public Private Partnerships in Western Europe and the US: New Growths from Old Roots, in *Public Private Partnerships: Policy and Experience*, edited by A. Ghobadian, D. Gallear, N. O'Regan and H. Viney. London: Palgrave, 221–250.

—— 2007. Triggering Change through Culture Clash: The UK Civil Service Reform Program, 1999–2005, in *Cultural Aspects of Public Management Reforms*, edited by K. Schedler and I. Proeller. Amsterdam: Elsevier, 323–350.

—— 2010. A Brief Intellectual History of the Public–Private Partnership Movement, in *International Handbook on Public–Private Partnerships*, edited by G. Hodge, C. Greve and A. Boardman. Cheltenham: Edward Elgar, chapter 3.

Bovens, M.A.P. and Zouridis, S. 2002. From Street-Level to System-Level Bureaucracies. *Public Administration Review*, 62(2), 164–174.

Bowerman, M. and Humphrey, C. 2002. Limiting the Scope of Central Government Audit: A Constitutional Problem or a Sensible Solution?, in *Innovations in Governmental Accounting*, edited by V. Montesinos and J.M. Vela. Dordrecht: Kluwer Academic Publishers, 331–341.

Boyne, G.A. 1996. Scale, Performance and the New Public Management: An Empirical Analysis of Local Authority Services. *Journal of Management Studies*, 33(6), 809–826.

—— 2002a. Concepts and Indicators of Local Authority Performance: An Evaluation of the Statutory Frameworks in England and Wales. *Public Money and Management*, 22(1), 17–24.

—— 2002b. Public and Private Management: What's the Difference? *Journal of Management Studies*, 39(10), 98–122.

—— 2003. Sources of Public Service Improvement: A Critical Review and Research Agenda. *Journal of Public Administration Research and Theory*, 13(3), 367–394.

—— 2010. Strategic Planning and Public Service Performance, in *Public Service Improvement: Theories and Evidence*, edited by R. Ashworth, G.A. Boyne and T. Entwistle. Oxford: Oxford University Press, chapter 4.

Boyne, G.A., Farrell, C., Law, J., Powel, M. and Walker, R.M. 2003. *Evaluating Public Sector Reforms*. Buckingham: Open University Press.

Boyne, G.A., Gould-Williams, J.S., Law, J. and Walker, R.M. 2002. Best Value: Total Quality Management for Local Government? *Public Money and Management*, 22(3), 9–16.

Boyne, G.A, James, O., John, P. and Petrovsky, N. 2010. Does Public Service Performance Affect Top Management Turnover? *Journal of Public Administration Research and Theory*, 20(suppl 2), 261–279.

Boyne, G.A, James, O. and Petrovsky, N. 2010. *When Do New Chief Executives Make a Difference to Policies and Performance? A Theoretical Model of Insider/Outsider Distinctiveness in the Public Sector*. Paper to the Mid-West Political Science Association, Chicago, 8 April.

Bozeman, B. 2007. *Public Value and Public Interest: Counterbalancing Economic Individualism*. Washington D.C.: Georgetown University Press.

Bradley, S., Johnes, G. and Millington, J. 2001. The Effect of Competition on the Efficiency of Secondary Schools in England. *European Journal of Operational Research*, 135(3), 545–568.

Braithwaite, V. and Levi, M. (eds) 1998. *Trust and Governance*. New York: Russell Sage Foundation.

Brand, U. and Sekler, N. 2009. Postneoliberalism: Catch-all Word or Valuable Analytical and Political Concept? Aims of a Beginning Debate. *Development Dialogue*, 51(January), 5–15.

Brandsen, T. and Pestoff, V. 2006. Co-production, the Third Sector and the Delivery of Public Services. *Public Management Review*, 8(40), 493–502.

Brans, M., De Visscher, C. and Vancoppenolle, D. 2006. Administrative Reform in Belgium: Maintenance or Modernisation. *West European Politics*, 29(5), 979–998.

Bray, M. and Neilson, D. 1996. Industrial Relations Reform and the Relative Autonomy of the State, in *The Great Experiment: Labour Parties and Public Policy Transformation in Australia and New Zealand*, edited by F. Castles, R. Gerritsen and J. Vowles. Auckland: Auckland University Press, 68–87.

Bray, M. and Walsh, P. 1998. Different Paths to Neo-Liberalism? Comparing Australia and New Zealand. *Industrial Relations*, 37(3), 358–387.

Brehm, J. and Gates, S. 1997. *Working, Shirking, and Sabotage: Bureaucratic Response to a Democratic Public*. Ann Arbor, MI: University of Michigan Press.

Briggs, C. 1999. The Transition and Decline of the ACTU during the 1990s: From a 'Governing Institution' to a 'Servicing Organisation'. *New Zealand Journal of Industrial Relations*, 24(3), 257–289.

—— 2004. The End of a Cycle? The Australian Council of Trade Unions in a Historic Perspective, in *Peak Unions in Australia*, edited by B. Ellem, R. Markey and J. Shields. Sydney: Federation Press, 236–260.

Broadbent, J. 2010. Achieving Efficiency and Effectiveness in Challenging Times. *Public Money and Management*, 30(1), 3–4.

Broadbent, J. and Laughlin, R. 1997. Evaluating the 'New Public Management' Reforms in the UK: A Constitutional Possibility. *Public Administration*, 75(3), 487–507.

—— 2002. Public Service Professionals and the New Public Management in Context: Control of the Professionals in the New Public Services, in *New Public Management: Current Trends and Future Prospects*, edited by K. McLaughlin, S.P. Osborne and E. Ferlie. London: Routledge, 95–108.

—— 2003. Control and Legitimation in Government Accountability Processes: The Private Finance Initiative in the UK. *Critical Perspectives on Accounting*, 14(1–2), 23–48.

Brown, A.D. and Humphreys, M. 1995. International Cultural Differences in Public Sector Management. *International Journal of Public Sector Management*, 8(3), 5–23.

Brudney, J.L., Fernandez, S., Ryu, J.E. and Wright, D.S. 2005. Exploring and Explaining Contracting Out: Patterns Among the American States. *Journal of Public Administration Research and Theory*, 15(3), 393–419.

Brunsson, N. 1989. *The Organization of Hypocrisy: Talk, Decisions and Actions in Organizations*. Chichester: Wiley.

—— 2000. *The Irrational Organization*. 2nd edition. Bergen: Fagbokforlaget.

—— 2006. *Mechanisms of Hope: Maintaining the Dream of the Rational Organization*. Malmö: Copenhagen Business School Press.

—— 2007. *The Consequences of Decision-Making*. Oxford: Oxford University Press.

—— 2009. *Reform as Routine: Organizational Change and Stability in the Modern World*. Oxford: Oxford University Press.

Brunsson, N. and Jacobsson, B. (eds) 2000. *A World of Standards*. Oxford: Oxford University Press.

Brunsson, N. and Olsen, J.P. 1993. *The Reforming Organization*. London: Routledge.

Brunsson, N. and Sahlin-Andersson, K. 2000. Constructing Organizations: The Example of Public Management Reform. *Organization Studies*, 21(4), 721–746.

Bryson, J. and Smith-Ring, P. 1990. A Transaction-based Approach to Policy Intervention. *Policy Studies*, 23(3), 205–229.

Buchanan, J. 1978. From Private Preferences to Public Philosophy: The Development of Public Choice, in *The Economics of Politics*, edited by J. Buchanan. London: Institute of Economic Affairs, 1–20.

—— 1987. The Constitution of Economic Policy. *American Economic Review*, 77(3), 242–250.

Buchanan, J. and Tullock, G. 1962. *The Calculus of Consent: Logical Foundations of Constitutional Democracy*. Ann Arbor, MI: University of Michigan Press.

Budge, I. 1996. *The New Challenge of Direct Democracy*. Cambridge: Polity Press.

Bukovansky, M. 2006. The Hollowness of Anti-corruption Discourse. *Review of International Political Economy*, 13(2), 181–209.

Burnham, J. and Pyper, R. 2008. *Britain's Modernised Civil Service*. Basingstoke: Palgrave Macmillan.

Burrage, M. and Torstendahl, R. 1990. *The Formation of Professions: Knowledge, State and Strategy*. London: Sage.

Butler, R. 1994. Reinventing British Government. *Public Administration*, 72(2), 263–270.

Byrkjeflot, H. 2005. The Making of a Health Care State? Recent Hospital Reforms in Norway. *Rokkan Rapport* 15. Bergen: Rokkansenteret.

Byrkjeflot, H. and Grønlie, T. 2005. Det regionale helseforetaket – mellom velferdslokalisme og sentralstatlig styring?, in *Helse-Norge i støpeskjeen – søkelys på sykehusreformen*, edited by S. Opedal and I. Stigen. Bergen: Fagbokforlaget, chapter 11.

Byrkjeflot, H. and Neby, S. 2008. The End of the Decentralised Model of Healthcare Governance? Comparing Developments in the Scandinavian Hospital Sectors. *Journal for Health Organization and Management*, 22(4), 331–349.

Cabinet Office 2003. *Better Policy-making: A Guide to Regulatory Impact Assessment*. London: Cabinet Office.

—— 2006a. *UK Government's Approach to Public Service Reform: A Discussion Paper*. London: Cabinet Office.

—— 2006b. *Public Bodies: A Guide for Departments*. London: Cabinet Office, Agencies and Public Bodies Team.

Campbell, C. and Halligan, J. 1992. *Political Leadership in an Age of Constraint: Bureaucratic Politics under Hawke and Keating*. St Leonards: Allen & Unwin.

—— 1993. *Political Leadership in an Age of Constraint: The Experience of Australia*. Pittsburgh, PA: University of Pittsburgh Press.

Campbell, C. and Szablowski, G. 1979. *The Super-Bureaucrats*. Toronto: Macmillan.

Campbell, C. and Wilson, G. 1995. *The End of Whitehall: The Death of a Paradigm?* Oxford: Basil Blackwell.

Capano, G. 2003. Administrative Traditions: Italian Administrative Reforms during the 1990s. *Public Administration*, 81(4), 781–801.

Caplan, B. 2007. *The Myth of the Rational Voter: Why Democracies Choose Bad Policies*. Princeton, NJ: Princeton University Press.

Cassese, S. 1995. Les succès et les échecs de la modernisation de l'administration Italienne. L'expérience du gouvernement Ciampi. *Revue Française d'Administration Publique*, 75(July–September), 377–386.

—— 1999. Italy's Senior Civil Service: An Ossified World, in *Bureaucratic Elites in Western Europe*, edited by E.C. Page and V. Wright. Oxford: Oxford University Press, 55–64.

—— 2002. Le nouveau régime de la haute fonction publique en Italie: une modification constitutionnelle. *Revue Française d'Administration Publique*, 104(4), 677–688.

Cawson, A. 1986. *Corporatism and Political Theory*. Oxford: Blackwell.

Centrelink 1999. *Submission to the Welfare Reform Review*. Commonwealth of Australia, December 1999. Canberra: Centrelink.

—— 2006. *Centrelink Annual Report 2005–2006*. Centrelink Communication Division, Canberra Business Centre, August 2006. Canberra: Centrelink. Available at: http://www.centrelink.gov.au/internet/internet.nsf/publications/ar0506.htm [accessed: 04/06/2010].

Chancellor of the Exchequer 1998. *Modern Public Services for Britain: Investing in Reform*. Cm 4011. London: The Stationary Office.

Chandler, J. 1991. Public Administration: A Discipline in Decline. *Teaching Public Administration*, 6(2), 39–45.

Chandler, T. and Feuille, P. 1991. Municipal Unions and Privatization. *Public Administration Review*, 51(1), 92–103.

Chapman, J. and Duncan, G. 2007. Is There Now a 'New Zealand Model'? *Public Management Review*, 9(1), 1–25.

Charles, M.B., de Jong, W.M. and Ryan, N. 2010. Public Values in Western Europe: A Temporal Perspective. *American Review of Public Administration*, forthcoming.

Cheung, A.B.L. 1997. Understanding Public Sector Reforms: Global Trends and Diverse Agendas. *International Review of Administrative Sciences*, 63(4), 435–457.

—— 2002. Public Enterprises and Privatization in East Asia: Paths, Politics and Prospects. *Public Finance and Management*, 2(1), 67–96.

—— 2003. Government Reinvention in Taiwan: Administrative Modernization and Regime Transition, in *Governance and Public Sector Reform in Asia: Paradigm Shifts or Business As Usual?*, edited by A.B.L. Cheung and I. Scott. London: Curzon Press, 90–116.

—— 2005. The Politics of Administrative Reforms in Asia: Paradigms and Legacies, Paths and Diversities. *Governance*, 18(2), 257–282.

—— 2009. Public Management Reform in Hong Kong, in *International Handbook of Public Management Reform*, edited by S.F. Goldfinch and J.L. Wallis. Cheltenham and Northampton, MA: Edward Elgar, 317–335.

Cheung, A.B.L. and Scott, I. 2003. Governance and Public Sector Reforms in Asia: Paradigms, Paradoxes and Dilemmas, in *Governance and Public Sector Reform in Asia: Paradigm Shifts or Business As Usual?*, edited by A.B.L. Cheung and I. Scott. London: Curzon Press, 1–24.

Chevallier, J. 2004. La Réforme de l'Etat, in *Administration Francaise*. Paris: ENA.

Chevallier, J. and Rouban, L. 2003. *La réforme de l'Etat et la nouvelle gestion publique: mythes et réalités*. Paris: École Nationale d'Administration (ENA).

Chi, K.S., Arnold, K.A. and Perkins, H.M. 2003. Trends in the State Government Management: Budget Reduction, Restructuring, Privatization, and Performance Budgeting, in *Book of the States*. Lexington, KY: Councils of State Governments, 419–443.

Cho, Y.H. and Kim, S. 2000. Administrative and Regulatory Reform of Korea in a Time of National Crisis. *International Journal of Public Administration*, 23(11), 1997–2016.

Christensen, J.G. 2009. Danish Public Management Reform Before and After NPM, in *International Handbook of Public Management Reform*, edited by S.F. Goldfinch and J.L. Wallis. Cheltenham: Edward Elgar, 279–299.

Christensen, J.G., Mouritsen, P.E. and Nørgaard, A.S. (eds) 2009. *De store kommissioner: Vise mænd, smagsdommere eller nyttige idioter?* Odense: Syddansk Universitetsforlag.

Christensen, J.G. and Pallesen, T. 2001a. The Political Benefits of Corporatization and Privatization. *Journal of Public Policy*, 21(3), 283–309.

—— 2001b. Institutions, Distributional Concerns, and Public Sector Reform. *European Journal of Political Research*, 39(2), 179–202.

Christensen, T., Fimreite, A.L. and Lægreid P. 2007. Reform of the Employment and Welfare Administrations: The Challenges of Co-coordinating Diverse Public Organizations. *International Review of Administrative Sciences*, 73(3), 389–409.

Christensen, T. and Lægreid, P. 1999. New Public Management: Design, Resistance, or Transformation? A Study of How Modern Reforms are Received in a Civil Service System. *Public Productivity and Management Review*, 23(2), 169–193.

—— 2001a. *New Public Management: The Transformation of Ideas and Practice.* Aldershot: Ashgate.

—— 2001b. A Transformative Perspective on Administrative Reforms, in *New Public Management: The Transformation of Ideas and Practice*, edited by T. Christensen and P. Lægreid. Aldershot: Ashgate, 13–39.

—— 2001c. New Public Management: Undermining Political Control?, in *New Public Management: The Transformation of Ideas and Practice*, edited by T. Christensen and P. Lægreid. Aldershot: Ashgate, 93–119.

—— 2002. New Public Management: Puzzles of Democracy and the Influence of Citizens. *Journal of Political Philosophy*, 10(3), 267–295.

—— 2005a. *Regulatory Reforms and Agencification.* Paper to the Third ECPR General Conference: Section on Regulation in the Age of Governance, Budapest, 8–10 September.

—— 2005b. Trust in Government: The Relative Importance of Service Satisfaction, Political Factors and Demography. *Public Performance and Management Review*, 28(4), 487–511.

—— (eds) 2006. *Autonomy and Regulation: Coping with Agencies in the Modern State.* Cheltenham: Edward Elgar.

—— (eds) 2007a. *Transcending New Public Management: The Transformation of Public Sector Reforms.* Aldershot: Ashgate.

—— 2007b. The Whole-of-Government Approach to Public Sector Reform. *Public Administration Review*, 67(6), 1059–1066.

—— 2008. NPM and Beyond: Structure, Culture and Demography. *International Review of Administrative Sciences*, 74(1), 7–24.

—— 2009. Public Management Reform in Norway: Reluctance and Tensions, in *International Handbook of Public Management Reform*, edited by S.F. Goldfinch and J.L. Wallis. Cheltenham: Edward Elgar, 300–316.

—— 2010. Increasing Complexity in Public Organizations: The Challenge of Combining NPM and Post-NPM, in *Governance of Public Sector Organizations: Proliferation, Autonomy and Performance*, edited by P. Lægreid and K. Verhoest. London: Palgrave Macmillan, 255–275.

Christensen, T., Lægreid, P., Roness, P. and Røvik, K.A. 2007. *Organization Theory and the Public Sector: Instrument, Culture and Myth*. London and New York: Routledge.

Christensen, T., Lie, A. and Lægreid, P. 2007. Still Fragmented Government or Reassertion of the Centre?, in *Transcending New Public Management: The Transformation of Public Sector Reforms*, edited by T. Christensen and P. Lægreid. Aldershot: Ashgate, 17–42.

—— 2008. Beyond New Public Management: Agencification and Regulatory Reform in Norway. *Financial Accountability and Management*, 24(1), 15–30.

Christensen, T., Lisheng, D. and Painter, M. 2008. Administrative Reform in China's Central Government: How Much 'Learning from the West'? *International Review of Administrative Sciences*, 74(3), 351–371.

Christensen, T. and Røvik, K.A. 1999. The Ambiguity of Appropriateness, in *Organizing Political Institutions*, edited by M. Egeberg and P. Lægreid. Oslo: Scandinavian University Press, 159–180.

Christiansen, P.M. 1998. A Prescription Rejected: Market Solutions to Problems of Public Sector Governance. *Governance*, 11(3), 273–295.

Clark, I.D. and Swain, H. 2005. Distinguishing the Real from the Surreal in Management Reform: Suggestions for Beleaguered Administrators in the Government of Canada. *Canadian Public Administration*, 48(4), 453–477.

Clarke, J. 2007. Unsettled Connections: Citizens, Consumers and the Reform of Public Services. *Journal of Consumer Culture*, 7(2), 159–178.

—— 2010. Citizen-Consumers: Hyphenation, Identification, Depoliticization?, in *The Voice of the Citizen Consumer: A History of Market Research, Consumer Movements, and the Political Public Sphere*, edited by K. Brückweh. Oxford: Oxford University Press, forthcoming.

Clarke, J., Gewirtz, S. and McLaughlin, E. (eds) 2000. *New Managerialism New Welfare?* London: Sage.

Clarke, J. and Newman, J. 1997. *The Managerial State: Power, Politics and Ideology in the Remaking of Social Welfare*. London: Sage.

—— 2007. What's in a Name? New Labour's Citizen-Consumers and the Remaking of Public Services. *Cultural Studies*, 21(6), 738–757.

Clarke, J., Newman, J., Smith, N., Vidler, E. and Westmarland, L. 2007. *Creating Citizen-Consumers: Changing Publics and Changing Public Services*. London: Sage.

Clinton, B. and Gore, A. 1997. *The Blair House Papers*. Darby, PA: Diane Publishing.

Coen, D. and Richardson, J. (eds) 2009. *Lobbying the European Union: Institutions, Actors, and Issues*. Oxford: Oxford University Press.

Commission of the European Communities 2001. *European Governance. A White Paper*. COM (2001) 428 final. Brussels, 25 July.

Common, R. 2001. *Public Management and Policy Transfer in Southeast Asia*. Aldershot: Ashgate.

Considine, M. and Lewis, J. 2003. Bureaucracy, Network or Enterprise? Comparing Models of Governance in Australia, Britain, the Netherlands and New Zealand. *Public Administration Review*, 63(2), 131–140.

Considine, M. and Painter, M. (eds) 1997. *Managerialism: The Great Debate*. Carlton South: Melbourne University Press.

Conway, P. and Nicoletti, G. 2006. *Product Market Regulation in Non-manufacturing Sectors in OECD Countries: Measurement and Highlights*. OECD Economics Department: Working Paper No. 530. Paris: OECD.

Cornforth, C. (ed.) 2003. *The Governance of Public and Non-profit Organisations: What Do Boards Do?* London: Routledge.

Cornwall, A. and Coelho, V. (eds) 2007. *Spaces for Change: The Politics of Citizen Participation in New Democratic Spaces*. London: Zed Books.

Cowell, R., Downe, J., Leach, S. and Bovaird, T. 2005. *Meta-evaluation of the Local Government Modernisation Agenda: Progress Report on Public Confidence in Local Government*. London: ODPM.

Cribb, J. 2006. Agents or Stewards? Contracting with Voluntary Organizations. *Policy Quarterly*, 2(2), 11–17.

CRIPO 2006. *Comparative Research into Current Trends in Public Sector Organization*. [Online] Available at: www.soc.kuleuven.be/io/cost [accessed: 31/05/2010].

Curristine, T. 2005. Performance Information in the Budget Process: Results of the OECD 2005 Questionnaire. *OECD Journal on Budgeting*, 5(2), 87–131.

Cyert, R.M. and March, J.G. 1963. *A Behavioral Theory of the Firm*. Englewood Cliffs, NJ: Prentice-Hall.

Czarniawska, B. 2010. Going Back to Go Forward: On Studying Organizing in Action Nets, in *Process, Sensemaking and Organizing*, edited by T. Hernes and S. Maitlis. Oxford: Oxford University Press, chapter 8.

Dahl, R.A. and Lindblom, C.E. 1953. *Politics, Economics, and Welfare*. New York: Harper & Row.

Danielsen, Å., Hagen, T.P. and Sørensen, R.J. 2004. Den norske sykehusreformen. Hva som er galt, og hvordan den kan forbedres? *Økonomisk forum*, 8, 36–42.

Dastmalchian, A.H., Lee, S. and Ng, I. 2000. The Interplay between Organizational and National Cultures: A Comparison of Organizational Practices in Canada and South Korea using the Competing Values Framework. *International Journal of Human Resource Management*, 11(2), 388–412.

Davies, J.S. 2009. The Limits of Joined-up Government: Towards a Political Analysis. *Public Administration*, 87(1), 80–96.

Davis, P. and West, K. 2009. What do Public Values Mean for Public Action? Putting Public Values in their Plural Place. *The American Review of Public Administration*, 39(6), 602–618.

Dawson, S. and Dargie, C. 1999. New Public Management: An Assessment and Evaluation with Special Reference to Health. *Public Management Review*, 1(4), 459–482.

Day, P. and Klein, R. 1987. *Accountabilities*. London: Tavistock.

De Bruijn, H. and Dicke, W. 2006. Strategies for Safeguarding Public Values in Liberalized Utility Sectors. *Public Administration*, 84(3), 717–736.

De Bruijne, M., Dicke, W. and Veeneman, W. 2009. Editorial. *International Journal of Public Policy*, 4(5), 367–368.

Deem, R., Hillyard, S. and Reed, M. 2007. *Knowledge, Higher Education, and the New Managerialism: The Changing Management of UK Universities*. Oxford: Oxford University Press.

De Jong, M. and Mamadouh, V. 2002. Two Contrasting Perspectives on Institutional Transplantation, in *The Theory and Practice of Institutional Transplantation: Experiences with the Transfer of Policy Institutions*, edited by M. De Jong, K. Lalenis and V. Mamadouh. Dordrecht: Kluwer Academic Publishers, 19–32.

Dell'Aringa, C., Della Rocca, G. and Keller, B. (eds) 2001. *Strategic Choices in Reforming Public Service Employment: An International Handbook*. Basingstoke: Palgrave.

Deloitte 2006. *Closing the Infrastructure Gap: The Role of Public-Private Partnerships*. Washington D.C.: Deloitte.

Deming, W.E. 1994. *The New Economics for Industry, Government, Education*. Cambridge, MA: MIT, Centre for Advanced Educational Services.

Dent, M. 2003. *Remodelling Hospitals and Health Professions in Europe*. New York: Palgrave Macmillan.

Denters, D. and Rose, L. 2005. *Comparing Local Governance*. Basingstoke: Palgrave.

Dewar, D. 1997. The Audit of Central Government, in *Current Issues in Auditing*, edited by M. Sherer and S. Tyrley. London: Paul Chapman Publishing, 320–335.

Dezalay, Y. and Garth, B.G. 2002. *The Internationalization of Palace Wars: Lawyers, Economists, and the Contest to Transform Latin American States*. Chicago, IL: University of Chicago Press.

Diamond, L. 2008. The Democratic Rollback: The Resurgence of the Predatory State. *Foreign Affairs*, 87(March–April), 36–48.

Dicke, L. and Ott, J. 2002. A Test: Can Stewardship Theory Serve as a Second Conceptual Foundation for Accountability Methods in Contracted Human Services? *International Journal of Public Administration*, 25(4), 463–487.

Dieffenbach, T. 2009. New Public Management in Public Sector Organisations: The Dark Sides of Managerialist 'Enlightenment'. *Public Administration*, 87(4), 892–909.

DiMaggio, P.J. and Powell, W.W. 1991. The Iron Cage Revisited: Institutional Isomorphism and Collective Rationality in Organizational Fields. *American Sociological Review*, 48(2), 147–160.

Dolmans, L.J.F. 1989. Naar supervisie en meer aandacht voor de doelmatigheid. De Algemene Rekenkamer tussen 1945 en 1988, in *Van Camere vander Rekennghen tot Algemene Rekenkamer. Zes eeuwen Rekenkamer. Gedenkboek bij het 175-jarig bestaan van de Algemene Rekenkamer*, edited by P.J. Margry, E.C. Van Heukelom and A.J.M. Linders. Den Haag: SDU's Gravenhage, 377–430.

Domberger, S. and Jensen, P. 1997. Contracting Out by the Public Sector: Theory, Evidence, Prospects. *Oxford Review of Economic Policy*, 13(4), 67–78.

Donaldson, L. 1995. *American Anti-Management Theories of Organisation: A Critique of Paradigm Proliferation*. New York: Cambridge University Press.

Downs, G. and Larkey, P. 1986. *The Search for Government Efficiency: From Hubris to Helplessness*. Philadelphia, PA: Temple University Press.

Drori, G.S. and Meyer, J.W. 2006a. Global Scientization: An Environment for Expanded Organization, in *Globalization and Organization: World Society and Organizational Change*, edited by G.S. Drori, J.W. Meyer and H. Hwang. Oxford: Oxford University Press, 50–68.

Drori, G.S. and Meyer, J.W. 2006b. Scientization: Making a World Safe for Organizing, in *Transnational Governance: Institutional Dynamics of Regulation*, edited by M.L. Djelic and K. Sahlin-Andersson. Cambridge: Cambridge University Press, 31–52.

Drori, G.S., Meyer, J.W. and Hwang, H. (eds) 2006. *Globalization and Organization: World Society and Organizational Change*. Oxford: Oxford University Press.

Drucker, P. 1976. The Coming Rediscovery of Scientific Management. Reprinted in *F.W. Taylor: Critical Evaluations in Business and Management*, edited by J. Wood and M. Wood. 2002. New York: Routledge, 351–358.

Dryzek, J.S. 2002. *Beyond Deliberative Democracy: Liberals, Critics, Constellations*. Oxford: Oxford University Press.

Dubnick, M. 2005. Accountability and the Promise of Performance: In Search of Mechanisms. *Public Performance and Management Review*, 28(3), 376–417.

Du Gay, P. 2000. *In Praise of Bureaucracy*. London: Sage.

—— 2005. *The Values of Bureaucracy*. Oxford: Oxford University Press.

Dunleavy, P. 1985. Bureaucrats, Budgets and the Growth of the State. *British Journal of Political Science*, 15(3), 299–328.

—— 1991. *Democracy, Bureaucracy and Public Choice: Economic Explanations in Political Science*. London: Harvester Wheatsheaf.

Dunleavy, P. and Hood, C. 1994. From Old Public Administration to New Public Management. *Public Money and Management*, 14(3), 9–16.

Dunleavy, P., Margetts, H., Bastow, S. and Tinkler, J. 2005. New Public Management is Dead: Long Live Digital-Era Governance. *Journal of Public Administration Research and Theory*, 16(3), 467–494.

Dunn, W.N. and Miller, D.Y. 2007. A Critique of the New Public Management and the Neo-Weberian State: Advancing a Critical Theory of Administrative Reform. *Public Organization Review*, 7(4), 345–358.

Dunsire, A. 1986. A Cybernetic View of Guidance, Control and Evaluation in the Public Sector, in *Guidance, Control and Evaluation in the Public Sector*, edited by F.X. Kaufman, G. Majone and V. Ostrom. Berlin and New York: Walter de Gruyter, 327–346.

Duyvendak, J.W, Knijn, T and Kremer, M. (eds) 2006. *People, Policy and the New Professionals*. Amsterdam: Amsterdam University Press.

Dwivedi, O.P. and Halligan, J. 2003. The Canadian Public Service: Balancing Values and Management, in *Civil Service Systems in Anglo-American Countries*, edited by J. Halligan. Cheltenham and Northampton, MA: Edward Elgar, 148–173.

Easton, B. and Gerritsen, R. 1996. Economic Reform: Parallels and Divergences, in *The Great Experiment: Labour Parties and Public Policy Transformation in Australia and New Zealand*, edited by F. Castles, R. Gerritsen and J. Vowles. Auckland: Auckland University Press, 68–87.

Ebbinghaus, B. and Visser, J. (eds) 2000. *Trade Unions in Western Europe since 1945*. Basingstoke: Palgrave Macmillan.

Egeberg, M. 2003. How Bureaucratic Structure Matters: An Organizational Perspective, in *Handbook of Public Administration*, edited by B.G. Peters and J. Pierre. London: Sage, 116–126.

Egeberg, M. and Trondal, J. 2009. National Agencies in the European Administrative Space: Government Driven, Commission Driven or Networked? *Public Administration*, 87(4), 779–790.

Eichbaum, C. and Shaw, R. 2010. New Zealand, in *Partisan Appointees and Public Servants*, edited by C. Eichbaum and R. Shaw. Cheltenham: Edward Elgar, 114–150.

Eisenhardt, K. 1989. Agency Theory: An Assessment and Review. *The Academy of Management Review*, 40(1), 57–74.

Eisenstadt, S.N. and Lemarchand, R. 1981. *Political Clientelism, Patronage and Development*. London: Sage.

Eklund, N. 2008. Administrative Reform in Sweden: Administrative Dualism at the Corssroad, in *Handbook of Administrative Reform: An International Perspective*, edited by J. Killian and N. Eklund. Boca Raton, FL: Taylor and Francis, 115–136.

Ekonomistyrningsverket 2007. *Resultat och styrning i statsförvaltningen*. ESV rapport 2007: 23. Stockholm: Ekonomistyringsverket.

Eliassen, K.A. and Sitter, N. 2008. *Understanding Public Management*. London: Sage.

English, L. 2003. Emasculating Public Accountability in the Name of Competition: Transformation of State Audit in Victoria. *Critical Perspectives on Accounting*, 14(1–2), 51–76.

—— 2007. Performance Audit of Australian Public Private Partnerships: Legitimizing Government Policies or Providing Independent Oversight? *Financial Accountability and Management*, 23(3), 313–336.

Entwistle, T. and Martin, S. 2005. From Competition to Collaboration in Public Services Delivery: A New Agenda for Research. *Public Administration*, 83(1), 233–242.

Erichsen, V. 1995. State Traditions and Medical Professionalization in Scandinavia, in *Health Professions and the State in Europe*, edited by T. Johnson, G. Larkin and M. Saks. London: Routledge, 187–199.

Etzioni, A. 1975. *A Comparative Analysis of Complex Organizations: On Power, Involvement, and their Correlates*. Revised and illustrated edition. New York: The Free Press.

Etzioni-Halevey, E. 1983. *Bureaucracy and Democracy: A Political Dilemma*. London: Routledge and Kegan Paul.

Eureval 2008. *Meta-study on Decentralised Agencies: Cross-cutting Analysis of Evaluation Findings*. Evaluation for the European Commission, Final Report, September 2008. Brussels: EU Commission.

European Court of Auditors 2008. *Report on Preliminary Analysis of Feedback from the External Survey (SAI's) on Performance Indicators*. Luxembourg: European Court of Auditors.

Eurydice 2000. *Two Decades of Reform in Higher Education in Europe: 1980 Onwards*. Eurydice Studies, Education and Culture. Brussels: European Commission.

—— 2008. *Higher Education Governance in Europe: Policies, Structures, Funding and Academic Staff*. Eurydice Studies, Education and Culture. Brussels: European Commission.

Evans, P.B. and Rauch, J.E. 2000. Bureaucratic Structure and Bureaucratic Performance in Less Developed Countries. *Journal of Public Economics*, 75(1), 49–71.

Evers, A. 2008. Hybrid Organisations: Background, Concepts, Challenges, in *The Third Sector in Europe*, edited by S. Osborne. London: Routledge, 279–292.

Fairbrother, P. and Griffin, G. (eds) 2002. *Changing Prospects for Trade Unionism: Comparisons between Six Countries*. London: Continuum.

Fairbrother, P. and Yates, C.A.B. (eds) 2003. *Trade Unions in Renewal: A Comparative Study*. London: Continuum.

Falaschetti, D. and Miller, G. 2001. Constraining the Leviathan: Moral Hazard and Credible Commitment in Constitutional Design. *Journal of Theoretical Politics*, 13(4), 389–411.

Farnham, D., Hondeghem, A. and Horton, S. (eds) 2005. *Staff Participation and Public Management Reform: Some International Comparisons*. Basingstoke: Palgrave Macmillan.

Farnham, D. and Horton, S. 1996. *Managing the New Public Services*. Basingstoke: Macmillan.

Farrell, M.J. 1957. The Measurement of Productive Efficiency. *Journal of the Royal Statistical Society*, 120(3), 253–290.

Feigenbaum, H.B. and Henig, J.R. 1994. The Political Underpinnings of Privatization: A Typology. *World Politics*, 46(January), 185–208.

Feigenbaum, H., Henig, J.R. and Hamnett, C. 1998. *Shirking the State: The Political Underpinnings of Privatization*. Cambridge: Cambridge University Press.

Ferarri, A. 2006. The Internal Market and Hospital Efficiency: A Stochastic Distance Function Approach. *Applied Economics*, 38(18), 2121–2130.

Ferlie, E., Ashburner, L., Fitzgerald, L. and Pettigrew A. 1996. *The New Public Management in Action*. Oxford: Oxford University Press.

Ferlie, E., Musselin, C. and Andresani, G. 2008. The Steering of Higher Education Systems: A Public Management Perspective, *Higher Education*, 56(3), 325–348.

Ferris, J. 1986. The Decision to Contract Out: An Empirical Analysis. *Urban Affairs Quarterly*, 22(2), 289–311.

Ferris, J. and Grady, E. 1986. Contracting Out: For What? With Whom? *Public Administration Review*, 46(4), 332–344.

Fimreite, A.L. and Lægreid, P. 2009. Reorganizing the Welfare State Administration. *Public Management Review*, 11(3), 281–297.

Fjeldstad, O.H. and Isaksen, J. 2008. *Anti-Corruption Reforms: Challenges, Effects and Limits of World Bank Support*. IEG Working Paper No. 7. Washington D.C.: World Bank.

Flesher, D.L. and Zarzeski, M.T. 2002. The Roots of Operational (Value for Money) Auditing in English Speaking Countries. *Accounting and Business Research*, 32(2), 93–104.

Flinders, M. 2005. The Politics of Public-Private Partnerships. *British Journal of Political and International Relations*, 7(2), 215–239.

—— 2008. *Delegated Governance and the British State: Walking without Order*. Oxford: Oxford University Press.

Flinders, M. and Buller, J. 2006. Depoliticization, Democracy and Arena Shifting, in *Autonomy and Regulation: Coping with Agencies in the Modern State*, edited by T. Christensen and P. Lægreid. Cheltenham: Edward Elgar, 81–109.

Flinders, M. and Smith, M.J. (eds) 1999. *Quangos, Accountability and Reform: The Politics of Quasi-government*. London: Macmillan.

Forssell, A. and Jansson, D. 1996. The Logic of Organizational Transformation: On the Conversion of Non-business Organizations, in *Translating Organizational Change*, edited by B. Czarniawska and G. Sevón. Berlin: Walter de Gruyter, 93–116.

Foster, C. 1992. *Privatisation, Public Ownership and the Regulation of Natural Monopoly*. Oxford: Blackwell.

Fountain, J.E. 2001. Paradoxes of Public Sector Customer Service. *Governance*, 14(1), 55–74.

Fox, D.M. 1986. *Health Policies, Health Politics: The Experience of Britain and America, 1911–1965*. Princeton, NJ: Princeton University Press.

Frank, T. 2009. Struktur, magt og legitimitet: En analyse af hvorfor og hvordan Kodeks for God Offentlig Topledelse anvendes af danske og hollandske topembedsmænd. Ph.D. thesis, September 2009. Aarhus: University of Aarhus, Department of Political Science.

Frederickson, H.G. 1997. *The Spirit of Public Administration*. San Francisco, CA: Jossey–Bass Publishers.

—— 1999. The Repositioning of American Public Administration. *Political Science and Politics*, 32(4), 701–711.

Frederickson, H.G. and Smith, K. 2003 *The Public Administration Primer*. Boulder, CO: Westview Press.

Freeman, R. 2000. *The Politics of Health in Europe*. Manchester: Manchester University Press.

Freeman, R. and Moran, M. 2000. Reforming Health Care in Europe. *West European Politics* (special issue on Recasting European Welfare States), 23(2), 35–58.

Freidson, E. 1970. *Professional Dominance: The Social Structure of Medical Care*. Chicago, IL: Aldine.

—— 1984. The Changing Nature of Professional Control. *Annual Review of Sociology*, 10, 1–20.

Frey, B. and Jegen, R. 2001. Motivation Crowding Theory. *Journal of Economic Surveys*, 15(5), 589–611.

Frey, B. and Osterloh, M. 2006. *Evaluations: Hidden Costs, Questionable Benefits, and Superior Alternatives*. Working Paper No. 302. Zurich: University of Zurich, Institute for Empirical Research in Economics.

Friedman, M. 1981. *Free To Choose*. Harmondsworth: Penguin Books.

Fumasoli, T. 2008. *Governance in Swiss Universities: A Comparative Analysis through Cantonal and Federal Laws*. Paper to the 5th EUREDOCS Conference: Modernising European Higher Education: Priorities, Ideas and Challenges, Porto, 23–25 May.

Fumasoli, T. and Lepori, B. 2010. Patterns of Strategies in Swiss Higher Education Institutions. *Higher Education*. [Online]. Published 8 April 2010, DOI 10.1007/s10734-010-9330-x. Available at: http://www.springerlink.com/content/15235q226217g281/ [accessed: 02/08/2010].

Funnel, W. 1997. The Curse of Sisyphus: Public Sector Audit Independence in an Age of Economic Rationalism. *Australian Journal of Public Administration*, 56(4), 87–105.

—— 2003. Enduring Fundamentals: Constitutional Accountability and Auditors-General in the Reluctant State. *Critical Perspectives on Accounting*, 14(1–2), 107–132.

Gailmard, S. 2010. Politics, Principal-Agent Problems, and Public Service Motivation. *International Public Management Journal*, 13(1), 35–45.

Gailmard, S. and Patty, J.W. 2007. Slackers and Zealots: Civil Service, Policy Discretion and Bureaucratic Expertise. *American Journal of Political Science*, 51(4), 873–889.

Gains, F. 2004. Adapting the Agency Concept: Variations within Next Steps, in *Unbundled Government: A Critical Analysis of the Global Trend to Agencies, Quangos and Contractualisation*, edited by C. Pollitt and C. Talbot. London and New York: Routledge, 53–74.

Gardner, M. and Palmer, G. 1997. *Employment Relations: Industrial Relations and Human Resource Management in Australia*. 2nd edition. Melbourne: Macmillan.

Gendron, Y., Cooper, D.J and Townley, B. 2001. In the Name of Accountability: State Auditing, Independence and New Public Management. *Accounting, Auditing and Accountability Journal*, 14(3), 278–310.

—— 2007. The Construction of Auditing Expertise in Measuring Government Performance. *Accounting, Organizations and Society*, 32(1–2), 101–129.

Gérard, R. 2008. Private and Public Ownership in Economic Theory, in *Privatization: Successes and Failures*, edited by R. Gérard. New York and Chichester: Columbia University Press.

Gerdtham, U-G., Lothgren, M., Tambour, M. and Rehnberg, C. 1999. Internal Markets and Health Care Efficiency: A Multiple Output Stochastic Frontier Analysis. *Health Economics*, 8(1), 151–164.

Gerring, J. and Thacker, S.C. 2005. Do Neoliberal Policies Deter Political Corruption? *International Organization*, 59(1), 233–254.

Ghobadian, A., Gallear, D., O'Regan, N. and Viney, H. (eds) 2004. *Public–Private Partnerships: Policy and Experience*. London: Palgrave Macmillan.

Gill, D. 2008. By Accident or Design: Changes in the Structure of the State of New Zealand. *Policy Quarterly*, 4(2), 27–32.

Gill, D., Pride, S., Gilbert, H. and Norman, R. 2010. *The Future State*. Working Paper No. 10/08. Wellington: Institute of Policy Studies.

Gilley, B. 2009. *The Right to Rule: How States Win and Lose Legitimacy*. New York: Columbia University Press.

Gilroy, L. 2010. Government Privatization 101. *Reason Foundation*, 16 March [Online] Available at: http://reason.org/news/show/local-government-privatization-101 [accessed: 09/08/2010].

Glynn, J.J. 1985. Value for Money Auditing: An International Review and Comparison. *Financial Accountability and Management*, 1(2), 113–128.

—— 1996. Performance Auditing and Performance Improvement in Government: Public Sector Management Reform, Changing Accountabilities and the Role of Performance Audit, in *Performance Auditing and Public Sector Modernization*. Paris: OECD, 125–136.

Gonzalez, M.M. and Trujillo, L. 2008. Reforms and Infrastructure Efficiency in Spain's Container Ports. *Transportation Research Part A – Policy and Practice*, 42(1), 243–257.

Good, D. 2003. *The Politics of Public Management*. Toronto: University of Toronto Press.

Goodsell, C.T. 2004. *The Case for Bureaucracy*. 4th edition. Washington D.C.: CQ Press.

Gornitzka, Å. and Sverdrup, U. 2010. Enlightened Decision Making. The Role of Scientists in EU Governance. [Online] Available at: http://www.arena.uio.no/publications/working-papers2010/papers/wp_05_10.xml [accessed: 04/10/2010].

Government Performance and Results Act (GPRA) of 1993, 103rd Congress, 1st Session.

Gow, J.I. 1994. *Learning from Others: Administrative Innovations among Canadian Governments*. Toronto: Institute of Public Administration of Canada and Canadian Centre for Management Development.

—— 2004. *A Canadian Model of Public Administration?* Ottawa: Canadian School of Public Service.

Gow, J.I. and Dufour, C. 2000. Is the New Public Management a Paradigm? Does it Matter? *International Review of Administrative Sciences*, 66(4), 573–597.

Graham, C. 2000. *Regulating Public Utilities: A Constitutional Approach*. Oxford: Hart.

Gray, R. Dillard, J. and Spence, C. 2009. Social Accounting as if the World Matters: An Essay in Postalgia and a New Absurdism. *Public Management Review*, 11(5), 545–574.

Greenaway, J. 1995. Having the Bun and the Halfpenny: Can Old Public Service Ethics Survive in the New Whitehall? *Public Administration*, 73(3), 358–374.

Greene, J.D. 1996. Cities and Privatization: Examining the Effect of Fiscal Stress, Location, and Wealth in Medium-Sized Cities. *Policy Studies Journal*, 24(1), 135–144.

Greener, I. 2000a. Theorising Path-Dependency: How Does History Come to Matter in Organizations? *Management Decision*, 40(5–6), 614–619.

—— 2000b. Understanding NHS Reform: The Policy-Transfer, Social Learning, and Path-Dependency Perspectives. *Governance*, 15(2), 161–184.

Green-Pedersen, C. and Wilkerson, J. 2006. How Agenda-Setting Attributes Shape Politics: Basic Dilemmas, Problem Attention and Health Politics Developments in Denmark and the US. *Journal of European Public Policy*, 13(7), 1039–1052.

Gregory, R. 1995. The Peculiar Tasks of Public Management: Towards Conceptual Discrimination. *Australian Journal of Public Administration*, 54(2), 171–183.

—— 1999. Social Capital Theory and Administrative Reform: Maintaining Ethical Probity in Public Service. *Public Administration Review*, 59(1), 63–75.

—— 2003a. All the King's Horses and All the King's Men: Putting New Zealand's Public Sector Back Together Again. *International Public Management Review*, 4(2), 41–58.

—— 2003b. Transforming Governmental Culture: A Sceptical View of New Public Management, in *New Public Management: The Transformation of Ideas and Practice*, edited by T. Christensen and P. Lægreid. Aldershot: Ashgate, 231–257.

—— 2006. Theoretical Faith and Practical Works: De-Autonomizing and Joining-Up in the New Zealand State Sector, in *Autonomy and Regulation: Coping with Agencies in the Modern State*, edited by T. Christensen and P. Lægreid. Cheltenham: Edward Elgar, 137–161.

—— 2007. New Public Management and the Ghost of Max Weber: Exorcised or Still Haunting?, in *Transcending New Public Management: The Transformation of Public Sector Reforms*, edited by T. Christensen and P. Lægreid. Aldershot: Ashgate, 221–243.

Gregory, R. and Hicks, C. 1999. Promoting Public Service Integrity: A Case for Responsible Accountability. *Australian Journal of Public Administration*, 58(4), 3–15.

Greve, C. 2008. *Contracting for Public Services*. Abingdon: Routledge.

Greve, C., Flinders, M.V. and van Thiel, S. 1999. Quangos: What's in a Name? Defining Quasi-Autonomous Bodies from a Comparative Perspective. *Governance*, 12(1), 129–146.

Greve, C. and Mörth, U. 2010. Public-Private Partnerships: The Scandinavian Experience, in *International Handbook in Public-Private Partnerships*, edited by G. Hodge, C. Greve and A. Boardman. Cheltenham: Edward Elgar, chapter 18.

Grey, C. and Garsten, C. 2001. Trust, Control and Post-Bureaucracy. *Organization Studies*, 22(2), 229–250.

Griffin, G. and Svensen, S. 2002. Unions in Australia: Struggling to Survive, in *Changing Prospects for Trade Unionism: Comparisons between Six Countries*, edited by P. Fairbrother and G. Griffin. London: Continuum, 21–55.

Grimsey, D. and Lewis, M. 2004. *Public-Private Partnerships: The Worldwide Revolution in Infrastructure Provision and Project Finance*. Cheltenham: Edward Elgar.

Gronroos, C. 2007. *Service Management and Marketing*. Chichester: Wiley.

Grosser, A. 1967. The Evolution of European Parliaments, in *A New Europe?*, edited by S. Graubard. Boston, MA: Beacon Press.

Gulick, L. and Urwick, L. 1937. *Papers on the Science of Administration*. New York: Columbia University.

Ha, Y.S. 2004. Budgetary and Financial Management Reforms in Korea: Financial Crisis, New Public Management, and Fiscal Administration. *International Review of Administrative Sciences*, 70(3), 511–525.

Haas, P. 1992. Epistemic Communities and International Policy Coordination. *International Organization*, 46(1), 1–35.

Hafferty, F.W. and Light, D.W. 1995. Professional Dynamics and the Changing Nature of Medical Work. *Journal of Health and Social Behaviour*, 35 (extra issue), 132–153.

Hajnal, G. 2004. *Administrative Culture and New Public Management Reforms in a Comparative Case Study*. Budapest: Budapest University of Economic Sciences and Public Administration.

Hajnal, G. and Kádár, K. 2008. *The Agency Landscape in Hungary: An Empirical Survey of Non-Departmental Public Bodies in 2002–2006*. Paper to the third meeting of Comparative Research into Current Trends in Public Sector Organization (CRIPO), Utrecht, June.

Hall, P.A. and Taylor, R.C.R. 1996. Political Science and the Three New Institutionalisms. *Political Studies*, 44(4), 936–957.

Halligan, J. 2003. Leadership and the Senior Service Reform in a Comparative Perspective, in *Handbook of Public Administration*, edited by B.G. Peters and J. Pierre. London: Sage, 98–108.

—— 2004. The Quasi-Autonomous Agency in an Ambiguous Environment: The Centre Link Case. *Public Administration and Development*, 24(2), 147–156.

—— 2005. Public Sector Reform, in *Howard's Second and Third Governments*, edited by C. Aulich and R. Wettenhall. Sydney: University of New South Wales Press, 21–41.

—— 2006. The Reassertion of the Centre in a First Generation NPM System, in *Autonomy and Regulation: Coping with Agencies in the Modern State*, edited by T. Christensen and P. Lægreid. Cheltenham: Edward Elgar, 162–180.

—— 2007a. Anglo-American Systems: Easy Diffusion, in *Comparative Civil Service Systems in the 21st Century*, edited by J.C.N. Raadschelders, T.A.J. Toonen and F.M. Van der Meer. Basingstoke: Palgrave Macmillan, 50–64.

—— 2007b. Reform Design and Performance in Australia and New Zealand, in *Transcending New Public Management: The Transformation of Public Sector Reforms*, edited by T. Christensen and P. Lægreid. Aldershot: Ashgate, 43–64.

—— 2007c. Reintegrating Government in Third Generation Reforms of Australia and New Zealand. *Public Policy and Administration*, 22(2), 217–238.

—— 2009. A Comparative Perspective on Canadian Public Administration within an Anglophone Tradition, in *The Evolving Physiology of Government: Canadian Public Administration in Transition*, edited by O.P. Dwivedi, T.A. Mau and B. Sheldrick. Ottawa: University of Ottawa Press, 292–311.

—— 2010a. The Fate of Administrative Tradition in Anglophone Countries during the Reform Era, in *Administrative Traditions: Inheritances and Transplants in Comparative Perspective*, edited by M. Painter and B.G. Peters. Basingstoke: Palgrave, forthcoming.

—— 2010b. Post NPM Responses to Disaggregation through Coordinating Horizontally and Integrating Governance, in *Governance of Public Sector Organizations: Proliferation, Autonomy and Performance*, edited by P. Lægreid and K. Verhoest. London: Palgrave Macmillan, forthcoming.

Halligan, J. and Adams, J. 2004. Security, Capacity and Post-Market Reforms: Public Management Change in 2003. *Australia Journal of Public Administration*, 63(1), 85–93.

Halligan, J. and Bouckaert, G. 2009. Performance and Trust: Developmental Paths and Optional Directions, in *Change and Continuity in Public Sector Organizations: Essays in Honour of Per Lægreid*, edited by P.G. Roness and H. Sætren. Bergen: Fagbokforlaget, 257–278.

Halligan, J. with Wills, J. 2008. *The Centrelink Experiment: Innovation in Service Delivery*. Canberra: ANU E Press.

Ham, C. 1997. *Health Care Reform: Learning from the International Experience*. Bristol: Open University Press.

Hanf, K. and Scharpf, F. (eds) 1978. *Interorganizational Policy Making*. London: Sage.

Hanney, S., Gonzales-Block, M., Buxton, M. and Kogan, M. 2003. The Utilization of Health Research in Policy-making: Concepts, Examples and Methods of Assessment. *Health Research Policy and System*, 1(2), 2–30.

Hansen, A.D. 2007. Governance Networks and Participation, in *Theories of Democratic Network Governance*, edited by E. Sørensen and J. Torfing. Basingstoke: Palgrave, chapter 15.

Hansen, H.F. 2005. Evaluation in and of Public-Sector Reform: The Case of Denmark in a Nordic Perspective. *Scandinavian Political Studies*, 28(4), 323–347.

Hansen, H.F. and Rieper, O. 2009. Institutionalization of Second-Order Evidence-Producing Organizations, in *The Evidence Book*, edited by O. Rieper, F.L. Leeuw and T. Ling. New Brunswick, NJ: Transaction Publishers, 27–49.

Hansen, M.B. 2010. Marketization and Economic Performance: Competitive Tendering in the Social Sector. *Public Management Review*, 12(2), 255–274.

Haque, M.S. 2001. Recent Transition in Governance in South Asia: Contexts, Dimensions, and Implications. *International Journal of Public Administration*, 24(12), 1405–1436.

—— 2003. Reinventing Governance for Performance in South Asia: Impacts on Citizenship Rights. *International Journal of Public Administration*, 26(8–9), 941–964.

Harbridge, R., Crawford, A. and Hince, K. 2002. Unions in New Zealand: What the Law Giveth …, in *Changing Prospects for Trade Unionism: Comparisons between Six Countries*, edited by P. Fairbrother and G. Griffin. London: Continuum, 21–56.

Harding, A. and Preker, A. 2003. A Conceptual Framework for the Organizational Reforms of Hospitals, in *Innovations in Health Service Delivery: The Corporatization of Public Hospitals*, edited by A. Preker and A. Harding. Washington D.C.: The World Bank, 23–78.

Hargrove, E.C. and Glidewell, J.C. (eds) 1990. *Impossible Jobs in Public Management.* Lawrence, KS: University Press of Kansas.

Harris, J. 1998. Scientific Management, Bureau-Professionalism, New Managerialism: The Labour Process of State Social Work. *British Journal of Social Work*, 28(6), 839–862.

Harrison, S. and McDonald. R. 2008. *The Politics of Healthcare in Britain.* London: Sage.

Harrison, S. and Waqar, I.U.A. 2000. Medical Autonomy and the UK State 1975 to 2025. *Sociology*, 34(1), 129–146.

't Hart, P. and Wille, A. 2006. Ministers and Top Officials in the Dutch Executive: Living Together, Growing Apart? *Public Administration*, 84(1), 121–146.

Hartley, J. and Moore, M.H. 2008. Innovations in Governance. *Public Management Review*, 10(1), 3–20.

Harvey, O. 1992. The Unions and the Government: The Rise and Fall of the Compact, in *Controlling Interests: Business, the State and Society in New Zealand*, edited by J. Deeks and N. Perry. Auckland: Auckland University Press, 59–77.

Haveri, A. 2006. Complexity in Local Government: Limits to Rational Reforming. *Public Management Review*, 8(1), 31–46.

Hawkins, K. 1992. *The Uses of Discretion.* Oxford: Clarendon Press.

Hay, C. 2007. *Why We Hate Politics.* Cambridge: Polity Press.

Hayes, K.J., Razzolini, L. and Ross, L.B. 1998. Bureaucratic Choice and Nonoptimal Provision of Public Goods: Theory and Evidence. *Public Choice*, 94(1–2), 1–20.

Heclo, H. 1978. Issue Networks and the Executive Establishment, in *The New American Political System*, edited by A. King. Washington D.C.: AEI, 87–124.

Hedmo, T. and Sahlin-Andersson, K. 2007. The Evolution of a European Governance Network of Management Education, in *Democratic Network Governance in Europe*, edited by M. Marcussen and J. Torfing. London: Palgrave Macmillan, 195–213.

Hefetz, A. and Warner, M. 2004. Privatization and its Reverse: Explaining the Dynamics of the Government Contracting Process. *Journal of Public Administration Review*, 14(2), 171–190.

Heinrich, C.J. 2002. Outcomes-based Performance Management in the Public Sector: Implications for Government Accountability and Effectiveness. *Public Administration Review*, 62(6), 712–722.

Held, D. 2006. *Models of Democracy.* 3rd edition. Cambridge: Polity Press.

Hellandsvik, P. 2001. *New Health Organization in Norway. Government-Run Hospitals. Consequences for Research and Health Services.* Paper to the Nordic Meeting for Deans and Teaching Hospitals, Reykjavik, Iceland, 31 August.

Hellowell, M. 2010. The UK's Private Finance Initiative: History, Evaluation, Prospects, in *International Handbook in Public-Private Partnerships*, edited by G. Hodge, C. Greve and A. Boardman. Cheltenham: Edward Elgar, chapter 14.

Henderson, J., Hulme, D., Jalilian, H. and Phillips, R. 2007. Bureaucratic Effects: 'Weberian' State Agencies and Poverty Reduction. *Sociology of Health and Illness*, 41(3), 515–533.

Henning, R. 2000. Selling Standards, in *A World of Standards*, edited by N. Brunsson and B. Jacobsson. Oxford: Oxford University Press, 115–124.

Henrichsen, C. 2010. Administrative Justice in a Scandinavian Legal Context: From a Liberal and a Social State to a Market State or a Milieu State, in *Administrative Justice*, edited by M. Adler. Oxford: Hart, forthcoming.

Henry, C. and Matheu, M. 2001. New Regulations for Public Services in Competition, in *Regulation of Network Utilities: The European Experience*, edited by C. Henry, M. Matheu and A. Jeunemaître. Oxford: Oxford University Press, 1–38.

Herreros, F. 2009. The State, in *Handbook of Social Capital: The Troika of Sociology, Political Science and Economics*, edited by G.T. Svendsen and G.L.H. Svendsen. Amsterdam: Edward Elgar, 179–196.

Hesse, J.J., Hood, C. and Peters, B.G. 2003. Paradoxes in Public Sector Reform: Soft Theory and Hard Case, in *Paradoxes in Public Sector Reform: An International Comparison*, edited by J.J. Hesse, C. Hood and B.G. Peters. Baden-Baden: Nomos, 9–24.

Hill, M. and Hupe, P. 2009. *Implementing Public Policy*. London: Sage.

Hirschman, A.O. 1970. *Exit, Voice and Loyalty: Responses to Decline in Firms, Organizations and States*. Cambridge, MA: Harvard University Press.

Hix, S., Noury, A.G. and Roland, G. 2007. *Democratic Politics in the European Union*. Cambridge: Cambridge University Press.

HM Treasury 2008. *Infrastructure Procurement: Delivering Long-Term Value*. London: HMSO.

Hodge, G.A. 2000. *Privatization: An International Review of Performance*. Boulder, CO: Westview Press.

—— 2010. Reviewing Public-Private Partnerships: Some Thoughts on Evaluation, in *International Handbook in Public-Private Partnerships*, edited by G. Hodge, C. Greve and A. Boardman. Cheltenham: Edward Elgar, chapter 5.

Hodge, G.A. and Greve, C. 2007. Public-Private Partnerships: An International Performance Review. *Public Administration Review*, 67(3), 545–558.

—— 2009. PPPs: The Passage of Time Permits a Sober Reflection. *Economic Affairs*, 29(1), 33–39.

Hodge, G.A., Greve, C. and Boardman, A. (eds) 2010. *International Handbook in Public-Private Partnerships*. Chelthenham: Edward Elgar, forthcoming.

Hodges, R. 1997. Competition and Efficiency after Privatization: The Role of the NAO. *Public Money and Management*, 17(1), 35–42.

Hodges, R. and Wright, M. 1995. Audit and Accountability in the Privatization Process: The Role of the National Audit Office. *Financial Accountability and Management*, 11(2), 153–170.

Hodgkinson, C. 1996. *Administrative Philosophy: Values and Motivations in Administrative Life*. Oxford: Pergamon.

Hofstede, G. 2001. *Culture's Consequences: Comparing Values, Behaviors, Institutions and Organizations across Nations*. Thousand Oaks, CA: Sage.

Hoggett, P. 2006. Conflict, Ambivalence and the Contested Purpose of Public Organizations. *Human Relations*, 59(2), 175–194.

Hogwood, B. 1998. Regulatory Institutions in the United Kingdom: Increasing Regulation in the 'Shrinking State', in *Changing Regulatory Institutions in Britain and North America*, edited by G.B. Doern and S. Wilks. Toronto, Buffalo, NY and London: University of Toronto Press, 80–107.

Holmberg, S., Rothstein, B. and Nasiritousi, N. 2009. Quality of Government: What You Get. *Annual Review of Political Science*, 12(June), 135–161.

Homedesa, N. and Ugalde, A. 2005. Why Neoliberal Health Reforms Have Failed in Latin America. *Health Policy*, 71(1), 83–96.

Hondeghem, A. and Depré, R. 2005. *De Copernicushervorming in perspectief: Veranderingsmanagement in de federale overheid*. Vanden Broele: Brugge.

Hondeghem, A. and Perry, J.L. 2009. EGPA Symposium on Public Service Motivation and Performance: Introduction. *International Review of Administrative Sciences*, 75(1), 5–9.

Hood, C. 1990. De-Sir Humphreyfying the Westminster Model of Bureaucracy: A New Style of Governance? *Governance*, 3(2), 205–214.

—— 1991. A Public Management for All Seasons. *Public Administration*, 69(1), 3–19.

—— 1995. The 'New Public Management' in the 1980s: Variations on a Theme. *Accounting, Organizations and Society*, 20(2–3), 93–109.

—— 1996a. Exploring Variations in Public Management Reform of the 1980s, in *Civil Service Systems in Comparative Perspective*, edited by H. Bekke, J.L. Perry and T.A.J. Toonen. Bloomington, IN: Indiana University Press, 268–287.

—— 1996b. United Kingdom: From Second Chance to Near-Miss Learning, in *Lessons from Experience: Experiential Learning in Administrative Reforms in Eight Democracies*, edited by J.P. Olsen and B.G. Peters. Oslo: Scandinavian University Press, 36–70.

—— 1998. *The Art of the State: Culture, Rhetoric, and Public Management*. New York: Oxford University Press.

—— 2002a. Control, Bargains, and Cheating: The Politics of Public-Service Reform. *Journal of Public Administration Research and Theory*, 12(3), 309–332.

—— 2002b. The Risk Game and the Blame Game. *Government and Opposition*, 37(1), 15–37.

—— 2004. *Controlling Modern Government: Variety, Commonality and Change*. Cheltenham: Edward Elgar.

—— 2005a. Public Management: The Word, the Movement, the Science, in *The Oxford Handbook of Public Management*, edited by E. Ferlie, L.E Lynn and C. Pollitt. Oxford: Oxford University Press, 7–26.

—— 2005b. The Idea of Joined-Up Government: A Historical Perspective, in *Joined-Up Government*, edited by V. Bogdanor. Oxford: Oxford University Press for the British Academy, 19–42.

—— 2006. Gaming in Targetworld: The Targets Approach to Managing British Public Services. *Public Administration Review*, 66(4), 515–521.

—— 2007. What Happens When Transparency Meets Blame-Avoidance? *Public Management Review*, 9(2), 191–210.

Hood, C. and Jackson, M. 1991a. *Administrative Argument*. Aldershot: Dartmouth.

—— 1991b. The New Public Management: A Recipe for Disaster. *Canberra Bulletin of Public Administration*, 64(May), 16–24.

Hood, C., James, O., Peters, B.G. and Scott C. (eds) 2004. *Controlling Modern Government: Variety, Commonality and Change*. London: Edward Elgar.

Hood, C. and Lodge, M. 2006. *The Politics of Public Service Bargains: Reward, Competency, Loyalty – and Blame*. Oxford: Oxford University Press.

Hood, C. and Peters, G. 2004. The Middle Aging of New Public Management: Into the Age of Paradox? *Journal of Public Administration Research and Theory*, 14(3), 267–282.

Hood, C., Rothstein, H. and Baldwin, R. 2001. *The Government of Risk, Understanding Risk Regulation Schemes*. Oxford: Oxford University Press.

Hood, C., Scott, C., James, O., Jones, G. and Travers, T. 1999. *Regulation inside Government: Waste-Watchers, Quality Police and Sleaze-Busters*. Oxford: Oxford University Press.

Horn, M. 1995. *The Political Economy of Public Administration: Institutional Choice in the Public Sector*. Cambridge: Cambridge University Press.

House, R.J. and Hanges, P.J. (eds) 2004. *Culture, Leadership and Organizations: The Globe Study of 62 Societies*. Thousand Oaks, CA and London: Sage.

Howard, J. 1997. Transcript of the Prime Minister, the Hon. John Howard, MP, Address at the official launch of Centrelink (Commonwealth Services Delivery Agency). Canberra: The Great Hall, Parliament House, 24 September.

Huczynski, A. 1993. *Management Gurus*. London: Routledge.

Huff, A. and Reger, R. 1987. A Review of Strategic Process Research. *Journal of Management*, 13(2), 211–236.

Hughes, O. 1998. *Public Management and Administration: An Introduction*. Basingstoke: Macmillan.

—— 2010. Does Governance Exist?, in *The New Public Governance?*, edited by S. Osborne. London: Routledge, 87–104.

Humphrey, C. and Olson, O. 1995. Caught in the Act: Public Services Disappearing in the World of 'Accountable Management'?, in *Issues in Management Accounting*, edited by D. Ashton, T. Hopper and R. Scrapens. 2nd edition. Exeter: Prentice Hall, chapter 17.

Hunn, D. 2000. *Ministerial Review into the Department of Work and Income*. Wellington: State Services Commission.

Huntington, S.P. 1974. Post-Industrial Politics: How Benign Will it Be? *Comparative Politics*, 6(2), 163–191.

Hutter, B.M. 2005. *The Attractions of Risk-based Regulation: Accounting for the Emergence of Risk Ideas in Regulation*. Discussion Paper No. 33. London: LSE: ESRC Centre for the Analysis of Risk and Regulation.

Huxham, C. and Vangen, S. 2005. *Managing to Collaborate*. London: Routledge.

Ikenberry, G.J. 1990. The International Spread of Privatization Policies: Inducements, Learning and 'Policy Bandwagoning', in *The Political Economy of Public Sector Reform and Privatization*, edited by E.N. Suleiman and J. Waterburry. Boulder, CO: Waterview Press, 88–110.

Ingraham, P.W. and Moynihan, D.P. 2001. *When Does Performance Information Contribute to Performance Information Use? Putting the Factors in Place*. Working

Paper, Maxwell School of Syracuse University, Campbell Public Affairs Institute.

INTOSAI 2004. *Implementation Guidelines for Performance Auditing: Standards and Guidelines for Performance Auditing Based on INTOSAI's Auditing Standard and Practical Experience*. Stockholm, July.

—— 2009. First Meeting of the INTOSAI Working Group on the Value and Benefits of SAIs. *International Journal of Government Auditing*, July, 25–27.

Jacobs, K. 1998. Value for Money Auditing in New Zealand: Competing for Control in the Public Sector. *British Accounting Review*, 30(4), 343–360.

Jacobsen, C.B. and Andersen, L.B. 2009. *Regulating Research: Crowding In or Crowding Out?* Paper to the 2009 EGPA Conference: The Public Service: Service Delivery in the Information Age, St. Julians, 2–5 September.

Jacobsen, D.R. and Roness, P.G. 2008. Corporatism, Administrative Policy and State Employees' Unions, in *The Organizational Dimension of Politics*, edited by U. Sverdrup and J. Trondal. Bergen: Fagbokforlaget, 145–168.

James, O. 2001. Business Models and the Transfer of Business-Like Central Government Agencies. *Governance*, 14(2), 233–252.

—— 2003. *The Executive Agency Revolution in Whitehall: Public Interest versus Bureau-Shaping Perspectives*. Basingstoke: Palgrave Macmillan.

—— 2004a. The UK Core Executive's Use of Public Service Agreements as a Tool of Governance. *Public Administration*, 82(2), 397–419.

—— 2004b. Executive Agencies and Joined-up Government in the UK, in *Unbundled Government: A Critical Analysis of the Global Trend to Agencies, Quangos and Contractualisation*, edited by C. Pollitt and C. Talbot. London and New York: Routledge, 73–93.

Jann, W. 2000. Verwaltungskulturen in internationalen vergleich. Ein überblick über den Stand der empirischen forschung. *Die Verwaltung*, 33(3), 325–349.

—— 2003. State, Administration and Governance in Germany: Competing Traditions and Dominant Narratives. *Public Administration*, 81(1), 95–118.

Jeffares, S., Sullivan, H. and Bovaird, T. 2009. *Beyond the Contract: The Challenge of Evaluating the Performance of Public-Private Partnerships*. Paper to the 13th Annual IRSPM Conference in Copenhagen, 6–8 April. Available at: www.irspm.cbs.dk [accessed: 13/08/2010].

Jensen, A. and Stelling, P. 2007. Economic Impacts of Swedish Railway Deregulation: A Longitudinal Study. *Transportation Research Part E: Logistics and Transportation Review*, 43(5), 516–534.

Jensen, L. and Fjord, D. 2010. Budget Reforms in Denmark: Unheralded but Nevertheless Effective, in *The Reality of Budgetary Reform in OECD Nations: Trajectories and Consequences*, edited by J. Wanna, L. Jensen and J. de Vries. Cheltenham: Edward Elgar, 193–220.

Jensen, M. and Meckling, W. 1976. Theory of the Firm: Managerial Behaviour, Agency Costs and Ownership Structure. *Journal of Financial Economics*, 3(October), 305–360.

Jespersen, P.K. 2005. *Mellem profession og management*. Copenhagen: Handelshøjskolens Forlag.

—— 2008. *Changing Professional Autonomy through Quality Development? Quality Development as Response to New Demands for Transparency in Medical Work in Denmark and Norway*. Paper to the 3rd Nordic Workshop on Health Management and Organization, Uppsala, Sweden, 4–5 December.

Jespersen, P.K. and Wrede, S. 2009. The Changing Autonomy of the Nordic Medical Professions, in *Nordic Health Care Systems: Recent Reforms and Current Policy Challenges*, edited by J. Magnussen, K. Vrangbæk and R. Saltman. Maidenhead: Open University Press, 151–179.

Johnson, C. 1995. *Japan: Who Governs?: The Rise of the Developmental State*. New York: W.W. Norton.

Johnson, G., Larkin, G. and Saks, M. (eds) 1995. *Health Professions and the State in Europe*. London: Routledge.

Johnson, S. 2009. The Quiet Coup. *The Atlantic*, May 2009. Available at: http://www.theatlantic.com/magazine/archive/2009/05/the-quiet-coup/7364/ [accessed: 04/08/2010].

Johnson, T. 1972. *Professions and Power*. London: Macmillan.

Jones, D.N. 2009. Matching Regulatory Arrangements with Public Values. *International Journal of Public Policy*, 4(5), 435–448.

Kaase, M. and Newton, K. (eds) 1995. *Beliefs in Government*. Oxford: Oxford University Press.

Katz, R.S. and Mair, P. 1995. Changing Models of Party Organization and Party Democracy: The Emergence of Cartel Parties. *Party Politics*, 1(1), 5–28.

—— 2009. The Cartel Party Thesis: A Restatement. *Perspectives on Politics*, 7(1), 753–766.

Kaufman, H. 1960. *The Forest Ranger: A Study in Administrative Behavior*. Baltimore, MD: Johns Hopkins Press.

—— 1976. *Are Government Organizations Immortal?* Washington D.C.: Brookings Institution.

—— 2001. Major Players: Bureaucracies in American Government. *Public Administration Review*, 61(1), 18–42.

Kaufmann, D. 2004. *Human Rights and Governance: The Empirical Challenge*. Paper presented at the New York University Law School, March 2004.

Kaufmann, D. and Kraay, A. 2002. Growth without Governance. *Economia*, 3(1), 169–229.

—— 2003. *Governance and Growth: Causality with Way? Evidence for the World*, in brief, February. [Online.] Available at: http://www.uoit.ca/sas/governeaceAndCorr/GovGrowth.pdf [accessed: 04/08/2010].

Kavanagh, D. and Richards D. 2001. Departmentalism and Joined-Up Government: Back to the Future? *Parliamentary Affairs*, 54(1), 1–18.

Keeling, D. 1972. *Management in Government*. London: Allen & Unwin.

Kelsey, J. 1995. *The New Zealand Experiment: A World Model for Structural Adjustment?* Auckland: Auckland University Press/Bridget Willaims Books.

Kernaghan, K. 2003. Integrating Values into Public Service: The Value Statement as Centerpiece. *Public Administration Review*, 63(6), 711–719.

—— 2009. Putting Citizens First: Service Delivery and Integrated Public Governance, in *The Evolving Physiology of Government: Canadian Public Administration in Transition*, edited by O.P. Dwivedi, T.A. Mau and B. Sheldrick. Ottawa: University of Ottawa Press, 249–269.

Kessler, D.P. and McClellan, M. 2000. Is Hospital Competition Socially Wasteful? *Quarterly Journal of Economics*, 115(2), 577–616.

Kettl, D.F. 1993. *Sharing Power: Public Governance and Private Markets*. Washington D.C.: Brookings Institution.

—— 2000. *The Global Public Management Revolution: A Report on the Transformation of Governance*. Washington D.C.: Brookings Institution.

—— 2003. Contingent Coordination: Practical and Theoretical Puzzles for Homeland Security. *American Review for Public Administration*, 33(3), 253–277.

—— 2004. *System under Stress: Homeland Security and American Politics*. Washington D.C.: CQ Press.

—— 2009. *The Next Government of the United States*. New York: W.W. Norton.

—— 2010. Governance, Contract Management and Public Management, in *The New Public Governance? Critical Perspectives and Future Directions*, edited by S. Osborne. London: Routledge, 239–254.

Kickert, W.J.M. 1993. Complexity Governance and Dynamics: Conceptual Explorations of Public Network Management, in *Modern Governance: New Government-Society Interactions*, edited by J. Kooiman. London: Sage, 191–204.

—— 1997. Public Governance in the Netherlands: An Alternative to Anglo-American 'Managerialism'. *Public Administration*, 75(4), 731–752.

—— 2000. *Public Management Reforms in the Netherlands*. Delft: Eburon.

—— 2007. Public Management Reforms in Countries with a Napoleonic State Model: France, Italy and Spain, in *New Public Management in Europe: Adaptation and Alternatives*, edited by C. Pollitt, S. van Thiel and V. Homburg. Houndmills: Palgrave Macmillan, 26–51.

—— (ed.) 2008. *The Study of Public Management in Europe and the US: A Comparative Analysis of National Distinctiveness*. London: Routledge.

—— 2010. Managing Emergent and Complex Change: The Case of Dutch Agencification. *International Review of Administrative Sciences*, 76(2010), 3.

Kickert, W.J.M. and Hakvoort, J.L.M. 2000. Public Governance in Europe: A Historical-Institutional Tour d'horizont, in *Governance in Modern Society: Effects, Change and Formation of Government Institutions*, edited by O. Van Heffen, W.J.M. Kickert and J.J.A. Thomassen. Dordrecht: Kluwer Academic Publishers.

Killerby, P. 2005. 'Trust Me, I'm from the Government': The Complex Relationship between Trust in Government and Quality of Governance. *Social Policy Journal of New Zealand*, 25(July), 1–15.

Kim, P.S. 2007. Transforming Higher-level Civil Service in a New Age: A Case Study of a New Senior Civil Service in Korea. *Public Personnel Management*, 36(2), 127–142.

Kim, S. and Vandenabeele, W. 2009. *A Strategy for Building Public Service Motivation Research Internationally*. Paper to the International Public Service Motivation Research Conference, Indiana University, 7–9 June.

Kimberly, R. and Pouvourville, G. 2003. *The Migration of Managerial Innovation: Diagnosis-Related Groups and Health Care Administration in Western Europe*. San Francisco, CA: Jossey-Bass Publishers.

Kimberly, R., Pouvourville, G. and D'Aunno, T. 2008. *The Globalization of Managerial Innovation in Health Care*. Cambridge: Cambridge University Press.

Kirkhart, K.E. 2000. Reconceptualizing Evaluation Use: An Integrated Theory of Influence. *New Directions for Evaluation*, 2000(88), 5–23.

Kirkman, B.L.A. 2006. A Quarter Century of Culture's Consequences: A Review of Empirical Research Incorporating Hofstede's Cultural Values Framework. *Journal of International Business Studies*, 37(3), 285–320.

Kirkpatrick, I., Jespersen, P.K. and Dent, M. 2009. Medicine and Management in a Comparative Perspective: The Case of Denmark and England. *Sociology of Health and Illness*, 31(5), 642–658.

Kirkpatrick, I. and Martinez-Lucio, M. (eds) 1995. *The Politics of Quality in the Public Sector*. London: Routledge.

Kjeldsen, A.M. 2010. *Antecedents of Public Service Motivation Revised: The Effect of Employment Sector and Level of Professionalism when Controlling for Work Task*. Paper to the International Research Society for Public Management (IRSPM), Bern, 7–9 April.

Klijn, E.H. 2002. Governing Networks in the Hollow State: Contracting-Out, Process Management or a Combination of the Two. *Public Management Review*, 4(2), 149–166.

Klijn, E.H., Edelenbos, J. and Steijn, A.J. 2010. Trust in Governance Networks: Its Impact and Outcomes. *Administration and Society*, forthcoming.

Klijn, E.H. and Koppenjan, J. 2000. Public Management and Policy Networks: Foundations of a Network Approach to Governance. *Public Management Review*, 2(2), 135–158.

—— 2004. *Managing Uncertanties in Networks*. London: Routledge.

Kluckhohn, C. 1951. The Study of Culture, in *The Policy Sciences*, edited by D. Lerner and H.D. Laswell. Stanford, CA: Stanford University Press, 86–101.

Koci, M. 2007. Culture and Public Management Reforms: A Review and Research Agenda on the Basis of Experiences in Switzerland, in *Cultural Aspects of Public Management Reforms*, edited by K. Schedler and I. Proeller. Amsterdam: Elsevier, 249–274.

Kodrzycki, Y.K. 1994. Privatization of Local Public Services: Lessons for New England. *New England Economic Review*, May–June, 31–46.

—— 1998. Fiscal Pressure and the Privatization of Local Services. *New England Economic Review*, January–February, 39–50.

Kogan, M., Bauer, M., Bleiklie, I. and Henkel, M. (eds) 2006. *Transforming Higher Education: A Comparative Study*. 2nd edition. Dordrecht: Springer.

Kogan, M. and Hanney, S. 2000. *Reforming Higher Education*. London and Philadelphia, PA: Jessica Kingsley.

Kooiman, J. 1999. Social-political Governance: Overview, Reflections and Design. *Public Management Review*, 1(1), 67–92.

Korunka, C., Scharitzer, D., Carayon, P. and Saintfort, F. 2003. Employee Strain and Job Satisfaction Related to an Implementation of Quality in a Public Service Organization: A Longitudinal Study. *Work and Stress*, 17(1), 52–72.

Krasner, S.D. 1988. Sovereignty: An Institutional Perspective. *Comparative Political Studies*, 21(1), 66–94.

—— 1999. *Sovereignty: Organized Hypocrisy*. Princeton, NJ: Princeton University Press.

Kumlin, S. and Rothstein, B. 2005. Making and Breaking Social Capital: The Impact of Welfare State Institutions. *Comparative Political Studies*, 38(4), 339–365.

Kuntz, L. and Vera, A. 2007. Modular Organization and Hospital Performance. *Health Services Management Review*, 20(1), 48–58.

Lægreid, P., Opedal, S. and Stigen, I. 2005. The Norwegian Hospital Reform: Balancing Political Control and Enterprise Autonomy. *Journal of Health Politics, Policy and Law*, 30(6), 1027–1065.

Lægreid, P., Roness P.G. and Rubecksen, K. 2006. Autonomy and Control in the Norwegian Civil Service: Does Agency Form Matter?, in *Autonomy and Regulation: Coping with Agencies in the Modern State*, edited by T. Christensen, and P. Lægreid. Cheltenham: Edward Elgar, 235–267.

Lægreid, P. and Verhoest, K. (eds) 2010. *Governance of Public Sector Organizations: Proliferation, Autonomy and Performance*. Basingstoke: Palgrave Macmillan.

Lægreid P. and Wise, L. 2007. Reforming Human Resource Management in Civil Service Systems, in *Comparative Civil Service Systems in the 21st Century*, edited by F. van der Meer, T. Thoonen and J. Raadschelders. London: Palgrave, 169–182.

Laing, A., Hogg, G. Newholm, T. and Keeling, D. 2009. Differentiating Consumers in Professional Services: Information Empowerment and Emergence of the Fragmented Consumer, in *The Consumer in Public Services: Choice, Values and Difference*, edited by R. Simmons, M. Powell and I. Greener. Bristol: Policy Press, 57–76.

Lalenis, K., De Jong, M. and Mamadouh, V. 2002. Families of Nations and Institutional Transplantation, in *The Theory and Practice of Institutional Transplantation: Experiences with the Transfer of Policy Institutions*, edited by M. De Jong, K. Lalenis and V. Mamadouh. Dordrecht: Kluwer Academic Publishers, 33–54.

Lamoreaux, N.R. 2004. Partnerships, Corporations, and the Limits on Contractual Freedom in U.S. History: An Essay in Economics, Law, and Culture, in *Constructing Corporate America: History, Politics, Culture*, edited by K. Lipartito and D.B. Sicilia. Oxford: Oxford University Press, 29–65.

Lane, J–E. 2000. *New Public Management: An Introduction*. London: Routledge.

—— 2009. *State Management: An Enquiry into Models of Public Administration and Management*. London: Routledge.

Lansbury. R. and Macdonald, D. 2001. Employment Relations in the Australian Public Sector, in *Strategic Choices in Reforming Public Service Employment: An International Handbook*, edited by C. Dell'Aringa, G. Della Rocca and B. Keller. Basingstoke: Palgrave, 216–242.

La Porta, R., Florencio Lopez-de-Silanes, A.S. and Vishny, R. 1999. The Quality of Government. *Journal of Law, Economics and Organization*, 15(1), 222–279.

Lapsley, I. 1997. The New Public Management Diaspora: The Health Care Experiment. *International Association of Management Journal*, 9(2), 1–14.

—— 2008. The NPM Agenda: Back to the Future. *Financial Accountability and Management*, 24(1), 7–96.

Lee, E.W.Y. and Haque, M.S. 2006. The New Public Management Reform and Governance in Asian NICs: A Comparison of Hong Kong and Singapore. *Governance*, 19(4), 605–626.

Lee, K.S., Chun, K.H. and Lee, J.S. 2008. Reforming the Hospital Service Structure to Improve Efficiency: Urban Hospital Specialization. *Health Policy*, 87(1), 41–49.

Leeuw, F.L. 1996. Performance Auditing, New Public Management and Performance Improvement: Questions and Answers. *Accounting, Auditing and Accountability Journal*, 9(2), 92–102.

Leftwich, A. 1993. Governance, Democracy and Development in the Third World. *Third World Quarterly*, 14(3), 605–624.

Le Grand, J. 2003. *Motivation, Agency and Public Policy: Of Knights and Knaves, Pawns and Queens*. New York: Oxford University Press.

—— 2007. *The Other Invisible Hand: Delivering Public Services through Choice and Competition*. Princeton, NJ: Princeton University Press.

Leibenstein, H. 1966. Allocative Efficiency vs X-Efficiency. *American Economic Review*, 56(3), 392–415.

Leisink, P. and Steijn, B. 2009. Public Service Motivation and Job Performance of Public Sector Employees in the Netherlands. *International Review of Administrative Sciences*, 75(1), 35–52.

Leišytė, L. 2007. University Governance and Academic Research: Case Studies of Research Units in Dutch and English Universities. Dissertation. Enschede: CHEPS.

Lepori, B. 2008. Research in Non-University Higher Education Institutions: The Case of the Swiss Universities of Applied Sciences. *Higher Education*, 56(1), 45–58.

—— 2010. *ERAWATCH Country Report 2009: Switzerland*. EUR23976 EN/29 – 2009. Brussels: European Commission.

Lepori, B. and Fumasoli, T. 2010. Reforms in Governance and Funding of Swiss Higher Education. Report for the EU Governance and Funding Project. Unpublished working paper, Lugano.

Lerner, A.P. 1944. *The Economics of Control*. New York: Macmillan.

Levi-Faur, D. 2005. The Global Diffusion of Regulatory Capitalism. *The Annals of the American Academy of Political and Social Science*, 528(March), 12–32.

Lewicki, R.J. and Bunker, B.B. 1996. Developing and Maintaining Trust in Work Relationships, in *Trust in Organizations: Frontiers of Theory and Research*, edited by R.M. Kramer and T.R. Tyler. Thousand Oaks, CA: Sage, 114–139.

Light, P.C. 1997. *The Tides of Reform*. New Haven, CT: Yale University Press.

Lijphart, A. 1984. *Democracies: Patterns of Majoritarian and Consensus Government in Twenty-one Countries*. New Haven, CT: Yale University Press.

Lindquist, E. 2006. *A Critical Moment: Capturing and Conveying the Evolution of the Canadian Public Service*. Ottawa: Canadian School of Public Service.

Ling, T. 2002. Delivering Joined-Up Government in the UK: Dimensions, Issues and Problems. *Public Administration*, 80(4), 615–642.

—— 2003. Ex Ante Evaluation and the Changing Public Audit Function: The Scenario Planning Approach. *Evaluation*, 9(4), 437–452.

—— 2007. New Wine in Old Bottles? When Audit, Accountability, and Evaluation Meet, in *Making Accountability Work: Dilemmas for Evaluation and for Audit*, edited by M.L. Bemelmans-Videc, J. Lonsdale and B. Perrin. New Brunswick, NJ: Transaction Publishers, 127–141.

Lipsky, M. 1979. *Street Level Bureaucracy*. New York: Russell Sage Foundation.

Llewellyn, N., Lewis, P. and Woods, A. 2007. Public Management and the Expansion of the Entrepreneurial Ethos? *Public Management Review*, 9(2), 253–268.

Löffler, E. 2003. The Administrative State in Western Democracies, in *The Sage Handbook of Public Administration*, edited by B. Guy Peters and J. Pierre. London: Sage, 478–488.

Lonsdale, J. 2000. Developments in Value-For-Money Audit Methods: Impacts and Implications. *International Review of Administrative Sciences*, 66(1), 73–89.

—— 2007. *Adding Value: Measuring the Impact of Performance Audit Work in the Education and Social Welfare Fields*. Paper to the Korean Evaluation Research Instutute-conference, Seoul, August 2007.

—— 2008. Balancing Independence and Responsiveness: A Practitioner Perspective on the Relationships Shaping Performance Audit. *Evaluation*, 14(2), 227–248.

Luhmann, N. 2000. *Organisation und Entscheidung*. Opladen: Westdeutscher Verlag.

Lundquist, L. 1991. *Förvaltning och demokrati*. Stockholm: Norstedts.

Lynn, L.E. 1990. Managing the Social Safety Net: The Job of Social Welfare Executive, in *Impossible Jobs in Public Management*, edited by E. Hargrove and J.C. Glidewell. Lawrence, KS: University Press of Kansas, 133–152.

Lynn, L.E., Heinrich, C. and Hill, C. 2001. *Improving Governance: A New Logic for Empirical Research*. Washington D.C.: Georgetown University Press.

Macinati, M.S. 2008. The Relationship between Quality Management Systems and Organizational Performance in the Italian National Health Service. *Health Policy*, 85(2), 228–241.

Mahony, N. 2008. Spectacular Political Experiments. Dissertation. Milton Keynes: The Open University.

Majone, G. 2001. Two Logics of Delegation: Agency and Fiduciary Relations in EU Governance. *European Union Politics*, 2(1), 103–122.

Mandell, E. and Keast, R. 2008. Evaluating the Effectiveness of Interorganizational Relations through Networks: Developing a Framework for Revised Performance Measures. *Public Management Review*, 10(6), 715–731.

Manning, N. 1997. Three Perspectives on Alternative Service Delivery. *Public Sector Management*, 7(4), 5–7.

—— 2001. The Legacy of the New Public Management in Developing Countries. *International Review of Administrative Sciences*, 67(2), 296–310.

—— 2006. *Where is Public Management Heading? Hopes and Expectations*. Paris: OECD.

Maor, M. 1999. The Paradox of Managerialism. *Public Administration Review*, 59(1), 5–18.

March, J.G. 1978. Bounded Rationality, Ambiguity and the Engineering of Choice. *Bell Journal of Economics*, 9(2), 587–608.

March, J.G. and Olsen, J.P. 1976. *Ambiguity and Choice in Organizations*. Bergen: Universitetsforlaget.

—— 1983. Organizing Political Life: What Administrative Reorganization Tells Us about Government. *American Political Science Review*, 77(2), 281–297.

—— 1989. *Rediscovering Institutions: The Organizational Basis of Politics*. New York: Free Press.

March, J. and Simon, H. 1958. *Organizations*. New York: Wiley.

Marcuccio, M. and Steccolini, I. 2005. Social and Environmental Reporting in Local Authorities: A New Italian Fashion? *Public Management Review*, 7(2), 155–176.

Marcussen, M. 2002. *OECD og idéspillet. Game Over?* Copenhagen: Hans Reitzels Forlag.

—— 2006. Institutional Transformation? The Scientization of Central Banking as Case, in *Autonomy and Regulation: Coping with Agencies in the Modern State*, edited by T. Christensen and P. Lægreid. Cheltenham: Edward Elgar, 81–109.

—— 2007. Central Banking Reform across the World: Only by Nights are All Cats Grey, in *Transcending New Public Management: The Transformation of Public Sector Reforms*, edited by T. Christensen and P. Lægreid. Aldershot: Ashgate, 135–154.

—— 2010a. *Den danske model og globaliseringen*. Frederiksberg: Samfundslitteratur.

—— 2010b. The Triumph and Despair of Central Banking, in *European Power Elites and the Consequences: Studies in the Social Construction of the EU*, edited by N. Kauppi and M.R. Madsen. London: Routledge, forthcoming.

Marcussen, M. and Ronit, K. 2009. *Globaliseringens udfordringer. Politiske og administrative modeller under pres*. Copenhagen: Hans Reitzels Forlag.

Marsh, D. and Rhodes, R. 1992. *Policy Networks in British Government*. Oxford: Clarendon Press.

Marson, B. and Heintzman, R. 2009. *Research to Results: A Decade of Research-Based Service Improvement in Canada*. Toronto: Institute of Public Administration.

Martinsen, D. and Beck Jørgensen, T. 2010. Accountability as a Differentiated Value in Supranational Governance. *American Review of Public Administration*, forthcoming.

Martinsen, D. and Vrangbæk, K. 2008. The Europeanization of Health Care Governance: Implementing the Market Imperatives of Europe. *Public Administration*, 86(1), 169–184.

Massey, A. and Pyper, R. 2005. *Public Management and Modernisation in Britain*. Basingstoke: Palgrave Macmillan.

Masujima, T. 2005. Administrative Reform in Japan: Past Developments and Future Trends. *International Review of Administrative Sciences*, 71(2), 295–308.

Mattei, P. 2009. *Restructuring Welfare Organizations in Europe: From Democracy to Good Management?* Basingstoke: Palgrave Macmillan.

Mauro, P. 1995. Corruption and Growth. *Quarterly Journal of Economics*, 110(3), 681–712.

Mayo, E. 1933. *The Human Problems of an Industrial Civilization*. New York: Macmillan.

McCourt, W. 2007. Impartiality through Bureaucracy? A Sri Lankan Approach to Managing Values. *Journal of International Development*, 19(3), 429–442.

McCourt, W. and Minogue, M. (eds) 2001. *The Internationalization of Public Management: Reinventing the Third World State*. Cheltenham: Edward Elgar.

McCrae, M. and Vada, H. 1997. Performance Audit Scope and the Independence of the Australian Commonwealth Auditor-General. *Financial Accountability and Management*, 13(3), 203–223.

McCrudden, C. 1999. Social Policy and Economic Regulators: Some Issues from the Reform of Utility Regulation, in *Regulation and Deregulation: Policy and Practice in the Utilities and Financial Services Industries*, edited by C. McCrudden. Oxford: Clarendon Press, 275–291.

McCubbins, M.D., Noll, R.G. and Weingast, B.R. 1989. Structure and Process, Politics and Policy: Administrative Arrangements and the Political Control of Agencies. *Virginia Law Review*, 75(2), 431–482.

McFarland, A. 2007. Neopluralism. *Annual Review of Political Science* 10(1), 45–66.

McLaughlin, K., Osborne, S. and Ferlie, E. (eds) 2002. *New Public Management: Current Trends and Future Prospects*. London: Routledge.

McNabb, D.E. 2009. *The New Face of Government: How Public Managers are Forging a New Approach to Governance*. Boca Raton, FL: Auerbach Publications.

McSweeney, B. 1994. Management by Accounting, in *Accounting as Social and Institutional Practice*, edited by A.G. Hopwood and P. Miller. Cambridge: Cambridge University Press, 237–269.

Megginson, W.L. 2005. *The Financial Economics of Privatization*. Oxford and New York: Oxford University Press.

Megginson, W.L. and Netter, J.M. 2001. From State to Market: A Survey of Empirical Studies of Privatization. *Journal of Economic Literature*, 39(2), 321–389.

Metcalfe, L. and Richards, S. 1991. *Improving Public Management*. London: Sage.

Meyer, J.W. and Rowan, B. 1977. Institutionalized Organizations: Formal Structure as Myth and Ceremony. *American Journal of Sociology*, 83(2), 340–363.

Meyer-Sahling, J-H. 2009. Varieties of Legacies: A Critical Review of Legacy Explanations of Public Administration Reform in East Central Europe. *International Review of Administrative Sciences*, 75(3), 509–528.

Micklethwait, J. and Wooldridge, A. 1996. *The Witch Doctors: Making Sense of the Management Gurus*. New York: Times Books.

Migué, J. and Belanger, G. 1974. Towards a General Theory of Managerial Discretion. *Public Choice*, 17(1), 27–43.

Miller, G.J. 1992. *Managerial Dilemmas: The Political Economy of Hierarchy*. Cambridge: Cambridge University Press.

—— 2005. The Political Evolution of Principal-Agency Models. *Annual Review of Political Science*, 8(June), 203–225.

Miller, P. and O'Leary, T. 1987. Accounting and the Construction of the Governable Person. *Accounting, Organizations and Society*, 12(3), 235–265.

Milward, H.B. and Provan, K. 2000. Governing the Hollow State. *Journal of Public Administration Research and Theory*, 10(2), 359–380.

—— 2003. Managing the Hollow State: Collaboration and Contracting. *Public Management Review*, 5(1), 1–18.

Ministry of Social Development. 2002. *Building Leadership for Social Development*. Briefing to the Incoming Minister 2002–2003. Wellington: Ministry of Social Development.

Mintzberg, H. 1996. Managing Government – Governing Management. *Harvard Business Review*, 74(3), 75–83.

Mishra, R. 1984. *The Welfare State in Crisis*. Brighton: Wheatsheaf.

Mizruchi, M.S. and Fein, L.C. 1999. The Social Construction of Organizational Knowledge: A Study of the Uses of Coercive, Mimetic, and Normative Isomorphism. *Administrative Science Quarterly*, 44(4), 653–683.

Moe, R. 1994. The 'Reinventing Government' Exercise: Misinterpreting the Problem, Misjudging the Consequences. *Public Administration Review*, 54(2), 111–122.

Moe, T. 1984. The New Economics of Organizations. *American Journal of Political Science*, 28(4), 739–777.

Mohan, J. 2002. *Planning, Markets and Hospitals*. London: Routledge.

—— 2003. The Past and Future of the NHS: New Labour and Foundation Hospitals. *History and Policy*. [Online.] Available at: http://eprints.soton.ac.uk/42795/ [accessed: 22/04/2010].

Molina, O. and Rhodes, M. 2002. Corporatism: The Past, Present, and Future of a Concept. *Annual Review of Political Science*, 5, 305–331.

Montin, S. 2000. Between Fragmentation and Coordination. *Public Management Review*, 2(1), 1–24.

Moon, M.J. and Ingraham, P. 1998. Shaping Administrative Reform and Governance: An Examination of the Political Nexus Triads in Three Asian Countries. *Governance*, 11(1), 77–100.

Mooney, G. and Neal, S. (eds) 2009. *Community*. Buckingham: Open University Press/McGraw Hill.

Moore, M.H. 1995. *Creating Public Value: Strategic Management in Government*. Cambridge, MA: Harvard University Press.

Moran, M. 1999. *Governing the Health Care State: A Comparative Study of the United Kingdom, the United States and Germany*. Manchester: Manchester University Press.

—— 2003. *The British Regulatory State: High Modernism and Hyper-Innovation*. Oxford: Oxford University Press.

Morgan, D.R. and Hirlinger, M.W. 1991. Intergovernmental Service Contracts: A Multivariate Explanation. *Urban Affairs Quarterly*, 27(1), 128–144.

Morgan, D.R., Hirlinger, M.W. and England, R. 1988. The Decision to Contract Out: A Further Explanation. *Western Political Quarterly*, 41(2), 363–372.

Morin, D. 2001. Influence of Value for Money Audit on Public Administrations: Looking Beyond Appearances. *Financial Accountability and Management*, 17(2), 99–118.

—— 2003. Controllers or Catalysts for Change and Improvement: Would the Real Value for Money Auditors Please Stand Up? *Managerial Auditing Journal*, 18(1), 19–30.

—— 2008a. Auditors General's Universe Revisited: An Exploratory Study of the Influence they Exert on Public Administration through their Value for Money Audits. *Managerial Auditing Journal*, 23(7), 697–720.

—— 2008b. *Being a Magistrate at the French Cour des Comptes: Balancing between Tradition and Modernity*. Paper to the 5th International Conference on Accounting, Auditing and Management in Public Sector Reforms, European Institute for Advanced Studies in Management (EIASM), Amsterdam, 3–5 September.

Morison, J. and Newman, D. 2001. On Line Citizenship: Consultation and Participation in New Labour's Britain and Beyond. *International Review of Law, Computers and Technology*, 15(2), 171–194.

Mörth, U. (ed.) 2007. *European Public-Private Collaboration: A Choice between Efficiency and Democratic Accountability?* Chelthenham: Edward Elgar.

Mosher, F. 1968. *Democracy and the Public Service*. New York: Oxford University Press.

Mott Macdonald 2002. *Review of Large Public Procurement in the UK*. London: Mott Macdonald.

Mouritsen, J. 1997. *Taellelighedens regime*. Copenhagen: Jurist och økonomforbundets forlag.

Moynihan, D.P. 2006. Ambiguity in Policy Lessons: The Agencification Experience. *Public Administration*, 84(4), 1029–1050.

—— 2008. The Normative Model in Decline? Public Service Motivation in the Age of Governance, in *Motivation in Public Management: The Call of Public Service*, edited by J. Perry and A. Hondeghem. Oxford: Oxford University Press, 247–267.

Moynihan, D.P. and Pandey, S. 2007. The Role of Organizations in Fostering Public Service Motivation. *Public Administration Review*, 67(1), 40–53.

Mueller, D. 1989. *Public Choice II*. Cambridge: Cambridge University Press.

Mulgan, R. 2001. Auditors-General: Cuckoos in the Managerialist Nest? *Australian Journal of Public Administration*, 60(2), 24–34.

—— 2003. *Holding Power to Account: Accountability in Modern Democracies*. New York: Palgrave Macmillan.

—— 2005. Joined-Up Government: Past, Present, and Future, in *Joined-Up Government*, edited by V. Bogdanor. Oxford: Oxford University Press, 175–187.

—— 2006. Government Accountability for Outsourced Services. *Australian Journal of Public Administration*, 65(2), 48–58.

Muller, P. 1992. Le modèle français d'administration, in *Administration française. Est elle en crise?*, edited by P. Muller. Paris: L'Harmattan, 11–32.

Müller, W. and Strom, K. 2003. *Coalition Governments in Western Europe*. Oxford: Oxford University Press.

Mungiu-Pippidi, A. 2006. Corruption: Diagnosis and Treatment. *Journal of Democracy*, 17(3), 86–99.

Murray, M. 1975. Comparing Public and Private Management: An Exploratory Essay. *Public Administration Review*, 35(4), 364–371.

Musgrave, R.A. 1959. *The Theory of Public Finance: A Study in Public Economy*. New York: McGraw Hill.

Musselin, C. 1997. State/University Relations and How to Change Them: The Case of France and Germany. *European Journal of Education*, 32(2), 145–164.

—— 2010. Universities and Pricing on Higher Education Markets, in *Changing Educational Landscapes: Educational Policies, Schooling Systems and Higher Education – A Comparative Perspective*, edited by D. Mattheou. Dordrecht: Springer.

Musselin, C. and Becquet, V. 2008. Academic Work and Academic Identities: A Comparison between Four Disciplines, in *Cultural Perspectives on Higher Education*, edited by J. Välimaa and O.-H. Ylijoki. Dordrecht: Springer, 91–108.

Nakamura, A. 1998. Japan's Central Administration at the Crossroads: Increasing Public Demand for Deregulation, Decentralization and De-Bureaucratization. *International Journal of Public Administration*, 21(10), 1511–1531.

NAO 2000. *Examining the Value for Money of Deals under the Private Finance Initiative*. London: National Audit Office.

—— 2003. *Improving Service Delivery: The Role of Executive Agencies*. Report by the Comptoller and Auditer General, HC 525 Session 2002–2003. London: National Audit Office.

—— 2007. *Evaluation of Regulatory Impact Assessments 2006–07*. London: National Audit Office.

Nath, N., Van Peursem, K., Lowe, A. 2005. *Public Sector Performance Auditing: Emergence, Purpose and Meaning*. Working Paper Series, the University of Waikato, Department of Accounting.

National Partnership for Reinventing Government 2001. *History of the National Partnership for Reinventing Government: Accomplishments, 1993–2000, A Summary*. Available at: http://govinfo.library.unt.edu/npr/whoweare/appendixf.html [accessed: 02/03/2010].

Neave, G. 1998. The Evaluative State Reconsidered. *European Journal of Education*, 33(3), 265–284.

Neave, G. and van Vught, F.A. (eds) 1991. *Prometheus Bound: The Changing Relationship between Government and Higher Education in Western Europe*. Oxford: Pergamon.

Needham, C. 2009a. Interpreting Personalization in England's National Health Service: A Textual Analysis. *Critical Policy Studies*, 3(2), 204–220.

—— 2009b. Policing with a Smile: Narratives of Consumerism in New Labour's Criminal Justice Policy. *Public Administration*, 87(1), 97–116.

Neveu, C. (ed.) 2007. *Cultures et practiques participatives*. Paris: L'Harmattan.

Newbery, D.M.G. 1999. *Privatisation, Restructuring and Regulation of Network Industries*. Cambridge, MA and London: MIT Press.

Newman, J. 2001. *Modernising Governance: New Labour, Policy and Society*. London: Sage.

Newman, J. and Clarke, J. 2009. *Publics, Politics and Power: Remaking the Public in Public Services*. London: Sage.

Newman, J. and Kuhlmann, E. 2007. Consumers Enter the Political Stage? The Modernization of Health Care in Britain and Germany. *European Journal of Social Policy*, 17(2), 99–110.

Newman, J. and Tonkens, E. (eds) 2010. *Summoning the Active Citizen: Participation, Responsibility and Choice in Western Europe*. Amsterdam: Amsterdam University Press, forthcoming.

Newman, K.L. and Nollen, S.D. 1996. Culture and Congruence: The Fit between Management Practices and National Culture. *Journal of International Business Studies*, 27(4), 753–779.

Nickel, P. and Eikenberry, A. 2006. Beyond Public vs. Private: The Transformative Potential of Democratic Feminist Management. *Administrative Theory and Praxis*, 28(3), 359–380.

Nickson, A. 1999. Does the NPM Work in Less Developed Countries? The Case of the Urban Water Supply Sector. *Journal of International Development*, 11(5), 777–783.

Niskanen, W.A. 1971. *Bureaucracy and Representative Government*. Chicago, IL: Aldine Atherton.

—— 1973. *Bureaucracy: Servant or Master?* Wolverhampton: William Gibbon & Sons.

Noblet, A.J. and Rodwell, J.J. 2009. Integrating Job Stress and Social Exchange Theories to Predict Employee Strain in Reformed Public Sector Contexts. *Journal of Public Administration Research and Theory*, 19(3), 555–578.

Nohria, N. and Eccles, R. 1992. *Networks and Organizations: Structures, Form and Action*. Boston, MA: Harvard Business School Press.

Nolan Committee on Standards in Public Life 1995. *Standards in Public Life*. First Report of the Committee on Standards in Public Life. London: HMSO.

Nordby, T. 2004. Patterns of Corporatist Intermediation, in *Nordic Politics: Comparative Perspectives*, edited by K. Heidar. Oslo: Universitetsforlaget, 98–107.

Norman, R. 1995. New Zealand's Reinvented Government: Experiences of Public Managers. *Public Sector*, 18(2), 22–25.

—— 2003. *Obedient Servants? Management Freedoms and Accountabilities in the New Zealand Public Sector*. Wellington: Victoria University Press.

Normanton, E. 1966. *The Accountability and Audit of Government: A Comparative Study*. Manchester: Manchester University Press.

Norris, P. 1999. *Critical Citizens: Global Support for Democratic Governance*. Oxford: Oxford University Press.

—— 2002. *Democratic Phoenix: Reinventing Political Activism*. Cambridge: Cambridge University Press.

North, D.C., Wallis, J.J. and Weingast, B.R. 2009. *Violence and Social Orders: A Conceptual Framework for Interpreting Recorded Human History*. Cambridge: Cambridge University Press.

Nye, J.S., Zelikow, P.D. and King, D.C. 1997. *Why People Don't Trust Government*. Cambridge, MA: Harvard University Press.

O'Brien, J. 1997. Occupational and Professional Identity as an Industrial Strategy in the New Zealand State Sector. *Journal of Industrial Relations*, 39(4), 499–517.

—— 2000. Union Strategy in a Decentralising Regulatory Environment: The Community and Public Sector Union and the National Tertiary Education Union, in *Research on Work, Employment and Industrial Relations 2000. Proceedings of the 14th AIRAANZ Conference, Newcastle, February 2000, NSW*, edited by J. Burgess and G. Strachan. Volume I. Newcastle: University of Newcastle, 160–169.

O'Brien, J. and Fairbrother, P. 2000. A Changing Public Sector: Developments at the Commonwealth Level. *Australian Journal of Public Administration*, 59(4), 59–66.

O'Brien, J. and Hort, L. 1998. Introduction: The State of State Employment. *Australian Journal of Public Administration*, 57(2), 46–48.

O'Brien, J. and O'Donnell, M. 1999. Government Management and Unions: The Public Service under the Workplace Relations Act. *Journal of Industrial Relations*, 41(3), 446–467.

OECD 1995. *Governance in Transition: Public Management Reforms in OECD Countries*. Paris: OECD.

—— 1996. *Ethics in the Public Service*. Paris: OECD.

—— 2000a. *Government of the Future*. Paris: OECD.

—— 2000b. *Building Public Trust: Ethics Measures in OECD Countries*. Paris: OECD.

—— 2001. *Citizens as Partners: Information, Consultation and Public Participation in Policy-Making*. Paris: OECD.

—— 2002a. *OECD Reviews of Regulatory Reform. Regulatory Policies in OECD Countries: From Interventionism to Regulatory Governance*. Paris: OECD.

—— 2002b. *Distributed Public Governance: Agencies, Authorities and Other Government Bodies*. Paris: OECD.

—— 2005. *Modernising Government: The Way Forward*. Paris: OECD.

—— 2008. *Public-Private Partnerships: In Pursuit of Risk Sharing and Value for Money*. Paris: OECD.

—— 2009a. *Government at a Glance*. Paris: OECD.

—— 2009b. *Measuring Government Activity*, edited by C. Pollitt, G. Bouckaert and W. Van Dooren. Paris: OECD.

O'Fairchellaigh, C., Wanna, J. and Weller, P. 1999. *Public Sector Management in Australia: New Challenges, New Directions*. 2nd edition. South Yarra: Macmillan.

Office of Public Service Reform 2002. *Reforming our Public Services: Principles into Practice*. London: Office of Public Service Reform.

Ofgem 2007. *Proposed Revised Guidance on Impact Assessment*. London: Office of Gas and Electricity Markets.

O'Flynn, J. 2007. From New Public Management to Public Value, Paradigmatic Change and Managerial Implication. *Australian Journal of Public Administration*, 53(3), 353–366.

Okuonzi, S.A. 2004. Learning from Failed Health Reform in Uganda. *British Medical Journal*, 329(7475), 1173–1175.

O'Leary, R., Bingham, L.B. and Gerard, C. 2006. Special Issue on Collobartive Public Management. *Public Administration Review* (December). Supplement to Volume 66.

Olsen, J.P. 1988. Administrative Reform and Theories of Organization, in *Organizing Governance: Governing Organizations*, edited by C. Campbell and B.G. Peters. Pittsburgh, PA: University of Pittsburgh Press, 233–254.

—— 1996. Norway: Slow Learner or Another Triumph of the Tortoise?, in *Lessons from Experience: Experiential Reforms in Eight Democracies*, edited by J.P. Olsen and B.G. Peters. Oslo: Scandinavian University Press, 180–213.

—— 2006. Maybe it's Time to Rediscover Bureaucracy? *Journal of Public Administration Research and Theory*, 16(1), 1–24.

—— 2007. *Europe in Search for Political Order*. Oxford: Oxford University Press.

—— 2008a. Institutional Autonomy and Democratic Government, in *Change and Continuity in Public Sector Organizations: Essays in Honour of Per Lægreid*, edited by P.G. Roness and H. Sætren. Bergen: Fagbokforlaget, 299–321.

—— 2008b. The Ups and Downs of Bureaucratic Organizations. *Annual Review of Political Science*, 11(June), 13–37.

—— 2009. Change and Continuity: An Institutional Approach to Institutions of Democratic Government. *European Political Science Review*, 1(1), 3–32.

Olson, O., Guthrie, J. and Humphrey, C. (eds) 1998. *Global Warning: Debating International Developments in New Public Financial Management*. Oslo: Cappelen Akademisk Forlag.

Ongaro, E. (ed.) 2008. Introduction: Public Management Reform in France, Greece, Italy, Portugal, Spain. Special Issue on 'Public Management Reform in Countries in the Napoleonic Tradition'. *International Journal of Public Sector Management*, 21(2), 101–117.

—— 2009. *Public Management Reform and Modernization: Trajectories of Administrative Change in Italy, France, Greece, Portugal and Spain*. Cheltenham: Edward Elgar.

Osborne, D. and Gaebler, T. 1992. *Reinventing Government: How the Entrepreneurial Spirit is Transforming the Public Sector*. Reading: Addison-Wesley.

Osborne, D. and Plastrik, P. 1998. *Banishing Bureaucracy: The Five Strategies for Reinventing Government*. New York: Penguin.

Osborne, S.P. 1997. Managing the Coordination of Social Services in the Mixed Economy of Welfare: Competition, Cooperation or Common Cause? *British Journal of Management*, 8(4), 317–328.

—— (ed.) 2001. *Public-Private Partnerships: Theory and Practice in International Perspective*. New York: Routledge.

—— 2006. The New Public Governance? *Public Management Review*, 8(3), 377–387.

—— (ed.) 2010a. *The New Public Governance? Critical Perspectives and Future Directions*. London: Routledge.

—— 2010b. Delivering Public Services: Time for a New Theory. *Public Management Review*, 12(1), 1-11.

—— 2010c. The (New) Public Governance: A Suitable Case for Treatment, in *The New Public Governance? Critical Perspectives and Future Directions*. London: Routledge.

—— 2010d. Public Governance and Public Services Delivery: A Research Agenda for the Future, in *The New Public Governance? Critical Perspectives and Future Directions*. London: Routledge.

Ostrom, V. and Ostrom, E. 1971. *Public Choice: A Different Approach to the Study of Public Administration. Public Administration Review*, 31(2), 203–216.

O'Toole, L.J. and Meier, K.J. 2004. Parkinson's Law and New Public Management? Contracting Determinants and Service-quality Consequences in Public Education. *Public Administration Review*, 64(3), 342–352.

O'Toole, L.J., Walker, R., Meier, K. and Boyne, G. 2007. Networking in Comparative Context. *Public Management Review*, 9(30), 401–420.

Ouchi, W. 1979. Markets, Bureaucracies and Clans. *Administrative Science Quarterly*, 25(1), 129–141.

Paarlberg, L.E., Perry, J.L. and Hondeghem, A. 2008. From Theory to Practice: Strategies for Applying Public Service Motivation, in *Motivation in Public Management: The Call of Public Service*, edited by J.L. Perry and A. Hondeghem. Oxford: Oxford University Press, 268–314.

Page, E.C. 2005. Joined-Up Government and the Civil Service, in *Joined-Up Government*, edited by V. Bogdanor. Oxford: Oxford University Press, 139–155.

Page, E.C. and Jenkins, W. 2005. *Policy Bureaucracy*. Oxford: Oxford University Press.

Painter, M. 1988. Public Management: Fad or Fallacy? *Australian Journal of Public Administration*, 47(1), 1–3.

—— 2002. Public Administration Reform in Vietnam: Problems and Prospects. *Public Administration and Development*, 23(3), 259–271.

—— 2003. The Politics of State Sector Reforms in Vietnam: Contested Agendas and Uncertain Trajectories. *The Journal of Development Studies*, 41(2), 261–283.

Painter, M. and Peters, B.G. (eds) 2010. *Tradition and Public Administration*. New York: Palgrave Macmillan.

Pallesen, T. 2004. A Political Perspective on Contracting Out: The Politics of Good Times. Experiences from Danish Local Governments. *Governance*, 17(4), 573–587.

—— 2006. The Politics of Contracting Out in School Districts: The Case of Washington State. *State and Local Government Review*, 38(1), 34–40.

Pallot, J. 1999. Service Delivery: The Audit Dimension. *Australian Journal of Public Administration*, 58(3), 43–49.

—— 2003. A Wider Accountability? The Audit Office and New Zealand's Bureaucratic Revolution. *Critical Perspectives on Accounting*, 14(1–2), 133–155.

Paradeise, C., Reale, E., Bleiklie, I. and Ferlie, E. (eds) 2009. *University Governance: Western European Comparative Perspectives*. Dordrecht: Springer.

Park, S.M. and Rainey, H.G. 2008. Leadership and Public Service Motivation in U.S. Federal Agencies. *International Public Management Journal*, 11(1), 109–142.

Parker, R. and Bradley, L. 2000. Organizational Culture in the Public Sector: Evidence from Six Organizations. *International Journal of Public Sector Management*, 13(2), 125–141.

Parker, S., Paun, A., McClory, J. and Blatchford, K. 2010. *Shaping Up: A Whitehall for the Future*. London: Institute for Government.

Parsons, T. 1964. The Professions and Social Structure, in *Essays in Sociological Theory*, edited by T. Parsons. Glencoe, IL: Free Press, 34–49.

Patapan, H., Wanna, J. and Weller, P. 2005. *Westminster Legacies: Democracy and Responsible Government on Asia and the Pacific*. Sydney: UNSW Press.

Paterson, J. 1988. A Managerialist Strikes Back. *Australian Journal of Public Administration*, 47(4), 287–295.

Paton, C. 2006. *New Labour's State of Health: Political Economy, Public Policy and the NHS*. Aldershot: Ashgate.

Pedersen, O.K. and Lægreid, P. 1994. En nordisk model?, in *Forvaltningspolitik i Norden*, edited by P. Lægreid and O.K. Pedersen. Copenhagen: Jurist- og Økonomforbundets Forlag, 249–275.

Peetz, D. 1998. *Unions in a Contrary World: The Future of the Australian Trade Union Movement*. Cambridge: Cambridge University Press.

Pendleton, A. 1999. Ownership or Competition? An Evaluation of the Effects of Privatization on Industrial Relations: Institutions, Processes and Outcomes. *Public Administration*, 77(4), 769–791.

Perellon, J. 2001. The Development of Quality Assurance Policy in Higher Education. A Comparative Analysis of England, the Netherlands, Spain and Switzerland. Dissertation. London, University of London, Institute of Education.

Perrow, C. 1986. *Complex Organizations: A Critical Essay*. New York: Random House.

Perry, J.L. 1996. Measuring Public Service Motivation: An Assessment of Construct Reliability and Validity. *Journal of Public Administration Research and Theory*, 6(1), 5–24.

Perry, J.L. and Hondeghem, A. 2008a. Editors' Introduction, in *Motivation in Public Management: The Call of Public Service*, edited by J.L. Perry and A. Hondeghem. Oxford: Oxford University Press, 1–14.

—— 2008b. Directions for Future Theory and Research, in *Motivation in Public Management: The Call of Public Service*, edited by J.L. Perry and A. Hondeghem. Oxford: Oxford University Press, 294–310.

Perry, J.L. and Wise, L.R. 1990. The Motivational Bases of Public Service. *Public Administration Review*, 50(3), 367–373.

Perry, P.L., Engbers, T. and Jun, S.Y. 2009. Back to the Future? Performance-Related Pay, Empirical Research, and the Perils of Persistence. *Public Administration Review*, 69(1), 39–51.

Peters, B.G. 1999. *Institutional Theory in Political Science: The 'New Institutionalism'*. London: Pinter.

—— 2001a. *The Politics of Bureaucracy*. London: Routledge.

—— 2001b. *The Future of Governing: Four Emerging Models*. 2nd edition. Lawrence, KS: University Press of Kansas.

—— 2008. *Bureaucracy and Democracy*. Paper to the SOG/IPSA Conference, New Public Management and the Quality of Government, Gothenburg, 13–15 November.

—— 2010. Meta-governance and Public Management, in *The New Public Governance? Critical Perspectives and Future Directions*, edited by S. Osborne. London: Routledge, 36–51.

Peters, B.G. and Pierre, J. (eds) 2004. *Politicization of the Civil Service in Comparative Perspective.* London: Routledge.

Peters, B.G. and Wright, V. 1996. Public Policy and Administration, Old and New, in *A New Handbook of Political Science*, edited by R.E. Goodin and H.D. Klingemann. Oxford: Oxford University Press, 628–641.

Peters, T.J. and Waterman, R.H. 1982. *In Search of Excellence: Lessons from America's Best-Run Companies.* New York: Harper & Row.

Petrie, M. 1998. *Organisational Transformation: The Income Support Experience.* New Zealand: Department of Social Welfare.

Pfeffer, J. 1981. *Power in Organizations.* Marshfield, MA: Pitman.

Pharr, S. and Putnam, R.D. 2000. *Disaffected Democracies: What's Troubling the Trilateral Countries?* Princeton, NJ: Princeton University Press.

Piattoni, S. (ed.) 2001. *Clientelism, Interests, and Democratic Representation: The European Experience in Historical and Comparative Perspective.* Cambridge: Cambridge University Press.

Pierre, J. (ed.) 2000. *Debating Governance: Authority, Steering, and Democracy.* Oxford: Oxford University Press.

—— 2004. Central Agencies in Sweden: A Report from Utopia, in *Unbundled Government: A Critical Analysis of the Global Trend to Agencies, Quangos and Contractualisation*, edited by C. Pollitt and C. Talbot. London and New York: Routledge, 203–214.

Pierre, J. and Painter, M. 2010. Why Legality Cannot be Contracted Out: Exploring the Limits of New Public Management, in *Reasserting the Public in Public Services: New Public Management Reforms*, edited by M. Ramesh, E. Araral Jr and X. Wu. New York: Routledge, 49–62.

Pierson, P. 2004. *Politics in Time: History, Institutions, and Social Analysis.* Princeton, NJ: Princeton University Press.

Pierson, P. and Skocpol, T. 2002. Historical Institutionalism in Contemporary Political Science, in *Political Science: The State of the Discipline*, edited by H. Milner and I. Katznelson. 2nd edition. Washington D.C.: ASPA, 693–721.

Pilkington, C. 1999. *The Civil Service in Britain Today.* Manchester: Manchester University Press.

Pillay, S. 2008. A Cultural Ecology of New Public Management. *International Review of Administrative Sciences*, 74(3), 373–394.

Pine, J. and Gilmore, J. 1999. *The Experience Economy: Work is Theatre and Every Business a Stage.* Cambridge, MA: Harvard Business School Press.

Pirie, M. 1988. *Privatization: Theory, Practice and Choice.* London: Wildwood House.

Poguntke, T. and Webb, P. 2005. *The Presidentialization of Politics: A Comparative Study of Modern Democracies.* Oxford: Oxford University Press.

Polidano, C. 1999. *The New Public Management in Developing Countries.* IDPM Public Policy and Management, Working Paper No. 13. Manchester: University of Manchester, Institute for Development Policy and Management.

Polidano, C. and Hulme, D. 2001. Towards a Post-NPM Public Management Agenda. *Public Management Review*, 3(3), 297–303.

Pollitt, C. 1990. *Managerialism and the Public Services: The Anglo-American Experience*. Oxford: Basil Blackwell.

—— 1995. Justification by Works or by Faith? Evaluation of New Public Management. *Evaluation*, 1(2), 133–154.

—— 1998. Managerialism Revisited, in *Taking Stock: Assessing Public Sector Reforms*, edited by B.G. Peters and D.J. Savoie. Montreal: McGill–Queens University Press, 45–77.

—— 2000. Is the Emperor in His Underwear? An Analysis of the Impacts of Public Management Reform. *Public Management*, 2(2), 181–190.

—— 2001a. Convergence: The Useful Myth. *Public Administration*, 79(4), 933–947.

—— 2001b. Clarifying Convergence: Striking Similarities and Durable Differences in Public Management Reform. *Public Management Review*, 3(4), 471–492.

—— 2002. The New Public Management in International Perspective: An Analysis of Impacts and Effects, in *New Public Management*, edited by K. KcLaughlin, S.P. Osborne and E. Ferlie. London: Routledge, 274–292.

—— 2003a. *The Essential Public Manager*. Maidenhead: Open University Press.

—— 2003b. Performance Audit in Western Europe: Trends and Choices. *Critical Perspectives on Accounting*, 14(1–2), 157–170.

—— 2003c. Joined-up Government: A Survey. *Political Studies Review*, 1(1), 34–49.

—— 2004. Theoretical Overview, in *Unbundled Government: A Critical Analysis of the Global Trend to Agencies, Quangos and Contractualisation*, edited by C. Pollitt and C. Talbot. London and New York: Routledge, 319–341.

—— 2006. *Blair's Re-Disorganization: Hyper-Modernism and the Costs of Reform – A Cautionary Tale*. Paper presented at the University of Canberra, 24 October.

—— 2007a. The New Public Management: An Overview of Its Current Status. *Administraţie Şi Management Public*, 8, 110–115.

—— 2007b. New Labour's Dis-Reorganization. *Public Management Review*, 9(4), 529–543.

—— 2008. *Time, Policy, Management: Governing with the Past*. Oxford: Oxford University Press.

—— 2009. Pathologies of the Neo-Liberal State: From Bureaucracy to Fragmentocracy? *Norsk Statsvitenskapelig Tidsskrift*, 9(2), 160–182.

Pollitt, C. and Bouckaert, G. 2004. *Public Management Reform: A Comparative Analysis*. 2nd edition. Oxford: Oxford University Press.

Pollitt, C., Caulfield J., Smullen, A. and Talbot, C. 2004. *Agencies: How Governments Do Things Through Semi-Autonomous Organizations*. Basingstoke: Palgrave Macmillan.

Pollitt, C., Girre, X., Lonsdale, J., Mul, R., Summa, H. and Waerness, M. 1999. *Performance or Compliance: Performance Audit and Public Management in Five Countries*. Oxford: Oxford University Press.

Pollitt, C. and Summa, H. 1997. Reflexive Watchdogs? How Supreme Audit Institutions Account for Themselves. *Public Administration*, 75(2), 313–336.

Pollitt, C. and Talbot, C. 2004. *Unbundled Government: A Critical Analysis of the Global Trend to Agencies, Quangos and Contractualisation*. London: Routledge.

Pollitt, C., van Thiel, S. and Homburg, V. (eds) 2007. *New Public Management in Europe: Adaptation and Alternatives*. Houndmills: Palgrave.

Pollock, A., Price, D. and Player, S. 2007. An Examination of the UK's Treasury Evidence Base for Cost and Time Overrun Data in UK Value-for-Money Policy and Appraisal. *Public Money and Management*, 27(2), 127–133.

Pollock, A., Shaoul, J. and Vickers, N. 2002. Private Finance and Value for Money in NHS Hospitals: A Policy in Search of a Rationale? *British Medical Journal*, 324(7347), 1205–1208.

Poole, M., Mansfield, R. and Gould-Williams, J. 2006. Public and Private Sector Managers Over 20 Years: A Test of the 'Convergence Thesis'. *Public Administration*, 84(4), 1051–1076.

Posner, B. and Schmidt, W. 1996. The Values of Business and Federal Government Executives: More Different than Alike. *Public Personnel Management*, 25(3), 277–289.

Powell, G.B. 2002. *Elections as Instruments of Democracy: Majoritarian and Proportional Visions*. New Haven, CT: Yale University Press.

Powell, W. 1990. Neither Market Nor Hierarchy: Network Forms of Organization. *Research in Organizational Behaviour*, 12(1), 295–336.

Power, M. 1997. *The Audit Society: Rituals of Verification*. Oxford: Oxford University Press.

—— 2005. The Theory of the Audit Explosion, in *The Oxford Handbook of Public Management*, edited by E. Ferlie, L.E Lynn and C. Pollitt. Oxford: Oxford University Press, 326–344.

Prachett, L. and Wingfield, M. 1996. Petty Bureaucracy and Woolly-Minded Liberalism? The Changing Ethos of Local Government Officers. *Public Administration*, 74(4), 639–656.

Premfors, R., Ehn, P., Halden, E. and Sundström, G. 2009. *Demokrati och byråkrati*. Lund: Studentlitteratur.

Proeller, I. and Schedler, K. 2005. Change and Continuity in the Continental Tradition of Public Management, in *The Oxford Handbook of Public Management*, edited by E. Ferlie, L.E. Lynn and C. Pollitt. Oxford: Oxford University Press, 695–719.

Propper, C., Burgess, S. and Green, K. 2004. Does Competition Between Hospitals Improve the Quality of Care? Hospital Death Rates and the NHS Internal Market. *Journal of Public Economics*, 88(7), 1247–1272.

Prosser, T. 1999. Theorising Utility Regulation. *Modern Law Review*, 62(2), 196–217.

Pugh, D. and Hickson, D. 1976. *Organisational Structure in its Contest: The Aston Programme I*. Farnborough: Saxon House.

Put, V. 2006. *De bril waarmee auditors naar de werkelijkheid kijken. Over normen die rekenhoven gebruiken bij het beoordelen van de overheid*. Brugge: Die Keure.

—— 2011. Norms in Performance Audits: Some Strategic Considerations, in *Performance Auditing: Contributing to Accountability in Democratic Government*, edited by P. Wilkins, J. Lonsdale and T. Ling. Cheltenham: Edward Elgar, forthcoming.

Put, V. and Turksema, R. 2011. Selection of Performance Audits Topics by Supreme Audit Institutions, in *Performance Auditing: Contributing to Accountability in Democratic Government*, edited by P. Wilkins, J. Lonsdale and T. Ling. Cheltenham: Edward Elgar, forthcoming.

Quah, J.S.T. 2007a. Administrative Reform in Singapore: An Evaluation of Public Service 21 (1995–2004), in *Public Administration in Transition: Essays in Honor of Gerald E. Caiden*, edited by D. Agyriades, O.P. Dwivedi and J.J. Jabbra. London: Vallentine Mitchell, 162–188.

—— 2007b. Administrative Reform and Governance in Singapore, in *The Repositioning of Public Governance: Global Experience and Challenges*, edited by G.E. Caiden and Tsai-Tsu Su. Taipei: Department of Political Science, National Taiwan University, 123–154.

Radaelli, C.M. 1999. *Technocracy in the European Union*. London: Longman.

Radaelli, C.M. and de Francesco, F. 2007. *Regulatory Quality in Europe: Concepts, Measures and Policy Processes*. Manchester: Manchester University Press.

Radaelli, C.M. and Meuwese, A.C.M. 2009. Better Regulation in Europe: Between Public Management and Regulatory Reform. *Public Administration*, 87(3), 639–654.

Radcliffe, V.S. 1999. Knowing Efficiency: The Enactment of Efficiency in Efficiency Auditing. *Accounting, Organizations and Society*, 24(4), 333–362.

Rainey, H.G. 1989. Public Management: Recent Research on the Political Context and Managerial Roles, Structures and Behaviors. *Journal of Management*, 15(2), 229–250.

—— 1993. Towards a Theory of Goal Ambiguity in Public Organizations, in *Research in Public Administration*, edited by J.L. Perry. Vol. II. Amsterdam: Elsevier, 121–166.

Rainey, H.G., Backoff, R. and Levine, C. 1976. Comparing Public and Private Organizations. *Public Administration Review*, 36(2), 233–244.

Ramo, J.C. 2004. *The Beijing Consensus*. London: The Foreign Policy Centre.

Rawson, D.W. and Wrightson, S. 1980. *A Handbook of Australian Trade Unions and Employees' Associations*. 4th edition. Canberra: Australian National University, Research School of Social Sciences.

Reichard, C. 2003. Local Public Management Reforms in Germany. *Public Administration*, 81(2), 345–363.

—— 2008. The Study of Public Management in Germany, in *The Study of Public Management in Europe and the US*, edited by W.J.M. Kickert. London: Routledge, 42–69.

Reichard, C. and Röber, M. 1993. Was kommt nach der Einheit? Die öffentliche Verwaltung in der ehemaligen DDR zwischen Blaupause und Reform, in *Der lange Weg zur Einheit*, edited by G.J. Glaeßner. Berlin: Aufbau, 215–245.

Renn, O. 2008. *Risk Governance: Coping with Uncertainty in a Complex World*. London: Earthscan.

Revelli, F. and Tovmo, P. 2007. Revealed Yardstick Competition: Local Government Efficiency Patterns in Norway. *Journal of Urban Economics*, 62(1), 121–134.

Rhodes, R.A.W. 1997. *Understanding Governance*. Buckingham: Open University Press.

—— 2000. Governance and Public Administration, in *Debating Governance*, edited by J. Pierre. Oxford: Oxford University Press, 54–90.

Richards, D. 2003. The Civil Service in Britain: A Case-study in Path Dependency, in *Civil Service Systems in Anglo-American Countries*, edited by J. Halligan. Cheltenham: Edward Elgar, 27–69.

Richards, D. and Smith, M. 2006. The Tensions of Political Control and Administrative Autonomy: From NPM to a Reconstituted Westminster Model, in *Autonomy and Regulation: Coping with Agencies in the Modern State*, edited by T. Christensen and P. Lægreid. Cheltenham: Edward Elgar, 181–202.

Rieder, S. and Lehmann, L. 2002. Evaluation of New Public Management Reforms in Switzerland: Empirical Results and Reflections on Methodology. *International Public Management Review*, 3(2), 25–43.

Riska, E. 1993. The Medical Profession in the Nordic Countries, in *The Changing Medical Profession: An International Perspective*, edited by F.W. Hafferty and J.B. Mckinlay. Oxford: Oxford University Press, 150–161.

Roberts, A.S. 1998. *The Paradox of Public Sector Reform: Works Better, Trusted Less?* SSRN eLibrary. Available at: http://ssrn.com/paper=1561904 [accessed: 01/03/2010].

Robson, W. 1928. *Justice and Administrative Law*. London: Macmillan.

Rodrik, D. 2007. *One Economics, Many Recipes: Globalization, Institutions and Economic Growth*. Princeton, NJ: Princeton University Press.

Rokkan, S. 1967. Norway: Votes Count but Resources Decide, in *Political Oppositions in Western Democracies*, edited by R.A. Dahl. New Haven, CT: Yale University Press.

Rombach, B. 1997. *Den marknadslika kommunen*. Stockholm: Nerenius och Santérus Förlag.

Rommel, J. and Christians, J. 2009. Steering from Ministers and Departments: Coping Strategies of Agencies in Flanders. *Public Management Review*, 11(1), 79–100.

Roness, P.G. 1993. Tenestemannsorganisasjonane si rolle i omforminga av offentleg sektor. *Nordisk Administrativt Tidsskrift*, 85(1), 5–27.

—— 2001. Transforming State Employees' Unions, in *New Public Management: The Transformation of Ideas and Practice*, edited by T. Christensen and P. Lægreid. Aldershot: Ashgate, 173–208.

—— 2007. Types of State Organizations: Arguments, Doctrines and Changes beyond New Public Management, in *Transcending New Public Management: The Transformation of Public Sectors Reforms*, edited by T.Christensen and P. Lægreid. Aldershot: Ashgate, 65–88.

Rose, R. 1974. *The Problem of Party Government*. London: Macmillan.

Rose-Ackerman, S. and Kornai, J. (eds) 2004. *Building a Trustworthy State in Post-Socialist Transition*. New York: Palgrave Macmillan.

Rosenbloom, D.H. 1998. *Understanding Management, Politics and Law in the Public Sector*. New York: McGraw-Hill.

Rosenthal, R. 1991. *Meta-Analytical Procedures for Social Research*. London: Sage.

Rothstein, B. 2005. *Social Traps and the Problem of Trust*. Cambridge: Cambridge University Press.

—— 2009. Creating Political Legitimacy: Electoral Democracy versus Quality of Governance. *American Behavioral Scientist*, 53(3), 311–320.

Rothstein, B. and Eek, D. 2009. Political Corruption and Social Trust: An Experimental Approach. *Rationality and Society*, 21(1), 81–112.

Rothstein, B. and Stolle, D. 2008. The State and Social Capital: An Institutional Theory of Generalized Trust. *Comparative Politics*, 40(4), 441–467.

Rothstein, B. and Teorell, J. 2008. What is Quality of Government: A Theory of Impartial Political Institutions. *Governance*, 21(2), 165–190.

Rouban, L. 1997. The Administrative Modernisation Policy in France, in *Public Management and Administrative Modernisation in Western Europe*, edited by W.J.M. Kickert. Cheltenham: Edward Elgar, 141–156.

—— 1998. *The French Civil Service*. Paris: La Documentation Française.

—— 2003. Réformer ou recomposer l'Etat? Les enjeux sociopolitiques d'une mutation annoncée. *Revue Française d'Administration Publique*, 1–2(105–106), 153–166.

Røvik, K.A. 2002. The Secrets of the Winners: Management Ideas that Flow, in *The Expansion of Management Knowledge: Carriers, Flows and Sources*, edited by K. Sahlin-Andersson and L. Engwall. Stanford, CA: Stanford University Press, 113–144.

—— 2007. *Trender og Translasjoner – Ideer som former det 21. århundrets organisasjon*. Oslo: Universitetsforlaget.

Royal Commission on Australian Government Administration 1976. *Report: Royal Commission on Australian Government Administration*. Canberra: A.G.P.S.

Rudd, K. 2009. The Global Financial Crisis. *The Monthly Magazine*, 42(February), 20–29.

Ruffner, M. and Sevilla, J. 2004. Public Sector Modernization: Modernizing Accountability and Control. *OECD Journal on Budgeting*, 4(2), 123–141.

Rutgers, M.R. 2009. The Oath of Office as Public Value Guardian. *The American Review of Public Administration [OnlineFirst]*, 4 November, 1–17.

Ryan, C. and Walsh, P. 2004. Collaboration of Public Sector Agencies: Reporting and Accountability Challenges. *International Journal of Public Sector Management*, 17(7), 621–631.

Ryan, N. 2000. *Public Confidence in the Public Sector*. A discussion paper prepared for the Office of the Auditor General of Western Australia. West Perth: Office of the Auditor General of Western Australia.

Sahlin-Andersson, K. 1994. Varför låter sig kommuner omvandlas, in *Organisationsexperiment i kommuner och landsting*, edited by B. Jacobsson. Stockholm: Nerenius och Santérus förlag.

—— 2001. National, International and Transnational Construction of New Public Management, in *New Public Management: The Transformation of Ideas and Practice*, edited by T. Christensen and P. Lægreid. Aldershot: Ashgate, 42–72.

Saint-Martin, D. 2000. *Building the New Managerialist State: Consultants and the Politics of Public Sector Reform in Comparative Perspective.* Oxford: Oxford University Press.

—— 2001. How the Reinventing Government Movement in Public Administration was Exported from the U.S. to Other Countries. *International Journal of Public Administration,* 24(6), 573–604.

—— 2004. Managerialist Advocate or 'Control Freak': The Janus Faced Office of the Auditor General. *Canadian Public Administration,* 47(2), 121–140.

Salamon, L. 2002. *The Tools of Government: A Guide to the New Governance.* New York: Oxford University Press.

Salmon, P. 1987. Decentralisation as an Incentive Scheme. *Oxford Review of Economic Policy,* 3(2), 24–43.

Samaratunge, R., Alam, Q. and Teicher, J. 2008. The New Public Management Reforms in Asia: A Comparison of South and Southeast Asian Countries. *International Review of Administrative Sciences,* 74(1), 25–46.

Sarker, A.E. 2006. New Public Management in Developing Countries: An Analysis of Success and Failure with Particular Reference to Singapore and Bangladesh. *International Journal of Public Sector Management,* 19(2), 180–203.

Savas, E.S. 1997. *Privatization.* New York: Chatham House.

—— 2000. *Privatization and Public-Private Partnerships.* New York: Chatham House.

Savoie, D.J. 1994. *Thatcher, Reagan, Mulroney: In Search of a New Bureaucracy.* Toronto: University of Toronto Press.

—— 1999. *Governing from the Centre: The Concentration of Power in Canadian Politics.* Toronto: University of Toronto Press.

—— 2003. *Breaking the Bargain: Public Servants, Ministers, and Parliament.* Toronto: University of Toronto Press.

—— 2008. *Court Government and the Collapse of Accountability in Canada and the United Kingdom.* Toronto: University of Toronto Press.

Sayre, W. 1958. Premises of Public Administration. *Public Administration Review,* 18(2), 102–105.

Schachter, H.L. 2007. Does Frederick Taylor's Ghost still Haunt the Halls of Government? A Look at the Concept of Governmental Efficiency in our Time. *Public Administration Review,* 67(5), 800–810.

Scharpf, F.W. 1997a. *Games Real Actors Play: Actor-Centered Institutionalism in Policy Research.* Boulder, CO: Westview Press.

—— 1997b. Economic Integration, Democracy, and the Welfare State. *Journal of European Public Policy,* 4(1), 18–36.

—— 1999. *Governing in Europe: Effective and Democratic?* Oxford: Oxford University Press.

Schedler, K. and Proeller, I. (eds) 2007. *Cultural Aspects of Public Management Reforms.* Amsterdam: Elsevier.

Schick, A. 1996. *The Spirit of Reform: Managing the New Zealand State Sector in a Time of Change.* A Report Prepared for the State Services Commission and the Treasury. Wellington: State Services Commission/the Treasury.

—— 1998. Why Most Developing Countries Should Not Try New Zealand Reforms. *The World Bank Research Observer*, 13(1), 123–131.

—— 2002. Agencies in Search of Principles, in *Distributed Public Governance: Agencies, Authorities and Other Government Bodies*. Paris: OECD, 33–52.

Schiffer, J.R. 1983. *Anatomy of a Laissez-faire Government: The Hong Kong Growth Model Reconsidered*. Hong Kong: University of Hong Kong, Centre of Urban Studies and Urban Planning.

Schillemans, T. 2008. Accountability in the Shadow of Hierarchy: The Horizontal Accountability of Agencies. *Public Organization Review*, 8(2), 175–194.

Schiller, C., Hensen, H. and Kuhnle, S. 2009. Global Health Policy: What Role for International Governmental Organizations?, in *The Role of International Organizations in Social Policy Ideas, Actors and Impact*, edited by R. Ervik, N. Kildal and E. Nilssen. Cheltenham: Edward Elgar, chapter 10.

Schmitter, P.C. 1974. Still the Century of Corporatism? *Review of Politics*, 36(1), 85–131.

Schofield, J. 2001. Time for a Revival? Public Policy Implementation: A Review of the Literature and an Agenda for Future Research. *International Journal of Management Reviews*, 3(3), 3245–3263.

Schrijvers, A. 1993. The Management of a Larger Town: Outcome Related Performance Indicators and Organizational Control in the Public Sector. *Public Administration*, 71(4), 595–603.

Schröter, E. 2000. Culture's Consequences? In Search of Cultural Explanations of British and German Public Sector Reform, in *Comparing Public Sector Reform in Britain and Germany*, edited by H. Wollmann and E. Schröter. Dartmouth: Aldershot.

Schubert, T. 2009. Empirical Observations on New Public Management to Increase Efficiency in Public Research: Boon or Bane? *Research Policy*, 38(8), 1225–1234.

Schwartz, R. and Mayne, J. 2005. Assuring the Quality of Evaluative Information: Theory and Practice. *Evaluation and Program Planning*, 28(1), 1–14.

Schwass, M. and Norman, R. 2007. *From Transactions to Outcomes: The Ministry of Social Development*. Australia and New Zealand School of Government case series. Wellington: The Australia and New Zealand School of Government (ANZSOG).

Scott, G. 2001. *Public Management in New Zealand: Lessons and Challenges*. Wellington: New Zealand Business Roundtable.

Scott, G., Bushnell, P. and Sallee, N. 1990. Reform of the Core Public Sector: New Zealand Experience. *Governance*, 3(2), 138–167.

Scott, W.R. 1992. *Organizations: Rational, Natural and Open Systems*. Englewood Cliffs, NJ: Prentice Hall.

Scott, W.R. and Davies, G. 2006. *Organizations and Organizing: Rational, Natural and Open Systems Perspectives*. 6th revised edition. Englewood Cliffs, NJ: Prentice Hall.

Self, P. 1985. *Political Theories of Modern Government: Its Role and Reform*. London: Allen and Unwin.

—— 2000a. *Rolling Back the State: Economic Dogma and Political Choice*. New York: St. Martin's Press.

—— 2000b. *Rolling Back the Market: Economic Dogma and Political Choice*. London: Macmillan.

Selznick, P. 1957. *Leadership in Administration: A Sociological Interpretation*. Berkeley, CA: University of California Press.

—— 1996. Institutionalism 'Old' and 'New'. *Administrative Science Quarterly*, 41(2), 270–277.

Sen, A. 1999. *Development as Freedom*. Oxford: Oxford University Press.

Shand, D. and Anand, P. 1996. Performance Auditing in the Public Sector: Approaches and Issues in OECD Member Countries, in *Performance Auditing and Public Sector Modernization*. Paris: OECD, chapter 2.

Shaoul, J. 2004. Railpolitik: The Financial Realities of Operating Britain's National Railways. *Public Money and Management*, 24(1), 27–36.

Shapiro, M. 1997. The Problems of Independent Agencies in the United States and the European Union. *Journal of European Public Policy*, 4(2), 276–291.

Shaw, R. 2005. New Zealand Public Management Reform and the Partnership for Quality Agreement, in *Staff Participation and Public Management Reform: Some International Comparisons*, edited by D. Farnham, A. Hondeghem and S. Horton. Basingstoke: Palgrave Macmillan, 214–229.

Shergold, P. 2004. Regeneration: New Structures, New Leaders, New Traditions. *Australian Journal of Public Administration*, 54(2), 3–6.

Simey, M. 1988. *Democracy Rediscovered: A Study in Police Accountability*. London: Pluto Press.

Simmons, R. 2009. Understanding the 'Differentiated Consumer' in Public Services, in *The Consumer in Public Services: Choice, Values and Difference*, edited by R. Simmons, M. Powell and I. Greener. Bristol: Policy Press, 57–76.

Simon, H.A. 1976. *Administrative Behavior: A Study of Decision-making Processes in Administrative Organization*. 3rd edition. London: Macmillan.

—— 1997. *Keynote Address*, presented to the American Society of Public Administration Annual Conference, Pittsburgh, July.

Simpson, H. 2009. Productivity in Public Services. *Journal of Economic Surveys*, 23(2), 250–276.

Skelcher, C., Mathur, N. and Smith, M. 2005. The Public Governance of Collaborative Spaces: Discourse, Design and Democracy. *Public Administration*, 83(3), 573–596.

Small, V. 1999. Labour Roasts New WINZ Spin. *New Zealand Herald*, 23 July.

Smith, A. and Norman, R. 1997. *George Hickton, Salesman: Change Manager Case Study*. Wellington: Victoria Link.

Smith, B.C. 2007. *Good Governance and Development*. Basingstoke: Palgrave.

Smith, J. 1991. The Public Service Ethos. *Public Administration*, 69(4), 515–523.

Smith, K.B. and Meier, K.J. 1995. *The Case against School Choice: Politics, Markets and Fools*. New York: M.E. Sharpe.

Smith, P.B. 2002. Culture's Consequences: Something Old and Something New. *Human Relations*, 55(1), 119–135.

Smith, P.B., Dugan, S. and Trompenaars, F. 1996. National Culture and Managerial Values: A Dimensional Analysis Across 43 Nations. *Journal of Cross-Cultural Psychology*, 27(2), 252–285.

Smith, R. and Weller, P. (eds) 1978. *Public Service Inquiries in Australia*. Queensland: University of Queensland Press.

Smith, W. 1997. *Utility Regulators: The Independence Debate, Public Policy for the Private Sector*, Note 127, October 1997. Washington D.C.: World Bank.

Smullen, A. 2007. Translating Agency Reform: Rhetoric and Culture in Comparative Perspective. Dissertation. Rotterdam: Erasmus University.

Söderlund, N., Csaba, I., Gray, A., Milne, R. and Raftery, J. 1997. Impact of the NHS Reforms on English Hospital Productivity: An Analysis of the First Three Years. *British Medical Journal*, 315(7116), 1126–129.

Sørensen, E. and Torfing, J. 2005. Democratic Anchorage of Government Networks. *Scandinavian Political Studies*, 28(2), 195–218.

―― 2008. *Theories of Democratic Network Governance*. Basingstoke: Palgrave Macmillan.

Sotiropoulos, D.A. 2004. Southern European Public Bureaucracies in Comparative Perspective. *West European Politics*, 27(3), 405–422.

―― 2006. *Patronage in South European Bureaucracies in the 1980s and 1990s: The Politicization of Central Public Administrations in Greece, Italy, Portugal and Spain*. Paper to the ECPR workshops, Nicosia, April 2006.

de Sousa, L. 2001. Political Parties and Corruption in Portugal. *West European Politics*, 24(1), 157–180.

Spanou, C. 1996. Penelope's Suitors: Administrative Modernization and Party Competition in Greece. *West European Politics*, 19(1), 97–124.

―― 2001. (Re)shaping the Politics-Administration Nexus in Greece. The Decline of a Symbiotic Relationship?, in *Politicians, Bureaucrats and Administrative Reform*, edited by B.G. Peters and J. Pierre. London: Routledge, 101–110.

Spence, J. 1980. *To Change China: Western Advisers in China*. New York: Penguin Books.

Spicer, B., Emanuel, D. and Powell, M. 1996. *Transforming Government Enterprises*. St. Leonards: Centre for Independent Studies.

Spulber, N. 1997. *Redefining the State: Privatization and Welfare Reform in Industrial and Transitional Economies*. Cambridge: Cambridge University Press.

Stambolovic, V. 2003. Epidemic of Health Care Reforms. *European Journal of Public Health*, 13(1), 77–79.

Statskontoret 2005. *Mot en modern och sammanhållen förvaltning. Erfarenheter från sex myndigheters samverkan i 15 projekt*. Rapport 2005: 125. Stockholm: Statskontoret.

Steen, T. and Rutgers, M. 2009. *There are Always Two Sides to the Coin: The Upshot of an Instrumental Approach Towards Public Service Motivation and the Oath of Office*. Paper to the International Public Service Motivation Research Conference, Bloomington, Indiana, 7–9 June.

Stein, R.M. 1990. *Urban Alternatives*. Pittsburgh, PA: University of Pittsburgh Press.

Stensöta, H.O. 2004. Den empatiska staten: jämställdhetens inverkan på daghem och polis 1950–2000. Dissertation. Göteborg: Göteborg University, Department of Political Science.

—— 2010. The Conditions of Care: Reframing the Debate about Public Sector Ethics. *Public Administration Review*, 70(2), 295–303.

Stephens, R. 1996. Social Services, in *A Study of Economic Reform: The Case of New Zealand*, edited by B. Silverstone, A. Bollard and R. Lattimore. Amsterdam: Elsvier, chapter 14.

Sterck, M., Scheeers, B. and Bouckaert, G. 2005. *The Modernization of the Public Control Pyramid: International Trends*. Leuven: Steunpunt Bestuurlijke Organisatie Vlaanderen.

Stevers, T.A. 1979. *De Rekenkamer*. Leiden and Antwerp: Stenfert Kroeze.

Stewart, J. and Walsh, K. 1992. Change in the Management of Public Services. *Public Administration*, 70(4), 499–518.

Stoker, G. 2005. Joined-Up Government for Local and Regional Institutions, in *Joined-Up Government*, edited by V. Bogdanor. Oxford: Oxford University Press, 156–174.

—— 2006a. Public Value Management: A New Narrative for Networked Governance? *American Review of Public Administration*, 36(1), 41–57.

—— 2006b. *Why Politics Matters: Making Democracy Work*. New York: Palgrave Macmillan.

Stolle, D. and Rothstein, B. 2007. Institutionelle Grundlagen des Sozialkapitals. *Kölner Zeitschrift für Soziologie und Sozialpsychologie*, Sonderheft 47, 113–140.

Stortingsmelding nr. 19. 2008–2009. *Ei forvaltning for demokrati og fellesskap*. Oslo: Det Kongelege Fornyings- og Administrasjonsdepartement.

Streeck, W. and Thelen, K. (eds) 2005. *Beyond Continuity: Institutional Change in Advanced Political Economies*. Oxford: Oxford University Press.

Strokosch, K. and Osborne, S. 2009. *Understanding the Co-production of Public Services: A New Approach and its Implications for Public Services Delivery*. Paper to the British Academy of Management Conference, University of Sussex, September 2009.

Strøm, K. 1990. A Behavioral Theory of Competitive Political Parties. *American Journal of Political Science*, 34(2), 565–598.

Studlar, D.T., MacAllister, I. and Ascui, A. 1990. Privatization and the British Electorate: Microeconomic Policies, Macroeconomic Evaluations, and Party Support. *American Journal of Political Science*, 34(4), 1077–1101.

Subirats, J. 1990. *Modernising the Spanish Public Administration or Reform in Disguise*. Working Paper No. 20. Barcelona: Autonomous University Barcelona.

Suleiman, E. 2003. *Dismantling Democratic States*. Princeton, NJ: Princeton University Press.

Sullivan, H. 2001. Modernisation, Democratisation and Community Governance. *Local Government Studies*, 27(3), 1–24.

Sun, M.T.W. 2008. Rhetoric or Action? An Assessment of the Administrative Reform in Taiwan. *Journal of Asian Public Policy*, 1(1), 52–70.

Svensen, S. and Teicher, J. 1999. Restructuring the Australian State? A Bipartisan Agenda. *Public Management*, 1(3), 329–348.

Swan, W. 2008. Address to the Per Capita Conference, Brisbane, 30 October 2008.

Swann, D. 1988. *The Retreat of the State: Deregulation and Privatisation in the UK and US*. London: Harvester/Wheatsheaf.

Swindell, D. and Kelly, J.M. 2000. Linking Citizen Satisfaction Data to Performance Measures: A Preliminary Evaluation. *Public Performance and Management Review*, 24(1), 30–52.

Taggart, P. 1995. New Populist Parties in Western Europe. *West European Politics*, 18(1), 34–51.

Talbot, C. 2004. The Agency Idea: Sometimes Old, Sometimes New, Sometimes Borrowed, Sometimes Untrue, in *Unbundled Government: A Critical Analysis of the Global Trend to Agencies, Quangos and Contractualisation*, edited by C. Pollitt and C. Talbot. London and New York: Routledge, 3–21.

—— 2007. *Second Report: The 2007 Pre-Budget Report*. Treasury Committee, House of Commons, 15 October.

Talbot, C. and Johnson, C. 2007. Seasonal Cycles in Public Management: Disaggregation and Re-aggregation. *Public Money and Management*, 27(1), 55–56.

Tanne, J.H. 2010. US House of Representatives Approves Historic Healthcare Reform Bill. *British Medical Journal*, 340(7748), 671.

Taylor, F.W. 1911. *The Principles of Scientific Management*. New York: Harper & Bros.

—— 1916. Government Efficiency. *Bulletin of the Taylor Society*, 2(5), 7–13.

Ter Bogt, H. and van Helden, J. 2000. Accounting Change in Dutch Government: Exploring the Gap between Expectations and Realizations. *Management Accounting Research*, 11(2), 263–279.

Terry, F. 1996. The Private Finance Initiative: Overdue Reform or Policy Breakthough? *Public Money and Management*, 16(1), 9–16.

Thaler, R. and Sustein, C. 2008. *Nudge: Improving Decisions about Health, Wealth and Happiness*. New Haven, CT: Yale University Press.

Thatcher, M. 1995. *Downing Street Years*. London: Harper Collins.

—— 2005. Independent Regulatory Agencies and Elected Politicians in Europe, in *Regulation through Agencies in the EU: A New Paradigm of European Governance*, edited by D. Geradin, R. Muñoz and N. Petit. Cheltenham: Edward Elgar, 47–66.

Thatcher, M. and Stone Sweet, A. 2002. Theory and Practice of Delegation to Non-Majoritarian Institutions. *West European Politics*, 25(1), 1–22.

The Economist 2009a. The Return of Economic Nationalism. 7 February, 9–10.

—— 2009b. There was a Lawyer, an Engineer and a Politician …. 18 April.

—— 2009c. The State of Economics. The Other-worldly Philosophers. 16 July.

—— 2009d. A 'New Normal' for the World Economy: After the Storm. 1 October.

—— 2009e. A Heated Debate: Why Political Orthodoxy Must Not Silence Scientific Argument. 28 November.

—— 2010. Spin, Science and Climate Change: Action on Climate is Justified, Not Because Science is Certain, but Precisely Because it is Not. 20 March.

The Harris Poll 2009. *Firefighters, Scientists and Doctors Seen as the Most Prestigious Occupations*. HarrisInteractive. [Online.] Avalilable at: www.harrisinteractive. com/vault/Harris-Interactive-Poll-Research-Pres-Occupations-2009-08.pdf. [accessed: 22/03/2010].

Thelen, K. 1999. Historical Institutionalism in Comparative Politics. *Annual Review of Political Science*, 2(1), 369–404.

The Treasury 1987. *Government Management: Briefing to the Incoming Government*, Volume 1. Wellington: The New Zealand Treasury.

van Thiel, S. 2001. *Quangos: Trends, Causes and Consequences*. Aldershot: Ashgate.

—— 2004. Quangos in Dutch Government, in *Unbundled Government: A Critical Analysis of the Global Trend to Agencies, Quangos and Contractualisation*, edited by C. Pollitt and C. Talbot. London and New York: Routledge, 167–183.

—— 2008. *The Empty Nest Syndrome: Dutch Ministries after the Separation of Policy and Administration*. Paper to the International Research Society for Public Management Conference (IRSPM) 12, Brisbane, Australia, 26–28 March.

van Thiel, S. and van Buuren, A. 2001. Ontwikkeling van het Aantal Zelfstandige Bestuursorganen 1993 en 2003: Zijn ZBO's uit de mode. *Bestuurswetenschappen*, 55(5), 386–404.

van Thiel, S. and CRIPO team 2009. *The Rise of Executive Agencies: Comparing the Agencification of 25 Tasks in 21 Countries*. Paper to the EGPA Conference, Malta, 2–5 September.

van Thiel, S. and Pollitt, C. 2007. The Management and Control of Executive Agencies: An Anglo-Dutch Comparison, in *New Public Management in Europe: Adaptation and Alternatives*, edited by C. Pollitt, S. van Thiel and V. Homburg. Basingstoke: Palgrave Macmillan, 52–70.

van Thiel, S. and Yesilkagit, K. 2008. *Good Neighbours or Distant Friends? Trust between Dutch Ministries and their Executive Agencies*. Paper for the ECPR Conference, Administration, Policy and Politics in Government Regulation, chaired by J.G. Christensen, Pisa, 6–8 September 2007.

Thompson, W. 2002. *Managing Change to Improve Public Services: Top Down or Bottom Up?* London: Office of Public Service Reform.

Thornthwaite, L. and Hollander, R. 1998. Two Models of Contemporary Public Service Wage Determination in Australia. *Australian Journal of Public Administration*, 57(2), 98–106.

Thuillier, G. and Tulard, J. 1984. *Histoire de l'Administration Française*. Paris: Presses Universitaires de France.

Tiebout, C. 1956. A Pure Theory of Local Expenditure. *Journal of Political Economy*, 64(5), 416–424.

Togeby, L., Andersen, J.G., Christiansen, P.M., Beck Jørgensen, T. and Vallgårda, S. 2003. *Magt og demokrati i Danmark. Hovedresultaterne fra Magtudredningen*. Århus: Aarhus Universitetsforlag.

Toonen, T.A.J. 2003. Administrative Reform, in *The Sage Handbook of Public Administration*, edited by B.G. Peters and J. Pierre. London: Sage, 467–477.

Torres, L. and Pina, V. 1999. An Empirical Study on the Performance of Supreme Audit Institutions in European Union Privatizations. *The European Accounting Review*, 8(4), 777–795.

—— 2002. Changes in Public Service Delivery in the EU Countries. *Public Money and Management*, 22(4), 41–48.

Tranvik, T. and Fimreite, A.L. 2006. Reform Failure: The Processes of Devolution and Centralization in Norway. *Local Government Studies*, 32(1), 89–107.

Treasury Committee 2007. *Second Report: The 2007 Pre-Budget Report*, 15 October. London: House of Commons.

Trondal, J., Marcussen, M., Larsson, T. and Veggeland, F. 2010. *Unpacking International Organisations: Dynamics of Compound Bureaucracies*. Manchester: Manchester University Press.

Tsebelis, G. 1990. *Nested Games: Rational Choice in a Comparative Perspective*. New York: Cambridge University Press.

Turner, M. 1998. Central-Local Relations in the Asia-Pacific: Convergence or Divergence?, in *Beyond the New Public Management: Changing Ideas and Practices in Governance* edited by M. Minogue, C. Polidano and D. Hulme. Cheltenham: Edward Elgar, 246–259.

—— 2002. Choosing Items from the Menu: New Public Management in Southeast Asia. *International Journal of Public Administration*, 25(12), 1493–1512.

Turvey, R. 2001. Introduction, in *Regulatory Review 2000/2001*, edited by P. Vass. Bath: University of Bath, Centre for the Study of Regulated Industries, 1–7.

van Twist, M.J., van der Steen, M., Marcel Karré, P., Peeters, R. and van Ostaijen, M. 2009. *Vernieuwende Verandering: Continuiteit en Discontinuiteit van vernieuwing van de rijksdienst*. The Hague: Ministry of Home Affairs.

Umeh, O.J. and Andranovich, G. 2005. *Culture, Development and Public Administration in Africa*. Bloomfield, CT: Kumarian Press.

UN and INTOSAI 2007. *The Value and Benefits of Audit in a Globalised Environment*. 19th UN/INTOSAI Symposium, Vienna, Austria, 28–30 March.

United Nations Economic and Social Commission for Asia and the Pacific 2006. *What is Good Governance?*, 24 December. [Online.] Available at: www.unescap.org/huset/gg/governance.htm; http://www.unescap.org/pdd/prs/ProjectActivities/Ongoing/gg/governance.asp [accessed: 04/08/2010].

Upton, S. 1999. The Role of the State. Institute of Policy Studies, Victoria University. *IPS Policy Newsletter*, 56(February), 8–15.

Vabø, M. 2010. Active Citizenship in Norwegian Elderly Care: From Activation to Consumer Activism, in *Summoning the Active Citizen: Participation, Responsibility and Choice in Western Europe*, edited by J. Newman and E. Tonkens. Amsterdam: Amsterdam University Press.

Vandenabeele, W. 2007. Towards a Theory of Public Service Motivation: An Institutional Approach. *Public Management Review*, 10(4), 545–556.

—— 2008. Development of a Public Service Motivation Measurement Scale: Corroboration and Extending Perry's Measurement Instrument. *International Public Management Journal*, 11(1), 143–167.

—— 2009. The Mediating Effect of Job Satisfaction and Organizational Commitment on Self-reported Performance: More Robust Evidence of the PSM–Performance Relationship. *International Review of Administrative Sciences*, 75(1), 11–34.

Van der Waal, Z. 2008. *Value Solidity: Differences, Similarities and Conflicts between the Organizational Values of Government and Business*. Amsterdam: V.U. University.

Van der Waal, Z. and Huberts, L. 2008. Value Solidity in Government and Business: Results of an Empirical Study on Public and Private Sector Organizational Values. *The American Review of Public Administration*, 38(3), 264–285.

Van der Waal, Z., Pekur, A. and Vrangbæk, K. 2008. Public Sector Value Congruence among Old and New EU Member-States? Empirical Evidence from the Netherlands, Denmark and Estonia. *Public Integrity*, 10(4), 317–333.

Van Deth, J.W. and Scarbrough, E. 1995. Perspectives on Value Change, in *The Impact of Values*, edited by J.W. Van Deth and E. Scarbrough. Oxford: Oxford University Press, 528–540.

Van de Walle, S. and Bouckaert, G. 2003. Public Service Performance and Trust in Government: The Problem of Causality. *International Journal of Public Administration*, 26(8–9), 891–913.

—— 2007. Perceptions of Productivity and Performance in Europe and the USA. *International Journal of Public Administration*, 30(11), 1–18.

Van de Walle, S., Kampen, J.K. and Bouckaert, G. 2005a. Deep Impact for High Impact Agencies? Assessing the Role of Bureaucratic Encounters in Evaluations of Government. *Public Performance and Management Review*, 28(4), 532–549.

Van de Walle, S., Thijs, N. and Bouckaert, G. 2005b. A Tale of Two Charters: Political Crisis, Political Realignment and Administrative Reform in Belgium. *Public Management Review*, 7(3), 367–390.

Van de Walle, S. and Roberts, A. 2008. Publishing Performance Information: An Illusion of Control?, in *Performance Information in the Public Sector: How it is Used*, edited by W. Van Dooren and S. Van de Walle. Basingstoke: Palgrave, 211–226.

Van de Walle, S., Van Roosbroek S. and Bouckaert, G. 2008. Trust in the Public Sector: Is there Any Evidence for a Long-term Decline? *International Review of Administrative Sciences*, 74(1), 45–62.

Van Dooren, W., Bouckaert, G. and Halligan, J. 2010. *Performance Management in the Public Sector*. London: Routledge.

Van Ham, H. and Koppenjan, J. 2001. Building Public-Private Partnerships. *Public Management Review*, 4(1), 593–616.

Van Loocke, E. and Put, V. 2009. *De impact van Performance Auditing: 'Slow and Subtle'?* Paper to the 8th Nederlands-Belgisch Politicologenetmaal, Nijmegen, 28–29 May.

Van Oosteroom, R. 2002. The Netherlands, in *Distributed Public Governance: Agencies, Authorities and Other Government Bodies*. Paris: OECD, 113–133.

Vargo, S., Maglio, P. and Archpru Akaka, M. 2008. On Value and Value Co-Creation: A Service Systems and Service Logic Perspective. *European Journal of Management*, 26(3), 145–152.

Vass, P. 1998. Regulatory Reform and Relations among Multiple Authorities in the United Kingdom, in *Changing Regulatory Institutions in Britain and North America*, edited by G.B. Doern and S. Wilks. Toronto, Buffalo, NY and London: University of Toronto Press, 236–260.

Verhoest, K., Peters, B.G., Bouckaert, G. and Verschuere, B. 2004. The Study of Organisational Autonomy: A Conceptual Review. *Public Administration and Development*, 24(2), 101–118.

Verhoest, K., Roness, P.G., Verschuere, B., Rubecksen, K. and MacCarthaigh, M. 2010. *Autonomy and Control of State Agencies: Comparing States and Agencies*. Basingstoke: Palgrave Macmillan.

Verschuere, B. 2009. The Role of Public Agencies in the Policy Making Process: Rhetoric versus Reality. *Public Policy and Administration*, 24(1), 22–46.

Vibert, F. 2007. *The Rise of the Unelected: Democracy and the New Separation of Powers*. Cambridge: Cambridge University Press.

Vickers, J. and Yarrow, G.K. 1988. *Privatization: An Economic Analysis*. Boston, MA: MIT Press.

Vidal, I. 2008. The Role of Social Enterprises in Europe: A Core Element or a Distraction in the Provision of Public Services?, in *The Third Sector in Europe: Prospects and Challenges*, edited by S. Osborne. Abingdon: Routledge, 309–326.

Vigoda-Gadot, E. and Yuval, F. 2004. The State of Bureaucracy: Public Opinion about the Performance of Government Agencies in Israel. *International Journal of Public Opinion Research*, 16(1), 63–80.

Vining, A. and Boardman, A.E. 1992. Ownership versus Competition: Efficiency in Public Enterprise. *Public Choice*, 73(2), 205–239.

—— 2005. Public-Private Partnerships in the UK and Canada: There Are No Free Lunches. *Journal of Comparative Policy Analysis*, 7(3), 199–220.

—— 2010. Assessing the Economic Worth of Public-Private Partnerships, in *International Handbook on Public–Private Partnerships*, edited by G. Hodge, C. Greve and A. Boardman. Cheltenham: Edward Elgar, chapter 8.

Vining, A. and Weimer, D. 1990. Government Supply and Government Production Failure: A Framework Based on Contestability. *Journal of Public Policy*, 10(1), 1–22.

Vrangbæk, K. 2008. Rapid Growth in Private Health Care. *Health Policy Monitor*, 12(October). [Online.] Available at: http://www.hpm.org/survey/dk/a12/4 [accessed: 02/08/2010].

—— 2009. Public Sector Values in Denmark: A Survey Analysis. *International Journal of Public Administration*, 32(5), 508–535.

Wade, R. 1990. *Governing the Market: Economic Theory and the Role of Government in East Asian Industrialization*. Princeton, NJ: Princeton University Press.

Walker, R.M. and Boyne, G.A. 2006. Public Management Reform and Organizational Performance: An Empirical Assessment of the U.K. Labour Government's Service Improvement Strategy. *Journal of Policy Analysis and Management*, 25(2), 371–393.

Wallis, J. and Gregory, R. 2009. Leadership, Accountability and Public Value: Resolving a Problem in 'New Governance'? *International Journal of Public Administration*, 32(3–4), 250–273.

Walsh, P. 1991. The State Sector Act 1988, in *Reshaping the State: New Zealand's Bureaucratic Revolution*, edited by J. Boston, J. Martin, J. Pallot and P. Walsh. Auckland: Oxford University Press, 52–80.

Walsh, P. and Brosnan, P. 1999. Redesigning Industrial Relations: The Employment Contracts Act and Industrial Relations, in *Redesigning the Welfare State in New Zealand: Problems, Policies, Prospects*, edited by J. Boston, P. Dalziel and S. St. John. Auckland: Oxford University Press, 98–116.

Walsh, P., Harbridge, R. and Crawford, A. 2001. Public Sector Industrial Relations in New Zealand, in *Strategic Choices in Reforming Public Service Employment: An*

International Handbook, edited by C. Dell'Aringa, G. Della Rocca and B. Keller. Basingstoke: Palgrave, 185–215.

Weaver, B.K. and Rockman, B.A. 1993. Assessing the Effects of Institutions, in *Do Institutions Matter? Government Capabilities in the United States and Abroad*, edited by R.K. Weaver and B.A. Rockman. Washington D.C.: Brookings Institution, 1–41.

Weber, M. 1947. *The Theory of Social and Economic Organization*. Translated by A. Henderson and T. Parsons. New York: The Free Press.

de Weert, E. 2004. The Academic Workplace. Country Report: The Netherlands, in *The International Attractiveness of the Academic Workplace in Europe*, edited by J. Enders and E. de Weert. Frankfurt: Gewerkschaft Erziehung und Wissenschaft, 290–309.

Weibel, A., Rost, K. and Osterloh, M. 2009. Pay for Performance in the Public Sector: Benefits and (Hidden) Costs. *Journal of Public Administration Research and Theory*, 20(2), 387–412.

Weick, K. 2001. *Making Sense of the Organization*. Malden, MA: Blackwell.

Weihe, G. 2005. *Public-Private Partnerships: Addressing a Nebulous Concept*. Working Paper No. 16. Copenhagen: Copenhagen Business School, International Center for Business and Politics.

Weiss, C. 1979. The Many Meanings of Research Utilisation. *Public Administration Review*, 39(5), 426–443.

West, K. and Davies, P. 2010. What is the Public Value of Government Action? Towards a (New) Pragmatic Approach to Value Questions in Public Endeavours. *Public Administration*, forthcoming.

Westerheijden, D., de Boer, H. and Enders, J. 2009. Netherlands; An 'Echternach' Procession in Different Directions; Oscillating Steps towards Reform, in *University Governance: Western European Comparative Perspectives*, edited by C. Paradeise, E. Reale, I. Bleiklie and E. Ferlie. Dordrecht: Springer, 103–126.

Wettenhall, R. 2005a. Agencies and Non-Departmental Public Bodies: The Hard and Soft Lenses of Agencification Theory. *Public Management Review*, 7(4), 615–635.

—— 2005b. The Public-Private Interface: Surveying the History, in *The Challenge of Public-Private Partnerships: Learning from International Experience*, edited by G. Hodge and C. Greve. Chelthenham: Edward Elgar.

Wheat, E.M. 1991. The Activist Auditor: A New Player in State and Local Politics. *Public Administration Review*, 51(5), 385–392.

Wiggan, I. 2009. Mapping the Governance Reform of Welfare to Work in Britain under New Labour. *International Journal of Public Administration*, 32(12), 1026–1047.

Wildawsky, A. 1979. *Speaking Truth to Power*. Boston, MA: Little Brown.

Williams, D.W. 2003. Measuring Government in the Early Twentieth Century. *Public Administration Review*, 63(6), 643–659.

Williamson, J. 1989. What Washington Means by Policy Reform, in *Latin American Readjustment: How Much Has Happened*, edited by J. Williamson. Washington D.C.: Institute for International Economics.

Williamson, O. 1975. *Markets and Hierarchies*. New York: Free Press.

—— 1985. *The Economic Institutions of Capitalism: Firms, Markets, Relational Contracting.* New York: Free Press.

Williamson, P.J. 1989. *Corporatism in Perspective: An Introductory Guide to Corporatist Theory.* London: Sage.

Wilsford, D. 1994. Path Dependency or Why History Makes It Difficult, but Not Impossible, to Reform Health Care Services in a Big Way. *Journal of Public Policy,* 14(3), 251–283.

Wilson, J.Q. 1989. *Bureaucracy: What Government Agencies Do and Why They Do It.* New York: Basic Books.

Wilson, W. 1887. The Study of Administration. *Political Sciences Quarterly,* 2(2), 197–222.

Winter, S. 2004. Implementation, in *The Handbook of Public Administration,* edited by B.G. Peters and J. Pierre. London: Sage.

Wollmann, H. (ed.) 2003. *Evaluation in Public Sector Reform.* Cheltenham: Edward Elgar.

Wood, J. and Wood, M. (eds) 2002. *F.W. Taylor: Critical Evaluations in Business and Management.* New York: Routledge.

Woodward, J. 1965. *Industrial Organisation: Theory and Practice.* London: Oxford University Press.

World Bank 1993. *The East Asian Economic Miracle: Economic Growth and Public Policy.* New York: Oxford University Press.

—— 2010. *The Worldwide Governance Indicator Project.* [Online.] Available at: http://info.worldbank.org/governance/wgi/index.asp [accessed: 19/03/2010].

Wright, B.E. 2001. Public-Sector Work Motivation: A Review of the Current Literature and a Revised Conceptual Model. *Journal of Public Administration Research and Theory,* 11(4), 559–586.

Wright, V. 1990. The Administrative Machine: Old Problems and New Dilemmas, in *Developments in French Politics,* edited by P.A. Hall, J. Hayward and H. Machin. Houndmills: Macmillan, 114–132.

—— 1994. Reshaping the State: The Implications for Public Administration. *West European Politics,* 17(3), 102–137.

Yeatman, A. 1987. The Concept of Public Management and the Australian State in the 1980s. *Australian Journal of Public Administration,* 46(4), 339–356.

Zhao, Y. and Peters, B.G. 2009. The State of the State: Comparing Governance in the United States and China. *Public Administration Review,* 67(1), 122–128.

Zmerli, S. and Newton, K. 2008. Social Trust and Attitudes toward Democracy. *Public Opinion Quarterly,* 72(4), 706–724.

Zullo, R. 2009. Does Fiscal Stress Induce Privatization: Correlates of Private and Intermunicipal Contracting, 1992–2002. *Governance,* 22(3), 459–481.

Zussman, D. 2002. Alternative Service Delivery, in *A Handbook of Canadian Public Administration,* edited by C. Dunn. Don Mills: Oxford University Press, 53–76.

Index

Other Research Companions available in Politics and International Relations:

The Ashgate Research Companion to Secession
Edited by Aleksandar Pavkovic and Peter Radan
ISBN 978-0-7546-7702-4

The Ashgate Research Companion to Non-State Actors
Edited by Bob Reinalda
ISBN: 978-0-7546-7906-6

The Ashgate Research Companion to Modern Warfare
Edited by George Kassimeris and John Buckley
ISBN 978-0-7546-7410-8

The Ashgate Research Companion to US Foreign Policy
Edited by Robert J. Pauly, Jr.
ISBN 978-0-7546-4862-8

The Ashgate Research Companion to Political Leadership
Edited by Joseph Masciulli, Mikhail A. Molchanov and W. Andy Knight
ISBN 978-0-7546-7182-4

The Ashgate Research Companion to Ethics and International Relations
Edited by Patrick Hayden
ISBN 978-0-7546-7101-5

The Ashgate Research Companion to Federalism
Edited by Ann Ward and Lee Ward
ISBN 978-0-7546-7131-2

The Ashgate Research Companion to the Politics of Democratization in Europe
Concepts and Histories
Edited by Kari Palonen, Tuija Pulkkinen and José María Rosales
ISBN 978-0-7546-7250-0